EUROPE
TRAVELBOOK™

THE GUIDE TO
PREMIER DESTINATIONS

SEVENTH EDITION

AAA

President & CEO: Robert Darbelnet
Executive Vice President, Publishing &
   Administration: Rick Rinner
Managing Director, Travel Information:
   Bob Hopkins

Director, Product Development & Sales: Bill Wood
Director, Publishing Marketing &
   Communications: Patty Wight
Business Manager: Linda Indolfi
Director, Purchasing & Corporate Services: Becky
   Barrett
Director, Business Development: Gary Sisco
Director, Tourism Information Development:
   Michael Petrone
Director, Publishing Operations/Travel Information:
   Jeff Zimmerman
Director, Manufacturing & Quality: Susan Sears
Director, GIS/Cartography: Jan Coyne
Director, Publishing/GIS Systems &
   Development: Ramin Kalhor
Manager, Business Line Publicity: Justin McNaull

Product Manager: Nancy Jones, CTC
Development Editor: Greg Weekes
Manager, Electronic Media Design:
   Mike McCrary
Art Director: Barbra Natali
Manager, Pre-Press /Photo Services & Product
   Support: Tim Johnson
Photo Researcher: Denise Campbell

Managers, Club Sales: Roberta Hodak and Tina
   Franzzo
Manager, Retail Sales: John Coerper
Manager, Retail Marketing: Laura Hartnett
Travel Services: Linda Marsh, CTC

Published by AAA Publishing, 1000 AAA Drive,
Heathrow, Florida 32746

Text © AAA Publishing 2006
All rights reserved.

Maps © Automobile Association Developments
Limited 1999, 2001, 2002, 2003, 2005

The *AAA Europe TravelBook – The Guide to Premier
Destinations* was created and produced for AAA
Publishing by AA Publishing, Basingstoke,
England.

Written by Des Hannigan, Sally Roy and Nia
Williams
Managing Editor: Sheila Hawkins
Seventh edition verified by Apostrophe S Ltd, Chris
Bagshaw, Lyndsay Bennett, Paula Canal, Dale
Cambre (AAA), Colin Follett, Sylvie Franquet,
Barbara Frye, Mike Gerrard, Tim Jepson, Tim
Locke, Regine Smith-Thyme
Page make-up by Keenes, Andover.

Cover photos
Main photo: Switzerland © Sime/eStock Photo
Spine: Canterbury, England
© Medioimages/imagestate

ISBN-13:   978-1-59508-101-8
ISBN-10:   1-59508-101-1

Cataloging-in-Publication Data is on file with the
Library of Congress.

Color separations by Keenes, Andover.
Printed and bound in Spain by Printer Industria
Grafica S.A., Barcelona.

A02502

View from beneath the Eiffel Tower in Paris, France

FOREWORD

Welcome to the seventh edition of the AAA Europe TravelBook!

If you are thinking about going to Europe, this book will help make your trip truly memorable and enjoyable. Although every traveler has a personal favorite European destination, for this book we've selected places that have special appeal, particularly if you're a first- or second-time visitor. Experience world capitals that have delighted visitors for centuries: the broad 18th-century boulevards, wonderful museums and superb food of Paris; London, where tradition and royal pageantry are juxtaposed with a lively arts scene; Prague's medieval grandeur, vibrantly emerging after decades of suppression; Rome, cradle of one of the world's great civilizations; and Vienna, with a magnificent opera house that is still a focus for world-renowned music.

But not all Europeans reside in big cities. Odense, in Denmark, welcomes visitors to the charming museum that was the birthplace of famed storyteller Hans Christian Andersen. York, in England, has an atmospheric old center, The Shambles, with ancient cobbled streets, leaning half-timbered shops and pubs, and the mighty towers of the grand York Minster cathedral. And for centuries the city of Santiago de Compostela, in Spain, has welcomed Christian pilgrims from the far corners of Europe to its monumental cathedral built around the reputed grave of St. James; pilgrims still come, drawn by the myth and beauty of this holy place.

This book will not only whet your travel appetite with lively text and striking photographs, it also provides a wealth of practical information that will enable both seasoned and novice travelers to get the most out of their trip. Included are tips about what you will need to bring and about getting around once you're there, maps to help you find your way, detailed descriptions of what to see, suggestions for where to stay and eat, and insider advice from specialist authors to increase your enjoyment of the fascinating cultures that make up Europe.

EUROPE TRAVELBOOK™
THE GUIDE TO PREMIER DESTINATIONS

CONTENTS

For conversion charts, see
the inside back cover

Map of Europe

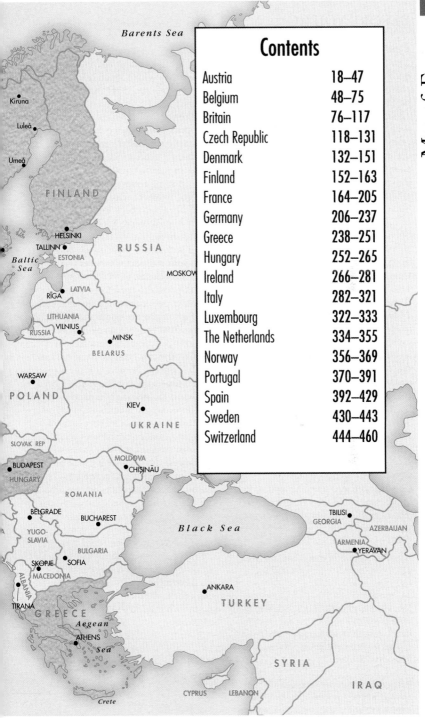

Map of Europe

Contents

Introduction to Europe

BEFORE YOU GO

Passports and Visas

The most important document you'll need to arrange before you travel is a passport. Passport application forms can be obtained at any AAA office. They also are available from many Federal, state or probate courts, many post offices, some libraries and some county and municipal offices authorized to accept passport applications. U.S. Passport Agencies have offices in major cities; check the Yellow Pages (U.S. Government, State Department, Bureau of Consular Affairs, Office of Passport Services) for the one nearest you. You also can request an application form from National Passport Information Center (NPIC) at 1-877-487-2778 or 1-888-874-7793 (TDD/TTY). Automated information is available daily 24 hours; operators for TDD/TTY are available Mon.–Fri. 8–8 (Eastern Time), excluding federal holidays.

Passport information and downloadable application forms are available on the Web site for Passport Information at www.travel.state.gov/passport_services.html. Travel warnings, consular information sheets, public announcements and publications information also can be accessed. Passport and consular/emergency services for Canadian citizens traveling abroad can be accessed at the Department of Foreign Affairs and International Trade Internet site at www.voyage.gc.ca.

The information in this guide has been compiled for U.S. citizens traveling as tourists.

Travelers who are not U.S. citizens, or who are traveling on business, should check with their embassies and tourist offices for information on the countries they wish to visit.

Entry requirements are subject to change at short notice, and travelers are advised to check the current situation before they travel.

Each person traveling must have a passport; apply early, since processing can take several months from the time of application until it arrives. Expedite Service is available for an extra charge. Before departure, make sure your passport is valid for at least six months prior to the expiration date; some European countries require this.

Keep your passport in a safe place, since you'll need it whenever you board an international flight, train or ferry. In some countries, you will be required to leave your passport with the hotel when you check in; this is to satisfy regulations requiring the hotel to register all foreign visitors with local police authorities. In addition, you must show your passport whenever you cash a traveler's check.

Passports also need to be shown whenever national borders are crossed, although in practice border controls have been relaxed between many European Union (E.U.) member countries. In Geneva, the city transportation system crosses national borders and the airport also straddles the border, so you'll need a passport simply to get around.

Photocopy the identification page; leave one copy with a friend in case of emergency, and carry one with you in case your passport is lost or stolen while traveling. If this occurs, inform local police immediately and contact the nearest U.S. embassy or consulate. The U.S. Department of State has a 24-hour traveler's hotline; phone (202) 647-5225.

In addition to a passport, some countries require a visa. Travel visas are not necessary when visiting any of the countries covered in this book, but if you'll be traveling to other nations, check their entry requirements before you leave home. AAA offices have visa information.

AAA and CAA members will want to visit www.aaa.com before setting out on their international travels. Check for merchants who will accept your AAA or CAA membership card in order to obtain member savings at more than 150,000 locations throughout the world. Members visiting their club's www.aaa.com Web site should look for the "Search for Savings" link under the Show Your Card & Save or Member Savings/Benefits sections, and then look for the "International" Search for Savings link.

Travel and Health Insurance

Before departing, make sure you are covered by insurance that will reimburse travel expenses if you need to cancel or cut short your trip due to unforeseen circumstances. You'll also need coverage for property loss or theft, emergency medical and dental treatment, and emergency evacuation if necessary. Before taking out additional insurance, check to see whether your current homeowner or medical coverage already covers you for travel abroad.

If you make a claim, your insurance company will need proof of the incident or expenditure. Keep copies of any police report and related documents, or doctor or hospital bills or statements, to submit with your insurance claim.

Weather and When To Go

The European continent occupies a far more northerly location than its overall moderate climate would suggest. Different factors affect the weather at any given destination. The warming influence of the Gulf Stream affects all countries with an Atlantic coastline, from Spain and Portugal north through the British Isles into Scandinavia. The North and Baltic seas also affect temperatures and precipitation of the coastal areas they border, causing unpredictable weather.

Another definer is altitude, and Europe's great mountain ranges affect local temperatures and rainfall as well. The Pyrenees divide the Iberian Peninsula and France, while the Alps form an immense natural barrier across Austria, Switzerland and northern Italy south into France, where they descend to the Mediterranean Sea at Monaco. This entire region is popular with winter

skiers, while summer visitors can expect clouds, mist and cool temperatures. The Apennines cut down the boot of Italy, also creating somewhat changeable conditions.

Destinations bordering the Mediterranean are ideal for summer vacations, with mostly sunny skies, warm temperatures and little rain. The flip side can be the heat – especially in southern Spain and Greece – so protect yourself from overexposure to the sun and carry drinking water for extended outdoor excursions. Winters in the Mediterranean region are cool and rainy, but temperatures are not usually severe and snow is rare in coastal areas.

Summer also is the main vacation season in central Europe, which has warm, mainly dry summers and cold winters with snow at higher elevations. The weather in spring is generally more unpredictable than in the fall.

The British Isles can have weeks of dry conditions in summer, although it's best to come prepared for rain; a collapsible umbrella should be an essential traveling companion. British winters are rainy, although temperatures are rarely extremely cold. Snow is uncommon except in the higher regions of northern England and Scotland.

Scandinavia has varying weather and overall lower temperatures. Daytime highs in the summer months rarely exceed 75 degrees Fahrenheit, and the coastal locations of Copenhagen, Oslo, Stockholm and Helsinki increase the probability of unsettled conditions. Winters are uniformly severe, with significant snowfall the rule.

European school vacations are a factor in planning when to travel. Schools in most countries are in session from September until early July, making May and June good months to visit.

What To Pack

Electrical appliances will require an adapter that changes the arrangement of the plug prongs, as well as an electrical voltage converter that will allow a normal 110-volt American appliance to take 220- to 240-volt

Introduction to Europe

European current. Two-in-one adapter/converters are available at some hardware stores.

Bring a first-aid kit with bandages, sunblock, insect repellent and over-the-counter remedies for minor ailments. Include written prescriptions for prescription medicines in case you need more or need to show the prescription to customs officials. Tissues will come in handy, as local restrooms in some areas will likely be below U.S. standards. European hotel rooms provide towels but often no washcloth, so pack one in case.

In light of the Sept. 11, 2001 terrorist attacks, check with your airline before including any type of knife.

WHILE YOU ARE THERE

Emergencies
See the Essential Information section, pages 461–537, for information about a specific country.

Health
Take sensible precautions during hot weather. Wear a hat, sunglasses and sunblock, especially if you are on or near the water. Drink plenty of fluids, and remember that alcoholic beverages and the caffeine in coffee, tea and some sodas has a dehydrating effect.

The tap water in northern Europe is generally safe to drink, although its high mineral content can cause minor upsets if you're not used to it. Bottled water, still or carbonated, is inexpensive and widely available. In an area where the tap water is unsafe, avoid ice cubes and salads with ingredients that are likely to have been washed in water.

Pharmacists are a good first source for dealing with minor health problems; a pharmacist will be able to direct you to a doctor if necessary. For advice pertaining to specific topics, see the "Health" subheading under individual countries in Essential Information.

Language
Traveling is always more enjoyable if you can converse a bit in the local language. "Yes," "no," "please" and "thank you," accompanied by a pleasant smile and polite manner, will go far toward oiling social wheels. Refer to the "Useful Words and Phrases" subheading under individual countries in Essential Information for a helpful list.

English is most likely to be spoken in Scandinavia, The Netherlands, Belgium, Luxembourg, Germany, Austria and Switzerland. In Britain and Ireland you may encounter strong regional accents, as well as unfamiliar words and expressions.

To some Europeans – particularly the French and the British – good manners are a social necessity. "Please" and "thank you" should be part of every request in Britain; in France, anyone you don't know personally (including the staff in stores and restaurants) should be addressed as "monsieur" ("sir"), "madame" ("madam") or "mademoiselle" ("miss").

If you're really stuck with communications, remember that hotel receptionists usually speak English, and are invariably helpful and friendly; you can ask them to phone for taxis and arrange for cleaning and similar personal services.

Media
Room televisions in the larger hotels have satellite or cable connections and broadcast BBC channels, the British Sky network or CNN. On the radio you may be able to pick up Voice of America, Radio Canada or BBC broadcasts.

In larger cities, American newspapers (usually previous-day editions) and magazines are widely available; the most common are *USA Today*, the international edition of the *New York Herald Tribune* and *Time* magazine. They can be purchased at airports and central train stations, as well as at newsstands, tobacconists and "stationers," shops that also sell books and stationery.

Money and Valuables
Having some of your funds in local currency is a necessity, but only carry what you'll need for a day or two. If it's lost or stolen you almost certainly won't

get it back, and if you have to convert a large amount back to dollars or to another foreign currency, you may have to pay again for exchange charges. Customs restrictions may apply if you need to carry large amounts of currency.

The euro (€) is the common currency of 12 European Union countries (Austria, Belgium, Finland, France, Germany, Greece, Ireland, Italy, Luxembourg, The Netherlands, Portugal and Spain). For additional information see the "Money" subheading under individual countries in Essential Information.

Currency exchange facilities are widely available in Europe. There are exchange offices at airports and central train stations, in the central business districts in cities, and at seaports and other international border crossing points. They are often open extended hours in summer and during vacations. Most hotel reception desks also will exchange currency. Exchange rates are normally displayed; local newspapers and the international editions of U. S. newspapers also provide the current rate of exchange. A commission may or may not be charged for each transaction. Although any commission is likely to be a little higher at hotels, it may be worth paying extra for the convenience.

Traveler's checks are reliable and safe. Keep a record of the check numbers you redeem, and carry numbers and receipts in a separate place in case you need to produce them in the event of loss. Be prepared to show your passport each time you cash in a check or offer one in payment. If you're going to be spending time in just one or two countries you may want to obtain traveler's checks in the local currency; traveler's checks in euros are recommended if traveling in the euro zone extensively. You can use them for purchases in stores, although you'll still need to show your passport.

Credit cards are an easy and trouble-free method of payment. American Express, MasterCard and VISA are the most widely accepted; check with your credit card company before departure if you have any doubt about its validity abroad. Keep a record of your card number in a separate place, and note the international phone number to report card loss in case yours is misplaced or stolen. You also can get cash advances with your credit card from an ATM, usually at favorable exchange rates.

Leave valuable jewelry at home; ostentatious displays mark you as a prospective target for theft. Make sure your luggage is lockable and labeled both outside and inside. Never leave your bags unattended. Train stations normally provide lockers or check desks where you can leave a heavy bag while sightseeing. If you're traveling by car, keep your doors locked in slow-moving traffic or when driving through busy urban areas, and put everything in the trunk while the car is parked.

If the worst happens and you do have belongings stolen, report the incident to the police immediately and get a written police report or statement to provide to your insurance company as evidence for your claim.

Personal Safety

Most of the rules for personal safety constitute common sense. Keep valuables (passport, money, checks, credit cards) hidden when you're on the move; a money belt or neck purse worn inside clothing is the safest option. Put money in different places so that if one bag is lost you have another source of funds. Fanny packs and pockets are not safe places to carry valuables. Any bag you'll be carrying with you during the day should have a secure fastener, with a sturdy strap that goes over your neck and crosses your body – not simply over the shoulder. This helps ensure that bulkier items (cameras, binoculars, etc.) will be safe from pickpockets and petty thieves in crowded urban areas or on buses or trains.

The big tourist attractions are prime territory for pickpockets, as are buses, trains, subways, markets and airports. Be on guard for people who "accidentally" bump into you, or watch while you use an ATM. In large cities, be on the lookout for gangs of youngsters who create a commotion and then steal bags from tourists while their attention is distracted.

Introduction to Europe

Introduction to Europe

People begging in the street can be quite persistent; walk quickly away without responding or making eye contact. Contact a police officer if anyone becomes particularly aggressive; police on city streets throughout Europe are usually very approachable and often speak a little English. In general, avoid walking alone after dark. In southern European city centers during the summer, however, you'll almost certainly encounter throngs of locals out walking and shopping late into the evening, refreshed by a few hours of afternoon siesta.

Phone Service

You can make international calls from most European telephones; for specific information see "Telephones" under individual countries in the Essential Information section. To place a call to another country, first dial the international code, then the country code, then the area code (minus any initial zero) and the local number. Sometimes you'll need to wait for another dial tone after dialing the international code. In some countries the telecommunications infrastructure is fairly fragile, and it may take two or three tries before you get through.

The easiest and least expensive way to make an international call is to use a calling card. Dialing the appropriate access number (numbers differ according to country) will connect you with an English-speaking operator who can place a collect call or a call credited to your card. To obtain a card and a list of country access numbers, contact your telephone service provider. If you use a pay phone, you may need to insert a coin in the local currency to get an outside line to make the call.

The convenience of making a phone call from your hotel room will be offset by the hefty surcharges tacked onto the bill. It's always less expensive to use the pay phone in the lobby; ask the hotel staff for assistance if you can't figure out how the phone works.

Some cell phones may be adaptable for use in Europe, but the operating frequencies are different; check with your service provider. Fax machines are available in the central business centers of cities and at some hotels. If you can't do without e-mail, there are cybercafés in major cities throughout Europe – handy places to stop for coffee and a bite to eat, as well as using the computers to send e-mail and check your favorite Web sites.

If you're staying in one country for a few days, it may be worthwhile to obtain a local prepaid telephone card, which can be used with phones that accept them. They can normally be purchased at small stores called "tobacconists" that also sell cigarettes, candy, snacks, magazines and sometimes postage stamps.

Travelers with Disabilities

Facilities for disabled visitors in northern and central European countries are generally very good, but old castles, palaces, cathedrals and historic houses may not be adapted for special access. The Mediterranean countries, Czech Republic and Hungary are improving, but if you need help it is advisable to check in advance with local tourist offices. The old central cores of European cities are often difficult to change or adapt to make them suitable for those with special needs. Expect steps and stairways in city centers (some stairways have no handrails), in addition to cobbled and uneven street and sidewalk surfaces.

Almost all of the old buildings in Europe – including those that house hotels and such attractions as museums and castles – are likely to contain stairways, narrow halls and doorways, and other access irregularities. Make certain that accessibility standards meet your requirements when reserving accommodations.

Often hotels will be able to provide a room with adequate access if they know your needs in advance. Call ahead to attractions and restaurants as well to ascertain the nature of their facilities. Motorized carts at airports will whisk you to and from arrival and departure gates.

GETTING AROUND

City Transportation

A good first stop when you arrive at your destination is either a central public transportation information center or the tourist information office (see the Essential Information boxes in the introduction to each featured city). Spend time here and obtain information on how to get around the city, including transportation maps and detailed city maps. You also may be able to purchase travel tickets for public transportation, including those valid for multiple rides or for one or more days; they will save you money and the inconvenience of having to buy a new ticket for every journey.

There are a variety of public transportation options in Europe:

- Subways (metro) are underground trains that travel through tunnels beneath city centers, emerging to ground level in less congested suburban areas, or to cross rivers.
- Private bus companies operate along designated routes in city centers; double-decked buses are common for carrying larger numbers of passengers. Long-distance buses are commonly known as "coaches" in Britain and Ireland.
- Trams are vehicles that travel on rails set into the street surface. They are often powered by overhead electric cables that run along the route. If you are walking or in a car, be especially careful of trams; they always have the right of way, and because they run quietly can appear with little warning.
- Trolley buses run on tires, but are powered by overhead electric cables running above the route. Like trams, they have right of way in traffic and run quietly.
- Funiculars are passenger cars that ascend and descend steep hills or cliffs on a track set into the ground, typically on slopes leading down to a beach but also in some cities, such as Lisbon, Barcelona or Budapest, where there are steep inclines.
- Cable cars are suspended from cables attached to the top of the cars. They are common at ski resorts, and also in some cities.
- Rack railways are a feature in Switzerland, where trains that climb steep mountains connect with a cog system between the rails that provides extra power up the slopes.

In many continental European countries, you buy a travel ticket at a ticket office, booth or ticket machine and validate it by pushing it into a special machine, either at the stop or on the vehicle, which will give the ticket a date and time stamp for the appropriate journey or time period. If you buy a tourist ticket valid for a number of days, you will usually need to validate it only once before you first use it.

Between Cities

Trains Most countries in Europe have a national train system, with trains operating across national borders. Service is generally efficient, although local routes with frequent stops can be slow. If your entire trip is going to be by train it may be worth obtaining a Eurail pass from your travel agent in the United States before you go (note that they are not on sale in Europe). Passes are valid for periods from a few days to three months. In addition, many national rail systems have their own passes for travel within a country; these also are available from travel agents in the United States and Canada, and also in Europe.

Tickets for most trains are available either in advance or just before travel. For special trains (some express trains – for instance, in Spain; overnight sleeper trains; the Orient Express; or the Eurostar trains between Britain, France and Belgium that travel through the tunnel beneath the English Channel) you may need to buy tickets a few days in advance to be sure of getting a seat. This is especially the case during busy vacation times.

Information about main city train stations is in the Essential Information box for each city.

Introduction to Europe

Introduction to Europe

Airlines Most countries have a national airline as well as independent operators that operate internationally, based on hub cities within the country. Additionally, smaller airlines serve smaller destinations, usually functioning within the country. Schedules, fares and availability are subject to frequent change. If you have a specific itinerary in mind, your travel agent is the best place to start for flight information.

For the best choice of flights and prices, reserve your tickets well in advance. Big airports in major cities – Paris, London and Rome, for example – will have the largest choice of flights, but also are the busiest. For this reason it can be a good idea to begin your trip at a smaller, less busy destination.

Ferries Services transport individual passengers as well as cars, and in some cases trains (the cars of the train actually travel on the boat). Ferry companies offering longer-distance journeys of two or three days have very comfortable ships, and they promote these services as "mini-cruises" that can make a relaxing interlude between busy city sightseeing sessions.

Ferries operate regularly in the Scandinavian archipelago and along the Norwegian fjords; among the Scottish islands; between Britain and Ireland, Scandinavia, Germany, The Netherlands, Belgium, France and Spain; and throughout the islands and coastal ports of the Mediterranean countries and islands.

Generally speaking, transfers from ports to city centers are less straightforward than from airports and train stations. If you intend to carry a lot of luggage, it may be advisable to ask tourist information offices about this when planning your trip.

European Customs and Immigration

Each country has its own customs import regulations; see the Essential Information section beginning on page 461. For the purposes of customs and duty-free allowances, the countries of the European Union are considered as one customs area, and there are no limits on goods for personal use when traveling between member countries. However, customs restrictions do apply when traveling between E.U. countries and non-E.U. countries. The E.U. member countries include all the countries in this book, with the exception of Norway and Switzerland.

At the immigration barrier in E.U. countries, travelers are separated into two lanes – one for E.U. citizens and one for non-E.U. citizens. Border controls between E.U. countries are gradually being relaxed. You will probably pass through an immigration desk when arriving in a new country by plane, train or ferry, but road barrier checkpoints within the E.U. have largely disappeared in recent years. There are still border controls in place between the E.U. and the rest of Europe, however.

DRIVING IN EUROPE

European Automobile Clubs

For the benefit of members traveling abroad, AAA maintains reciprocal agreements with motoring clubs in Europe. Presentation of your valid AAA membership card at participating motoring clubs allows you to receive services they provide to their own members. Operating philosophies and

AAA Travel Agencies

AAA Travel Agencies offer various member services to help simplify the logistics of international travel planning, especially for the first-time visitor. They can make airline reservations, book accommodations, set up escorted tours and independent travel packages, offer passport and visa assistance, arrange for car rentals and an official International Driving Permit, and provide fee-free VISA traveler's checks. AAA members also are eligible for discounts on selected hotels and motels and receive exclusive savings on cruising vacations.

facilities differ from country to country, however, so service may not be the same as back home. AAA members will need to visit their local club to obtain information about services that can be expected from a specific European motoring club.

Refer to the Essential Information pages for each country for motoring club contact details, as well as documentation requirements and driving regulations.

Car Rental

If you intend to drive across national borders tell the rental company. This will affect both the rate and the type of insurance documentation required. Some rental agencies may require several days' notice to supply a car available for travel to continental Europe. Most car rental companies in Europe will not rent to an individual under 21.

To rent a car you will need a valid U.S. driver's license and preferably an International Driving Permit, and you will probably be asked to show your passport. Depending on which rental company you use, you may be required to produce an additional credit card or further proof of identity for renting premium or luxury cars.

European cars are generally small and tend to have manual transmissions. Some rental companies offer vehicles equipped with air conditioning. Rates vary, but a AAA travel agent should be able to give you an accurate estimate. Reciprocal arrangements with European motoring clubs may not apply if you are driving a rental car (see the Driving section under Essential Information for each country). Be sure to inquire about local taxes; in France, taxes increase rental rates by up to one-third. Find out exactly what insurance coverage is included, and check whether you need a collision damage waiver (CDW) – you might already be covered through your personal car insurance policy or credit card company. A CDW may not cover certain types of damage; for example, in Greece damage to the

underside of a car caused by a rough road may not be covered.

AAA Travel Agencies can make rental car reservations, provide prepayment arrangements, or reserve a car for you for specified dates and destinations. Rates are generally lower if reservations are made in the United States prior to your departure. They also are guaranteed in U.S. dollars if you prepay; it is recommended that you reserve well in advance. If you plan to travel through several countries, make certain that the rental company has been informed, and that you have the necessary documents.

Hertz Affordable Europe offers discounts to AAA members on guaranteed low, competitive rates with 24-hour emergency roadside assistance, free unlimited mileage, free detailed maps and Computerized Driving Directions, Prestige Collection vehicles, a toll-free Help Line, Instant Return Service, cellular phone rentals, European Driver's Guides and Hertz #1 Club Gold. Hertz operates more than 7,200 locations worldwide in over 150 countries, including 2,000 locations throughout Europe. For reservations contact Hertz at (800) 654-3080, www.aaa.com or a AAA Travel Agency.

Green Card

If you drive a car in Europe you will need a Green Card (sometimes called an International Insurance Certificate) to prove that you have liability insurance. Most car rental agencies will provide this with the vehicle; most companies include it in the rental price.

A Green Card also is advised for motorists taking their own vehicle overseas; for additional information contact your automobile insurer.

International Driving Permit (IDP)

An International Driving Permit is a document containing your photograph and confirming that you hold a valid driver's license in your own country. It

Introduction to Europe

has a standard translation in several languages and is a useful document to carry if you plan to drive in Europe, even if it is not specifically required by the country. The permit is available from AAA Travel Agencies.

Driving Regulations

Driving in busy European cities can be a daunting prospect if you're not used to the road signs, driving habits and local regulations. If you are renting a car, be sure to get as much information about the country's driving conditions from the rental company as possible. They will usually be able to provide a chart of common road signs and an area road map. If you are visiting a city by car, park outside the city center, preferably close to a public transportation link, and proceed to the center by public transportation.

Check parking signs where you leave your car: insure there are no restrictions, that you pay for and display a parking sticker if necessary, and check closing times if you use a multistory parking garage. Because of congestion in city centers, parking regulations are strictly enforced.

If you enter central London by car during the week you will incur a daily congestion charge of £8. Vehicles entering the charging zone (basically all streets within the Inner Ring Road) must be registered; an area license permits drivers to enter and leave the zone an unlimited number of times within a particular day. The daily charge must be paid by 10 p.m. if not already prepaid; between 10 p.m. and midnight it goes up to £10. Payment can be made at pay stations, selected gas stations and retailers displaying the PayPoint logo. The zone charge is in effect Mon.–Fri. 7–6:30. For additional information phone 0845 900 1234; www.cclondon.com.

Specific driving regulations for each country are provided in the Essential Information section. In some European countries, police can levy on-the-spot fines for serious offenses – including speeding and drink-driving.

RETURNING TO THE UNITED STATES

Confirming Return Travel

If you are flying, it is advisable to contact the airport the day before leaving to be sure flight details are unchanged. Some carriers require you to reconfirm flights after an extended stopover of more than a few days; check the information that was supplied with your ticket. Allow plenty of time to get to the airport for check-in and clearing security.

Tax-free Shopping

Some major stores offer "tax-free shopping" to tourists. Although specific procedures differ slightly between countries, this enables you to make purchases and have them either sent to the airport of your departing flight, or directly to your home address. Such shopping saves the (often substantial) sales tax, but these items are still subject to any applicable U.S. import duty, plus postage and handling charges.

U.S. Customs

During your flight or voyage returning to the United States, you will be required to complete a customs declaration form. Returning to the United States you are allowed $800 worth of personal goods and gifts (including items purchased in duty-free shops); keep sales slips and have them ready for inspection. The duty-free exemption can include 100 cigars or 200 cigarettes, as well as one liter of wine, beer or liquor if you are 21 or over. (Tobacco products of Cuban origin are prohibited unless they were acquired in Cuba.) Any purchases in excess of the $800 exemption will be subject to duty. There is no restriction on the importing or exporting of currency.

For more information contact U.S. Customs and Border Protection, 1300 Pennsylvania Ave., N.W. Washington, DC 20229, phone (202) 354-1000 (www.cbp.gov) for a copy of the brochure *Know Before You Go*, which has details on customs requirements.

PREMIER
DESTINATIONS

*"IN whichever country of
Europe one dwells, one
feels that the other
countries are near..."*

From *The American Commonwealth*
by British politician and writer James Bryce

AUSTRIA

"THE country is wonderful. Mountains holding up cups of snow to the fiery sun..."

English novelist George Meredith, praising the Alps in a letter to Frederick A. H. Maxse, July 1861

Opposite: Snow-capped mountains dwarf a village and pastureland in the Leogang area of Austria

Austria

AUSTRIA

Small yet beautiful, Austria has unrivaled Alpine scenery, some of Europe's finest baroque architecture, and a long musical and cultural tradition. The Austrian people also are known for their warmth and hospitality toward visitors. Straddling the center of Europe, the country has exerted a critical influence on the region's history through the centuries, becoming a major player in world politics. Today, despite loss of territory and power after two world wars, Austria retains its status as the crossroads of modern Europe. The grandeur of the mountains draws visitors from all over the world, while the combination of efficiency and charm makes Austria one of Europe's most beguiling tourist destinations.

The Land

Austria is the most mountainous country in Europe, with more than 70 percent of the land occupied by the Alps and Alpine valleys. This section of the eastern Alps is characterized by massive mountain chains with sheer rock faces and jagged ridges broken by deep valleys. The Tyrol region, bordering the Swiss and Italian Alps in western Austria, is renowned for its stunning scenery and is a popular skiing and hiking area. Below the tree line the mountains are heavily forested, giving way to lush Alpine meadows, grazed in summer by gentle-faced cattle and carpeted with vivid wildflowers.

Picturesque villages sit amid the pastures and along the valley bottoms, each with distinctive churches, clusters of traditional shuttered houses and wooden farm buildings. The Danube (Donau) river dominates northeastern

MORE TOP DESTINATIONS IN AUSTRIA

- Baden E2 • Bad Ischl C2
- Eisenstadt E2 • Eisriesenwelt C2
- Graz D2 • Grossglockner Hochalpenstrasse C1 • Hallstatt C2
- Kitzbühel B2 • Maria Saal D1
- Melk D3 • Mondsee C2
- Ötztal A2 • Riegersburg E2
- Salzkammergut C2
- St. Anton A2 • Stein D3
- Wachau D3 • Zillertal B2

AUSTRIA

0   50   100 km

0   50 miles

3

N

GERMANY

2

Bodensee

Bregenz

Dornbirn   Bezau   Reutte   Lermoos   Pertisau   Achensee

A14   Feldkirch   Mittelberg   Schwaz

LIECHTEN-   Bludenz   Baad   INNSBRUCK

STEIN   Zürs   Lech   Ötztal   Igls   Zell am

  Brand   St Anton   Landeck   Oetz   Ziller

           Steinach   Mayrhofe

      Galtür   Sölden   A13

3312m ▲   3774m ▲   Obergurgl

Piz Buin   Wildspitze

SWITZERLAND

1   ITALY

A   B

Austria

Austria, and most of the country's people inhabit the rolling terrain around the river. The flat fields of the Vienna basin are intensely cultivated, producing grain, fruit and vines.

The Habsburg Legacy

Throughout six centuries of Habsburg rule, Austria dominated the politics of much of Europe. The Habsburg Empire spread from Spain to Hungary, with sons and daughters of the ruling families marrying into other European ruling houses and thus furthering its influence. Vienna, with its grandiose architecture, splendidly illustrates Austrian prestige, and the entire country is rich in buildings from the days of the empire.

The Viennese Court sent administrators and army officials into the provinces; they brought along Viennese customs, attitudes and manners, as did the nobility who spent time both in the capital and on their country estates. The high-handed approach of these outsiders throughout the provinces has left a legacy of mistrust of the Viennese still discernible today. Historically, too, because of the terrain, the different areas of Austria were immensely varied, each valley having its own dialect, dress, habits and way of life.

Crossroads of Europe

At the end of World War II, Austria was divided into four zones of occupation, with the Allied powers occupying most of the western half. With economic aid provided by the Marshall Plan after

The architecture and setting of the Old Town make Innsbruck a popular holiday destination

World War II, this area was able to industrialize more efficiently than the Soviet-occupied zone, and the east-west divide continued even after the Second Republic was founded in 1955 and independence was regained.

Present-day Austria shares a boundary with eight other European countries: Germany, Italy, the Czech Republic, Hungary, Slovakia, Slovenia, Switzerland and Lichtenstein. Its 8 million inhabitants live in nine provinces, each with its own very distinctive characteristics.

More than half the working population is employed in the service sector: education, tourism, administration and health. Traditional agriculture only continues thanks to large subsidies, and now employs less than 10 percent of the workforce. The vast majority of Austrians speak German or a German dialect. Austria was only slightly affected by the Protestant Reformation and is still a deeply Catholic country. Its glorious baroque churches are packed for Sunday Mass.

Proud Traditions

Despite sharing a common language, Austrians are very different from their German neighbors – more lighthearted, and generally more relaxed in their approach to life. They see themselves, correctly, as hospitable and cordial, thus defining the term *Gemütlichkeit*. This manifests itself in an easy friendliness to everyone, and it's one of the first things visitors notice. Every region sees itself as the best, and people proudly wear regional dress and enjoy traditional music and festivals. So when you encounter people wearing *Lederhosen* (leather pants) and *Dirndl* (bodiced dresses), it's for their benefit, not yours.

There's an elegance and ease to much Austrian life; cafés buzz with the chatter of people, *Bierkeller* (taverns) are packed with young and old, and streets are full of strolling crowds. Manners are conservative, even old-fashioned; this is a country where children open doors and give up seats for adults, and outside of the cities nearly every stranger is greeted with an amicable *"Grüss Gott."*

Environmental Issues

It's not only the tree-clad mountain slopes and verdant valleys that make Austria green; this is one of the most environmentally aware countries in Europe. Austria banned all nuclear power in the 1970s, and since then its green policy has made giant strides.

Heavy investment in public transportation has dramatically lessened

Austria

the use of cars. This is a huge benefit to visitors, making travel in Austria, with its seamless connections between different forms of public transportation, very easy. Despite the Alpine terrain, Austrians cycle a lot, and every town has bike routes and parks. Recycling is a way of life; there are many different types of garbage cans, each clearly labeled for the appropriate trash.

Sauerkraut and Strudel

Austrians take food seriously, and waiters are genuinely interested to know whether you've enjoyed a meal and alarmingly downcast if you can't cope with the vast portions served. Mealtimes are closer to American schedules than elsewhere, with lunch around noon and dinner any time after 6.

Each region has its own specialties, but the emphasis everywhere is on heavy soups, plenty of meat, *Knödel* (dumplings) and noodles, and cream, cream, cream. The latter appears in sauces, soups, coffee and whipped mounds decorating just about every dessert. Sauerkraut (pickled cabbage) frequently accompanies main courses, along with piles of potatoes, and salads are drenched in creamy dressings.

Austrians indulge their passion for coffee and cakes between meals, and you should certainly sample *Apfelstrudel* (apple strudel) and *Sachertorte*, a wickedly rich chocolate cake oozing apricot jam.

There are many different types of beer, and some excellent wines. You should also try *Schnapps*, a strong fruit or herb-based liqueur, drunk as a digestive aid. Coffee is the national drink, with cafés often serving as many as 20 or more different variations; hot chocolate is good, too. And on the healthy side, there are outstanding fruit and vegetable juices.

Summer and Winter

Austria offers visitors as much in the winter as in the summer. For Europeans, the Austrian Alps have been a favorite skiing destination for many years, with impeccably organized facilities, trails ranging from gentle slopes to world-class black runs, and wonderful après-ski dining and nightlife.

Summer sees the Alpine pastures at their best, and the whole country is crisscrossed with hiking trails through glorious mountain scenery. It's in summer, too, that the cities come alive, with strolling crowds, colorful flowers and a plethora of music and folk festivals. Spring starts late, so it's best to plan a visit in May or later. In early spring and again in autumn, you may experience the dreaded *Föhn* wind in western Austria; this is a fierce, warm, dry wind from the south that is notorious for making people generally tired and grumpy, so be prepared.

The traditional *Loden* jacket and *Dirndl* costume, worn at festival time

Austria

TIMELINE

15 BC to AD 50	Romans establish frontier provinces along the Danube and found legionary fortress of Carnuntum.
500–700	After final withdrawal of Romans, Alamanni and Bavarian tribes settle lower Alpine regions.
966	Austmark, established as a bulwark against attacks from the east, is first referred to as Ostarrichi.
1278	Founding of Habsburg Dynasty, beginning 640 years of power.
1493–1519	Foundations of the Habsburg world empire laid by marriage contracts of Maximilian I.
1699	Conquest of Hungary; Habsburgs gain hereditary right to the Hungarian throne in the male line.
1805–1806	Napoleon defeats the Austrians at Battle of Austerlitz; end of Holy Roman Empire.
1814–15	Congress of Vienna restructures the political map of Europe.
1914	Assassination of heir to Austrian throne at Sarejevo leads to outbreak of World War I; Austria fights on losing side.
1919	Dissolution of Austro-Hungarian monarchy; loss of territories.
1938	Hitler incorporates Austria into the German Reich.
1939–45	World War II; Austrians fight in German army; following defeat, Austria is divided into four zones of occupation.
1955	Full sovereignty and founding of Second Republic; Austria is admitted to the United Nations.
1986	Kurt Waldheim is elected president.
1995	Austria joins European Community.
1999	Austria enters European Monetary Union.

THE LAST OF THE KNIGHTS

Maximilian I ruled from 1493 until 1519; these years saw the establishment of his family, the Habsburgs, as hereditary emperors of the Holy Roman Empire and rulers of Austria and far beyond, a dynasty that continued until 1918. Maximilian, through two strategic marriages, gained control over Burgundy (a region in northern France) and the Low Countries. He married his son into the Spanish royal family, giving the Habsburgs rights over Spain, Naples and Spanish America and thus laying the foundations for the vast empire that was to come. Maximilian reformed the governmental administration, patronized the arts, loved hunting and jousting, and was known as "the last of the knights" who led Austria from the Middle Ages to the bright light of the Renaissance and the empire.

Stop at a sidewalk café on the Graben to absorb the atmosphere of Vienna

SURVIVAL GUIDE

- Always return greetings; hospitality is Austria's most important national characteristic, and people expect a reply to their welcoming *"Grüss Gott,"* meaning "God's greeting."
- For the opera, men should wear a jacket and tie; women, a dress, suit or smart pants.
- When going into churches, remember that it's disrespectful to show bare shoulders or upper arms.
- Take an umbrella; it can rain heavily, anywhere, at any time of year.
- For a day in the mountains, remember that the temperature drops as you gain altitude. Take warm clothes so you can layer, and if you're hiking, wear suitable footwear, and bring water and food.
- Austrians are very litter-conscious and streets are immaculately clean; do your part to leave them that way.
- It's considered polite to stand in line when waiting for a bus or at an attraction, and to defer to the elderly.

- Bedding in Austria consists of a large, puffy feather quilt in a cotton cover. This will be folded on your bed, waiting to be opened up at bedtime.
- Austrians eat and drink with gusto, and spirits as well as the noise level rise during the evening. Drunkenness, however, is considered uncouth.
- All cafés, bars and restaurants have coat hooks and umbrella stands, and it's considered more respectful to leave coats and umbrellas there rather than on your chair.
- It's acceptable to spend up to an hour lingering over one or two drinks in a café.
- Public restrooms are free, numerous and spotless; you'll find them in virtually all public buildings, and you can also use bathrooms in cafés and restaurants.
- Always cross the street at official crossings and wait for the green man signal. It's illegal, though seldom prosecuted, to cross anywhere else.

Vienna

VIENNA

For much of the 20th century, Vienna (Wien) had an air of fading grandeur, a city whose days of imperial glory had truly passed. But in the 1980s Vienna began to redefine itself, and continues to do so. In the last two decades population has increased for the first time since 1919; a vibrant youth culture has emerged; and the imperial architecture of the 18th and 19th centuries has been joined by exciting modern designs, such as the huge museum quarter built on the site of the emperor's former stables. In the 21st century Vienna seems to be shaking off its torpor and styling itself, once again, as a dynamic European cultural center.

Finding Your Way

Between 1857 and 1865 Emperor Franz Josef I had the bastions surrounding Vienna's Old Town (Innere Stadt) demolished, and laid out a vast boulevard known as the Ring. Within the Old Town and the Ring are Vienna's most important sights, including St. Stephen's Cathedral (Stephansdom, see page 32) and the Imperial Palace (Hofburg, see page 29).

It's possible to take in the main sights on foot, but the "Hop on, Hop off" buses are a flexible alternative, allowing you to hop on or off anywhere along their route. There are also trams and underground (U-Bahn) trains running through and around the area. A more expensive option is to hire a horse-drawn carriage (*Fiaker*) at Stephansplatz, Heldenplatz or Albertinaplatz. Be sure to agree on the price and length of trip before you begin your journey.

The Third Man

One of Vienna's favorite parks is the Prater, situated on the former imperial hunting grounds. It was opened to the public in 1766, and its attractions now include racing tracks, a fairground and a Ferris wheel built in 1897. This is where Joseph Cotten and Orson Welles had their confrontation high over the city in the 1949 film *Der dritte Mann (The Third Man)*.

Vienna

An outer ring road, the Gürtel (belt), links the city with major freeways. East of Vienna, the Danube river and the Danube canal cut through some 23 districts, and on the southern outskirts are the Vienna Woods (Wienerwald). Maps showing walking routes through the woods are available from the efficient information center at the corner of Albertinaplatz and Maysedergasse.

Architecture

Wandering Vienna's streets is a treat for lovers of architecture. Styles range from the Gothic pointed arches of St. Stephen's Cathedral and the neo-Gothic arcades of the New City Hall (Neues Rathaus) to the baroque of the 17th and 18th centuries.

Imperial 19th-century majesty is typified in buildings lining the Ring

Vienna

and also in the art nouveau edifices, known here as the "Secession" style because its practitioners seceded from the staid Association of Fine Artists in 1897. They went on to set up their own exhibitions in the Secession Building on Friedrichstrasse.

There also are modern styles, such as the shining glass curves of the 1900 Haas-Haus by Hans Hollein, opposite St. Stephen's; and a postmodern housing block by Friedensreich Hundertwasser, a Hansel-and-Gretel building of colored mosaics, in Kegelgasse.

Viennese Music

Vienna is proud of its long history as a center of classical music, and celebrates with a busy schedule of concerts, balls and café concerts. On the grand end of the scale is a series of annual balls, reaching its peak with February's Opera Ball at the State Opera (Staatsoper).

The city's classical music venues are worth seeing just for their extravagant decoration. The main sights are the State Opera (on Opernring); the

Konzerthaus (on Lothringerstrasse); the Musikverein (at Karlsplatz); and the Imperial Palace's Royal Chapel (Burgkapelle) where the Vienna Boys' Choir still sings at Sunday Mass.

Viennese Shopping

Expect high prices; you can get items of similar quality for up to a third less just over the border in Germany. Clothes are especially expensive – the best options are chain stores such as Humanic, in the mall at Vösendorf on the southern edge of the city (to get there, take the bus or tram from the Oper/Karlsplatz station).

Porcelain and glassware have been produced in Vienna for more than 200 years. Several outlets on Kärntnerstrasse (near the central Stephansplatz) sell good examples, including J & L Lobmeyr (No. 26), which has an exhibition of its early work on the top floor. The Old Town has plenty of window-shopping potential, and stores usually stay open until 7:30 one evening a week (either Thursday or Friday).

ESSENTIAL INFORMATION

TOURIST INFORMATION
Wien Tourismus
(Vienna Tourist Board)
• Albertinaplatz, corner of Maysedergasse (daily 9–7) ☎ 01 24 555 (information and hotel bookings); fax 01 24 555–666; www.info.wien.at

URBAN TRANSPORTATION
Vienna has a network of subway (U-Bahn) lines, trams (Strassenbahn) and buses. U-Bahn lines 1, 2 and 4 meet at central Oper/Karlsplatz. Subways are marked with a U on the city map. A rapid transit railroad, the S-Bahn (Schnellbahn), travels into the city center from the suburbs. Hopper buses 1A, 2A and 3A

stop near major Old Town sights. Pick up transportation maps at the Opern Passage/Karlsplatz U-Bahn information counter (☎ 01 79 09 10-10). Taxis can be ordered: ☎ 01 31 30-0, 01 40 10-0 or 60160.

AIRPORT INFORMATION
Vienna International Airport (☎ 01 7007 22233; 24 hours) is a 20-minute bus ride from the City Air Terminal, in the city center. Shuttle buses run regularly between the two sites (☎ 01 93000 2300) plus from the airport to Südbahnhof and Westbahnhof railroad stations. There also are S-Bahn trains (line 7) and the faster nonstop city airport train CAT (half-hourly) from the airport to the city center.

CLIMATE – average highs and lows for the month

JAN.	FEB.	MAR.	APR.	MAY	JUN.	JUL.	AUG.	SEP.	OCT.	NOV.	DEC.
2°C	3°C	9°C	14°C	19°C	22°C	25°C	24°C	20°C	14°C	7°C	4°C
36°F	37°F	48°F	57°F	66°F	72°F	77°F	75°F	68°F	57°F	45°F	39°F
-3°C	-2°C	2°C	5°C	9°C	13°C	15°C	15°C	12°C	6°C	2°C	-1°C
27°F	28°F	36°F	41°F	48°F	55°F	59°F	59°F	54°F	43°F	36°F	30°F

City Sights

Key to symbols

✚ map coordinates refer to the Vienna map on pages 26–27; sights below are highlighted in yellow on the map.

✉ address or location ☎ telephone number
🕐 opening times Ⓜ nearest subway 🚌 nearest bus or tram route 🍴 restaurant or café on site or nearby 🎟 admission charge: $$$ more than €5, $$ €2–€5, $ less than €2 ⓘ other relevant information

Albertina

✚ C2 ✉ Albertinaplatz 1 ☎ 01 534 83-0 🕐 Daily 10–6 (also Wed. 6–9 p.m.) Ⓜ U-Bahn: Stephansplatz 🚊 Tram D 🍴 Restaurant 🎟 $$$
ⓘ Guided tours Sat. and Sun. at 3:30 p.m.

Housed within the beautiful Hofburg (Imperial Palace), the Albertina is named after its founder, Duke Albert von Sachsen-Teschen (1738–1822), who lived in the palace at the end of the 18th century. The Albertina's collection of over a million drawings, prints and engravings dates from the 14th century and includes exquisite pieces by Raphael, Michelangelo, Goya, Cezanne and studies of children by Rubens. Also here is the world's most important collection of work by Albrecht Dürer, which includes Dürer's masterpieces *Hare* and *Clasped Hands*. An ultramodern study and research center uses a state-of-the-art storage system to protect the museum's invaluable collection.

Hofburg

Kaiserappartements ✚ C2 ✉ Michaelerplatz (entrance: beneath Michaelerkuppel cupola) ☎ 01 533 7570 🕐 Daily 9–5, Jul.–Aug.; 9–4:30, rest of year 🍴 Augustinerkeller Restaurant, see page 540 Ⓜ U-Bahn: Herrengasse, Stephansplatz or Volkstheater 🚌 H2A, 3A; tram D, J, 1, 2, 46, 49 🎟 $$$
Schatzkammer ✉ Schweizerhof ☎ 01 525 240 🕐 Wed.–Mon. 10–6 🍴 Augustinerkeller Restaurant, see page 540 Ⓜ U-Bahn: Herrengasse, Stephansplatz or Volkstheater 🚌 H2A, 3A; tram D, J, 1, 2, 46, 49 🎟 $$$

Blue and gold domes top the magnificent Hofburg (Imperial Palace), which took more than six centuries to build. The original fortress, built in 1275, made way for the Schweizerhof (Swiss Courtyard), whose Schweizertor (Swiss Gate) went up in the 16th century. Other sections were added during the 17th and 18th centuries, including the gorgeously decorated Hofbibliothek (Library) and the Hofreitschule (Riding School), where white Lipizzaner horses are put through their paces for visitors (see page 32). The Kaiserappartements (Imperial Apartments) were built in the 19th century, and new sections were added on as recently as 1913 to create today's enormous complex of 18 wings, 2,600 rooms and 19 courtyards. Many of the Habsburg trappings are on display, including the imperial crowns in the Schatzkammer (Treasuries). The first six

Spanning 600 years of architectural history, the Imperial Palace stands in its own lovely gardens

Neptune's Fountain stands proudly in the formal gardens of the impressive Schönbrunn Palace

rooms of the Kaiserappartements now house the Sisi Museum, dedicated to the life of Empress Sisi.

KIRCHE AM STEINHOF

🚩 Off the map ✉ Baumgartner Höhe 1, Penzing ☎ 01 91060 11204 🕐 Closed for restoration until 2006 🚌 47A, 48A 💵 $$

Huge copper angels guard the portico of the eccentric, domed Kirche am Steinhof (Steinhof Church), built 1904–1907 for people suffering from mental illness. Its white interior is full of light; colored glass, and windows by Secessionist artist Kolo Moser brighten the vault and side altars. Short benches have plenty of space in between so that patients taken ill could be helped out. Running water was provided in the stoop (entranceway) to lessen the risk of infection. A ceiling under the cupola gives the effect of a starry sky.

SCHLOSS BELVEDERE

🚩 D1 ✉ Rennweg 6A (Unteres Belvedere); Prinz-Eugen-Strasse 27 (Oberes Belvedere) ☎ 01 79557 134 🕐 Palace: Tue.–Sun. 10–6. Alpine Gardens (at Oberes Belvedere): daily 10–6; Apr.–Oct. (closed in bad weather) 🍴 Im Palais Schwarzenberg, see

page 540 🚇 Karlsplatz, Stadtpark 🚋 Tram 71 (Unteres Belvedere); bus 13A; tram D, O, 18 (Oberes Belvedere) 💵 $$$ ℹ️ Tours daily at 11 a.m.

The spectacularly baroque Schloss Belvedere (Belvedere Palace) was built for Austrian general and prince Eugene of Savoy, who led his army to many victories over the French. Begun in 1714, building was in two phases: the Unteres Belvedere (Lower Belvedere), where Eugene's military triumphs are celebrated in a ceiling fresco; and the Oberes Belvedere (Upper Belvedere), which housed his collection of paintings and later became the Imperial Picture Gallery. Archduke Franz Ferdinand, whose assassination sparked the events leading to World War I, lived here for 20 years until his death. The Belvedere is now devoted wholly to art, with Austrian baroque paintings on view in the lower palace, and medieval works in the Orangerie (Orangery); the Upper Belvedere has superb 19th- and 20th-century paintings, including *The Kiss* by Gustav Klimt and *Death and the Maiden* by Egon Schiele.

SCHLOSS SCHÖNBRUNN

🚩 A1 ✉ Schönbrunner Schlossstrasse 147 ☎ 01 81113 239 (palace); 01 8773 244 (coach collection); 01 877 9294 (zoo); 01 8775 087 (palm house) 🕐 Palace: daily 8:30–6, Jul.–Aug.; 8:30–5, Apr.–Jun. and Sep.–Oct.; 8:30–4:30, rest of year. Coach collection: daily 9–6, Apr.–Oct.; Tue.–Sun. 10–4, rest of year. Zoo: daily 9–6:30, May–Sep.; 9–6, in Apr.; 9–5:30, Mar. and Oct.; 9–5, in Feb.; 9–4:30, rest of year. Palm house: daily 9:30–5:30, May–Sep.; 9:30–4:30, rest of year 🍴 Tyrolean Restaurant in grounds of zoo 🚇 U4 Schönbrunn 🚌 10A; tram 10, 58, 60 💵 $$$ (palace, zoo and palm house); $$ (coach collection) ℹ️ Audio-guided tours. Concerts ☎ 01 812 50 04

The imposing size and symmetry of the Schloss Schönbrunn (Schönbrunn Palace), the imperial summer getaway, made the point that the Habsburgs were very wealthy and very powerful. There are 1,400 rooms: the original 1695 plan was to show that the Austrians would not be outdone by the French monarchs' glorious palace of Versailles. But the first design was not finished, and between 1744 and 1749 court architect Nikolaus Pacassi produced a new version. He was responsible for the geometric splendor of the long building

Beethoven's house on Probusgasse – he was drawn to the musical city of Vienna when he was only 20

CITY OF COMPOSERS

Many 17th- and 18th-century Habsburg rulers were music lovers and musicians: Leopold I was a composer, Charles VI was a violinist, and Maria Theresa played the double bass. Royal patronage drew some of the world's greatest composers to Vienna, including Beethoven and Brahms; Mozart gave his first public concert at age six in Schönbrunn's Hall of Mirrors.

The waltz is inextricably linked to Vienna thanks to Johann Strauss, the "Waltz King," and every New Year's Day the Vienna Philharmonic Orchestra plays his waltzes to a billion television viewers around the world. A gilded statue of Strauss, affectionately known as "Schoni," with jaunty moustache and playing his violin, stands in City Park (Stadtpark).

In 1498 Emperor Maximilian I engaged 12 young male choristers to sing with the court orchestra. Over the following centuries some of Austria's greatest composers served their apprenticeships with the choir, including Franz Schubert and Joseph Haydn. Schubert and Haydn would have been dressed in full imperial military uniforms, like the rest of the choir. The current naval-style dress wasn't implemented until 1919.

The elaborate and gilded Musikverein was built in the 19th century as a concert venue for the city's Society of the Friends of Music. (It's here that the Vienna Philharmonic performs its New Year concert.) In 1913 the hall was the scene of a brawl between conservatives and radicals of musical taste, at a concert performed by Arnold Schönberg.

Schönberg changed the face of modern musical composition by abandoning the standard eight-tone scale familiar to the Western ear and devising a complex 12-tone system. Together with his former pupils Alban Berg and Anton von Webern, he formed the Second Viennese School of Music and continued to compose according to his new scale, despite the hostile response of the Vienna audience.

Vienna

that overlooks ornamental gardens and fountains. In the park beyond there's a zoo and a glass-and-iron palm house. Inside the palace there is a coach collection and displays of Indian and Persian miniatures, Japanese and Italian art, 18th-century porcelain, and painted landscapes.

SPANISCHE HOFREITSCHULE

✚ D2 ✉ Michaelerplatz 1 ☎ 01 533 9031
🕐 Performance: selected Fri. at 6 p.m., some Sat. and Sun. at 11 a.m., Mar.–Jun. and Sep.–Dec. Training: Tue.–Sat. 10–noon, early Feb.–late Jun., Sep.–Oct. and Dec. Final rehearsal: selected Fri. at 10 a.m.
🚇 U-Bahn: Herrengasse, Stephansplatz or Volkstheater 🚌 48A, 57A; tram D, J, 1, 2, 46, 49 💵 $$$
❓ Check well in advance as performance times vary

In a glittering white arena of the Imperial Palace the white Lipizzaner horses of the Spanische Hofreitschule (Spanish Riding School) strut to the gavotte, quadrille and waltz and show off the leaping, rearing and trotting of the high school (*haute école*) of dressage. Originally the horses were brought from Spain and bred at a 16th-century stud farm at Lipica, Slovenia (hence their name).

Full performances, complete with music and uniformed riders, are booked well in advance, but same-day tickets for the less glamorous morning training sessions or a final rehearsal can be purchased at the visitor center, Michaelerplatz 1, Tue.–Sat. 9–5.

STEPHANSDOM

✚ D3 ✉ Stephansplatz ☎ 01 515 52-3530 🕐 For tourists: daily 9–11:30 and 1–4:30. 🍴 Do & Co Im Haas-Haus, see page 540 🚇 U-Bahn: Stephansplatz
ℹ Guided tours: Mon.–Sat. at 10:30 and 3, Sun. at 3. Catacomb tours: Mon.–Sat. 10–11:30 and 1:30–4:30

Stephansdom (St. Stephen's Cathedral) is an unmistakable landmark, with its black, yellow and green tiled roof and the 446-foot Gothic South Tower, known to locals as "Steffl," or "Little Steve." Relics of earlier churches are incorporated into the building, including the Giant's Door and the Tower of Heathens, supposedly the site of a pagan shrine. Inside, St. Stephen the Martyr is represented on a baroque 17th-century altar painting by Tobias Pock. The catacombs house an ossuary – a storage place for bones – where the remains of plague victims were kept.

UHRENMUSEUM

✚ D3 ✉ Schulhof 2 ☎ 01 5332 265 🕐 Tue.–Sun. 10–6 🚇 U-Bahn: Herrengasse or Stephansplatz
💵 $$ (Free on Sun., and Fri. before noon, except holidays)

In 1917 Vienna's city councilors set up a museum devoted to timepieces through the ages in Obizzi Palace. The little palace was once the home of Count Ernst Rüdiger von Starhemberg, who defended Vienna against the 1683 Turkish siege; it is tucked into a side street by the Am Hof Church. The Uhrenmuseum (Clock Museum) has more than 3,000 fascinating items on display, including an onion clock, a sand clock and an astronomical clock whose hand takes 20,904 years to complete one circuit.

St. Stephen's Cathedral towers above shoppers and sightseers in Stephansplatz

VIENNESE FLAVORS

Coffeehouses and pastry shops (*Konditoreien*) are two pretty good reasons for visiting Vienna. At the turn of the 20th century, artists, musicians and writers gathered in cafés to swap ideas, work, read or just sit, and some of their old haunts are still going strong. Stop by Bräunerhof (Stallburggasse 2, ☎ 01 512 38 93); Central (Herrengasse 14 ☎ 01 533 37 64-26); or the grand old Imperial (Kärtner Ring 16, ☎ 01 501 10-389), in the former city mansion of the Duke of Württemberg. Customers are generally left alone to linger in the grandiose surroundings, sipping one of the many coffee drinks.

A quiet corner to pause and sample Vienna's culinary delights

On average, Austrians drink about 423 pints of coffee a year, and the menu usually offers dozens of varieties. *Mocca* is black coffee; a *Kleiner* or *Grosser Brauner* has a little milk, a *Melange* has more; a *Fiaker* is mocca with rum or brandy; and an *Einspänner* is a mocca with whipped cream. The *café-Konditorei*, or pastry-shop-cum-café, is a showcase for Vienna's pastry makers. The most famous is Demel at Kohlmarkt 14, a must for visitors.

Wine made from the most recent grape harvest is known here as *Heuriger*, and this is also the name for the Viennese taverns that serve it. These *Heurigen* stand in their own vineyards in the Vienna Woods, and serve food – usually roast meat, cheese and salad – to soak up the wine. A small band is likely to be playing rousing folk music, and in summer there are often long tables and benches set outside. A bunch of fir twigs is traditionally hung outside the tavern door to show that it's open.

Viennese cooking is plain, simple and filling. It's collectively known as *Beisl* – a Yiddish word introduced by traditionally Jewish tavern owners. Dishes might include boiled beef (*Tafelspitz*), steak with crispy onions (*Zwiebelrostbraten*), chopped calves' heart and lungs in sauce (*Beuschel*) and – perhaps the best-known export – *Wiener Schnitzel*, a fried veal cutlet coated with egg and breadcrumbs. For dessert the popular choice is *Strudel*, fruit-filled baked dough with raisins and cinnamon (a perfect choice with a Viennese coffee).

INNSBRUCK

Strategically and beautifully situated on the Inn river, in the heart of the Alps, Innsbruck stands at a great European crossroads. The 19th-century construction of the east-west railroad through the Arlberg valley, in combination with the city's historic control of the north-south trade route through the Brenner Pass, placed it firmly on the trans-European map. Today, travelers from across Europe pass this way, and Innsbruck, with its excellent tourist facilities, is well worth more than a brief stop en route.

Innsbruck Through Time

Innsbruck has had a checkered past. By the 12th century a fortified town was growing up beside the bridge over the Inn river, near the site of an old Roman garrison. By the 1360s, when the Habsburgs had acquired the Tyrol region, the settlement had outgrown its original fortifying walls. Under Maximilian I, Emperor of the Germans from 1493 to 1519, Innsbruck was the Habsburg empire's administrative and cultural center.

The next 200 years encompassed a golden age that continued through the reign of Empress Maria Theresia from 1717 to 1780. When Napoleon conquered the Tyrol in the 1790s Innsbruck became part of Bavaria, but was handed back to Austria in 1814. The city became part of Italy following World War I and suffered much damage during World War II. But since then Innsbruck has prospered, and today it is a university city as well as a popular tourist destination.

Exploring Innsbruck

The center of Innsbruck is small, and it's likely your hotel will be within easy walking distance of the historic Old Town (Altstadt), a pedestrianized maze of picturesque streets. Attractions outside the city are served both by regular local buses and special tourist shuttles

A spectacular view across Innsbruck from the Stadtturm, the 187-foot-high Town Tower

Innsbruck

that take you right to where the action is. It's worth buying the Innsbruck Card, which gives you free entry to many museums and other attractions, plus free use of public transportation and four mountain cable-car systems, the latter otherwise very expensive. It's valid for 24, 48 or 72 hours and obtainable at the tourist office.

A Rich Culture

Because of its long history, Innsbruck is richly endowed with some marvelous buildings, churches and museums. The Old Town is a tiny area packed with handsome houses and narrow arcaded streets. Outside this ancient core you'll find splendid Renaissance, baroque and rococo architecture. Many of these fine buildings house Innsbruck's museums, some devoted to history and the arts, others offering insights into such subjects as Tyrolean railroads, bells and hunting. The cathedral and churches are packed with artistic treasures.

Landmarks along the 17th- and 18th-century street, Maria-Theresien-Strasse, include a column topped by a statue of the Virgin (the Annasäule, built 1706), and a resplendent arch, the Triumphpforte, built in 1765. Nowadays, six bridges span the Inn river – originally called the Innbrücke – from which the city gets its name, leading to the riverfront houses of the Mariahilf neighborhood. This area is also home to a botanic garden.

You can stroll beside the river, with mountains towering in the background, to the Hofgarten – a colorful garden first laid out in 1410 but refined by Archduke Ferdinand II in the 16th century. Southeast of the city center, overlooking the Inn valley, is Ferdinand's palace, Schloss Ambras.

Mountain Scenery

Dramatic mountains encircle the city of Innsbruck, their lower slopes scattered with picturesque villages. The surrounding countryside offers year-round opportunities for fresh air and exercise against a backdrop of some of Europe's loveliest upland scenery. The best way to experience this landscape is on foot, and the tourist office arranges daily guided hikes outside the city in the summer; you can even rent boots and a backpack. You can swim, ride, play golf, go rafting or summer skiing, or just enjoy the Alps

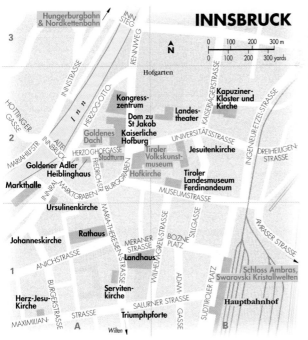

Innsbruck

from the comfort of a sightseeing airplane flight. Winter brings the skiing season, when sports fans flock to Innsbruck from all over the world and the city's architecture is particularly beautiful under a fresh blanket of snow.

Tyrolean Tastes

You can sample a wide range of Austrian and Tyrolean specialties at Innsbruck's restaurants, taverns and cafés (see page 541). The food is good and portions are generous, and you'll find the warm welcome that is so common all over Austria. In the summer, follow dinner with a cable-car ride up the Seegrube mountain to enjoy a drink while watching the sparkling lights of the city far below, or take a lantern-lit hike to a party held in a hillside hut.

Year round you can take in a Tyrolean folklore evening, which includes traditional dances, yodeling and a performance on the alphorn; during the summer, *Schuhplattler* dancers and brass bands perform in the center of town. Innsbruck's casino offers a more sophisticated evening, and there's always a choice of classical music, and often opera.

Woodcarvings and *Christkindl*

Some of Innsbruck's most appealing stores are tucked away in the narrow streets of the Old Town, where you'll find ethnic Austrian souvenirs, clothes, knitwear, antiques and interior design pieces. Woodcarvings make ideal presents, as do dried-flower garlands and baskets – charming decorations for Christmas and Easter – and intricately made national costumes.

Maria-Theresien-Strasse has a range of department, home furnishing and linen stores. Excellent bookstores offer English-language illustrated books about Austria, as well as beautiful calendars that make good gifts. The atmospheric Christmas market (*Christkindlmarkt*) sets up in the Old Town, its stalls brimming with gifts, traditional decorations, cookies and tempting sweetmeats.

ESSENTIAL INFORMATION

TOURIST INFORMATION
Innsbruck Tourismus
(Innsbruck Tourist Board)
• Burggraben 3 ☎ 0512 59850;
fax 0512 59850-107; www.innsbruck.info
• Accommodation reservation (same address)
☎ 0512 562000; fax 0512 562000-220
www.hotel@innsbruck.info

card from the tourist information office and also from some tobacconists. Validate your ticket when boarding the bus or tram, and press the illuminated button near the door to open the doors when you want to get off. Local bus drivers are particularly helpful. There are taxi stands throughout the city center, or you can call a taxi (☎ 0512 1718, 0512 5311).

URBAN TRANSPORTATION
Many of Innsbruck's main sights are grouped together within walking distance in and around the Old Town (Altstadt); use the excellent tram and bus service for venturing farther afield. You can buy a day-use ticket, book of tickets or weekly transportation

AIRPORT INFORMATION
Innsbruck Airport (☎ 0512 22525-0), with domestic and some European flights, is 2 miles west of the city center. Bus F runs throughout the day to the central railroad station and the city center, or you can pick up a taxi outside the terminal.

CLIMATE – average highs and lows for the month

	JAN.	FEB.	MAR.	APR.	MAY	JUN.	JUL.	AUG.	SEP.	OCT.	NOV.	DEC.
	1°C	4°C	10°C	15°C	20°C	23°C	25°C	24°C	20°C	14°C	8°C	2°C
	34°F	39°F	50°F	59°F	68°F	73°F	77°F	75°F	68°F	57°F	46°F	36°F
	-7°C	-4°C	0°C	4°C	8°C	11°C	13°C	12°C	9°C	4°C	0°C	-4°C
	19°F	25°F	32°F	39°F	46°F	52°F	55°F	54°F	48°F	39°F	32°F	25°F

CITY SIGHTS

Key to symbols

☩ map coordinates refer to the Innsbruck map on page 35; sights below are highlighted in yellow on the map.

✉ address or location ☎ telephone number ⏰ opening times Ⓜ nearest subway 🚌 nearest bus or tram route 🍴 restaurant or café on site or nearby 🎫 admission charge: $$$ more than €5, $$ €2–€5, $ less than €2 ℹ️ other relevant information

GOLDENES DACHL

☩ A2 ✉ Herzog-Friedrich-Strasse 15 ☎ 0512 581111 ⏰ Daily 10–6, May–Sep.; Tue.–Sun. 10–5, rest of year 🚌 O, K, L, N; tram 1, 3, 6 🎫 $$

Innsbruck's Goldenes Dachl (Golden Roof) is, in fact, an oriel (bay) window, added onto the front of the previous ducal palace to commemorate Emperor Maximilian I's marriage to Bianca Maria Sforza of Milan in 1493. Beautifully decorated with reliefs of the Emperor, it is roofed with more than 2,700 gilt copper tiles – hence its name. From here, Maximilian watched festivities in the square below. An informative audiovisual show and the "Maximilianeum" museum (behind the Goldenes Dachl) will fill you in on Maximilian's life and times.

HOFKIRCHE

☩ A2 ✉ Universitätsstrasse 2 ☎ 0512 584302 ⏰ Mon.–Sat. 9–5, Sun. 12:30–5 🚌 O, K, L, N; tram 1, 3, 6 🎫 $$

The Hofkirche (Court Church) of Innsbruck is one of Europe's least known but most impressive monuments. Built in the late Gothic style between 1553 and 1563, this three-aisled structure houses the tomb (now empty) of Maximilian I, among the finest existing works of German Renaissance sculpture. Twenty-eight larger-than-life-size bronze statues surround Maximilian's black marble sarcophagus, decorated with 24 reliefs showing scenes from the Emperor's life. These represent Maximilian's ancestors and contemporaries, and were created by the best artists of the time. Albrecht Dürer was responsible for several, including the figure of the legendary King Arthur of England, considered the finest

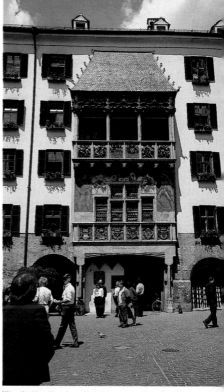

The Golden Roof recalls 15th-century Innsbruck

statue anywhere of a Renaissance knight. Elsewhere in the church you can see bronze saints and busts of Roman emperors, all figures destined for Maximilian's unfinished sarcophagus.

HUNGERBURGBAHN AND NORDKETTENBAHN

Hungerburgbahn ☩ Off the map ✉ Rennweg 41 ☎ 0512 292250 ⏰ Daily 8:10–6:10, Jul.–Sep.; 8:25–5:10, rest of year 🍴 Cafés and restaurants at top and bottom of car 🚌 J, D, E, 4; tram 1 🎫 $$
Nordkettenbahn ☩ Off the map ✉ Höhenstrasse 145 ☎ 0512 293344 ⏰ Daily 8:25–5:30, Jul.–Sep.; 8:40–5, May–Jun.; 9:10–5, Oct.; 8:55–4:30, rest of year (Also every Fri. until 11:30 p.m.) 🍴 Cafés and restaurants at top and bottom of car 🚌 J, N, D, E, 4; tram 1; Hungerburgbahn 🎫 $$$ (reduced fare Fri. after 9:30 p.m.)

These two connecting mountain transportation systems will take you effortlessly up the Nordkette to 6,250-foot Seegrube; from here you can go even higher, to 7,657-foot Hafelekar. The Hungerburgbahn is a steep funicular, built around 1906 to link lower and upper

Ride the funicular for dramatic views of Innsbruck and the surrounding mountains

example of a 16th-century bathroom, complete with sunken copper bath.

STADTTURM

⊞ A2 ⊠ Herzog-Friedrich-Strasse 21 ☎ 0512 5871133 🕐 Daily 10–8, Jun.–Sep.; 10–5, rest of year 🚉 0, L, K, N; tram 1, 3, 6 ✋ $$

For a bird's-eye view of Innsbruck, climb (there's no elevator) the 187-foot-high Stadtturm (Town Tower), built in 1442–1450 as a watchtower. The bulbous cupola was added in the 16th century.

SWAROVSKI KRISTALLWELTEN

⊞ Off the map ⊠ Kristallweltenstrasse 1, Wattens ☎ 05224 51080 🕐 Daily 9–6. Closed second and third week of Nov. 🍴 Restaurant and café 🚉 Bus to Watten every half hour from the Innsbruck railroad station ✋ $$$

One of the Innsbruck area's most visited attractions, Swarovski Kristallwelten (Swarovski Crystal Worlds) in Wattens, 9 miles east of Innsbruck, has to be experienced to be believed. This multi-media theme park centers around the magic of crystal and features moving walls, sculptures and sparkling crystals in underground caverns. You enter through the Giant, a leafy face on the side of a hill with glowing eyes and a water-filled mouth, to experience strange sights and sounds.

TIROLER VOLKSKUNST-MUSEUM

⊞ B2 ⊠ Universitätsstrasse 2 ☎ 0512 584302 🕐 Mon.–Sat. 9–5, Sun. 10–5. Closed holidays 🚉 0, L, K, N; tram 1, 3, 6 ✋ $$; free to all Dec. 24

The appealing Tiroler Volkskunstmuseum (Museum of Tyrolean Folk Art) is housed in a 1553 abbey and is a great introduction to the traditional way of life in the Tyrol. This large museum, with exhibits excellently labeled in English, has fascinating displays on every aspect of rural life, as well as complete Gothic and Renaissance house interiors. Don't miss the models of farmhouses or the charming Christmas nativity scenes, where Jesus' birth is depicted in busy Alpine villages.

Innsbruck; it's a fun ride to a pretty area with pleasant woodland walks and attractive outdoor cafés. From here, the Nordkettenbahn cable car runs up Hungerburg mountain over precipitous slopes to the Seegrube station, with ever-widening views over Innsbruck, the valley and the high Alpine peaks. A wonderful panorama of mountains awaits you at the top.

SCHLOSS AMBRAS

⊞ Off the map ⊠ Schlossstrasse 20 ☎ 01525 24743 🕐 Daily 10–5, Dec.–Oct. 🍴 Castle restaurant and café 🚉 K or tram 3, 6, or special Sightseer from Maria-Theresien-Strasse (Altes Landhaus) ✋ $$$

Schloss Ambras (Ambras Castle) lies outside Innsbruck, a beautiful 16th-century conversion of a medieval castle standing in a landscaped garden above the Inn valley. It was the home of Archduke Ferdinand from 1563 to 1595; an avid collector and patron of the arts, he built the superb Spanish Hall, with its colorful frescoes and beautiful ceiling, and amassed a collection of curiosities. They are displayed in the Wunderkammer (Wonder-room), a sort of early museum that offers great insight into the Renaissance mind. The castle also contains a fine armory and a large portrait gallery dedicated to the imperial Habsburg family, although most visitors find Ferdinand's wife's bathroom far more interesting. It is a perfect and rare

Spectacular descent in the Tyrol – snowboarding is gaining in popularity

WINTER SPORTS IN INNSBRUCK

Innsbruck and its surrounding villages offer superb skiing amid beautiful Alpine landscapes. Winter sports enthusiasts will find something for every taste, and some excellent all-inclusive deals can be arranged through the Innsbruck tourist office.

Skiing

You can ski at spots throughout the Innsbruck area as well as at surrounding resorts such as Kitzbühel and Arlberg-St. Anton. There are some 322 miles of well-maintained downhill runs served by 210 lifts. Every skill level is catered to, from gentle runs of hard-packed snow for families and beginners to extreme slopes and off-run skiing for experts. Special areas are designated for snowboarding and carving, and for the truly tough and experienced back-country skier there are superb high-altitude itineraries.

Cross-country skiing on the downhill runs is very popular in Europe, and 12 different cross-country areas are accessible, offering 186 miles of tracks. Ski and snowboard schools operate daily, and ski guides can be hired on a daily basis. Several areas have snowmaking equipment to supplement early winter snow. Access to the slopes is by a combination of bus, funicular, cable car, chairlifts and surface lifts. Free buses take skiers from the city center to their chosen ski area and collect them at the end of the day; these buses also run to Kitzbühel and St. Anton. Innsbruck's season runs from mid-December to mid-April.

Winter Fun

There are plenty of other activities besides hitting the slopes. With its Olympic facilities, Innsbruck offers skating and curling, or you can take a piloted bobsled ride down the Olympic run. Dog- and horse-drawn sleigh rides give you a chance to appreciate the winter beauty of the mountains, and tobogganing and winter walking provide a gentler pace. Various events are organized throughout the season, culminating on New Year's Day with torchlit celebrations in the Old Town and on the mountains.

i Information on ski packages is available from the tourist information office (✉ Innsbruck Tourismus, A-6021 Innsbruck, Burggraben 3, Austria ☎ 0512 59850; fax 0512 59850-107; www.ski-innsbruck.at)

Salzburg

SALZBURG

The little city of Salzburg, stretching along the Salzach river and tucked beneath Mönchsberg hill, is a delightful combination of medieval, Renaissance and baroque architecture, the birthplace of Wolfgang Amadeus Mozart and the gateway to some of

Austria's most splendid landscapes. Add to this friendly people, a relaxed way of life and one of the world's greatest music festivals, and it's easy to see why Salzburg is popular year-round with tourists. For fans of the movie *The Sound of Music,* there's the added bonus that the city was home to the von Trapp family; movie locations are scattered around the city and are easy to visit.

Mozart's Footsteps

Many visitors simply enjoy Salzburg's beauty, atmosphere and charm, although others come for specific reasons – to study the superb baroque architecture, listen to music or tread in Mozart's footsteps. Others flock here to follow *The Sound of Music* trail, and various tour companies run trips with English guides that take you to sites associated with the film.

For classical music lovers, festivals are the main draw (see page 42); the city is packed during festival season and it's hard to find accommodations. Salzburg's charming cityscape, however, can be enjoyed any time of year. Late spring and autumn are good times to visit, but whenever you come it will probably rain: Salzburg has a reputation for being the country's wettest city.

Getting Your Bearings

Salzburg is an easy city to negotiate. The historic center on both banks of the Salzach river is pedestrianized; you can walk from end to end in roughly half an hour, but you'll want to spend more time enjoying the medieval streets and spacious baroque squares. Most of what you'll want to see is on the left bank, with a few sights across the river.

Tourist offices sell the Salzburg Card, which provides free single admission to all museums and attractions, offers discounts on various services, and provides free access to public transportation. The card is valid for 24, 48 or 72 hours.

Various companies will take you on city tours or farther afield to see the landscape of the Salzkammergut, one of the loveliest parts of Austria. There are fascinating walking tours around Salzburg, concentrating on different aspects of the city. If you just want to sit back and relax, you can take a trip in a horse-drawn carriage (*Fiaker*); pick one up on the Residenzplatz.

Cosmopolitan Cuisine

You'll eat extremely well in Salzburg, which has dozens of restaurants, inns, taverns and cafés where you can enjoy anything from local and regional specialties to Japanese sushi. Traditional cooking is hearty and filling; plates of meat with solid dumplings, soups and spicy *Gulasch* (meat stew). The local specialty is *Salzburger Nockerl* (an egg dessert), and a variety of drinks and open wines (available by the glass) are also offered.

Make a point of lingering an hour or so in one of Salzburg's traditional cafés, which specialize in coffee and cream cakes served in elegant surroundings. Many cafés and restaurants have summertime beer gardens, some in beautiful settings.

Salzburg Souvenirs

Salzburg is filled with tempting stores, many of them lining the Getreidegasse (see page 44) and its surrounding streets, although there's a good cluster on the left bank of the river. The exquisite traditional women's clothes are appealing buys, but keep in mind that what looks lovely here might not look so good back home. Also look for attractive wooden carvings, delicate porcelain and crystal, and bright china and linens, all with an Austrian theme, as well as big European designer names. Don't forget Austria's well-organized tax-free shopping service.

Music and Marionettes

Although classical music is the heart of Salzburg's entertainment scene, it's not the only attraction; concerts take place year-round at venues around the city. Enjoy a traditional dinner in the Festung Hohensalzburg (Hohensalzburg Fortress, see page 43), followed by a Mozart serenade from musicians in period dress. The main festival season runs from late July through August, but there's something happening almost every month, including an autumn jazz festival and fairs in September and the weeks before Christmas. Adults can take in a visit to the city's casino, while children will enjoy watching a performance at the Marionette Theater.

Austrian Cafés

There's no better way to get the feel of the country than by spending an hour or so in a café, a quintessential Austrian experience. Café decor ranges from chandelier-hung baroque splendor to wood-paneled coziness, but the basic elements are always similar: excellent service, a vast range of coffees, and a wide choice of feather-light cream cakes and pastries, all indulged in by well-dressed locals chatting or reading the newspapers. Reading materials are provided by the establishment and hung on wooden poles. Cafés often serve beer and wine, and some offer savory snacks. Many have summertime terraces, the perfect place to write your postcards and rest your feet.

ESSENTIAL INFORMATION

TOURIST INFORMATION
Tourismus Salzburg
(Informationsstellen)
• Mozartplatz 5
☎ 0662 889 87-330; fax 0662 889 8732
• Hauptbahnhof: Bahnsteig 2a
☎ 0662 889 87-340
www.salzburg.info

URBAN TRANSPORTATION
Salzburg's small central core makes it possible to walk to everything you'll want to see. There are, however, good bus and trolley bus services covering the whole city. Buy your ticket before boarding, either at the machines at the main bus stops or from any tobacconist, and remember to validate it as soon as you board the bus. Validation machines are marked "Entwerter." There is no need to punch them again if you change buses. To open the doors

from either outside or inside the bus you must press the illuminated button beside the door. For service information call ☎ 0662 46 60. There are several taxi stands outside the historic center, or you can call Queen's Taxi (☎ 0662 17 15) or Salzburger Funktaxi (☎ 0662 81 11).
If you are driving to Salzburg, do not try to bring your car into the city center, where parking is an enormous problem. There are large, supervised parking lots outside the city where cars can safely be left, then take a shuttle bus service to the city center.

AIRPORT INFORMATION
Salzburg's W. A. Mozart Airport (☎ 0662 85 80-251), with domestic and some European flights, is about 4 miles west of the city center. Bus 2 runs every 15 minutes throughout the day to the railroad station, and there is a taxi stand outside the terminal.

CLIMATE – average highs and lows for the month

JAN.	FEB.	MAR.	APR.	MAY	JUN.	JUL.	AUG.	SEP.	OCT.	NOV.	DEC.
2°C	4°C	10°C	14°C	19°C	22°C	24°C	24°C	20°C	14°C	7°C	2°C
36°F	39°F	50°F	57°F	66°F	72°F	75°F	75°F	68°F	57°F	45°F	36°F
-5°C	-4°C	-2°C	2°C	8°C	12°C	13°C	13°C	9°C	4°C	-2°C	-3°C
23°F	25°F	28°F	36°F	46°F	54°F	55°F	55°F	48°F	39°F	28°F	27°F

CITY SIGHTS

Key to symbols

➕ map coordinates refer to the Salzburg map on page 40; sights below are highlighted in yellow on the map.
✉ address or location ☎ telephone number
🕐 opening times 🚌 nearest bus, tram, or funicular route 🍴 restaurant or café on site or nearby
🎫 admission charge: $$$ more than €5, $$ €2–€5, $ less than €2 ℹ other relevant information

DOM

➕ B2/C2 ✉ Domplatz ☎ Cathedral excavations: 0662 845 295-55; Museum 0662 844 189 🕐 Cathedral excavations: daily 9–5, Jul.–Aug. Museum: Mon.–Sat. 10–5, Sun. 11–6, early May–late Oct. 🚌 5, 6, 51, 55 🎫 Cathedral excavations $; Museum $$ ℹ Guided tours Sat. at 10:30

The ornate facade of the Dom (Cathedral), the first truly Italian-style church to be built north of the Alps, dominates the Domplatz, its four huge marble statues giving an indication of the interior splendors. There's been a cathedral here since the eighth century; today's structure is the third to occupy the site. It was built between 1614 and 1628, badly damaged during World War II, and completely restored by 1959. The huge interior, accommodating 10,000 people, is a riot of stucco, marble and gilding, the simple 14th-century font providing a serene contrast. You can visit the crypt to see the foundations of the medieval cathedral and the remains of the original Roman church, while the museum has superb treasures such as an eighth-century cross.

FESTSPIELHAUS

➕ B2 ✉ Hofstallgasse ☎ 0662 849 097 🕐 Guided tours daily at 9:30, 2 and 3:30, Jul.–Aug.; at 2 and 3:30, Jun. and Sep.; at 2:30, Jan. 7–May 31 and Oct. 1–Dec. 22 🚌 1, 5, 6, 51, 55 🎫 $$ ℹ Entry is only with a guided tour; tour times are subject to change if rehearsals are in progress. Check before you visit

Even if you're not musically inclined, Salzburg's Festspielhäuser (Festival Theaters) are well worth visiting. They stand on the site of the old court stables, the winter riding school that was converted to form the Kleines Festspielhaus (Little Theater). The Grosses Festspielhaus (Large Theater), built in 1960, runs right into Mönchsberg hill;

An architectural delight, the domes of Salzburg nestle beneath a grand mountain backdrop

vast amounts of rock were removed during its construction. The only way to see the theaters, unless you attend a performance, is by guided tour; this will give you a chance to experience the superb acoustics of the 2,000-seat Large Theater, said to be among the best in the world.

FESTUNG HOHENSALZBURG

➕ C1 ✉ Mönchsberg 34 ☎ 0662 842 430-11 🕐 Grounds: daily 9 a.m.–10 p.m., May–Aug.; 9–9, in Sep.; 9–5, rest of year. Interior: daily 9–7, May–Sep.; 9–5:30, rest of year. Rainer Museum: daily same hours as interior, May 1 to mid-Oct. only 🍴 Café and restaurant (see pages 42 and 542) in fortress 🚌 Festungsbahn funicular daily 9 a.m.–10 p.m. and later for concerts, May–Aug.; 9–9, in Sep.; 9–5, rest of year 🎫 Reduced combination ticket $$$

The massive Festung Hohensalzburg (Hohensalzburg Fortress) dominates Salzburg from Mönchsberg hill. This fortress was built, altered and extended between 1077 and 1681 by Salzburg's ruling archbishops. Walk up or take the funicular to admire the views before joining one of the guided tours, the only way to visit the interior. You'll see winding passages and ornate state rooms, including the Golden Room with its gilded tracery, and the Golden Hall, with a superb gold and blue coffered ceiling. The Rainer Museum displays instruments of medieval torture, weapons and coats of arms.

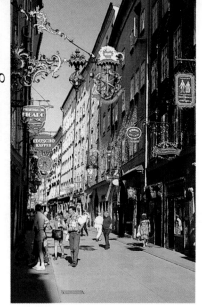

Medieval Getreidegasse, with its attractive
buildings and enticing stores

FRANZISKANERKIRCHE

➕ B2 ✉ Franziskanergasse 5 🕐 Daily 6:30
a.m.–7:30 p.m. 🚌 5, 6, 51, 55

A few steps from the cathedral stands the
Franziskanerkirche (Franciscan Church),
a peaceful and lofty building dedicated to
the Virgin that was Salzburg's parish
church until 1635. The nave, with its
Romanesque details, is the oldest part, its
dimness set off by the airy Gothic choir,
built in the 15th century. Be sure to go
behind the altar to admire the ring of
baroque chapels that encircle it.

GETREIDEGASSE

➕ B3 ✉ Getreidegasse 🚌 5, 6, 51, 55

The medieval street known as the
Getreidegasse runs through the center of
old Salzburg and is lined with stores, each
with a distinctive wrought-iron sign
hanging above. Most of the houses date
from the 15th through the 18th centuries
and were built by prosperous burghers for
their businesses and families. Passages run
through the buildings to connect with
picturesque courtyards and squares; these
are called *Durchhäuser*, meaning "through
the houses." Crowds throng the street and
its continuation, the Judengasse, and
there's no better place to soak up
Salzburg's unique atmosphere.

HAUS DER NATUR

➕ B3 ✉ Museumsplatz 5 ☎ 0662 842 653 🕐 Daily
9–5 🍴 Café in museum 🚌 10, 49, 60, 80, 95 💵 $$

A few hours in Salzburg's Haus der Natur
(Natural History Museum) provides a
splendid antidote to an excess of fine
architecture and Mozart. Popular with
families, the museum's more than 90 rooms
house a wide range of scientific and nature
displays, including a reptile zoo, European
animal exhibits and an excellent aquarium
complete with great white sharks. Children
of all ages will enjoy the Space Research
Hall, with its dioramas, models and mock-
up of a future space city.

MIRABELLGARTEN

➕ B4 ✉ Mirabellplatz 🕐 Daily 6:30 a.m.–dusk
🚌 1, 5, 6, 51, 55

The beautiful Mirabellgarten (Mirabell
Garden) spreads around the Schloss
Mirabell (Mirabell Castle), built in 1606
by Archbishop Wolf Dietrich as a home
for his mistress, Salome Alt. The terraces,
gardens, lawns and flower beds around the
house are a splendid example of baroque
garden design, where trees, shrubs and
flowers contrast with statues and
fountains to create a truly civilized
landscape. Concerts are held in the castle's
Marble Hall, one of the loveliest places to
hear Mozart's music.

MOZARTS GEBURTSHAUS

➕ B2 ✉ Getreidegasse 9 ☎ 0662 844 313
🕐 Daily 9–7, Jul.–Aug.; 9–6, rest of year 🍴 Café on
ground floor of museum 🚌 5, 6, 51, 55 💵 $$$
ℹ Last admission 30 minutes before closing

Wolfgang Amadeus Mozart was born in a
modest middle-class apartment in the
heart of Salzburg on Jan. 27, 1756. These
rooms are among Salzburg's most visited
sights, a place of pilgrimage for music
lovers from all over the world. Climb the
stairs to enter the Mozarts Geburtshaus
(Mozart's Birthplace), today a simple
museum containing family portraits and
mementos of the composer, including his
first violin. The next-door flat has been
filled with period furniture to give an idea
of the appearance of 18th-century living

MOZART AND THE SALZBURG FESTIVAL

Although Mozart spent much of his adult life in Vienna, his name is inextricably linked with his birthplace, Salzburg. Considered by many to be the world's greatest composer, Mozart's spiritual legacy to his native city is one of the world's greatest music festivals, the Salzburg Festival, and a year-round program of musical events.

Austrian musicians, this music festival attracts audiences and renowned performers from all over the world. Its main venues are the Festival Theaters complex (see page 43), but performances are held in buildings all over the city. The program always includes Mozart operas and orchestral works, but many other composers are featured, as well as plays – in particular *Everyman*, which is traditionally performed outside in the Domplatz.

If you want to attend the festival it is essential to book far ahead; reservations start in December, when you should also reserve your accommodations.

Mozart

Wolfgang Amadeus Mozart was born in Salzburg in 1756, the son of a respected court musician, himself a fine violinist whose treatise on violin technique is still respected. The boy soon showed signs of genius, playing a variety of instruments by sight and ear and starting to compose at an early age. Mozart's father touted his talented son all around the European courts, keeping a stern eye on his behavior, spending and morals, and thus storing up trouble for the pair's future relationship.

Eventually the small-town atmosphere of Salzburg, with its reliance on the bishops for employment, proved too stifling, and Mozart moved to Vienna, where he married Constanze. He composed prodigiously and was capable of writing scores as if by divine dictation, while chatting to his friends. Unfortunately, Mozart's genius did not extend to managing his finances; weighed down by money worries and stress, he died in 1791 and was buried in a pauper's grave.

The Salzburg Festival

The Salzburg Festival is held annually during the last week of July and most of August. Established in 1920 by Max Reinhardt, Richard Strauss and other

Salzburg Ticket Service ✉ Salzburg Information, Mozartplatz 5, A-5020 Salzburg, Austria ☎ 0662 840 310; fax 0662 842 476; www.salzburgticket.com

Mozart's Birthplace, on the third-floor apartment in Getreidegasse

Salzburg

quarters, where each room opens from its adjoining room and communal wooden balconies overlook a courtyard. One floor down, you can study stage sets and costumes from festival productions of Mozart's works while listening to his sublime music.

MOZART-WOHNHAUS

✚ B3 ✉ Makartplatz 8 ☎ 0662 874 227-40
🕐 Daily 9–7, Jul.–Aug.; 9–6, rest of year 🚌 15, 27,
51 🚋 $$$ ℹ Guided and self-guiding tours; last
admission 90 minutes before closing

In 1773 the Mozart family left their modest flat in Getreidegasse and moved across the river to Makartplatz to occupy a far more spacious and elegant apartment, now the Mozart-Wohnhaus (Mozart's House). The building was badly damaged in World War II and was finally renovated and reopened for the 240th anniversary of Mozart's birth in 1996. The result is a superb state-of-the-art museum with evocative displays of Mozart memorabilia.

A true picture of the composer emerges – a man who loved games and jokes, who had an earthy sense of humor and a difficult relationship with his father. Here are scribbled letters, musical manuscripts, instruments and books, all brought to life through an English-language commentary. Two rooms are devoted to audiovisual programs about Mozart's early life and his travels through Europe, which, given 18th-century roads, were impressive.

RESIDENZ

✚ B2–C2 ✉ Residenzplatz 1 ☎ Palace: 0662 8042-
2690. Art Gallery: 0662 840 451 🕐 Palace: daily 10–5
(times differ around Easter). Art Gallery: Tue.–Sun.
10–5, also occasional Mon. Closed 3 weeks in Nov.
and Dec. 24 🚌 5, 6, 49, 51, 55 🚋 Palace $$$; Art
Gallery $$$; reduced combination ticket $$$ ℹ Self-
guiding tours of Palace

The Residenzplatz is the triumphant architectural landmark of the inner city, splendidly adorned with an ebullient baroque fountain (the largest in central Europe) complete with horses and dolphins and topped by a conch-blowing triton. Opposite rises the Residenz (Archbishop's Palace), built 1595–1619 around three

courtyards. See the impressive baroque interiors on an audio-guided tour that leads through rooms of ornate decoration with stucco, gilding, marble and astonishing painted ceilings. Nothing gives a better sense of the scale of grandeur and luxury enjoyed by Salzburg's prince bishops. The palace also contains an art gallery. Concerts are held in the state rooms.

SALZBURGER MUSEUM CAROLINO AUGUSTEUM

✚ B3 ✉ Main Building: Museumsplatz 1. Toy
Museum: Bürgerspitalgasse 2 ☎ Main Building:
0662 620 808-200. Toy Museum: 0662 620 808-300
🕐 Main Building: daily 9–5 (also Thu. 5–8). Toy
Museum: daily 9–5 🚌 10, 49, 60, 80, 95 🚋 $$ (each
museum) ℹ Reduced combination ticket available
for both buildings

Salzburg's primary museum has collections housed in two buildings. The Haupthaus (Main Building) covers classical antiquities and art; the Spielzeugmuseum und Musikinstrumente (Toy Museum and Musical Instruments) has a charming collection of toys, dolls and musical instruments. You can trace Salzburg's history from Roman times and admire some lovely 17th-century paneled rooms. Among the highlights is a beautiful Celtic ewer. The toys and dolls, some 250 years old, include train sets and puppet theaters.

STIFTSKIRCHE ST. PETER

✚ B2 ✉ St. Peter-Bezirk 1 ☎ 0662 844 576
🕐 Church: daily 8–noon and 2:30–6:30. Catacombs:
Tue.–Sun. 10:30–5, May–Sep.; Wed.–Thu. 10:30–3:30,
Fri.–Sun. 10:30–4, rest of year 🍴 Stiftskeller
St.Peter, see page 542 🚌 1, 5, 6, 51 ,55
🚋 Catacombs $

The lovely Stiftskirche St. Peter (St. Peter's Church) was built between 1131 and 1147 but altered to its present rococo appearance in the 18th century. A simple Romanesque west door leads into a sumptuous interior, resplendent with 16 marble altars in its side chapels and decorated with green and pink molding and golden cherubs. See the monument to Mozart's beloved sister Nannerl before leaving to explore the charming old Friedhof (cemetery), with its flower-bedecked graves and monuments.

Salzburg

A DAY IN SALZBURG

Although several companies offer a variety of tours in and around Salzburg, the city is small enough to find your way around easily, so it makes sense to plan your own day's sightseeing.

A Mozart Morning

After a hearty Austrian breakfast, spend the morning concentrating on Wolfgang Amadeus Mozart, Salzburg's most famous son. His father, employed as a musician in the city, lived in a house on Getreidegasse, where Mozart was born in 1756. After visiting the house and its museum you may be ready for a cup of coffee; head for the Café Tomaselli in the Alter Markt. It was here that Mozart's widow came with her second husband to write the composer's biography in 1820.

Next, cross the Staatsbrücke and walk along the river to Mozart's House (Mozart-Wohnhaus) on Makartplatz, a far grander house where Mozart lived between 1773 and 1780 in a spacious apartment. Nearby you'll find the Mozarteum, the music university that holds the Mozart archives. The hut on the grounds is the Little Magic Flute House (Zauberflötenhäuschen) which once stood in Vienna. Here, Mozart composed the opera in less than five months.

An Afternoon in the Altstadt

Back across the river, have lunch and then spend the afternoon exploring the Old Town (Altstadt). Most sights are clustered around the trio of lovely squares known as the Residenzplatz, the Domplatz and the Mozartplatz. Behind the cathedral (Dom, see page 43), take the funicular up to the fortress of Hohensalzburg (see page 43).

After this, visit the fine Museum Carolino Augusteum. En route, stop at the Pferdeschwemme (literally, "horse-swim"), a frescoed fountain-cum-pool where horses once were led down sloping ramps to be washed. Leave time to enjoy the stores along Getreidegasse and in the alleys leading off it, where you'll find every imaginable Austrian souvenir.

A Salzburg Evening

No Salzburg visit would be complete without some music; many visitors enjoy special Mozart evenings, with dinner followed by a performance of the composer's works played by costumed musicians. Then wander back through the atmospheric streets to your hotel with music ringing in your ears. For the walk route, see the city map on page 40.

Take a *Fiaker* (horse-drawn carriage) for a leisurely view of old Salzburg

Breathtaking in evening light, Salzburg's medieval fortress towers over the city

BELGIUM

"THE buildings, streets, squares, all are picturesque; the houses, green, blue, pink, yellow, with richest ornaments..."

From English poet Dorothy Wordsworth's *Journal*, July 14, 1820

Opposite: The Carpet of Flowers festival takes place biennially in Brussels' Grand' Place

BELGIUM

Belgium is a young country in terms of "old" Europe. Its name derives from a prehistoric tribe, the Belgae, but there is no racial or cultural link with such a distant past. The country has been in the melting pot of European history for centuries and only achieved true national identity in 1830. Yet nowhere else on the Continent will you be so close to such a powerful sense of European history.

Influential Neighbors

The Belgium of today is a nation born out of a divided Europe, a remarkable survivor in spite of the differences in politics, territory and language that remain within its own borders. Too often it is seen as the administrative focus of the European Union, a country preoccupied with international politics and commerce. Geographically, it is tiny (about the size of Maryland) relative to the size of Europe's larger nations. The Netherlands lies to the north; Germany to the east; France to the south; and Luxembourg, an independent Grand Duchy linked historically to Belgium, adjoins it on the southeast.

The northwestern coastline of Belgium faces Britain across the narrow neck of the English Channel. The influences and interests of all of these countries have impacted on Belgium and, in the case of France and the Netherlands, have radically shaped the country's north–south linguistic and cultural divide.

Landscape of History

Apart from the canals in the north, Belgium has no outstanding landscape

features that define it in the way that Norway is defined by its fjords, Greece by its islands, Switzerland by its Alps or Britain by its surrounding seas. Yet Belgium has a very special, very powerful identity expressed through historic cities and a peerless artistic legacy. You will be seduced by medieval Bruges and old Brussels; feel a sense of history in Ghent, Antwerp and regional cities such as Leuven and Mechelen; and be enchanted by the castles in the

MORE TOP DESTINATIONS IN BELGIUM

- Alden Biesen D3
- Antwerpen C4
- Damme A4 • Kasteel Ooidonk B3
- Knokke-Heist A4 • Kortrijk A3
- Leuven C3 • Mechelen C3
- Oudenaarde B3
- La Roche-en-Ardenne D2
- Villers-la-Ville C3 • Ypres A3

Belgium

Ardennes region. The dazzling works of art of early Flemish Masters and medieval painters will fascinate you: prepare yourself for Jan van Eyck, Hans Memling and Peter Paul Rubens, as well as the Brueghels, Anthony van Dyck and Jacob Jordaens.

Belgium is about the landscape of history rather than of scenery. Yet outside the cities and towns lies a quietly charming countryside of fruitful farms, serene waterways and flower-filled meadows. On the immediate outskirts of Brussels is the Forêt de Soignes, a superb beech forest that is an oasis of peace. In the Haspengouw region to the west of Brussels are several historic castles, such as the stately Gaasbeek with its formal gardens and the 13th-century, moated Alden Biesen. A more somber yet compelling aspect of Belgium is enshrined in the poem *In Flanders Fields* by John McCrae (1872–1918). Throughout Europe's turbulent history

BELGIUM

a water park, Aqualibi, adjacent; just outside Bruges, at Boudewijnpark, is Europe's largest dolphinarium.

Exploring Belgium

Public transportation in Belgium is universally efficient, but the railroad network is by far the best way to travel. It is well integrated with systems in neighboring countries, and trains are frequent. Inter-city trains are fast and comfortable; local trains tend to be slower, and you may feel that some of the older equipment seems a little spartan and drab. Overall, however, the high standards that distinguish rail travel throughout northern Europe prevail. City transportation systems are also well run. Trams are a northern European institution, and the larger cities in Belgium have good tram and bus services. Brussels and Antwerp have well organized subway systems that visitors will find useful.

Renting a car will give you independence, but driving in Belgium can be a challenge due mainly to the small size of the country and, in part, to its congested urban nature. The road system is excellent, but because distances between built-up areas can be short, you are frequently faced with busy intersections. Traffic in Brussels and in the larger cities is hectic, and navigation can be complicated for visitors because road signs are in French and Flemish. Out on the road, along the east–west dividing line between French-speaking and Flemish-speaking Belgium, destination names on road signs change suddenly between French and Flemish.

Diverse Foods

Food in Belgium is often characterized as being French in quality and German in quantity. The reality is more subtle. Wallonian cuisine shares the French penchant for wine-based sauces, but

Dominating the surrounding park, the Atomium has become a symbol of Brussels

this northwestern corner of the Continent has seen conflict, none so bitter as World War I. Towns such as Mons and Ypres still resonate with memories, and you will find many memorials and graves in the now-healed landscape.

Beaches, Woodlands and Parks

Along Belgium's relatively short 60-mile coastline there are attractive sand dunes, beaches and resorts, lively towns such as Oostende, and exclusive and stylish places like De Haan or Knokke-Heist. And though there may be no dramatic mountains, the southern provinces of Namur and Liège embrace the hill country of the Ardennes, a varied and pleasant landscape of woods, river valleys and soft moorland where you can walk or enjoy bicycle rides around Dinant and Rochefort.

For gardens and floral displays, try the National Botanical Garden at Meise, near Brussels. If theme parks appeal to you, Belgium has a variety of venues to thrill children and adults alike. At Wavre, near Brussels, is Six Flags Belgium, a huge theme park with

Scene of one of the most famous battles in history, Waterloo lies 12 miles south of Brussels

traditional Belgian cuisine focuses particularly on beef and pork, and specializes in seafood in the west and game in the Ardennes.

In most good hotels you will find the generous buffet breakfasts that are an international staple, comprising a variety of cereals, cheeses and hams, along with fish and smoked meats. For lunch and dinner, be adventurous. Try *maatjes*, marinated raw herring swallowed whole, but not quite the raw experience it seems. Or settle for *mosselen*, Belgian mussels in a variety of tangy sauces. For a truly filling meal, try *waterzooi*, a traditional Flemish stew of fresh vegetables with rabbit, chicken or fish, or *paling in 't groen*, freshwater eels in a green herb sauce. And do not miss Ardennes pâté or the region's excellent smoked ham.

In spring look for asparagus with a butter-based sauce, chopped boiled egg and chopped ham. This goes nicely with one of Belgium's many excellent beers, which tend to be rich, mellow and smooth. In the Flemish and the Liège regions of Belgium the specialty is *jenever*, a grain spirit.

For those with a sweet tooth, Belgium's famous *chocolatiers* will be irresistible. The specialties are individually made pralines with liqueur or cream fillings, and truffles with the utterly indulgent ingredients of butter, cream and sugar. *Gaufres*, tasty waffles, are a Belgian treat that you can buy from street vendors.

Traditional Courtesy

Throughout Belgium, visitors will find the local people unfailingly helpful. This is a conservative country with a strongly Roman Catholic religious tradition, factors that make people courteous yet reserved. The language divide (see page 54) lends a certain rivalry to relations between Flemings and Walloons, yet such cultural diversity seems to make most Belgians amenable to and interested in visitors. The people may seem busy and preoccupied, but they will respond politely and matter-of-factly if you ask for advice or information about their country, which is, after all, a distillation of the most significant aspects of old and new Europe.

Belgium

TIMELINE

57 BC	Romans in northern Europe conquer Iron Age Belgae tribe territory, part of land now occupied by present-day Belgium.
AD 751	Carolingian Dynasty is formed; during reign of Charlemagne, Holy Roman Emperor, the Low Countries prosper.
993	King Baudouin I dies, and his brother, Albert II, becomes king.
1419	Central government established at Bruges; the city becomes a center of the cloth trade and a focus of early Flemish painters.
1519	Charles V of Spain is crowned Holy Roman Emperor; the Netherlands comes under Spanish control.
1581	The Netherlands divides into United Provinces of the Netherlands and Spanish Netherlands (Belgium).
1713	War of Spanish Succession ends; Austria controls Belgium.
1815	Congress of Vienna; Belgium and the United Provinces of the Netherlands form the Kingdom of the Netherlands, ruled from the Hague by the Dutch William of Orange.
1839	Belgian independence recognized by the (Dutch) Netherlands.
1914–18	Most of Belgium is occupied by Germany.
1940–44	Belgium again occupied by Germany.
1957	European Economic Community (now the European Union) establishes its headquarters in Brussels.
1967	NATO sets up headquarters in Brussels.
1992	Belgium signs the Maastricht Treaty, establishing the European Union.
2002	Belgium adopts the euro as its official currency.

LANGUAGE DIVIDE

There is a dramatic linguistic divide between north and south Belgium, a legacy of the country's formation from a southern French-influenced area and a northern Flemish-influenced area. In northern Belgium the dominant language is Flemish, a Germanic language similar to Dutch. In southern Belgium, in the area known as Wallonia, the prevailing language is a French dialect. Brussels lies within the Flemish half of Belgium and is officially bilingual, but within the city French is the dominant language.

Be careful in associating Flemish too closely with Dutch. Brugeans (residents of Bruges) will tell you that theirs is a far subtler language, with more lyrical twists and turns. And Ghentenaars (residents of Ghent) will tell you that they speak better Flemish than Brugeans; if you visit more remote rural districts you will find even more robust regional differences.

SURVIVAL GUIDE

- Flemish and French are both spoken in Brussels, where even street signs are in both languages. You can try out your French in Brussels and Wallonia and your Flemish in Ghent, Bruges and in the north; but to use either language in the wrong area may elicit a frosty reaction. Many Belgians speak English to a greater or lesser degree, and this is often the wisest option, particularly in Brussels.

- You will usually find that the Flemish and French proper names have similarities; for example, Bruges is Bruges (French) and Brugge (Flemish), Louvain is Louvain (French) and Leuven (Flemish). But there are problematic differences. For example, Ghent is Gand (French) but Gent (Flemish), and Mechelen is Malines (French) but Mechelen (Flemish). If in doubt, especially when checking train or bus destinations, confirm the destination with an English-speaking official.

- There are a few public restrooms in Belgian cities, but they are often not clean. Railroad and bus stations, restaurants and the bigger cafés have public bathrooms with attendants. You are expected to pay about 20 to 50 cents to use restrooms.

- In restaurants, the *menu* usually signifies the dish of the day. If you want to choose from a selection of dishes, ask for the *kaart* (Flemish) or the *carte* (French).

- In the rue des Bouchers area of Brussels, you may find that prominently displayed *menus* at reasonable prices become suddenly replaced as soon as you are seated. You may be repeatedly offered house specialties at inflated prices. If this is

Sample one of the 400 Belgian beers at a sidewalk café in the historic Grand' Place

not what you want, move on to another restaurant.

- For a quick snack, there are numerous fast-food outlets, stalls and, in large shopping precincts, café counter service. Apart from the universal hamburgers and french fries, there is usually a big selection of *broodjes*, baguettes crammed with mouthwatering fillings. Seasoned and smoked sausages are sold from street vendors in the northern areas of Belgium. *Gaufres*, tasty, vanilla-flavored waffles, are another treat, bought fresh from street stalls and spread with jam.

- Beer brewing is a Belgian specialty, and there are hundreds of different Belgian brews. Try a *bière* with your meal at a restaurant. It is perfectly in keeping with the cuisine, which incorporates beer in many dishes. The best Belgian beers can be as distinctive as wine.

Brussels

BRUSSELS

Brussels (Brussel or Bruxelles) takes most people by surprise. The city's name is so closely associated with the modern trappings of the European Union (E.U.) that for many it is synonymous with modern high-rise buildings and the world of suited bureaucrats. The real Brussels has a far more colorful and resonant life. It is an exciting, modern city, yet rich in beautiful medieval and art nouveau buildings, outstanding museums and galleries, and a cultural life vibrantly international in character.

Life in the City

You may feel intimidated at first by the hectic pace of the busy streets, but Brussels is genuine "old Europe" at heart – open, friendly and welcoming. Life between the busy boulevards is engagingly relaxed. There is a wonderful

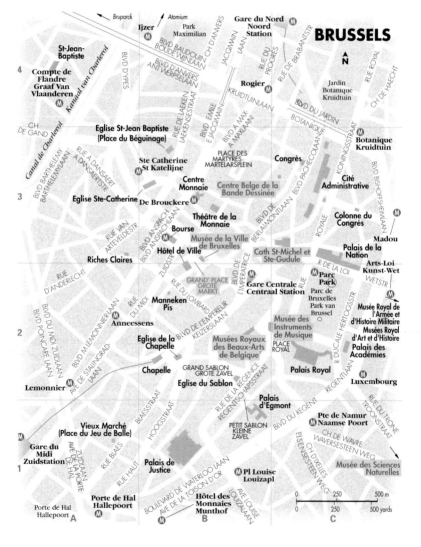

variety about Brussels, a sense of its being several urban "villages" within a whole.

The heart of the city lies within a barrier of encircling main roads known as the *petit ring*. You should be able to reach the inner city's finest features easily, and you should have no difficulty finding your way around; another option is to join one of the many guided tours. For areas outside the *petit ring* use the city's subway system, one of the easiest ways of getting around greater Brussels.

Medieval Townscape

Historic Brussels is celebrated by the breathtaking Grand' Place (Grote Markt, see pages 59 and 61), the best-preserved medieval townscape in Europe. North of here you will find the rue des Bouchers area, where narrow cobbled streets are lined with competing restaurants more reminiscent of Mediterranean cities. Nearby are the elegant, glass-roofed shopping malls of the 19th-century Galeries St.-Hubert.

A short distance west of Grand' Place, along rue au Beurre, is the massive neoclassical Bourse, the city's stock exchange, its front facing busy boulevard Anspach. Nearby is rue Neuve, a lively shopping street. Head west from boulevard Anspach and discover Brussels' very old heartland of place St.-Géry, with its covered market,

and place Ste.-Cathérine and place du Béguinage, old cobbled squares with slightly worn but still splendid baroque churches. Between St.-Géry and Ste.-Cathérine lies rue Antoine Dansaert, a street featuring chic clothing stores.

Sightseeing and Shopping

Outside the center there are other atmospheric and stylish areas: Le Sablon, near the southern edge of the *petit ring*, is convenient to the Royal Fine Arts Museums of Belgium (Musées Royaux des Beaux-Arts de Belgique, see page 60). The leafy place de Grand Sablon is the center of Brussels' antique trade, and it has some fine restaurants and antiques shops. Just south of Le Sablon is the busy and fashionable shopping street of avenue Louise, at the heart of the upscale area of Ixelles/Elsene. This is where many of the trendy shops and restaurants are.

There is so much to see in Brussels that you'll need to use your time efficiently to visit as many of the superb attractions as possible. Branch out beyond the *petit ring* to places like Heysel, 4 miles north of Grand' Place. Here stands the Atomium (due to reopen in January 2006), a vast model of a metal crystal, its steel spheres gleaming in the sun. At its foot the popular Mini-Europe presents scaled-down versions of Europe's most famous buildings. Visit the Parc du Cinquantenaire, Leopold II's 1880 celebration of the Golden Jubilee of the Belgian State. The park has a

Petit Julien

South of Grand' Place on rue du Chêne (reached via rue Charles-Buls and Stoofstraat) stands the famous *Manneken-Pis*, a bronze fountain statuette of a naked little boy happily urinating. *Petit Julien*, as he is properly called, dates from 1619 and has long been an irreverent and endearing symbol of "carefree" Brussels.

Banners fly at a colorful Belgian pageant

Cuisine and Culture

Make sure you enjoy classic Brussels cuisine at superb gourmet restaurants such as Comme Chez Soi (see page 543); or try a less pricey local *geuze* or *kriek* beer in any one of the café bars in and around Grand' Place and St. Géry. Sample Brussels' mussels, of course, but also enjoy *anguilles au vert*, freshwater eels in sauce, or *waterzooi*, fish or chicken stew with vegetables and creamy sauce, and spoil yourself with Belgian chocolate.

Enjoy great music in the superb national opera house, Théâtre de la Monnaie, or in one of the lively rock and jazz venues. There also are colorful street theaters, annual festivals and puppet theater events for kids.

central avenue, named after John F. Kennedy, that leads to a triumphal arch linking monumental halls. Several major museums are located here.

ESSENTIAL INFORMATION

TOURIST INFORMATION BRUSSELS
• Belgian Tourist Information Office 63 rue du Marché aux Herbes ☎ 02 504 0390; fax 02 504 0270; www.visitbelgium.com
• Hôtel de Ville, Grand' Place (Grote Markt) ☎ 02 513 8940; fax 02 514 4538
• Hall d'arrivées (arrivals hall) Brussels International Airport
• Hall TGV/Thalys/Eurostar, Gare du Midi/Zuidstation (South Station)

blue background. Brussels has subways, buses and an underground tram system (same ticket for all), as well as taxis. The subway lines have stations located near major attractions. For information on buses in Brussels call ☎ 070 220200; www.delijn.be or for trams and metro ☎ 02 515 2000; www.stib.be. Licensed, metered taxis can be hailed in the street or from a taxi stand at Grand' Place and at Gare Centrale; rates double when traveling outside the city. Call Taxi Bleues ☎ 02 268 0000.

URBAN TRANSPORTATION
Brussels has three main railroad stations: the Gare du Nord/Noordstation (Brussels North), Gare Centrale/Centraal Station (Brussels Central) and Gare du Midi/ Zuidstation (Brussels South). Eurostar service from London's Waterloo train station (2 hours, 45 minutes) arrives at Brussels South, as does the TGV/Thalys train (1 hour, 25 minutes) from Paris. For rail information call ☎ 02 528 2828. There are metro (subway) stops at all three stations. Subway stations are marked on the map as "M" and are identified at entrances by a white letter "M" on a

AIRPORT INFORMATION
Brussels International Airport is located at Zaventem, 8 miles northeast of the city. There is an Airport City Express train that runs to/from all of Brussels' main stations at 20-minute intervals (journey time 20 minutes), daily 5:30 a.m.–midnight. from the airport and 5:40 a.m.–11:10 p.m. from the city. There is a tourist information office in the arrivals hall (daily 8 a.m.–9 p.m.). Accommodations can be reserved here, and you can obtain information about Brussels and northern Belgium. For flight information call ☎ 0900 70000 (daily 7 a.m.–10 p.m.; toll call); www.brusselsairport.be.

CLIMATE – average highs and lows for the month

JAN.	FEB.	MAR.	APR.	MAY	JUN.	JUL.	AUG.	SEP.	OCT.	NOV.	DEC.
4°C	6°C	10°C	13°C	18°C	22°C	22°C	22°C	20°C	15°C	9°C	5°C
39°F	43°F	50°F	55°F	64°F	72°F	72°F	72°F	68°F	59°F	48°F	41°F
-1°C	0°C	2°C	5°C	8°C	11°C	12°C	12°C	10°C	7°C	3°C	0°C
30°F	32°F	36°F	41°F	46°F	52°F	54°F	54°F	50°F	45°F	37°F	32°F

CITY SIGHTS

Key to symbols

⊞ map coordinates refer to the Brussels map on page 56; sights below are highlighted in yellow on the map. ⊠ address or location ☎ telephone number ◷ opening times Ⓜ nearest subway 🚌 nearest bus or tram route 🍴 restaurant or café on site or nearby 💷 admission charge: $$$ more than €5, $$ €3–€5, $ less than €3 ℹ other relevant information

CATHÉDRALE ST.-MICHEL ET STE.-GUDULE

⊞ C3 ⊠ place Ste.-Gudule ☎ 02 217 8345 or 02 219 6834 (crypt) ◷ Cathedral: daily 8–6. Treasure Museum: Mon.–Fri. 10–12:30 and 2–5, Sat. 10–12:30 and 2–3:30, Sun. 2–5. Crypt: by appointment only Ⓜ Gare Centrale 💷 Cathedral free; Museum $, Crypt $

Work began on the Cathédrale St.-Michel et Ste.-Gudule (Cathedral of St. Michael and St. Gudula) in the 13th century. Architecturally, the building is a lesson in the various forms of Brabantine Gothic that evolved over the 300 years it took to complete the work. Inside the church, baroque style is lavishly celebrated by giant figures of the Apostles, while Renaissance influence shines from the exceptional stained glass of the 16th-century west window. The Romanesque remains of an 11th-century church can be seen down in the crypt.

CENTRE BELGE DE LA BANDE DESSINÉE

⊞ C3 ⊠ rue des Sables 20 ☎ 02 219 1980 ◷ Tue.–Sun. 10–6 (reading room: Tue.–Thu. noon–5, Fri. and Sun. noon–6, Sat. 10–6) 🍴 Museum restaurant Ⓜ Gare Centrale or Rogier 🚌 tram 92, 93, 94 💷 $$$ (includes reading room)

The Centre Belge de la Bande Dessinée (Belgian Center for Comic Strip Art) encompasses a dazzling celebration of the strip cartoon, the *bande dessinée*. The strip cartoon is closely associated with Belgium,

Guild House, Grand' Place

not least in the shape of Hergé's (Georges Rémi's) famous character Tin Tin, created in 1929. The form has strong design links to art nou-veau and it is an added delight that the museum building was designed in 1906 as a fabric shop by Victor Horta, the most distinguished of art nouveau architects.

GRAND' PLACE

⊞ B2–B3 ⊠ Grand' Place 🍴 La Taverne du Passage, see page 543 Ⓜ Bourse, Gare Centrale 🚌 Tram 23, 52, 56, 81 ℹ Audio tour can be rented from the tourist office ($$). Summer concerts; biennial (even years) Carpet of Flowers in mid-Aug.; annual medieval festival, the *Ommegang*, in early Jul.; Planting of the Maytree procession on Aug. 9

Brussels' Grand' Place (also see page 61), a UNESCO World Heritage Site, is an extravaganza of medieval architecture, as displayed in the numerous guild houses that complement the Place's awesome Hôtel de Ville (Town Hall, see page 61). Opposite stands the splendid La Maison du Roi (The King's House), which houses the City of Brussels Museum. At No. 10 La Maison de l'Arbre d'Or (the Golden Tree) is the Museum of Belgian Beer Brewers. At No. 13 is the Cacao and Chocolate Museum.

Tin Tin's space rocket from *Destination Moon*

MUSÉE HORTA

✚ Off the map ✉ rue Américaine 23–25 ☎ 02 543
0490 🕐 Tue.–Sun. 2–5:30 🚌 54, 60; tram 81, 82, 91, 92
✋ $$

This is not just a museum; it is the house
that Belgium's famed art nouveau
architect, Victor Horta, built for himself.
The art nouveau style, popular in Europe
and especially in Brussels between 1893
and 1918, typically used industrial
materials like steel and iron in the visible
parts of houses. The decoration was
inspired by nature, and decorative
mosaics, or sgraffito, were often used.
The house also features a beautiful glass
ceiling. This can be seen to good effect
from the stairwell, which is flooded with
natural light and topped by an area
known as the lantern. At the top of
another level in the house is a glass-
roofed conservatory housing a winter
garden. The furniture perfectly fits the
overall style, and the attention to detail
is stunning.

MUSÉE DES INSTRUMENTS DE MUSIQUE

✚ B2 ✉ rue Montagne de la Cour 2 ☎ 02 545
0130 🕐 Tue.–Fri. 9–5, Sat.–Sun. 10–5 🍴 Rooftop
restaurant 🚇 Merode or Schuman 🚉 Gare
Centrale 🚌 27, 38, 60, 71, 95, 96; tram 92, 93, 94
✋ $$; free to all first Mon. of the month after 1 p.m.

The Musée des Instruments de Musique
(Museum of Musical Instruments) is
housed in a former department store, one
of the most striking art nouveau buildings
in Brussels. The Old England store was
built in 1898 by architect Paul Saintenoy
in glass and steel. The airy and beautifully
adapted space holds one of the largest and
most varied collections of musical
instruments in the world. The collection
includes more than 7,000 items from
around the world, dating from antiquity
to the 20th century. Visitors are given
infrared headphones that allow them to
hear the sound of the musical instruments
on display.

On the top floor is a pleasant tearoom
-restaurant with a terrace commanding
great views over the place Royale and
Bussels.

MUSÉE DE LA VILLE DE BRUXELLES

✚ B3 ✉ rue du Poivre 1 (entrance from Grand'
Place) ☎ 02 279 4350 🕐 Tue.–Fri. 10–5, Sat.–Sun.
10–1 🚇 Bourse, De Brouckère or Gare Centrale
🚌 Tram 23, 52, 55, 56, 81 ✋ $

The Musée de la Ville de Bruxelles (City
of Brussels Museum) is a local celebration
of Brussels and has very little information
in English. It deserves a visit, however, for
its porcelain, pottery and tapestry
collections as well as its paintings,
including Pieter Brueghel the Elder's
splendid *The Marriage Procession*.

The museum is located on Grand'
Place in the handsome building known as
a Maison du Roi (the King's House). On
the top floor there is an entertaining
display of some of the 654 costumes
comprising the "wardrobe" of the
Manneken-Pis (see box page 57), which
have been donated by heads of state and
others since 1698.

MUSÉES ROYAUX DES BEAUX-ARTS DE BELGIQUE

✚ B2 ✉ Museum of Ancient Art: rue de la Régence
3; Museum of Modern Art: place Royal 1–2 ☎ 02 508
3211 🕐 Tue.–Sun. 10–5 🍴 Museum café 🚉 Gare
Centrale or Parc 🚌 27, 38, 60, 71, 95, 96; tram 92, 93,
94 ✋ $$ (includes both museums, free after 1 p.m.
first Wed. of each month)

The Musées Royaux des Beaux-Arts de
Belgique (Royal Fine Arts Museums of
Belgium) are housed in the former court of
Charles Lorraine. The entrance fee
includes both the Musée d'Art Ancien
(Museum of Ancient Art) and the Musée
d'Art Moderne (Museum of Modern Art);
the two are linked by a stretch of
underground passage.

The complex contains one of the most
comprehensive and exciting collections of
paintings in Europe, covering the 14th
century to the present day. Pieter Brueghel,
Pablo Picasso and Auguste Rodin are only
a few of the leading names of Flemish and
Western art represented here.

You'll enjoy the museum even more if
you rent the audio program for the Ancient
Art section (it's not available for the superb
Modern Art section).

GRAND' PLACE

The late medieval Grand' Place, or Grote Markt in Flemish, is one of the most glorious sights of urban Europe. A first glimpse of Grand' Place, whether by day or floodlit at night, should stop even the most jaded in their tracks. These are buildings that seem wrought from nature, yet their symmetry and elegance is ravishing. Any debate about the competing merits of traditional or Modernist architecture melts away in the face of such adventurous style. Even the bars on the ground-floor premises pale into insignificance.

What you see in Grand' Place today are some of the finest examples of Flemish Renaissance and Gothic architecture, most of which are 17th-century replacements of older wooden-framed guild houses. The originals were

Grandiose gables on the guild houses in Grand' Place recall the wealth of their creators

destroyed in 1695 during a devastating bombardment of Brussels by the troops of a spiteful Louis XIV. The citizens rebuilt the heart of their city in a bold act of defiance. The Town Hall (Hôtel de Ville) is the focus of Grand' Place (guided tours only, call 02 279 4355 for tour times). Its soaring tower dominates the Brussels skyline; its carved facade is crammed with dukes, duchesses, monks, saints and sinners.

The guild houses, which make up the other sides of the square, are named and represented by gilded statues, bas-reliefs, motifs and classical orders. They are a riot of exquisite forms and symbols. Look for No. 7, Le Renard (The Fox), the Haberdasher's guild house; and No. 6, Le Cornet (the Horn), the guild house of the Boatmen.

Opposite the Town Hall is La Maison du Roi (The King's House), known also as the Broodhuis (Bread House) and home to the City of Brussels Museum (Musée de la Ville de Bruxelles, see page 60). On the east side of Grand' Place is the restored facade of the house of the Dukes of Brabant, six individual houses united by the cool elegance of a single Renaissance facade.

Finally, in the southeast corner to the left of the Town Hall, is No. 10, L'Arbre d'Or (The Golden Tree). This is the headquarters of the Brewers' Guild, the Knights of the Mash Staff, and also houses a Brewery Museum. Next door is Le Cygne (The Swan), complete with a graceful swan motif and rounding off the magnificent Grand' Place with a flourish.

Bruges

BRUGES

In Bruges (Brugge), the survival of exquisite medieval buildings provides a vivid architectural record of 16th-century Europe. Yet that survival is the result of a commercial decline that lasted for nearly 400 years. By the early 16th century, the Zwin river, which linked Bruges and its elegant canals to the North Sea, could not be navigated because of silting; the successful cloth trade had declined, and local and foreign traders moved their businesses to the flourishing port of Antwerp. There was no wealth with which to modernize the venerable townscape. We can thank the rough handling of history for a city that delights with the completeness of its medieval street plan and its ornate buildings, now a UNESCO World Heritage Site.

Finding Your Way

If you arrive at Bruges railroad station you will find a small tourist information office on Stationsplein, outside the

"The Venice of the north" – take a leisurely boat trip on one of Bruges' canals

station to the right. It is only a short bus ride from Stationsplein to Bruges' grand central square, the Markt (see page 66), a good place to start sightseeing. A short walk along Breydelstraat, the street that begins at the southeast corner of the Markt, is the Burg (see pages 68–69), the historic heart of Bruges.

You can enjoy Bruges through guided tours, on foot, by bicycle, by bus or by canal boat (daily Mar.–Nov., weekends only rest of year). Trips on the famous horse-drawn carriages and trams of Bruges are enjoyable but expensive. The city is to explore on your own, however.

A City of Canals

A few steps south of the Burg, along the narrow alley known as Blind Donkey Street (Blinde Ezelstraat), will bring you to the colonnaded fish market, a lively scene Tuesday to Saturday mornings. From here proceed right to Huidenvettersplein, and then along Rosary Quay (Rozenhoedkaai) to the Dijver, a pretty, tree-lined walkway running alongside the canal. There is a splendid complex of museum buildings here, including the Groeningemuseum, with a wonderful collection of paintings by the Flemish Primitives, the Gruuthusemuseum, which displays decorative arts, and the Church of Our

Lady (Onze-Lieve-Vrouwekerk, see page 67).

Across the road from the church is the Hans Hemling Museum which occupies a medieval hospital. Nearby is the old Beguinage (Begynhof), and from there you can explore the city's ancient walls and gates. The many canals lend Bruges the nickname "the Venice of the north."

Cosmopolitan Tastes

Amid this historical splendor, modern Bruges has its own delights. The city's social life is centered on the Market Square and 't Zand, both lined with sidewalk cafés and bars. There is a Wednesday Market on the first square and a larger Saturday Market on the

Lace

Bruges has long been famous for its lace. Since the 16th century, lace makers here specialized in bobbin lace, a method that used weaving and plaiting with thread-loaded bobbins, with the threads pinned to the pattern. In Italy, they made needlepoint lace, a method of embroidering with buttonhole and other stitches.

Intricate work of the lace maker on Wollestraat

You will find every type of international restaurant, but try Belgian specialties such as *kalfsblanket*, veal ragout, or *lapin à la gueuze*, rabbit cooked in *gueuze* beer, or in winter, *hutsepot*, a hotpot of vegetables with lamb.

Lace, Chocolate and Music

If you like lace, do not miss the Gruuthuse lace shop on the Dijver for authentic work, or the many lace shops on Wollestraat, the street running south from the Markt. For antiques and craft shops, Mariastraat running south from Simon Stevinplein on Steenstraat is the place; and for mouthwatering *chocolatier*, try the local favorite, Speghelaere at Ezelstraat 92, where all the chocolates and marzipan are made on the premises.

latter. Between 't Zand and the Markt lie Bruges' busiest streets, Noordzandstraat and Zuidzandstraat, the latter leading into the shopping area of Steenstraat, with connecting squares and narrow streets harboring cafés and bistros. Eating out in Bruges is a diner's delight.

At night, Bruges lights up spectacularly; the buildings in the Markt and elsewhere are illuminated. Find out what's happening at Cultuurcentrum in St. Jakobsstraat, a venue for theater and music, or catch one of the summer concerts in the open-air stage on the Burg.

ESSENTIAL INFORMATION

TOURIST INFORMATION
Toerisme Brugge (Bruges Tourism)
• Burg 11 ☎ 050 448 686; fax 050 448 600; www.brugge.be
• Stationsplein, Bruges railroad station (contact details same as above)

URBAN TRANSPORTATION
Bruges railroad station lies just over a mile southwest of the Markt. The station is small, well kept and has standard facilities. For information call ☎ 050 302.424. There is also an efficient bus service that caters to the city and its environs (call ☎ 050 353 143 for information). If you'd prefer to take a taxi, cab stands are at the Markt (☎ 050 334 444) and at Stationsplein (☎ 050 384 660).

AIRPORT INFORMATION
Bruges does not have an airport; the nearest one is Brussels International Airport at Zaventem (see page 58). For flight information call ☎ 0900 70000 (daily 7 a.m.– 10 p.m.; toll call). Train connections for Bruges are made at Brussels' Nord/Noord (North), Centrale/Centraal (Central) and Midi/Zuid (South) stations.

CLIMATE – average highs and lows for the month

JAN.	FEB.	MAR.	APR.	MAY	JUN.	JUL.	AUG.	SEP.	OCT.	NOV.	DEC.
5°C	6°C	8°C	11°C	15°C	18°C	19°C	20°C	18°C	15°C	10°C	6°C
41°F	43°F	46°F	52°F	59°F	64°F	66°F	68°F	64°F	59°F	50°F	43°F
1°C	2°C	3°C	5°C	9°C	11°C	12°C	12°C	11°C	8°C	4°C	2°C
34°F	36°F	37°F	41°F	48°F	52°F	54°F	54°F	52°F	46°F	39°F	36°F

Bruges

CITY SIGHTS

Key to symbols

⊞ map coordinates refer to the Bruges map on page 62; sights below are highlighted in yellow on the map.

☒ address or location ☎ telephone number
⏰ opening times ▣ nearest bus route
🍴 restaurant or café on site or nearby
🍷 admission charge: $$$ more than €5, $$
€3–€5, $ less than €3 ⓘ other relevant information

BASILIEK VAN HET HEILIG BLOED

⊞ B2 ☒ Burg 10 ☎ 050 336 792 ⏰ Daily 9:30–noon and 2–6, Apr.–Sep.; 10–noon and 2–4 (except Wed. afternoon), rest of year 🍴 Breydel-Deconinck, see page 543 ▣ All buses to market 🍷 Chapels free; Museum $

The Basiliek van het Heilig Bloed (Basilica of the Holy Blood, see also pages 68–69) has been a place of pilgrimage for many centuries. The basilica consists of two chapels; the lower St. Basil's Chapel, which displays a Romanesque style, and the upper 15th-century Gothic Style chapel with the famous Relic of the Holy Blood. In the Middle Ages, this vial, containing two drops of holy blood, was considered one of the holiest relics in Europe. It is still exhibited every Friday.

BEGIJNHOF

⊞ B1 ☒ Wyngaardstraat ☎ 050 360 140 ⏰ Beguinage: daily sunrise–sunset. Beguine's House: Mon.–Fri. 10–noon and 1:45–5:30 (also 5:30–6 p.m. Jul.–Aug.), Sat 10–noon, Mar.–Nov.; Tue. 10:45–noon and 1:45–3:30, Wed.–Thu. 1:45–4:15, Sat. 10–noon, rest of year ▣ 1 🍷 Beguinage and church free; Beguine's House $

The Begijnhof (Beguinage) complex, a wonderful testimony to a more sedate, spiritual age, has retained its tranquil atmosphere. It was founded in 1245 to accommodate pious single women, many of them lace makers, who lived reclusive lives. These inhabitants, known as Beguines, abandoned the complex in the 1920s, but Benedictine nuns later settled in the Beguinage and still live here today. The 17th-century cottages surround a peaceful square. You can visit the Begijnhuisje (Beguine's House), a museum house that has old-style furnishings and a delightful little cloister. The Begijnhof Church of St. Elizabeth has a simple grace.

BELFORT

⊞ B2 ☒ Markt ☎ 050 448 711 ⏰ Tue.–Sun. 9:30–5 ▣ 1–10, 13, 15, 16 🍷 $$$ ⓘ Check with the tourist office for carillon recitals

Bruges' famous medieval Belfort (Belfry) dominates the Markt. You can reach the top of the 289-foot tower by climbing the 366 steps. Ascending it is a challenge but every step will be memorable. You may marvel at the vast number of bricks and the tons of mortar holding everything together, including the 27 tons that the 47-bell carillon weighs. Just below the belfry is the chamber containing the clock mechanism and copper carillon drum. The bells ring out at each

Springtime at the Begijnhof – a haven of peace and serenity

A detail from *The King Drinks* by Jacob Jordaens (1593–1678) on display in the Groeningemuseum

quarter hour. You have time to watch the ingenious system whir and click into life, like some great mechanical beast, before the final short climb to the belfry to enjoy the melodic, and surprisingly muted, peals and take in the stunning view.

GROENINGEMUSEUM

✚ B2 ✉ Dijver 12 ☎ 050 448 743 🕐 Tue.–Sun. 9:30–5 🍴 Den Dijver, see page 543 🚻 1 💷 $$$ (includes audio guide)

The Groeningemuseum is housed in a former Augustinian monastery on the Dijver and contains Bruges' superb civic collection of 15th- to 20th-century Flemish, Dutch and Belgian paintings. There are exceptional works here, including Jan van Eyck's *The Madonna with Canon Joris van der Paele*, the works of Pieter Pourbus and Hans Memling, and *The Last Judgement* by Hieronymus Bosch, a painting that demands close attention.

HUISBROUWERIJ DE HALVE MAAN "STRAFFE HENDRIK"

✚ B1 ✉ Walplein 26 ☎ 050 332 697 🕐 Guided tours daily 11–4, Apr.–Sep.; 11–3, rest of year 🚻 1 💷 $$ (includes a drink)

For relief from Bruges' cultural and artistic delights, step into the Huisbrouwerij de Halve Maan "Straffe Hendrik" (The Half Moon "Strong Henry" Brewery), where the local Strong Henry beer has been brewed since 1546 (the present building dates from 1856). Even the air of the brewery is so aromatic that it might make your head spin, although a visit to the roof will clear it. There is a guided tour of the interesting brewery museum and a complimentary drink of beer at the attractive bar to finish.

MARKT

✚ B2 ✉ Markt 🚌 Most buses 🏇 Horse-drawn carriage trips ($$$) and mini-bus tours ($$$) start from the Markt

The Markt (Market Square) is the bustling heart of Bruges. The Gothic buildings of the Provinciaal Hof, seat of the government of West Flanders, and the adjoining Central Post Office dominate the east side of the impressive square. The Belfry stands on the south side. The crow-stepped gables of a row of old guild houses, now painted in bright colors, catch the sun on the north side of the square. They stand behind a statue of Jan Breydel and Pieter de Coninck, Flemish heroes who led a 1302 uprising against French overlordship. The west side of the Markt has a mix of handsome buildings, including the 15th-century Maison Bouchoute and the Craenenburg House (now the Café Craenenburg) flanking the entrance to Sint Amandstraat.

MEMLING MUSEUM

✚ B1 ✉ Mariastraat 38 ☎ 050 448 770 🕐 Tue.–Sun. 9:30–5 🚻 1 💷 $$$

St. John's Hospital, founded in the 12th century, was one of the oldest surviving medieval hospitals in Europe, but it has been renovated into a spectacular background for Hans Memling's paintings. A German painter, Memling settled in Bruges in 1465 and soon was in great demand. The chapel, which contains magnificent 15th-century Memling panels and the St. Ursula Shrine, is the highlight of the complex, but the old hospital pharmacy is also worth a visit. Look out for the *Madonna with Child* and the *Lamentation of Christ*.

Bruges

The opulent mausoleum of Charles the Bold in the Church of Our Lady

ONZE-LIEVE-VROUWEKERK

🕂 B2 ✉ Mariastraat 🕐 Tue.–Fri. 9:30–12:30 and 1:30–5, Sat. 9:30–12:30 and 1:30–4, Sun. 1:30–5. No sightseeing during services 🍴 Den Dijver, see page 543 🚌 1 💶 Church free; Choir Gallery $

The Gothic gloom of the Onze-Lieve-Vrouwekerk (Church of Our Lady) is emphasized by mournful piped music. Notices exhorting *stilte* (silence) will keep you suitably hushed. Even Michelangelo's masterful sculpture the *Madonna and Child* seems constrained within the cold prison of its marble altar. Yet the church's powerful sense of sanctity and its outstanding works of sacred art overpower the initial feeling of gloominess. The pulpit, designed by Bruges artist Jan Antoon Garemijn, is a marvelous rococo extravaganza that will cheer you on your way to the choir and the magnificent, gilded Renaissance mausoleums of Mary of Burgundy and Charles the Bold.

PALEIS VAN DE BRUGSE VRIJE

🕂 B2 ✉ Burg 11A ☎ 050 448 260 🕐 Tue.–Sun. 9:30–noon and 1:30–5 🍴 Breydel-Deconinck, see page 543 🚌 1 💶 $ combined ticket with Gothic Hall in the Stadhuis; Courtyard free

The Paleis van de Brugse Vrije (Palace of the Liberty of Bruges; see page 68) is an 18th-century building. One wing houses Old Recorders' House, a 16th-century building once used to hold public records.

SINT-SALVATORSKATHEDRAAL

🕂 B2 ✉ Steenstraat 🕐 Cathedral: Mon. 2–5:45, Tue.–Fri. 8:30–11:45 and 2–5:45, Sat. 8:30–11:45 and 2–3:30, Sun. 9–10:15 a.m. and 3–5:45. Museum: Sun.–Fri. 2–5 🚌 1–5, 13, 89 💶 Cathedral free; Museum $ 🎵 Major concerts held in cathedral

Bruges' great churches reflect a sober Flemish style rather than Latin exuberance. But Sint-Salvatorskathedraal (St. Saviour's Cathedral) has many features to counteract its Gothic vastness. The high altar and the 15th-century choir stalls add a richly decorative note; the rood loft, beneath the organ case, contains a superb baroque sculpture of God the Father in white marble by Arthur Quellin the Younger. Visit the Cathedral Museum; among its treasures is the vivid realism of Dirk Bouts' 15th-century triptych *The Martyrdom of St. Hippolytus.*

STADHUIS

🕂 B2 ✉ Burg 12 ☎ 050 448 113 🕐 Tue.–Sun. 9:30–5 🍴 Breydel-Deconinck, see page 543 🚌 All buses to the Markt 💶 Gothic Hall $ (combined ticket with Paleis van de Brugse Vrije)

The Stadhuis (Town Hall) of Bruges stands in the Burg (see pages 68–69) and dates from the 14th century. It has been rebuilt over the years and has a superb carved facade. Inside is the splendid former council chamber, the Gotische Zaal (Gothic Hall).

A MEDIEVAL EXPERIENCE: THE BURG

The Burg is medieval Bruges at its most tangible. Once it was a jealously guarded enclave, walled and with locked gates. The northern side of this outstanding architectural complex contained the 10th-century Romanesque Church of St. Donation, demolished in 1799. A scale model of the church under the trees on the square, the Burgplein, is a reminder of a lost final flourish to the Burg. Also on the northern side, on Breydelstraat, is the handsome baroque facade of the Provost's House of St. Donation.

On the east side of the Burg is the Palace of the Liberty of Bruges (Paleis van de Brugse Vrije). This was once the ruling seat of the Bruges Vrije, a territorial precinct of Flanders. The building now houses the Bruges tourist information center in one wing. The other wing harbors a magnificent Renaissance chimney piece created in honor of Charles V, Count of Flanders and Holy Roman Emperor. The lower section is in black marble with an alabaster frieze depicting the biblical story of Suzanna and the Elders. The main section is in exquisitely carved wood and depicts the Emperor and fellow members of the Habsburg family, the male contingent endowed with startling Habsburgian codpieces.

To the right of the palace across narrow Blind Donkey Street (Blinde Ezelstraat) is the Town Hall of Bruges (Stadhuis). This exquisite building dates from the 14th century but has been rebuilt and renovated over the centuries. The turreted, Gothic facade is a lyrical evocation of the mason's craft. Inside is the council chamber, the Gothic Hall (Gotische Zaal), with

Procession of the Holy Blood

historical wall paintings and a handsome chimney piece. Its glorious vaulted ceiling is all gilded wooden arches with slender ribs and hanging keystones. Fortunate couples are married here.

To the right of the Town Hall in the southwest corner of the Burg is the most medieval building of all, the Basilica of the Holy Blood (Basiliek van het Heilig Bloed). In the building is a sacred vial said to contain drops of Christ's blood, brought to Bruges in 1150 from the Holy Land by Diederik von den Elzas, count of Flanders. The Holy Blood is still deeply venerated. Each Ascension Day in May or June, the relic is the focus of the most important event in West Flanders, the Procession of the Holy Blood (Heilig-Bloedprocessie), a theatrical costume pageant depicting religious events.

There is something strangely compelling about the Basilica of the Holy Blood. It has a medieval

Medieval elegance in lights – an evening meal in the atmospheric Burg after a long day of sightseeing

authenticity that is irresistible, even to the ungodly. The building contains an upper and lower chapel. You enter the lower chapel through a modest doorway and it is as if you are stepping straight into the Middle Ages.

The basilica dates from the 12th century and was built to house the relics of St. Basil. It has been partly restored, but is still one of the finest surviving examples of Romanesque architecture in Flanders. Squat pillars support the vaulted roof of the nave. Wall carvings are simple, almost primitive. The air is dense and exterior sounds are muffled and resonant.

Gothic Mood

You re-emerge into the daylight, pass through an enchanting Gothic doorway in the ornate facade of the main chapel and then mount a wide staircase beneath shallow vaults. The upper chapel is a breathtaking contrast to the somber Romanesque below the

stairs. It is lavishly decorated in a late Gothic style that overlays original Romanesque themes. A rococo white marble altar, barrel roof, luminous stained glass, carved wood, and gold and silver artifacts all create a mood that is reminiscent of the heavy decoration of Orthodox churches.

There is a delightful spherical oak pulpit with disk canopy but with no visible access. The secret is a small door to the side of the Holy Blood altar, which opens onto hidden stairs. The Holy Blood is contained within a crystal sheath with gold crown stoppers and is supported by gilded copper and silver angels. Adjoining the upper church is a small museum with the gold and silver reliquary for the Holy Blood.

Return to the 21st century by visiting the contemporary pavilion under the trees, designed by famed Japanese architect Toyo Ito and built in 2002; it's a reminder that Bruges acknowledges the present as well as the past.

GHENT

At first glance Ghent (Gent or Gand) seems slightly rough around the edges, a city lacking the sparkle of Luxembourg or the carefully preserved splendor of Bruges. Ghent has been an industrial and commercial center throughout its long history, and the fabric of the city has suffered because of this. But apart from the urban realities this is Belgium's "City of Flowers," containing some of the finest historical and cultural artifacts in Europe, along with architecture that encompasses soaring towers and exquisitely decorative domestic buildings. Its citizens, the friendly Gentenaars, are shrewd, down to earth and personable. Many speak some

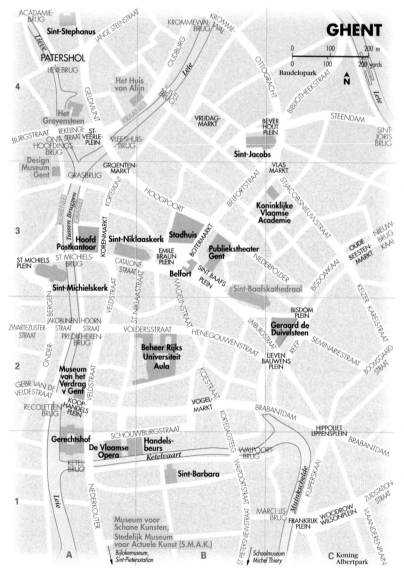

GHENT

| | 0 | 100 | 200 m |
| | 0 | 100 | 200 yards |

The towers of Ghent reflect the wealth of the city created during the 14th- and 15th-century cloth trade

English and are always ready to oblige the visitor with guidance and advice.

First Impressions

Ghent's main railroad station, Sint-Pietersstation (St. Peter's Station), is just over a mile south of the city center. The station can be a sobering experience for the first-time visitor. It is a busy place and has reasonable facilities, but there is not much information for new arrivals. Head to the heart of the city and the helpful tourist information center in the crypt of the Belfry (Belfort) in Botermarkt, Sint-Baafsplein.

Buses, trolley buses and trams leave regularly for Korenmarkt from a covered terminal on the east side of Sint-Pietersstation. Ghent's trams run along extremely narrow streets – a mildly alarming experience at first – but they do so with great efficiency. Do not be surprised to see the driver stop, get out and adjust the wing mirror of a parked car so that the tram may squeeze past.

The great central squares are the best places to get a handle on Ghent. Here are the powerful Gothic churches of Sint-Baafskathedraal (see page 74) and Sint-Niklaaskerk. Civic buildings between them include the Belfry (Belfort), the Cloth Hall (Lakenhalle) and the Town Hall (Stadhuis), with their distinctive mix of architectural styles. Take the glass elevator to the top of the Belfort for superb views of this remarkable city of towers and steeples.

Old Ghent

For a taste of old Ghent, go west from Sint-Niklaaskerk, past the neo-Gothic, neo-Renaissance flamboyance of the 1910 former post office, to the bridge of Sint-Michielsbrug that spans the Leie river. Look back from the bridge for a breathtaking view of the skyline. North of the bridge is Tussen Bruggen, once a busy harbor and still lined by the gabled buildings of Graslei and Korenlei.

North of Graslei is Groentenmarkt, a tree-shaded square flanked by the sturdy 15th-century Groot Vleeshuis (Great Butchers' Hall). Today the Groentenmarkt is the scene of a daily fruit and vegetable market except on Sundays, when there's an open-air art

Ghent

forum. A few steps farther is the Sint-Veerleplein, with a monumental baroque archway to the old fish market and handsome gabled houses. These are all overshadowed by the brooding mass of Het Gravensteen, the Castle of the Counts (see opposite page).

Across the street, to the east of Het Gravensteen, is the street of Kraanlei, a row of late medieval buildings lining a stretch of the Leie river. This is one of Ghent's finest streetscapes. From Kraanlei's far end, the Zuivelbrug (Zuivel Bridge) crosses the canal into the square of Vrijdagmarkt, where there is a big market on Fridays.

Shopping in Ghent

Ghent's main commercial and shopping area lies to the south of Korenmarkt and Botermarkt. The busy Veldstraat has stores of all types, but if you walk through the network of little streets just east of here, including Mageleinstraat, Sint-Niklaasstraat, Kortedagsteeg and Koestraat, you'll find numerous specialty shops. These include chic fashion boutiques, delicatessens, *chocolateries*, antiques and crafts shops, and Bloch, a patisserie and coffee shop that is second to none. At the heart of the area is the famous Kouter flower market, at its colorful best on Sundays, a vivid indication of Ghent's fame as the "City of Flowers."

Night Lights

Eating out in Ghent is an essential experience. Try such local specialties as *Gentse hazenpeper* (jugged hare) or *Gentse waterzooi van riviervis* (freshwater fish stew). There are intimate restaurants in the Patershol area north of Kraanlei. Enjoy Ghent by night, when the buildings are lit up and the streets hum with life. Spend an evening at Publiekstheater Gent (Ghent Public Theater) on Sint-Baafsplein; at De Vlaamse Opera on Schouwburgstraat; or at the trendy and busy Handelsbeurs on the Kouter, a venue for classical music and concerts.

ESSENTIAL INFORMATION

 TOURIST INFORMATION
Toerisme Stad Gent (Ghent Tourism)
• Raadskelder, Belfort (Belfry), Botermarkt 17A
☎ 09 266 5232; fax 09 266 5673; www.gent.be

 URBAN TRANSPORTATION
Ghent railroad station (Sint-Pietersstation) is 1 mile south of the city center. For information on train services phone ☎ 09 241 2840 (daily 7 a.m.–8 p.m.). Ghent's main bus and tram stations adjoin the railroad station. Most buses, trolley buses and trams also run from the Korenmarkt. For information, call Delijn ☎ 09 210 9311 (daily 6 a.m.–11 p.m.);

www.delijn.be/oostrlaanderen. There are taxi stands at the Korenmarkt and outside Sint-Pietersstation. For taxis, phone ☎ 09 222 2222 or 09 225 2525.

 AIRPORT INFORMATION
The nearest airport is Brussels International Airport at Zaventem (see page 58). For flight information, call ☎ 0900 70000 (daily 7 a.m.–10 p.m.; toll call). Train connections to Ghent can be made at Brussels' Nord/Noord (North), Centrale/Centraal (Central) and Midi/Zuid (South) stations. The trip from Brussels airport to Ghent takes about 30 minutes.

CLIMATE – average highs and lows for the month

JAN.	FEB.	MAR.	APR.	MAY	JUN.	JUL.	AUG.	SEP.	OCT.	NOV.	DEC.
5°C	6°C	9°C	11°C	17°C	21°C	22°C	22°C	20°C	15°C	9°C	5°C
41°F	43°F	48°F	52°F	63°F	70°F	72°F	72°F	68°F	59°F	48°F	41°F
0°C	1°C	2°C	5°C	8°C	11°C	12°C	12°C	11°C	7°C	4°C	2°C
32°F	34°F	36°F	41°F	46°F	52°F	54°F	54°F	52°F	45°F	39°F	36°F

CITY SIGHTS

Key to symbols

✚ map coordinates refer to the Ghent map on page 70; sights below are highlighted in yellow on the map.
✉ address or location ☎ telephone number
🕐 opening times 🚌 nearest bus, trolley bus, or tram route 🍴 restaurant or café on site or nearby
💷 admission charge: $$$ more than €5, $$ €3–€5, $ less than €3 ℹ️ other relevant information

DESIGN MUSEUM GENT

✚ A3 ✉ Jan Breydelstraat 5 ☎ 09 267 9999
🕐 Tue.–Sun. 10–6 🚌 Tram 1, 3 💷 $
The Design Museum Gent is a Ghent experience not to be missed. Housed in the handsome old Hotel de Coninck, and with a stunning contemporary extension, the museum exhibits Belgian decorative and applied art, crafts and design from the Renaissance to 20th-century art nouveau, art deco and contemporary work. The older part of the museum displays superb period interiors and has lucid explanations of baroque, rococo and classical styles. Look for the "banana skin" armchair.

GRASLEI EN KORENLEI

✚ A3 ✉ Graslei en Korenlei 🚌 16, 18, 38; trolley bus 3 🍴 Belgaqueen $$–$$$ see page 544
Graslei and Korenlei are the two wharves flanking the medieval harbor Tussen Bruggen (meaning "between the bridges") that lies to the north of the bridge of Sint-Michielsbrug. Their names relate to their role in the early grain trade; their flanking buildings were the trade and guild houses of the medieval period, carefully restored for the World Exhibition of 1913. The facades of these magnificent buildings offer an impression of Ghent in the days when the wharves were alive with the raucous, colorful world of medieval trade.

HET GRAVENSTEEN

✚ A4 ✉ Sint-Veerleplein ☎ 09 225 9306 🕐 Daily 9–6, Apr.–Sep.; 9–5 rest of year 🚌 3, 17, 38, 39; tram 1, 10, 11, 13, 40, 42 🍴 T'Buikske Vol $$–$$$ see page 544 💷 $$$ (includes museums) ℹ️ Last admission 45 minutes before closing

Medieval guild houses line the Leie

Magnificent Gravensteen (Castle of the Counts) has all the authentic menace of 12th-century feudalism. A visit to this well-restored building is irresistible, and merely passing through the shadowy, arched entrance feels like a commitment. The main castle is a series of intriguing rooms linked by winding staircases. In the upper rooms there are historical exhibitions, including the Wapenmuseum (Weapons Museum) with a collection of historical weapons and Gerechtsmuseum (Museum of Instruments of Torture), which displays tools of torture and execution.

HET HUIS VAN ALIJN

✚ A4–B4 ✉ Kraanlei 65 ☎ 09 269 2350; puppet theater: 09 269 2367 🕐 Tue.–Sun. 11–5 🚌 Tram 1, 10, 12 🍴 Museum tavern 💷 $$ ℹ️ Puppet shows Wed. and Sat. (also Thu. during school holidays) at 2:30 ($$)
The intriguing Het Huis van Alijn (Alijn House) owes much of its charm to its location among the old buildings of the 14th-century Kinderen Alijns Hospitaal (Hospial of the Alijns Children), on the canal-side street of Kraanlei. Children will be thrilled with the museum's marionette theater and other delights. The collections are spread throughout a number of quaint little houses surrounding a central square. The domestic and commercial life of Ghent through the ages is exhaustively represented in excellent set-piece tableaux and displays. The museum's puppet theater company 't Spelleke van de Folklore is based here, and performances are staged regularly.

Magnificent St. Bavo's Cathedral and Belfry

KRAANLEI

➕ A4 ✉ Kraanlei 🍴 De Hel, see page 544
🚊 Tram 1, 10, 11, 13

Kraanlei is one of Ghent's finest surviving canal-side streets. Its name derives from a wooden crane that was used to unload cargo. Today the baroque facades of Kraanlei's buildings, with touches of Gothic, are splendid survivors of an exuberant age of prosperity and Flemish culture. The houses have stepped gables and pediments. Look for Ghent's version of Brussels' *Manneken-Pis* (see page 57), perched above the door of a restaurant a few buildings from the beginning of the street. Halfway along is the Het Huis van Alijn (Alijn House; see page 73). Three of the finest facades are at the far end of Kraanlei and include the exquisite 17th-century house known as "The Flying Deer." A few steps north of Kraanlei takes you into the Patershol area, a warren of cobbled streets lined with tall buildings. Once the factory workers' district, Patershol is being rejuvenated, with restaurants, art galleries and refurbished apartments.

MUSEUM VOOR SCHONE KUNSTEN

➕ A1 ✉ Citadelpark ☎ 09 240 0700 🕐 Tue.–Sun.
10–6 🍴 Museum café 🚌 5, 9, 50, 51, 70–74, 76–78;
tram 1, 10, 13 💷 $

The Museum voor Schone Kunsten (Fine

Arts) is closed for renovation until 2006, but most of the collection can be seen in other museums in Ghent. Check the website www.mskgent.be for details regarding what is where. The exceptional collection includes works by Flemish and other European masters from the 14th to mid-20th centuries. Of special note are works by Hieronymus Bosch. Other superb works include Pieter Brueghel the Younger's *Wedding Feast* and Jef Lambeaux's monumental relief panel, *Human Passions*.

SINT-BAAFSKATHEDRAAL

➕ B3 ✉ Sint-Baafsplein ☎ 09 225 4985
🕐 Cathedral and crypt: Mon.–Sat. 8:30–6, Sun. 1–6,
Apr.–Oct.; Mon.–Sat. 8:30–5, Sun. 1–5, rest of year.
Mystic Lamb: Mon.–Sat. 9:30–5, Sun. 1–5, Apr.–Oct.;
Mon.–Sat. 10:30–noon and 2–4, Sun. 2–5, rest of year
🚌 16, 17, 18, 19, 38; tram 12, 41 💷 Cathedral and
altar free; Mystic Lamb $$ (includes audio guide)

The tall four-stage tower of Sint-Baafskathedraal (St. Bavo's Cathedral) dominates the east end of Botermarkt. Externally, the cathedral is a stern mix of Gothic styles beneath a patina of city grime. Inside is one of the great art treasures of the world, the multi-paneled *Het Lam Gods* (*The Mystic Lamb*) known as the Ghent Altar (see opposite page). Other treasures include the rococo pulpit in Carrara marble and Danish oak, with its carved staircases like twisted tree roots. The 12th-century Romanesque crypt of St. Baafs is full of religious artifacts and works of art.

STEDELIJK MUSEUM VOOR ACTUELE KUNST (S.M.A.K.)

➕ A1 ✉ Citadelpark ☎ 09 221 1703 🕐 Tue.–Sun.
10–6 (also first Wed. of the month) 🍴 Museum café
🚌 5, 50, 70–74, 76–78, 90 💷 $$$

Opposite the Museum of Fine Arts (see above) is the Stedelijk Museum voor Actuele Kunst (Municipal Museum of Contemporary Art), or S.M.A.K. Belgium's finest post-1945 art collection, it includes works by Andy Warhol, Francis Bacon, Joseph Beuys, David Hockney, Christo and Belgian artist Marcel Broodthaers, and often has outstanding temporary exhibitions.

DE AANBIDDING VAN HET LAM GODS – THE ADORATION OF THE MYSTIC LAMB

The famous Ghent Altar, *Het Lam Gods* (*The Mystic Lamb*), lives up to your highest expectations. A visit to Sint-Baafskathedraal (St. Bavo's Cathedral) and a view of the altar should not be missed. This luminous, enthralling work has the kind of impact that can change lives and attitudes.

The Ghent Altar is a polyptych, a painting made up of many panels. It is allegedly the work of two 15th-century Flemish painters, the brothers Hubert and Jan van Eyck. There are doubts over whether or not Hubert van Eyck even existed, although Jan van Eyck was unquestionably the most famous painter of his generation. He was a technical master who is credited with developing oil painting to such an extent that the paint he used has retained its vivid colors to this day, with a little help from restoration and refurbishment through the ages.

The Ghent Altar is composed of two rows of paintings, one above the other. The centerpiece in the upper row is of Christ the King, who is flanked by the Virgin Mary, St. John the Baptist, singing angels, a musician, and nude portraits of Adam and a pregnant Eve within the wing panels. The focus of the lower row is the Adoration of the Lamb of God. The flanking panels depict processions of the faithful, judges, knights, hermits and pilgrims. The painted wing panels fold over to enclose the central panels. All of this is presented in breathtaking color and luminosity against superbly detailed Flanders landscapes.

The altar has survived the dangerous meddling of history. Iconoclasts sought to destroy it. In the 1780s, Emperor Joseph II prudishly replaced the sensual nude figures of Adam and Eve with clothed versions. During World War II, German soldiers stole the work and hid it in a mine, from which it was liberated by American troops. Two panels were stolen in 1934; the thief demanded a ransom, but was refused. The panel depicting John the Baptist was later found wrapped in a blanket in Brussels Central railroad station. The panel of the Righteous Judges has never been traced and was replaced by a copy, painted by a Belgian artist, who incorporated his own likeness into one of the figures, a forgivable indulgence for any painter dreaming of immortality.

BRITAIN

"*A LITTLE foggy island in the north-west corner of Europe...*"

From *The Australians*, 1893, by Australian poet and essayist Francis Adams

Opposite: Colorful Tudor pond garden at London's Hampton Court Palace

Britain

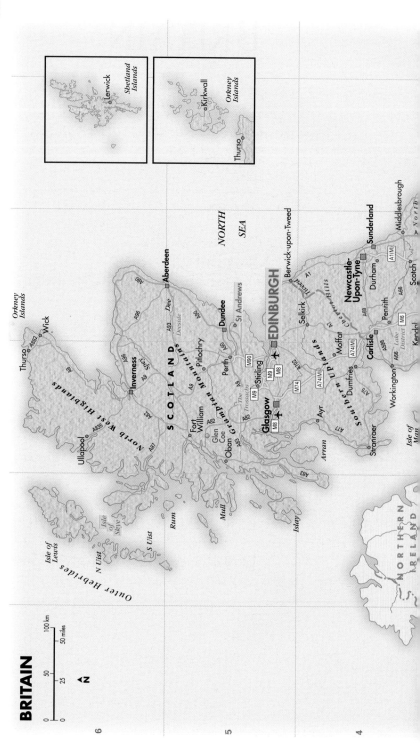

BRITAIN

N

0 — 50 — 100 km
0 — 25 — 50 miles

Orkney Islands

Shetland Islands

Lerwick

Orkney Islands

Kirkwall

Thurso

NORTH SEA

Outer Hebrides

Isle of Lewis

N Uist

S Uist

Isle of Skye

Rum

Mull

Islay

Ullapool

Thurso

Wick

Inverness

North West Highlands

Fort William

Glen Coe

Oban

SCOTLAND

Grampian Mountains

Deeside

Aberdeen

Dee

Pitlochry

Perth

Stirling

The Trossachs

Dundee

St Andrews

EDINBURGH

Berwick-upon-Tweed

Glasgow

Ayr

Arran

Southern Uplands

Dumfries

Moffat

Selkirk

Cheviot Hills

Tweed

A1

Newcastle-Upon-Tyne

Sunderland

Middlesbrough

Durham

Penrith

Carlisle

Workington

Stranraer

Lake District

Kendal

Isle of Man

NORTHERN IRELAND

Scotch

Britain

Britain

BRITAIN

Within this remarkable nation, an island barely 700 miles from north to south and less than 350 miles at its widest point, live nearly 60 million people. From this small island, a large percentage of the world's population inherited many of the linguistic and cultural influences that shaped their lives.

A Diverse Unity

England, Scotland and Wales – collectively known as Britain – each retain individual cultural characteristics. To complicate matters further for the visitor, there are distinct regions within regions, all reflecting the resilient and determined individuality that is typically British. If you spend any time traveling through Britain, you will find that the landscape and the customs of the people change dramatically, sometimes within only a few miles.

People have been arriving at all points around Britain's corrugated coastline for centuries, but London is the focus of the country as a whole. Here history, politics and culture meet in one of the most invigorating cities in the world. Beyond London lies provincial and rural England. You'll find a landscape of meadows, hedgerows and woods, its earth relentlessly farmed for centuries. But much of the countryside has retained, in between the maze of roads and highways, a semblance of Old England, and in treasured corners the beauty of the past is preserved.

At Canterbury, in Kent, is the great cathedral that drew tens of thousands of medieval pilgrims to the relics of the revered Thomas à Becket, the great English churchman. These pilgrims inspired the country's first great poet, Geoffrey Chaucer, to write his *Canterbury Tales*, as vivid a picture of the medieval world as you will find.

Yet before Chaucer and before Canterbury, the earliest Britons had raised their own pagan equivalents to the Christian cathedrals. At Stonehenge, and perhaps more hauntingly at Avebury in Wiltshire, in the heart of southern England, are the standing stones and burial chambers of Britons who commanded England centuries before Romans, Danes, Anglo Saxons and Normans ever did.

Britain Explained

The name "Britain" (or "Great Britain") refers to the countries of England, Scotland and Wales located on the main island of Britain. To include Northern Ireland, the correct name is the "United Kingdom." The United Kingdom is the official unified entity, governed by the central parliament in London and (nominally) by Queen Elizabeth II.

However, political boundaries are becoming increasingly blurred by the European Union. Member countries are subject to E.U. rules and regulations, and regions are now being encouraged in their efforts at self-determination, with the result that Scotland and Wales – historically uneasy with what they saw as an English parliament (and Queen) in London – now have their own national assemblies and a degree of autonomy. But the legacy of London remains, and when the British talk about "this country" they usually mean Britain.

Sunrise over ancient Britain – Stonehenge is a reminder of the achievements of early inhabitants

Village Greens and Seaside

Throughout scores of picturesque villages in southern and western England, you will find the essence of the country where people still play cricket on village greens, dance around maypoles on May Day and sell jars of local honey at village festivals – weather permitting, of course.

Yet England also boasts great cities and historic towns that bustle with life. The great seaport of Bristol is one. The Georgian city of Bath, where golden Cotswold stone and the classical elegance of 18th-century fashion conspired to create one of the world's most astounding cityscapes, seems consumed with golden light in the summer sun.

Miles of coastline fringe the English Channel. On the southern coast are the cliffs of Beachy Head, famous resorts like Brighton and Bournemouth, as well as long stretches of green and peaceful coast that run westward past Dorset's limestone cliffs and the red cliffs of Devon to the golden beaches of Cornwall.

From Oxford to the Lakes

North and west of London, in the counties of Oxfordshire and Warwickshire, are such cities as Oxford, university town par excellence, matched only by its rival Cambridge in the fen country of eastern England. Here, too, you will find the Cotswold Hills and the historic town of Stratford-upon-Avon.

Progress through the cultural heart of England is not an idyllic rural journey by any means. Yet the cities of

MORE TOP DESTINATIONS IN BRITAIN

● Avebury D2 ● Bath D1
● Caernarfon Castle C3
● Canterbury E1 ● Chester D3
● Cotswolds D2 ● Dartmoor C1
● Deeside D5 ● Glen Coe C5
● Isle of Skye B6 ● Lake District D4
● Snowdonia C3 ● St. Andrews D5
● St. Michael's Mount B1
● Stratford-upon-Avon D2
● Stonehenge D1 ● The Trossachs C5 ● Windsor Castle E2
● Yorkshire Dales D3

Scottish piper in full regalia

Manchester, Leeds, Birmingham and Liverpool are vibrant and exciting places, while historic cities such as Chester, on the Welsh Borders, and York in the east have managed to preserve their medieval townscapes. Beyond this great sprawl an unspoiled England survives. Derbyshire's Peak District, the Yorkshire Dales, the exquisite Lake District of Cumbria and the lonely heights of Northumbria seem to appear like magic in the landscape.

Wild Wales

Wales is renowned as a land of poetry and song and as a part of Britain that seems older than time. In these green borderlands, the ruined castles of Norman Britain survive, relics of a time when England failed to entirely subdue the "wild Welsh." Strongholds of the Anglo Norman conquerors, such as Caernarfon Castle, are reminders of a later age of determined feudalism. But in the beautiful countryside of central Wales, on the rugged west coast and in the great mountains of Snowdonia, the spirit of the ancient Welsh lives on, the powerful identity of modern Wales a token of that endurance.

North to the Highlands

North of Cumbria and Northumberland, the Southern Uplands guard Scotland's borderland, once infamous for its violent robber clans. It was this raw border country that gave courage to heroic Scottish patriots like Robert Bruce and William Wallace as they pitted themselves against England's might. And across these hills in 1745 marched Charles Edward Stuart – Bonnie Prince Charlie, the last of a moribund royal line – supported by the cream of the Highland clans in a doomed final gesture of defiance by Scotland against English domination.

North of the Southern Uplands are the Central Lowlands of Scotland, with the capital city of Edinburgh to the east and Glasgow, the great powerhouse of old industrial Scotland, to the west. Edinburgh is the historic distillation of all things Scottish, the political and cultural focus of the nation from a time when poet Robert Burns and novelist Walter Scott graced fashionable 18th-century salons, to the vigorous and progressive Edinburgh Festival of today.

Across the Forth river (Firth of Forth) from Edinburgh lies the region of Fife, often referred to as the "Kingdom of Fife," home to the university town and golfing mecca of St. Andrews. To the north and west are the Scottish Highlands, Britain's most dramatic landscape, and some of the last great wilderness areas of Europe.

At the edge of the Highlands are the Trossachs, Scotland's equivalent to England's Lake District, steeped in the history of real-life characters like Rob Roy Macgregor, inspiration for the classic novels of Sir Walter Scott. Farther north are the mountains of Aberdeenshire. Here, on Royal Deeside, sits Balmoral Castle, traditional retreat of the Queen and her family. Scotland's most spectacular mountain country lies to the far west and north, at the Pass of Glen Coe, and then for more than 100 miles northward along the west coast to Kintail

Britain

and Wester Ross. Out to sea is the Isle of Skye and the misty Hebrides, romantic islands at Britain's far western edge.

Seeing the Country

Britain's essence lies in its diversity and in the hidden corners between the most popular places. Traveling independently by train or bus is one way to explore off the beaten track, but you will need to plan carefully. Britain's long-distance bus network is generally good, but away from major cities and main roads service can vary greatly. Organized bus tours, on the other hand, will whisk you efficiently to all the major tourist sights. Traveling by car is another option; Britain is so diverse that you can drive for a few hours on a main highway and then veer off onto quieter byways.

London is a year-round destination, but outside the main summer season and major vacation periods, Britain's hidden corners are extremely quiet. May and June are good months to visit – the freshness of early June is invigorating in England's upland areas, northern Wales and the Scottish Highlands. Winter is another story, of course, but even in December and January Britain's larger cities are vibrant; London, Manchester, Liverpool, Cardiff, Edinburgh and Glasgow all pulse with British fashion and style.

Great classical music can be savored year-round in London, Manchester and Edinburgh. Attend world-class theater in Cardiff and Glasgow. Outstanding choirs fill England's cathedrals with truly heavenly music, and the open-air performances by Welsh and Cornish choirs are enchanting. Join the singing customers or listen to folk music at a neighborhood pub, or discover a colorful local festival or time-honored custom in a Devonshire hamlet or Yorkshire town.

The Taste of Britain

The same variety applies to shopping. The British were dismissed by Napoleon as a "nation of shopkeepers," but the intended slight is actually a compliment. The British engaged in trade the world over, and today that spirit of enterprise, curiosity, good business sense and eclectic style is maintained. Fashion salons rival those in France and Italy. Britain has some of the finest antiques shops, art galleries and auction houses in Europe. Traditional and modern styles are blended to produce some colorful and out-of-the-ordinary clothing and craft items, and it is often in the provinces that the best examples are found.

Not so long ago, British food was seen as typically uninspired and overcooked. But British nouvelle cuisine is exciting yet still essentially British, the ingredients fresh and flavorful. British beer has rediscovered great traditions, too; every English county has a lively range of local ales to back up the standard brews. In Scotland, sample the best from the country's range of whiskeys and superb single malts.

Cornish pasties – with tasty, savory fillings

Britain

TIMELINE

8000 BC	Mesolithic hunter-gatherers journey into southern Britain.
4000 BC	Neolithic "New Stone Age" people settle in southern Britain.
circa 500 BC	Iron age culture develops in Britain.
55–54 BC	Julius Caesar makes expeditions to Britain.
AD 43	Roman conquest of Britain begins; first settlement of London by Romans.
circa 400	Roman army and administration withdraws from Britain.
1066	Battle of Hastings; Norman Conquest of Britain.
1314	Battle of Bannockburn, in which England suffers disastrous defeat at the hands of Scotland's Robert Bruce.
1534	Henry VIII appoints himself head of the Church in England; beginning of English Reformation.
1649	King Charles I executed; British Commonwealth established.
1707	Scotland and England unite by Act of Union.
1776	American colonies declare independence from Britain.
1815	Battle of Waterloo; Napoleon defeated by combined European force led by Duke of Wellington.
1914–18	Britain plays major part in World War I.
1939–44	World War II begins; Winston Churchill becomes Prime Minister of Britain; D-Day, Allied forces invade Normandy.
1945	War ends; Churchill loses in national elections.
1973	Britain joins European Union.
2002	Celebrations held throughout Britain for Queen Elizabeth II's Golden Jubilee.

PROTECTED BY SEA

Britain's island location has protected it from invasion over the centuries. The country has experienced two definitive "invasions," by the Romans in the first century and by the Normans in 1066. Others tried their best. The Danes, or Vikings, steadily occupied eastern England during the ninth century but were later repulsed. The Anglo Saxons did not invade in the sense of armed occupation, but rather by a slow and steady immigration and integration after Roman withdrawal left chaos and uncertainty within the country. In later centuries Britain developed a powerful military and naval force, and although almost constantly at war with various European powers during the medieval period was itself never invaded. In more recent times both Napoleon and Hitler tried and failed to conquer. The English Channel and the surrounding seas have been Britain's greatest strategic blessing.

Royal pageantry at the annual Trooping the Colour, a celebration of the Queen's "official" birthday, held in June at the Horse Guards Parade in central London

SURVIVAL GUIDE

- If visiting London, try to see one of the city's pageants, such as Trooping the Colour on Queen Elizabeth's birthday, or the Lord Mayor's Show in November. For something altogether informal, join the fun at the fantastic Notting Hill Carnival at the end of August.

- In York, be careful where pedestrian zones end and traffic begins. Also, as in all major cities, watch out for pickpockets on crowded streets.

- Try Britain's various regional foods. The national dish – fish and chips – can be found almost anywhere. In London, seek out genuine East End whelks. In Cornwall, look for Cornish pasties (savory pastry), a true hand-held meal. In Wales, sample Caerphilly cheese; in Yorkshire, try beef and Yorkshire pudding; and don't miss steak-and-kidney pie in any English country pub. In Scotland, tackle haggis, tatties (potatoes) and neeps (turnips), or kippers (smoked herring) – all accompanied by a thick and creamy regional beer or a good strong cup of tea.

- Be prepared for dramatic changes in the weather. They say that Britain has no climate, it just has weather. The truth is that the country is caught between the extremes of northern and southern Europe, while its island nature allows vast amounts of condensed Atlantic sea water to be deposited as wind-blown rain at regular intervals. Expect rain, and if it comes, enjoy it; or, like the British do, blame the government.

- Make sure you always know what county of England you are in, and try not to confuse counties, especially not Yorkshire and Lancashire. Never refer to Welsh or Scottish people as English.

- In southwest England especially, enjoy a cream tea. This grand traditional indulgence consists of fresh, fluffy scones (biscuits) spread with jam and delicious, thick clotted cream. The cream is slathered on top of the jam or vice versa.

- The strength of the summer sun can deceive in Britain, often because a wind may be blowing or there are passing clouds. Guard against sunburn even if there is a cool breeze.

LONDON

London is one of the world's great experiences, a city that is always exhilarating, sometimes bewildering, sometimes exhausting, but never disappointing. This financial, commercial and political center is also a year-round tourist city. The excitement is palpable. There is a feeling that something is always happening, that you are in the middle of one of a handful of truly great cities.

London

London needs to be taken very much on its terms; if you do so, you will enjoy it thoroughly. It is an expensive and sometimes stressful place; admission prices to major attractions are steep and the crowds of fellow visitors can be huge.

There are excellent guided tours, and bus tours are an easy way to sample all London (and beyond) has to offer. Exploring independently can be hugely rewarding, however, provided you plan well. Many of London's attractions are some distance apart, and if you set out

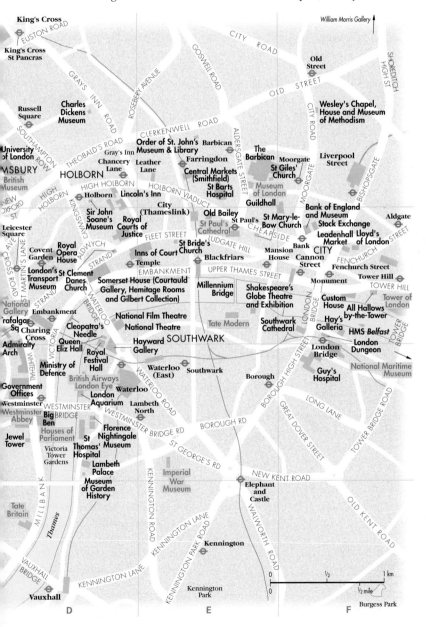

D   E   F

London

blindly determined to see everything you may end up frustrated and exhausted. Orient yourself by establishing two or three familiar focal points from which you can connect to other parts of the city.

Trafalgar Square to Big Ben

Trafalgar Square should be one of these focal points. It is the symbolic center of London; the towering pillar of Lord Nelson's column rises 172 feet into the London sky. At the base of the column are fountains and monumental guardian lions. All around the central square a constant throng of people is besieged by fluttering pigeons. Trafalgar Square is overlooked from the north by the National Gallery. At the southwest corner of the square is Admiralty Arch, through which you reach The Mall and progress toward Buckingham Palace.

Whitehall, London's "political" street, runs due south from Trafalgar Square. You'll see such landmarks as Big Ben, the clock tower of Westminster, as you walk past the Old Admiralty Building and the Horse Guards, where helmeted troopers in scarlet or blue sit immobile on their sleek, black, patient horses. Soon you pass the gates of Downing Street, where Britain's Prime Minister and Chancellor of the Exchequer have their homes. In the middle of Whitehall is the Cenotaph, a stark and simple memorial to the dead of two world wars. Beyond the Cenotaph, Whitehall merges with Parliament Street and then meets Bridge Street. To the left is Westminster Bridge and the River Thames; straight ahead are the Houses of Parliament and to the right is Westminster Abbey.

Piccadilly Circus to Covent Garden

Another prime focus of central London is busy Piccadilly Circus, with the elegantly poised statue of Eros at its center. You can reach Piccadilly from Trafalgar Square by walking along Pall Mall from in front of the National Gallery and then turning right up Haymarket. From Piccadilly you can plunge into London's world of great shopping. To the north lies Soho, the long-established heart of late-night London, slightly risqué but full of character. Here are some of the capital's best theaters, cafés and restaurants, a multitude of offbeat and specialty stores, and a resident population that maintains the area's tradition of eccentricity, style and eclectic fashion.

Soho spills eastward through the rather small Chinatown area around Gerrard Street to reach another of London's focal points, Leicester Square, lined with movie theaters and restaurants. To the east, along Cranbourne and Garrick streets, is Covent Garden, one of London's liveliest and most entertaining venues, featuring stores, cafés, restaurants and a nonstop show of street entertainers.

Beyond the Center

Once familiar with central London, you can start to venture beyond the focal points. This is where the city's excellent subway network, the Tube (London Underground), comes in handy. London buses also supply excellent service, but if you can master the subway system you can reach just about everything worth seeing. Use of the subway does mean you lose some grip of how London lies above ground; sometimes it is more rewarding if you walk to your destination, provided it isn't too far.

Head east from Trafalgar Square, by subway or on foot, along the Strand, Fleet Street and Ludgate Hill, to St. Paul's Cathedral. Then proceed east to the Tower of London and Tower Bridge.

Or go west from Trafalgar Square, beyond Buckingham Palace, to the great green space of Hyde Park and fashionable Knightsbridge, where you will find Harrods department store. Here, too, are three great London museums: the Victoria and Albert, the Science Museum and the Natural History Museum.

Something for Everyone

To get the most out of London during a short stay, pick and choose carefully. Visit museums in which you have a particular interest. Tackle shopping the same way. Attend a performance at the National Theatre on the South Bank, or take in a West End show. Eat out in style if you can afford it, or enjoy the atmosphere at one of London's many traditional pubs.

You will find a fascinating mix of people; this is one of the most cosmopolitan cities in the world. There can be a sharp edge to Londoners, but you will never be short of advice or direction. And when in doubt, remember that London policemen are perhaps the most helpful and courteous citizens of all.

London

CLIMATE – average highs and lows for the month

JAN.	FEB.	MAR.	APR.	MAY	JUN.	JUL.	AUG.	SEP.	OCT.	NOV.	DEC.
6°C	6°C	10°C	13°C	16°C	20°C	21°C	21°C	18°C	14°C	10°C	7°C
43°F	43°F	50°F	55°F	61°F	68°F	70°F	70°F	64°F	57°F	50°F	45°F
2°C	2°C	3°C	5°C	8°C	11°C	13°C	13°C	11°C	7°C	5°C	3°C
36°F	36°F	37°F	41°F	46°F	52°F	55°F	55°F	52°F	45°F	41°F	37°F

The Houses of Parliament, a spectacular example of 19th-century Victorian Gothic Revival architecture

CITY SIGHTS

Key to symbols

⊞ map coordinates refer to the London map on pages 86–87; sights below are highlighted in yellow on the map.

⊠ address or location ☎ telephone number

⊙ opening times ⦿ nearest subway ⊟ nearest bus route ⛴ riverboat � restaurant or café on site or nearby ⦿ admission charge: $$$ more than £6, $$ £2–£6, $ less than £2 ⓘ other relevant information

BRITISH AIRWAYS LONDON EYE

⊞ D2 ⊠ Jubilee Gardens, South Bank ☎ 08705 000600 ⊙ Daily 9 a.m.–10 p.m., Jun.–Aug.; 9:30–9, May–Jun. and Sep.; 9:30–8 rest of year. Hours subject to change ⦿ Waterloo ⊟ 11, 24, 211, RV1 ⛴ Waterloo Millenium Pier ⦿ $$$

Built as part of the city's millennial celebrations, the London Eye is a superb feat of construction. A huge Ferris wheel, it slowly rotates (once every 30 minutes), giving visitors a bird's-eye view across London from within 32 glassed capsules. At 450 feet high, it is the largest observation wheel in the world.

BRITISH MUSEUM

⊞ D4 ⊠ Great Russell Street ☎ 020 7323 8299 ⊙ Galleries: daily 10–5:30 (also Thu.–Fri. 5–8:30). Great Court: Sun.–Wed. 9–6, Thu.–Sat. 9 a.m.–11 p.m.) ffl Restaurant and cafés ⦿ Holborn, Russell Square, Tottenham Court Road or Goodge Street ⊟ 7, 8, 10, 19, 22B, 24, 25, 29, 38, 55, 68, 73, 91, 134, 188 ⦿ Free; possible charge for special exhibitions ⓘ Guided tours ($$$) at 10:30, 1 and 3

The British Museum, founded in 1753, is a treasure house of global artifacts, many of them the riches of Britain's imperial past. There are more than 6 million exhibits, including the Elgin Marbles, magnificent fifth-century BC relief sculptures taken from the Parthenon in 1801 by Thomas Bruce, the Earl of Elgin, and still the subject of Greek demands for their return.

Other highlights are the Rosetta Stone, key to the understanding of Egyptian hieroglyphics; the 2,000-year-old Lindow Man, whose preserved body was found in an English peat bog; the Mildenhall Treasure, a collection of Roman silver; and Anglo Saxon artifacts from a ship burial discovered at Sutton Hoo on England's eastern coast during the outbreak of World War II. Don't miss the Egyptian Galleries, the finest collection outside Egypt itself.

The Great Court opened in 2000, increasing the museum's public space by 50 percent. A massive glass roof now spans the central courtyard, making it the largest covered square in Europe. The area houses galleries, an education center, COMPASS (a multimedia information database) and, at its heart, the Reading Room, resplendent in blue and gold. This is where Karl Marx wrote *Das Kapital*; today visitors can sit at the leather-covered desks and take in the atmosphere.

HOUSES OF PARLIAMENT

➕ D2 ✉ St. Margaret Street ☎ 020 7219 4272 (House of Commons), 020 7219 3107 (House of Lords); 020 7219 3000 (both houses) 🕐 Mon.–Fri. (times vary; phone for details) Ⓜ Westminster 🚌 3, 11, 12, 24, 53, 77A, 148, 159, 211 ⛴ Westminster Millennium Pier 💲 Free; tours $$$

The Houses of Parliament, also known as the Palace of Westminster, are mainly to be admired from the outside. The present building replaced an older palace dating from the 11th century. Most of this earlier building burned down in 1834. The structure's linear form is doubly enhanced by the vertical thrust of Victoria Tower and the clock tower known as Big Ben. Inside access is limited because it is the workplace of British government. You can attend debates in the House of Lords and House of Commons on a first-come-first-served basis in a line for the "Strangers' Galleries" (public galleries) outside St. Stephen's Entrance. Tours of the Houses of Parliament are available to overseas visitors Mon.–Sat. during the summer recess (early Aug.–early Oct.); reserve in advance.

IMPERIAL WAR MUSEUM

➕ E2 ✉ Lambeth Road ☎ 020 7416 5320 🕐 Daily 10–6 🍴 Café Ⓜ Lambeth North 🚌 1, 3, 12, 45, 53, 59, 63, 68, 100, 159, 168, 171, 172, 176, 188, 344, C10 💲 Free; charge for exhibitions 🎧 Audio tours $$

Two vast guns stand in front of the handsome Ionic portico of the Imperial War Museum, where the story of 20th-century conflict is documented. The museum was formerly the infamous Bethlehem Royal Hospital, notorious asylum for the insane, and known as "Bedlam." There are more than 50 historic aircraft, tanks and other field weapons on display but the most fascinating exhibits involve the human element through re-creations of World War I trench warfare and the London Blitz. The cruel lessons of conflict are not shirked, especially in the permanent exhibition on the Holocaust.

KEW GARDENS

➕ Off the map ✉ Kew Road, Richmond ☎ 020 8332 5655 🕐 Open daily at 9:30 a.m.; closes between 4:15 and 7:30 depending on season 🍴 Restaurant and cafés Ⓜ Kew Gardens 🚌 65, 237, 267, 391 ⛴ Kew Pier (early Apr.–late Sep. only) 💲 $$$

The Royal Botanic Gardens at Kew, a World Heritage Site, date from 1759 and represent one of the finest collections of plants in the world, all contained within a 300-acre site. The vast Temperate House contains plants from every continent, and the architectural wonders are just as fascinating. Highlights include the Palm House, a billowing pavilion in glass and wrought iron that is a classic expression of creative 19th-century design. Scattered throughout the gardens are such interesting buildings as a 10-story pagoda and Kew Palace. The latter was built in 1631 by a Dutch merchant and was used as a country retreat by George III; it is a superb example of classical brickwork. Also here is Queen Charlotte's Cottage, given by George III to his wife Charlotte and a superb example of "cottage ornée" style.

LONDON ZOO

➕ Off the map ✉ Outer Circle, Regent's Park ☎ 020 7722 3333 🕐 Daily 10–5:30, early Mar.–early Oct.; 10–4:30, mid-Feb. to early Mar. and in late Oct.; last admission 1 hour before closing 🍴 Restaurant Ⓜ Camden Town 🚌 C2, 274 ⛴ Canal boat form Camden Lock 💲 $$$

London Zoo is irresistible for children but a treat for all. The 36-acre zoo has a strong conservation ethic and is working hard toward transforming the captive-animal emphasis of old-fashioned zoos. There are daily events and programs, including feeding time, "Animals in Action" and the Children's Zoo, where kids can handle docile animals. The "Web of Life" feature in the Millennium Conservation Centre explains how life-forms relate to one another. The spectacular Snowdon Aviary is a highlight, as is the Penguin Pool with its spiral ramp.

MADAME TUSSAUDS

➕ B4 ✉ Marylebone Road ☎ 0870 4003000 🕐 Mon.–Fri. 9:30–5:30, Sat.–Sun. 9–6 (extended hours during school holidays). Auditorium: Mon.–Fri. 12:30–5:30, Sat.–Sun. 10:30–6 🍴 Café Ⓜ Baker

London

Street 🚇 13, 18, 27, 30, 74, 82, 113, 139, 159, 274
💷 $$$; Chamber Live $$ 🎟 Reserve ahead by
credit card to avoid the sometimes hour-long line

A visit to Madame Tussauds' celebrated
wax model museum could be described as
blatant people-watching. The experience is
expensive, but where else can you peer up
the nose of a world leader or make faces at
the rich and famous? Just about everyone
is here: royalty, presidents, politicians,
celebrities, stars, heroes and villains.

Exhibits such as Blush and Premier
Night cast new light on the phrase
"rubbing shoulders with the rich and
famous." The Chamber of Horrors,
including the Live Chamber, has hideous
charm, although perhaps not for the very
young; the murderous are still menacing,
even in effigy, and you'll watch them
uneasily out of the corner of your eye.
Other attractions include The Spirit of
London, a quick trip through 400 years of
London's history as glimpsed from a
miniature city taxicab.

The adjacent Auditorium provides a
relaxing half-hour's mocked-up stargazing
and several space exhibits.

MUSEUM OF LONDON

🔲 E4 ✉ 150 London Wall ☎ 08704 443852 or 08704
443851 (recorded information) 🕐 Mon.–Sat. 10–5,
Sun. 11:30–5:50; last admission at 5:30 🍴 Café
🚇 Barbican or St. Paul's 🚌 4, 11, 8, 25, 56, 100, 172,
242, 501, 521 💷 Free; charge for special exhibitions

To really get a handle on London and its
utterly fascinating history, visit this
rewarding and enjoyable museum. The
story of the city from prehistoric times to
the present is told through set-piece
galleries focusing on important periods.
The Roman section is superb; its
reconstructed rooms, one with a fabulous
mosaic floor, and its sculptures are
particularly special highlights. Another
highlight is the Lord Mayor's State
Coach from the 1750s, a glittering golden
extravaganza that is still used during the
Lord Mayor's Show each November and
for the coronation of a new sovereign. The
Museum in Docklands (☎ 08704 44
3856), affiliated with the Museum of
London, brings to life dockland activity
through the ages.

NATIONAL GALLERY

🔲 D3 ✉ Trafalgar Square ☎ 020 7747 2885
🕐 Daily 10–6 (also Wed. 6–9 p.m.) 🍴 Restaurant
and café 🚇 Charing Cross or Leicester Square
🚌 3, 6, 9, 11, 12, 13, 15, 23, 24, 29, 53, X53, 77A, 88,
91, 109, 139, 159, 176, 453 💷 Free. The National
Gallery stages temporary exhibitions of major
artists, for which there is usually an admission
charge

London's National Gallery contains one of
the finest collections of Western European
art in the world. You may find most of the
world here on a busy day, but "the National"
seems able to absorb the crowds. The
collection is displayed chronologically in four
wings: the Sainsbury Wing (1250–1500),
West Wing (1510–1600), North Wing
(1600–1700) and East Wing (1700–1900).
You will need a floor plan to navigate.
Portable CD players are available (for a
suggested donation); the Gallery Guide
Soundtrack provides guidance.

Among the highlights not to miss are:
Leonardo da Vinci's *Virgin of the Rocks;*
Sandro Botticelli's *Venus and Mars;*
Titian's vivid and agile *Bacchus and
Ariadne;* Jan van Eyck's *The Arnolfini
Portrait;* Diego Velázquez's sensual
The Rokeby Venus; Rembrandt's
haunting *Self Portrait at the age of 34;*
Paul Cezanne's *Bathers;* and Vincent van
Gogh's *Sunflowers.*

The North Wing's octagonal Room 15
has glorious works by the great landscape
painters Claude Lorrain and J. M. W.
Turner. Head to the east wing for
Room 34, the Sackler Room, where you are
surrounded by the works of English
masters such as Thomas Gainsborough, Sir
Joshua Reynolds and John Constable.

NATIONAL MARITIME MUSEUM

🔲 Off the map ✉ Romney Road, Greenwich
☎ 020 8858 4422 or 020 8312 6565 (24-hour recorded
information) 🕐 Daily 10–6, Jul.–Aug.; 10–5 rest of
year; last admission 30 minutes before closing
🍴 Café in museum 🚇 Docklands Light Railway:
Cutty Sark 🚌 177, 180, 188, 199, 286, 380, 386
🚤 Riverboat to Greenwich Pier 💷 Free; charge for
special exhibitions

A visit to the world's largest maritime

COVENT GARDEN THROUGH TIME

London is an ever-changing city and, over the years, has evolved from surprising origins. A classic example of London's fascinating development is Covent Garden, today a lively focus of entertainment, dining and shopping. The area gets its name from being the medieval-era "Garden of the Convent," when vegetables were grown here for the kitchens at Westminster Abbey.

During the 17th century it was laid out as the finest square in London, complete with the Church of St. Paul and arcaded houses. The architect was Inigo Jones, who planned it in Italianate style, with the square known as the piazza. Then the owner of Covent Garden, the Earl of Bedford, decided to hold a market in the square. Commerce overcame culture; buildings were erected – first the older fruit and vegetable market and then the floral market. The Opera House building was added later.

In 1974 the market moved to new premises and the piazza market halls were renovated and filled with stores, cafés and restaurants that have transformed the old "Garden of the Convent" into a major leisure area.

Covent Garden Today

From Covent Garden subway station, turn right and walk southeast, past Crabtree & Evelyn (renowned for bath oils and soaps) on your right, into the heart of Covent Garden. This is an excellent place to browse and wander at your leisure. There are fashion boutiques for all tastes. These line the cobbled piazza, tastefully blending in with the Italianate architecture and elegant columns. Under the glass-and-iron roof of the renovated market building set in the middle of the square, you'll find stalls selling crafts, jewelry and clothing. There is a small branch of the much-loved London toy shop, Hamleys, on the northern side of the central market. In front of St. Paul's Church, on the western side of the market, street performers often entertain the crowds with comedy or magic tricks. It all adds to the exciting bustle of this area.

If you walk back toward the Covent Garden subway and head two blocks north, you will find yourself in the maze of small streets that intersect with Neal Street. Neal's Yard has a bohemian air, and there are some good places to buy vegetarian food or eat a light meal. Neal's Yard Dairy sells some of the best cheese in the country – it's all British or Irish made.

Back to traditional roots – selling flowers in the "Garden of the Convent"

Classical facade of St. Paul's Cathedral

visitors to go behind the scenes, watching scientists at work in new laboratories and viewing otherwise hidden parts of the museum's invaluable collection.

The Dinosaurs Gallery features a huge, animatronic *Tyrannosaurus rex*, complete with smelly breath. This is not quite Disney, but the main exhibits tell the dinosaur story through a mix of science and entertaining effect. The Earth Galleries deal with the world beneath our feet and are every bit as fascinating.

ST. PAUL'S CATHEDRAL

✚ E3 ✉ St. Paul's Churchyardl ☎ 020 7246 8348 ⏰ Mon.–Sat. 8:30–5 (last admission at 4). Closed during some services 🍴 Restaurant and café Ⓢ St. Paul's 🚌 4, 11, 15, 23, 25, 26, 100, 242 💷 $$$ ℹ Guided tours ($$) at 11, 11;30. 1;30 and 2; audio tours $$

St. Paul's Cathedral is one of Sir Christopher Wren's greatest achievements, and is easily reached from the Tate Modern on the South Bank by a walk over the Millennium Bridge. The twin towers and baroque elements of its facade and the crowning glory of its dome are still breathtaking. The airy, bright interior is full of stately monuments, memorials and statues. You can descend to the crypt or ascend heavenward up 530 steps, first to the famous Whispering Gallery, where you can whisper your thoughts for everyone else to hear, on to the Stone Gallery and then to the Golden Gallery for superb views over London.

SCIENCE MUSEUM

✚ A2 ✉ Exhibition Road ☎ 0870 870 4868 ⏰ Daily 10–6 🍴 Café Ⓢ South Kensington 🚌 9, 10, 14, 49, 52, 70, 74, 345, 360, 414, C1 💷 Free; IMAX cinema $$$; space flight simulator $$

Every aspect of science and technology is covered in this vast collection, and you will find everything from atoms to the *Apollo 10* command module. The museum's official guidebook will help you find your way around the seven floors. On display are George Stephenson's early locomotive, the *Rocket*, and Charles Babbage's enormous prototype computer.

museum offers insight into Britain's past maritime expertise. The Nelson Gallery celebrates the great admiral, with his bullet-pierced coat from the Battle of Trafalgar adding drama. In the glass-roofed Neptune Court is the gilded state barge created for Frederick, Prince of Wales in 1732. Themed galleries tell of early explorers, the age of ocean liners, naval costumes and the British Empire. Children can try their hands at things nautical in the All Hands and Bridge galleries, while all ages can test their knowledge in the Search Station zone.

NATURAL HISTORY MUSEUM

✚ A2 ✉ Cromwell Road (Life Galleries entrance), Exhibition Road (Earth Galleries entrance) ☎ 020 7942 5000 ⏰ Mon.–Sat. 10–5:50, Sun. 11–5:50; last admission at 5:30 🍴 Restaurant and cafés Ⓢ South Kensington 🚌 14, 49, 70, 74, 345, C1 💷 Free; charge for special exhibitions

The Natural History Museum shouldn't be missed and is a great favorite with children. There are thought to be 70 million plus objects in the collection (but not all on display), from the tiniest of preserved insects to a reconstructed blue whale. The museum is divided into two sections, the Life Galleries and the Earth Galleries. In the former, the Darwin Centre allows

The Tower of London recalls some of the most dramatic times of British history over 900 years

The huge Flight Gallery contains ranks of aircraft, and in the East Hall's Power Gallery great steam engines from the Industrial Revolution hiss and revolve. Many of the exhibits have a hands-on element. Check for any special events or demonstrations on the day you visit. The Wellcome Wing is a groundbreaking complex of up-to-the-minute exhibits that give visitors the chance to interact with and explore current scientific issues.

TATE BRITAIN

D1 ⊠ Millbank (also entrances: Atterbury Street and John Islip Street) ☎ 020 7887 8000 or 020 7887 8008 (24-hour recorded information) Daily 10–5:50; last admission at 5 Restaurant and café in gallery Pimlico 2, 3, 36, 77A, 88, 159, 185, 507, C10 Tate Boat: Tate Britain to Tate Modern Free; special exhibitions $$$ Guided tours (free), events, talks and films

Tate Britain exhibits the world's greatest collection of British art from 1500 to the present in a mixture of historical and thematic displays. Works by artists as diverse as Barbara Hepworth, William Hogarth and David Hockney are on display. The Turner Collection in the Clore Gallery comprises 300 oil paintings and 30,000 sketches and watercolors by J. M. W. Turner.

TATE MODERN

E3 ⊠ Bankside (entrances: river walkway or Holland Street) ☎ 020 7887 8000 or 020 7887 8008 (24-hour recorded information) Daily 10–6 (also Fri.–Sat. 6–10 p.m.); last admission 45 minutes before closing Restaurant and café Southwark 45, 63, 100, 344, 381, RV1 Tate Boat: Tate Britain to Tate Modern Free; special exhibitions $$$

Housed in the former Bankside Power Station, on the south bank of the River Thames, the Tate Modern opened in 2000. Britain's national museum of modern art features an international collection from 1900 to the present. It includes works by major figures such as Salvador Dalí, Pablo Picasso, Henri Matisse, Edvard Munch, Piet Mondrian, Jackson Pollock, Andy Warhol and Roy Lichtenstein, as well as such contemporary artists as Damien Hirst. In a break with tradition, the collection is presented in themed groups rather than chronologically or by school. Adventurous and often controversial conceptual works and installations also are a feature.

You can approach the Tate Modern in style from north of the river by walking across the Millennium Bridge, a pedestrian-only bridge that slices straight across the Thames.

The simple memorial to World War I victims lies beneath the soaring arches of Westminster Abbey

TOWER OF LONDON

✚ F3 ✉ Tower Hill ☎ 0870 750 8080 or 0870 756 6060 (recorded information) ◷ Tue.–Sat. 9–5, Sun.–Mon. 10–6, Mar.–Oct.; Tue.–Sat. 9–5, Sun.–Mon. 10–5, rest of year 🍴 Restaurant and café 🚇 Tower Hill 🚌 15, 25, 42, 78, 100, D1 🚢 Riverboat to Tower Millennium Pier ✋ $$$

There are crowds of visitors here most of the year, and you may find yourself being hurried through some of the sections. It is an astonishing place all the same, steeped in history. Many of the nation's most daring personalities ended up here, as prisoners or as reluctant "guests"; or, like Henry VIII's wives Anne Boleyn and Catherine Howard, on a final trip to the executioner's block. Tours conducted by the Yeoman Warders, or "Beefeaters," give an excellent introduction, after which you can wander at will to ponder the Bloody Tower, Traitors' Gate, the Tower Ravens and the execution site at Tower Green.

VICTORIA AND ALBERT MUSEUM

✚ A2 ✉ Cromwell Road ☎ 020 7942 2000 or 0870 906 3883 (24-hour recorded information) ◷ Daily 10–5:45 (also Wed. and last Fri. of the month 5:45–10) 🍴 Restaurant and cafés 🚇 South Kensington 🚌 14, 74, C1 ✋ Free; charge for some exhibitions and events ℹ Free guided introductory tours daily at 10:30, 11:30, 1:30 and 3:30 (also Wed. at 4:30); British Gallery tours daily at 12:30 and 2:30; special themed tour Wed. at 7:30 p.m.

The "V&A," as it is affectionately known, is recognized as being the world's greatest repository of applied and decorative art, containing a ravishing collection of jewelry, silverware, glass, ceramics, textiles, dress, furniture, sculpture, paintings, books, prints and photographs from all over the world. The British Galleries, a chronological survey of British art and design from 1500 to 1900, are an attraction in themselves. The Europe galleries alone are a day's work. The Asia, Ceramics, Glass, Sculpture and the Fashion, Jewellery and Accessories galleries, along with the superb art collection, are all worth seeing. The Silver galleries display European silver from 1400 to 1800.

WESTMINSTER ABBEY

✚ D2 ✉ Broad Sanctuary ☎ 020 7654 4900 ◷ Mon.–Fri. 9.30–4:45 (also Wed. 4:45–7 p.m., late Mar.–late Oct.; 4:45–6, rest of year), Sat. 9:30–2:45; last admission 1 hour before closing. Cloisters: daily 8–6. Abbey Museum, Pyx Chamber and Chapter House: daily 10:30–4 🚇 Westminster or St. James's Park 🚌 3, 11, 12, 24, 53, 77A, 88, 159 ✋ Abbey $$$. Cloisters, Abbey Museum, Pyx Chamber and Chapter House free ℹ Abbey tours $$; audio tour $$

Westminster Abbey has been the ceremonial site of almost every British coronation, from William the Conqueror in 1066 to Queen Elizabeth II in 1953. Monarchs buried here include Henry VII, Elizabeth I and Mary, Queen of Scots. The abbey is full of monuments and memorials to famous people. A tour of the many Coronation treasures offers insight into the grandeur of the occasion. The present abbey dates, in part, from the 13th century and is a powerful expression of English Gothic style, with French elements.

Henry VII's chapel has a style of airy elegance that represents Gothic at its finest. Tiered sculptures line the walls, and the lofty roof is hung with exquisite fan vaulting. The Tomb of the Unknown Warrior commemorates the hundreds of thousands of British servicemen killed in World War I. In the south transept is Poets' Corner, resting place of Chaucer, Robert Browning and Alfred Tennyson, among others.

Looking from St. James's Park to the exuberant Victoria Monument and Buckingham Palace beyond

A ROYAL STROLL

Royal London begins at Admiralty Arch, at the southwest corner of Trafalgar Square. The arch dates from 1911 and was erected as part of a general celebration of Queen Victoria's life and reign. Beyond the arch is The Mall, a broad open avenue that runs southwest, directly toward Buckingham Palace. It was first laid out by Charles II in the 1660s as part of St. James's Park. It is open to traffic, but as soon as you pass beneath Admiralty Arch the city's character becomes less frantic.

Keep to the sidewalk on the left of the avenue and you'll soon pass a statue of the seafarer Captain James Cook. St. James's Park spreads out to the left – a great sweep of open lawns, trees and gardens with a lake at its heart. The right (north) side of The Mall is lined with stately buildings. First is Carlton House Terrace, broken halfway by the Duke of York's Steps that lead up to the Duke of York's Column. At St. James's Palace, sentries guard the Tudor Tower. Next to the palace is Clarence House, the London residence of the Prince of Wales and the Duchess of Cornwall. Five of the rooms are open to the public from early August to mid-October (tickets must be reserved in advance; ☎ 020 7766 7303).

On your way to the large open area in front of Buckingham Palace is Lancaster House (a building now used by the government). In front of the palace is the spectacular bronze and marble Victoria Monument, erected in 1911 and constructed with more than 2,300 tons of marble. The exuberant bronze winged Victory crowns the monument.

Beyond the monument and behind a barricade of railings and gates stands Buckingham Palace. The "royal standard" (the Queen's flag) flies when the Queen is in residence. The Changing of the Guard takes place daily at 11:30 a.m. from early April through July, and on alternate days the rest of the year (weather permitting).

Nineteen of Buckingham Palace's state rooms are open from late August until late September, when the royal family are not in residence (ticket office in Green Park or ☎ 020 7321 2233). The Royal Mews are worth a visit for their state carriages and splendid horses. For the walking route, see the city map on pages 86–87.

Horse Guards ride along The Mall

Edinburgh

EDINBURGH

Edinburgh is Scotland in microcosm. In this lively capital city, buildings do not overpower the spectacular landscape of hills and crags that march across the southeastern horizon. Yet Edinburgh's buildings – from the old houses of the Royal Mile to the elegant Georgian terraces and crescents of the New Town – are outstanding complements to the city's natural setting. Few other capitals seem to reflect the history and culture of their country so potently.

Edinburgh's famous castle sits high on a craggy promontory, Castle Rock, made inaccessible on three sides by steep cliffs and with a long descending ridge on its fourth side. The city's layout is linear, a pattern set by Castle Rock and Castle Ridge, down which the Royal Mile descends to the Palace of Holyroodhouse. North of the Royal Mile lies a shallow valley once covered by swampy Nor' Loch, and now occupied by the lovely Princes Street Gardens, with Waverley Station, the city's main railroad station, at their eastern end. Above the gardens and to the north is Edinburgh's main

thoroughfare, Princes Street, its south side uncluttered by buildings and thus serving as a splendid place from which to view the castle and Old Edinburgh.

First Impressions

Most visitors arrive by train at Waverley Station. From the station you emerge onto Waverley Bridge

Greyfriars Bobby

This Skye terrier's devotion to his dead master is enshrined in Edinburgh folklore. The famous Greyfriars Bobby was a trained police dog who worked with his master, Constable John Gray, guarding livestock at Edinburgh's city market, the Grassmarket, during the 1850s. When Gray died at age 45 he was buried in Greyfriars churchyard, and his devoted terrier took up what began a 14-year vigil by his grave. Bobby was cared for and beloved by everyone in the neighborhood. A statue of Greyfriars Bobby stands at the junction of Candlemaker Row and the George IV Bridge, near the church gate and opposite a pub named after the faithful hound.

Edinburgh

and get an immediate first impression of the city's visual drama. The castle and the dark soaring back walls of the buildings that enclose the Royal Mile rise to the south like extensions of the cliffs of Castle Rock. To the north is Princes Street. Here, the Scott Monument, a towering Gothic steeple, dominates one view; the bulk of the Balmoral Hotel, itself castle-like, dominates the other. These buildings are spectacularly illuminated at night.

From Waverley Bridge you can take an instant Edinburgh Tour open-top bus tour that will introduce you to the city. Details about city transportation are available from Lothian Buses City Centre Travelshops at Hanover Street, Shandwick Place and Waverley Bridge. Next door is The Hub, Edinburgh's Festival Centre. You can also find out about various other guided tours from the Edinburgh and Scotland Information Centre on Princes Street, only a minute or so from Waverley

Station. They include historical walking tours and highly entertaining Witchery Tours, or ghost tours, that take you through the Old Town's maze of historic lanes and courtyards.

Two Edinburghs

Exploring the city on your own is straightforward. Old Edinburgh is the southern part, encompassed by the castle and the Royal Mile; beyond them are the areas of Southside, the Grassmarket and Canongate. To the south of the Royal Mile you will find the Royal Museum, the Museum of Scotland (see page 102) and the Edinburgh Festival Theatre, a venue presenting fine drama and opera. Edinburgh Castle and the Royal Mile are Old Edinburgh's main attractions. You can easily spend an entire day here, and amid the souvenir shops and tourist spots there is a potent sense of history embodied by the splendid clutter of tall old sandstone buildings. Also take time for a walk in

Edinburgh

Holyrood Park, a green world of spectacular craggy hills, lochs and glens that is a genuine slice of Highland Scotland.

North of Waverley Bridge is Edinburgh's New Town, where Old Edinburgh expanded during the 18th century as part of a typically Georgian exercise in town planning. Above Princes Street is George Street, with handsome Charlotte Square and St. Andrew Square at either end. The elegance and unity of Georgian architecture – an exhilarating contrast to the equally splendid Royal Mile – can be appreciated at such locations as Queen Street Gardens, the Royal Circus (a circular residential street), Great King Street and Drummond Place – all north of George Street – as well as around Moray Place, west of Queen Street Gardens.

Life in Edinburgh

George Street and Princes Street, and the short connecting streets between them, are Edinburgh's main shopping streets. On Princes Street you will find an Edinburgh institution, Jenners, a department store that sells luxury items and has a wonderful food hall. This street also has branches of House of Fraser, Debenhams, and Marks and Spencer.

Edinburgh is crowded during the summer, but the cultural feast of the Edinburgh International Festival, in the second half of August and early September, is well worth taking in. There also are good alternatives outside the festival season – modern Scottish drama at the Traverse Theatre, or musical performances at Usher Hall.

Stylish Edinburgh restaurants offer distinctive Scottish dishes like wild salmon, Aberdeen Angus beef or game such as grouse. Local residents are friendly and down to earth, always willing to help visitors. Traditional Scottish reticence is replaced here by a style that reflects sophistication without pretension, and by pride in the city's internationalism. And with a historic return to the Royal Mile by Scotland's recently formed governing body, the Scottish Parliament, Edinburgh has entered the new millennium with renewed stature and optimism.

ESSENTIAL INFORMATION

 TOURIST INFORMATION
Edinburgh and Scotland Information Centre
• 3 Princes Street ☎ 08452 255121 (U.K. only); 001 44 1506 832121 (from the U.S.); www.edinburgh.org
• Edinburgh International Airport (walk-in visitors only).

 URBAN TRANSPORTATION
The main train station is Waverley Station on Princes Street (☎ 08457 550033). A good bus network services Edinburgh. For bus information contact Lothian Busses City Centre Travelshops at Hanover Street, Shandwick Place or Waverley Bridge (☎ 0131 555 6363, 24 hours). Taxis can be hailed on the street; there are also stands at Waverley Station and on Waverley Bridge, or call Central Taxis (☎ 0131 229 2468) or City Cabs (☎ 0131 228 1211).

 AIRPORT INFORMATION
Edinburgh International Airport, at Turnhouse, is 8 miles west of the city center. Buses run to and from Waverley Station every 10 minutes, every 15 minutes off peak times; journey time 20 minutes. Taxis also serve the airport. For airport information ☎ 08700 400007.

CLIMATE – average highs and lows for the month

JAN.	FEB.	MAR.	APR.	MAY	JUN.	JUL.	AUG.	SEP.	OCT.	NOV.	DEC.
5°C	6°C	7°C	10°C	13°C	16°C	18°C	17°C	15°C	12°C	9°C	6°C
42°F	43°F	45°F	50°F	55°F	61°F	64°F	63°F	59°F	54°F	48°F	43°F
1°C	1°C	2°C	4°C	6°C	9°C	11°C	11°C	9°C	6°C	4°C	2°C
34°F	34°F	36°F	39°F	43°F	48°F	52°F	52°F	48°F	43°F	39°F	36°F

Dramatically perched on a volcanic crag, Edinburgh Castle dates back to the 12th century

CITY SIGHTS

Key to symbols

🔳 map coordinates refer to the Edinburgh map on pages 98–99; sights below are highlighted in yellow on the map.

✉ address or location ☎ telephone number

🕐 opening times 🚌 nearest bus route

🍴 restaurant or café on site or nearby

👜 admission charge: $$$ more than £6, $$ £2–£6, $ less than £2 ℹ️ other relevant information

CALTON HILL

Calton Hill 🔳 D2–D3
Nelson Monument ✉ Calton Hill ☎ 0131 556 2716 🕐 Mon. 1–6, Tue.–Sat. 10–6, Apr.–Sep.; Mon.–Sat. 10–3, rest of year 🚌 35 👜 $$

Calton Hill, at the east end of Princes Street, is crowned with neoclassic buildings that have earned Edinburgh the nickname "The Athens of the North," but their dark stonework hardly matches the bare, bright brilliance of the Parthenon or the Temple of the Winds. There are great views of Princes Street, Edinburgh Castle and Arthur's Seat from this hilltop, as well as Holyrood Park and the Salisbury Crag. You can also climb the 143 steps of the tall monument to Admiral Horatio Nelson for an even better view from its top. Note: This site should be avoided at dusk and after dark.

EDINBURGH CASTLE

🔳 B1–C1 ✉ Castlehill ☎ 0131 225 9846 🕐 Daily 9:30–6, Apr.–Oct.; 9:30–5, rest of year. Last admission 45 minutes before closing 🍴 Cafés 🚌 23, 27, 28, 35, 41, 45 👜 $$$

You can tackle Scotland's most visited attraction in several ways. There are official guided tours, which are entertaining and informative. A self-guiding audio tour is a good option that helps focus the mind amid inevitable crowds. Brace yourself for the One O' Clock Gun, a 25-pounder that blasts off a single blank charge from the Half Moon battery at 1 p.m. daily, except Sunday. Castle highlights are the 12th-century St. Margaret's Chapel; the Stone of Scone; the Vaults, where the mighty 500-year-old siege gun, Mons Meg, stands in grim splendor like some huge black beast; and the Great Hall, with its glorious hammer beam roof and masses of weaponry. The Honours of the Kingdom exhibition is an evocative journey through history that culminates with a display of Scotland's luminous Crown Jewels in the Crown Room.

Hikers enjoy the view of Edinburgh from Arthur's Seat in Holyrood Park, 822 feet above the city

GEORGIAN HOUSE

🔲 B2 ✉ 7 Charlotte Square ☎ 0131 226 3318
🕐 Daily 10–7, Jul.–Aug.; 10–5, Apr.–Jun. and
Sep.–Oct.; 11–3 in Mar. and Nov. Last admission 45
minutes before closing 🚌 All city center buses
💷 $$

The Georgian House is the showplace of
New Town's Charlotte Square and one of
the most prestigious addresses in
Scotland. Built in 1796 by Robert Adam,
this masterpiece of urban design was
once home to the chief of the Lamont
clan. There are three floors open to the
public, all full of delectable furnishings
and beautiful paintings. The basement
houses the original wine cellar and
kitchen.

HOLYROOD PARK

🔲 E1 ✉ Queen's Drive 🚌 35 💷 Free
Few cities are blessed with such a
marvelous open space as Holyrood Park,
or Queen's Park, as it is also known. The
park is dominated by the dramatic
Salisbury Crags and by Arthur's Seat, a
high, rounded hill. You can enter the
park from the bottom of the Royal Mile
(see pages 104–105), just beyond the
Palace of Holyroodhouse. The park's
high ground is encircled by a public road,
the Queen's Drive, but the area is better
enjoyed on foot. A broad, slanting path

slices up the slopes below Salisbury
Crags. It takes you high above the city,
and the views are outstanding. Arthur's
Seat can also be climbed, but it is a
challenging hike; hiking boots are
recommended. However, you can keep to
the low ground of the park and still enjoy
the splendid sights.

MUSEUM OF SCOTLAND AND ROYAL MUSEUM

🔲 D1 ✉ Chambers Street ☎ 0131 247 4422
🕐 Mon.–Sat. 10–5 (also Tue. 5–8), Sun. noon–5
🍽 Restaurant and cafés 🚌 23, 27, 28, 41, 42, 45
💷 Free ℹ Free guided tours

The long-established Royal Museum is a
splendid 19th-century building enclosing
a vast space framed by elegant ironwork,
with galleries rising through several
floors. Here are traditional displays
covering the natural world, science and
industry, and the decorative arts.
Alongside the Royal Museum stands an
adventurous new building, the Museum
of Scotland, a dramatic modern design in
golden stone that tells the story of
Scotland from its geological beginnings
to the 20th century. The complex contains
several levels, each displaying a particular
era of Scotland's history. Ask the
atttendant at the information desk for
floor plans and advice on finding your way
around the galleries.

NATIONAL GALLERY OF SCOTLAND

➕ C2 ✉ The Mound ☎ 0131 624 6200 🕐 Daily 10–5 (also Thu. 5–7) 🚌 City center buses 💷 Free; special exhibitions $$ ℹ Free shuttle bus between the five National Galleries of Scotland in Edinburgh

The National Gallery is a large, 19th-century neoclassic building with a good selection from all periods, including the splendid *Trinity Altarpiece*, by Hugo van der Goes, and the seductive *Venus Anadyomene*, by Titian. Most of the major names in 17th-century European art are represented; there are some fine landscapes by Claude Lorrain, and Nicholas Poussin's *Seven Sacraments* is on view. There is a powerful work by Frederick Edwin Church, *Niagara Falls from the American Side*. Scottish painting is well represented by Gavin Hamilton and Allan Ramsay. Look for *Edinburgh Castle and the Nor' Loch*, by Alexander Nasmyth, for some idea of what Old Edinburgh looked like before the Nor' Loch was drained and replaced by Princes Street Gardens. Sir Henry Raeburn's *The Rev. Robert Walker Skating on Duddingston Loch* and Sir George Harvey's *The Curlers* are wonderfully lively and very typical Scottish narrative works.

PALACE OF HOLYROODHOUSE

➕ E2 ✉ Canongate, Royal Mile ☎ 0131 556 5100 🕐 Daily 9:30–6, Apr.–Oct.; 9:30–4:30, rest of year; last admission 45 minutes before closing 🚌 35 💷 $$$ ℹ Closed for state functions. Phone for details

Queen Elizabeth II's official residence in Scotland, ancient Holyroodhouse was part of the Abbey of Holyrood, but much of the present palace was built for King Charles II. The severe neoclassicism of the courtyard block reflects the distinctly English fashion of the time; nevertheless it exudes Scottish history. The State Apartments of Charles' palace are luxurious and grand, crammed with artifacts and paintings elegantly displayed beneath superb stucco ceilings. Deep in the Historical Apartments is the bedchamber of Mary, Queen of Scots and the adjoining closet where, in 1566, her secretary and confidante, David Rizzio, was stabbed to death by associates of the Queen's delinquent husband, Lord Darnley. You can view the palace by guided tour only, but you'll be led by knowledgeable and entertaining staff. The Queen's Gallery, in an adjacent building, has exhibitions of art from the Royal collections.

ROYAL BOTANIC GARDEN EDINBURGH

➕ Off the map ✉ 20A Inverleith Row ☎ 0131 552 7171 🕐 Daily 10–7, Apr.–Sep.; 10–6, Mar. and Oct.; 10–4 rest of year 🍴 Café 🚌 8, 17, 23, 27 💷 Free; Glasshouse $$ ℹ Guided tours Apr.–Sep. at 11 and 2 ($$)

The Royal Botanic Garden Edinburgh is just north of the New Town. Rhododendrons are the highlight of Scotland's premier garden, at their colorful best from late April to early June. Other attractions are the Glasshouses, where orchids, palms and other exotics flourish in defiance of Scotland's less than tropical climate; the Chinese Hillside; and a decidedly Scottish heather garden.

ST. GILES' CATHEDRAL

➕ D2 ✉ Royal Mile ☎ 0131 225 9442 🕐 Mon.–Fri. 9–7, Sat. 9–5, Sun. 1–5, May–Sep.; Mon.–Sat. 9–5, Sun. 1–5, rest of year 🍴 Restaurant 🚌 23, 27, 28, 35, 41, 42, 45 💷 Free (donation suggested $) ℹ Guided tours (free)

St. Giles' Cathedral (or the High Kirk of Edinburgh) is the seat of Scotland's Presbyterian religion and a powerful feature of the Royal Mile (see pages 104–105). The Kirk is an uneasy mix of medieval Gothic and Georgian Gothic, the latter grafted on in the early 19th century; the interior reflects an enthusiastic Victorian restoration. There are some superb external features, including the 19th-century west door and the late medieval tower and spire, a dramatic sight on Edinburgh's skyline. Inside, St. Giles' has many fine features and memorials. A 20th-century addition is the Thistle Chapel, built in 1911 as a private chapel for the Knights of the Most Holy Order of the Thistle. Richly carved stonework enlivens the interior of the chapel, and the lierne vaulting of the roof, with its carved bosses, is outstanding. Look near the entrance door for the tiny bagpipe-playing angel.

Edinburgh

STROLL DOWN THE ROYAL MILE

Edinburgh's Royal Mile is the epitome of Old Edinburgh. Made up of four linked streets – Castlehill, Lawnmarket, High Street and Canongate – it descends the sloping back of a long, steep-sided ridge from Edinburgh Castle (see page 101) at the west end to the Palace of Holyroodhouse (see page 103) at the east end. On either side of the Royal Mile are tall buildings, riddled with courtyards and passageways known as "closes" and separated by narrow streets known as "wynds", all of it a delight to explore. All the way down the Royal Mile historic buildings punctuate the general streetscape, and there are numerous stores, cafés, restaurants and pubs.

You can begin a relaxed descent of the Royal Mile from the entrance to the Castle Esplanade, starting with Castlehill. Attractions beckon from either side. On the left is the Edinburgh Old Town Weaving Company, with its masses of tartan cloth and working mill. On the right is the Scotch Whisky Heritage Centre. Next on the left and well worth a visit is the fascinating Camera Obscura and World of Illusions, where moving images of the surrounding area are projected onto a white viewing table. The street is narrow here but opens up just past the powerful Highland Tolbooth, a handsome Gothic building with the tallest spire in Edinburgh. It is now The Hub, Edinburgh's Festival Centre, home of the Edinburgh International Festival and a focus of the city's cultural life. At this point, the Royal Mile becomes the much wider Lawnmarket, once the city's linen market.

Keep to the left side of the street, where steps rise from street level to the

The start of the atmospheric Royal Mile, marked by tall, narrow, sandstone buildings

pavement. There are several stores here selling woolen and tartan goods. Soon you come to Gladstone's Land, a 17th-century merchant's house now restored by the National Trust for Scotland. The house's Painted Chamber is stunning. Just a bit farther is the entrance to Lady Stair's Close. A narrow alleyway leads to an open square and to Lady Stair's House, now The Writers' Museum, a quiet little corner housing memorabilia associated with Scotland's finest writers, including Robert Burns, Robert Louis Stevenson and Sir Walter Scott. The spiral stairs have an uneven step halfway up, a common trick in medieval houses aimed at tripping an intruder in the dark.

The Lawnmarket reaches a junction with Bank Street and the street called George IV Bridge, where the Royal Mile becomes High Street. Here you will find a remarkable concentration of historic buildings. On the east corner with Bank Street is the High Court, with a bronze statue of Scottish philosopher David Hume in front of it. Next to the High Court is Edinburgh City Chambers,

Edinburgh

At the foot of the Royal Mile on the fringe of Old Edinburgh, Holyroodhouse is the official Scottish residence of Queen Elizabeth II

with an arcaded entrance screen. Opposite is St. Giles' Cathedral (see page 103). Behind St. Giles is Parliament Square and the old Parliament House, seat of the Scottish Parliament until the union with England in 1707.

High Street then descends gently to a junction with North and South Bridge Street. Stay on the north side of High Street, past the entrances to various alleys, and look for Chalmer's Court. Go through the entrance and down the steps to the preserved apse of the 15th-century Trinity College Church, home to the Brass Rubbing Centre.

On the other side of High Street opposite Chalmer's Court is the entertaining Museum of Childhood. Farther down High Street, just before the junction with Jeffrey Street and St. Mary's Street, is the John Knox House, a celebration of the 16th-century religious reformer who brought the Protestant Reformation to Scotland with more than a whiff of fire and brimstone. Beyond Jeffrey Street the Royal Mile becomes Canongate and

narrows once more. Halfway down Canongate is the old Tolbooth, with its wonderful clock and conical-roofed towers. Canongate Tolbooth was once a courtroom and jail and is now The People's Story, an exhibition of Edinburgh life. Just opposite is The Museum of Edinburgh, a beautifully restored late 16th-century building containing an excellent collection of Edinburgh artifacts.

Diagonally opposite the Museum of Edinburgh is the 17th-century Canongate Kirk and Kirkyard, which has a wonderfully bright interior. The church has close royal connections; the royal family worship here when they are in residence at nearby Holyroodhouse, and the royal coat of arms can be seen on one of the church benches, or pews. A short distance past the church the Royal Mile passes the new Scottish Parliament building to the right, and continues as Abbey Street to end its progress through Scottish history at the gates of the Palace of Holyroodhouse. For the walking route, see the city map on pages 98–99.

With the spires of Christ Church and Merton College in the background, a rowing "eight" carries on Oxford student sporting traditions

OXFORD

Oxford, 56 miles northwest of London, is a typical English market town at heart. It is located within a hollow amid low hills at the gentle confluence of the River Thames and River Cherwell. What makes Oxford exceptional is its university, the oldest in the English-speaking world, an institution that is represented not by a single campus but by 39 independent colleges that are scattered throughout the city. They represent elegant seats of learning, but are also blessed with beautiful buildings.

The history of Oxford is said to have begun with the founding of a priory by the Saxon St. Frideswide, near where the River Thames and River Cherwell meet. Christ Church Cathedral supplanted the priory, and in time wealth from the medieval wool trade led to the founding of other religious houses, where learning was revered. Scholars were drawn to Oxford, and from these beginnings the university evolved.

Unless you're a student, Oxford is more of a journey through history and great architecture than through academia. For the visitor, the experience may seem faintly voyeuristic. You visit the colleges, picking your way through elegant quadrangles, chapels, arched passageways, gardens and libraries, and at times you may feel you are intruding on a select world of academic privilege and of cultural paradigms.

Yet the physical integration of Oxford's colleges with the realities of Oxford as a city dispel any sense of intrusion. This is a living, working city that retains its own identity and commercial life. Take a ride on a Guide Friday open-top bus to see the principal sights, leaving the bus where and when you like, or take a guided walking tour of historic Oxford or of the colleges. Stroll by the Thames or take a river cruise.

Oxford's Colleges

You can walk around central Oxford in under an hour, but it is the density and

Oxford

complexity of colleges and great buildings that is so absorbing. The heart of the university lies between High Street and Broad Street and is enclosed by the colleges of Brasenose, All Souls, Hertford and Exeter. The University Church of St. Mary the Virgin (see page 110) is on High Street. Behind St. Mary's is Radcliffe Square, which has the elegant 18th-century Renaissance rotunda of the Radcliffe Camera (chamber) at its heart. On the east side of the square is All Souls College. On the west side is Brasenose College, named after a traditional brass "mask" door knocker and a treasured college possession; a replica can be seen on the great oak doors.

From Radcliffe Square you can walk into the Schools Quadrangle of the Bodleian Library, with its superb Jacobean entrance tower and decorative inner walls. Through the arch on the north side of the quadrangle is the Sheldonian Theatre, where the

Encaenia (the ceremony to confer honorary degrees) and the degree ceremony for Oxford graduates are held.

The Radcliffe Square area is the heart of the university, but try to visit some of the colleges when their grounds are open to the public. Include Christ Church (see page 109), the largest and most famous of the colleges, and do not miss nearby Merton College, reputedly the oldest of them all and certainly one of the finest, with its delightful gardens, ancient quadrangle, medieval library and chapel. Adjoining Merton Street, cobbled and quiet, is one of the finest parts of the city. Merton counts among its alumni 14th-century religious reformer John Wycliffe, poet T. S. Eliot and actor-singer Kris Kristofferson. Then head east toward Magdalen (pronounced "Maudlin") and its superb tower, Cloister Quad, gardens and riverside walks. Magdalen alumni include playwright Oscar Wilde and actor Dudley Moore.

Oxford

The Market Town

Oxford itself is famous for automobile manufacturing, and is the home of the Morris Oxford and the T-series MG sports car. They were produced at Oxford's Cowley factories, built up by William Richard Morris, later Viscount Nuffield, a self-made man who founded Oxford's Nuffield College among his numerous charitable acts. Visit the Museum of Oxford and discover the history of the city, and take in the Pitt Rivers Museum and the Oxford University Museum of Natural History. Climb to the top of Carfax Tower for great views of Oxford.

The streets radiating from Carfax constitute Oxford's main shopping area. Cornmarket has a range of well-known stores. Off Cornmarket's east side is Golden Cross, where Shakespeare's plays are said to have been performed. Just beyond is the celebrated covered market, with excellent food stalls and other outlets.

Oxford's university population and townspeople exhibit a fascinating contrast of lifestyles. In medieval times this duality led to occasional bloody

The Original Alice

The children's books *Alice in Wonderland* and *Alice Through The Looking Glass* were inspired by Oxford life. Charles Lutwidge Dodgson, a lecturer and ordained deacon at Christ Church, wrote the books during the latter part of the 19th century. Dodgson formed an intense friendship with Alice Liddell, the young daughter of the Dean of Christ Church. He entertained her and her sisters with his stories of Wonderland, and they were later published under the pseudonym Lewis Carroll. Alice's Shop, ✉ 83 St. Aldates ☎ 01865 723793 ❹ Daily 11–5, sells Alice memorabilia.

battles, but although today's students are noted for their often boisterous post-exam antics, Oxford is an eminently civilized place where the traditions of "town and gown" rest easily side by side.

ESSENTIAL INFORMATION

TOURIST INFORMATION
Oxford Tourist Information Centre
• 15–16 Broad Street
☎ 01865 726871;
www.visitoxford.org

URBAN TRANSPORTATION
Oxford railroad station, Botley Road (☎ 08457 484950) offers regular train connections to and from London. Central Oxford is a 10-minute walk from the station. Local bus services in and around the city are frequent. Two companies provide all local services: The Oxford Bus Company (☎ 01865 785400) and

Stagecoach Oxford (☎ 01865 772250). Taxi stands are located at the railroad station, Carfax and the Gloucester Green bus station. Call 001 Taxis (☎ 01865 240000).

AIRPORT INFORMATION
London's Heathrow and Gatwick airports (see page 89) have bus connections to and from Oxford; buses depart every half hour, daily 24 hours. For information call Oxford Express (☎ 08706 082608). Birmingham Airport has daily rail (☎ 08457 484950) and bus (☎ 08705 808080) connections to and from Oxford.

CLIMATE – average highs and lows for the month											
JAN.	FEB.	MAR.	APR.	MAY	JUN.	JUL.	AUG.	SEP.	OCT.	NOV.	DEC.
7°C	7°C	10°C	13°C	16°C	16°C	21°C	18°C	18°C	14°C	10°C	8°C
45°F	45°F	50°F	55°F	61°F	61°F	70°F	64°F	64°F	57°F	50°F	46°F
3°C	3°C	4°C	5°C	8°C	10°C	13°C	13°C	11°C	8°C	6°C	4°C
37°F	37°F	39°F	41°F	46°F	50°F	55°F	55°F	52°F	46°F	43°F	39°F

CITY SIGHTS

Key to symbols

✚ map coordinates refer to the Oxford map on page 107; sights below are highlighted in yellow on the map.

✉ address or location ☎ telephone number

🕐 opening times 🚌 nearest bus route

🍴 restaurant or café on site or nearby

🖐 admission charge: $$$ more than £6, $$ £2–£6, $ less than £2 ℹ other relevant information

ASHMOLEAN MUSEUM

✚ A3 ✉ Beaumont Street ☎ 01865 278000 🕐 Tue.–Sat. 10–5 (also Thu. 5–7, Jun.–Aug.), Sun. noon–5 🍴 Café 🚌 2A, 2B, 2C, 7B, 7D, 7 (Kidlington) 🖐 Free

The Ashmolean is a fascinating museum of grand oddities and elegant art, housed in a neoclassic building dating from the 1840s. The oldest museum in Britain, founded in 1683, the Ashmolean's extensive collection includes much medieval material; Greek, Roman and Egyptian artifacts; and fine Asian porcelain. The upper floor has a dazzling collection of Italian Renaissance paintings as well as early 20th-century art.

CHRIST CHURCH

✚ A1–B1 ✉ St. Aldates ☎ College and cathedral: 01865 276942; Picture Gallery: 01865 276172 🕐 College and cathedral: Mon.–Sat. 9–5, Sun. 1–5. Picture Gallery: Mon.–Sat. 10:30–5, Sun. 2–5, Apr.–Sep.; Mon.–Sat. 10:30–1 and 2–4:30, Sun. 2–4:30, rest of year 🚌 City center buses 🖐 College and cathedral $$; Picture Gallery $ ℹ May close on short notice. Check with tourist office

Oxford's largest college, Christ Church, is the most visited of all the university's colleges. Entry is gained through a turnstile by the War Memorial Gardens in the street known as St. Aldates, where college "bulldogs," immaculately dressed custodians in bowler hats, cheerfully order you around.

The present cathedral dates from the 12th century. Among its many fine features are exquisite stained-glass windows. Tom Quad is Christ Church's glorious central

Above: Porcelain figures in the Ashmolean

quadrangle; Mercury Pond, with Mercury Fountain at its center, adds an elegant accent. The figure of Mercury sports tiny patches of well-watered moss and often sprouts neckties and other "dress" donated by students. The entrance to Tom Quad and to Christ Church is the mighty gate tower, Tom Tower, that holds a massive seven-ton bell, Great Tom. Visit Christ Church's vaulted Great Hall, the Picture Gallery of Old Masters paintings and drawings, and Canterbury and Peckwater quadrangles.

MUSEUM OF OXFORD

✚ A1 ✉ Town hall, St. Aldates ☎ 01865 252761 🕐 Tue.–Fri. 10–4, Sat. 10–5, Sun. noon–4 🚌 City center buses 🖐 $ ℹ Audio tours

The Museum of Oxford, housed in the Town Hall, has well-arranged displays and gives an excellent account of Oxford's history. Everyone who played a part in the making of Oxford is here, from prehistory through the Roman, Saxon and Norman periods to the present day. The realities of town life from both sides of the track are depicted through 19th-century house interiors from residential and working-class districts. "Looking for Alice" explores the lives of Lewis Carroll and Alice Liddell (see box, page 108).

THE OXFORD STORY

✚ A2 ✉ 6 Broad Street ☎ 01865 728822 🕐 Daily 9:30–5, Jul.–Aug.; Mon.–Sat. 10–4:30, Sun. 11–4:30, rest of year 🚌 City center buses 🖐 $$$

The Oxford Story explores the history of Oxford University complete with sights, sounds and smells. You enter from Broad Street, watch a video introduction and then are transported gently up a steep ramp on a 25-minute "dark" ride, gliding past displays about the university, its history and the personalities associated with it, accompanied by persuasive commentary. The interactive "Innovate" exhibit links the university's present-day work with scientific research for the future.

Oxford

OXFORD UNIVERSITY MUSEUM OF NATURAL HISTORY

✚ Off the map ✉ Parks Road ☎ 01865 272950
🕐 Daily noon–5 🚌 6A 🎟 Free

The Oxford University Museum of Natural History is housed in a 19th-century building in Italianate Gothic style, its facade embellished with carvings. The interior is a single open space, surrounded by an ambulatory and forested with slender iron columns that support a wrought-iron vault and glass roof. Exhibits range from dinosaur skeletons to minerals and fossils. Visitors can access the Pitt Rivers Museum from the rear of the building.

PITT RIVERS MUSEUM

✚ Off the map ✉ South Parks Road (enter through the Oxford University Museum of Natural History)
☎ 01865 270927 🕐 Daily noon–4:30 🚌 6A
🎟 Free ℹ Audio guided tours ($)

This fascinating museum is a marvelous example of 19th-century museum culture. It displays the often wildly eccentric collection of Lieutenant General Augustus Henry Lane Fox Pitt Rivers, who served throughout the British Empire and

Wrought-iron arches over dinosaur skeletons at the Oxford University Museum of Natural History

gathered many artifacts along the way. The collection reflects the general's intense interest in tribal cultures and is an invaluable comment on the human condition worldwide. The museum also displays unusual objects brought back by early anthropologists and explorers, including Captain Cook. The collection includes ritual masks, shrunken heads and weird magical objects.

UNIVERSITY CHURCH OF ST. MARY THE VIRGIN

✚ B2 ✉ High Street ☎ 01865 279111
🕐 Mon.–Sat. 9–6, Sun. noon–6, Jul.–Aug.; Mon.–Sat. 9–5, Sun. noon– 5, rest of year 🍴 Café in adjoining Old Convocation House 🚌 City center buses
🎟 Church free; tower $

St. Mary the Virgin is both the parish church of Oxford and the university's church. It forms the southern side of Radcliffe Square. The early 14th-century tower rises above Oxford's dreaming spires, domes and cupolas. The south porch, facing High Street, is a 17th-century addition that trumpeted Italian influence with its twisted columns and heavily decorated segmental arch. The interior of the church is filled with monuments and wall tablets. You can plod up the tower as far as the base of the spire for fine views over Oxford. The climb is narrow and steep, and the up and down flow of people can cause traffic jams, although there is a resting place with benches in the bell room about halfway up.

UNIVERSITY OF OXFORD BOTANIC GARDEN

✚ C1 ✉ Rose Lane ☎ 01865 286690 🕐 Daily 9–6 (last admission 5:15), May–Sep.; 9–5, Mar.–Apr. and Oct.; 9–4:30 rest of year 🚌 City center buses 🎟 $$

The University of Oxford Botanic Garden was founded as a "physic garden" in 1621 and is Britain's oldest botanic garden. In imitation of the herbal gardens of Europe, it is a delightful enclave with a collection of more than 7,000 plant species. The River Cherwell and Magdalen College's tower enhance the setting, and the original layout survives today. South of the main garden is a less geometrically designed display created in the 1940s. There also are splendid greenhouses with 100-year-old cacti.

Anne Hathaway's cottage, just west of Stratford, the childhood home of William Shakespeare's wife

SHAKESPEARE'S STRATFORD-UPON-AVON

Stratford-upon-Avon was the birthplace of William Shakespeare and today the town is something of a shrine to the poet-playwright, its numerous Tudor and Jacobean half-timbered houses enhancing the Shakespearean theme. Shakespeare's Birthplace on Henley Street has been restored with late 16th-century furnishings and is full of fascinating memorabilia. Another fine old building is the Elizabethan Harvard House, which, although having no connection to Shakespeare, is interesting as the birthplace of John Harvard, who founded Harvard College in Massachusets.

After an intriguing life, Shakespeare died in 1616 at the early age of 52 in a house called New Place in Stratford. The original house was demolished by the owner in 1759 because he found visitors a nuisance. The foundations remain and are adjoined by the Elizabethan-style Knott Garden and Nash's House, the superbly restored 17th-century home of Thomas Nash, husband of Shakespeare's granddaughter, Elizabeth Hall.

Another famous Stratford building is Holy Trinity Church, located on the banks of the River Avon. Here you will see the remarkable alabaster bust of Shakespeare, modeled on a wax impression of the playwright's face at his death. Nearby is Shakespeare's tomb and those of his wife, Anne Hathaway, and his daughter, Suzanna. On the banks of the River Avon to the north of the church is the Royal Shakespeare Theatre, where the Royal Shakespeare Company performs the Bard's plays.

Arrange day trips to Stratford at the Oxford Tourist Information Centre or through Cotswold Roaming.

Tourist Information Centre ✉ 15–16 Broad Street, Oxford OX1 3AS ☎ 01865 726871
Cotswold Roaming ✉ P.O. Box 784, Headington, Oxford OX3 9YS ☎ 01865 308300;
www.oxfordcity.co.uk/cotswold-roaming/

Walk along the city walls for a view of York Minster, Britain's largest medieval Gothic cathedral

YORK

Two thousand years of English history are written across the face of York. Within the old city's walls, and within sight and sound of the magnificent York Minster cathedral, narrow, cobbled streets, ancient remains, medieval buildings, historic churches, and award-winning museums sit happily alongside modern stores, restaurants and hotels.

York is a small town at heart. It began life as a riverside encampment established by an ancient British tribe, the Brigantes. In turn, Brigantes were usurped in AD 71 by Roman invaders who made York their empire's northern European capital. Anglo Saxons, who established York as a center of early Christianity, followed the Romans. In AD 867, the settlement was captured by the Danes – the plundering Vikings of romantic history.

In subsequent centuries York fell under the control of the Normans, who laid the first substantial foundations of the present minster and built the original city walls. During the 16th and 17th centuries, religious and dynastic struggles kept the city in the national forefront, at a time when poverty, plague and famine often made ordinary life harsh and terrible. The more enterprising world of the 18th and 19th centuries and the emergence of York as the railroad capital of northern England made the city a fashionable commercial center, one that was only lightly touched by the more brutal aspects of the Industrial Revolution. Today visitors walk on hallowed ground that has supported more than 2,000 years of human achievement, as well as misery.

Sightseeing in York

Many parts of central York are pedestrian-only, and though crowds may throng the narrow streets, people have precedence over vehicles. In the nicest areas of old York there is no stream of roaring traffic pinning you to the sidewalk. You go with the flow, but there is no rush-hour element even during the busiest times of day.

York's flavor can be captured via a York City SightSeeing or Guide Friday open-top double-decker bus or in a horse-drawn carriage. The inner city can be explored on one of numerous city tours, led by local experts. Or you can take a "ghost walk," complete with an entertaining guide and actors making impromptu, phantom appearances in dark alleys. Leisurely daytime guided walks take in the city walls and ancient streets.

You could also explore on your own. Central York is not large, and you're never far from the next fascinating building, museum or attraction. Few houses in York rise above two or three stories, and the sun finds its way into hidden corners, lighting the upper parts of old buildings. Take time as you stroll

to appreciate the colorful facades and architectural features, like Stonegate's little red devil above the corner with Coffee Yard Lane.

The many different people who colonized York left an engaging but confusing legacy of local words. The word "bar" means gate and refers to the magnificent stone gateways, such as Bootham Bar and Monk Bar, that punctuate the city walls. On the other hand, the Viking word "gate," as in Stonegate and Petergate, means street.

Walk part of the city walls for a superb overview of York. Try the section from Monk Bar (location of the fascinating Richard III Museum), at the north end of Goodramgate, to

York

Bootham Bar at the west end of High Petergate. The views of York Minster along this stretch are outstanding.

Visit such main attractions as York Minster and JORVIK, but do not neglect other sights – like the hands-on ARC (Archaeological Resource Centre) in St. Saviour's Church and The York Dungeon on Clifford Street, both great fun for children. Enjoy the talented street entertainers and the many festivals and events staged here each year.

Shopping in Old York

Shopping in York is fun. Streets such as Stonegate and The Shambles are overflowing with specialty stores, including antique shops, art and craft galleries, bookstores, jewelers, tea blenders and boutiques. Every major chain store is represented in the main shopping areas of Coney Street, St. Mary's Square and Parliament Street.

A huge variety of eateries will tempt you, from traditional English tea and coffee houses – such as Betty's Café Tea Rooms in St. Helen's Square and The Earl Grey Tea Rooms in The Shambles

Minster

The Old English word "Minster" was used in medieval England as a variant of the word "monastery." It was sometimes used to describe the church attached to a monastery, which was used for worship by the monks. Through time the word became associated with certain cathedral churches, like York Minster.

– to dozens of restaurants. Authentic English pubs include Stonegate's Ye Old Starre Inne and the 15th-century Black Swan, on Peasholme Green.

York is essentially English at heart, but its northern regional identity makes it very different from London and southern England. Expect friendliness and helpfulness from locals, but be prepared for that matter-of-fact approach for which Yorkshire people are famous. You will be given facts rather than fiction and guidance rather than gossip to help you get the best out of the heartland of historic England.

ESSENTIAL INFORMATION

TOURIST INFORMATION
York Tourist Information Centres
• De Grey Rooms, Exhibition Square
☎ 01904 621756
• York Railway Station, Station Road
☎ 01904 621756
York Tourism Bureau
• 20 George Hudson Street (not open to visitors)
☎ 01904 554455; www.visityork.org

URBAN TRANSPORTATION
York railroad station, Station Road
(☎ 08457 484950). Local services are run by Great North Eastern Railways

(☎ 08457 225225). York bus station is on Rougier Street. For information ☎ 01904 551400. There are taxi stands at York railroad station (☎ 01904 623332) and at Duncombe Place, near York Minster.

AIRPORT INFORMATION
Leeds and Bradford International Airport (☎ 0113 250 9696; www.lbia.co.uk), 11 miles northwest of Leeds, is an hour's drive from York. Manchester airport (☎ 0161 489 3000; www.manchesterairport.co.uk) is 56 miles southwest by road, but has direct train services to York.

CLIMATE – average highs and lows for the month

JAN.	FEB.	MAR.	APR.	MAY	JUN.	JUL.	AUG.	SEP.	OCT.	NOV.	DEC.
6°C	7°C	9°C	13°C	16°C	19°C	21°C	20°C	18°C	14°C	9°C	7°C
43°F	45°F	48°F	55°F	61°F	66°F	70°F	68°F	64°F	57°F	48°F	45°F
0°C	1°C	2°C	4°C	7°C	10°C	12°C	11°C	10°C	7°C	4°C	2°C
32°F	34°F	36°F	39°F	45°F	50°F	54°F	52°F	50°F	45°F	39°F	36°F

CITY SIGHTS

Key to symbols

✚ map coordinates refer to the York map on page 113; sights below are highlighted in yellow on the map. ✉ address or location ☎ telephone number ⏱ opening times 🍴 restaurant or café on site or nearby 💷 admission charge: $$$ more than £6, $$ £2–£6, $ less than £2 🛈 other relevant information

FAIRFAX HOUSE

✚ C1 ✉ Castlegate ☎ 01904 655543 ⏱ Mon.–Thu. and Sat. 11–5, Sun. 1:30–5; last admission at 4:30 💷 $$ 🛈 Guided tours Sat. only at 11 and 2

This elegant house was lavishly decorated by Viscount Fairfax in 1759, but was neglected in later years. It was bought in 1980 by the York Civic Trust, which carried out an inspired restoration. Today, Fairfax House is one of the finest examples of an 18th-century town house in England. Enjoy the sumptuous plasterwork ceilings, damask hangings, marble fireplaces and magnificent furnishings.

JORVIK

✚ C2 ✉ Coppergate ☎ 01904 643211 ⏱ Daily 10–5, Apr.–Oct.; 10–4, rest of year 🍴 Café 💷 $$$

This very popular attraction reveals the archeological remains of Viking York, or Jorvik, unearthed here from 1976 to 1981. Deep underground, you're shuttled back in time 1,000 years to a reconstructed Viking street complete with thatched houses, lifelike figures and the evocative sounds and smells of everyday life. Traveling in a "time capsule" back to the year AD 975, you "fly" across the city, over streets and backyards, to discover how a Viking settlement of 10,000 people functioned on this very site.

MERCHANT ADVENTURERS' HALL

✚ C2 ✉ Fossgate ☎ 01904 654818 ⏱ Mon.–Thu. 9–5, Fri.–Sat. 9–3:30, Sun. noon–4, Apr.–Sep.; Mon.–Sat. 9–3:30, rest of year 💷 $$

This medieval Guild Hall is the finest of

The opulent salon in Fairfax House

its kind to survive in Europe. Its brick and timber-framed exterior, the vast, open timber work of the Great Hall and the interior paneling effortlessly transport visitors from the present into a convincing medieval environment. The hall was built from 1357 to 1361 by a religious fraternity that evolved into a merchants' guild, which survives today as a charitable organization and guardian of this outstanding building.

NATIONAL RAILWAY MUSEUM

✚ Off the map ✉ Leeman Road ☎ 01904 621261 ⏱ Daily 10–6 🍴 Restaurant and café 💷 Free; charge for special exhibitions

For travel enthusiasts young and old, this atmospheric museum – the largest of its kind in the world – offers vivid insight into 200 years of transportation history. There are displays of over 60 steam, diesel and electric locomotives, including a working replica of George Stephenson's famous 1829 *Rocket;* the wonderful *Mallard*, still the fastest steam engine in the world; and the only Shinkansen (Bullet Train) outside Japan.

YORK ART GALLERY

✚ B3 ✉ Exhibition Square ☎ 01904 687687 ⏱ Daily 10–5 💷 Free

The excellent collection in this small, friendly and informative gallery provides an overview of 600 years of Western European art from the Italian Renaissance to the contemporary scene. There are a number of paintings by York

York

artist William Etty, who had a liking for exuberant nudes. There also is a collection by leading 20th-century potters such as Bernard Leach and Shoji Hamada.

YORK CASTLE MUSEUM

✚ C1 ✉ The Eye of York, Tower Street ☎ 01904 687687 🕐 Daily 9:30–5 🍴 Café 💰 $$ ℹ Hands-on family activities during school vacations

This museum is housed in two former prisons. Behind the handsome neoclassic facade of the building is an outstanding collection of exhibits illustrating the social history of York, and of Britain, over the past 400 years. Walkways lead past vivid reconstructions of complete Victorian and Edwardian streets, lined with old stores full of authentic contents. Allow several hours to get the most out of the experience, which also includes a visit to the condemned cell that once held legendary highwayman Dick Turpin.

YORK MINSTER

✚ B3 ✉ Minster Yard ☎ 01904 557216 🕐 Minster: Mon.–Sat. 7–6:30, Sun. noon–6:30. Undercroft, Treasury and Crypt: Mon.–Sat. 9–5, Sun. noon–5, Easter–Oct. 31; Mon.–Sat. 9:30–5, Sun. noon–5, rest of year. Tower: Mon.–Sat. 9–5:30, Sun. noon–5:30, Easter–Oct. 31; Mon.–Sat. 9:30–30 minutes before dusk, rest of year 🍴 Restaurant 💰 $$. Undercroft, Treasury and Crypt $$. Tower $$ ℹ Free tours. Closed to visitors during major services

York cathedral's present foundations were laid by the Normans in the 12th century. A visit to the Minster is a historical experience as well as a religious one; the walls are crowded with dramatic monuments and the architectural features are superb.

Past the broad introductory nave is the central crossing, where north and south transepts, nave and choir all meet below the soaring vaulted roof of the central tower, 200 feet above. The choir is full of intricate design and ornamentation. At the east end of the church you will find the Lady Chapel and the great East Window – as big as

Tower and spires of York Minster

a tennis court and the largest medieval stained-glass window in the world.

Also visit the intriguing Crypt, where the pillars are from the original Norman church. In the Chapter House, look for the wickedly irreverent figures of priests and prelates scattered among the carvings above the encircling stalls. The Undercroft has displays of Roman and Norman remains and church silver.

Consider climbing the 275 spiral steps of the great 234-foot tower, but do so only if you're in good physical condition; it can prove to be a small Everest for some.

YORKSHIRE MUSEUM

✚ A3–B3 ✉ Museum Gardens ☎ 01904 687687 🕐 Daily 10–5 🍴 Café 💰 $$ ℹ Events and changing exhibitions at various times; opening times vary

This eclectic treasure house includes some of the finest Roman, Viking, Anglo Saxon and medieval artifacts in Europe. The grounds feature handsome gardens that contain York's oldest ruin, the Multangular Tower, part of fourth-century Roman fortifications.

The luminous Middleham Jewel, a 15th-century sapphire set within a gold pendant, is a major exhibit. Also of interest is a collection of sea dragons from the Jurassic period. The museum building incorporates part of the ruins of medieval St. Mary's Abbey. This section, with its haunting reconstructions and medieval music, is a delight.

York

WALK THROUGH THE PAST

York's appeal stems largely from the survival of its central streets in their original form. While many cities and towns had their centers remodeled over the years, central York was spared wholesale change. Plans to demolish the city walls during the Victorian period were resisted, and within the precise boundaries of those restored walls the narrow streets and interlocking alleys and courtyards make up one of the best preserved late medieval cities in Europe.

Many of York's old houses are not the original buildings; they have been rebuilt or restored over time. But their styles are medieval, and so venerable is the layout of central York that when you walk down Stonegate you follow the exact line of the Roman approach road to the imperial encampment of AD 71.

The most famous of York's ancient thoroughfares is The Shambles, a narrow street overhung by timber-framed houses. Its name derives from the butchers' shops and slaughterhouses once located here. Todays The Shambles is a delight. It typifies York's medieval character, but in times past this would have been a filthy, raucous, rough-and-

ready place that would horrify modern sensibilities. Today it can be enjoyed for its quaintness, free of medieval realities. Don't miss bustling Newgate Market (open daily) between Parliament Street and The Shambles, where – within the rules of modern hygiene and legality – some of the liveliness of medieval times still survives.

To get the most out of old York, explore the interlocking alleys that connect the center. Wander at will with a city map, which will show you the main landmarks, but investigate the twists and turns of the numerous passages leading off Stonegate, Petergate, Davygate and Church Street. They'll land you unexpectedly in the bustle of St. Helen's Square, with its handsome Mansion House and Guildhall, or in King's Square, where old gravestones make up part of the paving. Brimming with charming little shops, cafés and restaurants, old York exudes unforgettable character.

A rainy night in The Shambles, where medieval buildings overhang cobbled lanes

CZECH REPUBLIC

"NOT all the seductions of Vienna…nor the dominion of a German bureaucracy have broken the stubborn heart of the Czech…"

From *A History of Europe*, by English historian H. A. L. Fisher

Opposite: The 15th-century Astronomical Clock dominates the front of the Old Town Hall in Prague

Czech Republic

CZECH REPUBLIC

Since 1989, the Czechs have been embracing change and finding their footing as a new republic. In that year, the Velvet Revolution saw Czechoslovakia discard 40 years of Communist rule without firing a single shot. At the start of the 21st century, the country is coping with the difficulties and benefits of adapting to Western capitalism and establishing a new social and economic order.

Bohemia and Moravia

Most visitors to the Czech Republic head straight for Prague, but there is plenty to enjoy in the country's diverse landscapes. Locked between Poland, Germany, Slovakia and Austria, the republic takes in two regions: Bohemia, itself surrounded by a ring of mountains, and the lowlands of Moravia. Both have suffered adversely from the effects of heavy industrialization – acid rain and deforestation among them – but both also have areas of real beauty.

In southern Bohemia, such medieval towns as České Budějovice (home of Budweiser beer) and Český Krumlov, with its great 13th-century castle, recall a time when kings and lords were eager to build in one of Europe's richest regions. To the west are famous spa towns best known by their German names: Karlsbad (Karlovy Vary) and Marienbad (Mariánské Lázně).

In Moravia, wedged between the western uplands and the eastern White Carpathian mountains, the city of Brno gives access to the Punkevní jeskyně (Punkva Caves).

Czech Culture

Despite the hijacking of the term "bohemian" by the West to mean "unconventional," the Czechs are generally rather reserved. Beyond this, though, is a friendliness and genuine interest in other cultures. Young Czechs often speak English, and are tuned in to Anglo-American pop culture.

Love of arts and literature is not confined to Prague. Václav Havel, the

The face of the modern Czech Republic – President Václav Klaus

first post-Communist president, was better known among Czechs as a poet and playwright. Music has a special place in Czech life, too – from oompah-style brass bands to the classical tradition that produced such composers as Antonín Dvořák.

Overall, most people who travel around the Czech Republic will be struck by the diversity of this small nation. As the republic embraces capitalism, there is a certain amount of anxiety as well as hope. A visit to this society in transition between two worlds is sure to be rewarding.

CZECH REPUBLIC

| 0 | 20 | 40 | 60 | 80 km |
| 0 | 10 | 20 | 30 | 40 | 50 miles |

POLAND

N

Jeseník
Hrubý Jeseník
1491m
Pradĕd
Krnov
Nízký Jeseník
Šumperk
Opava
Ostrava
Karviná
Šternberk
Moravia
Havířov
Odra
Olomouc
E442
Nový Jičín
Frýdek-Místek
Prostějov
Punkevní jeskyně
Přerov
Valašské Meziříčí
Rožnov pod Radhoštěm
Vyškov
Lešná
Vsetín
Moravský kras
Kroměříž
Zlín
Slavkov u Brne
Uherské Hradiště
Karpaty
Hodonín
Strážnice
E65
Bílé
SLOVAK REPUBLIC
Lednice
Břeclav

D   E

MORE TOP DESTINATIONS IN THE CZECH REPUBLIC

● České Budějovice B1
● Český Krumlov B1 ● Český ráj C3
● Karlovy Vary A3 ● Krkonoše C3
● Mariánské Lázně A2
● Olomouc D2
● Punkevní jeskyně D1 ● Šumava A1–B1 ● Telč C1 ● Vranov C1

TIMELINE

AD 872   The Přemysl Dynasty begins its 421-year rule of Bohemia.

929   "Good" King Wenceslas is assassinated by his brother, Boleslav, and made the country's patron saint.

1346   Devout Charles IV, Holy Roman Emperor, is crowned king of Bohemia and ushers in its Golden Age.

1415   Religious reformer Jan Hus is burned at the stake in Constance; four years later, in Prague, his supporters throw Catholic councilors from town hall windows and start the Hussite Wars.

1583   The Habsburg court moves to Prague.

1848   The Habsburgs suppress an uprising of Czech nationalism.

1914   Czechs are forced to fight for the Austrian Habsburgs in World War I, but thousands desert to the Russians.

1918   With the defeat of Austria-Hungary, the new state of Czechoslovakia is proclaimed.

1938   Czechoslovakia is forced to hand over Sudetenland to Hitler.

1945   Slovakia and the Czech lands are liberated by the Red Army and the United States; the Communist Party seizes power in 1948.

1968   The First Secretary, Alexander Dubček, introduces "socialism with a human face" in the reforms of the "Prague Spring"; in August, Soviet troops invade Czechoslovakia.

1989   "Velvet Revolution"; Václav Havel elected president of Czechoslovakia.

1993   Czechoslovakia splits into Czech and Slovak republics.

1999   Czech Republic becomes a NATO member.

2004   Czech Republic joins the European Union.

THE VELVET REVOLUTION

On Nov. 17, 1989, a week after the fall of the Berlin Wall, there was an officially sanctioned demonstration in Prague to mark the Nazi suppression of Czech universities. It soon turned into a protest march against the authorities, and was forcefully put down by riot police. A rumor began that the police had killed one demonstrator. In fact, it wasn't true, but the story was enough to fuel public anger. People poured into the streets night after night, watched by television viewers across the world. Alexander Dubček was brought back from obscurity in Bratislava to address the crowds. Václav Havel headed a newly established Civic Forum, and on December 10 a new government was formed, with the Communists reduced to a minority. Less than three weeks later, Havel was installed as president.

Clean, fast and cheap – Prague's excellent subway system is a good way to get around

SURVIVAL GUIDE

- Czech pronunciation is difficult, but worth mastering if only for place names. Some Czechs – particularly young city dwellers – may speak excellent English. A grasp of German is also useful.

- The cuisine is heavily meat-based – dumplings with pork and duck are popular dishes – and can be quite flavorful. This is the home of light beer, and the products of České Budějovice (Budweis) and Plzeň (Pilsen) are only the most famous among a multitude of local varieties.

- It's worth looking through bookstores, despite the language barrier, as the illustrated books are a treat. For souvenirs, take home Bohemian crystal, porcelain, lacework, garnets and prints.

- Easter is as important a holiday as Christmas, and is marked by the bizarre fertility ritual of boys whipping girls' legs with birch twigs.

- On St. Nicholas' Eve (Dec. 5), neighborhood St. Nicholas figures walk the streets with an angel and a devil, giving candy to good children

and coal to bad. Christmas dinner is traditionally carp – sold live at street stalls to be eaten on Christmas Eve with potato salad and schnitzel.

- Prague is even busier than usual in May and early June, when it hosts the Prague Spring International Music Festival: Reserve accommodations several weeks in advance for this period.

- Public transportation is an enjoyable way of seeing the republic. Almost every town has a railroad station (*nádraží*), and side trips are cheap. The fast trains (*rychlík*) stop at major cities; local trains (*osobní vlak*) are slow, stop everywhere and usually have only second-class carriages.

- The Czech Republic suffers from a shortage of hotels and hostels, although this is fast changing. Many historic hotels have been overhauled, and there's been a surge of new accommodations in converted buildings. A sign saying *Zimmer frei* ("rooms available") indicates a bed and breakfast in a private home.

Prague

PRAGUE

Nothing can prepare you for the beauty of Prague. Its title of "Golden City" barely conveys the color and elegance of its historic center: painted medieval and Renaissance facades glinting pink and green and silver in the sun; a jumble of rust-red rooftops; mellow stone, turquoise domes, steel-gray Gothic spires. Prague's buildings and streets span 1,000 years. Wandering the cobbled passageways and alleys thus becomes the highlight of any visit.

Compass Bearings

Central Prague is made up of four towns, joined together in 1784. On the west bank of the Vltava river are Hradčany and the Lesser Quarter (Malá Strana); on the east bank are the Old Town (Staré Město) and New Town (Nové Město). In the 19th century the Jewish ghetto, Josefov, was also incorporated into the Old Town. Beyond this core is a circle of suburbs, but the main historic sights are within the substantially traffic-free center.

Nerudova

A steep street climbs from Malostranské Square, near Prague Castle, in the Lesser Quarter. This street, Nerudova, was named after journalist and writer Jan Neruda. He wrote stories about daily life in 19th-century Prague, and was born at No. 47, near the top. Eighteenth-century houses line the street, identified by intricately crafted signs; numbers weren't introduced until the 1770s. Look for The Three Fiddles (No. 12), The Green Lobster (No. 43) and Neruda's home, The Two Suns.

Prague Castle

The two banks of the Vltava are connected by a series of 15 bridges, the oldest of which, the Charles Bridge (Karlův most), is a magnet for tourists, performers and vendors. On the west bank, Hradčany, the area around Prague Castle and its hill, is the major attraction.

PRAGUE

HRADČANY

Královská zahrada

Mičovna

Chotkovy sady

Belvedér

CHOTKOVA

4   Pražský hrad

Katedrála sv Víta

Bazilika sv Jiří

Starý Královský palác

Ledeburský palác

Ledeburská zahrada

VALDŠTEJNSKÁ

Valdštejnský palác

M

Schwarzenberský palác-Vojenské muzeum

Šternberský palác

Kostel sv Tomáš

TOMÁŠSKÁ

LETENSKÁ

Loretánská kaple, Strahovský klášter

UVOZ NERUDOVA

Lichtenštejnský palác

MALOSTRANSKÉ NÁM

Malostranská radnice

Vojanovy sady

ULI ZUCEHO

MINARE

Morzinský palác

Chrám svatého Mikuláše

MOSTECKÁ

Schönbornská zahrada

Vrtbovská zahrada

MALTÉZSKÉ NÁM

Kostel Panny Marie pod řetězem

3   Seminářská zahrada

Kostel Panny Marie Vítězná

KARMELITSKÁ

Muzeum hudebních nástrojů

Státní ústřední archív

Kampa

MALÁ STRANA

Muzeum tělesné vychovy a sportu

Certovka

Petřín

UJEZD

Lanova dráha

Petřínské sady

Hladová zed'

VÍTĚZNÁ

2   Kinského zahrada

NÁMĚSTÍ KINSKÝCH

JANÁČKOVO NÁBŘEŽÍ

ZBOROVSKÁ

Národopisné muzeum

HOLEČKOVA

ŠTEFÁNIKOVA

EL PEŠKOVÉ

VODNÍROVSKÁ

Dětský ostrov

ARBESOVO NÁM

0   100   200   300 m
0   100   200   300 yards

1

V BOTANICE

N

Letohradek Portheimka

A   KARTOUZSKÁ

Kostel sv Václava

MATOUŠOVA

PRESLOVA

ZBOROVSKÁ

B

Prague

It includes (along with the castle itself) Golden Lane (Zlatá ulička), with tiny houses originally occupied by the Emperor's gatekeepers; the Gothic Mihulka Powder Tower (Prašná věž Mihulka), where alchemists once tried to create gold; and the palaces surrounding Hradčany Square (Hradčanské náměstí).

Old and New Prague

Across the river in the Old Town is the Old Town Square (Staroměstské náměstí). Here are the sprawling Old Town Hall (Staroměstská radnice, see page 130), the white Church of St. Nicholas (Chrám svatého Mikuláše) and the dark towers of Týn Church.

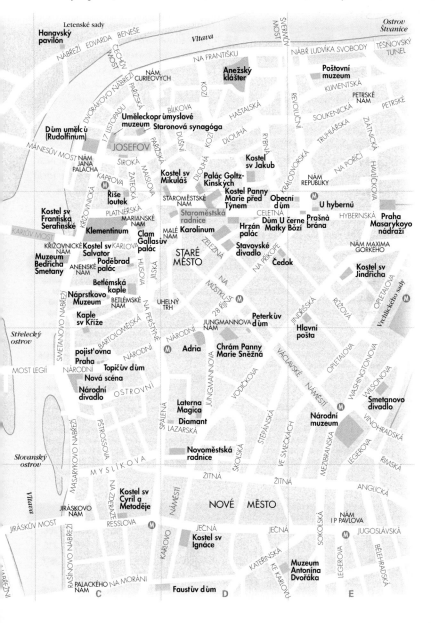

Letenské sady
Hanavský pavilón
NÁBŘEŽÍ EDVARDA BENEŠE
Vltava
Ostrov Štvanice
ŠVERMŮV MOST
NÁBŘ LUDVÍKA SVOBODY
TĚSNOVSKÝ TUNEL
NA FRANTIŠKU
NÁM. CURIEOVÝCH
Anežský klášter
Poštovní muzeum
KLIMENTSKÁ
PETRSKÉ NÁM
PETRSKÉ
SOUKENICKÁ
REVOLUČNÍ
Dům umělců (Rudolfinum)
Uměleckoprůmyslové muzeum
Staronová synagóga
JOSEFOV
HAŠTALSKÁ
DLOUHÁ
DUŠNÍ
RYBNÁ
TRUHLÁŘSKÁ
ZLATNICKÁ
MÁNESŮV MOST
NÁM JANA PALACHA
ŠIROKÁ
PAŘÍZSKÁ
Kostel sv Jakub
KRÁLODVORSKÁ
NA POŘÍČÍ
HAVLÍČKOVA
KAPROVA
MAISLOVA
DLOUHÁ
KOZÍ
NÁM REPUBLIKY
Kostel sv Mikuláš
Palác Goltz-Kinských
Řiše loutek
STAROMĚSTSKÉ NÁM
Kostel Panny Marie před Týnem
Obecní dům
U hybernů
Kostel sv Františka Serafinské
PLATNÉŘSKÁ
MARIÁNSKÉ NÁM
Staroměstská radnice
CELETNÁ
Dům U černé Matky Boží
Prašná brána
HYBERNSKÁ
Praha Masarykovo nádraží
Klementinum
MALÉ NÁM
Karolinum
Hrzán palác
Stavovské divadlo
NÁM MAXIMA GORKÉHO
KARLŮV MOST
Kostel sv Salvator
KARLOVA
Clam Gallasův palác
ZELEZNÁ
Čedok
NA PŘÍKOPĚ
Kostel sv Jindřicha
KŘIŽOVNICKÉ NÁM
Muzeum Bedřicha Smetany
ANENSKÉ NÁM
Poděbrad palác
HUSOVA
JILSKÁ
STARÉ MĚSTO
RŮŽOVÁ
OPLETALOVA
Betlémská kaple
Náprstkovo Muzeum
BETLÉMSKÉ NÁM
NA PERŠTÝNĚ
UHELNÝ TRH
NA MŮSTKU
INDŘISKÁ
Vrchlického sady
Kaple sv Kříže
28 ŘÍJNA
Peterkův dům
Hlavní pošta
Střelecký ostrov
BARTOLOMĚJSKÁ
NÁRODNÍ
JUNGMANNOVA NÁM
OPLETALOVA
pojišt'ovna
Adria
Chrám Panny Marie Sněžná
VÁCLAVSKÉ NÁMĚSTÍ
WASHINGTONOVA
WILSONOVA
MOST LEGIÍ
Praha
NÁRODNÍ
Topičův dům
JUNGMANNOVA
VODIČKOVA
Nová scéna
Národní divadlo
OSTROVNÍ
Smetanovo divadlo
Laterna Magica
Diamant
ŠPÁLENÁ
ŠTĚPÁNSKÁ
Národní muzeum
VINOHRADSKÁ
Slovanský ostrov
MASARYKOVO NÁBŘEŽÍ
PŠTROSSOVA
LAZARSKÁ
Novoměstská radnice
ŠKOLSKÁ
VE SMEČKÁCH
MEZIBRANSKÁ
LEGEROVÁ
RIMSKÁ
MYSLÍKOVA
ZITNÁ
ZITNÁ
ANGLICKÁ
Vltava
NA ZDERAZE
Kostel sv Cyril a Metoděje
NÁMĚSTÍ
NOVÉ   MĚSTO
SOKOLSKÁ
NÁM I P PAVLOVA
JUGOSLÁVSKÁ
JIRÁSKOVO NÁM
RESSLOVA
KARLOVO
JEČNÁ
JEČNÁ
LEGEROVÁ
BĚLEHRADSKÁ
JIRÁSKŮV MOST
Kostel sv Ignáce
KATEŘINSKÁ
KE KARLOVU
Muzeum Antonína Dvořáka
RAŠÍNOVO NÁBŘEŽÍ
PALACKÉHO NÁM
NA MORÁNI
Faustův dům
C   D   E

Prague Castle and the spires of St. Vitus' Cathedral

This is where street artists perform. The hub of the New Town is Wenceslas Square (Václavské náměstí), a busy boulevard renowned as the focus of protests during the Velvet Revolution.

Locals love their music – as Mozart found out, when he triumphed here after only moderate success in Vienna. Classical music seems to be everywhere in Prague, advertised in listings guides and on posters across the city. Tickets are reasonably priced and the performances can be superb.

Czech Beer and Puppets

Restaurants and cafés fill up quickly in Prague, so it's a good idea to make reservations. There's a wide range of options, from American and Italian to Lebanese and Japanese. Don't leave the city without tasting at least one Czech beer. Prague's own brews include Staropramen and U Fleků.

The best shopping is in the maze of arcades under the buildings of Wenceslas Square, along the pedestrian-only street Na Příkopě and also along Celetná. There are interesting craft shops on Karlova, near the Charles Bridge. Puppets make ideal gifts – they're works of art, not just playthings. For a huge selection of books in several languages, try Palác Knih at Václavské náměstí 41.

ESSENTIAL INFORMATION

TOURIST INFORMATION
Pražská informační služba (Prague Information Service)
• Staroměstská radnice (Old Town Hall), Staroměstské náměstí 1
• Na Příkopě 20
• Praha hlavní nádraží (Prague railroad station)
• Karlův most (Charles Bridge) – Apr.–Oct. only
• ☎ Central information number 12 444 (in English; 8 a.m.–7 p.m.)
www.prague-info.cz

URBAN TRANSPORTATION
Prague has three subway lines: A (green), B (yellow) and C (red). Stations are indicated by the letter "M" (marked in a red circle on the city map). Trains run frequently every day between 5 a.m. and midnight. Trams and buses are frequent, (4:30 a.m. to midnight with some night services). Buses run outside the city center. One ticket can be used for the subway, buses and trams. For bus information call ☎ 900 144 444. Use caution when taking taxis – make sure the taxi has a meter registering the fare, or else agree on a price before you get into the cab. Avoid taking taxis at a stand, especially one near a tourist spot or a nightclub.

AIRPORT INFORMATION
Praha-Ruzyně Airport, 10 miles north-west of the city, is a bus ride from the center. Airport bus No. 119 runs to Dejvická and 179 to Nové Butovice subway stations; shuttle buses run to náměstí Republiky. Shuttle services also run to the main hotels. Call for flight information (☎ 220 113 314 or 220 113 321), or call Czech Airlines (ČSA) ☎ 220 104 310.

CLIMATE – average highs and lows for the month

	JAN.	FEB.	MAR.	APR.	MAY	JUN.	JUL.	AUG.	SEP.	OCT.	NOV.	DEC.
	2°C	2°C	8°C	12°C	18°C	20°C	22°C	23°C	18°C	12°C	5°C	2°C
	36°F	36°F	46°F	54°F	64°F	68°F	72°F	73°F	64°F	54°F	41°F	36°F
	-4°C	-4°C	0°C	2°C	7°C	10°C	13°C	12°C	9°C	0°C	0°C	-2°C
	25°F	25°F	32°F	36°F	45°F	50°F	55°F	54°F	48°F	32°F	32°F	28°F

City Sights

Key to symbols

⊞ map coordinates refer to the Prague map on pages 124–125; sights below are highlighted in yellow on the map.

⊠ address or location ☎ telephone number
🕐 opening times Ⓜ nearest subway 🚌 nearest bus or tram route 🍴 restaurant or café on site or nearby 💰 admission charge: $$$ more than 110Kč, $$ 70Kč–110Kč, $ less than 70Kč ⓘ other relevant information

Chrám svatého Mikuláše

⊞ A3 ⊠ Malostranské náměstí 🕐 Daily 9–5, Mar.–Oct.; 9–4, rest of year. Tower: daily 10–6, Mar. 24–Oct. 31 Ⓜ Malostranská 🚌 Tram 12, 22, 23 💰 $ ⓘ Guided tours of the tower are available

Mozart played the 2,500-pipe organ here in 1787; he couldn't have chosen a more grandiose setting than the Chrám svatého Mikuláše (St. Nicholas' Church). It was constructed in the 18th century to celebrate Catholic counter-Reformation propaganda. It's a frenzy of decoration: pink-and-green mock-marble pillars; a 16,146-square-foot ceiling fresco; a copper statue of St. Nicholas; and huge sculptures of the four church fathers, including St. Cyril killing the devil.

Josefov

⊞ C4 ⊠ Jewish Museum: U Staré školy 1 ☎ 224 819 456 🕐 Jewish Museum sites: Sun.–Fri. 9–6, Apr.–Oct.; 9–4:30, rest of year. Closed Jewish holidays. Old-New Synagogue: Sun.–Thu. 9:30–6, Fri. 9:30–5, Apr.–Oct.; Sun.–Thu. 9:30–5, Fri. 9:30–4, rest of year Ⓜ Staroměstská 🚌 Tram 17, 18 💰 Jewish Museum $$$; Old-New Synagogue $$$

Walls went up around Prague's Jewish community in 1254, in keeping with a church law that Christians and Jews should live apart. But the walls did nothing to protect the inhabitants of the ghetto from centuries of persecution. In 1389, 3,000 were massacred in a pogrom, and at regular intervals, kings passed laws forcing Jews to wear particular clothes or colors to identify them.

Even in the face of such vicious discrimination, the ghetto developed as a center of learning, and some members were able to buy occasional privileges for the community

Inside the dome of St. Nicholas' Church

from the imperial court. In 1784 Joseph II abolished residence restrictions (the area was later named after him). Over a century later, most of its slums were demolished.

In the confined space of the Starý židovský hřbitov (Old Jewish Cemetery), 100,000 people are buried. Crooked gravestones lean and overlap; pebbles and prayers are still left on them as tributes. At the entrance, the Old Gravediggers' Hall has an exhibition of drawings by children held here before being sent by the Nazis to Auschwitz concentration camp; about 15,000 children passed through. By the end of World War II, Prague's Jewish population had been virtually wiped out. A museum devoted to the Holocaust is housed in the Pinkasova synagóga (Pinkas Synagogue).

The oldest building is the 13th-century Staronová synagóga (Old-New Synagogue), where legend has it the clay man, or Golem, created by Rabbi Löw in 1580 to serve and guard the ghetto, is still kept in the attic. The Rabbi had to return his creation to clay after it ran rampant through the streets. This and other synagogues around the cemetery survived World War II because of Hitler's perverse plan to create a museum dedicated to a vanished race. The synagogues collectively (apart from the Old-New Synagogue) form the Židovské muzeum (Jewish Museum) and can all be visited on one ticket.

The 17th-century cloisters of the Loreta shrine

KARLŮV MOST

➕ B3–C3 ✉ Staré Město/Malá Strana 🚊 Tram 12, 22, 23 to Malostranské náměstí

Karlův most (Charles Bridge) is much more than just a river crossing. A walk across the 1,700-foot span takes you past 30 sculptures, plus countless courting couples, puppeteers, musicians, souvenir sellers and tourists, and offers a breathtaking view both of the river and of the city's domes and looming spires. It was the work of Petr Parléř, who also created much of St. Vitus' Cathedral, and was built in 1357 to link the Old Town with the Lesser Quarter. Known until 1870 as the Stone or Prague Bridge, it has 16 sandstone arches but was originally relatively plain. The first ornament, a bronze crucifix, was added in 1657. Over the following 60 years statues were erected, evenly spaced along the parapets; they include St. John of Nepomuk (with the spangled halo), who was thrown from the bridge in 1393 after taking the side of the church in a dispute with the king.

LORETÁNSKÁ KAPLE

➕ Off the map ✉ Loretánské náměstí 7, Hradčany ☎ 220 516 740 🕐 Tue.–Sun. 9–12:15 and 1–4:30 🍴 U Ševce Matouše, see page 548 🚊 Tram 22, 23 to Pohořelec 💲 $$

As part of its campaign to win worshipers back to Catholicism after the Reformation, the church made much of the cult of the Virgin Mary, and the ornate Loretánská kaple (Loreta Chapel) is one result. It was built in 1626 around a replica of Mary's house, supposedly flown by angels from Nazareth to Loreto in Italy, and it soon became a site of pilgrimage. Don't miss the painting of St. Starosta, who grew a beard to repel her suitor and was crucified by her infuriated father.

PETŘÍN

➕ A3 ✉ Petřín Lookout Tower: Petřínské sady. Funicular railway: Újezd, Malá Strana 🕐 Lookout Tower: daily 10–10, May–Aug.; daily 10–7, in Apr. and Sep.; daily 10–6, in Oct.; Sat.–Sun. 10–5, rest of year. Funicular: daily 9 a.m.–11:30 p.m., Apr.–Oct. (to 11:20 p.m rest of year) 🚊 Tram 22, 23 to Pohořelec 💲 Tower $; Funicular $

Woods and orchards cover this hill on the city's western bank, and a funicular railway, the lanová dráha na Petřín, takes passengers up and down. The carriages were installed in 1891, the same year that the Petřínská rozhledna (Petřín Lookout Tower) was constructed at the top, both great Czech achievements. Steps (299 of them) lead to the tower's viewing platform.

PRAŽSKÝ HRAD

➕ A4 ✉ Hradčany ☎ 224 373 368 🕐 Castle precincts: daily 5 a.m.–midnight, Apr.–Oct.; 5 a.m.–11 p.m., rest of year. Castle sights: daily 9–5, Apr.–Oct.; 9–4, rest of year. Castle gardens: daily 10–6, Apr.–Oct. 🍴 U Ševce Matouše, see page 548; U Zlaté hrušky, see page 548 🚊 Tram 22, 23 to Pražský hrad 💲 Castle $$$ (ticket valid 3 days); gardens free ❓ Guided tours in English $$$

Looming over the city and the river, Pražský hrad (Prague Castle) has been a symbol of Czech authority since the first fortress was built on this high, rocky site in the ninth century. The name actually refers to a complex of palaces, courtyards, churches and streets, all spread across the hill known

KAFKA

Franz Kafka's diminutive house on Golden Lane

Franz Kafka wrote two of the 20th century's most significant novels – *The Trial* and *The Castle* – but he died practically unknown, having made his friend, Max Brod, promise to destroy all his writings. It's only because Brod broke his promise that Kafka is read throughout the world today.

His tales of helpless individuals caught in the workings of massive bureaucracy were inspired by the overgrown Habsburg administration. They came to represent the menace and detachment of authority in general, and the term "Kafkaesque" was coined to describe a seemingly ordinary but surreal and dangerous world of systems with their own life and logic.

Kafka was born in Prague, and moved with his family from house to house around Old Town Square, where his father was a haberdasher. He studied law and worked as an insurance clerk, writing his stories by night. The city appears throughout his writings. *The Castle* was inspired by Prague Castle; his story *The Great Wall of China* was based on the "Hunger Wall" on Petřín Hill, built as part of a 14th-century job creation scheme and funded by money expropriated from Jews. Kafka rented a house on Golden Lane (Zlatá ulička), but his health was poor and he died of tuberculosis at the age of 41. His grave can be seen at the New Jewish Cemetery (Židovské hřbitovy) in the Žižkov district. He left behind a third, unfinished novel, *Amerika*, and many short stories.

The most famous, *Metamorphosis*, related the story of Gregor Samsa, who awakens to find himself transformed into a giant insect and to his family becomes an object first of horror, then of pity and finally of contempt. The theme of a bewildered victim of inexplicable events is characteristic of Kafka's style.

The author also recorded his wanderings around Prague, his relationship with his father and with Felice Bauer (to whom he was twice engaged), and his tortured nights of writing in his diaries, which also were posthumously published.

The Communist regime subsequently suppressed Kafka's work, but he is now, finally, acknowledged and honored in the city he described as "a little old mother with sharp claws: she won't let go."

The Astronomical Clock on the Old Town Hall

as Hradčany. A long flight of broad steps (usually lined with souvenir sellers) climbs to the castle itself, a mixture of styles spanning 450 years of restoration and guarded by a series of courtyards. At the entrance to the outer courtyard, two soldiers stand at attention under grotesque and threatening statues of the Titans. The guard is changed every hour on the hour. In the second courtyard, entered through the 17th-century Matthias Gate, are the castle's art gallery and information center. Finally, you reach the courtyard of Katedrála sv Víta (St. Vitus' Cathedral), which took 600 years to complete, only finished in 1929. The royal palace, to the right, is a maze of rooms centered around the 15th-century Vladislav Hall, where mounted knights would trot down the Riders' Staircase to take part in indoor jousting matches.

STAROMĚSTSKÁ RADNICE

🞠 D3 ✉ Staroměstské náměstí 1 ☎ 224 482 909 🕓 Tue.–Sun. 9–6, Mon. 11–6, Apr.–Oct.; Tue.–Sun. 9–5, Mon. 11–5, rest of year 🚇 Staroměstská 🚋 Tram 17 to Staroměstská 🖐 $ ℹ Guided tours offered by Prague Information Service (see page 126)

Since a merchants' house was earmarked by the city council in 1338, the Staroměstská radnice (Old Town Hall) has gradually expanded and taken over a whole row of houses. A tower and chapel were added; features range from the original carved facade to the 19th-century house known as "At the Cock." Its main attraction is the intricate Astronomical Clock high on one wall, which gives the time, month, season, zodiac signs, course of the sun and Christian holidays. On the hour a skeleton appears and chimes the bell, followed by the Twelve Apostles parading from their little doors above the clock face.

ŠTERNBERSKÝ PALÁC

🞠 A4 ✉ Hradčanské náměstí 15 ☎ 233 090 570 or 220 514 596 🕓 Tue.–Sun. 10–6 🍴 Kavárna ve Šternberské paláci, in the palace 🚋 Tram 22, 23 to Pražský hrad 🖐 $$$

Tucked into an alley off Hradčany Square is Šternberský palác (Sternberg Palace), a town house built for Count Sternberg in 1698. It has a fine collection of Old Masters. Highlights include *The Feast of the Rosary*, by German Renaissance painter and engraver Albrecht Dürer, and *Adam and Eve,* by painter, etcher and woodcut-designer Lucas Cranach the Elder.

STRAHOVSKÝ KLÁŠTER

🞠 Off the map ✉ Strahovské nádvoří 1/132, Hradčany ☎ 220 516 671 🕓 Daily 9–noon and 1–5 🍴 Peklo ("Hell") restaurant in the cellars 🚋 Tram 22, 23 to Pohořelec 🖐 $$

The baroque spires of Strahovský klášter (Strahov Monastery) dominate the hilltop west of Hradčany: the monastery's name means "to watch over," and it has guarded this site since the 12th century. Elaborately decorated library halls store more than 130,000 books and manuscripts; the oldest, the *Strahov Gospels*, is displayed at the entrance. The upper floor of the cloisters is now a gallery of artworks returned to the monks by former Communist rulers.

EXCURSION TO KUTNÁ HORA

When silver and copper ore deposits were found on this hill 40 miles southeast of Prague, a town shot up virtually overnight, taking the appropriate name of Kutná Hora, or "Mining Mountain." That was in the late 13th century, and soon a royal mint was set up, hammering out the silver coin known as *pražské groše* in its workshops. Also constructed was a royal palace known as the Italian Court, a reference to the Florentine advisers of King Wenceslas II (1283– 1305). The town flourished on its mining proceeds, and even managed to recover after being taken over by one force after another during the Hussite Wars. But by the end of the 16th century the mountain was all mined out and the town fell into decay, suffering the final blow with a disastrous fire in 1770.

The 14th-century Italian Court at Kutná Hora, built on the proceeds from mining

The handsome Cathedral of St. Barbara was paid for by miners and dedicated to their patron saint. For its design they turned to the prestigious architect of Prague's St. Vitus' Cathedral, Petr Parléř, who rose to the occasion with distinctive tent-like spires and flying buttresses. In the side chapel, frescoes show the coin makers and the miners at work.

Sculptures line Barborská ulice, a street leading to an impressive 15th-century house built for a profiteer who ran an illegal private mining operation. It's now the Mining Museum, and behind it is the medieval mine itself, consisting of 820 feet of tunnels; a horse-drawn winch at the entrance drew out the bags of ore. The royal mint is gone (although it is still possible to make out its outline); parts of the Italian Court – including the chapel, adorned with art nouveau frescoes – can be visited.

Some 2 miles north of town in Sedlec is the kostnice, an ossuary (storehouse for bones) originally owned by Cistercian monks. During the 19th century its 40,000 human bones were put to artistic use by František Rint, who made them into bells and other items.

Contact a tourist information office for details of public transportation to Kutná Hora and Sedlec. Agencies organizing tours from Prague to Kutná Hora include:
Martin Tour ☒ Štěpánská 61, 110 00-Praha (Prague) 1 ☎ 224 212 473; fax 224 225 437; www.martintour.cz
For more information contact: Kutná Hora visitor information ☒ Palackého náměstí . 377, Kutná Hora ☎ 327 512 378; Kostnice ☎ 327 561 143

DENMARK

"C*OPENHAGEN is the best–*
built city of the north. "

From *Travels into Poland, Russia, Sweden, etc.*
by English historian and travel writer William Coxe

Opposite: *The Little Mermaid*, Copenhagen's most enduring symbol

Denmark

DENMARK

Denmark was the cradle of ancient Scandinavia. Talk of the first Vikings and you talk of Danes. It was from this fragmented mosaic of peninsulas and islands between mainland Europe and the Swedish-Norwegian landmass that those consummate seamen first struck out in search of plunder and new territory. Denmark is the smallest of the four Scandinavian nations, yet the Danes have made their country one of the most advanced and progressive in the world.

Danish Archipelago

The Kingdom of Denmark is just over 200 miles long, and the Jutland peninsula (the primary landmass) is only 75 miles wide. Nowhere in Denmark is much higher than 100 feet

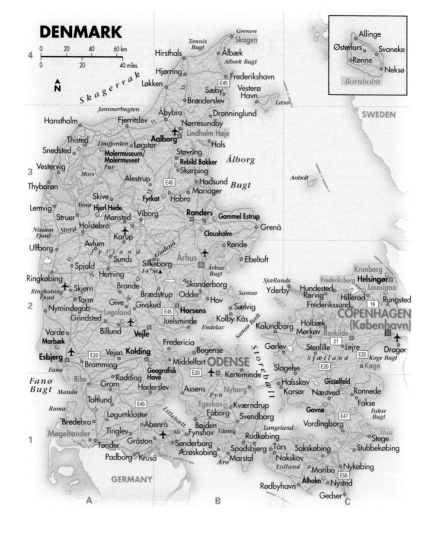

above sea level, and the country's highest point – Yding Skovhøj in central Jutland – is only 567 feet in elevation. Jutland's narrow southern border is with Germany; its west coast adjoins the North Sea.

East of Jutland, and with barely a sliver of water in between, is Denmark's second-largest island, Funen (Fyn). East of Funen is Zealand (Sjælland), the largest island, its northeastern edge a stone's throw from the Swedish coast and home to the capital, Copenhagen (København). Zealand and Funen lie like natural fortresses across the Kattegat, the channel separating Denmark from Sweden. This strategic position across the entrance to the Baltic Sea has always placed the country at the maritime heart of northern Europe.

The Jutland Peninsula

Copenhagen is the magnet for visitors, but the rest of this disparate and fascinating country has much to offer. Far western Jutland has an invigorating coastal landscape of long, sandy beaches backed by broad dunes and moorland. This landscape is repeated in north Jutland beyond the dividing waters of the Limfjord and all the way to the Skagen peninsula, the birdlike beak of land that thrusts into the sea at Denmark's northern edge. In north Jutland, outside the city of Aalborg, are evocative traces of Scandinavia's Viking culture at Lindholm Høje, a remarkable Viking burial ground of nearly 700 graves, many marked by stones in the shape of long ships.

The heathland of the west coast of central Jutland gives way in the east to a fertile undulating countryside of small farms and woodland, interspersed with country towns and pretty villages. On the east coast is Århus, a sophisticated and historic university city and

Attractive half-timbered houses in Rønne, on the Danish island of Bornholm

Denmark's second largest. Here you will find the mighty Århus Cathedral and the intriguing Den Gamle By, the Old Town and its dozens of restored, timber-framed buildings. South of Århus is a great stretch of woodland where you can enjoy peace and quiet along walking, bicycling and horseback riding trails. Southwest of Århus is the

MORE TOP DESTINATIONS IN DENMARK

● Århus B2 ● Bornholm C4
● Egeskov B1 ● Frederiksborg C2
● Køge C2 ● Kronborg C2
● Legoland A2 ● Lindholm Høje B3
● Louisiana C2 ● Møgeltønder A1
● Møn C1 ● Nyborg B1 ● Ribe A1
● Roskilde C2 ● Skagen B4

Denmark

town of Billund and Denmark's famous Legoland, the country's most visited attraction outside of Copenhagen. Beyond all the plastic bricks is the farming country of south Jutland, with such fascinating towns and villages as the ancient settlement of Ribe, which has a handsome cathedral, cobbled streets and gabled houses. The little village of Møgeltønder, in the far southwest, has a superb frescoed church and charming thatched houses.

Country of Islands

Denmark is a world of islands. There are more than 400 of them scattered around the country's coasts and across the Kattegat and the Baltic Sea. About 100 islands are inhabited. Funen (Fyn) is hailed as the "Garden of Denmark" because of its rich alluvial soils, legacy of the glacial debris left by retreating ice sheets.

The capital of Funen is Odense, the birthplace of Hans Christian Andersen. Funen has a gentle rural nature overall, its lush farmland complemented by a pleasant southern coastline and by good beaches on the peaceful island of Langeland, off the southeast coast.

Funen is connected to Denmark's largest island, Zealand, by a typically Danish feat of remarkable engineering. The 11-mile-long Great Belt rail and road fixed link bridge island hops, via the island of Sprogø, across the Great Belt (Storebælt) channel.

The ferry connection, used by visitors prior to 1998, was more romantic, but Scandinavian efficiency finally triumphed with a tunnel and bridge combination. A similar joint Danish-Swedish project, linking Copenhagen to Malmö across an artificial island built in the middle of the Øresund, was completed in 2000, thus laying the foundations for a new cultural and economic region.

Historic Zealand

Copenhagen may dominate Zealand, but the whole island is a treasure house of Danish history. North Zealand has much to offer in terms of historic buildings: the lakeside setting of magnificent Frederiksborg Castle (Frederiksborg Slot); and Elsinore Castle (Kronborg Slot) at Helsingør, the awe-inspiring setting for Shakespeare's *Hamlet*, overlooking the Øresund and the Swedish coast.

Just west of Copenhagen is Roskilde, Denmark's medieval capital, with a splendid cathedral housing the decorated crypts of 38 Danish kings and queens. In southern Zealand is the city of Køge, whose medieval center survives; at Trelleborg, on the west coast where the new rail bridge slices across the Great Belt, are the remains of the finest Viking ring fort in Denmark. Finally, just off the south coast of Zealand are the islands of Møn, Falster and Lolland, all linked to the main islands by bridges. Of these, Møn is the most interesting because of its chalk cliffs, a startling contrast to Denmark's almost uniform flatness.

Exploring Denmark

Denmark is one of the most accessible European countries. Its compact size and the smooth transition from island to island that modern engineering has accomplished makes exploring various regions by car an easy option once you are clear of Copenhagen's urban center.

This compactness makes traveling by public transportation almost as convenient. Fast, comfortable trains can whisk you from Zealand to Funen, and then on to Jutland, in a few hours. The efficient and extensive rail network offers stiff competition to long-distance bus services in Denmark, although buses are less expensive than trains.

Legoland, where millions of tiny Lego bricks have been made into an amazing model world

Denmark's climate is typical of a maritime environment, and the low elevation means there are no great extremes of temperature. Summers are pleasantly mild, but there can be wet spells; in winter snow is likely at times, but much less so than in the other Scandinavian countries.

Denmark is different in other ways as well, yet in matters of food and drink it remains engagingly – and tastily – Scandinavian. Danes relish the same hearty sandwich feast, here called the *smørrebrød,* that you find in Norway and Sweden, complete with its garnished mixes of delicious meat and seafood.

Beer is a Danish specialty, and the famous Danish breweries of Carlsberg and Tuborg produce some of the most popular brews in the world.

You will find that Danes are generally helpful and friendly. In rural areas and in provincial cities such as Odense, people are unfailingly so, but in Copenhagen there may be a sharper edge to people's attitudes. At times you may detect an apparent reserve on the part of Danish people. It is not a negative sentiment; the Danes are supremely accomplished, and beneath the reserve is a fierce national pride in their enduring country.

Denmark

TIMELINE

4000 BC   Neolithic settlers begin developing a farming economy.

500 BC to AD 500 Iron Age people set up trading centers in Jutland and Funen.

AD 793   Danish Vikings raid England's east coast, plundering the
                      monastery of Lindisfarne, and penetrate deep into mainland
                      Europe along the northern rivers.

circa 925   Gorm the Old becomes first king of a united Denmark.

1167   Founding of Copenhagen by Absalon, Bishop of Roskilde.

1588   Christian IV becomes king of Denmark and promotes the
                      construction of great Renaissance buildings, particularly in the
                      city of Copenhagen.

1611–60   Periodic wars with Sweden.

1814   Union with Norway ends after 278 years.

1849   New constitution abolishes absolute monarchy, establishing a
                      two-chamber parliament.

1914–18   Denmark is neutral during World War I.

1940   Denmark is invaded by the German army in spite of its
                      declared neutrality; the Danish Resistance carries out a
                      vigorous campaign against Germany.

1945   Denmark is liberated. A postwar reconstruction program begins.

1949   Denmark joins NATO.

1973   Danish people vote to join the European Economic Community.

1998   Opening of the fixed link rail and road bridge across the
                      Storebælt (Great Belt).

2000   Inauguration of the rail and road fixed link bridge across the
                      Øresund.

A TALENTED ROYAL LADY

Denmark's current queen, Margrethe II, was born in 1940. She was the
eldest daughter of King Frederik IX, who had no sons. After a favorable
1953 referendum, the Danish constitution, which allowed only for a male heir
to the throne, was amended to enable female succession. Margrethe became
queen at the age of 32, after Frederik's death in 1972. She is Denmark's first
female monarch since the 15th century. Queen Margrethe qualified as an
archeologist after studying at Copenhagen, Århus, Cambridge and Paris. She is
a talented artist, illustrating an edition of J. R. R. Tolkien's fantasy *Lord of the
Rings* and designing stamps for the Danish postal service. The queen has also
designed theatrical costumes and stage settings for the Danish Royal Theatre.
An accomplished linguist, Queen Margrethe has translated the work of the
French novelist Simone de Beauvoir, a task in which she worked with her
husband, French-born Prince Henrik.

Denmark

SURVIVAL GUIDE

- If you drive or cycle through Denmark, ask the tourist office for details about the "Marguerite Route," which is a series of linked routes (2,100 miles long) along quieter roads through the most scenic parts of the country. Signs display a daisy (marguerite) motif on a brown background. A map, free from the Danish Tourist Board, indicates the route.

- Danes celebrate Midsummer Eve (Sankt Hans) on June 23. Bonfires are lit throughout the country on the longest day of the year.

- In Denmark *morgenmad* is the word for breakfast, while *frokost* is lunch. *Smørrebrød,* the tasty Scandinavian open-faced sandwich, remains a lunchtime favorite; but try *frikadeller,* delicious fried meat or fish patties with salad and potatoes; or dip into the heftier *koldt bord,* a buffet-style selection. For main meals, enjoy *kogt torsk,* poached cod in mustard sauce, or old-fashioned *Skipper labskovs,* Danish stew.

- Delicious Danish pastries are called *wienerbrød* and come in a variety of shapes and tasty flavors. In every town and large village you will find a bakery selling pastries.

- Amber is a Danish specialty, the "Danish gold." The Amber Specialist (28 Frederiksberggade, Copenhagen, ☎ 33 11 88 03) is the place to look in Copenhagen, but you will find distinctive amber jewelry in stores throughout the country. If you're shopping for a colorful Scandinavian sweater go to Sweater Market (15 Frederiksberggade, Copenhagen, ☎ 33 15 27 73), Europe's largest sweater store.

- Denmark, like Sweden, is noted for its distinctive furnishing designs. The style known as "Danish Modern" is a classic merging of the functional with the aesthetic. Visit Illums Bolighus (Amagertorv, Copenhagen, ☎ 33 14 19 41) for some of the finest examples.

- Unlike the northern Scandinavian countries, Denmark has a far more relaxed approach to the sale of liquor. You can buy wines, spirits and beers in grocery stores, and you may find that prices are lower than in Norway, Sweden or Finland.

- Traditionally formal, Danes have become more relaxed about what to wear when eating out. Smart, casual clothes, especially during the warm summer months, are acceptable for dining at most Danish restaurants.

Standing guard at the Amalienborg Palace

Copenhagen

COPENHAGEN

Copenhagen (København) is where the European experience becomes Scandinavian. This is a magnificent city, far more a "Wonderful Copenhagen" than even the Danny Kaye song implies. It is a city of towers and steeples that are elegant and sculptural, as well as monumental. It is a city that draws you in along

Universitet Bibl

Frilandsmusee (Lyngby)

FREDERIK BAJERS PLADS

Rigshospitalet

Fælled Parken

Experimentarium; Tuborg Bryggerierne Dyrehaven (Bakken)

LILLE TRIANGEL

Garnisons Kirkegård

De gamles By

Blegdams Hospitalet

Holmes Kirkegård

Østerport Station

Nørre Hospitalet

Østre Anlæg

OSL PLAI

Mosaisk Kirkegård

SKT HANS TORV

Tinghus

Den Hirschsprungske Samling

Statens Museum for Kunst

Assistens Kirkegård

Danmarks-tekniske Høskole

SOLVTORVET

Danmarks-tekniske Høskole

SKT PAULS PLADS

Kommuneet Hospital

Palmehus

Geologisk Museum

DSB

BLÅGÅRDS PLADS

Botanisk Have

Rosenborg Slot

Marmorkir (Frederikskirke

Botanisk Museum

Kongens Have

C L Davids Samling

Arbejdermuseet

Musikhistorisk Museum

Radiohusets Koncertsal

Nørreport Station

KULTORVET

Rundetårn

Kongens Mytorv Station

KONGENS

Charlottenb

HERMES TRIERS PLADS

Søpavillionen

Ørsteds-parken

Telefonhus

GRÅBRØDRE PLADS

Forum Station

JULIUS THOMSENS PLADS

Universitet

BISPE-TORVET

FRUE PLADS

Helligånds-kirken

Nikolaj Kirke

Kongel Teater

SKT MARKUS PLADS

Tekn Inst

JARMERS PLADS

Vor Frue Kirke

GAMMEL-TORV

VIMMELSKAMAGERT (STRØGET)

DANASVEJ

NYTORV

HØJBRO PLADS

Thorvaldsens Museum

Tycho Brahe Planetarium

Vesterport Station

SAS

Scala

Domhuset

Lurblowers

RÅDHUS PLADSEN

Rådhuset

CHRISTIANSBORG SLOTSPLEIN

Holmens Kirk

Christiansborg Slot

Børsen

Tivoli

National-museet

DANTES PLADS

Ministerialbygn Det kongelige Bibliotek

Tøjhusmuseet

Københavns Bymuseum

BANEGÅRDS PLADS

KIRKEPLADS

VESTERBRO TORV

Hovedbanegården

Ny Carlsberg Glyptotek

Central Postbygning

OTTO MONSTEDS PLADS

Carlsberg Bryggerierne

Postterminal

AMAGER

Godsbanegården

Statens Serumimstit

A   B   C

pedestrian-only streets that lead in and out of delightful squares. It is a city with museums and attractions, restaurants, cafés and entertainment that place it among the finest of European capitals.

Copenhagen originated, like so many other Scandinavian towns and cities, as a small fishing village, its occupants taking advantage of the sheltered waters around Slotsholmen Island, the island that is now home to the Danish National Parliament (Folketing), and the Christiansborg Palace (Christiansborg Slot). By the 12th century Slotsholmen had been fortified in keeping with the settlement's growing commercial status, a status signified by its name, Kømandshavn, the "port of the merchants," later amended to København. By the middle of the 15th century, Copenhagen was the recognized capital of Denmark.

The city's status was enhanced by the construction of many fine buildings during the reign of Christian IV of Denmark in the 17th century, and by the 19th century Copenhagen had emerged as a major European capital. Development continued during the 20th century, and at the start of the new millennium Copenhagen stood as a mature and hugely successful city.

First Impressions

The initial impression visitors have of Copenhagen is of a city overpowered by traffic. To reach the central City Hall Square (Rådhuspladsen) from Copenhagen's central railroad station (Hovedbanegården), visitors pass Tivoli and then negotiate busy downtown streets. Hans Christian Andersens Boulevard, a broad and howling stream of traffic, is as far removed from Andersen's fairy-tale world as can be imagined. Keep your eyes open for cyclists as well as cars. The broad expanse of City Hall Square, a relaxed, traffic-free environment, leads to a refreshing world of lively streets, colorful squares and hidden corners, where pedestrians are the priority.

There is a lot to see in Copenhagen. Some attractions, such as Rosenborg Castle and the National Museum of Fine Arts, are some distance from City Hall Square. Even the famous statue of *The Little Mermaid* is a long walk along the waterfront from the central parts of the city. Getting around is easy, however, if you take advantage of the various guided walking tours that are available. Other sightseeing tours go by bus and by harbor or canal boats. The city's bus service is extremely efficient and comprehensive, complemented by a driverless subway (metro) system, the first stage of which opened in 2002 and which by 2007 will extend to the aiport. Because of the city center's pedestrian-only status, however, exploring on your own here is a pleasure.

Strøget and Beyond

Start at City Hall Square. Look up at the Unibank building, where you will see a unique bronze weathervane featuring a girl who appears on her bicycle when the weather is fine, and with an umbrella when it rains.

The sequence of streets known collectively as Strøget begins at City Hall Square, at the narrow Frederiksberggade. Amid the many stores and restaurants fascinating side streets lead to antiques and specialty outlets; vistas suddenly reveal the city's impressively grand architecture and fashionable people.

City on the Water's Edge

At the far end of Strøget, cross the big, bustling square of Kongens Nytorv (New Royal Market) to reach Nyhavn (New Harbor), the old harbor inlet, now an area of fashionable restaurants. Visit Amalienborg Plads (Amalienborg Square) and Amalienborg Palace, then head east to waterside Larsens Plads; from this square a pleasant walk north takes you to *The Little Mermaid*.

Nearby is the Frihedsmuseet (Museum of Danish Resistance), a celebration of resistance against the Nazis. These attractions all spotlight Copenhagen's lure for visitors: its astonishing variety.

ESSENTIAL INFORMATION

TOURIST INFORMATION
Wonderful Copenhagen (Copenhagen Tourist Information)
• Written inquiries: Gammel Kongevej 1, DK-1610 København V
• Personal callers: Bernstorffsgade 1 ☎ 70 22 24 42; fax 70 22 24 52; www.visitcopenhagen.dk

URBAN TRANSPORTATION
Copenhagen's main railroad station is Hovedbanegården, on Bernstorffsgade. For information call ☎ 33 14 17 01. The station has modern facilities, including stores, and is a few minutes from the city center. Copenhagen has a very good network of bus routes. City buses leave

from Rådhuspladsen. For information call ☎ 36 13 14 15. For details and information about transport on the subway (metro) call ☎ 33 11 17 00. Taxis have fixed rates. For service, call ☎ 35 35 35 35.

AIRPORT INFORMATION
Copenhagen Airport is at Kastrup, 6 miles south of the city center on the island of Amager. An Airport Express train runs from Hovedbanegården every 10 minutes (hourly 1:20– 4:20 a.m.; journey time approximately 12 minutes). Airport buses leave every 15 minutes from outside Hovedbanegården, on Bernstorffsgade. For airport information, call ☎ 32 47 47 47.

CLIMATE – average highs and lows for the month

JAN.	FEB.	MAR.	APR.	MAY	JUN.	JUL.	AUG.	SEP.	OCT.	NOV.	DEC.
3°C	3°C	5°C	10°C	15°C	19°C	20°C	20°C	16°C	11°C	7°C	4°C
37°F	37°F	41°F	50°F	59°F	66°F	68°F	68°F	61°F	52°F	45°F	39°F
-2°C	-2°C	0°C	2°C	7°C	11°C	13°C	12°C	10°C	7°C	3°C	0°C
28°F	28°F	32°F	36°F	45°F	52°F	55°F	54°F	50°F	45°F	37°F	32°F

Copenhagen

CITY SIGHTS

Key to symbols

⊞ map coordinates refer to the Copenhagen map on pages 140–141; sights below are highlighted in yellow on the map.

☒ address or location ☎ telephone number
◎ opening times 🚇 nearest subway (metro) or
S-train station 🚌 nearest bus route 🚢 water bus
🍴 restaurant or café on site or nearby 🎟 admission
charge: $$$ more than DKr25, $$ DKr12–DKr25, $ less
than DKr12 ℹ other relevant information

AMALIENBORG PLADS

⊞ D3 ☒ Amalienborg Plads ☎ Royal collections:
33 12 08 08 ◎ Royal collections: daily 10–4,
May–Oct.; Tue.–Sun. 11–4, rest of year 🚇 Kongens
Nytorv 🚌 1, 6, 9, 10 🚢 901, 902 🎟 Palace $$$

The royal heart of Copenhagen is the octagonal Amalienborg Plads (Amalienborg Square), with a statue of King Frederick V at its center, rococo palaces on four sides, and broad avenues leading off the other four. The Danish royal family spends most of autumn and winter in the palaces. Their very private presence gives the square a rather detached, lifeless atmosphere except during the colorful changing of the guard, daily at noon when the Queen is in residence.

On the northwest corner of the square is the Amalienborg Palace, containing a charming collection of royal memorabilia and a sequence of reconstructed rooms that illustrate the life of the royal Glücksburg family from the mid-19th to mid-20th centuries.

CHRISTIANSBORG SLOT

Christiansborg Slot ⊞ C2 ☒ Christiansborg
Slotsplads 🚇 Kongens Nytorv 🚌 1, 2, 2A, 6, 8, 9, 10,
19, 28, 29, 31 37, 41, 42, 43, 550S, 650S
Slotsholmen ruins ☎ 33 92 64 94 ◎ Daily 10–4,
May–Sep.; Tue., Thu. and Sat.–Sun. 10–4, Jan.–Dec.;
Tue.–Sun. 10–4, rest of year 🎟 $$
Kongelige Repræsentationslokaler ☎ 33 92 64 92
◎ Guided tours in English daily at 11, 1 and 3,
May–Sep.; Tue., Thu. and Sat.–Sun. at 3, rest of year
🎟 $$$
Kongelige Stalde og Kareter ☎ 33 40 26 77 ◎ Fri.–Sun.
2–4, May–Sep.; Sat.–Sun. 2–4, rest of year 🎟 $$
Teatermuseet ☎ 33 11 51 76 ◎ Tue.–Thu. 11–3,
Sat.–Sun. 1–4 🎟 $$$

Tøjhusmuseet ☎ 33 11 60 37 ◎ Tue.–Sun. noon–4
🎟 $$$ (free on Wed.)
Christiansborg Slotskirke ☎ 33 92 64 71 ◎ Daily
noon–4, Easter, Jul. and in mid-Oct.; Sun. noon–4,
rest of year 🎟 Free

The monumental complex that makes up Christiansborg Slot (Christiansborg Palace) dominates the island of Slotsholmen. It presents a rather stern face to the city approaching across the encircling canal from Strøget and Højbro Plads (Højbro Square). A visit here may take you all day. The vast west wing houses the Danish Parliament (Folketing), the Supreme Court and the Foreign Office, built between 1907 and 1916 to replace a more stylish building that burned down in 1884. Also here is the Kongelige Repræsentationslokaler (Royal Reception Rooms), with lavishly decorated rooms, and grand Renaissance Hall.

Below the palace are the preserved ruins of Bishop Absalon's Castle, dating from 1167; and its successor, Copenhagen Castle. Museums around the royal riding grounds include Kongelige Stalde og Kareter (Royal Stables and Coaches), the Teatermuseet (Theater Museum) and the Tøjhusmuseet (Royal Danish Arsenal Museum).

The Christiansborg Slotskirke (Christiansborg Palace Church), dating from 1826 but devastated by fire in 1992, reopened in 1997. It is used on royal and state occasions.

Den Lille Havfrue

Most visitors don't leave Copenhagen without seeing *The Little Mermaid* (*Den Lille Havfrue*), the most popular expression of Hans Christian Andersen's fairy-tale world. Some may find the experience disappointing. Designed in 1913, she languishes in rather stark isolation at the northern end of the city's waterfront. Sadly, vandals have damaged *The Little Mermaid* by sawing off her arm and her head on separate occasions. The original molds survive, however, making the *Mermaid* – in one sense – forever renewable.

The great marble dome of Marmorkirken

MARMORKIRKEN

🏛 D3 ✉ Frederiksgade 4 ☎ 33 15 01 44 🕐 Church: Mon.–Thu. 10–5 (also Wed. 5–6), Fri.–Sun. noon–5. Dome: tours daily at 1 and 3, mid-Jun. to Aug. 31; Sat.–Sun. at 3, rest of year 🚇 Kongens Nytorv 🚌 1, 6, 9 💰 Church free; Dome $$

Frederikskirken (Frederick's Church), known universally as Marmorkirken (Marble Church), seems out of place in a Copenhagen of slender, convoluted steeples and towers. The church was begun in 1749 as a final flourish to the nearby Amalienborg Palace, but was not completed until 1894. Modeled on St. Peter's in Rome, its dome measures 100 feet in diameter.

The nave is circular and is surrounded by a circular walkway, above which there is a whispering gallery with superb acoustics. Try whispering, and see how far the sound carries. The paneled frescoes on the inside of the dome are glowingly painted and gilded.

NATIONALMUSEET

🏛 C2 ✉ Ny Vestergade 10 ☎ 33 13 44 11 🕐 Tue.–Sun. 10–5 🍴 Museum restaurant 🚉 S-train København H 🚌 1, 2, 5, 6, 8, 10, 28, 29, 30, 32, 33, 550S, 650S 💰 $$$ (free on Wed., excluding special exhibitions)

Copenhagen's Nationalmuseet (National Museum) is one of the finest of its kind in Europe. There is a lot to see, so use the floor plan to get your bearings. The museum has outstanding exhibits on Danish history, with such superb Bronze Age artifacts as burial remains in oak coffins, a golden sun chariot and the silver Gundestrip cauldron. Among Iron Age finds are the magnificent North Slesvig Golden Horns. There is a collection of *lur*, the horn instruments that were used for ceremony and communication. Other major collections cover the Middle Ages and the Renaissance, Egyptian and classical antiquities, and human cultures. There is also a children's museum and a theater.

NY CARLSBERG GLYPTOTEK

🏛 B1 ✉ Dantes Plads 7 ☎ 33 41 81 41 🕐 Tue.–Sun. 10–4 🍴 Museum café 🚉 S-train København H 🚌 1, 2, 5, 6, 8, 10, 28, 29, 30, 32, 33, 550S, 650S 💰 $$ (free on Wed. and Sun.)

A splendid winter garden with huge palm trees is the unexpected focal point of the New Carlsberg Glyptotek, one of the country's finest art museums. Carl Jacobson, the owner of the Carlsberg breweries who founded the museum, was mostly interested in ancient art from the Mediterranean, and Danish and French art from the 19th century onwards. Highlights are the Etruscan collection, one of the largest outside Italy, and French sculpture (including a superb Rodin collection) and paintings. The French collection, housed in a specially designed structure, includes paintings by the main Impressionists and 40 works by Paul Gauguin. The museum is currently undergoing extensive renovation which is due for completion by June 2006.

ROSENBORG SLOT

🏛 C3 ✉ Øster Voldgade 4A ☎ 33 15 32 86 🕐 Daily 10–5, Jun.–Aug.; daily 10–4, May and Sep.; daily 11–3, in Oct.; Tue.–Sun. 11–2, Jan.–Apr. and Nov. 1 to mid-Dec. 🍴 Castle café/restaurant 🚇 Metro/S-train Nørreport 🚌 4E, 10, 14, 16, 31, 32, 42, 43, 72E, 79E, 173E, 150S, 184, 185, 350S 💰 $$$

The early 17th-century Rosenborg Slot (Rosenborg Castle) is an outstanding example of Renaissance architecture and style; it stands at the edge of the lovely Kongens Have, the King's Gardens. The lavishly decorated rooms reflect the regal styles of Danish monarchs from Christian IV to Frederick IV. There are superb marbled ceilings, late 17th-century Dutch tapestries, gilded mirrors, silver lions that seem poised to leap, gold and enamelware, and beautiful ceiling paintings. The Royal Treasury is in the castle basement; here the Danish Crown Jewels and other royal treasures glow in the delicate light.

RUNDETÅRN

✚ C3 ⊠ Købmagergade 52A ☎ 33 73 03 73
🕐 Tower: Mon.–Sat. 10–8, Sun. noon–8, Jun.–Aug.; Mon.–Sat. 10–5, Sun. noon–5, rest of year. Observatory: Tue.–Wed. 7–10 p.m., mid-Oct. to late Mar.; Sun. 1–4, mid-Jun. to mid-Aug. 🚇 Metro/S-train Nørreport
🚌 5, 7, 14, 16, 17, 24, 43, 84 💰 $$

The Rundetårn (Round Tower) is on Købmagergade, one of the city's liveliest streets. A visit is a must for anyone fit enough to trek up the covered, cobbled ramp that winds its way for 685 feet and through seven and a half turns to the top of the 115-foot landmark. Peter the Great of Russia is said to have ridden his horse up the ramp while the Czarina followed in a horse-drawn carriage. Today, everybody walks; keep to the outside for the easiest angle. From the top there are marvelous views of Copenhagen's red-tiled roofs and far-flung outskirts. The Round Tower dates from 1642 and was built by Christian IV as an observatory. It still functions as such and at certain times (see above) the public has access to the astronomical telescope.

STATENS MUSEUM FOR KUNST

✚ C4 ⊠ Sølvgade 48–50 ☎ 33 74 84 94
🕐 Tue.–Sun. 10–5 (also Wed. 5–8) 🍴 Museum café
🚇 Metro/S-train Nørreport or S-train Østerport
🚌 6A, 14, 40, 42, 43, 184, 185, 150S 💰 $$$ (free on Wed.) ℹ Audio guide available

A huge number of works are on display at the Statens Museum for Kunst (National Museum of Fine Arts). International and Danish art from the 13th century to 1900, shown in the old building, includes superb 17th-century Dutch paintings by Pieter Brueghel, Rembrandt, Jacob Jordaens and Jacob van Ruisdael; 19th-century Danish painting is represented by Golden Age artists such as Christoffer Eckersberg and

Fanciful facade at the ever-popular Tivoli

Christen Købke, and by the Skagen painters, Theodor Philipsen and the Funen Painters. Twentieth-century art, displayed in the new building, includes major works by Henri Matisse *(Odalisque)*, Max Ernst, the Cobra Group (*Springtime* by Asger Jorn), Georges Braque and Pablo Picasso, as well as other modern works.

TIVOLI

✚ B2 ⊠ Vesterbrogade 3 ☎ 33 15 10 01 🕐 Daily 11–11 (also Thu. and Sat. 11 p.m.–midnight and Fri. 11 p.m.–1 a.m.), Apr.–Sep. and mid-Nov. to Dec. 31
🍴 32 restaurants 🚇 S-train København H 🚌 1, 2, 6, 8, 10, 11, 12, 13, 14, 16, 28, 29, 30, 34, 40, 67, 68, 69, 150S, 250S, 550S, 650S 💰 $$$

Copenhagen's famous Tivoli is unmissable, except during the winter months when the gardens are closed. (They are open during the Christmas holidays, however.) At the heart of the city, the 21-acre park is given over to entertainment: flower gardens, lakes, theater, concert hall, carnival rides, amusements, food and drink, and above all people-watching. There is an entrance fee, and separate charges for carnival rides and indoor attractions (you can buy a pass). Tivoli is never dull; it is lit brilliantly at night and there are fireworks shows every Saturday, plus some Wednesdays, holidays and special days.

ODENSE

Odense seems to radiate the persuasive charm of a story by its most famous son, Hans Christian Andersen. Even factory chimneys on the outskirts of the city are gaily painted and are thus less stark against the sky, and the surviving medieval buildings of the Old Town are enchanting. Above all, the city makes a refreshing change from the urban bustle of Copenhagen. Odense's wealth of museums and attractions are worthy of a city several times its size.

An important regional capital and university town, Odense retains its provincial charm, and is rightly celebrated as the birthplace of Hans Christian Andersen and Denmark's great composer Carl Nielsen.

The Modern City

You will relax as soon as you arrive at Odense's modern railroad station, on Østre Stationsvej. Street life is busy here and the traffic is just as heavy as in any city, but directly across the road is Kongens Have, the old Royal Park. The park provides a peaceful introduction to Odense and takes you pleasantly along tree-shaded paths past the Odense Theater and the Funen Art Museum into the heart of the city. The center of Odense is at Flakhaven, a pedestrian-only area in front of the redbrick Town Hall (Rådhuset), the interior of which can be viewed on a guided tour. The friendly and helpful Odense Turist Bureau is to the left of the Town Hall.

All buses leave from central stops near the Town Hall, but you will have little need of public transportation in

Odense unless you travel outside the city. Most attractions are a short walk from the center, and it is very easy to find your way around.

From Flakhaven turn left along the street Vestergade, which takes you into the pleasant, pedestrian-only heart of modern Odense. Here you will find a variety of stores, including top fashion boutiques. Visit Inspiration Zinck (Nos. 82–84 Vestergade ☎ 66 12 96 93) for the best in Danish design and handicraft. Step down the adjoining street of Jernbanegade to Målet's bar and restaurant for a *smørrebrød*, Denmark's popular and delicious lunchtime snack, an open slice of rye bread heaped with sliced meat or fish and loaded with different garnishes.

The Old Town

Going east from the Town Hall takes you across the traffic-laden street Thomas B. Thriges Gade and into Odense's Old Town. Here in Hans Jensens Stræde is the Hans Christian Andersen House (entrance on Bangs Boder), amid a little complex of cobbled streets and doll-like houses

that was once the poor quarter of the city. Nearby is the Carl Nielsen Museum, which adjoins the Odense Concert Hall. Charming as this area is, the best of Old Odense is a couple of streets away, where the medieval thoroughfares of Overgade and Nedergade retain many of their enchanting old buildings.

Pause at the entrance to Nedergade and look down the side street leading down to the river. This is Paaskestræde, location of the Old Poor House, with its rippled red-tile roof and scalloped cornice above the first floor. Hans Christian Andersen went to school here, and the wording on the wall is his touching comment: "Here I went with my wooden shoes to the poor school."

The combination of old and new is what makes Odense such a delight. The city's human scale, its sense of healthy provincialism and its vigorous regional culture are all enhanced by the international cachet of Hans Christian Andersen and Carl Nielsen. What you will find refreshing is that the locals have retained a friendly, unaffected nature in the face of all this.

ESSENTIAL INFORMATION

TOURIST INFORMATION
Odense Turist Bureau
(Odense Tourist Bureau)
• Rådhuset, Vestergade 2 ☎ 66 12 75 20; fax 66 12 75 86; www.visitodense.com

URBAN TRANSPORTATION
Odense's railroad station or Østre Stationsvej (☎ 70 13 14 15) has modern facilities and is about a 10-minute walk from the city center. Odense's main attractions are within a small area of the city center, but if you

need bus information, call ☎ 63 11 22 33. For taxi service, call Odense Taxa ☎ 66 15 44 15.

AIRPORT INFORMATION
Odense Airport operates domestic flights only. The nearest international airport is Billund Airport, on Jutland, ☎ 76 50 50 50. There are coach connections between Billund Airport and Odense, arriving at Turisholdepladsen, Dannebrogsgade. For information about coach connections call ☎ 64 71 29 10 or 64 71 50 30.

CLIMATE – average highs and lows for the month

JAN.	FEB.	MAR.	APR.	MAY	JUN.	JUL.	AUG.	SEP.	OCT.	NOV.	DEC.
3°C	3°C	5°C	10°C	15°C	19°C	20°C	20°C	17°C	12°C	7°C	4°C
37°F	37°F	41°F	50°F	59°F	66°F	68°F	68°F	63°F	54°F	45°F	39°F
-2°C	-2°C	0°C	3°C	7°C	10°C	13°C	13°C	10°C	7°C	3°C	0°C
28°F	28°F	32°F	37°F	45°F	50°F	55°F	55°F	50°F	45°F	37°F	32°F

Windmill at the imaginative open-air museum of Funen Village, near Odense

CITY SIGHTS

Key to symbols

🗺 map coordinates refer to the Odense map on page 146; sights below are highlighted in yellow on the map.

✉ address or location ☎ telephone number

🕐 opening times 🍴 restaurant or café on site or nearby 🎟 admission charge: $$$ more than DKr25, $$ DKr12–DKr25, $ less than DKr12 ℹ other relevant information

BYMUSEET MØNTERGÅRDEN

✚ C2 ✉ Overgade 48–50 ☎ 65 51 46 01
🕐 Tue.–Sun. 10–4 🎟 $$

Housed in a marvelous old building – with redbrick, red-timber framing and a red-tiled roof – the Bymuseet Møntergården (City Museum Møntergården) tells the story of Odense's past through a number of clever and interesting exhibits. Behind the main building is a lovely yard with a huge tree in the center. On one side of the yard is a series of preserved domestic interiors from the 17th and 18th centuries and up to the 1950s. In keeping with Odense's charm, the museum has a wonderful air of quiet authenticity often absent in big-city institutions.

CARL NIELSEN MUSEET

✚ C3 ✉ Claus Bergs Gade 11 ☎ 65 51 46 01
🕐 Thu.–Fri. 2–6, Sun. noon–4, Jun.–Aug.; Thu.–Fri. 4–8, Sun. noon–4, rest of year 🎟 $$

Already blessed with Hans Christian Andersen, Odense also boasts Denmark's most famous composer, Carl August Nielsen, as another native son. Nielsen was born in 1865 at nearby Nørre Lyndelse and began his musical career as a trumpeter in a local band. His most famous works are his six symphonies, his opera *Saul and David* and choral works such as *Spring of Funen*. The Carl Nielsen Museum is a restful place housed in an extension of the Odense Koncerthus. It tells the story of the composer's life through displays of artifacts. Pause at key points, don earphones and drift away listening to Nielsen's music. His wife, Anne Marie Broderson, was an accomplished sculptress, and there are displays of her work.

DANMARKS JERNBANEMUSEUM

🚩 B3 ✉ Dannebrogsgade 24 ☎ 66 13 66 30 🕐 Daily 10–4 🍴 Museum café 💵 $$$ ℹ Steam-train trips during school holidays

Danmarks Jernbanemuseum (Denmark's Railway Museum) is ideally located next to Odense railroad station and is the biggest museum of its kind in Scandinavia. It features a reconstructed early 19th-century station and locomotives, including luxurious royal carriages. Add to this a model train section, trips on a mini train and a section on ferries and you might not get out of the station.

DEN FYNSKE LANDSBY

🚩 Off the map ✉ Sejerskovvej 20 ☎ 65 51 46 01 🕐 Daily 10–7, Jun.–Aug.; Tue.–Sun. 10–5, Easter –May 31 and Sep.–Oct.; Sun. and holidays 11–3, rest of year (restricted access to exhibits) 🍴 Museum café 💵 $$$ (increased charge mid-Jun. to mid-Aug. and 1 week mid-Oct.; free Sun., Nov.–Mar.) ℹ Living history events in summer

The open-air museum of Den Fynske Landsby (The Funen Village) gives colorful insight into rural life on the island of Funen during the 18th and 19th centuries. More than 20 thatched, timber-framed buildings are arranged like a farming village complete with duck pond, smithy, water mill and windmill. Farming continues during the summer months, and harvesting, beer brewing and craftwork are conducted as part of village life. There are particularly imaginative tableaux detailing the lives of a poor and a well-off 19th-century villager.

FYNS KUNSTMUSEUM

🚩 B2 ✉ Jernbanegade 13 ☎ 65 51 46 01 🕐 Tue.–Sun. 10–4 💵 $$$

The Fyns Kunstmuseum (Funen Art Museum) is located in an elegant, classical building and contains a superb collection. The museum has a distinctive atmosphere of serenity that is missing from some major galleries. Most of the works are by Danish artists from the 17th century to the present. Highlights include Jens Juel's vivid *The Open-Mouthed One* and P. S. Krøyer's *Italian Field Workers*, with its interesting preponderance of left-handed men – a little art puzzle. H. A. Brendekild's big painting *Finished,* with its prostrate worker in a vast, flat field, portrays the hard life of peasant workers in old Funen. By contrast, a real charmer is Gustava Emilie Grüner's *Group Portrait of the Family Leunbach,* with its cheerful, inviting faces. The museum also has some fine sculptures and a small collection of contemporary abstract art.

HANS CHRISTIAN ANDERSENS HUS

🚩 B2 ✉ Bangs Boder 29, 5000 Odense C ☎ 65 51 46 01 🕐 Daily 9–6, mid-Jun. to Aug. 31; Tue.–Sun. 10–4, rest of year. Closed Christmas vacation 💵 $$$

The new Hans Christian Andersens Hus (Hans Christian Andersen Museum) brings to life the story and brilliant works of Odense's famous son. The museum describes Andersen's extraordinary life and the intensity of character that shaped his work. You are taken on a historical journey of one man, and introduced to his world and influences, tracing the great storyteller's development from humble beginnings as a cobbler's son to world-wide fame as a published author.

Exhibitions throughout the museum show other aspects of the man including his artistic qualities. The museum's completion coincided with the 2005 bicentennial Hans Christian Andersen celebrations. The writer's original home and alleged birthplace is located at the heart of a charming complex of old single-story houses, once the "poor quarter" of Odense.

Odense

SANKT KNUDS DOMKIRKE

B2 ☒ Flakhaven ☎ 66 12 03 92 🕐 Mon.–Sat. 9–5, Sun. and holidays noon–5, Apr.–Oct.; Mon.–Sat. 10–4, Sun. and holidays noon–5, rest of year 💲 Free

The elegant Gothic style of Sankt Knuds Domkirke (St. Canute's Cathedral), Funen's cathedral, reflects the importance of early medieval Odense and the homage paid to King Knud (Canute), who – with his brother Benedikt (Benedict) – was slaughtered in 1086 by Jutland farmers in a rather drastic protest against royal taxes. The church has some powerful artifacts, not the least its splendid rococo pulpit and its altarpiece, a dazzling wood triptych with exquisite carvings and gold leaf that is one of the finest pieces of religious art in northern Europe. Down the stairs, in the atmospheric and chilly crypt, are two reliquaries containing the reputed skeletons of Knud and Benedikt, macabre but endearing somehow in their gaunt way.

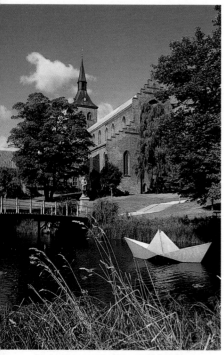
Tranquil scene at St. Canute's Cathedral

TIDENS SAMLING

A2 ☒ Brandts Passage 29–2 sal ☎ 65 91 19 42 🕐 Daily 10–5 🍴 Museum café 💲 $$$

For a museum with a difference, Tidens Samling (Time Collection) is hard to beat. It is located in a spacious loft area, where half the space is used to house exhibitions that always have an imaginative, cultural or fashion theme. The second half is home to the permanent Time Collection – a series of set-piece interiors from various periods from 1900 to the 1970s, each one crammed full of interesting authentic artifacts and furnishings.

The result is delightful – a unique look at changing domestic style. One of the many charming aspects of the Time Collection is that you can step into the displays, relax in the chairs, poke through the drawers, or do a bit of sock-mending. There is even a period-style coffee bar. Occasional fashion shows are done with absolute flair.

The Martyred King

The violent death of the 11th-century Danish King Knud (Canute), a descendant of Canute, one-time king of England, did Odense a favor. The king and his brother, Benedikt, were slaughtered in Odense's old Church of St. Alban's on July 10, 1086, by Jutland peasant farmers angered by excessive taxes the king levied to finance war with England. Fourteen years later Pope Paschalis II canonized the king as St. Knud the Holy. In an ironic twist, Benedictine monks from England settled in Odense and successfully promoted the town as a place of pilgrimage to the murdered ruler. The reputed skeletons of Knud and Benedikt can still be seen in Sankt Knuds Domkirke.

Statue of the writer, on the boulevard in Copenhagen that bears his name

The house where Andersen spent his formative years – now a museum

HANS CHRISTIAN ANDERSEN

Odense's most famous son left his native city at an early age. Yet Odense is still associated with Hans Christian Andersen. From humble beginnings – his mother was a washerwoman, his father a shoemaker – Andersen's astonishingly fertile imagination and creativity led him on extensive travels throughout Europe and established him as Denmark's major literary figure. He was born in 1805 in Odense, but it is not certain in which location. By the age of seven Andersen was inspired after visiting the theater in Odense; by 14 he was in Copenhagen, where he tried unsuccessfully to join the Royal Theater Company.

Andersen was a man of complex sensitivities whose relationships were profound and often difficult, although he was never short of friends and benefactors. He was essentially a poet and dramatist, and his early works reflect this. He had the urge to travel, typical of a lonely and introverted artist, and his first, self-published book was about a journey he made on foot through Denmark. In 1835 he published *Fairy Tales, Told for Children*. Plays, novels and travel accounts followed, along with a continuing output of the fairy tales that were to make his name.

Andersen's fairy tales were far more profound than mere fantasy, however charming. He was a powerful moralist, an intensely humane man who understood the human condition and injected into his stories remarkable life lessons. Famous tales such as *The Emperor's New Clothes, The Little Mermaid, The Ugly Duckling, The Tinder Box* and *The Nightingale* have entered the consciousness of generations of readers worldwide, for their literary elegance as much as their theatricality.

Andersen remained an intense and sometimes troubled man. He was a friend and associate of kings and of the famous. He never married, though he was deeply in love at times, not least with the Swedish singer Jenny Lind. He died at 70 in 1875. In the Denmark of his day Andersen was criticized and diminished for what was seen as his absorption with the wider European world. As always with genius, however, his work transcended time. In Odense the spirit of this remarkable man is vividly present, at the Hans Christian Anderson Museum and also in quieter corners of the Old Town.

FINLAND

"T HE appearance of the town is entirely modern, in some respects suggesting America rather than Europe. "

An early reference to Helsinki, from *Russia with Tehran, Port Arthur and Peking* by German travel publisher Karl Baedeker

Opposite: Sauna house on a lake edge near Jyvaskyla, Finland

FINLAND

Finland, one of the world's great survivors, is a small nation that has had to contend with harsh nature and belligerent neighbors in an often hostile northern European world. For centuries Finland was trapped between the aggressive ambitions of Sweden and Russia, and then in the 20th century between the Eastern and Western protagonists of the Cold War. The country's emergence as a self-confident, modern nation, with its historic identity intact, is a celebration of steady nerve, political shrewdness and tenacity.

The striking Sibelius monument, located in Sibelius Park in Helsinki

Land of Forests and Lakes

Finland is bordered on the east by Russia, on the northwest by Sweden and on the north by Norway. Most of Finland is less than 600 feet high, and over 70 percent of the country supports coniferous spruce and pine. The northern areas are covered with peat bog, and there are almost 188,000 lakes and nearly 180,000 islands. All of Finland is a seemingly endless blanket of trees, water and wide skies.

The main "lake district" of Saimaa in the east is a paradise of woodland and navigable rivers and lakes, punctuated by rugged cliffs and a glittering mosaic of islands and lakeside towns and villages. Apart from the special nature of the Finnish landscape, the main cities and towns – Helsinki, Turku, Tampere, Porvoo, Savonlinna, Oulu and Rovaniemi – have much to offer the visitor. They are as modern as any other European urban center, yet retain a deep-seated Finnish identity.

The Islands and Lapland

The mirror image of the inland water world is Finland's coastal region. Off Finland's southwestern coast is the Saaristomeri archipelago, with its thousands of islands and little rock islets known as "skerries." Farther out lie the Åland Islands, stepping stones to Sweden. You can explore the archipelago by ferry or steamship, or stay on shore at the beaches of Yyteri, near Pori, on the coast to the north.

In northern Finland, in the great wilderness of Lapland, you can learn about the life and culture of the Sami people in Rovaniemi's Arctic Center (Arktikum). The adventurous can go white-water rafting on the Tornionjoki river, follow one of the numerous hiking routes or head into the mountains of the northwest, where Finland's highest peak, Haltitunturi, reaches 4,300 feet.

Traveling in Finland

Traveling by car is a good way to see rural Finland. There are excellent road systems around Helsinki and between the main towns, but in rural areas some roads may be only dirt tracks.

Finland

Sunset over Lake Kallavesi, in the lakeland region at the heart of Finland

Finland's state railroad, Valtion Rautatiet, serves the whole country (except the extreme north), with the most frequent service in the south. Bus service is also good, and the east-west network in central and southern Finland is especially efficient.

The Finnish climate is far more amiable than you might expect from such a northern country. In spite of being in the same latitude as Alaska and Siberia, Finland and the whole Scandinavian peninsula enjoy a much milder climate owing to the influence of the Gulf Stream. There can be very warm dry spells in summer.

The Finnish people have a well-developed sense of irony, which may emerge in the form of jovial self-disparagement, especially among the young. The Finns know when to keep quiet and may appear to be unwilling to talk very much. But throughout the country you will be welcomed, and helped, with courtesy and kindness.

FINLAND

NORWAY · Karigasniemi
Kilpisjävi · Inari · Inarijärvi · Ivalo
E75
Lokan tekojärvi
Muonio · Sodankylä
E8 · Lapland
Arctic Circle · Kemijärvi
SWEDEN · Rovaniemi · E63
Kemi · Kuusamo
E75 · 20
Oulu/Uleåbog
Raahe
Oulujärvi · Kajaani
Gulf of Bothnia
Kokkola/Karleby
Jacobstad/Pietarsaari · Iisalmi
E63
Vaasa/Vasa · Kuopio
E75 · Varkaus · Joensuu
Helvetinjärven Kansallispuisto · Jyväskylä · Savonlinna
Pori/Björneborg · Tampere · Mikkeli
Rauma · Saimaa · Imatra
Hämeenlinna · Lahti · Loviisa/Lovisa · Lappeenranta
Järvenpää · Kotka
Turku/Åbo · Espoo/Esbo · E12 · Porvoo/Borgå
Åland/Ahvenanmaa · Hangö/Hanko · **HELSINKI (Helsingfors)**
A · 0 · 100 · 200 · 300 km
0 · 100 · B · 200 miles

MORE TOP DESTINATIONS IN FINLAND

- Åland A1 • Helvetinjärven Kansallispuisto A2 • Lapland B3
- Loviisa B1 • Porvoo B1 • Rauma A1
- Rovaniemi B3 • Saimaa B1
- Savonlinna B2 • Tampere A1
- Turku A1 • Vaasa A2

TIMELINE

4000 BC	Sami peoples move into northern Finland from the east.
1600 BC	Development of Iron Age culture and emergence of the Finno-Ugric language.
1100	Finland is occupied by four tribal elements: the Sami in the north, Karelians in the east, Tavastians in the central lakes and Finns in the southwest.
1249	Swedish Birger *Jarl* conducts a "Christian Crusade," thinly disguised as Swedish colonization of southwest Finland.
1290s	Invasions by Russia lead to Swedish–Russian conflicts.
1555	Finland is made a Swedish duchy; beginning of 250 years of Swedish influence.
1807	Czar Alexander I of Russia occupies Finland.
1917	Finland becomes an independent republic.
1939–44	Finland declares neutrality but Russia invades; Finland declares itself a "co-belligerent" with Germany in resisting Russian attacks; Britain declares war against Finland.
1992	The 1948 Treaty of Friendship, Cooperation and Mutual Assistance between Finland and Russia is dissolved.
1995	Finland becomes a member of the European Union.
2000	Helsinki is designated as a European City of Culture; Tarja Halonen becomes the first female president of Finland.

A BRIDGE BETWEEN EAST AND WEST

Finland's 20th-century relationship with Russia has often been misunderstood. The term "Finlandization" was used disparagingly by some to describe the country's carefully orchestrated policy toward its giant neighbor, but Finland's sensitive geographic position dictated this policy. For centuries, Russia competed with Sweden for domination over Finland. After 1807, Russian influence prevailed. Finland's declaration of independence in 1917 led to an uneasy relationship between the two countries, and resulted in bitter conflict during World War II. After the war, Finland was forced to tread a careful path between the Cold War policies of East and West. The Finnish politician who did the most to maintain national identity under these circumstances was Urho K. Kekkonen, who was the country's president from 1956 to 1981. Kekkonen's pragmatism and his careful balancing act between East and West earned him much criticism from Western politicians. But Finland remained essentially a Scandinavian country while maintaining "friendly coexistence" with Russia. Finland's rapid emergence, post-Cold War, as a democratic, pluralist and modern society is a testament to the wisdom of Kekkonen's strategy. It is said that he frequently conducted discussions with visiting Russian politicians in the relaxation of a traditional sauna, where everyone feels happily equal.

SURVIVAL GUIDE

- For Finnish and international fashion in Helsinki, try Marimekko, with locations at Pohjoisesplanadi 2 and 31, the Forum Shopping Mall and Eteläesplanadi 14. For exclusive silkwear look for Marja Kurki's scarfs in Stockmann department store. For traditional jewelry and Finnish national clothing, you cannot beat Kalevala Koru, Unioninkatu 25.

- Driving with dimmed headlights in the daytime is compulsory in Finland. When driving in rural Finland, look out for elk and reindeer on roads.

- You will find that consumer goods are generally more expensive in Finland than in the rest of Europe, although prices are coming down. Accommodations and eating out are also more expensive.

- Many hotels have saunas, but most are electrically heated. The traditional Finnish "smoke" sauna is heated by a wood-burning stove and is said to be the real experience. For information on traditional saunas, contact the Finnish Sauna Society, Vaskiniementie 10, FIN-00200 Helsinki ☎ 09 686 0560, fax 09 679 180.

Sampling some local dishes in a Helsinki café

- In Helsinki you will find numerous "grill kiosks," little huts selling fast food in the form of hamburgers, french fries, meat-filled pies and grilled sausages (*grillimakkara*). The kiosks are good for daytime snacks, but late at night they often attract loud, drunken revelers.

- On the weekend between June 20 and 26 there are midsummer celebrations throughout the country. After the long, dark nights of winter, Finns celebrate Midsummer's Day with gusto.

- For lunchtime snacks there are the ubiquitous baguettes, often with tasty fillings. Also try such Finnish favorites as salted salmon or herring slices with new potatoes, or typical minced meat dishes such as *metsästäjänpihvi* (minced meat in mushroom sauce).

- There is a state monopoly on the sale of alcohol, apart from medium-strength beers, which can be bought in some grocery stores. Wine and spirits can be bought only in state-controlled outlets known as ALKO (stores not open on Sunday). Restaurants usually serve alcohol.

- Public restrooms in Finland are generally clean and modern. Signs are *Naiset* for ladies and *Michet* for men.

HELSINKI

Helsinki (sometimes referred to in Swedish as Helsingfors) will take your breath away. It does so quite literally in the frozen winter, but even then it can have days of glorious weather – blue skies and pure white panoramas. In summer, the city will delight you even more with its stunning architecture and its blue Baltic waters.

City of the Sea

As with Oslo, the best way to approach Helsinki is by sea. The Lutheran Cathedral (Tuomiokirkko) and the Uspenski Cathedral (Uspenskin Katedraali) stand out against the skyline behind the handsome row of waterfront buildings that include the 19th-century City Hall and Presidential Palace. In front of them is Market Square, crammed with vendors selling everything from fish to handicrafts.

You miss this introduction to the city if you arrive by plane, bus or train, but the 19th-century railroad station is a striking example of Helsinki's remarkable architecture. Bus and railroad stations are close to the heart of things and only a few streets from Senate Square and the bustle of Mannerheimintie, the city's main street.

Finlandssvenska

The form of Swedish spoken in Finland is *Finlandssvenska*, "Finland's Swedish." Today about six percent of Finnish residents speak Swedish exclusively. Most of Finland's signs and street names are in Finnish and Swedish. Unless you are fluent in either language, you are best sticking to English, Finland's "second language."

Helsinki is an accessible city that is easy to explore independently. Trams and buses serve all parts of the city, but the subway system, *Metro*, is a single service line of little help to visitors.

The heart of summertime Helsinki is the tree-lined Esplanade (Eteläesplanadi) that runs west from Market Square (Kauppatori) and

Helsinki

South Harbor (Eteläsatama) to Mannerheimintie. There is a bandstand next to the renowned Kappeli restaurant (see page 550), where you can sample tasty Finnish specialties such as salmon soup (*lohikeitto*). The streets bordering the Esplanade have many stylish boutiques, such as Marimekko and Annikki Karvinen, as well as colorful cafés and restaurants. Stop for coffee and pastries at Café Kafka, in the Swedish Theater at the west end of the Esplanade.

Quiet Corners

For green spaces and seashore walks go south from the Esplanade, past the University Observatory and past the

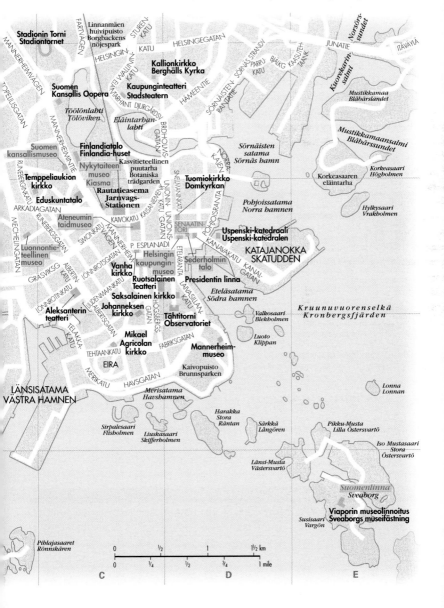

Helsinki

austere Russian Embassy, to reach Kaivopuisto Park. Beyond lies the seashore road of Ehrenströmintie, where moored yachts enhance the views of numerous islands. Or go north from the square in front of the railroad station to Kaisaniemi Park and the University Botanical Gardens, and on to the tree-fringed sea inlets beyond. Walk up Mannerheimintie to see the monumental Parliament House and Finlandia Hall; then go west to Temppeliaukio Church, a copper-domed church carved out of rock.

Despite Helsinki's reputation for long, dark winters, there is much to reward the visitor throughout the year. Enjoy the restaurants, listen to the music of Jean Sibelius in Finlandia Hall or attend world-class performances at the Finnish National Opera.

You will find fewer English speakers here than in other Scandinavian countries, but Helsinkians are proud of their heritage and are eager to help visitors enjoy this cultured and self-confident Baltic city.

"Smoke" Sauna

Sauna is a way of life for Finns – apart from being healthy and relaxing, it's a social, cultural – and, some say – almost religious practice. A sauna is an insulated room that is traditionally heated by a wood-burning stove. In a "smoke" sauna, steam is generated by throwing water on the hot stones of the stove, and the correct mix of steam and heat, known as *löyly*, fills the room in which you sit naked. Plunging into icy lakes or rolling in the snow between bouts of *löyly* is also an option.

ESSENTIAL INFORMATION

TOURIST INFORMATION
• Helsinki City Tourist & Convention Bureau, Pohjoisesplanadi 19 ☎ 09 169 3757; fax 09 169 3839; www.hel.fi/tourism
• Helsinki Expert (Hotel Booking Center), Helsinki railroad station ☎ 09 2288 1400; fax 09 2288 1499; www.helsinkiexpert.fi

URBAN TRANSPORTATION
Helsinki's railroad station is located on Kaivokatu. It is the terminus for main train services throughout the country and to Russia. For information ☎ 0600 41 902. Helsinki's bus, tram and subway network is operated by Helsingin Kaupungin Liikennelaitos (HKL). The city bus terminal is undergoing major reconstruction until 2006, during which time buses will arrive and depart from surrounding streets. Main tram stops are on Kaivokatu. For city bus, tram, metro and local train information call ☎ 0100 111 (from within Helsinki only; Mon.–Fri. 7–7, Sat.–Sun. 9–5). Long distance buses continue to

depart from the bus terminal but arrival points have been moved to Mannerheimintie and Arkadiankatu. For information call ☎ 0200 4000. Helsinki has a small subway system serving mainly suburban areas. Stations have a sign marked "M." Taxis have a yellow dome light and are free when it is lit. There is a taxi stand at the railroad station. Call the Helsinki Taxi Center at ☎ 0100 0700.

AIRPORT INFORMATION
Helsinki-Vantaa Airport is 12 miles north of the city. The airport is a modern, well-appointed complex with every facility. Finnair buses run to and from the airport to the Finnair City Terminal, Asema-ankio 3, near Helsinki railroad station. The service is every 20 minutes, daily 5:45 a.m.–1:10 a.m., and the journey takes about 30 minutes.
Slower, but less expensive, regular bus services (Nos. 615 and 415) also run between the airport and the city center. For information on flight arrivals and departures call ☎ 0200 14636.

CLIMATE – average highs and lows for the month

JAN.	FEB.	MAR.	APR.	MAY	JUN.	JUL.	AUG.	SEP.	OCT.	NOV.	DEC.
-3°C	-3°C	1°C	7°C	14°C	18°C	21°C	19°C	13°C	7°C	2°C	-1°C
27°F	27°F	34°F	45°F	57°F	64°F	70°F	66°F	55°F	45°F	36°F	30°F
-9°C	-9°C	-5°C	0°C	5°C	9°C	12°C	10°C	6°C	2°C	-2°C	-7°C
16°F	16°F	23°F	32°F	41°F	48°F	54°F	50°F	43°F	36°F	28°F	19°F

Helsinki

CITY SIGHTS

Key to symbols

⊞ map coordinates refer to the Helsinki map on pages 158–159; sights below are highlighted in yellow on the map.

⊠ address or location ☎ telephone number

◷ opening times ▣ nearest bus or tram route

⛴ ferry 🍴 restaurant or café on site or nearby

💷 admission charge: $$$ more than €4, $$ €1.5–€4,

$ less than €1.5 ⛉ other relevant information

ATENEUMIN TAIDMUSEO

⊞ C3 ⊠ Kaivokatu 2 ☎ 09 1733 6401 ◷ Tue.–Fri. 9–6 (also Wed.–Thu. 6–8 p.m.), Sat.–Sun. 11–5 🍴 Museum café ▣ All buses to Rautatientori Square bus terminus; tram 2, 3, 4, 6 💷 $$$ (free Wed. 5–8 p.m.)

The Ateneumin taidmuseo (Ateneum Art Museum) is housed in a handsome 19th-century building. Vincent van Gogh, Amedeo Modigliani and Paul Cézanne are represented, among many other international figures from the 19th century to the 1960s; but it is the significant collection of Finnish art, from the 18th century to the mid-1960s, that enhances the museum. There are some powerful works by realist painters Fanny Churberg and Albert Edelfelt, such as Edelfelt's gossiping group, *Women of Ruokalahti on the Church Hill*. Finland's master Akseli Gallen-Kallela dominates with works such as the seductive *Aino-Taru*, *The Aino Myth* and the earthy and very Finnish *A New House*. Gallen-Kallela pupil Hugo Simberg's mildly disturbing and surrealistic *The Wounded Angel* is another highlight. Wäinö Aaltonen's bronze of the Finnish runner Paavo Nurmi overpowers Room 24.

HELSINGIN KAUPUNGINMUSEO

⊞ D3 ⊠ Sofiankatu 4 ☎ 09 169 3933 ◷ Helsinki City Museum: Mon.–Fri. 9–5, Sat.–Sun. 11–5; "Street Museum": daily 24 hours 🍴 Nuevo, see page 550 ▣ Tram 1, 2, 3B, 3T, 4, 💷 Helsinki City Museum $$ (free Thu.); "Street Museum" free

The Helsingin kaupunginmuseo (Helsinki City Museum) is located in the "Street Museum" of Sofiankatu. The City Museum has branches throughout the city, including the nearby Sederholm House (see below). The main museum has an exhibition on Helsinki's history. The open-air "Street Museum" portrays changing styles of street architecture and accessories. Start at the harbor end and walk on cobbled surfaces past old street lamps and artifacts. You start in the late 18th century and finish in the 1930s.

LUONNONTIETEELLINEN MUSEO

⊞ B3 ⊠ Pohjoinen Rautatiekatu 13 ☎ 09 1912 8800 ◷ Tue.–Fri. 9–5, Sat.–Sun. 11–4 🍴 Museum café ▣ 16, 13, 21v; tram 3B, 3T 💷 $$$

The venerable Luonnontieteellinen museo (Natural History Museum) is guarded by a very handsome bronze elk, just one of the animals in the museum's vast and old-fashioned collection of mammals, birds, insects and minerals. The museum's mammal hall is one of the best in Europe, a series of tableaux showing exotic beasts and Finnish wildlife in their native habitats.

NYKYTAITEEN MUSEO KIASMA

⊞ C3 ⊠ Mannerheiminaukio 2 ☎ 09 1733 6501 ◷ Wed.–Sun. 10–8:30, Tue. 9–5 🍴 Museum café ▣ 16, 13, 21v; tram 4, 10 💷 $$$ (free Fri. 5–8:30 p.m.)

The Nykytaiteen museo Kiasma (Museum of Contemporary Art Kiasma) is one of the newest buildings in Helsinki. Its bold postmodern design, by American architect Steven Holl, has aroused some controversy. The exhibitions of conceptual art and often radical installations are at the forefront of European contemporary art and emphasize the sophistication of Finnish culture.

SEDERHOLMIN TALO

⊞ D3 ⊠ Aleksanterinkatu 16–18 ☎ 09 169 3625 ◷ Sun.–Thu. 11–4, Jan. 1 to mid-Jun. and mid-Aug. to Dec. 31 ▣ Tram 1, 2, 3B, 3T, 4, 💷 $$ (free Thu.)

The Sederholmin talo (Sederholm House) is a rare survivor of old Helsinki and is said to be the city's oldest stone house (built in 1757). What distinguishes this

The Lutheran Cathedral in Senate Square

rather unassuming building is the story it tells of its one-time owner, Johan Sederholm, an 18th-century Finnish businessman who rose from poverty to great wealth and distinction.

SENAATINTORI

⊞ D3 ✉ Senaatintori ☎ Lutheran Cathedral: 09 709 2455 ⏰ Lutheran Cathedral: Mon.–Sat. 9–6, Sun. noon–6 (also 6 p.m.–midnight, Jul.–Aug.) 🚃 Tram 1, 2, 3B, 3T, 7 � Summer festivals and events

Senaatintori (Senate Square) is the focus of the Russian Imperial style. This form of architecture was encouraged by Tsar Alexander I in his bid to make Helsinki a stylistically eastern capital after it was annexed by Russia from Sweden in 1809. The square and its major buildings were designed by C. L. Engel.

Helsinki's Lutheran Cathedral dominates Senate Square and the city skyline. The cathedral, also by Engel and completed in 1852, is essentially classical but has Byzantine elements. Its domes are copper-sheathed and gilded, the only accents in an otherwise blinding whiteness. The buildings that flank the square and cathedral include the Senate House, University Building and University Library.

SEURASAAREN ULKOMUSEO

⊞ A4 ✉ Seurasaari ☎ 09 4050 9660 (09 4050 9574 in winter) ⏰ Buildings: daily 11–5 (also Wed. 5–7), Jun.–Aug.; Mon.–Fri. 9–3, Sat.– Sun. 11–5, mid-May to May 31 and mid-Sep. to Sep. 30; Sat.–Sun. 11–5,

mid-Sep. Park: daily, all year 🍴 Museum café 📷 24; tram 4, then a 10-minute walk 💰 $$ (park free) ❶ Guided tours in English daily at 11:30 and 3:30, Jun.–Aug.

The Seurasaaren ulkomuseo (Seurasaari Open-Air Museum) is a collection of Finnish regional buildings dating from the 17th century. Located on Seurasaari Island, it is easily reached from central Helsinki. Most of the 85 buildings on the site date from the 18th and 19th centuries and include a manor house, traditional farmhouses and a church.

SUOMEN KANSALLISMUSEO

⊞ C4 ✉ Mannerheimintie 34 ☎ 09 40 501 (ticket office: 0 40 50 9400) ⏰ Tue.– Wed. 11–8, Thu.–Sun. 11–6 🍴 Museum restaurant 🚃 Tram 4, 7A, 7B, 10 💰 $$$ (free Tue. 5:30–8 p.m.)

The Suomen kansallismuseo (National Museum of Finland) dates from the early 20th century and is an excellent example of the art nouveau, or *Jugend* style of architecture. There are exhibits on Finnish history and many artifacts, including a Stone Age sculpture of an elk's head from around 3000 BC. The throne of Alexander I is on display, from which he proclaimed Finnish "incorporation" with Russia in 1809.

SUOMENLINNA

⊞ E1 ✉ Suomenlinna ☎ Visitor Center: 09 684 1880 ⏰ Visitor Center: daily 11–6, May–Aug.; 11–4, in Sep.; Tue.–Sun. 11–4, rest of year 🍴 Restaurants and cafés 📷 Ferries leave regularly from Kauppatorilta 💰 Site free; Visitor Center $$$; other museums $$ ❶ Guided tours daily at 10:30, 1 and 3, Jun.–Aug.

The historic fortress of Suomenlinna, a UNESCO World Heritage Site, is built on six interconnecting islands and was once dubbed the "Gibraltar of the North." First used by Sweden in 1748 under the name Sveaborg ("Sweden's Fortress"), the island was surrendered to Russia in 1808. It remained in Russian control until 1918, when newly independent Finland renamed it Suomenlinna ("Finland's Fortress"). The museums on Suomenlinna include the Suomenlinna Museum, the Military Museum, the Customs Museum, and a Doll and Toy Museum.

IMPERIAL CITY: THE BUILDINGS OF HELSINKI

Engel's Lutheran Cathedral (top), and the House of Estates – seat of government until 1906

Helsinki has some of the finest buildings in northern Europe, with the architectural heart of the city being Senate Square. Here, in the early 19th century, Berlin-born Carl Ludvig Engel was commissioned to create a new Helsinki in neoclassic Russian Imperial style. On its high podium, the gleaming white Lutheran Cathedral is the focus of the square. Leave the square at its northeastern corner and stroll up Snellmaninkatu a short distance to where the Bank of Finland (Suomen Pankki) faces the House of Estates (Säätytalo), built in the classical style with gilded Corinthian capitals.

Another great architectural theme in Helsinki is art nouveau, or *Jugend* as it is known in Finland. This style drew its motifs from Finnish culture and tradition; its materials are the timber and rough-faced granite of the country used in naturalistic ways. *Jugend* architecture is best seen in residential areas such as Eira, on the southern peninsula of the city, and on the little island to the east of the harbor, Katajanokka. The island is guarded by the magnificent Uspenski Cathedral, the most impressive expression of Orthodoxy you are likely to find in northern Europe.

Jugend architecture is characterized by turrets, castellated features and carved motifs. Yet the buildings remain elegant and restrained. Take a walk down Eira's streets of Huvilakatu and Laivurinkatu. On Laivurinkatu, look for No. 25, the Villa Johanna. Walk down Luotsikatu and Kauppiaankatu, a short distance east of the cathedral, where there are numerous examples of *Jugend* to compare with Senate Square's classicism and with the city's more modern buildings. Finlandia Hall and the Museum of Contemporary Art Kiasma maintain Helsinki's international reputation for architectural excellence.

FRANCE

"WE have come five hundred miles by rail through the heart of France. What a bewitching land it is!"

From *The Innocents Abroad* (1869),
by Mark Twain

Opposite: A Gothic abbey crowns the summit of Le Mont-St.-Michel, on the Normandy coast

FRANCE

France is the largest country in western Europe, geographically one of the most diverse, and certainly among the most beautiful. Its cities contain some of the greatest treasures in Europe; its countryside is prosperous and well tended. The French combine practicality with romance; they lead a stylish life, eat delicious food and bask in a pleasant climate.

Historically, France has developed the notion of equality for all and, while retaining its sense of tradition, remains a forward-looking country. Over the past half-century, for instance, the French have forged ahead in modern technology. France is a country of contrasts, making it a delight to explore.

France Today

France was among the first European countries to permanently dispense with its monarchy. Apart from a couple of brief periods, it has been a republic almost as long as the United States. The French Revolution gave a

MORE TOP DESTINATIONS IN FRANCE
• Aigues-Mortes D1 • Avignon D2 • Bayonne B1 • Beaune D3 • Bordeaux B2 • Carcassonne C1 • Carnac A4 • Cirque de Gavarnie B1 • Cirque de Navacelles D2 • Colleville-sur-Mer B5 • Grasse E2 • Grotte de Lascaux C2 • Honfleur B4 • Megève E3 • Le Mont-St.-Michel B4 • Pont du Gard D2 • Rocamadour C2

France

tremendous sense of patriotism to all French men and women, which continues to the present day.

Despite the apparently never-ending political ups and downs, French people have a strong sense of national pride

The Renaissance château at Azay-le-Rideau – one of the grand sights of the Loire Valley

and unity; they are essentially one people and one country. Every town and village in France flies the flag (*tricolore*) with pride, and displays a bust of Marianne in its town hall, the beautiful woman who epitomizes the spirit of France.

The French despair of their politicians, grumble at their government and taxation, and are quite capable of unruly demonstrations against the most surprising things, but *au fond*, at heart, they remain proud and devoted admirers of their country.

La Belle France

La belle France – beautiful France – is indeed truly beautiful. Hexagonal in shape, each of its six sides acts as a natural boundary. The English Channel and the rolling Atlantic guard the west coasts, the Pyrenees and Alps the southwest and southeast borders, the Mediterranean laps along the southern coast and the mighty Rhine river forms a barrier against Germany in the northeast. Within this area lies a huge variety of landscape, with plains, arable

flatlands, forested hills, vine- and olive-growing terraces, lush river valleys, inhospitable mountain massifs and a combined coastline stretching for almost 2,000 miles.

As you travel around France you'll notice how sparsely populated the land is compared to most other European countries. Miles go past without a sign of a town or village, yet the land is mostly cultivated, forested or tended in some way. France has always been an agricultural country, and today is the largest agricultural producer and exporter in the European Union.

Cities, Towns and Villages

In a country as geographically varied as France there is bound to be a diverse range of architecture, as styles evolved to suit the environment. In southern rural areas, the population lived in easily defensible communities and worked the fields daily, leaving a legacy of picturesque hilltop villages, with narrow streets for shelter against the fierce sun. In the mountains the design was dictated by the climate, and cozy wooden chalets evolved, with steep or flat roofs depending on the region.

The whole country in general enjoyed great prosperity during the 17th and 18th centuries, and in most of the major cities there are architectural reminders of this time, in the shape of churches, fine civic buildings, spacious squares and well-planned streets. Before the French Revolution, the aristocracy spent several months a year on their estates and built fine fortified houses and beautiful châteaux in which they lived.

This wonderful mixture of style still exists, and the French have been far more successful than some other European nations at preserving the historic centers of their towns. The second half of the 20th century saw some truly imaginative and innovative civic building projects in major cities, which you'll certainly notice.

The French Character

Other Europeans have a peculiar relationship with the French people, in which there may be more than a touch of envy. The French have much to boast about, and are rightly proud of their culture. As a result, they have gained a reputation with their neighbors for being arrogant. They are often accused of seeing themselves as decidedly superior to every other nation. For years the French have been criticized and stereotyped for their attitude. But the minute a foreigner steps on French soil he or she is once more seduced: by the country, the overwhelming charm of the people, the way of life.

Lifestyle

The French strike a happy balance between the work-driven culture of northern Europeans and the wonderfully alluring, but overly relaxed, southern European approach to life.

This is a prosperous country with a high standard of living, where both men and women hold down prestigious and influential jobs in every sector. It is also a highly efficient country with an excellent infrastructure, making things very easy for visitors. Public transportation is first-rate, with Europe's best and fastest train system. If you're driving, you'll find the roads fast and in good condition, although you should be aware of the sometimes erratic national driving style. Hotels are comfortable, restaurants provide good value, and tourism is a well-organized, thriving industry.

All this is augmented by the innate French sense of style, which is obvious the minute you arrive. This is evident in everything from the way produce is artfully stacked in market stalls to the sensible layout of an airport. You'll find a relaxed approach to most problems, but note that the wheels of daily life are oiled with a high level of politeness. Even if you don't speak the language, bear in mind that courtesy is extremely important in everyday dealings.

Yachts moored in Nice, on the French Riviera

The national game of *boules* is taken very seriously by its devotees, and is also fun to watch

People work hard in France, but indulge in relaxation as well. In the evenings they enjoy themselves over a lengthy meal or sit for hours in cafés. French citizens have always backed their country's achievements in culture and the arts, so there's a lively arts scene everywhere. You'll also find that almost everyone has strong views on a wide range of artistic, political and economic events, which they're eager to share.

Religion

France is nominally a Catholic country, with the church separated from the state since 1905. More than 80 percent of its 60 million inhabitants have been baptized into the Catholic church, although only a small percentage regularly attend church. There are approximately one million Protestants, who for historical reasons tend to be more active churchgoers. Immigrants from France's former colonies make up a large proportion of the considerable number of Muslims, while the Jewish population in France never recovered its numbers after World War II. Every town and village has one or more churches with Sunday and daily services.

Pastimes

The French take relaxation seriously. They enjoy sports, both as spectators and participants, with soccer the national favorite. The nation was elated when France won the 1998 World Cup and the European Football Championship in 2000. Tennis and golf are other popular sports, both with good facilities for tourists, and you'll find challenging golf courses all over France. Resort areas offer a huge range of pastimes, from tennis to sailing to organized hiking.

With the Alps on their doorstep, many people ski, especially during early February when children are out of school and families head for the slopes.

You may often see *boules* being played. This is a game where players attempt to surround a small target ball on the ground by throwing larger, heavier balls from a specified distance.

The mountains around Chamonix are among the best spots for Alpine skiing

Pleasures

Food and drink are among the national pleasures of France, and much time is spent shopping for and preparing food. Although modern life has taken its toll, fast food, frozen meals and "grazing" items are not considered mealtime options. If the French can't be bothered to cook, they can pick up exquisite, freshly prepared dishes from a *traiteur*, a type of delicatessen. Desserts are rarely homemade, bought instead from a *pâtisserie* (cake shop), ensuring that every mouthful is of the highest quality. Every region has its own food specialties, and these are taken so seriously that some foodstuffs have an *appellation controlée* label, similar to the labeling used for wine, meaning that the product must be from the area for which it is known.

French wines need no introduction, and visitors can enjoy winery visits and tastings in all the wine-producing areas. Champagne is kept for special occasions, while everyday drinks include many varieties of beer and the *pastis* family – an aniseed-flavored spirit diluted with water so it turns milky.

Material pleasures are important in France, where shopping is an art form. This is the country that produces cognac, internationally famous scents, and some of the world's most desirable clothes and accessories. You'll find that prices won't differ hugely from those back home, but the satisfaction is great from buying luxuries in their native land.

Expect a wealth of experience and pleasure in France: natural beauty, historic cities and good value despite the relatively high cost of living.

Exquisite chocolate confection

France

TIMELINE

15,000 BC	Lascaux cave paintings; first works by tribal group in area now covered by modern France.
3000 BC	Carnac stones erected.
58 BC	Julius Caesar invades Gaul.
AD 500	Frankish King Clovis unites tribes to form France.
800	Charlemagne crowned first Holy Roman Emperor.
1431	Joan of Arc burned at the stake; resulting patriotism gives France national identity.
1763	France loses North American possessions to England at end of Seven Years War.
1789	Start of French Revolution; monarchy overthrown and republic established.
1804	Napoleon proclaimed emperor; Napoleon defeated at Waterloo in 1815.
1874	First exhibition of Impressionist art.
1889	Eiffel Tower built for Paris Exhibition; beginning of *Belle Époque* era.
1914–18	France allies with Britain, Russia and United States against Germany and Austro-Hungary to fight World War I.
1939–45	France swiftly defeated by Germans in World War II; Charles de Gaulle leads Free French Army from England.
1958	France becomes a founder member of European Community.
1985	French agents blow up Greenpeace ship, the *Rainbow Warrior*, in Auckland, New Zealand.
1998	France wins soccer World Cup; country erupts in euphoria.
1999	France is among the first countries to adopt euro currency.
2003	The French government votes against military intervention in Iraq and takes no part in the coalition action.

IMPRESSIONISM

By the 1870s a group of Parisian artists had become increasingly bored with the traditional, studio-based, graphic style of most paintings. They were obsessed with light and its effect on landscape and objects at different times of day; painting outside, they worked on several canvases at a time as the light changed throughout the day. Among these artists were Monet, Manet, Pissarro, Renoir, Dégas and Sisley. In 1874 they held their first public exhibition, where their work was ridiculed. One critic was particularly scathing about Monet's painting *Impression of a Sunrise*, and so the name of the movement was born. Literary figures such as Zola and Flaubert supported Impressionism, feeling they could do with words what artists were doing with paint, and gradually public opinion was won over.

Sunday morning entertainment at the bandstand in the Luxembourg Gardens, Paris

SURVIVAL GUIDE

- You will find that many French people speak English, although they are not very willing to do so. It's polite to master the phrase "*parlez-vous anglais?*" to use before asking a question; you will notice a much better response.

- Politeness is highly regarded in France, so preface requests with "*bonjour*" (hello) and always say "*merci*" (thank you).

- French people can be among the world's best dressed, with a casual style that's difficult to emulate. Make an effort in France to be well groomed, as a smart appearance will ensure better service everywhere.

- The French government has introduced new laws governing smoking in public places, but they are frequently ignored. Smoking is often tolerated throughout restaurants and other public areas.

- It's a good idea to count your change in shops and markets, and make sure taxi meters are set at zero when starting a journey.

- It's probable you'll find a bidet in your bathroom, an appliance that looks like a toilet with faucets. This is designed for washing intimate body areas – although it's handy for washing socks, as well!

- Restrooms in museums, restaurants and many public places are generally modern, but in rural areas the toilet may consist of two floor-level porcelain plaques, on which the user squats. This often flushes automatically at high pressure, so watch out for your shoes.

- The French are notoriously inconsiderate drivers, giving little leeway to other road users. If you are driving long distances, use the highway system. You have to pay a toll (*péage*), but it's safer and less crowded.

- Sodas and soft drinks are very expensive in France; a beer (*bière*) often costs less then a Coke.

- Ice water and ice in drinks is not served routinely in France. Ask for *des glaçons* if you want ice. Legally, restaurants are obliged to serve tap water if you ask for it.

- French coffee is strong, so if you want a weaker cup ask for a *café américain*. Unless you ask for milk (*lait*) or cream (*crème*), it will always be served black (*noir*).

PARIS

It's hard to be indifferent to historic, hectic, elegant Paris. With all its moods, this is a city that can exhilarate you, exasperate you and leave you speechless with wonder, but it won't leave you cold. Paris is beautiful no matter when you visit: the quality of light ranges from crystalline brilliance to mellow gold; distant sounds mingle with bustling main streets; and with each season a new scent blows in to announce its arrival.

Getting Your Bearings

It would take months to explore all of Paris, so resign yourself to the idea that you're not going to be able to see everything on just one trip to this great city. Some people prefer to familiarize themselves with the city by wandering the different neighborhoods; others will try to see as many attractions as possible. Consider which style best suits you and then plan ahead.

You'll probably be surprised by the compressed scale; the 2 million inhabitants of inner Paris all live within an area bounded by the 21-mile Boulevard Périphérique that encircles the city. Even so, be prepared to walk considerable distances, even within the museums, some of which are on a grand scale. Your first stop should be the main tourist office on the Champs-Élysées; here you can get excellent maps, leaflets and information on excursions and events, and buy a Carte Musée-Monuments (Museum and Monument Pass). It's valid for one, three or five days, and entitles you to unlimited entry at 60 museums and monuments in Paris and the Île-de-France. If you visit as few as three museums or monuments on a one-day pass you will save money.

Tours and Excursions

Taking a city tour is an excellent way to get your bearings. Most tours cover the main sights on either side of the Seine river and take about two hours. An alternative is to take a bus run by Paris L'Open Tour, a choice of three routes that cover the city center, Bastille-Bercy and Montmartre with stops along the way, allowing you to get on and off to do your own sightseeing. Tickets are valid for one or two days, and there's English commentary. You may want to take a tour outside Paris; obvious choices are the fabulous Palace of Versailles, or the old royal hunting lodge of Fontainebleau and its surrounding forest. If you'll be spending your entire stay in Paris, consider taking a day trip to the châteaux of the Loire Valley, Chartres and its cathedral, or the magical island of Le Mont-St.-Michel in Normandy.

Parisian Neighborhoods

Most Parisians mentally split their city into two neat halves – Left Bank (Rive

Intriguing stores entice browsers in the atmospheric Latin Quarter – on the Left Bank

Gauche) and Right Bank (Rive Droite) – with the sinuous curve of the Seine dividing them. Traditionally, the Right Bank has stood for order and elegance, typified by the monumental architecture running from the Louvre up to the Arc de Triomphe; while the Left Bank is an altogether more raffish place. This is too simplistic, however. Paris, in fact, is a series of extremely individual *quartiers*, districts, each with its own personality, style and charm.

Riverbanks and Bridges

More than 30 bridges criss-cross the Seine, and the banks, known as *quais*, offer lovely views of the city. The best stretch of riverside for walking lies between the Pont de la Concorde (Concorde Bridge), leading to the place de la Concorde, and the Pont de Sully (Sully Bridge), at the eastern end of the Île St.-Louis. Browse in the *bouquinistes* (secondhand bookseller) stalls that line the riverbank, or simply revel in the subtly blended colors of sky, river, trees and stone. Several companies operate cruises on the Seine, an ideal way to enjoy the river.

Parisians

As inhabitants of a capital city, Parisians are surprisingly able to combine the inevitable pace of big-city life with the ability to switch off and spend hours strolling, window-shopping or endlessly chatting in a café. This is the quintessential image of the chic Parisian. To get a good taste of another side of life in the city, however, you should visit a neighborhood market: food shopping is a serious

Paris

business. One characteristic you will notice is how much people seem to read: there are countless bookstores, and métro (subway) commuters seem to always have their noses in a book. Your overall impression may be that the pace of life here is hurried, and the people can seem brusque, but they can also be charming, particularly to those enthusiastic about their city.

Shopping

The selection in the stores makes shopping irresistible for some. Haute couture stores cluster mainly around the Faubourg St.-Honoré and avenue Montaigne, with boutiques selling ready-to-wear (*prêt-à-porter*) designer outfits. Paris has a number of department stores; the best known are Galeries Lafayette and Printemps, both located on the monumental boulevard Haussmann, and La Samaritaine on rue de Rivoli near the Pont Neuf. Make a point to visit some of the covered shopping arcades, built in the 18th and early 19th centuries; Galerie Colbert and Galerie Vivienne are among the most attractive. Food stores are a must. Head for the world-famous Fauchon, 26 place de la Madeleine; Androuët, the ultimate cheese shop; and Lionel Poilâne, 8 rue du Cherche-Midi, Paris' most famous baker.

ESSENTIAL INFORMATION

TOURIST INFORMATION
Office de Tourisme et des Congrès de Paris (Paris Convention and Visitors Bureau)
• Gare de Lyon (Mon.–Sat.) • Gare du Nord (daily) • Tour Eiffel (May–Sep. only) • Montmartre (daily) • Opera-Grands Magasins 11 rue Scribe (Mon.–Sat.) • Carousel du Louvre (daily) • 25 rue des Pyramides (daily) For all tourist offices ☎ 08 92 68 30 30 (toll call); www.parisinfo.com

URBAN TRANSPORTATION
The easiest way to get around Paris is by the métro (subway), which runs daily 5:30 a.m.–12:30 a.m. The RER (Réseau Express Régional), a suburban express train, connects with the métro inside Paris. Tickets are available singly or in *carnets* (books) of 10; they are available at the stations and from tobacconists (*tabacs*) and must be validated before boarding. Keep your ticket, as there are heavy fines for travelers without tickets. The Paris Visite card, valid for 1, 2, 3 or 5 consecutive days, is interchangeable with the métro, bus, and SNCF (main line) trains within the Ile-de-France, enabling you to get to Versailles and Fontainebleau. Buses run daily 6:30 a.m.–8:30 p.m. (some routes until 1:30 a.m. or later); tickets are interchangeable with the subway. Bus stops have route maps and show the route number

of the buses stopping at each. For information on public transportation in English, phone ☎ 08 92 68 41 14 (toll call). A special tourist bus, the Balabus, operates on Sundays and holidays noon–8 from mid-April through September; stops are marked "Balabus (Bb)." Taxis can be hailed on the street or from stands around the city, and are identifiable by the light on the roof, illuminated when the taxi is free. From late Mar. to early Nov. you can take the Batobus (☎ 01 44 11 33 99) on the Seine to get around; this boat runs between the Eiffel Tower and the Jardin des Plantes daily 10–7 (also 7–9 p.m., Jul.–Sep.), with stops at the main tourist attractions.

AIRPORT INFORMATION
Paris has two international airports, Roissy-Charles-de-Gaulle (CDG, ☎ 01 48 62 22 80) and Orly (☎ 01 49 75 15 15). Most U.S. visitors arrive at CDG. It is 14 miles north of Paris; taxis are available at both terminals (terminal 2 serves Air France only). Roissybus buses (☎ 08 20 82 08 20) run at 12-minute intervals daily 5:45 a.m.–11:30 p.m. into central Paris, and RER trains every 8 minutes daily 4:55 a.m.–midnight (journey time 45 minutes). Orlybus buses serve Orly, 8 miles south of Paris, every 15 minutes daily 5:45 a.m.–11:30 p.m.; RER trains leave every 20 minutes daily 5:45 a.m.–11:15 p.m.

CLIMATE – average highs and lows for the month

JAN.	FEB.	MAR.	APR.	MAY	JUN.	JUL.	AUG.	SEP.	OCT.	NOV.	DEC.
6°C	7°C	10°C	13°C	18°C	21°C	24°C	24°C	20°C	14°C	9°C	8°C
43°F	45°F	50°F	55°F	64°F	70°F	75°F	75°F	68°F	57°F	48°F	46°F
2°C	2°C	4°C	5°C	9°C	12°C	14°C	14°C	12°C	8°C	4°C	2°C
36°F	36°F	39°F	41°F	49°F	54°F	57°F	57°F	54°F	46°F	39°F	36°F

The neoclassic Arc de Triomphe towers over the busy thoroughfare of the Champs-Élysées

CITY SIGHTS

Key to symbols

⊞ map coordinates refer to the Paris map on pages 174–175; sights below are highlighted in yellow on the map.

⊠ address or location   ☎ telephone number
◉ opening times   Ⓜ nearest subway (métro) or RER
▣ nearest bus route   🍴 restaurant or café on site or nearby   🎟 admission charge: $$$ more than €12, $$ €4–€12, $ less than €4   ℹ other relevant information

ARC DE TRIOMPHE

⊞ A3   ⊠ place Charles-de-Gaulle   ☎ 01 55 37 73 77
◉ Daily 10 a.m.–11 p.m., Apr.–Sep.; 10 a.m.– 10:30 p.m., rest of year. Last admission 30 minutes before closing   Ⓜ Métro/RER Charles de Gaulle-Étoile
🎟 $$ (free first Sun. of the month)

The Arc de Triomphe is a splendid starting point for a day's sightseeing; the view from the top allows you to appreciate the grandeur of Paris' city planning. Commissioned by Napoleon, the 164-foot-high Arc is now dedicated to the Unknown Soldier of World War I; the eternal flame burns beneath. Twelve avenues radiate from it, giving the surrounding square its original name of place de l'Étoile (the star); today it's called place Charles-de-Gaulle, in memory of the famous general. There are 284 steps to the top, and no elevator.

CATHÉDRALE NOTRE-DAME

⊞ D2   ⊠ 6 place du Parvis de Notre-Dame
☎ Cathedral: 01 42 34 56 10. Towers: 01 53 10 07 00
◉ Cathedral: Mon.–Fri. 8–6:45, Sat.–Sun. 8–7:45 (no visits during religious services). Towers: Mon.–Fri. 9–7:30, Sat.–Sun. 9 a.m.–11 p.m. Last admission 45 minutes before closing   Ⓜ Cité; RER Châtelet or St.-Michel Notre-Dame   🎟 Cathedral free; Tower $$; free first Sun. of the month, Oct.–Mar.

The great Gothic Cathédrale Notre-Dame (Cathedral of Our Lady), built between 1163 and 1345, stands on the Île de la Cité, the oldest part of Paris. The outside elevation is as impressive as the lofty interior; admire the twin towers, massive buttresses and the symmetry of the facade. Arrive early to climb one of the towers, and to view the paintings and the rose windows.

CENTRE NATIONAL D'ART ET DE CULTURE GEORGES POMPIDOU

⊞ D3   ⊠ place Georges Pompidou   ☎ 01 44 78 12 33   ◉ Wed.–Mon. 11–10 (museum and exhibitions close at 9 except the Level 6 exhibition, which closes at 11 p.m. Thu.). Ticket counter closes an hour before galleries close   🍴 Restaurant   Ⓜ Hôtel de Ville, Rambuteau; RER Châtelet-Les-Halles   🎟 Center free; musée $$ (free first Sun. of the month)

This controversial modern art center, opened

Paris

in the 1970s, quickly earned itself the nickname "the refinery," due to its similarity to an oil refinery. The architectural team of Richard Rogers and Renzo Piano designed it as the first post-modernist public building to show its structural elements on the outside. It's home to a movie theater, library and exhibition space, but its chief draw is the Musée National d'Art Moderne (National Modern Art Museum), which displays contemporary art from 1905 to the present day, including Salvador Dali's *Six Apparitions of Lénine*; Pablo Picasso's early cubist *Femme Assise*; and pop art by Andy Warhol.

CHAMPS-ÉLYSÉES

� B3 ✉ avenue des Champs-Élysées 🚇 Concorde, Champs-Élysées-Clémenceau, Franklin-D-Roosevelt, George V or Charles de Gaulle-Étoile

The stately and much-loved Champs-Élysées (Heavenly Fields) runs from the place de la Concorde (see page 184) to the Arc de Triomphe, and divides neatly into two sections, with the Rond-Point being the halfway mark. The lower section, nearest Concorde, is bordered with grass and chestnut trees, behind which stand the Grand and Petit Palais, both devoted to the arts. Above the bustling and lively Rond-Point are stores, offices, movie theaters and sidewalk cafés.

CITÉ DES SCIENCES ET DE L'INDUSTRIE

Cité des Sciences et de l'Industrie 🔳 E4 ✉ 30 avenue Corentin Cariou ☎ 01 40 05 80 00. Bookings: 08 92 69 70 72 🕐 Tue.–Sun. 10–6 (also Sun. 6–7 p.m.) 🍴 Restaurant 🚇 Porte de la Villette 💲💲 Cité de la Musique ✉ 221 avenue Jean-Jaurès ☎ 01 44 84 44 84 🕐 Music Museum: Tue.–Sat. noon–6, Sun. 10–6 🍴 Restaurant 🚇 Porte de Pantin 🎵 Concert Hall free; Music Museum 💲💲

On the northeast edge of Paris stands a modern park, La Villette, scattered with sculptures and fountains, and devoted to science and music. Once home to the city's slaughterhouses, the site has been remodeled and converted to house the ultra-modern Cité des Sciences et de l'Industrie (City of Sciences and Industry). You would need a day to do it justice, but if time is short, make sure you visit the main exhibition, Explora, focusing on life, natural resources and technological development. Go to the Géode, a movie theater with a hemispheric screen; the Cinaxe, a multisensory movie theater; or let the kids enjoy interactive games in Cité des Enfants (Children's City). Nearby is the Cité de la Musique, a complex devoted to music; it houses the Musée de la Musique (Music Museum).

CONCIERGERIE ET STE.-CHAPELLE

Conciergerie 🔳 C2 ✉ 1 quai de l'Horloge ☎ 01 53 40 60 80 🕐 Daily 9:30–6, Mar.–Oct.; 9–5, rest of year 🚇 Cité; RER St.-Michel Notre-Dame 💲💲 (free first Sun. of the month, Oct.–Mar.). Last admission 30 minutes before closing ℹ️ Guided tours in English Ste.-Chapelle ✉ 4 boulevard du Palais ☎ 01 53 40 60 80 🕐 Daily 9:30–6, Mar.–Nov.; 9–5, rest of year 🚇 Cité; RER St.-Michel Notre-Dame 💲💲 (free first Sun. of the month, Oct.–Mar.) ℹ️ Guided tours in English

The Conciergerie gained a sinister reputation during the 1790s, when Marie Antoinette, queen of France, and the infamous revolutionary Robespierre were imprisoned here. It is the only remaining part of the original royal complex on the Île de la Cité, a superb Gothic building, with twin round entrance towers and a distinctive roofline. Inside, its huge vaulted hall is the

Biblical scenes in the stained glass at Ste.-Chapelle

Notre-Dame, encircled by the Seine

highlight, along with reconstructed prison cells. Nearby stands the soaring Ste.-Chapelle, commissioned by Louis IX in 1245 to house the Crown of Thorns and a fragment of the True Cross. Built as two chapels, the upper was reserved for the royal family. Here, slender pillars divide the 50-foot-high stained-glass windows, also dating from the 13th century and showing scenes from the Old and New Testaments.

LA DÉFENSE

A4, off the map ⊠ La Défense ☎ Grande Arche: 01 49 07 27 57 🕐 Grande Arche: daily 10–6:30 🍴 Restaurant 🚇 Métro/RER Grande Arche de la Défense 💷 Grande Arche $$ ℹ Last ascent 30 minutes before closing.

It's well worth the journey out to Paris' prestigious modern business district, with its shopping center, IMAX movie theater and the Centre of New Industry and Technology (CNIT). A pedestrian esplanade leads to the Grande Arche de la Défense, the city's triumphant architectural celebration of the French Revolution's bicentennial. Take the glass elevator 360 feet to the top of the Arche, a stark and elegant hollow white marble cube, and a great view unfolds across Paris to the Arc de Triomphe (see page 178) and the obelisk in the place de la Concorde (see page 184).

ÎLE DE LA CITÉ

C2/D2 ⊠ Île de la Cité 🚇 Cité

One of the loveliest parts of Paris, the Île de la Cité is the ancient heart of the city; in medieval times it was the monarch's capital

and a religious and intellectual center. Here you'll find famous monuments, including Notre-Dame (see page 178) and Ste.-Chapelle (see page 179), impressive civic buildings such as the Palais de Justice, and pleasant streets and squares.

ÎLE ST.-LOUIS

D2 ⊠ Île St.-Louis 🍴 Nos Ancétres les Gaulois, see page 551 🚇 Pont Marie

Pont St.-Louis will lead you straight from the Île de la Cité on to the Île St.-Louis, ideal for a peaceful stroll, a light lunch and some expensive shopping. Once two islands, this largely residential area was developed in the 17th century, when most of its lovely streets and houses were built; since then little seems to have changed.

JARDIN DES TUILERIES

B3/C3 ⊠ place de la Concorde ☎ 01 40 20 90 43 🕐 Daily 7:30–7 🚇 Concorde or Tuileries 💷 Free

The Jardin des Tuileries (Tuileries Gardens) is a good place to recharge your batteries after the rigors of a visit to the Louvre. Designed by Le Nôtre, it's an excellent example of a 17th-century formal garden, its long central *allée* (alley) carrying the eye from the Louvre buildings and fountains to the expanse of the place de la Concorde.

LE MARAIS ET PLACE DES VOSGES

Musée National Picasso E2/E3 ⊠ 5 rue de Thorigny ☎ 01 42 71 25 21 🕐 Wed.–Mon. 9:30–6, Apr.–Sep.; daily 9:30–5:30, rest of year 🍴 Restaurant 🚇 St. Paul; RER Châtelet-Les Halles 💷 $$ (free first Sun. of the month) ℹ Guided tours ($$) in English at 11 a.m. on the first Mon. of the month

Maison de Victor Hugo E2 ⊠ 6 place des Vosges ☎ 01 42 72 10 16 🕐 Tue.–Sun. 10–6; last admission 30 minutes before closing 🍴 Le Grizzli, see page 551 🚇 Bastille or St.-Paul 💷 Free (charge for temporary exhibitions)

For many people, le Marais is the loveliest part of Paris. Its charm lies in the combination of architecture, atmosphere, the crowds that wander its streets, and its restaurants and shops. In the early 17th

THE FRENCH REVOLUTION

All over Paris there are reminders of France's 1789 Revolution, when the monarchy was swept away and equal rights for all citizens were established under the law. America's own Revolutionary War served as the catalyst for events in France.

By the end of Europe's Seven Years War in 1763, France had lost all its North American possessions. Louis XVI of France, thirsting for revenge, was happy to offer arms and troops to help American colonists during their struggle against the English. These soldiers came home inspired by the American ideals of liberty and equality, taking what was, in France, an intellectually led and tiny movement to a larger grass-roots level.

The palace at Versailles (top), home to the ill-fated Louis XVI, and the place de la Concorde, where he was beheaded in front of vast crowds

The Causes

France had enjoyed a Golden Age during the 17th and much of the 18th centuries; power became centralized in the hands of the monarchy, the country prospered and Paris became a center of art and sophistication. But this was at the expense of most of the population, whose standard of living dropped lower and lower. Meanwhile the nobility, deprived of any real political power, threw itself into a reckless and hedonistic lifestyle. The gap between rich and poor grew ever wider; time was ripe for republican ideas to bear fruit.

The Events

In 1789 the Third Estate, representing France's commoners, declared itself a National Assembly and demanded social and constitutional reform. On July 14 a Parisian mob stormed the Bastille prison, a hated symbol of royal power. Matters moved quickly, and within weeks France was in the grip of revolution as peasants across the country rose in revolt against the nobility and clergy.

In August, the Declaration of the Rights of Man was signed and the cry *"Liberté, égalité, fraternité"* (liberty, equality, brotherhood) was heard all over France. These high ideals soon degenerated into a bloodbath resulting in more than 40,000 people being executed. This period, aptly known as the "Terror," was halted only by Napoleon's rise to power.

Henri de Toulouse-Lautrec immortalized the dancers of the Moulin Rouge cabaret in his art

century Henri IV launched development by building the place des Vosges, Paris' oldest square. Its brick-and-stone facades, arcades and central garden make it one of the world's most harmonious and beautiful examples of city planning. Surrounding it are fine mansions built along streets such as the rue des Francs-Bourgeois – forming an unspoiled enclave of superb domestic architecture. The area also boasts some excellent and informative museums, among them the Carnavalet Museum; the National Picasso Museum; and Victor Hugo's House, once the writer's home, on the place des Vosges.

MONTMARTRE

📍 C4 ✉ Montmartre ☎ Basilique du Sacré-Cœur: 01 53 41 89 00 🕐 Basilique du Sacré-Cœur: daily 6 a.m.–10:30 p.m. (crypt and dome 10–5:45) 🚇 Anvers, Abbesses or Lamarck-Caulaincourt 🎫 Basilique du Sacré-Cœur free (crypt and dome $$)

Over-commercialized and crammed with tourists, Montmartre still draws thousands of visitors daily. The neighborhood, once famous for its 40 or more windmills, gained a Bohemian reputation in the late 19th century when artists and writers moved in, among them Pierre-Auguste Renoir, who portrayed the area in some of his liveliest paintings. Later came a new wave of talent, when Montmartre became home to Pablo Picasso and fellow cubist painters. The place du Tertre is the hub of the quarter;

nearby is the Basilique du Sacré-Cœur (Sacred Heart Basilica), an ornate 19th-century church whose domes are a familiar landmark on the skyline.

MUSÉE CARNAVALET

📍 D2 ✉ 23 rue de Sévigné ☎ 01 44 59 58 58 🕐 Tue.–Sun. 10–6. Last admission 30 minutes before closing 🍴 Restaurant 🚇 St. Paul or Chemin Vert 🎫 Free; temporary exhibitions ($$)

The Musée Carnavalet (Carnavalet Museum) combines a chance to see the interior of one of the finest houses in the Marais with a fascinating introduction to the history of Paris itself, from pre-Roman times to the present day. Built in 1540 and remodeled in the 17th century, this beautiful Renaissance mansion was the home of Madame de Sévigné, a famous hostess and literary figure during the reign of Louis XIV. Parts of the museum still feel like her home, where the sumptuous furnishings give some idea of the luxury of upper-class life. Allow enough time to study the models showing Paris' development, as well as the reconstructed rooms and quantities of interesting porcelain, silver and objets d'art.

MUSÉE DU LOUVRE

📍 C3 ✉ rue de Rivoli (main entrance: Pyramide, Cour Napoléon) ☎ 01 40 21 53 17 🕐 Wed.–Mon. 9–6:45 (also Mon., Wed. and Fri. part of museum, 6:45–9:45 p.m.) 🍴 Restaurants 🚇 Palais-Royal Musée du Louvre 🎫 $$ ($ after 3 p.m. and all day Sun.; free first Sun. of the month) 🎧 Self-guiding audio tours ($$) and guided tours ($$) in English are available (free to age under 26, Wed. and Fri. evenings). Sections are sometimes closed on a rotating basis, so call ahead to check.

The Musée du Louvre (Louvre Museum) started life as a palace in the 1190s. Demolished, rebuilt and extended over the centuries, this vast royal residence on the Seine assumed its present form by the 18th century, when the court of Louis XIV moved to the palace at Versailles.

The Revolutionary government of 1793 transformed it into a museum to house the royal collections, and over the years donations and purchases have enabled it to be augmented.

By the 1980s the collections had outgrown their home and President François Mitterrand launched the project known as the "Grand Louvre" to renovate and extend the existing museum space. Architect I. M. Pei was commissioned to design a new entrance in the central Cour Napoléon. Below his stunning glass Pyramide lies a vast new foyer giving access to the main museum areas, named Richelieu, Denon and Sully. The Louvre still seems confusing on arrival, but it is excellently signposted in French and English. It is best to go early, study the plan before you start and then decide what you want to see.

The museum is divided into seven departments, ranging from Egyptian, Greek, Etruscan, Roman and Oriental antiquities through a huge and outstanding painting collection, to sculpture, objets d'art, prints and drawings. Most visitors head straight for the most famous pieces, with Leonardo da Vinci's enigmatic and mysterious *Mona Lisa* topping the list (now in a prominent position in the refurbished *Salle des Etats*). Another great work of art to admire is the *Virgin of the Rocks*, also by da Vinci, a work in better shape and just as representative of

his genius. The Louvre also has six wonderful paintings by Georges de la Tour, the 17th-century French painter of candlelit night scenes. Take time, too, for Jan Vermeer's light-infused *Lacemaker;* Veronese's *Marriage Feast at Cana*, the largest work in the Louvre, full of fascinating detail; and Raphael's *Beautiful Gardener,* one of the sweetest of all his Virgins.

Two superb classical sculptures draw crowds: the *Winged Victory of Samothrace*, a second-century BC marble figure, full of movement and tension and standing dramatically at the top of a grand staircase; and the *Venus de Milo*, a serene Hellenistic figure of the goddess Aphrodite from the fourth century BC. Contrast these two with Michelangelo's *Slaves*, sculpted nearly 2,000 years later but clearly inspired by classical work.

MUSÉE D'ORSAY

C2 1 rue de la Légion d'Honneur 01 40 49 48 14 Tue.–Sun. 9–6, Jun.–Sep.; Tue.–Sat. 10–6, Sun. 9–6 (also Thu. 6–9:15 p.m. rest of year) Restaurant and snack bar Solférino; RER Musée d'Orsay $$ (reduced fee on Sun.; free first Sun. of the month) Guided tours ($$) at 11:30 and 2:30. Audiotape ($$) about the collection's masterpieces available in English

The architecturally controversial Musée d'Orsay (Orsay Museum) was opened in

The glass pyramid at the Louvre was constructed to celebrate the bicentennial of the French Revolution

1986 in the old railroad station, the Gare d'Orsay. Whatever your view, the wonderful art collection inside cannot fail to impress. The whole field of visual arts – painting, sculpture, architecture and design – from 1848 to 1914 is represented.

The major draw is the superb Impressionist and post-Impressionist collection on the upper and middle levels. Here hangs Edouard Manet's *Olympia*, a portrait of a naked prostitute that caused a sensation when it was painted in 1863. Also in the gallery is a series of garden scenes by Alfred Sisley and Camille Pissarro, where the light is so wonderfully expressed that you can almost tell what time of day it was. You'll find world-famous paintings such as Edouard Manet's *Déjeuner sur l'Herbe*, and Claude Monet's radiant light-filled images of Rouen Cathedral and his water gardens at Giverny. Here too are James McNeill Whistler's portrait of his mother, glowing examples by Renoir, and Edgar Degas' pert little dancers.

PLACE DE LA CONCORDE

✚ B3 ✉ place de la Concorde 🚇 Concorde
Nothing better epitomizes the self-confidence, wealth and flair of 18th-century France than the place de la Concorde, scene of Louis XVI's execution in 1793. No matter how many photos you've seen, nothing can prepare you for the scale of this elegant square, with its sweeping views up the Champs-Élysées (see page 179) and down to the Louvre (see page 182), and

---

What's On Where

Brochures published both weekly and monthly help you track down evening entertainment in Paris. English-language publications include *Where Paris*, *What's On* and *Time Out* (monthly) and the weekly *Pariscope*, which has an English section. These list an enormous selection of entertainment, including temporary events, shows and festivals. You can find them at tourist offices and English-language bookstores.

---

from the Madeleine to the Assemblée Nationale across the river. The octagonal square is lavishly decorated with statues, while in the center rises the slender shape of a 3,000-year-old Egyptian obelisk, flanked by two fountains.

LE QUARTIER LATIN AND VICINITY

Jardin du Luxembourg ✚ C2 ✉ rue de Medicis/rue de Vaugirard 🕐 Daily between 7:30 and 8:15 a.m. to between 5 and 9:55 p.m., depending on season 🚇 Odéon; RER Luxembourg

Panthéon ✚ D1–D2 ✉ place du Panthéon ☎ 01 44 32 18 00 🕐 Daily 10–6:30, Apr.–Oct.; 10–6, rest of year. Last admission 45 minutes before closing 🚇 Cardinal-Lemoine or Jussieu; RER Luxembourg 🎟 $$

The area around the Sorbonne, Paris' ancient university, has long been known as the Quartier Latin (Latin Quarter) because until the 1789 Revolution, Latin was the language spoken by students. Centered around the place St.-Michel and its tree-lined boulevard, this maze of medieval lanes, stores and cafés is always thronged with young people. Cross the boulevard to admire the Jardin du Luxembourg (Luxembourg Garden), then move on to the Panthéon, where great Frenchmen, including Voltaire and Victor Hugo, are buried.

TOUR EIFFEL

✚ A3 ✉ Champ de Mars ☎ 01 44 11 23 23 🕐 Daily 9 a.m.–midnight, mid-Jun. to Aug. 31; 9:30 a.m.–11 p.m. (stairs: 9:30–6), rest of year 🍽 Two restaurants in the Tower 🚇 Bir-Hakeim; RER Champ de Mars Tour Eiffel 🎟 Elevator: 1st floor $, 2nd floor $$, 3rd floor $$$; Staircase: 1st and 2nd floor $$ 🛈 Last admission 30 minutes before closing

When it was built by engineer Gustave Eiffel in 1889, the Tour Eiffel (Eiffel Tower) was, at almost 1,000 feet, the tallest man-made structure in the world. Part of the World Exhibition, it was an instant success, quickly becoming a familiar symbol of Paris. You can take an elevator to each of its three levels, the views widening at each stage. Mail a letter from the first-floor post office here, and the postmark will be "Paris Tour Eiffel."

EATING AND DRINKING IN PARIS

Your hotel will probably provide you with breakfast (normally at an extra charge), consisting of juice, freshly baked baguettes and a selection of croissants and *viennoiseries* (assorted pastries). However, a basic Continental breakfast can be had at most street cafés for a fraction of the price, and usually with a genuine Parisian atmosphere.

Main Meals

Lunch is generally served from midday until 2:30, and dinner from 7:30 until after 10. If you want either earlier, head for a *brasserie*, where you'll get simple, freshly cooked meals, and drinks and snacks throughout the day. Bistros are more modest than restaurants, although not always cheaper. You'll get the best value anywhere by choosing from the *menu* (often called *la formule*), where you'll get a choice of three or four courses for a fixed price. Some noted restaurants also serve what they term a *menu gastronomique*, which will include small portions of many of the famous house specialties. If you order water, you'll probably get bottled mineral water (still or carbonated), for which you'll be charged. Wine can be fairly expensive, but all restaurants serve their own house wine in carafes, which is often good value. A typical meal will include a starter, frequently some type of salad; a main course with vegetables; and cheese, followed by the dessert.

Snacks, Fast Food and Picnics

If you want a light lunch head for the cafés, which usually have tables outside when the weather's nice. They serve sandwiches and other snacks, and hot, cold and alcoholic drinks. A popular lunch place in Paris is the *bar à huîtres* (oyster bar), where other seafood also is available. There also are plenty of burger joints, as well as the *boulangerie* (bakery), where you can get a variety of savory pastries to take out. For those with a sweet tooth, a *pâtisserie* (cake shop) is the place for a mouthwatering range of cakes and pastries. Summer weather may tempt you to plan a picnic: you can put together a wonderful feast at your neighborhood market.

LYON

France's second largest city has much to offer; it's a place where history and tradition, excellent civic facilities and architectural merit combine with commercial importance to give a real big-city feel on a very human level.

The City and the Presqu'Île

Lyon's sprawl may be daunting if this is your first visit, but the city's major tourist attractions are in a surprisingly compact area. Public transportation is excellent, so it should take little time for you to get your bearings. Lyon's name is derived from the Latin *Lugdunum*, the capital of Roman Gaul, which was founded at the top of Fourvière, before spreading down the hill above the confluence of two great rivers known today as the Rhône and the Saône. After Rome fell, the medieval town gradually established itself, spreading out slowly to occupy the narrow spit of land immediately above the rivers' junction. This became known as the Presqu'Île (the isthmus), and here the city grew in the 17th and 18th centuries; it was only later that it expanded farther to the north and east. For visitors, the main sights are almost all either along the west bank of the Saône or on the Presqu'Île, the oldest parts of the city.

Exploring Lyon

Most visitors use the metro system, or subway, to travel around. Although it will get you from place to place effortlessly, you'll get a better sense of the city's layout if you set out on foot, and walking can actually be quicker. The hill of Fourvière (see page 190) is a useful landmark; if it's on your left you're heading north, right and you're walking south. For orientation purposes remember that the Saône is the river immediately below Fourvière, while the Rhône lies on the other side of the Presqu'Île. Lyon is remarkably hilly, especially the climb up Fourvière and the slopes of the Croix-Rousse district (see pages 189–190), so a trip to these places

Lyon

probably merits the short metro or bus ride. The tourist office offers an excellent one-, two- or three-day pass called the Lyon City Card. This moderately priced ticket gives you unlimited travel on the bus, trolley bus, tram and metro network, a river cruise (April through October), free admission to Lyon's best museums, a guided tour, a self-guiding audio tour of the Fourvière Basilica, access to the observatory, a lunchtime music concert, a 10 percent discount at Galeries LaFayette Lyon Part-Dieu, and a mass of literature to help make the most of your stay. The Lyonnais – with their reputation for common sense, wit and kindness – are helpful and friendly, and are usually happy to assist strangers.

Enjoying the Sights

Lyon, like so many historic cities, needs to be explored at leisure. Wander through picturesque neighborhoods, sit in cafés, pause in the lovely squares and linger on the bridges to admire the river scene. If pressed for time, consider taking a tour. The tourist office can provide details for both bus and walking tours, and cruises run during the summer. This prosperous city is well endowed with museums, some of which are remarkably esoteric. If you're an avid old-film fan, period automobile freak or if medical history or the discovery of electricity rivets you – you'll not be disappointed. Lyon also has child-friendly attractions, including a museum of automation history, a puppet museum

Contemporary centerpiece on place Louis Pradel, on the Presqu'Île

Lyon

and a huge and well-presented natural history museum.

La Cuisine

Ask any French citizen what he or she thinks is Lyon's main attraction and the answer will probably be *"la cuisine"* (the food). This is a city where eating is taken very seriously indeed. There are hundreds of restaurants, ranging from very simple to world class, and then there is the wine. North of Lyon, miles of famous vineyards produce quality reds and whites, with names to excite a wine lover – Mâcon, Pouilly, Fleurie and Beaujolais, to name but a few. Wine enthusiasts may consider an excursion to the wine country; the tourist office can help with this.

Souvenirs of Silk

Lyon has all the shopping you would expect from a city of its size and importance. The smartest stores lie in and around rue Président Edouard Herriot, and in the streets near place Bellecour and place des Terreaux, on the Presqu'Île. All the big international names are here, from jewelers, fashion designers and interior decorators to the best of shoe, leather, china and glass stores. The modern city center, around Part-Dieu railroad station, is home to downtown malls and chain stores, and there also are branches of France's top department stores. Lyon has its own specialties, with silk topping the list, and you'll find lovely scarves, ties and fabrics to take home.

On the Town

Lyon has plenty to offer in the way of evening entertainment. Opera, ballet, classical concerts, theater, jazz, rock and movies all thrive, with constantly changing programs; listings are available from the tourist office. There are dozens of bars playing live music; cabaret restaurants; nightclubs and floor shows; discos and karaoke bars; English, Irish and Australian pubs; a casino – the list goes on and on.

ESSENTIAL INFORMATION

TOURIST INFORMATION
Office du Tourisme et des Congrès du Grand Lyon (Lyon Convention and Visitors Bureau)
• place Bellecour ☎ 04 72 77 69 69;
fax 04 78 42 04 32; www.lyon-france.com

URBAN TRANSPORTATION
Central Lyon is well served by an extensive bus, trolley bus, tram and subway (metro) system. The subway runs daily 5 a.m.– 12:15 a.m. and is easy to use. You can pick up subway, bus and tram maps from station service booths and tourist offices. Subway stations are marked with an "M" on the city map. Tickets, available singly (valid for one or two hours'

travel) or in *carnets* (books) of 10, are interchangeable between the metro, bus and tram systems. A one-day travel pass *(Ticket Liberté Journée)* gives unlimited access to the transport system and is good value. For information ☎ 04 78 71 70 00. Remember to validate tickets before boarding. Taxis can be hailed or called. Try Lyon International Taxi ☎ 04 78 88 16 16 or Allo Taxi, ☎ 04 78 28 23 23.

AIRPORT INFORMATION
Lyon-Saint Exupéry Airport (☎ 08 26 80 08 26, toll call) is 13 miles from the city, about 30 minutes by taxi. A shuttle bus (Satobus) connects the airport with the city center every 20 minutes. For information ☎ 04 72 68 72 17.

CLIMATE – average highs and lows for the month

JAN.	FEB.	MAR.	APR.	MAY	JUN.	JUL.	AUG.	SEP.	OCT.	NOV.	DEC.
5°C	8°C	12°C	14°C	20°C	23°C	27°C	26°C	22°C	17°C	10°C	7°C
41°F	46°F	54°F	57°F	68°F	73°F	81°F	79°F	72°F	63°F	50°F	45°F
0°C	1°C	3°C	5°C	10°C	14°C	17°C	16°C	12°C	8°C	4°C	2°C
32°F	34°F	37°F	41°F	50°F	57°F	63°F	61°F	54°F	46°F	39°F	36°F

The restored old quarter on the right bank of the Saône is the focus of Lyonnais chic

CITY SIGHTS

Key to symbols

🞧 map coordinates refer to the Lyon map on page 186; sights below are highlighted in yellow on the map.

✉ address or location ☎ telephone number 🕐 opening times Ⓜ nearest subway 🚌 nearest bus or tram route 🍴 restaurant or café on site or nearby 💷 admission charge: $$$ more than €12, $$ €4–€12, $ less than €4 ℹ other relevant information

CATHÉDRALE ST.-JEAN

🞧 A2 ✉ place St.-Jean ☎ Cathedral: 04 78 42 28 25. Choir School: 04 78 92 82 29 🕐 Cathedral: Mon.–Fri. 8–noon and 2–7, Sat.–Sun. and holidays 8–noon and 2–5; Choir School: Daily 8:30–12.10 p.m. and 1:45–7 (closed during Sun. mass) Ⓜ Vieux Lyon 💷 Free

Post-Roman Lyon grew up around the site of the Cathédrale St.-Jean (St. John's Cathedral), a serene and lofty building with a flamboyant Gothic facade, flanked by a lovely Romanesque 11th-century choir school. Much of the interior dates from the 14th and 15th centuries. The rose windows in the transept are older; their glowing colors first illuminated the center of St. John's in the 1200s.

CENTRE D'HISTOIRE DE LA RÉSISTANCE ET DE LA DÉPORTATION

🞧 B1 ✉ 14 avenue Berthelot ☎ 04 78 72 23 11 🕐 Wed.–Sun. 9–5:30 Ⓜ Jean Macé 🚌 4, 11, 12E, 17, 18, 23, 39, 43, 47,53, 96; tram T2 (Centre Berthelot) 💷 $

World War II saw a highly organized, fearless and active resistance movement in Lyon, so it's fitting that the city should have created the fascinating Centre d'Histoire de la Résistance et de la Déportation (Center of the History of the Resistance and Deportation). Permanent and temporary displays, documents, audiovisual guides and videos commemorate the past as well as educating the young.

CROIX-ROUSSE

🞧 A3 ✉ Croix-Rousse Ⓜ Croix-Rousse ℹ You can arrange a guided tour at the tourist office

The slopes of the Croix-Rousse (Red Cross) area rise at the north end of the Presqu'Île, the neck of land between the Saône and Rhône rivers. This fascinating area was mainly occupied by religious institutions before the French Revolution, but the institutions were dissolved in 1789, leaving the area open to redevelopment by the silk industry. Today it is a UNESCO World Heritage Site and one of the liveliest, earthiest areas of Lyon.

FOURVIÈRE

✚ A3   ✉ Roman theaters: 6 rue de l'Antiquaille, Fourvière   ☎ 04 72 38 81 90   ◷ Daily 7 a.m.–9 p.m., mid-Aug. to mid-Sep.; 7–7, rest of year
🍴 Restaurant de Fourvière   ◎ Vieux Lyon then Fourvière funicular   ⏚ Free

One of your first impressions upon arriving in Lyon will be the hill of Fourvière, the site of Roman *Lugdunum*, with its amphitheaters (France's oldest, begun in 15 BC), a 2nd-century odeum (a small, roofed theater) and remains of a craft district. The hill rises above the Saône river, topped by the ornate mass of the 19th-century Basilique Notre-Dame de Fourvière and what appears to be a scaled-down copy of the Eiffel Tower – actually the Tour Metallique (Metal Tower), built in 1894 and now a radio and television transmitter. Take the funicular to the top and enjoy the fabulous views across the city.

MAISON DES CANUTS

✚ B3, off map   ✉ 10–12 rue d'Ivry   ☎ 04 78 28 62 04   ◷ Mon.–Sat. 10–6:30   ◎ Croix-Rousse   🚌 2, 6, 13, 33, 45, 61   ⏚ $$

The Maison des Canuts (Silkweavers' House) is a museum-cum-workshop devoted to the history of silk and silk weavers (*canuts*) in the heart of the Red Cross area. Here you can enjoy a video, browse through old machinery displays and watch silk-weaving demonstrations on traditional looms.

MUSÉE DE LA CIVILISATION GALLO-ROMAIN

✚ A2   ✉ 17 rue Cléberg   ☎ 04 72 38 81 90   ◷ Tue.–Sun. 10–6, Mar.–Oct.; 10–5, rest of year   ◎ Vieux Lyon then Fourvière funicular   ⏚ $

Housed in an innovative underground building designed by B. H. Zehrfuss, the 17-room Gallo-Roman Museum of Civilization displays objects found in Lyon.

Highlights include the "Claudius Tablet," part of a bronze tablet inscribed with a speech given by Emperor Claudius to the Senate in AD 48, and the Circus Mosaic, which vividly portrays a chariot race.

MUSÉE DES BEAUX-ARTS

✚ B3   ✉ 20 place des Terreaux   ☎ 04 72 10 17 40   ◷ Wed.–Thu. and Sat.–Mon. 10–6, Fri. 10:30–8   🍴 Museum restaurant   ◎ Hôtel de Ville   🚌 1, 3, 6, 13, 18, 19, 44   ⏚ $

The elegant mass of the Musée des Beaux-Arts (Museum of Fine Arts) dominates one side of the spacious place des Terreaux, with the impressive Hôtel de Ville (Town Hall) at right angles to it. The building was formerly the Benedictine convent of St.-Pierre, rebuilt between 1659 and 1685, and it opened as a museum in 1803. The museum has exhibits from Egypt and the ancient world, and collections of pottery, porcelain, glass and sculpture. Track down the Lalique glass display and the charming animal figurines, including a cumbersome yet graceful polar bear by 19th-century sculptor François Pompon. In the entrance foyer Pietro Perugino's *Ascension of Christ*, one of the artist's finest works outside Italy, is a fitting introduction to what's in store.

MUSÉE GADAGNE

✚ A3   ✉ 1 place du Petit Collège   ☎ 04 78 42 03 61   ◷ Wed.–Mon. 10:45–6   🍴 Comptoir du Bœuf, see page 551   ◎ Vieux Lyon   🚌 1, 3, 9, 18, 19, 31, 40, 44   ⏚ $ ⛨ Guided tours at 3 p.m. third Sun. of the month. Main galleries closed through 2006; ground-floor galleries open

The Musée Gadagne (Gadagen Museum) comprises two museums, the Musée Historique de Lyon (Lyon Historical Museum) and the Musée International de la Marionnette (International Puppet Museum), housed in one of Old Lyon's stateliest Renaissance mansions, the 15th-century Hôtel de Gadagne. The first museum traces Lyon's history from the Middle Ages to the 19th century. Guignol, the famous French puppet, hails from Lyon and is loved all over France for his wit, sarcasm and nagging wife; you can see Guignol, plus a worldwide cast of friends, in the charming puppet museum.

LA CUISINE LYONNAISE

Lyon is said to have more restaurants per capita than any other city in the world; no wonder that even other Frenchmen will admit, *"on mange bien à Lyon"* ("you eat well in Lyon").

Geography helps: the city stands at an agricultural crossroads, benefiting from prime beef from Charolles, wine from Beaujolais and superb dairy products from the Dauphiné. The commercial fruit and vegetable gardens of France supply the freshest ingredients, and better *boulangers* (bakers) and *pâtissiers* (cake-makers) than the Lyonnais are hard to find. Here you can spend happy hours practicing the art of *lèche-vitrines*, literally "licking the windows," but in reality window-shopping for food. Have a look in the *boucheries* (butchers), *traiteurs* (delicatessens) like you've never seen before, and *épiceries* (grocer shops) piled high with olive oil, vinegar, honey and jam. Afterward, go to the morning markets (except Monday) on the quai St.-Antoine along the river and drool over the gleaming vegetables, glistening fish and mounds of fruit. Then you can find a restaurant and eat – *bon appetit!*

Lyon has a long tradition of professional kitchens being managed by women, a legacy from times when all restaurants were family-run and *Maman* (mother) did the cooking. Such restaurants, known as *bouchons*, still exist, and are usually small and friendly, with visible kitchens. You can count on authentic Lyonnais dishes accompanied by straightforward wines, which are served in small jugs called *pots*, holding a standard amount. Some restaurants are renowned, and it's often necessary to book ahead.

Choice galore – one of the many sidewalk cafés offering Lyon's fine cuisine

What should you eat? The cooking is classic French, with quality ingredients, subtle sauces, properly aged meat and perfectly ripe cheeses. *Boudin blanc*, a veal sausage, is a specialty, as are *quenelles*, lighter-than-air poached fish dumplings served with Lyon's classic crayfish-based *sauce Nantua*. Tripe, pigs' feet and brains may not be what you're used to, but try them. *Pommes Lyonnaises* (potatoes fried with onions) are eaten worldwide, but try *gratin dauphinois* (potatoes baked in butter, cream, garlic and mustard) as well. Leave room for a dessert, such as a luscious fruit tart; *île flottante*, a dish with floating islands of meringue on a custard lake; sinful chocolate mousse; or the simplicity of *fromage blanc* – a fresh cream cheese eaten with sugar and cream.

MUSÉE DES TISSUS ET MUSÉE DES ARTS DECORATIFS

A1   ✉ 30–34 rue de la Charité   ☎ 04 78 38 42 00
🕐 Musée des Tissus: Tue.–Sun. 10–5:30; Musée des Arts Decoratifs: Tue.–Sun. 10–noon and 2–5:30
🍴 Chabert et Fils, see page 551   🚇 Ampère Victor Hugo   💰 $$ ℹ️ Musée des Tissus: guided tours 3 p.m. Sun. and first Thu. of month

The Musée des Tissus (Fabric Museum) is appropriately located in Lyon – home of some of the most beautiful silk and innovative production the industry has seen. A fine 18th-century mansion houses the collection, which has fabrics from all over the world, dating from as early as the fifth century. The Far Eastern silks and embroideries are exquisite, but the Lyon silk and costumes steal the show. These intricate pieces – including designs by Philippe de Lassalle, the greatest master of them all – are still stunningly vivid. Also exhibited are articles of clothing, featuring Mariano Fortuny's Greek-influenced gowns, as wearable today as they were in the 1920s. The Musée des Arts Décoratifs (Museum of Decorative Arts) is packed with furniture, china and glass.

PARC DE LA TÊTE D'OR

✚ B3, off the map   ✉ place Général-Leclerc   ☎ 04 72 69 47 60   🕐 Daily 6 a.m.–11 p.m. in summer, 6 a.m.–9 p.m. in winter
🚌 4; tram T2
💰 Free

Rose lovers should visit the superb 262-acre Parc de la Tête d'Or (Golden Head Park), home of Lyon's botanical gardens, which are beautifully landscaped around a lake. The *roseraie* (rose garden) has more than 60,000 bushes and 350 varieties, all thriving and filling the summer air with an overwhelming scent.

PLACE BELLECOUR

✚ B2   ✉ place Bellecour   🍴 Chabert et Fils, see page 551   🚇 Place Bellecour

The sweeping expanse of the place Bellecour – the old place Royale – is one of Europe's biggest squares. In the center is a bronze equestrian statue of Louis XIV; within the park are gravel paths and shade trees, making this a splendid oasis of calm in the heart of the busy Presqu'Île.

VIEUX LYON

✚ A2   ✉ Vieux Lyon   🍴 Comptoir du Bœuf, see page 551   🚇 Vieux Lyon   ℹ️ Guided walking tours available with audiocassette or English-speaking guides. Apply at the tourist office

Until the 1960s, Vieux Lyon (Old Lyon) was a run-down, derelict area. Happily, both the French government and the city of Lyon stepped in with funds to save this historic quarter, the largest Renaissance-era urban area in France and now a UNESCO World Heritage Site.

Here the medieval cathedral town grew and prospered as an international trade and banking center. Rich merchants and bankers built superb, ornately detailed houses along the narrow streets comprising the St.-Paul, St.-Jean and St.-Georges neighborhoods. They still stand today, rescued and restored, with their spick-and-span mullioned windows, vaulted walkways, towers and galleries. Many streets are linked by the passages known as *traboules*, which wind through courtyards and under other buildings; the name is derived from the Latin words *trans ambulare*, meaning "to walk through." Today Old Lyon hums with new life; there are studios, boutiques, and bars and restaurants, thronged in summer with both locals and visitors.

Louis XIV on horseback in the place Bellecour

Silkworms feed on mulberry leaves, which are prevalent in southern France

LYON AND THE SILK TRADITION

Nearly 5,000 years ago the Chinese discovered that the cocoon of an insignificant moth could be gently unraveled in a continuous thread and woven to produce a light and luxurious fabric. This fabric is silk, still one of the softest and most desirable of all textiles.

Silk made its way overland from China to Europe by the 12th century, and by the 1600s Lyon had become the center for European silk production. (The silkworm, *Bombyx mori*, also came to Europe and is now a domesticated insect with a ravenous appetite for mulberry leaves, which grow well in southern France and elsewhere.) The industry thrived, producing sophisticated weaves to supply France's rich and demanding upper classes. Sumptuous designs in dazzling colors were achieved on hand looms; silk damask, patterned silks and brocades, and figured silk velvets poured out of the workshops of Lyon.

In 1804, Joseph-Marie Jacquard invented the mechanical loom, which enabled patterns to be programed using a punch-card system. These very large looms were moved from the Old Town into special buildings in the Red Cross area (see pages 189–190) that were designed to accommodate their size. The silkweavers (*canuts*), who also moved, were paid an abysmally low price for each pattern, with the middleman scooping the profits. Social unrest finally erupted in 1831, after a three-year struggle by the *canuts* to get better pay and conditions.

By 1870 the industry had recovered and Lyon silk was considered to be among the best fabrics in the world. The creation of artificial silk and other man-made fibers in the 20th century brought an end to large-scale silk production. Lyon's 30,000 weavers dwindled, and today there are only a handful of workshops where people still weave manually; hand-woven weaves are in high demand and are used to help restore the interiors of France's historic buildings.

If you're interested, follow the silk trail in Lyon, from the Old Town to the slopes of the Red Cross district, where you can visit silk workshops and working hand looms. Be sure not to miss the Fabric Museum (see opposite page), keeping in mind that the most a skilled worker could hope to weave was three to four inches a day.

Nice

NICE

Nice, France's fifth-largest city and its biggest tourist resort, is perfectly situated on the sweeping Bay of Angels (Baie des Anges). With hills as its backdrop, it is blessed with gorgeous surroundings, a superb climate, a historic past and friendly people. Until 1860 Nice belonged to the County of Savoy, which became part of Italy in 1870, and to this day both the way of life and the inhabitants seem to combine the best of both cultures: Italian charm and flair tempered with a strong dash of Gallic sophistication.

The City

The Greeks built their settlement on the hills above the bay, and 300 years later the Romans settled here. The modern city stands on the same spot and has spread down to the flat land along the sea. Sheltered to the east and west by substantial promontories, and with the Maritime Alps to the north, Nice has its own microclimate, with mild winters and perfect summers. Over the centuries city planners have taken advantage of these conditions, resulting in one of the most graceful and flower-filled cities in Europe – the average Frenchman's retirement-home fantasy.

In recent years, Nice has marketed itself as a convention center and vacation hot spot, attested by the variety of hotels. It has more museums than any other French city outside of Paris, and plenty of festivals and events throughout the year.

Getting Around

Nice is a big city, with several districts – each of which you'll want to experience. The best way to orient yourself is to take a bus or taxi to an area, then explore on foot. Start with the

atmospheric and picturesque Old Town (Vieille Ville, see page 198), which you'll probably want to visit more than once. The seafront stretches nearly 4 miles west of the Old Town, with the famous Promenade des Anglais running along much of it. Behind the promenade and situated around the place Masséna is the commercial and business center, punctuated by peaceful gardens. The upscale residential suburb of Cimiez lies on the hill behind the old port and is home to several excellent museums. As you explore,

Nice

notice how the ambience varies, from the earthy gaiety in the streets of the Old Town to the haute couture you'll find along the Promenade des Anglais. You can see the different parts of Nice in style by hiring a *calèche* (horse-drawn carriage), or by taking the tourist train that trundles around the old quarter.

Flavors of the South

The French- and Italian-influenced cuisine of Nice is complemented by the sunny flavors of southern France. Look for an array of fish and seafood.

Vegetable dishes include *salade Niçoise* (made with lettuce, anchovies, tomatoes, hard-boiled eggs and black olives) and *ratatouille* (Mediterranean vegetable stew), which were created here. Also try *mesclun*, a bitter selection of wild leaves. Stuffed vegetables and zucchini flowers fried in batter accompany grilled fish and meat. *Estocaficada* is a Niçois dish made from dried Norwegian cod and tomatoes. *Socca*, a type of pancake made from chickpeas, and *pissaladière*, an onion and anchovy tart, make good light lunches. The area produces several

Nice

wines, Château de Bellet and Villars among them, and there's an international selection of wines and beer.

Local Wares and Souvenirs

Nice combines the temptations of big-city chain stores and designer outlets with local markets, antiques shops and souvenir stores. Department stores and big-name labels are found around place Masséna, while local products are sold in the Old Town. Traditional brightly printed cottons, scents from the hills around Grasse, food, oils and wines make lovely gifts, but the best souvenirs from Nice are traditional carved figurines, known as *santons*.

Carnaval

Nice has a clutch of dynamic theaters, concert halls and an opera, as well as movie theaters, nightclubs, a casino and a host of cabaret restaurants, live-music bars and throbbing discos. The best place to learn about what's going on is through *La Semaine des Spectacles* or *L'Officiel des Loisirs* (on sale at newsstands). Enjoy the local festivals, popular no matter what time of year. The big one is the *Nice Carnaval et Bataille de Fleurs* (Nice Carnival and Battle of Flowers) in February.

Beaches

Nice has public beaches, but to spend a day in the sun as the Niçois do, go to one of the city's 15 private beaches (open April through October). Included in the fee is an outdoor lounge chair and sun-shade umbrella, changing rooms, freshwater showers, a range of activities and access to a private bar/restaurant. The beaches are covered in pebbles here, not sand, and topless sunbathing is the rule rather than the exception on the French Riviera.

ESSENTIAL INFORMATION

TOURIST INFORMATION
Office de Tourisme et des Congrès de Nice (Nice Convention and Visitors Bureau)
• 5 Promenade des Anglais, fax 04 92 14 48 03; www.nicetourisme.com
• SNCF railroad station, avenue Thiers, fax 04 93 16 85 16
• Nice-Ferber, Promenade des Anglais (western end), fax 04 93 92 08 27
• Terminal 1, Aéroport Nice Côte d'Azur, fax 04 93 21 44 50
• Tourist information line ☎ 08 92 70 74 07 (24 hrs)

URBAN TRANSPORTATION
Sunbus operates all over the city; maps are available from their headquarters (Sun Boutique "Grand Hôtel," 10 avenue Félix-Faure ☎ 04 93 13 53 13) or from any tourist office. Buy your ticket, or SunMaxi or Souleu book of tickets (books of tickets valid for different numbers of days), at a kiosk before you board; don't forget to validate your ticket. A SunPass offers unlimited travel for 1, 5 or 7 days and is a good deal. Buses run until 1:10 a.m. Taxis can be found at city-center cab stands (Esplanade Masséna, Promenade des Anglais and place Garibaldi are probably the most convenient locations); or call Allo Taxi Riviéra (☎ 04 93 13 78 78).

AIRPORT INFORMATION
Aéroport Nice-Côte d'Azur (☎ 08 20 42 33 33 for inquiries in English) is west of the city. International flights leave from terminal 1; Paris and other French destinations are served by terminal 2. A shuttle bus (No. 23) runs every half-hour from terminal 1 to the SNCF railroad station in town daily 6 a.m.–9 p.m. Taxis can be found near the airport exits, and take about 15 to 20 minutes to reach the city.

CLIMATE – average highs and lows for the month

JAN.	FEB.	MAR.	APR.	MAY	JUN.	JUL.	AUG.	SEP.	OCT.	NOV.	DEC.
13°C	13°C	14°C	17°C	20°C	24°C	25°C	27°C	24°C	20°C	17°C	13°C
55°F	55°F	57°F	63°F	68°F	75°F	77°F	81°F	75°F	68°F	63°F	55°F
5°C	6°C	8°C	9°C	13°C	17°C	19°C	20°C	17°C	13°C	9°C	6°C
41°F	43°F	46°F	48°F	55°F	63°F	66°F	68°F	63°F	55°F	48°F	43°F

CITY SIGHTS

Key to symbols

⊞ map coordinates refer to the Nice map on pages 194–195; sights below are highlighted in yellow on the map.

⊠ address or location ☎ telephone number

◉ opening times ⊟ nearest bus route

🍴 restaurant or café on site or nearby

💳 admission charge: $$$ more than €12, $$ €4–€12, $ less than €4 ⓘ other relevant information

CATHÉDRALE ORTHODOXE RUSSE ST.-NICOLAS

⊞ B2 ⊠ avenue Nicolas II ☎ 04 93 96 88 02 ◉ Tours: Mon.–Sat. 9–noon and 2:30–6, Sun. 2:30–5:30, Apr.–Oct.; Mon.–Sat. 9:30–noon and 2:30–5:30, Sun. 2:30–5:30, rest of year. Closed Sun. morning and during religious services ⊟ 5, 7, 14, 15, 17 💳 $ ⓘ Religious services: Sat. 6 p.m. (5:30 p.m. Nov.–Feb.), Sun 10 a.m.

The Cathédrale Orthodoxe Russe St.-Nicolas (St. Nicholas' Russian Orthodox Cathedral), an exuberant pink-and-gray church with six green onion-shaped cupolas and an ornate exterior, looks out of place in southern France. Tzar Nicolas II built it from 1903 to 1912, and inside is a dazzling collection of treasures and memorabilia relating to the Russian presence in Nice.

CIMIEZ

Franciscan Church, Monastery and Museum ⊞ D4
⊠ place du Monastère ☎ 04 93 81 00 04
◉ Church, Monastery and Museum: Mon.–Sat. 10–noon and 3–6 ⊟ 15, 17, 20, 22, 25 💳 Free
ⓘ Concerts in monastery cloisters in Aug.

Site Archéologique Gallo-Romain ⊞ D4 ⊠ 160 avenue des Arènes ◉ Wed.–Mon. 10–6 ⊟ 15, 17, 20, 22, 25 💳 $$ (free on the first and third Sun. of the month) **Jardin des Arènes de Cimiez** ⊞ D4
⊠ avenue des Arènes ◉ Daily dawn–dusk ⊟ 15, 17, 20, 22, 25 💳 Free

Cimiez is a smart residential area packed with interesting attractions, including the Matisse Museum, a 16th-century Franciscan church and monastery, a small museum and cloister devoted to St. Francis, and the cemetery where artists Henri Matisse and Raoul Dufy are buried. The Roman site has been excavated, revealing the remains of an amphitheater and public baths. The attached museum holds the treasures uncovered.

The entrance to the remarkable Museum of Modern and Contemporary Art

MUSÉE D'ART MODERNE ET D'ART CONTEMPORAIN (MAMAC)

⊞ D2 ⊠ Promenade des Arts ☎ 04 93 62 61 62
◉ Tue.–Sun. 10–6 ⊟ 1, 2, 3, 5, 6, 7, 9, 10, 16, 17, 25
ⓘ Musem café 💳 $$ (free on the first and third Sun. of the month)

The Musée d'Art Moderne et d'Art Contemporain (Museum of Modern and Contemporary Art), or MAMAC, is an impressive museum constructed of four gray marble towers linked by glass walkways. The collection, founded by Nice artist Yves Klein, includes new realism, minimalism and pop art, with works by Roy Lichtenstein and Andy Warhol. Look for Klein's innovative *Mur du Feu* (*Wall of Fire*).

MUSÉE MATISSE

⊞ D4 ⊠ 164 avenue des Arènes de Cimiez ☎ 04 93 81 08 08 ◉ Wed.–Mon. 10–6 🍴 Café/restaurant
⊟ 15, 17, 20, 22, 25 💳 $$ ⓘ Guided tours ($) in English Thu. at 3:30 p.m. and first Sun. of the month at 4 p.m.

Drawings, paintings, hangings, gouache cutouts, engravings and sculptures covering the working life of this remarkable artist are displayed at the Matisse Museum. The collection, presented to the city by Henri Matisse and his widow, traces the artist's evolution through such movements as Impressionism and Fauvism. These stunning artworks are housed in a 17th-century Genoese-style villa.

Nice

MUSÉE NATIONAL MESSAGE BIBLIQUE MARC CHAGALL

⊞ C3　✉ avenue Dr. Ménard　☎ 04 93 53 87 20
🕐 Wed.–Mon. 10–6, Jul.–Sep.; 10–5 rest of year　🚌 15
💳 $$

The Marc Chagall Bibilical Message Museum is a dramatic modern gallery, designed by A. Harmant, that houses Chagall's own donations to the city and is the world's most important single collection of his work. The 17 canvasses that make up the *Biblical Message* were painted between 1954 and 1967 and depict the artist's own interpretation of the Bible's story. Other rooms display the 39 gouaches, 105 etchings and copper plates, and 200 sketches that Chagall used to help create the finished pieces.

PLACE MASSÉNA AND VICINITY

⊞ C1　✉ Promenade des Anglais　🕐 Gardens: daily dawn–dusk　🚌 3, 7, 10, 22　💳 Gardens free

The Niçois regard the elegant, arcaded place Masséna as the heart of their city. Around the square, with its sparkling fountain representing the planets, are broad boulevards, and a mile of gardens run around both of its sides. Take time to see the palms and roses at the Jardin Albert 1er (Albert I Garden), Nice's oldest gardens, and the Jardins Suspendus du Paillon (Hanging Gardens of Paillon), a stepped garden filled with azaleas, camellias and aromatic pines.

PROMENADE DES ANGLAIS

⊞ A1–B1　✉ Promenade des Anglais　🚌 3, 7, 10 22
🚩 Nice *Carnaval et Bataille de Fleurs* (Feb.); *Fête Nationale* fireworks display (Jul. 14); *Nuits Estivales*, summer music evenings (Jul. and Aug.)

Early in the 19th century the English discovered that France's sheltered Mediterranean coast had mild winters, and soon they flocked here in large numbers. Afternoon strolls were fashionable, but the rocky, six-foot-wide path along the shore was hardly suitable for gentle walks. In 1820 the Reverend Lewis Way organized the construction of a sweeping promenade, planted with palm trees and decked with flowers. Not surprisingly, the locals soon called it the Promenade des Anglais (the Englishmen's Walk). Today a busy highway cuts between the sea and the ornate exteriors of the *belle époque* luxury hotels. Even amid the sprawl of ugly concrete apartment blocks, the palms, flowers, strolling crowds and views remain unchanged – a superb background for Nice's festivals.

VIEILLE VILLE

⊞ D1　🕐 Fruit and vegetable markets: Tue.–Sun. morning. Antiques market: Mon. Flower market: Tue.–Sat. all day, Sun. morning. All located on cours Saleya　🚌 6, 9, 12

Until the 1970s Nice's Vieille Ville (Old Town) was a decaying slum, with neglected buildings and narrow streets. Today it's one of the liveliest, most colorful neighborhoods in the city, brimming with life, shops, bars – and noise, with interesting old houses, baroque churches, and 17th- and 18th-century civic buildings lining its streets. The cours Saleya is the hub of the quarter, an elongated square that is the home of Nice's famous fresh produce and antiques markets.

Strolling along the Promenade des Anglais

PARKS, GARDENS, TREES AND FLOWERS

Many Mediterranean cities have lovely *parcs* (parks) and *jardins* (gardens), but none more so than Nice. The green swath cutting through the city's heart is only one example, and every street is decked with tubs, planters and window boxes filled with colorful flowers.

Flowers at a colorful market stall in Old Nice

Parks

Formal parks lie within the city center, forming a green oasis for locals and visitors; the Jardin Albert 1er, L'Esplanade du Paillon and the Espace Masséna are good examples. Also in the city center, the wooded Parc du Château features winding paths and cascading water. The wilder Jardin des Arènes de Cimiez is a beautifully tended olive grove, the wind rustling the silver-gray foliage on the shapely trees.

Lovely, aromatic Aleppo pine trees, planted in 1866, abound in the Parc Forestier du Mont-Boron; they line almost 7 miles of trails that are edged with wild carnations and tiny orchids. Views from this park are spectacular: to the east is St.-Jean Cap Ferrat, and to the west is Nice's own Bay of Angels.

Gardens

Avid gardeners should head for Nice's Jardin Botanique (Botanic Garden), with a comprehensive and classic collection of Mediterranean flora. The Parc Floral Phoenix is another garden attraction focusing on tropical plants and fruit trees. A vast greenhouse – packed with numerous exotic and rare orchids, among other delights – dominates the 17-acre site.

Trees and Flowers

Most of Nice's trees and flowers are common to all Mediterranean countries, where this vegetation thrives in lime-rich, sandy or poor soil, can withstand months of summer heat and drought, and can endure an occasional wet or cold spell in winter. Olives, palms and pines are native; citrus trees, bougainvillea, mimosa, gerbera and many succulents have been introduced. Roses love Mediterranean conditions, which is why you'll see bigger and brighter ones here than anywhere else. If you're in the countryside – nature's own glorious garden – in April, May or June, you'll find spreads of wildflowers to rival any city park.

STRASBOURG

Strasbourg's tiny historic center, circled by arms of the Ill river, could easily lull a visitor into thinking that there was little more to the city than picturesque streets, a breathtakingly beautiful cathedral and a huge number of restaurants. But beyond its medieval core lie grandiose 19th-century civic buildings, an ancient university and the gleaming buildings housing European institutions, since Strasbourg is the seat of the European Parliament. It's a prosperous, cosmopolitan city, a beguiling blend of ancient and modern, Teutonic and French.

A Visitor's Strasbourg

For tourists, modern everyday Strasbourg need not intrude upon enjoyment of the old city. Aim to stay within the old, mostly pedestrian quarter; it's a delightful place to walk around, with an impressive choice of

hotels, bars and restaurants. There's a large presence of European parliamentary officials, many of whom speak English, and the range of English-language tourist literature is excellent.

Strasbourg's appeal lies in its combination of history, architecture and culture. First impressions are of a very German city, the timbered houses and cobbled streets reminiscent of villages across the Rhine river, a little to the east. But the atmosphere is definitely French, with the style and way of life that it implies. Lying so near the German border, however, Strasbourg is a favorite destination for day and weekend visits, and you'll see and hear many Germans.

Exploring the City

Undoubtedly, it's best to explore Strasbourg on foot. Apart from visiting the wonderful cathedral, museums and fine churches, most visitors spend time simply strolling the streets. You'll find hidden corners and buildings waiting to

Strasbourg

be photographed around every turn, so take your time. Water plays a large part in the city's layout; the center is encircled by water, divided into different channels and crossed by graceful bridges. Old mills and fortifications along the river bear witness to the city's historic importance, while the mighty Rhine, the German border, lies only a stone's throw away.

If you're interested in architecture, you could follow one of several marked routes through the heart of the old city center (see Petite France, page 204). The tram can be useful for saving your legs, and taxis are easily available. There's also the peaceful boat trip around the center (see page 205).

Sample Alsace wines in the Old Town

Eat, Drink and Enjoy

Strasbourg and Alsace is one of the few areas in Europe that produces both notable wines and beers, and it also is home to some of the finest cooking in France. There are strong German influences here, giving the cuisine a different character from typical French fare. History has played a part in this, and it's a pleasure to see the past so clearly reflected at the table – the popular dish *choucroute*, for instance, is really the same thing as sauerkraut.

But don't be fooled. There's much more to the cuisine in Strasbourg than German cooking; you'll find Italian, Chinese, Lebanese, Tex-Mex, Moroccan and others. With all these options, make sure you don't overlook the opportunity to try some real Strasbourg specialties (see page 553). Stop in a *winstub,* a small family-run restaurant often housed in an historic building, where you'll be able to sample the best of local cooking and flavors.

Alsace produces some notable wines, mainly whites, which are similar in character to the best of German wines.

They are traditionally labeled with the name of the grape rather than the place of origin. Riesling, Gewürztraminer, Pinot Blanc and Muscat are all reliable varieties to look for. Beer also is big in Alsace, the home of Heineken and Kronenbourg, two of Europe's biggest sellers. Other smaller local breweries produce excellent beer.

Evening Diversions

Strasbourg has a rich cultural life, with its own orchestra participating at the renowned International Music Festival in June; in late September through early October there's the annual *Musica,* a festival of contemporary music. Opera, theater, jazz and dance performances are held year-round and are widely advertised. In summer, most tourists are drawn to the nightly folklore displays of music and dance held in some of the old city's most picturesque squares.

Malls and Markets

Shopping in Strasbourg is a real pleasure, with an excellent choice of the world's best-known designer names,

Timber-framed buildings line cobbled streets in the old part of the city

jewelers, antiques shops and international bookstores clustered around the center of the old city. Across the river, Centre Halles is a fair-sized shopping mall housing France's familiar chain stores. The weekly market takes place on Wednesdays in the place Kléber – stalls of fresh produce, cheese and meat jostle with inexpensive and cheerful clothes and household goods. Souvenir shops sell Alsatian handicrafts; pottery, lace and carved wood are worth looking at.

ESSENTIAL INFORMATION

TOURIST INFORMATION
Office de Tourisme de Strasbourg (Strasbourg Tourist Office)
• 17 place de la Cathédrale
☎ 03 88 52 28 28; fax 03 88 52 28 29
• place de la Gare ☎ 03 88 32 51 49
• Pont de l'Europe ☎ 03 88 61 39 23
• Aéroport ☎ 03 88 64 50 15;
www.ot-strasbourg.fr

URBAN TRANSPORTATION
Walking is a pleasure in Strasbourg, although the modern trams are useful at the start or end of the day. Buy tickets from machines located at stops, and validate them before boarding. Outer Strasbourg is served by an efficient bus service, which you can use to visit the European Institutions (again, validate your ticket). Transportation maps are available at the railroad station and the tourist office (for information call ☎ 33 88 77 70 70). Taxis are plentiful and reasonably priced; find them at the station, place Kléber or place Gutenberg, or call for one (Taxis 13 ☎ 03 88 36 13 13).

AIRPORT INFORMATION
Strasbourg-Entzheim International Airport (☎ 03 88 64 67 67), with connections to most major European cities, is about 10 minutes south of the city by car. A shuttle bus runs 5:10 a.m.–11:15 p.m. every 15 minutes Mon.–Fri., Sat. a.m. and Sun. p.m., and every 30 minutes Sat. p.m. and Sun. a.m. to Baggersee tram station (journey time 25 minutes), where tram line A connects with the city center.

CLIMATE – average highs and lows for the month

JAN.	FEB.	MAR.	APR.	MAY	JUN.	JUL.	AUG.	SEP.	OCT.	NOV.	DEC.
4°C	5°C	10°C	15°C	19°C	22°C	24°C	24°C	20°C	14°C	8°C	4°C
39°F	41°F	50°F	59°F	66°F	72°F	75°F	75°F	68°F	57°F	46°F	39°F
-2°C	-2°C	1°C	5°C	9°C	12°C	14°C	13°C	10°C	6°C	2°C	0°C
28°F	28°F	34°F	41°F	48°F	54°F	57°F	55°F	50°F	43°F	36°F	32°F

City Sights

Key to symbols

➕ map coordinates refer to the Strasbourg map on page 200; sights below are highlighted in yellow on the map.

✉ address or location ☎ telephone number

🕐 opening times 🚌 nearest bus or tram route

🍴 restaurant or café on site or nearby

🍷 admission charge: $$$ more than €12, $$ €4–€12, $ less than €4 ⓘ other relevant information

Cathédrale Notre-Dame

➕ B2 ✉ place de la Cathédrale 🕐 Cathedral: daily 7–11:30 and 12:40–7. Platform: Mon.–Fri. 9–5:30, Sat.–Sun. 10–5:30, Apr.–Oct.; Mon.–Fri. 9–4:30, Sat.–Sun. 10–4:30, rest of year. Cathedral closed during Mass 🍴 Au Bon Vivant, see page 553 🚌 11, 14, 21, 24; tram A, D 🍷 Cathedral free; platform $; clock $

A superb example of Gothic architecture, the Cathédrale Notre-Dame (Cathedral of Our Lady) dominates old Strasbourg; its single steeple soars to 466 feet. Built between 1176 and 1439, it stands in a cobbled square on the site of an earlier basilica. A team of masons from Chartres worked on it in the 13th century, creating superb statuary and a harmonious interior, subtly lit by fine stained-glass windows. The main facade, a riot of sinuous, graceful biblical figures and saints, was completed half a century later. A platform constructed in the late 14th century to connect the two towers is reached by 329 stairs.

The astronomical clock in the south transept is a huge timepiece with a planetary dial constructed in the 1540s. Its automated figures perform daily at 12:30 (entrance at the south doorway noon–12:20), when the Apostles march before Christ, a cock crows and beats its wings, and the seven ages of man can be seen. The cathedral's loveliest sculpture is the *Pilier des Anges* (*Pillar of the Angels*), a wondrously carved pillar entwined with the four evangelists and trumpeting angels, all heralding the Last Judgment.

Les Grandes Places

➕ B1–B2 ✉ place Kléber, place Gutenberg, place de la Cathédrale 🚌 11, 14, 21, 24; tram A, B, C, D ⓘ Christkindelsmärik, last week in Nov. through Dec.

Top: The single-steepled Cathedral of Our Lady, embellished with statuary

Above: Flying the flags – Strasbourg is the center of the European Union

Strasbourg is scattered with *grandes places* (large squares). The main three – place Kléber, place Gutenberg and place de la Cathédrale – are all within a five-minute walk of each other. The cathedral square, with its cobblestones and timber-framed houses, is distinctly medieval; 18th-century Kléber square has an elegant spaciousness; and Renaissance-style place Gutenberg nicely bridges the architectural time gap. From late November through December, all three squares are the backdrop for Strasbourg's famous *Christkindelsmärik* (Market of the Child Jesus), a month-long street market dating from 1570.

Musée Alsacien

➕ B1 ✉ 23–25 quai St.-Nicolas ☎ 03 88 52 50 01 🕐 Wed.–Mon. noon–6 (also Sun. 10–noon), Apr.–Jun. and Sep.–Dec.; Wed.–Mon. 10–6, Jan.–Mar. and Jul.–Aug. 🍴 Au Petit Tonnelier, see page 553 🚌 10; tram A, D 🍷 $, combination ticket with Musee des Beaux-Arts and Musee de l'Oeuvre $$; free to all first Sun. of the month

If you only have time to visit one museum, it should be the Musée Alsacien (Alsation Museum) – a charming regional venue housed in a disorderly canal-side

Strasbourg

building. Not only does it give a chance to see the interior courtyards and inside of a 15th-century house, but it's crammed with attractive displays, all illustrating traditional Alsatian life. There are complete rooms and workshops, colorful pottery and glass, regional costumes and much more. Look for the votive pictures – naive religious paintings commissioned as prayer and thanks to God, and illustrating farm animals, children and loved ones.

MUSÉE ARCHÉOLOGIQUE

✚ C1 ✉ 2 place du Château ☎ 03 88 52 50 00 🕐 Wed.–Mon. 10–6 🍴 Aux Armes de Strasbourg, see page 553 🚃 10, 11, 14, 21, 24; tram A, D ✋ $ (free first Sun. of the month)

Strasbourg is proud of the Musée Archéologique (Archeological Museum), one of France's most important museums of its kind. Imaginatively laid out, it's housed in the basement of the Rohan Palace, and takes the visitor through Alsace from 600,000 BC to AD 800. There are interesting prehistoric sections, but more appealing are the reminders of everyday life in Roman Gaul.

MUSÉE D'ART MODERNE ET CONTEMPORAIN

✚ A1–A2 ✉ 1 place Hans-Jean Arp ☎ 03 88 23 31 31 🕐 Tue.–Sat. 11–7, Thu. noon–10 p.m., Sun. 10–6 🍴 Museum restaurant 🚃 4, 10; tram B, C ✋ $$ (free first Sun. of the month)

Opened in 1998, the Musée d'Art Moderne et Contemporain (Modern and Contemporary Art Museum) is an airy building across the water from the Old Town. It covers painting and sculpture from 1870 to the present day. The room devoted to Gustave Doré gives a fine introduction to his work.

MUSÉE DES BEAUX-ARTS

✚ C1 ✉ 2 place du Château ☎ 03 88 52 50 00 🕐 Wed.–Mon. 10–6 🍴 Aux Armes de Strasbourg, see page 553 🚃 10, 11, 14, 21, 24; tram A, D ✋ $, ombination ticket with Musee Alsacien and Musee de l'Oeuvre $$; free to all first Sun. of the month

The elegant first-floor rooms of the Palais Rohan (Rohan Palace) house the Musée des Beaux-Arts (Fine Arts Museum), a comprehensive provincial collection covering European paintings from the Middle Ages to 1870. Memling's *Polyptich of Vanity* steals the show, although the museum is justly proud of *La belle Strasbourgeoise,* by Nicolas de Largillière – a portrait of an enigmatic local lady. The ground floor of this same Renaissance building is home to the separate Strasbourg's Musée des Arts Décoratifs (Decorative Arts Museum).

MUSÉE DE L'ŒUVRE NOTRE-DAME

✚ B1 ✉ 3 place du Château ☎ 03 88 52 50 00 🕐 Tue.–Sun. 10–6 🚃 10, 11, 14, 21, 24; tram A, D ✋ $, combination ticket with Musee Alsacien and Musee des Beaux-Arts $$; free to all first Sun. of the month

The Musée de l'Œuvre Notre-Dame (Museum of the Works of Our Lady) occupies a building used from the 14th to 16th centuries for cathedral maintenance. In addition to the rambling warren of fine rooms and staircases, there are courtyards, one of which is planted with medicinal herbs and plants similar to a 13th-century garden. Some of the cathedral's most precious sculptures are kept here, giving the public a chance to admire the elegance of 14th-century Gothic sculpture. The streamlined *Seven Wise Virgins* is a highlight, as is the nearby group of singularly unintimidating lions from the cathedral's main facade.

PETITE FRANCE

✚ A1 ✉ place Benjamin-Zix 🚃 10; tram A, D 🍴 Le Baeckeoffe d'Alsace, see page 553

As you stroll around Strasbourg, sooner or later you'll reach the picturesque Petite France (Little France). On the banks of the Ill river, at the west end of the historic center, cobbled streets are lined with lovely medieval and Renaissance timbered houses, dripping with colorful geraniums and shaded by ancient trees. Little France got its name in the 16th century, when sufferers of syphilis were isolated here, to keep them well away from "worthier" citizens.

Cruising down the Ill river – a perfect way to see the city

A DAY IN STRASBOURG

You awake early in the morning, and your time in this wonderful old city is limited. Here's what to do:

Spend an hour or so strolling around the historic center, visiting one of the daily produce markets and taking some photos in the morning light. Bakers and *pâtisserie* (cake) shops will be open, and you may be tempted to nibble on something as you go. Around mid-morning head for the Ill river, near the Palais Rohan, and buy your ticket for one of the 70-minute boat tours of Strasbourg. On the tour you can sit back and listen to the English commentary about the city's history and important monuments. The tour circles the central island, passing churches, fine buildings and flower-hung, timber-framed houses before heading upstream to give you a glimpse of the modernistic glass and steel palaces housing the buildings connected with the European Union.

Head next for the cathedral, timing your visit so that you'll be there at 12:30, when the marvelous astronomical clock (see page 203) swings into action. For lunch there is a wide choice of pretty outdoor eating places. Try a local specialty, such as *tarte flambée* (onion tart) or a beautifully presented *salade composée* (chef's salad).

If you enjoy museums, the afternoon's the time for checking out two of the best. At the top of the list is the Alsation Museum (Musée Alsacien), closely followed by the Gothic treasures in the Museum of the Works of Our Lady (Musée de l'Œuvre Notre-Dame). After this, you may be ready for a drink at a sidewalk café.

Evenings in Strasbourg feature a special dinner in one of the dozens of superb restaurants; be sure to eat a local dish, or follow the set menu, which is bound to be good. Afterward you can go to the movies (in English), a concert, enjoy a folklore display or simply stroll through the atmospheric old streets, and have a nightcap at a music bar. For nightowls, there are discos and clubs that stay open into the early hours.

🛈 Boat tours leave from the landing stage near the Palais Rohan daily on the half-hour 9:30 a.m.–10 p.m., May.–Oct.; 9:30–9, in Apr.; 9:30–5, rest of year. Call Bateaux Strasbourg-Fluvial (☎ 03 88 84 13 13) for details. 💲 $$. Consult the tourist office about the 3-day inclusive "Strasbourg Pass" and for evening events.

GERMANY

" I N Germany one breathes in love of order with the air... "

From the 1900 novel *Three Men on the Bummel* by English writer Jerome K. Jerome

Opposite: Tree-clad gorges and dramatic river views of Bad Schandau, in southern Saxony

Germany

GERMANY

N
NORTH
SEA

GERMANY

Germany

Germany is not easily summed up. Before 1871 there was no single, unified German state: the area was made up of several territories, loosely knit together in alliance. Their local languages and loyalties still have first claim on many Germans' hearts.

After World War II, the country was split between two opposed powers: the West, whose territory was known as the Federal Republic of Germany; and the Soviets, who created the German Democratic Republic (G.D.R.). In 1989, faced with popular protests and a retreating Soviet authority, the G.D.R.'s government opened the Berlin Wall, which had divided the city's eastern and western zones since 1961. A year later the country was reunited, and a new Germany was born. But within its unified political boundaries, this is still a nation of diversity, where the people and cultures vary as dramatically as the landscapes.

MORE TOP DESTINATIONS IN GERMANY

- Bamberg C2 • Berchtesgaden D1
- Bodensee (Lake Constance) B1
- Dresden D3 • Freiburg B1
- Goslar C4 • Hamburg C5
- Heidelberg B2 • Lübeck C5
- Mecklenburgische Seenplatte D4
- Regensburg D2 • Rheintal B2
- Sächsische Schweiz E3 • Trier A2
- Tübingen B1 • Ulm C1

Germany

Traveling in Germany

Germany's 16 administrative states
(*Bundesländer)* extend from the tail of
Denmark south to the Swiss and
Austrian Alps; the Netherlands,
Belgium, Luxembourg and France
border on the west, Poland and the
Czech Republic on the east. Each state
has enough of interest for the visitor to
occupy a whole vacation in its own right,
and Germans are themselves often
tourists in their own country, especially as
westerners and easterners explore each
other's previously unknown territories.

Traveling – by automobile or by
public transportation – is not a problem,
despite the country's size. The road
network in western Germany is excellent,
from the highways (*Autobahnen)* to
minor roads. In the east, roads were in
poorer condition for many years, but
there have been recent improvements.

The biggest culture shock to drivers
is likely to be the speed of traffic. There
is no official upper limit on highways,
and many drivers ignore the
recommended 130 k.p.h., the equivalent
of which is 80 m.p.h. Driving etiquette
is taken seriously, though: you can be
stopped and fined for swearing or
making rude gestures.

Taking the train is a convenient
way to cover large areas. The quickest
and most comfortable trains are the
InterCityExpress (ICE), InterCity (IC)
and EuroCity (EC) trains linking
major centers – but the InterRegio (IR)
trains connecting smaller towns are
also fast.

The North and the Baltic

Northern Germany has a maritime
character. Schleswig-Holstein, a
province Germans and Danes have
often fought over, is made up of two
former dukedoms and shares the
coastline with Lower Saxony. Together
they take in a shore ranging from the
fjords and hills of the Baltic coast to the
wind-lashed North Sea beaches. Inland,
the countryside is wide, rolling
farmland and peat bogs; offshore, the
North Friesian islands are favorite
summer destinations, with beaches and
brisk sea air. The inhabitants of coastal
Friesland have maintained their own
separate culture and language.

Northern Germany's cities were a
force to be reckoned with in the Middle
Ages. In the interests of trade and
power, they banded together to form
the Hanseatic League, a protected
market that monopolized trade between
the North and Baltic seas. The league's
merchants made huge fortunes and had
impressive houses and churches built
in seaports such as Hamburg, Lübeck
and Bremen.

Some of their legacies have survived
– or at least have been rebuilt after the
heavy bombing raids of World War II.
The Gothic/Renaissance architecture of
Bremen's Town Hall and Lübeck's
Music Academy, both converted from
merchant homes, still suggests the
affluence and style of the region's
medieval heyday.

Lower Saxony has many features
that are quintessentially German. Its
historic center, Hannover, is a thriving
commercial city; towns such as
Hildesheim and Wolfenbüttel, the
latter with its painted, half-timbered
facades, have been immaculately
restored after wartime damage.

The winter sports resort of Goslar,
once a silver- and lead-mining town,
has picture-book streets and squares
lined with Gothic, Renaissance and
baroque buildings, some inscribed with
gold lettering, others featuring curving,
sinuous slate roofs. To the east are the
Harz Mountains, on the old East/West
border, where witches are said to
celebrate their Sabbath on
Walpurgisnacht, the eve of May Day.

Sumptuous Renaissance and baroque style draws the crowds to Linderhof Castle in Bavaria

The Rhine

The great 820-mile Rhine flows from the Swiss Alps across the western regions of Germany, through the ancient city of Koblenz and the former seat of West German government, Bonn, and through the industrial country of Ruhr toward Rotterdam. Its valleys and those of its tributaries, the Mosel, Main, Nahe and Neckar, have been producing wines (mainly white) since Roman times. Castles with fairy-tale Gothic towers loom over the river, built for their powerful princes' protection and profit, which was gleaned from tolls on passing river traffic.

On the Lorelei rock, above the twisting Rhine gorge, the beautiful siren Lorelei is said to lure sailors to their death with her enchanting song. This is a romantic, myth-laden part of the country, and a river cruise is one of the most popular ways of seeing it.

The East

After years of restricted travel, border guards and obsessive document checking, eastern Germany is now completely open to visitors. When the Berlin Wall came down, East Germans poured into the West, eager to boost incomes, and some West Germans raised their voices against the sudden influx and resulting unemployment and uneasiness. After the initial euphoria of reunification came the backlash of mutual resentment and offshoots of xenophobia. Integration has pressed on, nevertheless, and financial investment in the east (another grievance to some western taxpayers) has brought new business and better facilities, although there is still a marked difference compared to the affluent west. English is less likely to be spoken here.

One of eastern Germany's highlights is Dresden, which re-created itself after devastation by more than 2,000 Allied

Germany

Bavarian craftsmanship – the astrological clock on the Old Town Hall in Munich

bombers in 1945. Fine 18th-century buildings surround its Brühlsche Terrace, an elevated section on the bank of the Elbe river, and the nearby baroque Zwinger pavilions house a marvelous collection of museums. Leipzig, the famous medieval university town, also is worth visiting, with its pedestrian-only center and attractive gardens and squares.

Weimar, once the home of poet and dramatist Johann Wolfgang von Goethe, composers Franz Liszt and Richard Strauss, and philosopher Friedrich Nietzsche, has a core of lovely historic buildings, parks and boulevards. The gentle hills and red-roofed villages of the Thüringian Forest form a stretch of popular walking country, despite some parts suffering the effects of industrial pollution; the region has a growing industry of family-run lodgings and restaurants.

The Black Forest and Bavaria

Two states make up southern Germany: Baden-Württemberg in the southwest and Bavaria in the southeast. As the name suggests, Baden-Württemberg is itself made up of two distinct areas: mainly Catholic Baden, where the inhabitants are said to be amiable and easy-going, and traditionally Protestant Württemberg (Swabia), where the work ethic is strongly established and the Swabian dialect is spoken.

Lovers of the outdoors flock to the Black Forest (Schwarzwald), a swath of highlands reaching over 3,900 feet and encompassing attractive villages, lush valleys, orchards and meadows as well as woods. Clock-making has been a successful industry here since the 1660s, and cuckoo clocks are on sale at every gift shop. The other notable local product is Black Forest cake – the

Germany

authentic and superior original is called *Schwarzwälder Kirschtorte*.

East of the Black Forest is a range of limestone cliffs and hills known as the Swabian Jura, where castles peer down at the Danube (Donau) river as it begins its long journey to the sea. Pleasant resorts surround the "Swabian Ocean," Lake Constance (Bodensee), which straddles the German-Austrian-Swiss border. The Neckar river flows through Swabia's vineyards and past romantic Heidelberg, where students and tourists really do raise huge beer tankards over tavern tables, as they did in Sigmund Romberg's operetta *The Student Prince*.

Clichés also come true in southern Bavaria. Here the people are characterized by their detractors as loud and brash, and by their admirers as humorous, warm and fun-loving. They are often seen in traditional leather trousers (*Lederhosen*) or embroidered dresses, and are primarily Catholic and conservative: the standard daily greeting here is *"Grüss Gott,"* or "God's greeting."

Between the Bavarian capital, Munich (München), and the magnificent Alpine peaks lie the wooded hills, pretty villages, lakes and castles that attract so many visitors from all over the world to this part of the country. The spectacular Alpine Road takes in the mountain scenery and passes the theatrical 19th-century castles of Linderhof, Herrenchiemsee and Neuschwanstein – all three are almost always packed to the brim with sightseers.

Northern Bavaria has its own character. In fact, not everyone here appreciates being labeled "Bavarian": this is the region known as Franconia (Franken), and its main city is Nuremberg (Nürnberg). Architecture and art come into their own here.

During the late Middle Ages and early Renaissance, artists such as Lucas Cranach and Albrecht Dürer were prominent in Germany, and Nuremberg's wonderful German National Museum displays some of their best work. A more sinister aspect of the city's past is recalled in the giant stadium and Hall of Congress, built for Hitler's mass rallies, and preserved as chilling memorials to that era.

The hugely popular Romantic Road, running from ancient Würzburg and the Franconian wine country all the way to the Alps, 217 miles south, links several unspoiled medieval towns. On the way, it passes Rothenburg ob der Tauber, one of the loveliest old towns in Germany – and as a result one of the most crowded. Also on the route are the old walled, half-timbered town of Dinkelsbühl and the splendid Renaissance city of Augsburg.

Spa Towns

Health and fitness are national preoccupations, apparent in the German love of soccer, skiing and tennis, and in the spa towns that thrive all over the country. At these spas Germans reap the benefits of medicinal waters and enjoy the other facilities, which can include mud baths, saunas and steam treatments.

Germany's oldest casino is one of the features of Baden-Baden, a celebrated spa town with graceful 19th-century hotels. Other spas also are worth investigating. Bad Ems, in the Rhineland's picturesque Lahn valley, was 19th-century ruler Kaiser Wilhelm's personal favorite. A steam train travels from Bad Doberan, near Rostock in eastern Germany, to the country's oldest seaside resort, Ostseebad Heiligendamm, founded in 1793. Bad Kissingen, Bavaria's most popular spa, is on the banks of the Saale river.

Germany

TIMELINE

800–700 BC	Celtic tribes settle around the Rhineland.
AD 800	Franks overrun the territory; Charlemagne, the Frankish king, is crowned Holy Roman Emperor.
1273	Rudolf of Habsburg is elected king, founding the 600-year Habsburg dynasty.
1517	Martin Luther precipitates the Reformation.
1740	Frederick the Great is crowned king of Prussia.
1871	Franco-Prussian War ends with states united under the Prussian Kaiser Wilhelm and chancellor, Otto von Bismarck.
1914–19	Habsburg claims to the Balkans lead to World War I; the Treaty of Versailles demands huge war reparations and surrender of territories from defeated Germany.
1930	The Nazis gain power in elections.
1933	Adolf Hitler is made chancellor; under Hitler's dictatorship, millions of Jews and minorities are persecuted and killed.
1939	Hitler invades Poland; Britain and France declare war.
1945	Allied forces enter Berlin; Hitler kills himself.
1949	Western occupying powers create the Federal Republic of Germany; Russia forms the German Democratic Republic.
1961	The Berlin Wall is built.
1990	A year after the demolition of the wall, East and West Germany reunite; Germany leads support for a politically and economically integrated European Union.
1999	Government moves to Berlin. Parliament meets in the newly refurbished, glass-domed Reichstag.

MAD KING LUDWIG

Ludwig II of Bavaria lost all interest in running his kingdom after it was drawn first into war and then into the German Empire by the Prussian Chancellor, Otto von Bismarck. The late 19th-century ruler was left with nothing to do but amuse himself, which he did by having three flamboyant castles built – Herrenchiemsee, Linderhof and Neuschwanstein – and watching them take shape through his telescope. Ludwig found other ways to spend his money, too, supporting Richard Wagner while he wrote his operas, but eventually he ran out of cash altogether. This and his eccentric manner made him an increasing liability to the Bavarian government. Its ministers plotted with Ludwig's uncle Luitpold to depose him and certify him insane. Only days later, Ludwig and his doctor drowned in the Starnberger See, a boating lake near Munich – whether by accident or design, no one knows.

SURVIVAL GUIDE

- Formality is important to Germans. Don't address people by their first names unless invited to; always use *Herr* (Sir) or *Frau* (Madam) at first.
- Job titles are used frequently in social exchange; doctors, for instance, are addressed as *Frau Doktor* or *Herr Doktor*.
- Local dishes, particularly in southern Bavaria, use the classic German ingredients of *Sauerkraut* (pickled cabbage), *Wurst* (sausage), dumplings, pork and potatoes. German cooking (*Gutbürgerliche Küche*) can be sampled at a *Gasthaus*, a restaurant serving simple meals.
- German wine is mainly white. *Tafelwein* is table wine, less expensive and harsher than the quality stuff; *Deutscher Tafelwein* is guaranteed to be wholly German, rather than a mix of different countries' grapes. *Qualitätswein* is the better product, from a specified range of vineyards. Some of the best grapes are *Riesling*, the fruity *Müller-Thurgau* and the spicy *Gewürztraminer*.
- Brewing is big business in Germany. *Bock* is a strong beer, light or dark, popular in Bavaria; *Weissbier* is pale wheat beer; and *Malz*, an unfermented black malt beer.
- *Imbiss* (snack) stands are found everywhere and sell hamburgers, meatballs, sausages and other fast food.
- Stores in the main cities are usually open from 9 or 9:30 a.m. until 7 or 8 p.m. Few close on Saturday afternoons, but some stay open until 6 p.m.
- Germany has a long tradition of toy-making, particularly china dolls and the famous Steiff teddy bears.
- Beer and wine festivals take place all over the country. Munich's September/October *Oktoberfest* is the best known, and the *Weinfeste*, celebrations held in the Rhine-Mosel area, also are worth attending.
- Dinkelsbühl's 10-day *Kinderzeche* festival, held in July, recalls the Thirty Years' War, when local children persuaded Swedish soldiers not to ransack their town. It features plays, a pageant and the boys' battalion, the *Knabenbataillon*, dressed in 18th-century military garb.
- The music of Richard Wagner is performed in the summer *Bayreuth Festival*, northeast of Nuremberg near the composer's former home. Tickets are snapped up a year in advance, and must be reserved by mail; for information and an application form contact Bayreuther Festspiele, Festspielhügel-Kartenbüro, Postfach 100262, 95402 Bayreuth, Germany, ☎ 0921 7878-0; www.bayreuther-festspiele.de. The order must be sent by Oct. 15.

Traditionally decorated beer mugs

Germany

Berlin

BERLIN

No other city better illustrates the upheaval in late 20th-century Europe than Berlin. For nearly 30 years it was, for all intents and purposes, two cities. Tourists posed on the Western side of the Berlin Wall, and those who crossed the East–West boundary at Checkpoint Charlie did so with the trepidation of travelers to another planet.

Then, in 1989, Berlin changed virtually overnight. The wall has all but vanished; Checkpoint Charlie is a museum; the No Man's Land that lay between the two zones is now the site of a new complex of ministries, offices, stores and hotels, providing facilities for the German parliament and government. Reunified Berlin is an exciting, restless place, reinventing itself at a fast pace.

Berlin Flavors

There are many restaurants and cafés in Berlin, serving every imaginable kind of food. The most popular restaurant areas are around Savignyplatz and Hardenbergstrasse and on the Ku'damm, and all buzz late into the night. Berlin has a larger Turkish community than any other city outside Turkey, and many live in the old quarter of Kreuzberg, where inexpensive Turkish meals are served in dozens of restaurants, especially in the neighborhood of Kottbusser Tor.

Kaffee und Kuchen (coffee and cakes) is an institution, usually indulged at about 4 p.m., but it doesn't come cheap. The café that started it all – Café Kranzler, which opened in 1835 – still operates on the Ku'damm.

Heavy, hearty German food can be sampled all over the city, in restaurants or in a tavern (*Kneipe*). There are more than 4,000 taverns, many offering *Hackepeter* (meatloaf), *Aal grün* (eel in parsley sauce) and *Solei* (pickled eggs).

If you find the traditional fare daunting, try the lighter new German cuisine (*neue Deutsche Küche*) at restaurants such as Trio, on Klausenerplatz.

Beer is, of course, a favorite beverage. One custom is to have a *Korn* – a light beer with a *Schnapps* chaser; another, a summer choice, is *Berliner Weisse mit Schuss*, light beer turned pink with raspberry liqueur or green with extract of woodruff.

Berlin

Music and Cabaret

In the 1920s Berlin had a reputation for "divine decadence," as portrayed in the 1972 film *Cabaret*. The cabaret tradition has been revived, albeit in a milder form, and there are clubs all over the city; there also are folk, jazz and other music venues. For the latest details consult *Berlin Tut Gut* (from tourist offices), which has English-language listings, or the *Berlin Das Magazin* (*Berlin – The Magazine*, published three times a year). The busiest district for entertainment is in Scheunenviertel.

The Berlin Philharmonic, perhaps the world's best-known orchestra, has its home at the Philharmonie, in the Kulturforum, a complex of concert halls and museums near Potsdamer Strasse. The Berlin Symphony Orchestra performs in the 19th-century Konzerthaus Berlin (Berlin Concert

House), at Gendarmenmarkt. Berlin's oldest opera house (built 1743) is the Staatsoper (State Opera), a fine baroque concert hall on Unter den Linden – its glittering list of past directors includes Felix Mendelssohn Bartholdy.

Store of the West

One of Europe's biggest department stores – second only to Harrods of London – is found in Berlin: the KaDeWe (Kaufhaus des Westens, or Store of the West), on Tauentzienstrasse, is open Mon.–Fri. 10–8, Sat. 9:30–8.

A branch of the Paris flagship, Galeries Lafayette, is on Friedrichstrasse, near the designer shops on the same street. In the leisure and shopping complex Europa-Center, not far from KaDeWe, there are 99 stores, cafés and bars.

Berlin porcelain makes a perfect souvenir. It's been produced here since 1763, when the Royal Porcelain Factory (K.P.M.; for tours call 030 390 090) opened, and the factory's main store is on the Ku'damm.

Street markets flourish in this city; on weekends try Tiergarten, Am Zeughaus or John F.-Kennedy-Platz, and the popular Saturday morning Winterfeldmarkt on Winterfeldtplatz is a lively affair.

Berlin Classicism

Sculptor, painter, set designer and architect Karl Friedrich Schinkel left his mark all over Berlin. After designing the Prussians' military medal, the Iron Cross, he was commissioned to create a series of civic buildings, including the National Theater, the museums on Museum Island and St. Nicholas' Church in Potsdam. He mixed his own Romantic tastes with the royally approved Classical style to form "Berlin Classicism," and gave his undivided attention to every detail, right down to the doorknobs.

ESSENTIAL INFORMATION

TOURIST INFORMATION
Berlin Tourismus Marketing GmbH (Berlin Tourist Marketing Board)
• Europa-Center, Budapester Strasse 45
• Brandenburger Tor (Brandenburg Gate), Pariser Platz
• Fernsehturm (TV-Tower), Alexanderplatz, Panoramastrasse 1A
• ☎ 030 25 00 25, 00 49 30 25 00 25 (from abroaad), fax 030 25 00 24 24, www.berlin-tourist-information.de

URBAN TRANSPORTATION
There are two city rail networks: the subway (U-Bahn) and the city railroad (S-Bahn), and tickets are interchangeable. The S-Bahn is marked on the Berlin city map as an "S" in a red circle. Buy tickets (valid for all forms of transport) in the station foyer and validate them in the machine on the platform. Trains run daily 5 a.m.–12:30

a.m.; U-Bahn lines 9 and 12 and S-Bahn line 7 run all night Friday and Saturday. Bus route 100 runs through the center from Bahnhof Zoo (Zoo station) in the west to Unter den Linden in the east. The main bus terminal is Funkturm (☎ 030 3010 0171). Trams are mainly confined to eastern parts of the city. Taxi stands are all over the city. Use only metered cabs (☎ 030 261 026 or 030 210 101).

AIRPORT INFORMATION
Berlin has three international airports: Tegel (northwest), Schönefeld (southeast) and Tempelhof (south). Bus 109 runs from Tegel to Zoologischer Garten. From Schönefeld S-Bahn lines 9 and 45 and from Tempelhof U-Bahn line 6 all run to the city center. For airport information ☎ 0180 500 0186.

CLIMATE – average highs and lows for the month

JAN.	FEB.	MAR.	APR.	MAY	JUN.	JUL.	AUG.	SEP.	OCT.	NOV.	DEC.
2°C	3°C	8°C	12°C	18°C	21°C	23°C	23°C	18°C	13°C	7°C	3°C
36°F	37°F	46°F	54°F	64°F	70°F	73°F	73°F	64°F	55°F	45°F	37°F
-3°C	-3°C	0°C	2°C	7°C	11°C	13°C	13°C	10°C	5°C	2°C	-1°C
27°F	27°F	32°F	36°F	45°F	52°F	55°F	55°F	50°F	41°F	36°F	30°F

Berlin

CITY SIGHTS

Key to symbols

⊞ map coordinates refer to the Berlin map on pages 216–217; sights below are highlighted in yellow on the map. ✉ address or location ☎ telephone number ⊙ opening times Ⓜ nearest subway 🚌 nearest bus or tram route 🍴 restaurant or café on site or nearby 💵 admission charge: $$$ more than €4, $$ €2–€4, $ less than €2 ℹ other relevant information

ALEXANDERPLATZ

⊞ E3 ✉ Alexanderplatz ☎ Fernsehturm: 030 242 3333. St. Marien-Kirche: 030 242 4467 ⊙ Fernsehturm: daily 9 a.m.–1 a.m., Mar.–Oct.; 10 a.m.–midnight, rest of year. St. Marien-Kirche: Mon.–Thu. 10–4, Sat.–Sun. noon–4 🍴 Zum Nussbaum, see page 554, or restaurant in Fernsehturm Ⓜ U-Bahn/S-Bahn to Alexanderplatz 🚌 100, 157, 148, 348, TXL; tram 2, 3, 4, 5, 6, N54, N92 💵 Fernsehturm $$$; St. Marien-Kirche: free ℹ St. Marien-Kirche: guided tours Mon.–Tue. at 1, Sun. at noon

Alexanderplatz, the marketplace known to Berliners as "Alex," was the heart of the old city. Rebuilt after World War II in a bleak style, it is now scheduled for renovations. Two old buildings have survived: the Rotes Rathaus (Red City Hall), built from 1861 to 1869 in Italian Renaissance style; and the St. Marien-Kirche (St. Mary's Church), built from 1270 to 1340 and Berlin's second-oldest parish church. At the center of the square, Fernsehturm, a 1,207-foot television tower, includes a revolving restaurant and a viewing platform at the top.

BAUHAUS-ARCHIV

⊞ C2 ✉ Klingelhöferstrasse 14 ☎ 030 254 0020 ⊙ Wed.–Mon. 10–5 🍴 Café on site Ⓜ U-Bahn to Nollendorfplatz 🚌 100, 129, 187, 341 💵 $$

After World War I Walter Gropius founded an architectural movement in Weimar, stressing function above beauty and encouraging collaboration between art and industry. The Bauhaus (Building House) school greatly influenced 20th-century design, but was condemned by the Nazis and eventually closed in Berlin in 1933. The Gropius-designed Bauhaus-Archiv (Bauhaus Archive), built in 1979, shows examples of the style – from chairs to models of buildings – and explains the aims of the Bauhaus artists.

Symbol of reconciliation – East meets West at the Brandenburg Gate

BERLINER DOM

⊞ D2 ✉ Am Lustgarten ☎ 030 2026 9119 ⊙ Mon.–Sat. 9–8, Sun. noon–8 🍴 Restaurant in Fernsehturm, see page 554 Ⓜ U-Bahn/S-Bahn to Alexanderplatz; S-Bahn to Hackescher Markt 🚌 100, 200, 348; tram 1, 2, 3, 4, 5, 6, 13, 15, 53 💵 $$$ (guided dome tour extra) ℹ Guided tours of dome: for information www.berliner-dom.de

Berliner Dom, Berlin's Protestant Cathedral, completed in 1905, is a monument to imperial wealth and power and contains approximately 90 sarcophagi and tombs of the royal Hohenzollern dynasty in its vault.

BRANDENBURGER TOR

⊞ D2 ✉ Pariser Platz 🍴 Borchardt, see page 554 Ⓜ S-Bahn to Unter den Linden 🚌 100, 200, 348

Built from 1788 to 1791 as an "arch of peace," the Brandenburger Tor (Brandenburg Gate) was modeled after the entrance to the Acropolis temple in Athens. A sculpture of the goddess Viktoria and her chariot, added to the top in 1789–93, was stolen by Napoleon in 1806. On its return, Karl Friedrich Schinkel added a triumphal wreath and iron cross to the goddess' staff. During the East-West split, it stood in No Man's Land. Now a symbol of reconciliation, it forms a backdrop for pop concerts.

A Henry Moore sculpture at the Kulturforum

HAUS AM CHECKPOINT CHARLIE

✚ D2 ✉ Friedrichstrasse 43–45 ☎ 030 253 7250
🕐 Mauermuseum: daily 9 a.m.–10 p.m. 🍴 Café on
site 🚇 U-Bahn to Kochstrasse, Stadtmitte 🚌 129
✋ $$$

The crossing point of the Berlin Wall,
known as Haus am Checkpoint Charlie
(House at Checkpoint Charlie), is now a
tourist attraction. The Eastern border
guards' hut was taken down in 1990 and
moved to the Deutsches Historisches
Museum on Unter den Linden. The site has
a display (Mauermuseum) of paraphernalia
and photographs illustrating the effects of
the wall and various escape attempts. A
video on the history of the wall includes
a look at the graffiti artists who decorated
the Western side.

KAISER-WILHELM-GEDÄCHTNIS-KIRCHE

✚ B2 ✉ Breitscheidplatz ☎ 030 218 5023
🕐 Church: daily 9–7; Memorial Hall and Ruined Tower:
Mon.–Sat. 10–4 🍴 Berliner Stube, see page 554
🚇 U-Bahn/S-Bahn to Zoologischer Garten; U-Bahn to
Kurfürstendamm 🚌 100, 109, 145, 146, 149, 200, 204,
245, 249, 349 ✋ Free

The landmark Kaiser-Wilhelm-
Gedächtnis-Kirche (Kaiser William
Memorial Church) is worth visiting as a
memorial to the devastation of World War
II. The 19th-century Romanesque hall was
all that remained of Kaiser Wilhelm II's
church after the 1943 air raids; it has been
left as it was, and a modern octagonal chapel
and hexagonal blue stained-glass tower were

added to it from 1959 to 1961. Inside, the
church displays a cross of nails donated by
Coventry, in Britain – another city
devastated by bombs.

KULTURFORUM

✚ C2 ✉ Gemäldegalerie and Kunstgewerbemuseum:
Matthäikirchplatz. Musikinstrumenten-Museum:
Tiergartenstrasse 1. Neue Nationalgalerie: Potsdamer
Strasse 50 ☎ Gemäldegalerie: 030 266 2951;
Musikinstrumenten-Museum: 030 254 81-0
🕐 Gemäldegalerie: Tue.–Sun. 10–6 (also Thu. 6–10
p.m.); Kunstgewerbemuseum: Tue.–Fri. 10–6, Sat.–Sun.
11–6; Musikinstrumenten-Museum: Tue.–Fri. 10–6,
Sat.–Sun. 10–5; Neue Nationalgalerie: Tue.–Fri. 10–6
(also Thu. 6–10 p.m.), Sat.–Sun. 11–6 🍴 Cafés on site
🚇 U-Bahn/S-Bahn to Potsdamer Platz; U-Bahn to
Mendelssohn-Bartholdy-Park 🚌 129, 148, 200, 248,
348 ✋ Gemäldegalerie, Kunstgewerbemuseum and
Neue Nationalgalerie $$$ (3-day ticket for all state
museums); Musikinstrumenten-Museum $$;
Gemäldegalerie free to all Thu. 6–10 p.m.

This complex of galleries, halls and
museums, all angles and curves, was designed
in the 1960s. The Gemäldegalerie (Picture
Gallery) displays European art from the
13th to the 18th centuries; look for works by
16th-century Dutch master Pieter Brueghel
and the collection of Italian Renaissance art.
The glass-and-steel Neue Nationalgalerie
(New National Gallery) includes works by
Salvador Dalí, Paul Klee and others.

A highlight of the Kulturforum
complex (built 1978–85) is the
Kunstgewerbemuseum (Arts and Crafts
Museum), where gold, silver, glass,
porcelain and jeweled arts and crafts are
displayed. The star item is the eighth-
century Burse Reliquary, a casket
glittering with silver, pearls, gems and
gold inlay. Next door to the Philharmonie
und Kammermusiksaal der Philharmonie,
the Musikinstrumenten-Museum
(Museum of Musical Instruments) has
everything from ancient bagpipes to
synthesizers.

MUSEUMSINSEL

✚ D3 ✉ Museumsinsel ☎ 030 2090 5577 🕐 Tue.–
Sun. 10–6 (also Thu. 6–10 p.m.) 🍴 Borchardt, see
page 554 🚇 U-Bahn/S-Bahn to Friedrichstrasse;
S-Bahn to Hackescher Markt 🚌 100, 147, 200, 348;

THE BERLIN WALL

On August 13, 1961, the German Democratic Republic began work on an "Anti-Fascist Protection Wall." Relations between the Eastern and Western sectors of Berlin had never been easy. The Soviets closed off their access routes in 1948, so supplies had to be flown in from the West in a year-long airlift. There had been popular protests against the Soviet authorities, and a steady exodus of East Berliners to the West. Finally the Eastern government decided to mark its boundary with bricks and barbed wire.

The border was based on a 1920 map of Berlin, and this was the course taken by the wall, without regard for any houses, or streets that might be in the way. The houses on Bernauer Strasse (Bernauer Street), which happened to be on the route, became part of the barrier, and their exits were bricked up. Residents tried to jump to freedom from the upper windows; 20 people were shot down. One guard took a last opportunity to leap over the temporary barbed wire entanglement when the wall was under construction. Those who didn't make it across were cut off from the West and from their friends and families as the 13-foot barricade took shape.

After the escape of 30 people through a tunnel from a bakery cellar in 1964, a large part of Bernauer Street was demolished, and a No Man's Land was created, guarded by dogs and 302 watchtowers. Booby traps were sunk into the Teltow canal, at the point where the border crossed the Spree river, after Günter Litfin was shot trying to swim his way to the West, on August 24, 1961. As the restrictions increased, the escapes grew more daring. One steamship's crew got the

Ray of hope – a segment of the Berlin Wall (top) and colorful fragments after its demolition in 1989

captain drunk and shut him in his cabin before sailing to the western bank. A homemade hot-air balloon was used to float over the wall. But the risks were very high: 239 people were killed in these attempts, including 25 guards.

At 9:15 p.m. on November 9, 1989, under pressure from an increasingly impatient crowd, border guards lifted the barriers and let Easterners cross the border freely for the first time since 1961. Fittingly, the first to cross were residents of Bernauer Street.

tram 1, 2, 3, 4, 5, 6, 7, 13, 52, 53   🎫 $$$ (3-day ticket for all state museums); Thu. 6–10 free

The first of a group of imposing museum buildings was begun on an island in the Spree river in 1830. In 1841, Frederick William IV designated the area a "space for art and science," and now many of Berlin's antiquities, dispersed during World War II, are being brought together for display in the complex. Altes Museum (Old Museum) was restored after its destruction in 1943. It is being stocked with ancient sculpture and art, as is the Pergamonmuseum, whose main exhibit is the 52-foot Pergamon Altar, from a 164 BC royal temple in Bergama, Turkey. The Bode Museum (closed until Oct. 2006) displays medieval sculpture, art and coins, while 19th-century German art is in the Alte Nationalgalerie (Old National Gallery). The Neues Museum (New Museum) presents the history of humankind; it is currently being restored and is scheduled to reopen in 2010.

SCHLOSS CHARLOTTENBURG

➕ A3   ✉ Luisenplatz   ☎ 030 320 911   🕐 Old Palace: Tue.–Fri. 9–5, Sat.–Sun. 10–5; New Wing: Tue.–Fri. 10–6, Sat.–Sun. 11–6   🍴 Alt Luxemburg, see page 553   🚇 U-Bahn to Richard-Wagner-Platz or Sophie-Charlotte-Platz; S-Bahn to Westend   🚌 145, 210   🎫 Combination ticket for all buildings $$$

When work started on the Schloss Charlottenburg (Charlottenburg Palace) in 1695, it was designed as a rural home for Sophie-Charlotte, wife of the future King Frederick I of Prussia. Over the next 100 years it grew into a sprawling palace with royal apartments, dazzling rooms such as the

Statue of Frederick the Great on Unter den Linden

White Hall and Golden Gallery, and gardens in formal French and landscaped English style, sloping down toward the Spree river.

TIERGARTEN

➕ C2   ✉ Surrounds of Strasse des 17 Juni   🚇 S-Bahn to Tiergarten   🚌 TXL, 100, 123, 200, 248, 341

Once a hunting ground well stocked with boar and deer, the Tiergarten (Animal Garden) is a 524-acre park in the center of the city, with woodlands, lakes and waterways, gardens and open-air concerts. Landscaping first began in 1818. The park is divided by the wide avenue Strasse des 17 Juni, where an 1873 Siegessäule (victory column) crowned with a golden goddess commemorates Prussian successes against Denmark, Austria and France.

TOPOGRAPHIE DES TERRORS

➕ D2   ✉ Niederkirchnerstrasse 8   ☎ 030 2548 6703   🕐 Daily 10–8, May–Sep.; 10–6, rest of year   🚇 U-Bahn/S-Bahn to Potsdamer Platz; S-Bahn to Anhalter Bahnhof   🚌 129, 248, 341   🎫 Free

The grim Topographie des Terrors (Topography of Terror) occupies the site of the former Nazi secret police headquarters, where prisoners were interrogated and tortured. Photographs trace the emergence of Nazism, and a nearby viewing platform overlooks the enormous Regierungsviertel (Government Quarter), where the Third Reich had its administrative offices.

UNTER DEN LINDEN

➕ D2   ✉ Deutches Historiches Museum: Unter den Linden 2   ☎ Museum: 030 203 040   🕐 Museum: Daily 10–6   🍴 Borchardt, see page 554   🚇 S/U-Bahn Friedrichstrasse   🚌 100, 157, 200, 348; tram 2, 3, 4, 5, 6   🎫 Museum $$

Unter den Linden (Under the Lime Trees) was laid out in 1648 as a route to the Tiergarten. It runs from the Brandenburg Gate to Museum Island and the river, and is lined with baroque and neoclassic buildings. The 1695 Zeughaus (Arsenal) houses the Deutsches Historisches Museum (German History Museum). An equestrian statue of Frederick the Great at the eastern end was turned by the Communist regime to ride toward the East rather than the West.

Popular day trip – the extravagant Sanssouci Palace, where Frederick the Great spent his summers

AN EXCURSION TO POTSDAM

Visits to several palaces can be combined on a trip to Potsdam, southwest of Berlin. The setting for the 1945 Potsdam Conference, at which Allied leaders redrew the European map, is Cecilienhof Palace (Schloss Cecilienhof), a mock-Tudor 1916 building now partly used as a hotel. It was built for Kaiser Wilhelm II; although his nation was two years into a war with Britain, the Kaiser chose to have it built in the style of an English country house. The royal Hohenzollern family lived here until 1945. The conference hall, delegates' studies and the reception rooms used by Churchill, Truman and Stalin are unchanged and can all be seen.

The palace that really draws crowds to Potsdam is the Sanssouci Palace (Schloss Sanssouci), on the town's western outskirts. This summer retreat was where Frederick the Great could enjoy life "without care" (*sans souci*). A green dome tops the single-story, yellow rococo facade; inside the richly furnished rooms are full of artworks and ornaments. Sanssouci Park has lovely gardens, an 18th-century Chinese teahouse and the third Potsdam palace: Frederick's New Palace (Neues Palais), with its vast marble hall and indoor grotto decorated with shells.

The town of Potsdam also is worth seeing. St. Nicholas' Church (Nikolaikirche) is one of Karl Friedrich Schinkel's classical monuments. In the Old Town, sculptures of rearing horses mark the site of the former royal stables, and the 17th-century Marstall building is now a movie museum. Built in 1732, the New Town became the focus of Potsdam's exiled French Huguenot (Protestant) community. Some redbrick, gabled houses survive in the Dutch Quarter; they were built for Dutch construction workers who came to build the New Town.

☎ Cecilienhof Palace, Sanssouci Palace and New Palace: 0331 969 4200 🕐 Cecilienhof and Sanssouci Palaces: Tue.–Sun. 9–5, Apr.–Oct.; 9–4, rest of year; Sanssouci Park: daily dawn–dusk; New Palace: Sat.–Thu. 9–5, Apr.–Oct.; 10–4, rest of year 🚌 692, 695 or the S-Bahn (Potsdam Stadt). Tour operators in Berlin offer day trips by bus (inquire at the tourist office) 🎟 Cecilienhof Palace $$; Sanssouci Palace $$$ (guided tour only); New Palace $$

Surrounded by soaring spires and shaded by trees, Cologne's cafés serve a variety of delicious fare

COLOGNE

The two spires of Cologne (Köln) Cathedral soar above the Rhine, reminders of its past glory as a center of pilgrimage and the biggest city in medieval Germany. Despite the destruction of most of its central core in World War II, the city has retained and restored considerable evidence of its long and distinguished past. Today Cologne is thriving again, in business, trade, the arts and education, and its renowned sense of fun adds to the character that makes this one of Germany's most attractive cities.

Old Town

Cologne's Old Town (Altstadt) forms a vast semicircle on the west bank of the Rhine (Rhein) river, hemmed in by the Ring, a long boulevard that changes names along its route. It extends along the line of the former city fortifications and passes the old city gates of Eigelsteintor, Hahnentor and St. Severinstor. Within this area, the Cathedral (Dom, see page 227) is the main attraction and, in fact, the most visited monument in Germany. The railroad station and a group of major museums are within easy reach of it.

The Gothic-Renaissance Town Hall (Rathaus, see page 228) stands at the heart of the Old Town, just south of the Old Market Square; to the east, toward the river, is the 12th-century church of Gross St. Martin (see page 227), one of 12 wonderful pre-Gothic churches still standing in the city. These sights form the old core. Head across the river via the bridges Deutzer Brücke or Hohenzollern Brücke for a look back at an unrivaled view of historic Cologne.

Cafés and Taverns

There are 24 breweries here, more than in any other German city. All produce the local beer, *Kölsch*, which is light and clear and served in tall, slim glasses. Beer halls, known in the local dialect as *Weetschaften*, also serve food at very reasonable prices. Specialties at these establishments include rolls with cheese (*Halve Hahn*) or rye bread with black sausage (*Kölsche Kaviar*).

You will find plenty of restaurants in the historic center, ranging from the traditional *Gasthaus* (tavern) to trendy bistros, and the range of cuisines includes Japanese, French, Burmese, Chinese, Turkish and East European. Wine bars and cellars are another source of refreshment, serving some of the excellent wines from the Rhine valley. There are many cafés in which to stop for the ubiquitious *Kaffee und Kuchen* (coffee and cakes).

Karneval and Concerts

To see Cologne at its most boisterous, come before Easter for Carnival (*Karneval*) week. Precise dates change every year, but the fun always reaches its peak before Ash Wednesday, in

Cologne

time for the abstinence of Lent. On the Thursday before the seventh Sunday prior to Easter, the festival begins in a morning ceremony at Alter Markt (Old Market Square), and everyone gears up for the three "Crazy Days" (*Tolle Tage*) – Thursday, Sunday and Monday. There are costume balls at night, and more informal revelry on the streets and in the taverns. On Sunday there's a procession of floats, and on Monday a spectacular parade provides the lively and colorful climax.

For the rest of the year, there is a choice of calmer entertainment at the city's main cultural centers. Concerts are performed at the Philharmonie, in the Wallraf-Richartz/Ludwig museums building on Bischofsgartenstrasse. Other concerts take place regularly in

Cologne

the city's churches, and are usually free. Opera is staged at the Opernhaus. Cologne has a famous puppet theater – the Puppenspiele – but dialogue is in the local *Kölsch* dialect.

Listings for movies, theater and concerts are published in the magazines *Kölner Illustrierte* and *StadtRevue*, *Köln-Magazin*. Nightclubs and discos are concentrated on the streets around Gross St. Martin; in the St. Severin quarter, Südstadt; and in the university quarter – the Quartier Lateng, in the southwest part of the city.

Eau de Cologne

Probably the most appropriate souvenir to take home from Cologne is a bottle of *eau de Cologne*, first distilled from flower blossoms in the 18th century and intended as an aphrodisiac. Known here as *Kölnisch Wasser*, it's made by about 20 businesses, including one of the originals, Farina, which has been in operation since 1709. Stores all over the city sell it, but the Old Town is the best place to browse for gifts. An all-day market takes place Friday in Old Market Square. On spring weekends (April and May) the same square is completely taken over by hundreds of flower stalls. Wine markets set up in New Market in May and late June. Just before Lent Cologne celebrates Carnival, and all shops close during the "Crazy Days."

Crazy Days

On the first of the Crazy Days (*Tolle Tage*) of Carnival, a procession takes place based on the local legend of Jan and Griet. Jan von Werth worked for a farmer and was very much in love with Griet, who refused him, hoping to find a wealthy husband. In desperation, Jan went off to fight in the Thirty Years War. However, he came back many years later as a highly honored hero who went on to become a general.

ESSENTIAL INFORMATION

TOURIST INFORMATION
Köln Tourismus (Cologne Tourist Office)
• Unter Fettenhennen 19, in front of the cathedral ☎ 0221 30400; fax 0221 2213 0410; www.koelntourismus.de

URBAN TRANSPORTATION
Cologne has an integrated transportation system. Trams travel through the Old Town, some above ground (east–west lines), some underground (north-south lines); they also share some lines with freight trains. Subway stations are marked on the Cologne city map by the letter "U" in a red circle. Tickets are sold individually or for groups of up to

5 persons (valid 9 a.m.–3 a.m.); you can also buy a 7-day travel card. The bus and railroad stations are next to the cathedral. For information call Cologne transportation information, ☎ 0180 350 4030.

AIRPORT INFORMATION
The Cologne/Bonn airport is 20 minutes by bus from the city center. Bus 170 travels to and from the airport and the main railroad station every 15 or 30 minutes daily 5:30 a.m.–11:45 p.m. Suburban (S-Bahn) trains operate from the airport to the city center, and InterCity-Express (ICE) trains take passengers to destinations across Germany. Taxis operate from the airport to the city center. For flight information, call ☎ 02203 400 (24 hours).

CLIMATE – average highs and lows for the month

JAN.	FEB.	MAR.	APR.	MAY	JUN.	JUL.	AUG.	SEP.	OCT.	NOV.	DEC.
3°C	4°C	10°C	14°C	19°C	22°C	24°C	24°C	20°C	14°C	8°C	3°C
37°F	39°F	50°F	57°F	66°F	72°F	75°F	75°F	68°F	57°F	46°F	37°F
-2°C	-2°C	0°C	4°C	8°C	12°C	14°C	13°C	10°C	6°C	3°C	0°C
28°F	28°F	32°F	39°F	46°F	54°F	57°F	55°F	50°F	43°F	37°F	32°F

CITY SIGHTS

Key to symbols

🔲 map coordinates refer to the Cologne map on page 225; sights below are highlighted in yellow on the map.
🔲 address or location 🔲 telephone number 🔲 opening times 🔲 nearest subway 🔲 nearest bus or tram route 🔲 restaurant or café on site or nearby 🔲 admission charge: $$$ more than €4, $$ €2–€4, $ less than €2 🔲 other relevant information

DOM

🔲 B3 🔲 Am Hof 🔲 Cathedral: 0221 9258 47-30; Treasure Chamber: 0221 2728 0-10 🔲 Cathedral: daily 6 a.m.–7:30 p.m. Treasure Chamber: daily 10–6. Tower: daily 9–6, May–Sep.; 9–5, Mar.–Apr. and Oct.; 9–4, rest of year 🔲 Brauhaus Sion, see page 554 🔲 Lines 5, 12, 16, 18 to Dom/Hbf 🔲 Cathedral free (guided tours $$$); Treasure Chamber $$; Tower $

It took more than 600 years to complete the Dom (Cathedral), a Gothic masterpiece that incorporated the original architects' plans right to the end. The purpose of the project (begun in 1248) was to provide an appropriately grand setting for the relics of the Three Magi, which were snatched from Milan and kept here in a golden shrine. The final result is majestic, with intricately worked masonry serving to lighten the great mass of the facade and the two 515-foot spires – at the time they were built, the tallest structures in the world.

The golden shrine is, of course, the main focus of the interior, but there are many other treasures. In the south ambulatory chapel, the altarpiece of the *Adoration of the Magi* is a superb work by Stefan Lochner, one of the 15th-century artists of the Cologne School. In the north chapel is the 11th-century Gero Crucifix. One of the church's most inspiring features is the stained glass, ranging from the 13th-century Bible Window in the ambulatory to the Bavarian windows in the nave, donated by King Ludwig I in the 19th century.

GROSS ST. MARTIN

🔲 B3/C3 🔲 An Gross St. Martin 🔲 0221 1642 5650 🔲 Mon.–Fri. 10:15–6, Sat. 10–12:30 and 1:30–6, Sun.

The glorious Gero Crucifix in Cologne Cathedral

2–4 🔲 Päffgen in der Altstadt, see page 555 🔲 Lines 5, 12, 16, 18 to Dom/Hbf 🔲 Tram 7, 9 to Heumarkt 🔲 Free

From its consecration in 1172 until the 19th century, the church of Gross St. Martin was the most distinctive feature of Cologne's skyline. Its tower, with four turrets at the corners, makes an interesting contrast to the lacy stonework of the cathedral's spires. Originally this was a monastery church, built for Benedictine monks from Ireland and Scotland.

MUSEUM FÜR ANGEWANDTE KUNST

🔲 B3 🔲 An der Rechtschule 🔲 0221 2212 3860 🔲 Tue.–Sun. 11–5 🔲 Lines 5, 12, 16, 18 to Dom/Hbf 🔲 Café 🔲 $$$

The Museum für Angewandte Kunst (Museum of Applied Art) has an exquisite collection of applied arts ranging from medieval to contemporary times. One of the most interesting pieces is the Nikolaus Kanne, created around 1660 in Hamburg. There is also a fine collection of art nouveau works.

Museum Schnütgen

✚ B2 ✉ Cäcilienstrasse 29 ☎ 0221 2212 3620
🕐 Tue.–Fri. 10–5, Sat.–Sun. 11–5 🍴 Brauhaus Sion, see page 554 🚇 Lines 3, 4, 12, 16, 18 to Neumarkt
🚊 Tram 1, 2, 7, 9 to Neumarkt 💵 $$

Some of the best medieval religious art and furnishings in the city can be seen at the Schnütgen Museum, which occupies the deconsecrated church of St. Cäcilien. Among other treasures are original carvings from the cathedral altar and some beautiful ivory pieces. The carved *memento mori* (reminders of mortality) are chilling depictions of human bodies in a state of decay.

Rathaus

✚ B3 ✉ Rathausplatz ☎ 0221 2212 4502
🕐 Mon.–Thu. 8–4 (also Tue. 4–6), Fri. 8–noon
🍴 Restaurant in Ratskeller 🚇 Lines 5, 12, 16, 18 to Dom/Hbf 🚊 Tram 1, 7, 9 to Heumarkt ℹ Contact Tourist Office to book guided tours (see page 226)

The Rathaus (Town Hall) is a Cologne landmark at the heart of the Old Town. A flamboyant, octagonal, 15th-century tower tops off the 14th-century body of the building. The Renaissance *loggia* (porch) was added in the 1570s. Under a glass pyramid in front of the hall is a 12th-century Jewish bathhouse, the *Mikwe*. There was once a ghetto here, where the city's Jewish community lived until they were expelled in 1424.

Römisch-Germanisches Museum

✚ B3 ✉ Roncalliplatz 4 ☎ 0221 2212 4438
🕐 Tue.–Sun. 10–5 🚇 Lines 5, 12, 16, 18 to Dom/Hbf
💵 $$$ ℹ During special exhibitions, hours and admission may vary

For hundreds of years Cologne was under Roman rule; city status was granted in AD 50 by Emperor Claudius. The Römisch-Germanisches Museum (Roman-Germanic Museum) depicts daily life in the Roman Empire through locally excavated items. The main exhibit is the astonishing 230-foot Dionysus Mosaic, once part of a third-century Roman villa: it shows Dionysus, god of wine, indulging in drunken revelry. An older exhibit is the 49-foot-high tomb of a legionnaire called Poblicius, who died

about AD 40. There's a display of third- and fourth-century glass designs from Cologne, as well as a collection of jewelry found at Frankish burial sites.

St. Ursula

✚ B4 ✉ Ursulaplatz 24 ☎ 0221 133 400
🕐 Mon.–Sat. 10–noon and 3–5, Sun. 3–5
🍴 Bosporus, see page 554 🚇 Lines 5, 12, 16, 18 to Dom/Hbf 💵 Free

North of the city center is the church of St. Ursula; it was named after the daughter of a fourth-century king of Britain, who was said to have been killed in the city by Huns, along with her 11,000 virgin companions. The popularity of the cult of St. Ursula contributed to the city's development as a center of pilgrimage, and she appears in the Cologne coat of arms. The church sacristan can provide visitor access to the baroque Goldene Kammer (Golden Chamber).

Wallraf-Richartz-Museum/Museum Ludwig

✚ B3/C3 ✉ Wallraf-Richartz-Museum: Martinstrasse 39. Museum Ludwig: Bischofsgartenstrasse 1
☎ Wallraf-Richartz-Museum: 0221 2212 7694.
Museum Ludwig: 0221 2212 6165 🕐 Wallraf-Richartz Museum: Tue. 10–8, Wed.–Fri. 10–6, Sat.–Sun. 11–6; Museum Ludwig: Tue.–Sun. 10–6, (10 a.m.–11 p.m. first Fri. of the month) 🚇 Lines 5, 12, 16, 18 to Dom/Hbf
💵 $$$ (each museum) ℹ During special exhibitions, hours and admission may vary

Cologne's major collection of German and international art is here, with works through the 19th century shown in the first-floor Wallraf-Richartz-Museum, and 20th-century art shown in the Museum Ludwig, which occupies the rest of the building. At the Wallraf-Richartz you can study the work produced in Cologne in the 15th century, when the city was at the forefront of artistic development. In particular, look for the triptychs by the artist known as the Master of St. Bartholomew, one of the last of the Cologne School, whose brightly colored paintings resemble carvings.

Many 20th-century greats are represented in the Ludwig Museum, including Otto Dix and Max Ernst; the section on pop art has works by Andy Warhol and Roy Lichtenstein.

Cologne

An Excursion to Bergischer Dom

Bergischer Dom (Altenberger Dom), about 11 miles northeast of Cologne, is set on the Dhünn river in the woods of the hilly country called Bergisches Land. The original church of this former Cistercian monastery was built using stone from the manor of the Count of Berg, who left it to the monks after moving his headquarters elsewhere in 1133. It took a little more than 100 years to finish building the present monastery, which was begun in 1259 – only seven years after work had started on the cathedral in Cologne (which took more than six centuries to complete).

The end result is one of Germany's best examples of 13th-century Gothic style: no elaborate embellishments and no tower, but a marvelous sense of space and light, enhanced by the simple, silvery stained-glass windows in the chancel. The west window representing *Holy Jerusalem (Das Himmlische Jerusalem)* is the biggest stained-glass window in the country. There are tombs of the past counts of Berg in the north transept.

During the Napoleonic Wars in the late 18th and early 19th centuries, the church fell into disuse and was in danger of crumbling. Luckily, King Frederick William IV took an interest in its restoration, and it was opened again to worshipers on the condition – laid down by the king – that both Catholics and Protestants could attend. This holds true today, and on Sundays both Catholic and Protestant congregations from the city come here for services. The outbuildings now house restaurants; at any of these *Küchenhof*, you can ask for the key to

the oldest standing part of the monastery, the 13th-century chapel Markuskapelle. One of the most exquisite features of the whole complex is the choir surrounded by chapels, viewed most rewardingly from the slope east of the monastery.

It takes an hour to reach Bergischer Dom from Cologne's center: the underground trams (U-Bahn lines 4, 15, 16, 18, 19) take you to Wiener Platz for a connection with bus 434.

Guided excursions from Cologne can be arranged by the Cologne tourist information office (Köln Tourismus – see Essential Information box, page 226). Free guided tours are given Sat. at 11 a.m., Sun. and holidays at 1 and 3:30 p.m.; www.altenbergerdom.de

Fine stonework in the Bergischer Dom

Munich

MUNICH

The capital of Bavaria is one of Germany's most appealing and popular cities. Even though Munich (München) is the country's third-largest city, with a cosmopolitan society and culture, it has also retained a village-like atmosphere with parks and a pedestrian-only center. It's only an hour from the Alps, and also has the easygoing feel of a Mediterranean town. Even on the briefest German tour, Munich is a city not to be missed.

Munich on Foot

Central Munich is compact and attractive, and easy to explore on foot. Long pedestrian streets (Neuhauser Strasse and Kaufingerstrasse) run from the main railroad station and from Karlstor, one of the city gates, to Marienplatz, the square at the heart of the Old Town. Here you can watch the mechanical characters of the carillon (*Glockenspiel*) at the front of the New Town Hall (Neues Rathaus, see page 234) and visit the twin-towered cathedral. To the north of the square is the tree-lined Maximilianstrasse, which leads to the Bavarian Parliament building and the Residenz (palace). Great art collections – the Old and New Picture Galleries and the Modern Art Picture Gallery – are a short distance northwest of the city center; to the south are the history museum and, on an island in the Isar river, one of the world's foremost museums of science and technology, the German Museum (Deutsches Museum, see page 233).

Bavarian Eateries

There are innumerable restaurants and cafés in Munich, and its large foreign population ensures a wide range of cuisines. At specifically Bavarian cafés, the Munich *Weisswürste* (white veal sausage with parsley) is a staple, served in hot water to be peeled and covered in mustard before eating. This delicacy is usually eaten before noon. Meals are generally early in Munich, as people start work at 7 or 8 a.m. Lunch can begin at 11:30 but is often substantial, and the "lunch hour" can last until 2 p.m. Dinner is served between 6:30 and 11 p.m., but locals tend to stick to a light supper, or *Abendbrot*. The Schwabing district, north of the city

Munich

center, is a busy area of sidewalk cafés and taverns. Snack bars (*Lokal* or *Schnellimbiss*) and even butcher shops (*Metzgereien*) sell tasty meatloaf and sausages all day. And don't leave the city without visiting one of the beer gardens.

Music and Film

Munich is a major European cultural center, with thriving movie and publishing industries and a proud musical tradition. Three symphony orchestras are based here, and the Residenz provides an impressive venue – either in the concert hall or, in summer, in the courtyard. Opera and ballet are staged at the Bavarian State Opera, where the July Opera Festival is the highlight of the city's calendar. The main cultural center is the modern Gasteig, home of the Munich Philharmonic Orchestra; students from the Richard Strauss

Munich

Conservatory give free lunchtime or early-evening recitals in the Small Concert Hall during the week. The annual International Film Festival takes place at the Gasteig in late June and early July – the high point of a series of festivals devoted to the movies.

Munich tends to shut down early, but Schwabing has many cabarets, theaters and live music venues ranging from rock to folk to jazz – including the well-known Jazzclub Unterfahrt at Einsteinstrasse 42.

Boutiques and Markets

There's good window-shopping all over the old center of Munich, especially along the pedestrian-only Neuhauser Strasse and Kaufingerstrasse. Maximilianstrasse is a browser's paradise, lined with designer fashion boutiques, art galleries and jewelers. More stores abound in the arcades and lanes leading off Residenzstrasse. Antiques, less

City of Monks

Munich's city emblem is the *Münchener Kindl*, or "little monk," recalling its origins as a monastic settlement. The first recorded mention of *Munichen*, "the home of monks," was in AD 777. The city itself was founded nearly 400 years later by Henry the Lion, Duke of Saxony.

expensive fashion and secondhand stores are concentrated in the student area of Schwabing, and Bavarian crafts are sold in the streets that run off Max-Joseph-Platz. Munich's famous (and expensive) open-air food market, Viktualienmarkt, with its formidable women vendors and fresh goods ranging from local cheese to Alpine flowers, sets up south of the Marienplatz every day except late Saturday afternoon and Sunday.

ESSENTIAL INFORMATION

TOURIST INFORMATION
Fremdenverkehrsamt München (Munich Tourist Office)
• Sendlinger Strasse 1 ☎ 089 23 39 65 00; fax 089 23 33 02 33; www.muenchen-tourist.de
• Hauptbahnhof, Bahnhofplatz 2
• Neues Rathaus (New City Hall), Marienplatz

URBAN TRANSPORTATION
A U-Bahn (subway) and S-Bahn (suburban) train network covers the city center and beyond. The U-Bahn is marked on the city map by the letter "U" in a red circle, the S-Bahn by the letter "S" in a red circle. Trains run daily 5 a.m.–1 a.m. Buy tickets from machines at Münchner Verkehrs-und Tarifverbund (MVV) stations, MVV sales desks, newsstands, and aboard buses and trams. You can purchase tickets individually, in strips or for 1, 3 or 7 days: multiple

tickets are valid for buses and trams, too. Validate your ticket in the automatic stamping machine as you board, except for tickets bought from machines on trams (these will stamp automatically). One ticket is good for up to four bus/tram or two train stops; two tickets for additional stops. For MVV information ☎ 089 21 03 30. Taxi stands can be found all over the city. Call Taxi-München, ☎ 089 21 61-0, or IsarFunk Taxizentrale, ☎ 089 45 05 40.

AIRPORT INFORMATION
The international airport, Flughafen München Franz-Josef-Strauss, is 19 miles north of the city center. S-Bahn (lines 1 and 8) trains run 24 hours a day to the main railroad station (Hauptbahnhof), a 36-minute journey; airport buses run to the station from the North Terminal daily 6:20 a.m.–9:40 p.m., a 45-minute journey. For flight information ☎ 089 97 52 13 13.

CLIMATE – average highs and lows for the month

JAN.	FEB.	MAR.	APR.	MAY	JUN.	JUL.	AUG.	SEP.	OCT.	NOV.	DEC.
2°C	3°C	8°C	11°C	17°C	20°C	22°C	23°C	19°C	13°C	7°C	3°C
36°F	37°F	46°F	52°F	63°F	68°F	72°F	73°F	66°F	55°F	45°F	37°F
-4°C	-4°C	0°C	2°C	7°C	10°C	12°C	12°C	8°C	4°C	0°C	-3°C
25°F	25°F	32°F	36°F	45°F	50°F	54°F	54°F	46°F	39°F	32°F	27°F

Munich

CITY SIGHTS

Key to symbols

🗓 map coordinates refer to the Munich map on pages 230–231; sights below are highlighted in yellow on the map. ✉ address or location ☎ telephone number ⏰ opening times Ⓜ nearest subway 🚌 nearest bus or tram route 🍴 restaurant or café on site or nearby 🎟 admission charge: $$$ more than €4, $$ €2–€4, $ less than €2 ℹ other relevant information

ALTE PINAKOTHEK

🗓 B4/C4 ✉ Barer Strasse 27 ☎ 089 23 80 52 16 ⏰ Tue.–Sun. 10–5 (also Tue. 5–10 p.m.) Ⓜ U-Bahn to Königsplatz 🚌 Tram 27 🎟 $$$ ℹ Combination ticket for all three Pinakothek museums available

Over 850 pre-18th-century paintings are being rehoused in the huge Alte Pinakothek (Old Picture Gallery), built in 1836 to store the expanding royal art collection. The museum has been extensively restored over the last 50 years. Among the treasures are works by Albrecht Dürer and the world's best collection of work by Peter Paul Rubens.

ASAMKIRCHE

🗓 B2 ✉ Sendlinger Strasse 32 ⏰ Daily 8–5:30 Ⓜ U-Bahn to Sendlinger Tor 🚌 31, 56; tram 17, 18, 20, 21, 27

The Asamkirche (Asam Church) is a stunning example of baroque architecture. Built as a private chapel 1733–46 by architect and sculptor Egid Quirin Asam and his brother Cosmas Damian Asam, it was opened to the public in 1746. Every inch is decorated with gold leaf, sculptures and frescoes. One of Asam's works is at the altar, showing the crucified Christ in God's embrace – *The Throne of Mercy*.

BMW MUSEUM

🗓 B4 ✉ Petuelring 130 ☎ 089 38 22 33 07 ⏰ Daily 9–5 Ⓜ U-Bahn to Olympiazentrum or Petuelring 🚌 36, 43, 81, 136, 184 🎟 $$ ℹ Last admission at 4

The BMW Museum occupies a half-spherical silver structure next to the Bavarian Motor Works headquarters – itself a striking building with four silver cylinders. Cars, motorcycles, videos and slides illustrate the history of the automobile and its place in our lives, and visitors can even design their own cars with the aid of computer graphics.

DEUTSCHES MUSEUM

🗓 D1 ✉ Museumsinsel 1 ☎ 089 21 79-1 ⏰ Daily 9–5 🍴 Café on site Ⓜ U Bahn to Fraunhoferstrasse; S-Bahn to Isartor 🚌 Tram 18 🎟 $$$

One of the biggest science and technology museums in the world, the German Museum has more than 17,000 items on display, and deals with everything from lightning demonstrations to space travel to hydraulics to the first German submarine. Audiovisual displays and hands-on exhibits add to the fun.

ENGLISCHER GARTEN

🗓 D3, E3, D4, E4 ✉ Kutscherei Hans Holzmann ⏰ Daily 24 hours 🍴 Beer gardens, cafés and restaurants in park Ⓜ U-Bahn to Odeonsplatz, Universität, Giselastrasse or Münchener Freiheit 🚌 53; tram 17

Stretching along the bank of the Isar river, the landscaped park Englischer Garten (English Garden) was created in 1789 on a former hunting ground. Today it is busy with street entertainers and people lunching, boating and taking in the fresh air. Boats can be rented at the Kleinhesseloher See, and there is a beer garden, the Seehaus, near the lake. Enjoy good city views from the circular "temple," the *monopteros*; other popular attractions are the Chinese Tower and beer garden, the Japanese Tea House and the carousel.

Early touring car at the BMW Museum

The onion domes of Munich's cathedral

FRAUENKIRCHE

C2 ✉ Frauenplatz 1 ☎ 089 29 00 82-0
🕐 Church: Sat.–Thu. 7–7 (also Thu. 7–8:30 p.m.),
Fri. 7–6; South tower: Mon.–Sat. 10–5, Apr.–Oct.
🚇 U-Bahn/S-Bahn to Marienplatz 🚌 52; tram 19
💰 Church free: south tower $$

Munich's twin-towered cathedral (Church of Our Dear Lady), a famous city landmark, was built between 1468 and 1488, but was left without a roof. In 1524 its green onion domes were "temporarily" added – and have been there ever since. Near the entrance is a footprint in the floor, said to be that of the devil, who stamped with glee thinking that the architect had forgotten to put in the windows. In fact, the windows can't be seen from where the devil was standing – but they are there. The south tower can be climbed.

HAUS DER KUNST

D3 ✉ Prinzregentenstrasse 1 ☎ 089 211 27-0
🕐 Daily 10–8 (also Thu. 8–10 p.m.) for exhibitions
only 🍴 Café in gallery 🚇 U-Bahn to Odeonsplatz
or Lehel 🚌 53; tram 17 💰 $$$; exhibition admission
varies

The Haus der Kunst (House of Art) was opened by the Nazis in 1937 as a white-columned building known to its detractors as the *Weisswurst* (white sausage) gallery. It was part of Hitler's campaign against modern artists such as Paul Klee and Max Beckmann: While their work was ridiculed in an exhibition of "degenerates" in the Hofgarten, this gallery showed state-approved art. Work denounced by the Third Reich is shown in a series of exhibitions.

LENBACHHAUS

B3 ✉ Luisenstrasse 33 ☎ 089 23 33 20 00
🕐 Tue.–Sun. 10–6 🍴 Café in gallery 🚇 U-Bahn to
Königsplatz; tram 27 💰 $$$

Home of aristocratic painter Franz von Lenbach, the Lenbachhaus is now an art gallery. It shows the progression of art in Munich from the 15th and 16th centuries to the 19th-century Romantics. Highlights of the collection are works by the Munich Expressionists, the so-called *Blaue Reiter* (Blue Rider) group of the 20th century, with more than 90 abstract paintings and 900 other works by Wassily Kandinsky – the world's largest assemblage of his art.

NEUE PINAKOTHEK

B4–C4 ✉ Barer Strasse 29 ☎ 089 23 80 51 95
🕐 Wed.–Mon. 10–5 (also Wed. 5–10 p.m.) 🍴 Café in
gallery 🚇 U-Bahn to Königsplatz, Theresienstrasse
🚌 Tram 27 💰 $$$ ℹ️ Combination ticket for all
three Pinakothek museums available

Across the street from the Renaissance-style Alte Pinakothek (Old Picture Gallery, see page 233) is Neue Pinakothek (New Picture Gallery), a modern building featuring art from the late 18th to the 20th centuries. It covers French and German Impressionists, Romantic and rococo paintings, and the art nouveau style known in Germany as *Jugendstil*.

NEUES RATHAUS

C2 ✉ Marienplatz 8 ☎ 089 23 300 0 🕐 Tower:
Daily 9–7, May–Oct. and Dec.; Mon.–Thu. 9–4:30, Fri.
9–1, rest of year 🍴 Ratskeller, see page 555 🚇 U-
Bahn/S-Bahn to Marienplatz 🚌 52 💰 Tower $$

A forest of neo-Gothic turrets, towers, spurs and gargoyles, the 19th-century Neues Rathaus (New Town Hall) sprawls around six courtyards on the north side of Marienplatz. On its central tower (Rathausturm) is a 43-bell clock (Glockenspiel), which comes to life every day at 11 a.m. (also at noon and 5 p.m., Mar.–Oct.) as life-size figures from Munich's history come dancing out to its four melodies. The *Schäfflertanz*, a dance which celebrates the end of the plague in 1517, is performed by dancers in the city streets every seven years (next due in 2012).

Wilhelm V of Bavaria founded Munich's Hofbräu brewery in 1589 to brew a dark ale more to his liking than the local beer. At this time, beer was a drink restricted to the Bavarian upper classes: they had made it their own preserve after losing their vineyards in a series of bad winters. In 1828, the brewery became an inn, and the delights of its beer were made accessible to all.

HOFBRÄUHAUS

ends on the first Sunday in October. Barbecues, processions and music all play their part in this annual jamboree, but beer is the main ingredient.

If the Hofbräuhaus is too crowded, there are other options all over town, plus numerous beer gardens where you can even bring your own food. The *Oktoberfest* action takes place on the fairground at Theresienwiese, west of the city.

Whether you drink at the Hofbräuhaus or elsewhere, make sure you don't sit at the regulars' table (*Stammtisch*). You'll know you're there if the waitress refuses to take your order!

The huge beer hall and its tree-shaded courtyard has been the scene of political upheaval and violence in recent history. The Nazi party held its early mass meetings here, and a fight broke out during one of Adolf Hitler's speeches that became known as the Battle of the Hofbräuhaus.

Nowadays, there is nothing sinister about the hall's fame: tourists flock to the long benches, listen to the Bavarian brass bands and drink beer served by traditionally dressed waitresses. They no longer practice the customary quality test for *Bock* beer, though, which is probably just as well. The test apparently consisted of drinkers sitting at one of the Hofbräuhaus' beer-soaked benches and consuming *Bock* beer for hours at a time, staying put even while nature took its course. If, at the end of the session, they stuck to the benches when they tried to get up, the beer was reckoned to be thick enough and ready to sell.

The Hofbräuhaus is the city's most popular beer hall and fills up very quickly, especially during the world-famous, 16-day *Oktoberfest*, a beer festival that

Service with a smile at Munich's most famous beer hall

Munich

ODEONSPLATZ

⊞ C3 🍴 Halali, see page 555 🚇 U-Bahn to
Odeonsplatz 🚌 53

This regal square was laid out for Ludwig I
early in the 19th century and marks the
beginning of two great Munich boulevards –
Ludwigstrasse and Prinzregentenstrasse. The
Feldherrnhalle (Military Commanders' Hall)
was added as a tribute to the Bavarian army,
and is guarded by two bronze lions.
Overlooking Odeonsplatz is the lovely
baroque, golden-stone Theatinerkirche, the
church where Wittelsbach family members
were laid to rest. The immaculate gardens of
Hofgarten are next to the square.

OLYMPIAPARK

⊞ A4 ✉ Spiridon-Louis-Ring 21 ☎ 089 30 67-0
🕐 Olympiapark: daily 24 hrs.; Olympiastadion: daily
8:30–6, mid-Apr. to mid-Oct.; 9–4:30 rest of year (except
during events); Olympiaturm: daily 9 a.m.–midnight (last
admission at 11:30 p.m.) 🍴 Revolving restaurant,
Olympiaturm 🚇 U-Bahn to Olympiazentrum 🚌 36, 41,
43, 81, 136, 184; tram 20, 21, 27 💶 Olympiapark free;
Olympiastadion: $$; Olympiaturm $$

The park built for the 1972 Olympics has
become a focus for strollers, joggers and
swimmers. Its television tower, the
Olympiaturm, is the highest reinforced
concrete tower in Europe, and has a platform
and revolving restaurant with fantastic Alpine
views. A tour train takes visitors around
Olympic Lake; Olympic Hill, made of
wartime debris; and the Olympic Village.
You also can visit the Olympiastadion
(Olympic stadium).

Ceiling detail at the fabulous Residenz

PINAKOTHEK DER MODERNE

⊞ C3 ✉ Barer Strasse 40 ☎ 089 2 38 05 3-60
🕐 Tue.–Sun. 10–5 (also Thu.–Fri. 5–8)
🚇 U-Bahn to Königsplatz 🚌 53; tram 27 💶 $$$
ℹ Combination ticket for all three Pinakothek
museums available; free to all Sun.

Opened in 2003, this is one of the most
important art museums in Germany. The
light, airy building, innovative in design and
architecture, displays 20th- and 21st-
century art including works on paper.

RESIDENZ

⊞ C2, D2, C3, D3 ✉ Residenzstrasse 1/Max-Joseph-
Platz 3 ☎ 089 29 06 71 🕐 Daily 9–6, Apr. 1 to mid-
Oct.; 10–4 rest of year 🍴 Spatenhaus, see page 555
🚇 U-Bahn to Odeonsplatz; U-Bahn/S-Bahn to
Marienplatz 🚌 52, 53; tram 19 💶 $$$

The 112 rooms of the Wittelsbach
dynasty's dazzling palace are a treasure-
trove of artworks, ornaments, furnishings
and statues – too much to take in during
just one visit. Highlights include the
vaulted Antiquarium, built in 1568; the
rococo Cuvilliés Theater; the crown jewels
in the Treasury; and the Ahnengalerie
(Ancestral Portrait Gallery).

SCHLOSS NYMPHENBURG

⊞ A4 ☎ 089 17 90 86 68 🕐 Palace: daily 9–6, Apr. 1
to mid-Oct.; 10–6 rest of year. Gardens: daily
dawn–dusk 🍴 Schlosscafé Palmenhaus, see page
555 🚇 U-Bahn to Rotkreuzplatz 🚌 51; tram 17
💶 All attractions $$$; Castle and Gallery $$;
Marstallmuseum $$

For centuries the mighty Wittelsbach family
ruled Bavaria. Schloss Nymphenburg
(Nymphenburg Palace) was built as their
summer villa by Agostino Barelli between
1664 and 1674. Every generation of
Wittelsbachs subsequently added to his
creation, and the palace now measures 1,640
feet from end to end. In the central section is
the Schönheitsgalerie, or Gallery of Beauties
– 36 paintings of beautiful women produced
between 1827 and 1850 for Ludwig I. The
former palace stables house the
Marstallmuseum, a museum of porcelain
and a collection of state carriages and sleighs,
and in the 1734 Amalienburg hunting lodge
there is a Hall of Mirrors.

A WALK ALONG PRINZREGENTENSTRASSE

This grand old boulevard runs east from the 17th-century Court Garden (Hofgarten), with its beautiful fountains and Renaissance arcades. A startling modern addition, the steel-and-glass Staatskanzlei, houses the Bavarian State Chancellery. Prinzregentenstrasse was laid out at the end of the 19th century and named for Prince Luitpold, who ruled as regent after his nephew, Ludwig II, had been declared mad and deposed.

Fountain in the Hofgarten

Today it takes visitors through one of the city's main museum and gallery quarters. Running past the southern end of the English Garden, the boulevard first reaches the Haus der Kunst (House of Art, see page 234), formerly a gallery of Nazi-approved art. It exhibits the kind of work the Nazis had condemned. Next door is the Bavarian National Museum (Bayerisches Nationalmuseum), in a turn-of-the-20th-century building incorporating many different architectural styles.

The next notable monument is the former Prussian embassy, now the Schack-Galerie, named for one of the 19th century's great patrons of the arts, Count Schack. His own collection of paintings is represented by such artists as Franz von Lenbach and Arnold Böcklin, who relied on the count for their livelihoods. The gallery is open Wed.–Sun. 10–5.

Prinzregentenstrasse continues across the Isar river and past the *Angel of Peace* (*Friedensengel*), a golden monument to peace, erected to commemorate the end of the Franco-Prussian War. Nowadays citizens gather on New Year's Day to enjoy fireworks displays and the view of Munich. Farther along, past the Europaplatz, is the Villa Stuck, a 19th-century house built in a mix of styles by artist Franz von Stuck. Von Stuck was part of the 1890s *avant-garde* school known as the Munich Secession, and his own work is displayed inside (currently closed for restoration).

The boulevard continues east to the Prinzregententheater (☎ 089 21 85 02), which stages drama, concerts and musicals. It was designed in 1900 to emulate the neoclassic Wagner Festival Theater in Bayreuth and sits on Prinzregentenplatz, where there is a U-Bahn station; trains travel back to Odeonsplatz and the Hofgarten. For the walking route, see the city map on pages 230–231.

GREECE

"MIGHTY indeed are the marks and monuments of our empire we have left. Future ages will wonder at us, as the present age wonders at us now..."

From *The Peloponnesian War*, circa 400 BC, by Athenian historian Thucydides

Opposite: Verdant olive groves on the fertile Lasithi plateau in eastern Crete

GREECE

Somewhere, subconsciously, we all feel we have a stake in Greece. The language, political systems, values and ethics of the Western world are inextricably connected to this beautiful country's ancient civilization. Visitors often arrive with high expectations and romantic notions, muddled snippets of myths, history and hearsay mingled in their minds. Those experiencing the country for the first time are likely to be captivated. Greece evokes strong feelings, and even months of travel would scarcely be enough to do this stunning country justice.

The Land

There are more than 160 inhabited islands in Greece, scattered on three sides of the mainland. Some are studded with pine and eucalyptus, and some are arid or mountainous. Most are blessed with idyllic beaches and picturesque villages, and many have superb ancient sites, Frankish castles or Venetian fortifications.

You could spend years discovering them all, so spare at least a few days to visit one or two. Greek islands are a vital part of the country and have bedazzled travelers for centuries. There are regular

Greece

ferry services to the main islands in summer, but services to more remote islands are less regular and can be challenging – but worth the effort – to organize. Check the website www.gtp.gr, which lists monthly ferry routes.

Much of mainland Greece is very mountainous. The slopes of Olympus and Parnassus are carpeted with wildflowers in spring, offering superb vistas and rewarding hiking, as do the eerie and stony landscapes of the Máni and the steep-sided gorges and wild coastline of Crete.

Public transportation, especially by bus, is regular and reliable, and car rental is simple to arrange. If you do rent a car, be prepared for some poorly surfaced roads, and avoid driving in cities and larger rural towns if possible.

Traditional Culture

Greece has one of Europe's most vigorous cultures, perpetuated through architecture, crafts, music and dance. Traditional customs permeate everyday life, despite the growing impact of Western consumer values. If you can, see traditional dancing and listen to the music – the real thing is often easier to find in rural areas.

As in many other Mediterranean countries, much of life is lived in the full gaze of the public eye, hence the strolling crowds and packed cafés.

The Greeks and You

Tourism is not a slick operation in Greece; everything works, things eventually happen, but not necessarily with streamlined efficiency. So relax, slow down and you'll get much more out of your trip.

The Greeks have been dealing with foreign incursions for centuries, so they took the late 20th-century tourist influx in stride. The classical Greek tradition of hospitality to strangers is still strong,

which makes for a relaxed attitude toward visitors, particularly when you go off the beaten track.

Hospitality often takes the form of innumerable personal questions, among which "How much do you earn?" is usually near the top of the list. Don't be offended, as this is considered an acceptable and friendly exchange. If someone offers you something – a drink, some fruit, a flower – accept it graciously, as the donor is acting out a tradition that goes back thousands of years.

Greeks have a strong code of honor, which makes Greece a safe country to visit. It's highly unlikely you'll be cheated in any way, and you can safely walk most streets at night without worrying. Society has changed beyond recognition in the last 40 years, and young Greeks are far more emancipated than their parents. Female virtue – especially in rural areas – is still held in high regard. As a result, young Greek males may occasionally pester foreign girls in the often mistaken belief that they will respond more readily to their advances.

There's still a large rural class in Greece, and outside cities and tourist areas you'll see black-garbed figures laboring in tiny fields as they have for centuries, their lifestyle a million miles from that of city dwellers.

MORE TOP DESTINATIONS IN GREECE

- Chaniá B1• Delfoí B2
- Kefalloniá A2 • Léros C2
- Máni B1 • Metéora A3
- Monemvasía B1
- Mykínes B2• Mykonos C2
- Naxos C2 • Óros Píndos A3
- Samothráki B3 • Skópelos B2
- Thíra/Santorini C1 • Ydra B2

Greece

TIMELINE

776–700 BC   City-states established; first Olympic Games.

499–400 BC   Persian Wars; Golden Age of classical Greek culture;
Peloponnesian Wars against Sparta.

336–323 BC   Alexander the Great conquers the known world.

146 BC   Greece becomes a Roman province.

AD 394   Christianity established throughout the Roman Empire; the
Olympic Games finish and the Delphic Oracle is closed.

476–1453   Greece ruled from Constantinople; fall of Constantinople in
1453; Greece ruled by Turks for next 400 years.

1821–29   Greek War of Independence; Greece becomes an independent
modern state.

1917–18   Greece sides with Allies in World War I.

1940–44   Axis occupation during World War II.

1945–60   Many Greeks emigrate to the United States and Australia;
others flood into Athens from the countryside.

1974   Conflict with Turkey over Cyprus; situation remains tense into
the 21st century.

1975   Tourist boom begins with foreigners visiting classical sites,
islands and coastal resorts.

1981   Greece joins European Community; community funding
catapults much of the country into mainstream Europe.

1996   Macedonian claims by former Yugoslavs seen as implicit threat
to northern Greek region of Macedonia.

2001   Greece adopts the euro as its new national currency (euro bills
and coins appeared in 2002).

2004   Athens hosts the 2004 Olympic Games.

THE GOLDEN AGE OF CLASSICAL GREECE

The peace following the defeat of the Persians in the fifth century BC marked the start of a cultural, artistic and intellectual blossoming for Athens and the other city-states. Much of what truly epitomizes "the glory that was Greece" dates from this era. The great architectural triumphs, the start of drama and comedy, and the first steps in philosophical thought can all be traced to Athens at this time. The Acropolis took the form whose remains are seen today, decorated by Pheidas' sublime marbles, and subtly harmonious temples were built everywhere. The names Sophocles, Euripides, Aristophanes, Socrates and Plato are familiar worldwide; it's worth remembering that they lived and worked in this tiny state in the eastern Mediterranean more than 2,500 years ago.

Greece

SURVIVAL GUIDE

- Athens is best avoided during the sweltering summer months, when temperatures can soar, noise levels are high around the clock, and the ever-present pollution is at its worst.

- Head for restaurants and *tavernas* where locals eat; the food will be good. If you don't understand the menu in a *taverna* you may be invited into the kitchen for a look – choose what you want and point! In some areas of Greece there is an enduring belief that hot food harms the stomach, and food may therefore be served lukewarm. However, the preference for hot food is normally catered to.

- Remember to *never* flush toilet tissue down the toilet – it goes in the basket provided. You'll flood the bathroom if you put paper down the narrow pipes. This applies to *all* toilets throughout Greece. Public restrooms are few and far between, and many of them leave much to be desired.

- Greeks prefer to be cool and comfortable rather than stylish, but usually don't wear shorts in the city. It's respectful to cover bare shoulders and upper arms in churches. Topless and nude sunbathing are widely but discreetly practiced.

- Taxis outside main cities are fairly inexpensive, but in Athens drivers may hike rates for foreign visitors. Ask what the destination fare is before getting into a taxi or compare fares before deciding which one you'll use. On arrival by ferry or plane, if you already have a hotel reserved, resist being talked into going to another hotel.

- Don't rent a scooter; more tourists have accidents on them than by any other means.

- At important sites you may be approached by guides wanting to be paid for their services; some are good, others barely speak English. If you want guide service, use an official one or take a tour.

- There's a plethora of attractive, handmade items to buy in Greek stores and markets. Most prices are fixed, but you can try a little gentle haggling in markets.

- Be careful after it rains, when marble-surfaced walkways in Athens become very slippery. Also look out for unguarded holes on sidewalks, especially in poorly lit areas at night.

Parliamentary guard in traditional uniform

ATHENS

Athens is one of the Mediterranean's great cities, boasting some of the world's most treasured relics; it's also noisy, crowded and polluted, with sprawling, unattractive suburbs. Summertime heat and the lack of green, shady spots can be oppressive, but the city is exhilarating, fascinating and stimulating, as much for its past as its present. Accept it and enjoy it for the colorful place it is.

Tackling Athens

You'll probably spend most of your visit in Athens' tiny historical center. Base yourself near Syntagmatos Square or Pláka, which are only a 10- to 15-minute walk from most of the main tourist sights. Try to plan your day carefully, getting an early start, so you can lie low during the heat of the afternoon. If you need information or advice, you will find that most people connected with tourism speak English, ranging from a few words to polished and idiomatic speech.

Athens

Moving around the historic center on foot is easy, but is occasionally challenging at busy street crossings. Be aware that where there are no traffic lights local drivers rarely take note of pedestrian crossings; wait for a clear gap in traffic before crossing. City buses and trolley buses are often packed and may be delayed by traffic jams. Taxis are convenient for excursions out of the city, as is the greatly improved metro (subway) system. The main road systems into the city have also been improved.

ATHENS

AVEROF

LEÓFOROS ALÉXANDRAS

N

IPOKRÁTOUS

Gípedo
Panathinaïkoú

Lykavittós

VASÍLISSIS SOFÍAS

PAPADIAMANTOPOÚLOU

Ágios
Geórgios

KOLONÁKI

ILÍSIA

Mouseío
Kykladikis
Téchnis

Evangelismós

Ethnikí
Pinakothíki

ILISÍON

Polemikó
Mouseío

Vizantinó
Mouseío

KONSTANTÍNO

SPYROU

VAS ALÉXANDROU

Álsos
Syngroú

LEÓFOROS VAS GEORGÍOU II

MERKOÚRI

FORMÍONOS

YMITTOÚ

LEÓFOROS VAS

ERATÓSTHENOU

Stádio

ARCHIMDOUS

EFRÁNOROS

EFTIKHÍDOU

CHREMONÍDO

FILOLAOÚ

EMPEDOKLEOUS

YMITTOÚ

Profítis
Ilías

NIKOFORÍDI NIK

PAGKRÁTI

ANALIPSEOS

D   E

Much of this work was carried out in preparation for the 2004 Olympic Games.

Athenian Flavors

Sitting at a shady café table, lingering over a gargantuan lunch, munching sunflower seeds, melon, pistachio and pine nuts, or eating ice cream as you stroll on balmy evenings are true Athenian pleasures.

In a country where hospitality to strangers is one of the bedrock rules of society, it's not surprising that eating and drinking socially play an important role. Eating establishments are known as *estiatorio* (restaurants) or *tavernas* (less expensive, simpler and often family-run).

Greek food is delicious and healthy – fresh salads with feta cheese and olives, fantastic hors d'oeuvres (*mezédhes*), grilled meats, moussakas, and tasty stews and vegetables, perhaps washed down with *retsina*, the barrel-stored, pine-resonated white wine.

Dessert is normally fresh local fruit; if you want something sweeter, head for a *zaharoplastío*, a café serving the honey-soaked pastries much loved by the Greeks.

Festivals and Theater

Athens has theater, movies, dance, galleries and nightlife; everything changes rapidly, so pick up a free copy of such English-language magazines as *Athens Today* or *Athens News* to find out schedules.

In summer, the main tourist attractions are the amazing sound-and-light show at the Acropolis (from April through October) and the Hellenic Festival, which runs from June through September. The festival offers a wonderful program of excellent cultural events, although it's most famous for classical Greek theater.

The delicious Greek salad, topped with feta cheese and oregano

The Greek Alphabet

At first it may be daunting to see Greek script everywhere, but it won't be a major inconvenience. All street signs are in both Greek and Roman letters, as are signs to museums and most restaurants and shops. Public transportation is usually signed in Greek. But you'll get the hang of it and will feel a real sense of achievement when you do.

Ceramics and Honey

There's a wide range of shopping in Athens, from international labels to traditional Greek products. In Kolonáki and on and around Ermoú Street, the smartest retail areas, you'll find familiar merchandise.

Ethnic buys are another matter, with much to hunt down around Pláka and vicinity. Leather and woolen goods, traditional ceramics and tapestries, felt slippers, fruity olive oil,

honey and pistachios are all excellent buys. For something special, check out jewelry or religious stores; Greece has a long tradition of fine gold craftsmanship, and traditional icons are still made. Watch for Athens' kiosks (*períptera*) – much more than newsstands, they sell everything from snacks and drinks to bus tickets, simple medicines and telephone cards. In central Athens some are open 24 hours a day.

ESSENTIAL INFORMATION

TOURIST INFORMATION
• Tsoha 7, Ambelokipi ☎ 210 870 7000; www.gnto.gr
• Athens International Airport Arrivals Hall ☎ 210 353 0445

bus and trolley bus tickets on board and subway tickets at entrances to platforms. The Athens Urban Transport Organization's (OASA) website, www.oasa.gr, is very useful for locating bus, trolley bus and metro routes.

URBAN TRANSPORTATION
The easiest way to get around Athens is to walk or take one of the numerous yellow taxis. Taxis are hailed on the street and often shared; you pay for your segment of the journey, so check the meter when you get in. Alternatively, your hotel can arrange a taxi for you. Buses, trolley buses and the metro (subway) operate daily 5 a.m.–midnight; tickets are available at kiosks and are interchangeable with subway tickets, which can be bought at stations. Validate

AIRPORT INFORMATION
Athens International Airport (Eleftherios Venizelos) is at Spáta, 17 miles east of Athens (☎ 01 353 0000). Three 24-hour express bus lines (connecting with the metro) serve the airport: No. 94 to Ethniki Amyna; No. 95 to Syntagma Square; No. 96 to Piréas. Tickets cost €2.90 and allow unlimited 24-hour travel on the metro, bus and trolley bus. The city also is easily accessible by taxi.

CLIMATE – average highs and lows for the month

JAN.	FEB.	MAR.	APR.	MAY	JUN.	JUL.	AUG.	SEP.	OCT.	NOV.	DEC.
13°C	13°C	15°C	19°C	24°C	30°C	31°C	32°C	28°C	23°C	17°C	14°C
55°F	55°F	59°F	66°F	75°F	86°F	88°F	90°F	82°F	73°F	63°F	57°F
6°C	6°C	7°C	11°C	15°C	20°C	22°C	22°C	19°C	15°C	11°C	8°C
43°F	43°F	45°F	52°F	59°F	68°F	72°F	72°F	66°F	59°F	52°F	46°F

Room with a view – a quiet place to stop for a picnic

Stunning under floodlights, the Acropolis rises serenely above the city

CITY SIGHTS

Key to symbols

🗺 map coordinates refer to the Athens map on pages 244–245; sights below are highlighted in yellow on the map.

✉ address or location ☎ telephone number
🕐 opening times Ⓜ nearest subway 🚌 nearest bus or tram route 🍴 restaurant or café on site or nearby
💰 admission charge: $$$ more than €4, $$ €2–€4, $ less than €2 ℹ other relevant information

AGORÁ

🗺 B2 ✉ Adrianou or Theorias ☎ 210 321 0185
🕐 Tue.–Sun. 8:30–3 Ⓜ Thiseío or Monastiráki
💰 $$

The stately civic center and marketplace of ancient Athens is at the foot of the Acropolis, to which it was linked by the Panathenaic Way. Today the site is a jumble of atmospheric, tree-shaded ruins, and you'll need to use your imagination to visualize its glorious heyday. Dominating one end is the virtually reconstructed, fifth-century BC Doric temple known as the Thiseío. Opposite, the two-story Stoá Attálou, a second-century BC arcade, has been restored by the American School of Archeology to give an idea of the glory of these ancient public buildings. It contains a museum with finds from the site.

AKRÓPOLI

🗺 B2 ✉ Akrópoli ☎ 210 321 0219; Museum: 210 323 6665 🕐 Daily 8:30–3, Apr. 1 to mid-Oct.; 8:30–3:, rest of year. Closed holidays 🍴 Psaras, see page

556 Ⓜ Akropoli 🚌 1, 5, 9, 230, 231 💰 $$$
✉ 4 Stadiou

The Akrópoli (Acropolis) should top your sightseeing list. This naturally defensible rock was the sacred focal point of ancient Athens, and what you see today dates mainly from the fifth century BC, an era of peace and prosperity and the true "Golden Age" of Greece.

You reach the summit through the Propylaia, a magnificent stepped gateway, with the graceful little temple of Athena Nike to your right. Ahead rises the great Doric temple of the Parthenón; built using no perpendicular lines, its columns actually taper, giving the whole structure a feeling of lightness. It was decorated by leading Athenian sculptors and dedicated to the goddess Athena Parthenos, whose statue by the sculptor Pheidias stood inside. To the left of the Parthenón stands the Erechtheion, shrine to Athena and Poseidon, and said to be the place where the goddess created the first olive tree. The roof of the south portico is supported by six caryatids, stately maidens dressed in pleated tunics.

At the foot of the Acropolis you can see two Roman theaters, the Théatro Iródou Attikoú and the Théatro Dionysou.

ETHNIKÓ ARCHAIOLOGIKÓ MOUSEÍO

🗺 C4 ✉ 44 Patission ☎ 01 821 7717 or 01 821 7724
🕐 Tue.–Sun. 8–7, Mon. 12:30–7, Apr. 1 to mid-Oct.; Tue.–Sun. 8–5, Mon. 10:30–5, rest of year 🍴 Café in museum Ⓜ Omonia 🚌 2, 3, 11, 13, 15, 022, 035
💰 $$$

For lovers of classical art the Ethnikó Archaiologikó Mouseío (National Archeological Museum) is one of the world's top sights. The museum reopened in June 2004 following a complete refurbishment. This vast and varied collection covers all the finest from ancient Greece, with the bonus of an exceptional Egyptian collection. The museum needs a full day to do it justice.

The best approach is to concentrate on only the prime examples. Head first for the treasures from the royal tombs at Mycenae, dating from 1500 BC; they include exquisite gold funerary masks, necklaces and filigree flowers. Next, take in the sixth-century BC *kouros*, vibrant statues of nude male athletes; Aristodikos' superbly tactile athlete is one of the finest ever carved. Move on to admire the huge statue of Poseidon and the little jockey urging on his horse, both found in the sea in 1927. There's also a stunning bronze by the famous sculptor Praxiteles in room 28. Upstairs you'll find frescoes from Santorini (Thira), buried 3,500 years ago during a volcanic eruption, showing charming riverside scenes. Next door are the fascinating pottery collections; look for the rare *lekythoi* (white-ground clay ware), and the exquisite red and black Attic vases.

ETHNIKÓS KÍPOS

✚ C2 ✉ Amalias ☎ Museum: 210 721 1178
🕐 Daily dawn–dusk (museum: Tue.–Sun. 9–3
🚇 Omonia, Viktorias 🚌 1, 2, 4,11,12, 022, 025, 026

The green and somber Ethnikós Kípos (National Gardens) provide a wonderful oasis of cool. Laid out in the 19th century by Queen Amalia, this is a true southern Mediterranean garden – no colorful flowerbeds, but deep shade and sylvan green. With plenty of benches and cafés, the gardens are a good place for a picnic. Within the grounds is a botanical museum with samples of all the gardens' plants, many rare.

Greek head at the National Archeological Museum

GOULANDRIS MOUSEÍO KYKLADIKÍS TÉCHNIS

✚ D2 ✉ 4 Neophytou Douka ☎ 210 722 8321
🕐 Wed.–Fri. and Mon. 10–4, Sat. 10–3 🚇 Syntagma, Evengelismas 🚌 3, 7, 13, 022, 060 ✋ $$

The beautifully presented Goulandris Mouseío Kykladikís Téchnis (Museum of Cycladic Art), which houses a superb collection of prehistoric artifacts from the Aegean islands, was established in 1986. The collection, once the private property of the shipowning Goulandris family, dates from the Cycladic civilization, which flourished on the Greek islands from 3000 until 2000 BC. The figures, carved from local marble, could be taken for 20th-century work; elegant and minimalist, yet full of powerful feeling.

LYKAVITTÓS AND KOLONÁKI

✚ D3 ✉ Kolonáki 🕐 Funicular: daily 9:15 a.m.–11:45 p.m. 🍴 Terrace café at top 🚌 022, 060 ✋ $$

From Kolonáki Square, the hub of one of Athens' smartest shopping areas, the slopes of Lykavittós (Lykabettus) rise steeply to the 912-foot-high summit, one of the city's great vantage points. You can walk up or take the funicular to enjoy panoramic views over the city, from the Acropolis down to the sea at Piréas. Aim to get there for sunset, and leave time to visit the whitewashed chapel of Agios Giorgios (St. George) at the top.

MONASTIRÁKI

✚ B2 ✉ Monastiráki 🕐 Museum of Greek Ceramics: 210 324 2066 🕐 Market open daily, but largest on Sun. Museum: Wed.–Mon. 9–2:30 🚇 Monastiráki ✋ $

This bustling area surrounds Monastiráki square, named after a former monastery on this site. Today the square's focal point is the 18th-century Tzistarakis Mosque, a relic of Turkish rule, which houses the Keramiki Silogi (Museum of Greek Ceramics). However, most people head straight for

The great Doric temple of the Parthenon, the crowning glory of the Acropolis

Monastiráki's famous flea market, where you can find anything from clothes and kebabs to icons and compact discs. Sunday is the big day.

MOUSEÍO AKRÓPOLEOS

➕ B2 ✉ Akrópoli ☎ 210 321 4172 🕐 Daily 8–7:30, Apr. 1 to mid-Oct.; 8–5, rest of year
🍴 Psaras, see page 556 Ⓜ Akrópoli 🚌 1, 5, 22, 23, 230, 231 💳 $$$ (included in Acropolis entrance)

Tucked behind the Parthenon is the Mouseío Akrópoleos (Acropolis Museum), housing a fine collection of sculptures found on the Acropolis. The original caryatids from the Erectheion are best known, but spend time admiring the superb fragment of a horse and rider and the splendid marble hound, straining forward, in room IV.

OLYMPÍEION ZEUS AND PÝLI ADRIANOÚ

➕ C1 ✉ 2 Vasilissis Olgas ☎ 210 922 6330
🕐 Daily 8:30–3 Ⓜ Akrópoli 🚌 1, 4, 11, 040, 057
💳 $

Along with the Tower of the Winds in the Roman Agora, Olympíeion Zeus and Pýli Adrianoú (Temple of Olympian Zeus and Hadrian's Arch) are Athens' most impressive Roman legacy. Both of these structures were completed around AD 130 by the Emperor Hadrian; the temple as a shrine to this paramount Roman god, and the arch to mark the boundary between the old Greek city and Hadrian's new one. Fifteen massive columns remain of what was once Greece's largest temple.

PIRÉAS

➕ Off the map Ⓜ Piréas

Piréas is a town in its own right, although it's only five stops on the subway from Athens' center. It's a noisy, bustling port, one of the biggest in the Mediterranean, and many of the inter-island boats leave from its harbor. It boasts a magnificent cathedral, rebuilt after World War II; a fine archeological museum; and Greece's naval museum. Sunday is a good day to browse in the flea market.

PLÁKA

➕ B2 ✉ Pláka Ⓜ Syntagma, Monastiraki 🚌 9, 11, 15, 025, 026

Visitors return time and again to the picturesque Pláka neighborhood, at the foot of the Acropolis. The maze of colorful narrow streets, flower-bedecked squares and huge range of stores and *tavernas* may be touristy, but also radiate charm. Bustling Kidhathineon and Adrianoú, the main streets, teem with street life and are lined with mainly 19th-century, colorfully painted houses. Don't miss the dazzling white alleys that comprise Anafiotika, on the northern slopes of the Acropolis. This area was built in the 1840s by masons from the Cycladic islands, and it still retains a village atmosphere.

PLATÉIA SYNTAGMATOS

➕ C2 ✉ Syntagmatos Ⓜ Syntagma 🚌 1, 2, 4, 5, 022, 025, 026 ℹ Changing of the guard at varied times Mon.–Fri., at 11 a.m. on Sun.

Noisy, crowded, Platéia Syntagmatos (Constitution Square) is the heart of modern Athens, where you'll find hotels, offices, banks, restaurants, cafés and myriad jostling Athenians. The vast neoclassic edifice at the top is the Voulí (Parliament Building), once the royal palace. In front of it is the Tomb of the Unknown Soldier, patrolled around the clock by the Evzones, a guard of honor whose dress uniform features a short pleated kilt and pom-poms on their shoes. The central, pedestrianized area was refurbished in 2004.

The Athenian Treasury and Sacred Way at Delphi

AN EXCURSION TO DELPHI

The sacred site of Delphi (Delfoí), 93 miles northwest of Athens, is the obvious choice for a day trip. The greatest shrine of the ancient Greek world, the center of their earth, lies in an unrivaled position below the great peaks of Mount Parnassós. Dedicated to the god Apollo, in ancient times Delphi was independent – belonging to no state – so enemies could worship there together. It was famed for its oracle, which gave enigmatic and prophetic advice through the medium of a priestess.

In return for this, petitioners brought gifts and erected treasure houses to hold them; ancient writers referred to the marble and precious stones of the sanctuary. For centuries, pilgrims trudged through the mountains to bathe in the sacred Castalian spring and worship here, but in the fourth century Christianity triumphed and the last oracle slipped away. Below the site, olive groves spread down to the sea, the ground is carpeted with flowers and the sky is full of birds.

The French excavated Delphi in the 1890s, and today it lies on a series of terraces below Parnassós. The paved Sacred Way leads past treasure houses – one sensitively reconstructed – to the Temple of Apollo. Six columns still stand, giving an idea of its former size and grandeur. Up the hill you'll find the 5,000-seat theater, and higher still, the marvelously evocative athletic stadium, set amid pine trees. To visit the ruins of the Sanctuary of Athena, leave the main site and cross the modern road. Use the columns of the fourth-century BC Tholos, undoubtedly the most photographed of all Delphi's wonders, as your guide.

Delphi Museum

The adjacent museum contains the finds from Delphi, some of the finest in Greece. Sculptures from the Temple of Apollo, two superb examples of archaic *koroi* (statues), ivory, jewelry and pottery are all here. The highlight is the bronze *Charioteer*, dating from 478 BC, an artistic and technical masterpiece.

✚ See page 240, grid reference B2   ✉ Delphi
☎ 226 508 2312   🕐 Daily 7 a.m.–9 p.m., Apr.–Oct.;
Tue.–Fri. 8:30–6:45, Sat.–Sun. 8:30–3, rest of year
💺 $$ ℹ A guided excursion is the easiest way to visit Delphi
Excursion Operators
Chat Tours (✉ I9 Xenofontos Street, off Amalias Avenue ☎ 210 323 0872) is an experienced tour operator in Athens.

HUNGARY

*"*B*EYOND the river the hills…behold they lead to Heaven.*"*

By early 20th-century Hungarian poet Árpád Tóth

Opposite: View across the rooftops from the Firewatch Tower in Sopron, western Hungary

Hungary

HUNGARY

Hungary is situated at the heart of Europe. Surrounded by Austria, Slovakia, the Ukraine, Romania, Serbia and Montenegro, Croatia and Slovenia, it has absorbed the cultures of such peoples and conquerors as the Romans, Magyars, Turks and Habsburgs. Its majestic capital, Budapest, sits on the Danube river, which has brought trade and settlers through the country on its course from Austria to Serbia. For centuries Hungary has been a nation in flux, its territories expanding or diminishing through a series of invasions, occupations and liberations. It is today undergoing yet more change after emerging from 40 years of life behind the Iron Curtain.

Landscape of History

Northern, western and southern Hungary are different worlds. In the north, beyond the urban centers of Budapest and Miskolc, are the uplands and their wide, rolling, forested hills. The vineyards here produce famous Tokay and Bull's Blood wine.

In the west there are strong links with Western European culture. The rich farmlands are punctuated with historic towns that are packed with Renaissance and baroque buildings. In the south the landscape changes completely. Vast, flat grasslands form the Great Plain (*puszta*), dotted with tiny farmsteads and presided over by the capital, Debrecen. In the far south, the medieval city of Pécs preserves many relics of its 143 years under Turkish rule.

Making Contact

The Hungarian language, related to Finnish and Estonian, can be daunting for visitors. English may be spoken in the tourist areas, but German is more frequently used. When you find a common language, however, you will discover that Hungarians are courteous, generous and formal. Hungary is a multiracial nation, and despite its proximity to the Balkan region, considers itself to be West European.

Hungarian Heritage

Hungarians have strong folk traditions and customs, especially music and dance. You can enjoy them at a dance

Hungary

house (*táncház*); there are several in Budapest. Bands usually include bagpipes and a hurdy-gurdy, and the dancing is fast and furious.

In Kiskunság National Park, between the Danube and the Tisza rivers, a horse-drawn buggy takes visitors to see farmsteads, long-horned cattle and curly-horned Podokan sheep. There also are displays at Hortobágy National Park – Hungary's first national park.

In the Cserhát hills of the north, the village of Hollókő sits at the foot of a 13th-century castle. The village is home to the Palóc people, who speak a distinct regional dialect and wear colorful embroidered costumes and elaborate headdresses. For another insight into Hungary's heritage, visit the famous Király thermal baths in Budapest and enjoy the luxury of a Turkish-style bath or massage.

MORE TOP DESTINATIONS IN HUNGARY

- Balatonfüred B2
- Bugac-Puszta C1 • Eger D3
- Fertőd A2 • Gödöllő C3
- Hollókő C3 • Hortobágy Nemzeti Park D3 • Kecskemét C2
- Mátra C3 • Pécs B1 • Sopron A2
- Szabadtéri Néprajzi Múzeum C3
- Szentendre C3 • Tihany B2
- Tokaj D3 • Visegrád C3

Hungary

TIMELINE

13 BC	The Roman province of Pannonia is established on the west bank of the Danube; nomadic tribes occupy the east.
AD 896	Seven Magyar tribes cross the Carpathian Mountains and invade the Hungarian plains.
1000	King Stephen is crowned and makes Hungary a centralized, Christian state.
1526	Sultan Suleiman I and his Turkish army defeat the Hungarians at Mohács; most of the country is brought under his rule.
1686	Habsburg troops recapture Buda, on the west bank of the Danube (later united with Pest, on the east).
1896	The Great Exposition celebrates the 1,000th anniversary of the Magyar Conquest.
1919	Hungary briefly becomes a Bolshevik republic.
1920	Under the Treaty of Trianon, Hungary loses two-thirds of its territory to Czechoslovakia, Yugoslavia and Romania, and comes under the rule of an Austro-Hungarian regent.
1939	Hungary enters World War II as a German ally.
1944	German occupation; most of the Jewish population is deported.
1948	Communists take power.
1956	Rebellion against Communist rule is crushed by Soviet troops.
1989	Hungary opens its borders to Austria and the Iron Curtain begins to lift.
1990	Free elections are won by a center-right coalition.
1999	Hungary officially joins NATO.
2004	Hungary joins the European Union.

THE GOOD OLD DAYS

Hungary enjoyed two "golden ages" – one in the 15th century and another in the 19th. Under 15th-century ruler King Matthias, the son of a Transylvanian general, the nation expanded its borders and established its court in Vienna. Matthias patronized some of Europe's most brilliant scholars, and employed the best Italian artists to work on his palace in Visegrád. Ruins were unearthed here in the 1930s. His reign became a byword for good government. When he died, say Hungarians, justice died with him. The man known as "the greatest Hungarian" ushered in a second age of achievement. In the 19th century Count István Széchenyi modernized the country, laying surfaced roads, introducing steamships and founding an academy of sciences. He also linked Buda and Pest with the Chain Bridge, and stopped the regular cycle of floods around the Tisza river by building dams that regulated its flow.

SURVIVAL GUIDE

- Hungarian cuisine's best-known export, *gulyás* (goulash), is made with beef, onions, potatoes, paprika, tomatoes and garlic. Salami is a familiar item, as is *lecso*, a mix of peppers, tomatoes, onions and bacon fried in pork fat. Pastries also are specialties, sold in the *cukrászda* (pastry shop). Try *palacsinta*, thin pancakes filled with chocolate or curd cheese.

- Rural Hungarians produce and sell beautifully crafted items such as embroidered blouses and carved wood furniture. You can buy these in city stores, at national parks and from street sellers like the brightly costumed Transylvanian (Romanian) Hungarians.

- Wine is another good Hungarian buy, sold by dealers in the main vineyards, such as Eger. Many give tastings in their barrel-lined cellars.

- Go to street markets in the main towns and cities, such as the popular morning flea market on the southwest outskirts of Pécs. This is one of the biggest open-air markets in the country, selling antiques, crafts and food. On Sundays it also sells livestock, and the place is packed with country people.

- Some of the most fascinating ethnic communities have inevitably become big tourist magnets. Hollókő is filled with visitors for the August Palóc Festival and for Easter – an important celebration everywhere, marked with processions, egg-painting and a ceremony involving splashing girls with water or perfume.

- Summer festivals attract crowds to Pécs and Sopron in June, and on St. Stephen's Day on August 20. There are fireworks, fairs and processions all over Hungary.

A miscellany of merchandise on display at one of the many antiques shops in Budapest

- The state railroad, Hungarian Railways (Magyar Államvasutak – MÁV), travels to most of the country. There are special tourist passes offering unlimited use of the network for 7 or 10 days: contact MÁV (✉ Andrássy út 35, Budapest VI ☎ 1 461 5400).

- Accommodations are not limited to city hotels. The Danube bend, a spectacular deep gorge north of Budapest, is lined with attractive towns where many private homes offer rooms. The resorts around Lake Balaton are another option.

- For overnight stays on the Great Plain, try the Hortobágy Club Hotel in Hortobágy National Park (✉ H-4071 Hortobágy-Máta, Czinege utca 1 ☎ 52 369 020) or Pongrácz-Major Hotel near Kesckemét (✉ H-6041 Kerekegyháza, Kunpuszta 76 ☎ 76 361 073).

Budapest

BUDAPEST

Until the 19th century, two communities faced each other across the Danube. Royal, medieval Buda, with its majestic architecture, stood on the hilly western bank; and modern

Pest, a flat area of busy boulevards, was on the east bank. Then the Chain Bridge (Széchenyi lánchíd) was built and Budapest, "Queen of the Danube," was created, linking the western and eastern landscapes of Hungary: the green uplands behind Buda, and the flat fields of the Great Plain beyond Pest.

BUDAPEST

N

Óbuda

ÚJLIPOTVÁROS

4   RÓZSADOMB

Margit-sziget

Centenáriumi emlékmű

MARGIT HÍD

TERÉZVÁROS

Nyugati pályaudvar

VÍZIVÁROS

MOSZKVA TÉR

Néprajzi Múzeum

Országház

LIPÓTVÁROS

OKTOGON

3   Hadtörténeti Múzeum

VÁRHEGY

Mátyás templom

Halászbástya

Budavári Labirintus

KOSSUTH LAJOS TÉR

SZABADSÁG TÉR

Magyar Állami Operaház

Zeneakadémia

LISZT FERENC TÉR

Szent István-bazilika

ROOSEVELT TÉR

DEÁK FERENC TÉR

Déli pályaudvar

Várszinház

Magyar Nemzeti Galéria

ERZSÉBET TÉR

Pest Vigadó

VÖRÖSMARTY TÉR

Zsidó Múzeum

2   KRISZTINAVÁROS

Budai Vár

BUDA

Budapesti Történeti Múzeum

P E S T

Városháza

BELVÁROS

NAPHEGY

TABÁN

Belvárosi Plébánia templom

FERENCIEK TERE

Magyar Nemzeti Múzeum

DÖBRENTEI TÉR

KÁLVIN TÉR

1   SASHEGY

Citadella

GELLÉRT-HEGY

Jubileumi park

FŐVAM TÉR

Nagy-vásárcsarnok

SZT GELLÉRT TÉR

Duna

0   200   400   600   800 m
0   200   400   600   800 yards

A   B   C

Budapest

Crossing the Divide

The best place to get a feel for the capital's character and history is at Buda. Here you will find the oldest and grandest architecture, a cluster of museums and galleries, and countless cafés and bars. You can survey the whole city from Gellért Hill (Gellért-

hegy), and visit Castle Hill (Várhegy), a renovated medieval quarter reached by funicular railroad from the Buda end of Chain Bridge (Budavári Sikló). This is where you'll find the Buda Castle (Budai Vár) and the Fishermen's Fortress (Halászbástya).

Pest has a much more contemporary feel; its main landmark is the Gothic parliament building (Országház) dominating the riverbank. Also worth visiting are the Hungarian State Opera House (Magyar Állami Operaház) and the Museum of Fine Arts (Szépművészeti Múzeum). Between the riverbanks is tranquil Margaret Island (Margit-sziget), providing a haven of gardens in the middle of the Danube.

Local Flavors

In the late 19th and early 20th centuries Budapest ranked with Vienna and Paris as part of European café society, drawing artists and intellectuals to argue, work and read newspapers. After World War II, few of these hubs of creative life remained. The Café Restaurant New York, at Erzsébet körút 9–11, manages to preserve the aura associated with those days; it is currently closed for renovations.

Traditionally, Hungarian meals rely on the staples of spices, meat and cream and include intriguing specialties such as *túrós csúsza* (pasta with curd and sour cream). Since 1989 the range of international restaurant options has increased immeasurably.

Budapest at Night

The main home of opera and ballet is the Hungarian State Opera House (Magyar Állami Operaház, Andrássy út 22), a massive neo-Renaissance confection. Classical concerts take place in the art nouveau Academy of Music (Zeneakadémia), at Liszt Ferenc tér 8.

There are many clubs, rock venues

Panoramic view of Budapest from the top of Gellért Hill

bars and discos, and rock bands have emerged from their underground status of the Communist years. The English-language magazines *Budapest Week* (weekly) and *Budapest Panorama* (monthly) have entertainment listings.

Shopping

Pedestrian-only Váci utca, on the Pest side of the river, is the perfect place to start shopping trips, and to look for antiques and art bargains. Other main boulevards in central Pest also are lined with stores. In Buda, there's a good browsing area around Móricz Zsigmond körtér.

A well-known flea market (Ecseri) sets up at Nagykrősi út from Monday to Saturday. It's also a pleasure to wander among the heaped food stalls of the renovated Nagy-vásárcsarnok (Central Market Hall) on Fővám Körút. The market is open all day Monday to Friday and on Saturday until 2 p.m.

ESSENTIAL INFORMATION

TOURIST INFORMATION
8th Budapesti Turisztikai Sol Szolgáltató Kht (Tourism Office of Budapest)
• Sütő utca ☎ 1 438 8080
• Liszt Ferenc tér 11 ☎ /fax 1 322 4098
• Szentháromság tér ☎ 1 488 0453; fax 1 488 0474
• Nyugati palyaudvar (Western Railroad Station) ☎ 1 302 8580.
• Written inquiries to:H-1364 Budapest, PF 215
Fax 1 266 7477; www.budapestinfo.hu

URBAN TRANSPORTATION
Subway lines are color coded: yellow (M1), red (M2) and blue (M3). Buy tickets from the counter (*pénztár*) until 8 p.m., then from the section called *forgalmi ugyelét*. Trains run daily 4:30 a.m.–11:30 p.m. Buses with red or black numbers and no letter stop all over the city; avoid the express buses, which have a letter "E."

Trams and trolley buses also have an extensive network. Tickets are available from transport terminals, subway stations, vending machines or newsstands. For public transport information ☎ 1 461 6571. Subway stations are marked with an "M" on the city map. Make sure that taxis display a sign, and check that the meter is on and running. The biggest city company is Fötaxi (☎ 1 222 2222).

AIRPORT INFORMATION
Ferihegy Airport is 15 miles southeast of the city. The Air Traffic and Airport Authority (LRI) runs Centrum buses between the city (Erszébet tér bus station) and the airport every 30 minutes (5:30 a.m.–10 p.m.; journey time 45 minutes). Airport Minibuses (also run by LRI) travel to any requested destination (go to the Airport Minibus Service desk on arrival). Bus 93 runs to Kőbánya-Kispest subway station. For flight details ☎ 1 296 7155; general inquiries ☎ 1 296 9696.

CLIMATE – average highs and lows for the month

JAN.	FEB.	MAR.	APR.	MAY	JUN.	JUL.	AUG.	SEP.	OCT.	NOV.	DEC.
2°C	4°C	10°C	15°C	22°C	24°C	26°C	26°C	22°C	15°C	7°C	3°C
36°F	39°F	50°F	59°F	72°F	75°F	79°F	79°F	72°F	59°F	45°F	37°F
-4°C	-3°C	1°C	5°C	10°C	14°C	15°C	15°C	11°C	6°C	1°C	-3°C
25°F	27°F	34°F	41°F	50°F	57°F	59°F	59°F	52°F	43°F	34°F	27°F

City Sights

Key to symbols

🔲 map coordinates refer to the Budapest map on pages 258–259; sights below are highlighted in yellow on the map.

✉ address or location ☎ telephone number
🕐 opening times 🚇 nearest subway 🚌 nearest bus, trolley bus, or tram route 🍴 restaurant or café on site or nearby 🎫 admission charge: $$$ more than 1,000Ft, $$ 600Ft–1,000Ft, $ less than 600Ft
ℹ other relevant information

Budai Vár

🔲 B2 ✉ Várhegy 🚌 For all attractions: 5, 16, 78, Várbusz (Castle Bus) from Moszkva tér; tram 18; funicular from west end of Chain Bridge
Budapesti Történeti Múzeum ✉ Szent György tér 2
☎ 1 225 7815 🕐 Wed.–Mon. 10–6, Mar.–Oct.; 10–4, rest of year 🎫 $$; free Wed.
Kortárs Művészeti Múzeum ☎ 1 375 9175
🕐 Tue.–Sun. 10–6 🎫 $; free to all Tue.
Magyar Nemzeti Galéria ☎ 1 212 7356 🕐 Tue.–Sun. 10–6, early Mar. to early Dec.; 10–4, rest of year
🍴 Gallery café 🎫 Free, temporary exhibitions $.
ℹ Guided tours
Országos Széchényi Könyvtár ☎ 1 224 3700
🕐 Tue.–Fri. 9–9, Sat. 9–8 🎫 $; free Wed.
Budai Vár (Buda Castle) looks down over the Danube from the southern end of Várhegy (Castle Hill). Little is left of the earliest castle, which was built in the 13th century. What remains is in the cellars and underground passages, now part of the Budapesti Történeti Múzeum (Budapest History Museum), in Wing E. Before the building was flattened during World War II, it was an amalgam of 18th- and 19th-century Habsburg architecture. This is the version that has been carefully restored.

The Magyar Nemzeti Galéria (Hungarian National Gallery) collection of Hungarian art is housed in the Central Wings B, C and D, under a landmark dome.

A walk from here through a peaceful garden square and past the lovely Matthias Well fountain takes you to the West Wing (F) and the Országos Széchényi Könyvtár (National Széchényi Library), which stores approximately 2 million books.

Take a back seat for a view of Buda Castle

Contemporary art is displayed in the Kortárs Művészeti Múzeum (Museum of Contemporary Art – Ludwig Museum), in Wing A.

Statues outside the palace include Prince Eugene of Savoy, who routed the Turkish armies; King Matthias, in the west courtyard; and a mythical bird called the Turul.

Budavári Labirintus

🔲 B3 ✉ Uri utca 9 ☎ 1 212 0207 🕐 Daily 9:30–7:30 🚌 16, Várbusz (Castle Bus) 🎫 $$
A maze of catacombs extends for 16 miles under Várhegy (Castle Hill), made up of caverns linked by passageways originally built for use by the Turkish military. Only a tenth of the Budavári Labirintus (Buda Castle Labyrinth) complex can be visited, but even this gives a vivid impression of a strange, enclosed, underground world. Waxworks illustrate the history of Hungary from the misty past to the golden Renaissance age of King Matthias. During the siege of Budapest in World War II, thousands of people took shelter down here while above their heads the city was destroyed.

Magyar chiefs stand guard in Heroes' Square

GELLÉRT-HEGY

➕ B1 ✉ Between Erzsébet híd (Elizabeth Bridge) and Szabadság híd (Freedom Bridge) 🍴 Panorama, see page 557 🚌 7, 7A, 8, 78, 86, 112; tram 18, 19, 47, 49

Bishop Gellért failed to convert the pagan Magyars to Christianity; legend has it they stuck him in a barrel and threw him into the river from this 771-foot-high limestone cliff. His statue stands at the bottom of Gellért-hegy (Gellért Hill). At the top is the Citadella (Citadel), a stronghold built after the 1848–49 War of Independence to watch over the restive citizens. The Szabadság szobor (Freedom Monument), also at the top, was erected by the Russians in 1947. Before the fall of Communism, the monument featured a Soviet soldier as well as the now lone woman brandishing a palm leaf.

HALÁSZBÁSTYA

➕ B3 ✉ Szentháromság tér, Várhegy 🕐 Daily 24 hours 🍴 Alabárdos, see page 557 🚌 16, Várbusz (Castle Bus) from Moszkva tér 🎟 Free

Halászbástya (Fishermen's Fortress) is one of the city's greatest tourist draws: a fairy-tale, seven-towered rampart in pale stone wedged into the eastern rim of Castle Hill. The architect, Frigyes Schulek, designed the fortress as part of the city's millennial celebrations of Magyar nationhood in 1896. There are great river views, and plenty of souvenir stalls and shops.

HŐSÖK TERE

➕ D4 ✉ Andrássy út 🚇 Hősök tere 🚌 4; trolley bus 79

At the end of the grand Andrássy út and at the entrance to Városliget (City Park) is magnificent Hősök tere (Heroes' Square), part of the city's 1896 millennial celebrations. On either side are the Műcsarnok (Palace of Arts) and the Szépművészeti Múzeum (Museum of Fine Arts, see page 264); between them is a monument to Hungarian successes. Perched on a 118-foot-high column is the Archangel Gabriel; guarding the foot of the column are statues of the seven fierce and triumphant Magyar chiefs, with Árpád, their leader, in the center. They are flanked by colonnades bearing the figures of Fame, Knowledge, Peace and War; between the columns are more Hungarian icons, including King Stephen (who would later be sainted).

MAGYAR ÁLLAMI OPERAHÁZ

➕ C3 ✉ Andrássy út 22; tours begin at Hajós utca entrance ☎ 1 331 2550 or 1 332 8197 (tours) 🕐 Tours daily at 3 and 4 (duration 40 minutes) 🍴 Müvész, see page 557 🚇 Opera 🚌 4 🎟 Tour $$

The Magyar Állami Operaház (Hungarian State Opera House) building has beautiful marble-work, gold leaf and frescoes. Opened in 1884, it celebrates the musical world with statues of composers Wolfgang Mozart, Guiseppe Verdi, Richard Wagner and Ludwig van Beethoven, which stand on the stone cornice of the front terrace. Pride of place goes to Hungarians Franz Liszt and opera composer Ferenc Erkel, whose statues flank the entrance. Inside the building an enormous bronze chandelier hangs over the auditorium, which is decorated with Greek gods.

MAGYAR NEMZETI MÚZEUM

➕ D2 ✉ Múzeum körút 14–16 ☎ 1 338 2122 or 1 327 7768 (tours) 🕐 Tue.–Sun. 10–6 🍴 Empire, see page 557 🚇 Astoria or Kálvin tér 🚌 7, 7A, 9, 15, 78; tram 47, 49 🎟 Free, temporary exhibitions $$

Five collections form the Magyar Nemzeti Múzeum (Hungarian National Museum), Hungary's largest museum, covering an area of 861,111 square feet. They include

The Chain Bridge crosses the Danube, linking Buda and Pest

archeology, medieval and modern displays, a numismatic collection and historical portraits. The great prize among the exhibits is St. Stephen's 11th-century crown, which was stolen by Hungarian fascists after World War II and kept in the United States until President Jimmy Carter ordered its return. The upper part of the crown, a gold cap set above the jeweled headband, may date even earlier. Other curiosities are the inscribed brick from a 13th-century monk's tomb and the tent of a Turkish commander taken at the siege of Vienna in 1683.

MÁTYÁS-TEMPLOM

➕ B3 ✉ Szentháromság tér 2 ☎ 1 355 5657 🕓 Religious visits: daily 6 a.m.–8 p.m.; tourists generally Mon.–Fri. 9–5, Sat. 9–1, Sun. 1–5 🚌 16, Várbusz (Castle Bus) from Moszkva tér 💰 Religious visits free; tourists $

Fifteenth-century King Matthias was married twice in the Mátyás-templom (Matthias Church), which had already been in existence for two centuries. It later served the Turks as a mosque, and was subsequently remodeled in the 19th century in striking neo-Gothic style. Medieval touches have been reproduced in the interior, along with dramatic features such as the soaring 262-foot spire. The tombs of 12th-century monarch Béla III and his wife, Anne of Châtillon, are in the Trinity Chapel near the main door.

ORSZÁGHÁZ

➕ B3 ✉ Kossuth Lajos tér 1–3 ☎ 1 441 4904, 1 441 4412, 1441 4415 or 1 441 4138 🕓 English guided tours daily at 10, noon and 2. Tours subject to parliamentary sessions 🍴 Empire, see page 557 🚇 Kossuth tér 🚌 15; tram 2; trolley bus 70, 78 💰 $$$

Bristling with neo-Gothic spires and turrets, the Országház (Parliament) building sits on the eastern bank of the Danube, covering an area of nearly 200,000 square feet. Its magnificent red dome is 315 feet high and rises above a 16-sided hall between the upper and lower houses of parliament.

SZENT ISTVÁN-BAZILIKA

➕ C3 ✉ Svent István tér ☎ 1 317 2859 🕓 Church: daily 7–7. Chapel: Mon.– Sat. 9–5, Sun. 1–5. Dome: daily 10–6, Apr.–Oct. 🚇 Bajcsy-Zsilinsky út or Deák tér, Arany János utca 🚌 15; trolley bus 70, 72, 78 💰 Free; dome $

Budapest's biggest church, Szent István-bazilika (St. Stephen's Basilica), took 55 years to finish, and its dazzling interior includes 90 pounds of 24-carat gold, as well as frescoes, paintings and tapestries by Hungarian artists. Transylvanian and Hungarian heroes are represented by 88 statues, and the most cherished item – the mummified right hand of St. Stephen – is displayed in a glass case. Its 315-foot-high dome provides good views of the city.

Budapest

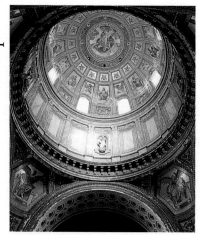

The golden dome of St. Stephen's Basilica

SZÉPMŰVÉSZETI MÚZEUM

🏛 D4 ✉ Dósza György út 41 ☎ 1 363 2675
◉ Tue.–Sun. 10–5:30 🚇 Hősök tere 🚌 4, 20, 30;
trolley bus 75, 79 💷 $$

The Szépművészeti Múzeum (Museum of Fine Arts) is a neoclassic temple built to celebrate the millennial anniversary of the Magyar nation and to house the nation's art. Its exhibits are now restricted to foreign work and include ancient Egyptian mummy cases and a world-renowned collection of old masters. Of particular note are works by Spanish artists El Greco and Pablo Picasso.

VÁROSLIGET

Magyar Mezőgazdasági Múzeum 🏛 E4
✉ Vajdahunyad vára ☎ 1 363 1117 ◉ Tue.–Sun.
10–5 (also Sat.–Sun. 5–6), Mar.–Oct.; Tue.–Sun. 10–4
(also Sat.–Sun. 4–5), rest of year 🍴 Gundel, see
page 557 🚇 Széchenyi fürdő 🚌 4, 20, 30; trolley
bus 70, 72, 75, 79 💷 $
Fővárosi Nagycirkusz 🏛 E4 ✉ Állatkerti út 12
☎ 1 343 8300 ◉ Telephone for details or ask at the
tourist office 🍴 Gundel, see page 557
🚇 Széchenyi fürdő 🚌 4; trolley bus 70, 72, 79
💷 $$
Közlekedési Múzeum 🏛 E4 ✉ Városligeti körút 11
☎ 1 273 3840 ◉ Tue.–Sun. 10–5 (also Sat.–Sun. 5–6),
May–Sep.; Tue.–Sun. 10–4 (also Sat.–Sun. 4–5),
Jan.–Apr.; Sat.–Sun. 10–5, rest of year 🍴 Gundel,
see page 557 🚇 Széchenyi fürdő 🚋 Tram 1; trolley
bus 70, 72, 74 💷 Free
Állatkert 🏛 D4 ✉ Állatkerti Körút 6–12 ☎ 1 363

3710 ◉ Daily 9–7, May–Aug.; 9–6, Apr. and Sep.;
9–5, Mar. and Oct.; 9–4, rest of year 🍴 Gundel
🚇 Széchenyi fürdő 🚌 4; trolley bus 72 💷 $
Vidámpark 🏛 E4 ✉ Állatkerti Körút 14–16 ☎ 1 363
2660 ◉ Daily 10–8, Apr.–Sep.; Sat.–Sun. 10–7, rest of
year 🍴 Gundel 🚇 Széchenyi fürdő 🚌 4; trolley bus
72 💷 Free entrance (rides $)
Petőfi Csarnok/Repüléstörténeti Múzeum 🏛 E4
✉ Zichy Mihály utca 14–16 ☎ 1 251 7266; Aviation
Museum 1 363 0809 ◉ Tue.–Sun. 10–5 (also Sat.–Sun.
5–6), mid-May to mid-Oct. 🍴 Gundel 🚇 Széchenyi
fürdő 🚋 Tram 1; trolley bus 70, 72, 74 💷 $

Beyond the bustling boulevards of Pest is Városliget (City Park). It was laid out in the 18th century and has acquired several extras over the years. The oddest is Vajdahunyad vára (Vajdahunyad Castle), built for the 1896 World Exhibition. Based on a Transylvanian fortress, its popularity ensured permanent survival. Inside the walls is the Magyar Mezőgazdasági Múzeum (Hungarian Agricultural Museum). The Állatkert (zoo), with art nouveau animal houses, is another favorite. There's also the Fővárosi Nagycirkusz (circus) and a slightly faded Vidámpark (amusement park).

In the park's southeast corner are the Közlekedési Múzeum (Transportation Museum) and the Petőfi Csarnok youth center, where local youth come to hear pop music and watch open-air movies in the summer. The hall contains the Repülési Múzeum (Aviation Museum), which exhibits the space capsule flown by the first Hungarian cosmonaut.

The Danube Esplanade

Running alongside the river on the Pest bank, between Chain Bridge (Széchenyi lánchíd) and Elizabeth Bridge (Erzsébet híd), is the tree-lined Danube Esplanade (Duna-korzó). In the 19th century, this was the most fashionable place to be seen. Café tables were set out in the evening, and gypsy bands played by lamplight under the stars. The elaborate Pesti Vigadó (Pest Concert Hall) is a legacy of that era, and still a venue for classical music concerts.

Esztergom's cathedral entrance, dominated by eight Corinthian pillars

EXCURSION TO ESZTERGOM

Hungary's largest cathedral towers over the stunning scenery of the Danube Bend at Esztergom, former royal city and the birthplace of King Stephen I (975–1038). There has been a settlement here, guarding the western approach to the gorge, since Roman times. Medieval Esztergom was destroyed by the Turks in 1543, but the city rose again, and it now boasts a center full of baroque buildings.

The cathedral is by far the most imposing: it is 328 feet from the floor to the top of its huge, glittering dome. It includes one of the world's biggest paintings – an altarpiece based on the work of 16th-century Italian artist Titian. The white marble altar itself was designed in 1519 and made by expert craftsmen from Florence, Italy.

Among other treasures are the impressive Renaissance interior of the Bakócz Chapel and a gold and enamel Gothic cross known as the Calvary of Matthias Corvinus. The dome offers a spectacular view over Esztergom and its surroundings.

The present version of the cathedral was begun in the 1820s: Hungarian composer Franz Liszt celebrated its

reconsecration in 1856 with a mass. Long before this second lease of life, Esztergom was the seat of the Hungarian Primate – head of the nation's Catholic Church – and an important royal base. King Stephen was crowned in a church on the site in AD 1000, and the remains of a royal palace are housed in the Castle Museum (Vár Múzeum) next door.

Two other museums are worth a visit. The Museum of Christian Art (Keresztény Múzeum) has a superb collection of medieval religious paintings and works by Italian artists such as Duccio di Buoninsegna, Lorenzo di Credi and Giovanni di Paolo. The Danube Museum (Duna Múzeum) features displays that clearly illustrate (despite Hungarian-only captions) the role of the river and its effects on the life of the town.

Esztergom is 41 miles north of Budapest. Buses travel from Budapest's Árpád híd bus station, and there is a regular service from Nyugati (Western) railroad station.

For tour information contact Gran Tours (✉ H-2500 Esztergom, Széchenyi tér 25 ☎ 33 417 052; fax 33 413 756).

IRELAND

"THERE lay the green shore of Ireland, like some coast of plenty."

On arriving in Ireland, from *English Traits*, 1856, by essayist and philosopher Ralph Waldo Emerson

Opposite: This view of the mountains and lakes of Killarney is known as "Ladies View"

Ireland

IRELAND

People long for Ireland in a way that they pine for few other countries. Call it romantic, call it sentimental, but there is something about this remarkable country that tugs at the heartstrings of even those who have no Irish blood. The beauty of the country, its powerful Gaelic traditions and the irrepressibly romantic and creative nature of the Irish people underscore this potent appeal. This is a country that is not without problems, however, and its political and religious divide has had far-reaching, universal impact.

Mists of Time

Ireland claims with pride that it was a "land of saints and scholars" when the rest of Europe was deep in the Dark Ages. It is often described as a Celtic country, with all the myth-making that goes along with that term. The Celts are seen as being a distinctive lost race of Iron Age people who, in the face of first Roman and then Anglo Saxon aggression, retreated into Scotland, Ireland, Wales and Cornwall in England, from where they passed down the

cultural values of their time. They did not call themselves Celts, and the term may be only a convenient label, but what is certain is that the influence of the earliest Bronze Age and Iron Age cultures survives on the peripheries of the British Isles. This is especially true in Ireland, where the evocative Gaelic language, still heard today, is its greatest expression.

There are thousands of prehistoric sites in Ireland: on the remote western seaboard, on the Beara peninsula, in County Kerry, and at exceptional places such as the Brù na Bòinne burial complex, in County Meath north of Dublin. Even where they are ruinous and vestigial, these ancient sites are hauntingly evocative.

You will find within the same landscape the music, song, wit and drama of Ireland that have been enshrined in hundreds of films, songs, dances and stories. A sense of the past is intense here; it has shaped Ireland in a seminal way, for better or for worse.

From Dublin to Kerry

Dublin is the boisterous heart of Ireland, the "family home." It should not be missed, of course, but Dublin will only whet your appetite for the rest of the country. Save time to explore other areas for the essential Irish experience. South of the capital lie the Wicklow Mountains, with the popular Glendalough at their heart – half religious site, wholly spectacular from a scenic point of view.

Farther south lies the fascinating Viking town of Wexford, from where the long, rambling southern coast of Ireland runs through endless great bays toward the distant west (and the most spectacular scenery). The western coast stretches for nearly 180 miles north to south, but measures much more if all the sinuous indentations, bays, river

---

MORE TOP DESTINATIONS IN IRELAND

- Aran Islands A2
- Beara Peninsula A1
- Blarney Castle B1 ● The Burren A2
- Clifden A2 ● Dingle A1
- Galway A2 ● Giant's Causeway C4
- Glendalough C2 ● Kilkenny B2
- Killarney A1 ● Brù na Bòinne C3

Ireland

IRELAND

ATLANTIC OCEAN

SCOTLAND

Malin Head
Rathlin I.
Giant's Causeway
Rathmullan
Letterkenny
Coleraine
A26
Dungloe
N13
Londonderry
Ardara
Ballybofey
Strabane
N14
NORTHERN
Ballymena
Donegal
Cookstown
IRELAND
Antrim
Omagh
M2
Belfast
Ballyshannon
Lough Erne
A5
Lough Neagh
Newtownards
N15
Bundoran
M1
Sligo
Enniskillen
Armagh
Mourne Mts
Erris Head
Donegal Bay
Monaghan
A1
Newcastle
Bangor Erris
Ballina
Colloney
Clones
Castleblayney
Newry
807m
Carrick-on-Shannon
Cavan
N2
Dundalk
Swinford
Boyle
N4
Carrickmacross
Castlebar
N5
N3
Monasterboice
IRISH SEA
Westport
Longford
Mellifont Abbey
Drogheda
Claremorris
Roscommon
Kells
Newgrange
Lough Mask
Cong
Lough Ree
REPUBLIC OF
Trim
Navan
M1
Skerries
Clifden
Tuam
Athlone
Royal Canal
Hill of Tara
Lucan
Ballynahinch Lake
Lough Corrib
Mullingar
N6
DUBLIN
Galway
Ballinasloe
Clonmacnois
Grand Canal
Castletown
Dun Laoghaire
Galway Bay
Coole Park
Loughrea
Tullamore
Bog of Allen
House
Bray
Aran Islands
The Burren
Thor Ballylee
Birr
IRELAND
Kildare
Naas
Powerscourt
Cliffs of Moher
Lough Derg
Portlaoise
N7
Glendalough
N11
N18
Roscrea
Athy
N9
927m
Wicklow
Craggaunowen
Ennis
Durrow
Carlow
Rathdrum
Kilrush
Bunratty
Nenagh
Thurles
N8
Nore
Arklow
Ballybunion
Adare
Limerick
Rock of Cashel
Kilkenny
N10
Gorey
Listowel
N21
Tipperary
N24
Cashel
Barrow
Enniscorthy
Tralee
Abbeyfeale
Mitchelstown Caves
Cahir
Carrick-on-Suir
New Ross
Wexford
Slea Head
Dingle
Castleisland
N20
Clonmel
N9
N25
Rosslare Harbour
Killorglin
Mallow
Fermoy
Lismore
Waterford
Dunganstown
Glenbeigh
1041m
Blackwater
Dungarvan
Tramore
Carnsore Point
Cahirciveen
N22
Macroom
Blarney
Waterville
RING OF KERRY
Kenmare
Blarney Castle
N25
Youghal
Parknasilla
Cork
Cobh
WALES
Beara Pen.
Clonakilty
Kinsale
Bantry
Skibbereen
Mizen Head
St George's Channel

0   40   80   120 km
0   20   40   60 miles

A   B   C

mouths, peninsulas and islands are taken into account.

Try to visit the far southwest. Take in the charming historic city of Kilkenny on the way; and visit Cork, the Irish Republic's second largest city, where you can kiss the nearby Blarney Stone if you feel that you should. Beyond Cork lies the glorious Beara peninsula. The bigger Iveragh peninsula is part of exquisite County Kerry to the north, land of the great mountains of Macgillycuddy's Reeks and the delightful lakes, and town, of Killarney.

Islands and Lakes

North of County Kerry lies the lovely Dingle peninsula and County Clare. Clare's southern half is mundane, but becomes increasingly spectacular the farther north you go, past the huge, echoing Cliffs of Moher and into the limestone country of the Burren, with its natural pavements of moonscape rock, dramatic stone burial chambers and hill forts.

In the pubs of Clare you will encounter the heart-stopping, foot-tapping essence of Irish music and

The great open spaces of the peat country as seen from Sligo Bay

song, in an environment that preserves the best of the past with energy, vitality and lyricism.

Off Clare's northwestern coast are the stunning Aran Islands, the magic names of Inishmor, Inishmaan and Inisheer resonating with all things Irish. Beyond Clare is Galway Bay and Galway city, the latter a lively, unfailingly charming place on the threshold of the Gaeltacht, the major area of Gaelic-speaking Ireland. Here, the mountains of Connemara and the broad lakes Loughs Corrib and Mask match an astonishing coastline of raw, rocky wilderness that lies to either side of the romantic town of Clifden.

Inland, Ireland also has much to offer. The heart of the country is a green bowl of rich farmland, of lakes, rivers and isolated ranges of rounded hills. Landlocked Ireland is outshone by the stupendous coastline of the far west, but it is a charming country full of character and tradition, where you will hear talk of horses and history and where lakes and rivers throng with fish.

Traveling North

Farther north is the remote county of Mayo, where you can follow the pilgrims' route up the Holy Mountain of Croagh Patrick, if you feel fit enough for the grueling four-hour clamber over rough rocks. Beyond Mayo are Sligo and Donegal, and golden beaches and tumbling Atlantic surf. Lakes and remote peninsulas enhance north Donegal, where the coast turns east toward the beautiful yet troubled city of Londonderry, gateway to Northern Ireland and the six counties of Ulster.

This British-ruled area has been riven for decades by sectarian violence and a divisiveness that is still struggling to resolve itself. Ulster's image has suffered much from "the Troubles" (the resumption of political violence since 1969), yet the beauty of its coast and countryside is of classic Irish quality.

"Organ-pipe" cliffs of the Giant's Causeway – County Antrim

The Giant's Causeway area, on County Antrim's north coast, is an astonishing landscape of perfectly formed hexagonal rock sections. Farther east lies the seaside town of Ballycastle, beyond which are the towering cliffs of Fair Head and then the green and peaceful Antrim Glens. South of Antrim lies Belfast, Ulster's capital, a city that has shown a grim face for far too long, and one that might yet be recognized, along with all of Ulster, for its majority of law-abiding, determined and hardworking citizens and for its deeply rooted Ulster-Irish traditions.

The Gaelic Lifestyle

In Dublin you will find museums, stores, theaters and restaurants to match those anywhere else in Europe, all suffused by the richness of Irish culture and by a modern sophistication.

In parts of rural Ireland things are different. You may come across an easygoing attitude, a relaxed approach reflecting the fact that the Irish have been around for a long time and often see no reason to rush things. At the same time, you may find yourself swept off your feet in places like beautiful, bustling Galway city, where a vigorous student population adds a contemporary note to the Gaelic culture most young people continue to embrace.

If you travel through Ireland, you will find the Irish hospitable and friendly. Often, if you ask a local for directions to a nearby site or place in town, you will be taken there rather than given complicated directions.

The Irish are fired by an all-consuming curiosity and have an almost total lack of pretension. They are a people whose history has often been terrible, bleak and unforgiving. Yet they have survived as the inheritors of a bewitching country that lies off the western edge of the Continent but is also an integral part of modern Europe.

Ireland

TIMELINE

circa 3000 BC	Neolithic, Stone Age farmers construct sacred burial chambers at Brù na Bòinne.
AD 430	Saint Patrick begins the conversion of Ireland to Christianity.
circa 795	Vikings settle on the River Liffey, thereby founding Dublin.
1170	Powerful Anglo-Irish hegemony established in Ireland.
circa 1610	Large areas of Ulster are confiscated by the English Crown.
1845–51	The Great Famine; a million Irish people die and a million emigrate, chiefly to America.
1921	Anglo-Irish Treaty partitions Ireland into the Irish Free State and mainly Protestant Ulster, which remains under British rule.
1948	Irish Free State is declared a republic.
1969	Beginning of "the Troubles" in Northern Ireland.
1972	Republic of Ireland joins the European Community.
1985	The Anglo-Irish Agreement is signed by British Prime Minister Margaret Thatcher and the Irish Prime Minister Garrett Fitzgerald.
1998	"Good Friday" agreement paves the way for a Northern Ireland Assembly.
2002	Republic of Ireland adopts the euro as its currency.

DIVIDED IRELAND

Ireland has been a divided country for long, bitter centuries. The reasons are complex and lie in historical developments over hundreds of years. The larger, southern part of modern Ireland is the Republic of Ireland, *Poblacht na h' Eireann* – mainly Roman Catholic, with a small minority of Protestants and a strong Irish Gaelic culture and identity. After years of stagnation, the nation is now enjoying economic success and modernization, partly through its early embracing of the European Union.

The smaller, northern part of Ireland is Ulster, or Northern Ireland, part of the United Kingdom of Great Britain. It is mainly Protestant, with a substantial Roman Catholic minority, and has a culture and identity that is essentially Irish, but with strong British elements. Ulster Protestants consider themselves Irish but wish to maintain a union with Britain. In Ulster, Roman Catholics, many of whom wish to be thought of as Northern Irish, are seen by many Protestants as representing a rival religion as well as representing southern Irish Republicanism. The tensions of this duality in Ulster gave rise to violent conflict that over some 30 years caused immeasurable suffering. Through the peace process, the 1998 "Good Friday" agreement created a devolved legislative Assembly for Northern Ireland and a framework for multiparty power-sharing. Violence was largely eliminated, but continued political conflict led to a temporary reversion to direct British rule.

SURVIVAL GUIDE

- If you visit Dublin in the early spring, try to be there on March 17, St. Patrick's Day, when the city is bursting with activity.

- If you're interested in shopping for Celtic crafts, don't miss the Kilkenny Design Centre in Kilkenny. This is the city's finest showcase for stylish Irish housewares, glass, books, fashion and jewelry. The upstairs restaurant serves generous portions of delicious homestyle food.

- Ireland is rapidly modernizing its road system, but there are still some very poor public roads, especially in the rural parts of the country. Look for unexpected potholes on otherwise smooth surfaces.

- Politics in Ireland is a very serious subject. It is best not to get involved in too much political discussion, especially in Northern Ireland. The subject is hugely complex and emotive. In the Republic of Ireland you should avoid referring to the "United Kingdom" or the "British Isles." The republic is emphatically a separate country. Speak of Ulster as Ulster or as Northern Ireland.

- Be aware that there is a no-smoking policy throughout the Republic of Ireland in all public places.

- Visit the local pubs in rural Ireland, especially in Clare, where in towns like Ennis you will find some of the greatest Irish music of all.

- Visit popular places such as Glendalough in County Wicklow, Killarney in Kerry and the Cliffs of Moher in Clare outside the peak season of July and August. Glendalough, especially, can become jammed with traffic.

- Enjoy the beautiful and often remote beaches of Ireland's west coast, but always be careful if you go swimming. Tides are very strong and there can be unexpected currents.

- Road signs in some parts of Ireland now show Gaelic spellings for towns and villages instead of English spellings. The conversion process will continue for some years and affects the counties of Galway, Kerry, Cork, Donegal, Waterford, Mayo and Meath.

- Ireland's Roman Catholic churches are extremely important places to the communities they serve, and you'll usually find someone praying if you visit. Be as discreet as possible when walking around the interiors of churches, and especially when in front of the altar. People may not take kindly to photographs being taken inside churches.

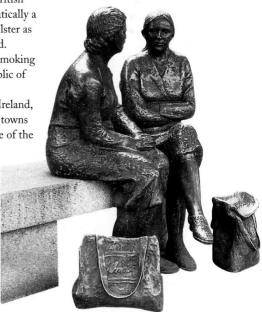

Shoppers frozen in time

Ireland

Dublin

DUBLIN

All roads seem to lead to Dublin in the end; it is a homecoming city where the visitor will feel as welcome as the Irish do. Dublin is celebrated today as one of Europe's most vibrant, colorful cities, something that Dubliners have always known. It is a rich distillation of all things Irish – music, conversation and laughter amid the city's lively streets, buzzing pubs and magnificent Georgian buildings.

Finding Your Way

The Dublin tourist office is located in the handsome old church of St. Andrew's, just southwest of Trinity College in the city center. Here you can obtain information about guided summer walking tours. Central Dublin is a reasonably easy and rewarding place to explore on foot. The main museums and notable buildings are concentrated in more fashionable south Dublin, but there are not-to-be-missed attractions across the River Liffey in north Dublin. A good starting point is the famous

O'Connell Bridge, where Dublin begins with a rush.

Take time to adjust to the breezy pace of it all. To the north is O'Connell Street – the "broadest street in Europe." Lively shopping streets such as Abbey Street Lower and Earl Street North lead off to either side. On Earl Street you will find a genial, roguish statue of James Joyce, Ireland's most famous writer and the masterful chronicler of Dublin life. Go down Earl Street and turn left onto Marlborough Street to visit St. Mary's Pro-Cathedral, a magnificent neoclassic building.

Opposite Earl Street is very busy Henry Street, with the huge ILAC Shopping Centre and the adjoining fruit and vegetable market on Moore Street. This whole area leading down to Smithfield Village has been the subject of recent refurbishment. The women who work the stalls are famous for their lively Joycean banter. On O'Connell Street, just before Henry Street, is one of the landmarks of the Easter Rising of 1916, when Irish nationalists staged an uprising against British rule and took over the General Post Office, opposite which is the dramatic Spire Monument, unveiled in 2002.

At the north end of O'Connell Street, by the Parnell Monument, is Parnell Square; on the square's north side is the Hugh Lane Municipal Gallery of Modern Art (see page 279) and the Dublin Writers Museum (see page 277).

The Heart of Dublin

South of O'Connell Bridge is the brimming heart of Dublin. From the south side of the bridge, walk down Westmoreland Street to College Green, a frantic concentration of traffic that initially detracts from the stupendous buildings that surround it. Admire the neoclassic splendor of the Bank of

Ireland and the elegant entrance to Trinity College, through which you can escape to the crowded but relaxing college campus. Otherwise, carefully cross College Green to the south and then continue past the buxom statue of Molly Malone, heroine of the famous "Cockles and Mussels" refrain, wheeling her cart in the midst of Dublin shoppers. The statue has become cheerfully known, through irrepressible Dublin wit, as "The Tart with the Cart."

Ahead lies pedestrian-only Grafton Street, crammed with interesting stores and delightful side streets on both sides; plus a variety of street performers. Head east to Leinster House, seat of Irish government, and to the National Museum and National Gallery.

Beyond these lie the 18th-century Georgian splendors of Merrion Square and Fitzwilliam Street. Alternatively, go west from Grafton Street along store-lined Wicklow Street, then on to Dublin Castle and Christ Church Cathedral; or head back north across Dame Street and into Temple Bar, the rejuvenated old riverside district that is the exciting focus of Dublin by night.

The Ha'penny Bridge

Dublin's Ha'penny Bridge, over the River Liffey, is best reached from Temple Bar by going down the narrow Merchant's Arch – look closely for the symbols of nearby stores carved into the pavement. The bridge dates from 1816 and is made of cast iron; its elegant arches are lit up at night. It was officially named the Wellington Bridge after the British Duke of Wellington, but gained its popular name from the half-penny toll once charged for crossing it.

Elegant 18th- and 19th-century Georgian architecture frames Ha'penny Bridge on the Liffey

Vary your Dublin experiences. Enjoy Temple Bar's restaurants and lively streets like Crow Street and Crown Alley, or visit St. Patrick's Cathedral on Patrick Street, where Jonathan Swift, author of *Gulliver's Travels,* was dean. Enjoy outstanding drama at Dublin's Abbey Theatre on Abbey Street, or classic Irish entertainment at the Olympia on Dame Street. Above all, visit Dublin's famous pubs (see page 281) for great music and talk. There is a quicker, sharper edge to the Irish here, as befits a busy, cosmopolitan city.

ESSENTIAL INFORMATION

TOURIST INFORMATION
Dublin Tourism Centre
• Suffolk Street ☎ 01 605 7700;
www.visitdublin.com
Also at: • 14 Upper O'Connell Street
• Baggot Street Bridge
• Arrivals Hall, Dublin Airport

URBAN TRANSPORTATION
Dublin has two main railroad stations: Heuston Station, Kingsbridge, is where services from southern and western Ireland terminate. Connolly Station, on Amiens Street, is where ferry connections arrive and the termination point for trains from the southeast, north and northwest, including Belfast. The Dublin Area Rapid Transit (DART) railroad line runs north to Howth and south to Greystones. Connolly Station and Pearse Station, and Tara Station are convenient city center stops. LUAS Green Line tram system (St. Stephen's Green to Sandyford) and Red Line (Connolly to Tallaght) brings passengers from the suburbs into the center. For train information call ☎ 01 850 366 2221. For DART call ☎ 01 703 3592. There is a good citywide bus service run by Dublin Bus (Bus Átha Cliath), 59 Upper O'Connell Street (☎ 01 873 4222); buses daily 7 a.m.–11:30 p.m. Nightlink service Mon.–Wed. 12:30 a.m.–2 a.m., Thu. 12:30 a.m.–3:30 a.m., Fri.–Sat. 12:30 a.m.–4:30 a.m. Countrywide services leave from the main bus station, Busáras, on Amiens Street. Dublin taxis are expensive and difficult to hail on the street. Stands are at O'Connell Street, St. Stephen's Green, College Green and Dame Street. Call ☎ 1800 727 272 (toll-free).

AIRPORT INFORMATION
Dublin Airport is 7 miles north of the city. A tourist office is in the arrivals hall. Aircoach runs a bus service to the city center every 15 minutes, 4:30 a.m.–midnight; the journey takes 30 minutes ☎ 01 844 7118. The Dublin Bus Airlink runs to/from Busáras. A slower, regular bus service (No. 41) runs to/from Eden Quay.

CLIMATE – average highs and lows for the month

JAN.	FEB.	MAR.	APR.	MAY	JUN.	JUL.	AUG.	SEP.	OCT.	NOV.	DEC.
8°C	8°C	9°C	11°C	14°C	17°C	19°C	18°C	16°C	13°C	10°C	8°C
46°F	46°F	48°F	52°F	57°F	63°F	66°F	65°F	61°F	55°F	50°F	46°F
3°C	3°C	4°C	5°C	7°C	10°C	12°C	12°C	10°C	8°C	5°C	4°C
37°F	37°F	39°F	41°F	45°F	50°F	54°F	54°F	50°F	46°F	41°F	39°F

Dublin

CITY SIGHTS

Key to symbols

🔲 map coordinates refer to the Dublin map on page 274; sights below are highlighted in yellow on the map.

✉ address or location ☎ telephone number

🕐 opening times 🔵 nearest DART station

🚌 nearest bus route 🍴 restaurant or café on site or nearby 💰 admission charge: $$$ more than €6, $$ €4–€6, $ less than €4 ℹ️ other relevant information

CHRIST CHURCH CATHEDRAL

Christ Church Cathedral 🔲 A2 ✉ Christchurch Place ☎ 01 677 8099 🕐 Mon.–Fri. 9:45–4:30, Sat. 10–4:30, Sun. 12:45–2:45 🚌 50, 78A 💰 $$

Dvblinia ✉ St. Michael's Hill ☎ 01 679 4611 🕐 Daily 10–5, Apr.–Sep.; Mon.–Sat. 11–4, Sun. 10–4:30, rest of year 🍴 Tea rooms on site 🚌 50, 78A 💰 $$

Dublin's great cathedral dates from the 12th century, but much of the surviving building is a 19th-century refurbishment in Gothic Revival style. The interior has numerous fine memorials and features, but the most authentic parts of Christ Church are the late 12th-century transepts and the ancient crypt, one of the largest medieval crypts in Europe. It is 175 feet long. Thickets of rough stone pillars support the entire weight of the massive building above; the air is dense with age. Weird monuments and artifacts lurk menacingly in niches and dark corners. They include battered statues of English kings, medieval carved stones and oddities such as a mummified cat and rat, thought to have become trapped during a chase through organ pipes. Linked to the cathedral by a covered stone bridge is Synod Hall, where the colorful exhibition "Dvblinia" details Dublin's history from the medieval period.

DUBLIN CASTLE

🔲 B2 ✉ Dame Street ☎ 01 677 7129 🕐 Mon.–Fri.10–4, Sat.–Sun. 2–4:45 🍴 Castle restaurant 🚌 49, 54, 56A, 77A, 123 💰 $$ ℹ️ Guided tours only; advance reservations are required. State apartments may be closed at times for official functions

Dublin Castle dates from the early 13th century but has been largely rebuilt and

Ornate interior decoration at Dublin Castle

expanded. It is a powerful and at times brooding reminder of the past. Look for deep scars in the stonework of the Guardroom, at the main (north) entrance leading to the cobbled upper yard. They are the result of repeated bayonet sharpening, an eerie symbol of 950 years of British rule. The state apartments that are open to the public include St. Patrick's Hall, the Throne Room, the State Drawing Room and the Picture Gallery, all of which have sumptuous decorations and furnishings. A reconstruction during the 1980s uncovered original 10th-century Viking defenses, a fascinating other world. The castle's Chapel Royal is a glorious neo-Gothic indulgence dating from 1814. Its exterior bristles with pointed Gothic motifs and 90 or so carved heads of historical figures. The interior has lavish plaster vaulting and superb carved oak galleries.

DUBLIN WRITERS MUSEUM

🔲 B3 ✉ 18 Parnell Square North ☎ 01 872 2077 🕐 Mon.–Sat. 10–6, Sun. 11–5 🍴 Museum restaurant 🔵 DART Connolly Station (10 mins walk) 🚌 10, 11, 11A, 11B, 13, 13A, 16, 16A, 19, 19A 💰 $$$ ℹ️ Combined ticket with James Joyce Museum and The Shaw Birthplace available

Literary Dublin in all its glory is represented by this engrossing museum's large collection of documents, artifacts, portraits and general memorabilia of famous Irish writers, including Oscar Wilde and Samuel Beckett. The combined buildings that contain the

Dublin

Ireland's most controversial novelist, James Joyce, was one of world literature's most important figures. Joyce was an innovator of the highest order, a writer of dazzling intellect. He was born in 1882 into a Dublin Catholic family of some gentility, although poverty overtook the family while Joyce was in his teens. He was educated at Ireland's leading Jesuit school and then at Catholic University College in Dublin.

JAMES JOYCE

central character, Leopold Bloom, through the streets of Dublin. The novel developed new literary forms in its exploration and use of language and in its epic structure. It was published in Paris in 1922 but was banned for obscenity in Britain and in the United States until 1936. *Finnegan's Wake* was published in 1939 and carried the "stream of consciousness" style of writing to revolutionary limits.

Joyce rebelled early against the tenets of his class and religion and against Ireland's prevailing politics and culture, both of which he felt were too "nationalistic." He left Ireland in 1904 with Nora Barnacle, who became his lifelong partner. After a visit in 1912, Joyce never returned to Ireland and remained in Europe until his death in Zurich in 1941.

Joyce wrote several books of poetry and novels; his most famous novels were *Ulysses* and *Finnegans Wake*. *Ulysses* was a monumental work, an allegorical saga describing the daylong wandering of its

Joyce is a national hero in Ireland, something that would have amused this complex and essentially solitary man. The James Joyce Cultural Centre is at No. 35 North Great George's Street in north Dublin. And each year on June 16 Dublin celebrates Bloomsday, during which there are guided walks, readings and numerous events based on Leopold Bloom's progress through the Dublin of *Ulysses*. Visits to famous Dublin pubs play a lively part in the festivities; participants dress in Edwardian clothes from the period featured in the novel and readings and other celebrations of *Ulysses* are staged.

A portrait of the artist by Jeffrey Morgan (top) and the James Joyce Martello Tower at Sandycove in south Dublin, which houses a small museum of Joycean memorabilia

museum date from the late 18th century and are themselves an experience. There is magnificent stucco, especially in the first-floor rooms. The colonnaded main salon, now the Gallery of Writers, has busts and paintings of famous names, a decorative ceiling and boisterous friezes.

GUINNESS STOREHOUSE

➕ Off the map ✉ St. James's Gate ☎ 01 408 4800
🕐 Daily 9:30–8, Jul.–Aug.; 9:30–5, rest of year
🚌 123 🍴 Café and bars 💲 $$$

Dublin without Guinness is like the earth without air. You can sample Guinness in its creamy, lip-smacking originality in the city's multitude of pubs (see page 281), but to reach the heart of things visit the enlightening and entertaining Guinness Storehouse, located in an original hop store at the brewery. Admission includes a pint of the famous stout in the Gravity bar, which has great views of the city.

HUGH LANE MUNICIPAL GALLERY OF MODERN ART

➕ B3 ✉ Parnell Square North ☎ 01 874 1903
🕐 Tue.–Thu. 9:30–6, Fri.–Sat. 9:30–5, Sun. 11–5
🍴 Gallery café 🚊 DART Connolly Station (10 mins walk) 🚌 10A, 11, 11A, 11B, 13A, 16, 16A, 19, 19A, 122,
💲 Free; Francis Bacon's studio $$$ (free to all Tue. 9:30–noon)

The Hugh Lane Gallery is located in the delightful Charlemont House. The collection, bequeathed by Sir Hugh Lane to Dublin Corporation in 1905, comprises 19th- and 20th-century Irish and international painters, including Claude Monet, Sir John Everett Millais and Edgar Degas. There are several outstanding works, not the least of which is Renoir's *Les Parapluies*. Notable Irish artists include Jack B. Yeats, and there are contemporary Irish works and temporary exhibitions, often of daring conceptual art. The gallery also has a fine collection of stained glass and is a venue for music recitals, poetry readings and lectures. Francis Bacon's studio was gifted to the gallery in 1998. Painstakingly removed from its London home, the studio was reconstructed here and opened to the public in 2001. An audiovisual display documents the process.

Compelling atmosphere at Kilmainham Gaol

KILMAINHAM GAOL

➕ Off the map ✉ Inchicore Road ☎ 01 453 5984
🕐 Daily 9:30–5, Apr.–Sep.; Mon.–Sat. 9:30–4, Sun. 10–5, rest of year. Last tour begins 1 hour before closing 🍴 Tea room on site 🚌 51B, 51C, 78A
💲 $$ (includes guided tour)

The notorious Kilmainham Gaol (prison) has been the scene of great misery. Kilmainham opened in 1796 and until 1924 when it closed, just about every famous name in the struggle for Irish independence and statehood was a "guest" at one time. They included Robert Emmet, Charles Stewart Parnell and Eamon DeValera. Fourteen leaders of the 1916 Easter Rising were executed in the prison yard. Explore the warren of gloomy cells and chilly corridors. Guided tours give a graphic picture of Irish history.

NATIONAL GALLERY

➕ C2 ✉ Merrion Square West (entrance also on Clare Street) ☎ 01 661 5133 🕐 Mon.–Sat. 9:30–5:30 (also Thu. 5:30–8:30), Sun. noon–5:30; last admission 30 minutes before closing 🍴 Gallery restaurant
🚊 DART Pearse Station (5 mins walk) 🚌 Cross-city buses 💲 Free; charge for some exhibitions ℹ️ Free guided tours Sat. at 3, Sun at 2:15, 3 and 4

Ireland's national art collection eschews quantity for quality, and this fine building holds a collection that represents all major schools of European art. The Shaw Room, dedicated to early benefactor George Bernard Shaw, is an elegant statement in its own right. Painters represented include

The National Gallery under the shadow of its founder, William Dargan

Titian, Francisco de Goya and Nicolas Poussin. Thomas Gainsborough and J. M. W. Turner are here as well, and there are strong collections of leading Irish artists such as Nathanial Hone, Jack B. Yeats and Roderic O'Conor. The gallery has computer facilities to find information about its paintings.

NATIONAL MUSEUM OF ARCHAEOLOGY AND HISTORY

✚ C2 ✉ Kildare Street ☎ 01 677 7444 🕐 Tue.–Sat. 10–5, Sun. 2–5 🍴 Museum restaurant 🚆 DART Pearse Station 🚌 Most cross-city buses 🎫 Free; guided tours $

Part of the National Museum of Ireland, this museum is part of a splendid complex of buildings that date from the 1890s. Together with the National Library opposite, the complex forms the approach to Leinster House, the seat of the Irish Government. Exhibits,which date from 7000 BC to the 20th century, include outstanding examples of Celtic and medieval art and the finest collection of prehistoric gold artifacts in Europe. Highlights include the Tara Brooch, the Derrynaflan and the Ardagh Chalice.

ST. STEPHEN'S GREEN

✚ C2 ✉ St. Stephen's Green ☎ 01 475 7816 🕐 Mon.–Sat. 8–dusk, Sun. 10–dusk 🚆 DART Pearse Station, St. Stephen's Green LUAS 🚌 Most cross-city buses

The delightful St. Stephen's Green has been a public park since 1664, when Dublin Corporation set aside 27 acres of open ground, albeit for use by its more well-to-do citizens. Access was by payment only until 1880, when the park was made free to all. There are numerous statues and busts of famous Irish men and women, including James Joyce, Robert Emmet, Wolfe Tone and Sir Arthur Guinness. The park is surrounded by some of the finest buildings in Dublin. They include the Shelbourne Meridien Hotel and the Roman Catholic University Church, with a neo-Byzantine interior.

TRINITY COLLEGE

Campus ✚ C3 ✉ College Green ☎ 01 608 1000 🕐 Daily 🚌 All cross city buses 🎫 Free ✚ Walking tours depart from inside the Front Gate daily beginning at 10:15 a.m. May to early Oct. 🎫 $$$
Old Library ✉ College Green 🕐 Mon.–Sat. 9:30–5, Sun. 9:30–4:30, Jun.–Sep.; Mon.–Sat. 9:30–5, Sun. noon–4:30, rest of year. Closed 10 days from late Dec. to early Jan. 🚌 All cross-city buses 🎫 $$$
Dublin Experience ✉ College Green 🕐 Daily 10–5, mid-May to Sep. 30 (shows on the hour, every hour) 🚌 All cross-city buses 🎫 $$

Dublin's Trinity College is an outstanding architectural and cultural oasis at the heart of a busy city. It was founded in 1592, but all of the present buildings date from after 1700. Enter the complex from College Green, between statues of poet Oliver Goldsmith and orator Edmund Burke, and then go through the Corinthian facade of the Palladian Regent House. This leads into cobbled Parliament Square, lined with grand buildings and dominated by a tall campanile. Trinity's Old Library and its Long Room contain some outstanding artifacts, including the ninth-century *Book of Kells,* an illuminated manuscript of the four gospels of the New Testament. Another attraction is the Dublin Experience, a 1-hour audiovisual overview of the city, housed in the modern Arts and Social Science Building.

DUBLIN'S PUBS

Irish pubs are fueled by good drink, but they are rooted in the gregarious nature of the Irish, and in lively gossip. Many pubs also are outstanding folk music venues, inevitable in a country so well suited to such spontaneous music.

A local favorite is the Brazen Head, at 20 Lower Bridge Street, hailed as the oldest pub in Dublin. Davy Byrnes, on Duke Street just off busy Grafton Street, has an art deco lounge with lively murals that were painted by Irish playwright Brendan Behan's father-in-law. For Victorian authenticity try the Stag's Head, on Dame Court.

You can hear great Irish music with your Guinness in some of the busy Temple Bar pubs like Gogarty's, on the corner of Fleet and Anglesea streets. One of the best Dublin music pubs is O'Donoghue's, on Merrion Row down from St. Stephen's Green. This was the favored haunt of the Dubliners folk group in its 1960s heyday, and the city's best folk musicians regularly raise the roof here.

Other good traditional pubs are Doheny & Nesbits on Lower Baggott Street; The Palace on Fleet Street; O'Neill's, at the corner of Pearse and Shaw streets; and old-fashioned Mulligan's on Poolbeg Street, a last outpost of Joycean Dublin amid the chilly lifelessness of modern office blocks. South of St. Stephen's Green at the corner of Camden Street Upper and Harcourt Road is The Bleeding Horse, formerly a blacksmith's shop and a church; its warren of little rooms are called "snugs."

If you want Dublin sophistication try the Horse Shoe Bar in the Shelbourne Hotel or the Morrison Bar in the Morrison Hotel, where trendy Dubliners meet for drinks overlooking the River Liffey at Ormond Quay. For

Guinness in lights (top), and behind the bar at one of Dublin's 800 pubs

a down-to-earth atmosphere visit Joxer Daly's on Dorset Street Upper in north Dublin, where Old Dublin reigns unchanged. These are just a small selection from the multitude of Dublin's pubs.

ITALY

*"LUMP the whole thing!
Say that the Creator made
Italy from designs by Michael
Angelo."*

From Mark Twain's 1869 novel *The Innocents Abroad*

Opposite: The village of Altagnana nestles on a hillside beneath Italy's magnificent Alpi Apuane

Italy

ITALY

SWITZERLAND

AUSTRIA

Sluderno-Schluderns
Merano-Meran
Cortina d'Ampezzo

Courmayeur
Aosta
Lago Maggiore
Baveno
Stresa
Lago di Como
Bellagio
Como
Bergamo
Bréscia
Molveno
Adamello 3554m
Édolo
A22
Trento
Bolzano-Bozen
Dolomiti
Belluno
A23
E55
Udine
Pordenone
Asolo
Treviso
Cividale di Friuli
SLOVENIA
Monfalcone
Trieste

4061m
Gran Paradiso
Ivréa
Novara
A8
E64
A4
Milano
Verona
Vicenza
VENICE (Venezia)
A5
E25
Vercelli
Pavia
A1
A4
Asola
E70
Padova
Mantova
Rovigo
Golfo di Venézia

Turin (Torino)
A32 E70

FRANCE
Pinerolo
A6
E717
Asti
Alba
A26
Cúneo
Alessandria
A7
E25
Piacenza
Parma
E70
Cremona
A21
A22
Reggio nell'Emilia
A13
Po
Ferrara
E76
Ravenna

Génova
Savona
A10
E80
Portofino
Rapallo
A12
La Spézia
A15
E33
Módena
Bologna
ADRIATIC

San Remo
Impéria
Bordighera
Golfo di Génova
Portovénere
Massa
Pistóia
Prato
A1
E35/E76
Faenza
A14
E45
Rímini
SAN MARINO
Pésaro

MONACO
Viaréggio
Lucca
Pisa
FLORENCE (Firenze)
Urbino
Ancona

Livorno
San Gimignano
Volterra
Siena
Arezzo
Cortona
Perúgia
Gúbbio
Loreto
E55

Isola d'Elba
Montepulciano
Grosseto
Todi
Assisi
Spoleto
Ascoli Piceno

Corse (Corsica)
FRANCE
Orvieto
Sovana
E35/E45
Terni
Téramo
L'Aquila
Pescara
A24
Chieti
A14
Vaste

Piombino
Viterbo
Rieti
Civitavécchia
A12
Tivoli
Subiaco
Avezzano
A25
Campobasso

Costa Smeralda
Ólbia
ROME (Roma)
Frosinone
A1
Cassino
E45
Benev

Sássari
Latina
Anzio
Terracina
Caserta

Alghero
Nuoro
NAPLES (Napoli)
1277m
Vesuvius

Oristano
Lago Omodeo
Sardegna (Sardinia)
Ísola d'Ischia
Ísola di Capri
Pompeii
Amalfi
Sorrento
Ravell
Paest

TYRRHENIAN SEA

Sant' Antioco
Cágliari

MEDITERRANEAN SEA

Erice
Palermo
Cefalù
A20
Trápani
Segesta
A29
A19
3323
Mt Etna
Selinunte
Caltanissetta
Enna
Agrigento
Piazza Armerina

Sicilia (Sicily)
Ragusa

ALGERIA
A

TUNISIA
B

C

5 4 3 2 1

ITALY

Few countries have as much to offer as Italy (Italia), with its warm and passionate people; varied and beautiful landscape; a rich artistic, historic and cultural heritage; some of the world's best food and wine; and a stylish and relaxed philosophy on life. Italy has something for everyone, whether the visitor is seeking great cities, tiny villages, idyllic countryside or beautiful beaches.

Bella Italia

Of all European countries, Italy is the one to which many travelers return time and again, their love affair blossoming with each trip. Whether your visit is a chance opportunity or the dream of a lifetime, Italy will fulfill and exceed your expectations, capture your heart and senses, and send you away longing to return.

From the Alps in the north, through the prosperous and fertile heartland to the stark beauty of the deep south, Italy is blessed with some of the world's most beguiling landscapes. The northern half features Tuscany's classic olive, vine and cypress-studded rolling countryside; the dramatic peaks of the Dolomites

MORE TOP DESTINATIONS IN ITALY

- Agrigento C1 • Assisi C4
- Lago di Garda B5 • Molveno B5
- Paestum D2 • Piazza Armerina D1
- Portovénere B4 • Ravello D2
- Ravenna C4 • San Gimignano B4
- Sovana C3 • Siena B4 • Urbino C4
- Verona B5 • Vieste D3

Italy

(Dolomiti); pine-clad white cliffs and turquoise seas; and the eerie loveliness of mist-laden mornings in the great river valleys. The south is equally lovely, with an arid and fierce beauty during the long hot summers, when the intense color of the sea offsets the bleached ocher mountains.

Most of Italy is mountainous, the long spine of the Apennines (Appennini) running almost from top to bottom and stretching virtually from coast to coast. Some hilly areas are immensely fertile, as in Tuscany and Umbria in central Italy, while in other places, such as Basilicata and Calabria in the south, the combination of altitude and extreme climate can make the land unproductive.

The largest area of flatland is the great plain of the Po river valley in the north, which extends down the eastern seaboard, an agriculturally rich and productive swath. Much of upland Italy is wooded, and there is a wide variety of indigenous plants.

Diverse Regions

Until 1870 Italy was a collection of separate and disparate states with a complex history, which does much to explain the diversity of people and attitudes. Camillo Cavour (statesman and first prime minister of a united Italy) remarked after unification in 1860, "We have made Italy, now we must make Italians." This aim still seems to await fruition, such is the gulf between the different regions. Italy has been a republic since 1946, the 21 regions (*regioni*) enjoying a large degree of self-government; some, such as Sicily and Sardinia, are semi-autonomous.

Italians would be the first to agree that there is no such thing as "an Italian." Ask an Italian where he's from and the answer will be "from Tuscany, from Rome, from Naples, from Sicily,"

but rarely "from Italy." Primary loyalties are firmly local and regional. The Italian character, attitudes, outlook and prejudices have been formed by the native region, not by the country as a whole. So the fiery Sicilians are light years away from the Milanese and their urbane efficiency, the cool and rational Tuscans or the abrasive Romans.

Language has also played a part. Modern Italian, rich, elegant and musical, derives from Tuscan, a medieval dialect used by Dante and Petrarch and firmly based on Latin. But throughout Italy there are some 1,500 diverse dialects, which were in daily use until widespread literacy and access to television. There are still some elderly people who have difficulty speaking modern Italian, although mass media are rapidly weakening dialects.

The considerable geographic differences between the north and south have produced another element of regionalism – a very real economic and cultural divide between the halves of the country. The cooler, more fertile north is richer, more advanced and more successful than the arid and impoverished south.

The People

All Italians do seem to share the same attitude toward life, one that is instantly apparent to foreigners. Life is for living, for enjoying, for savoring. There's always time to pause to chat, time for kindness, time to laugh; passions run high but anger is quickly over and forgotten. Pause in any Italian piazza and listen to the voices; there are no strident tones or harsh and ugly notes. Watch the way Italians treat children or the elderly, without condescension but with respect for their age. Problems are solved with little fuss on a personal level, although the labyrinth of Italian bureaucracy might drive visitors crazy.

Opposite: The medieval Campo, in the heart of Siena

Italy

Despite having one of the world's lowest national birthrates, family ties are exceptionally close, with children often living with their parents into their 30s, and elderly people are still mainly cared for at home. The mother's role is pivotal; Italian men, it is said, spend their whole lives searching for a woman to live up to their mother.

If you want to attract the opposite sex, you have to look good. This helps explain the importance of the *bella figura*, literally "beautiful form," but meaning infinitely more. Italians have an innate sense of style, and it matters greatly that clothes, cars and personal possessions are stylish and contemporary. *Bella figura* dictates that these must all be admired, and what better way to display them than during that great Italian tradition, the *passeggiata*? This nightly outdoor perambulation occurs in every village, town and city in the land, when citizens exit en masse from their homes, strolling through the streets, exchanging news and gossip, but above all admiring and hoping to be admired in return.

Country of Contrasts

A rich historical and cultural past has shaped the townscape in Italy. Cities, towns and villages are crammed with fine buildings, churches and works of art, a legacy of pre-Unification days. But over the past century, and notably since World War II, there has been huge development and growth in urban areas, with unattractive spreads of industrial buildings and blocks of soul-less apartments on the outskirts of countless towns. Every town still retains its central piazza, with civic buildings and a church grouped around or near it.

In many rural areas, people have traditionally lived in villages rather than on the land they work, traveling daily to the fields, so in some areas isolated country farmhouses are rare. There has sometimes been a huge gulf between the urban and rural populations, possibly due to the very early development of Italian towns.

The middle class was a late arrival in Italy and only really emerged during the great economic boom of the '50s and '60s. Even now there are still large numbers of agricultural workers and small shareholders, working the land as it has been worked for centuries, while their cousins may be employed in hi-tech industries.

Exploring Italy

Prosperous Italy has one of Europe's highest standards of living, making traveling easy and pleasurable. Tourism is a major industry, so you'll find English widely spoken in city hotels and restaurants, although not away from the main tourist areas.

Italian engineering prowess has produced an excellent road network, with both toll roads and good highways. Minor roads are often unsurfaced. Italians drive fast and aggressively but mostly safely, and once you're accustomed to the style of driving you should have no problems. All major cities have an airport, with frequent internal flights. Trains are cheap and punctual, although cross-country routes can be slow and complicated; it's safer to stick to the inter-city services. Buses connect even the smallest villages.

Italian hotels are all rated and inspected by regional authorities; regardless of the price range, they are spotlessly clean. Bathtubs are rare except in deluxe establishments, and showers frequently dribble when turned on; water is precious in many parts of the country. Air-conditioning is becoming more widespread but is by no means universal, and buildings can

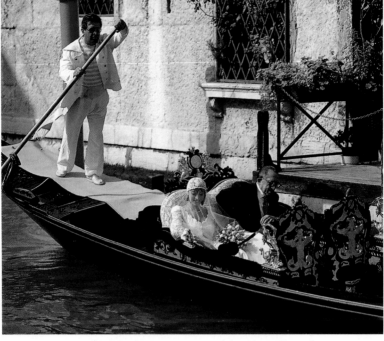

A wedding party makes its way through Venice in a specially decorated gondola

be stifling in summer. By law, heating in public places is not turned on until November 1.

Culinary Traditions

Italian cooking is regional and simple, relying on the superb quality of the ingredients, and you'll find wonderful dishes wherever you go. In a country where frozen food is only now becoming widespread, menus are dictated by the seasons, with a rich variety of dishes punctuating the different months.

The various types of restaurant can be confusing. The terms *ristorante, osteria* and *trattoria* are fairly interchangeable; *tavola calda* and *pizzeria* imply something a bit more humble. Lunch has traditionally been the main meal, but there is a trend toward making dinner the extravaganza. The evening menu often consists of *antipasto* (hors d'oeuvre), the first course (*primo*) of pasta, soup or rice, the meat or fish second course (*secondo*) with its accompanying *contorni* (vegetables) or *insalata* (salad), followed by *formaggio, dolce* or *frutta* (cheese, dessert or fruit). If a meal this size seems a bit daunting, choose just a couple of courses.

Many Italians automatically drink wine with their meals. *Denominazione d'Origine Controllata* (DOC) is a method of classification that guarantees the origin of the wine, and that it has been made following the guidelines for a particular area. However, it is no indication of quality.

Pastimes

The favorite Italian pastimes are probably eating, drinking and talking; preferably all together. Immensely sociable people, Italians tend to relax en masse, making group activities of every type very popular. Soccer is the national sport, and almost every Italian male either attends or follows Sunday matches. Deeply traditional, Italians prefer their pleasures to be family-oriented; a Sunday drive, a day at the beach or a gentle stroll, accompanied by a non-stop stream of chatter, constitute most people's idea of leisure.

Italy

TIMELINE

3000–1800 BC	First traces of migratory peoples in peninsula.
700–300 BC	Etruscan federation exists alongside Roman republic.
264–146 BC	Punic Wars against Carthage.
AD 200–400	Decline of Roman Empire.
550–770	Peninsula fragmented with different areas under Byzantine, Papal, Lombard and Frankish influence.
1300–1400	Emergence of the city-states in north; Renaissance era.
1500–1848	Fragmentation of peninsula under foreign domination.
1848–61	Struggle for unification, with brief republic established in 1848; kingdom of Italy proclaimed in 1861.
1870	Rome and the Papal States become part of a unified Italy.
1915–18	Italy sides with Allies during World War I.
1940	Italy enters World War II on Axis side.
1943	Fall of Mussolini and armistice with Allies; Mussolini reinstated by Germany as head of puppet republic; Rome liberated in 1944.
1946	Italian Republic established.
1957	Treaty of Rome; Italy becomes a founding member of European Community, now called the European Union.
1985–2000	Corruption is rife, but Italy flourishes as desire for political and institutional reform grows.
2005	Cardinal Joseph Ratzinger is elected the 265th pontiff, Pope Benedict XVI, following the death of Pope John Paul II.

THE ETRUSCANS

Travelers in central Italy will frequently come across signs of the Etruscans in monuments, tombs and museums. For centuries historians have questioned exactly who they were. This enigmatic race preceded the Romans and were at the height of their power from 800 to 400 BC. They formed a confederacy of 12 cities, built towns, passed laws, traded overseas and believed firmly in an afterlife. A lively and imaginative people, they also had highly developed cultural, political and social systems. The Romans, admirers of Etruscan culture, absorbed much of it as they rose to power. By the third century BC the Romans had virtually assimilated the entire nation, along with much of its language, customs and religious beliefs. Today only the monuments remain, particularly those to the Etruscan dead. Wonderful finds have been made in these tombs – jewelry, vases, sculpture and frescoes. They are preserved in museums all over ancient Etruria, the name given to the area they inhabited. You can visit Etruscan sites at Tarquinia and Cerveteri, both a short distance north of Rome, and see the finest Etruscan collection in the world at the Villa Giulia museum in Rome.

SURVIVAL GUIDE

Italy

- The fashion-conscious Italians spend much time and thought on looking good. Dressing appropriately means no shorts in cities. If you do show too much leg or arm, you won't be allowed to enter churches.

- Inevitably, Italy's star attractions in Rome, Venice, Florence and other major cities become packed during the hot summer. Get out early to avoid the main rush or, better still, visit in the late fall or winter when it's quieter and cooler.

- Nowadays, many of the major sights in the larger cities throughout the country stay open all day, but in rural towns everything closes down still from around 12:30 until 4:30 or 5 while most of the population eats a large lunch and has a siesta. Plan your day around this, remembering that museums, churches, galleries and stores will all be closed for several hours.

- Italians enjoy wine, which they drink with meals, but they disapprove of people who drink to excess.

- It is unusual to eat dinner before 7:30 or 8, and lunch is served from around 12:30 to about 2:30. Vegetarians will find plenty of choices in most restaurants. As for children, Italians genuinely love them, and most restaurants – even upscale ones – welcome them. Italian coffee is extremely strong, so if you want it weaker just ask for a *caffè americano*.

- Bars are much more than the name suggests. They are open from dawn until midnight or later, and offer coffee, tea, soda, snacks and pastries, as well as alcohol. All bars have restrooms and a public telephone.

- Smoking is common in some public places but this may change as a popular bill banning smoking in public places becomes law in several countries in the EU.

- One of the joys of Italy is shopping in little local stores and at the colorful street markets. However, shopping habits are slowly changing and out-of-town shopping centers are becoming more common. Shop and market prices are fixed.

- Facilities for visitors with disabilities are improving, but are not yet as good as those back home. If you need help it's best to check ahead with local tourist offices.

Italians make serious choices at a colorful city market

Rome

ROME

There's almost too much to Rome (Roma); too much history, too much art, too much noise, confusion, traffic. This is an overwhelming city in every way, with splendors and frustrations in equal measure. Nowhere else will your

senses be assaulted by such a glorious mélange of ancient, medieval, Renaissance, baroque and modern sights. Expectations run high, and every visitor comes with preconceptions of sun-filled days of *dolce vita* and romantic strolls through ancient streets. Put them aside, take it slow, accept Rome not as you think it should be, but as it is, and you'll discover a city that is virtually impossible to describe.

Mapping the City

It's a good idea to stay as centrally located as you can, but avoid the unwholesome area around the central railroad station, Stazione Termini, and keep in mind that few areas of the city

offer peace and quiet. You'll quickly realize that Rome has no discernible center, although Piazza Venezia, dominated by the vast, wedding cake-like monument of Victor Emmanuel II, is a good place to orient yourself. From here, the Via del Corso stretches north, and to the south lies the Forum (Foro Romano), the heart of classical Rome.

Between the Corso and the Tiber (Tevere) river lies the *centro storico*, or historic center, a maze of narrow medieval streets and Renaissance squares and one of the city's most beguiling areas. On the other side of the Corso are Rome's most elegant shopping streets, more sun-dappled piazzas, some lovely green spaces and the charms of the Via Vittorio Veneto, with its luxury hotels and galaxy of smart cafés. Across the river lies Trastevere, filled with charming streets and squares and noted for its excellent restaurants. To the north is Vatican City (Città del Vaticano), home of the Pope and St. Peter's Basilica (Basilica di San Pietro).

Seeing the Sights

It would take months to see all of Rome, so before you arrive, decide where your priorities lie. It's a mistake to rush out, exhausted from travel, and see the Vatican on your first day; instead wander around the back streets or linger over a cup of coffee before you plunge into serious sightseeing. If you're not a sightseer, enjoy the street life and the stylish stores and restaurants.

It's best to tackle the highlights early in the day, before the crowds and heat intensify and while you're still fresh. Make a point of resting during the early afternoon; most stores and attractions are closed then anyway, and you can venture out again refreshed and relaxed in the late afternoon. If time is short and you want to see a lot, think about taking a tour; your hotel will be able to

Running repairs at the fountain in Piazza Navona

advise you. Other options include walking tours with local experts to explore off-the-beaten-track areas or a boat trip on the Tiber river.

Peace and Quiet

Tranquility is in short supply in Rome, but there are moments when it seems within reach. In addition to the Villa Borghese (see page 300), other green spaces exist around the city, where the roar of the traffic is at least muted. One of the best is the Palatine Hill (Palatino) above the Forum, a good place to picnic after a morning's sightseeing, with scattered ruins, cypresses and wildflowers. The Botanical Garden (Giardino Botanico) in Trastevere provides cool shade amid the 7,000 species of plants, while the park Colle Oppio, with its strolling mothers and babies, is a good bet after a morning at the Colosseum.

Roman Cuisine

Romans enjoy dining out, and there are plenty of restaurant choices. Trastevere and the streets around Piazza Navona are packed with eateries; as always in Italy, look for places patronized by locals. Roman specialties center heavily

around the less attractive parts of animals, such as offal, brains and tripe, but staples like grilled meat and the delicious *saltimbocca alla Romana* (veal scaloppine cooked with prosciutto and sage) are easy to find. Pasta dishes include spicy *rigatoni all'amatriciana* (pasta with bacon, chili and tomato), and the delicious and familiar *spaghetti alla carbonara*, with bacon, egg and fettuccine.

Artichokes are a great Roman specialty, eaten either deep fried or raw; look for asparagus in early summer. Desserts are simple, but Roman ice cream is mouthwatering, and it's worth forgoing restaurant desserts and opting instead for a *gelateria*. Pizzas are excellent. Local wines come from the hills outside Rome, in an area known as the Castelli Romani; Frascati is the best known. You'll also find wines from all over Italy, as well as herbal aperitifs and liqueurs.

Boutiques and Markets

Shopping can be a pleasure in self-indulgent Rome, where there is a superb range of luxurious silk, linens,

Roman Fountains

Lovely fountains are scattered around Rome, and their beauty will stick in your mind when much else has faded. They provide cool places for a few minutes of rest, and the soothing sound of splashing water somehow manages to make itself heard over the noise of Rome's frenetic traffic. Be sure to pause at the Fontana delle Naiadi in Piazza della Repubblica, with its bronze nymphs; the dolphin-decorated Fontana del Tritone in Piazza Barberini; and the charming tortoise fountain, the Fontana delle Tartarughe, in Piazza Mattei.

Rome

leather and accessories. Shoes, bags, handmade evening wear, and exquisite china and porcelain are found in the smartest stores clustered around the Via Condotti and the Via Frattina, just off the Piazza di Spagna. You'll find moderately priced shops along the Via del Corso and the Via Nazionale; knitwear and sweaters are good buys. Rome also has several department stores, including the upscale La Rinascente in Piazza Colonna; Upim and Standa are inexpensive and cheerful chain stores with plenty of surprisingly stylish buys. If you enjoy markets, head for the daily food and vegetable market in the lovely Campo dei Fiori, or the many smaller street markets dotted around the city.

Nightlife

Romans consider a restaurant meal the pinnacle of evening entertainment, but there are other events going on as well. Pick up a copy of *Roma c'è* or *Trovaroma* for up-to-date information. There are plenty of music bars and discos. Opera is a good option, either at the Teatro dell'Opera or outdoors in summer at the Villa Borghese gardens. Rome has a clutch of movie theaters showing films in their original language. Concerts and recitals are frequently held in the city's churches.

ESSENTIAL INFORMATION

TOURIST INFORMATION AND CALL CENTER

☎ 06 3600 4399 (English speaking)
• Via Parigi 5 ☎ 06 488 991
• Largo Goldoni ☎ 06 6813 6061
• Piazza San Giovanni in Laterano ☎ 06 7720 3535
• Via Nazionale ☎ 06 4782 4525
• Piazza delle Cinque Lune ☎ 06 6880 9240
• Piazza Pia ☎ 06 6880 9707
• Piazza San Pietro ☎ 06 6988 2019
• Stazione Termini ☎ 06 4890 6300
• Via Marco Minghetti ☎ 06 678 2988
• Piazza Sonnino (Trastevere) ☎ 06 5833 3457
www.romaturismo.com

URBAN TRANSPORTATION

Public transportation in Rome consists of orange buses and trams and a two-line subway system. Subway stations are marked on the Rome city map by the letter "M" in a red circle. Bus tickets must be purchased from automatic machines before boarding, or from shops and newsstands displaying an ATAC or COTRAL sticker. They are valid for any number of bus trips plus one subway trip within a 75-minute period, and must be validated at the rear of the vehicle when boarding. The *biglietto integrato* is valid for a day's unlimited travel on buses, trams, the subway and the suburban train service. A weekly pass, the *carta integrata Settimanale*, also is available. Taxis are white, and park next to the stands with a blue-and-white sign; they do not stop on the street. You can call a taxi from Radio Taxi (☎ 06 3570, 06 4984 or 06 88177) or Radio Taxi Eurocosmo (☎ 06 8805461); the meter will start running straight after your call. Check that the meter is set at zero if you begin your ride at the taxi stand. Do not trust anyone offering a private taxi service.

AIRPORT INFORMATION

Rome has two airports: Leonardo da Vinci, at Fiumicino (west of the city); and Ciampino, south of Rome, which handles charter flights. The easiest link with Leonardo da Vinci is by train from Stazione Termini (the central railroad station); trains leave every 30 minutes 5:52 a.m.–11:52 p.m. Trains also run from the airport to Fara Sabina and Tiburtina train stations, but you will have to make a connection. There is a nightly bus service between the airport and Tiburtina Station. To reach Rome from Ciampino, take the subway line A to Anagnina and connect with the COTRAL bus service; both are scheduled to run daily 6:50 a.m.–11:40 p.m., or COTRAL bus to Ciampino station and then train to Rome Termini.

CLIMATE – average highs and lows for the month

	JAN.	FEB.	MAR.	APR.	MAY	JUN.	JUL.	AUG.	SEP.	OCT.	NOV.	DEC.
	13°C	13°C	15°C	17°C	21°C	25°C	28°C	28°C	26°C	21°C	17°C	14°C
	55°F	55°F	59°F	63°F	70°F	77°F	82°F	82°F	79°F	70°F	63°F	57°F
	4°C	4°C	5°C	8°C	12°C	16°C	19°C	19°C	17°C	13°C	8°C	5°C
	39°F	39°F	41°F	46°F	54°F	61°F	66°F	66°F	63°F	55°F	46°F	41°F

The Colosseum – the world's largest surviving structure from Roman antiquity

City Sights

Key to symbols

⊕ map coordinates refer to the Rome map on pages 292–293; sights below are highlighted in yellow on the map.

⊠ address or location ☎ telephone number

◉ opening times Ⓜ nearest subway station

🚉 nearest railroad station 🚌 nearest bus or tram route 🍴 restaurant or café on site or nearby

💶 admission charge: $$$ more than €6, $$ €3–€6, $ less than €3 ⓘ other relevant information

Basilica di San Pietro

⊕ A3 ⊠ Piazza San Pietro, Città del Vaticano ☎ 06 6988 4676 or 06 6988 2019 ◉ Daily 7–7, Apr.–Sep. Ⓜ Ottaviano 🚌 23, 64, 98, 492 💶 Admission free ($$ for elevator to terrace/steps to dome)

The spiritual heart of Catholicism, the Basilica di San Pietro (St. Peter's Basilica) stands on the site of the saint's burial place. This is architectural grandeur on a triumphant scale, from the sweeping colonnades branching from the magnificent facade to the soaring dome above the twisted columns of Giovanni Bernini's High Altar *baldacchino*. There's much that dates from 1506 to 1626, when Donato di Angelo Bramante and Bernini were the principal architects. Near the end of his life, Michelangelo designed the

dome, from which there are superb views; inside you can see the sublime *Pietà*, one of his earliest works. The right nave contains a bronze statue of St. Peter, his right foot worn away by pilgrims' caresses.

Colosseo

⊕ D2 ⊠ Piazza del Colosseo ☎ 06 7005 5469; 06 3996 7700 for advance booking ◉ Daily 9 a.m.–one hour before sunset Ⓜ Colosseo 🚌 11, 13, 15, 27, 30, 60, 75, 81, 85, 87, 110, 118, 186, 673 💶 $$$ (includes Palatino)

The massive Colosseo (Colosseum) dates from AD 72, and the design has never been bettered. This is a functional stadium that once seated 55,000, but it can be cleared in less than 20 minutes; its sophisticated "backstage" facilities allowed the arena to be flooded for mock sea battles. Most ancient entertainment featured animals, slaves and gladiators, but few Christians were martyred here. During the Middle Ages the Colosseum was a source of building stone, which explains the missing sections.

Fontana di Trevi

⊕ C3 ⊠ Piazza di Trevi Ⓜ Spagna or Barbarini 🚌 52, 53, 61, 62, 63, 71, 80, 85, 160, 492, 850

Among Rome's delightful fountains, none is more famous than the Fontana di Trevi (Trevi Fountain), tucked into a tiny piazza that makes its impact all the more dramatic. There's been a fountain here since Roman times; the present example dates from 1732 and takes its name from the three roads – *tre vie* – that converged here. Throw two coins in the fountain before you leave Rome; legend claims that the first coin grants a wish and the second guarantees your return.

FORO ROMANO E PALATINO

⊞ C2 ⊠ Via dei Fori Imperiali ☎ 06 3996 7700
🕐 Daily 9 a.m.–one hour before sunset Ⓜ Colosseo
🚌 11, 27, 81, 85, 87, 186 🎫 Foro Romano free;
Palatino $$$ (includes Colosseo)

Heart of the Roman Empire, the Foro Romano (Roman Forum) contained all of the ancient city's most important political, religious and municipal buildings. Today it's a romantic jumble of tumbled columns and walls set amid cypresses and wildflowers. It's worth spending time here, tracking down the fine second-century Arch of Septimius Severus, the Temple of Antoninus and Faustina (AD 141), the stately columns of the fourth-century Portico of the Dei Consentes, and the House of the Vestal Virgins, home of the guardians of the sacred fire. On the Palatino (Palatine), overlooking the Roman Forum, the ruins of the homes of wealthy Romans, emperors and aristocrats also may be explored.

MUSEI CAPITOLINI

⊞ C2 ⊠ Piazza del Campidoglio 1 ☎ 06 6710 2475
🕐 Tue.–Sun. 9–7:45 🚌 44, 46, 64, 70, 81, 110 🎫 $$$

The two *palazzi* housing the great classical collection of the Musei Capitolini (Capitoline Museums) are set on either side of a Michelangelo-designed square. Look for the *Dying Gaul* and the tautly muscled *Discobolus* (Discus Thrower). Bronzes include the famous fifth-century BC *Capitoline Wolf Suckling Romulus and Remus* and, finest of all, the superb equestrian statue of *Marcus Aurelius*. Paintings include some major works by Titian and Paolo Veronese.

MUSEI VATICANI

⊞ A3 ⊠ Viale Vaticano, Città del Vaticano ☎ 06
6988 3332 🕐 Mon.–Sat. 8:45–4:45, last Sun. of month

Rome's magical Trevi Fountain

8:45–1:45, Mar.–Oct.; 8:45–1:45, rest of year
Ⓜ Ottaviano 🚌 19, 32, 49, 81, 98 🎫 $$$; free to all last Sun. of month

The Musei Vaticani (Vatican Museums) make up the world's largest museum complex, with around a dozen self-contained museums in 1,400 rooms. It would take days to see everything, so it makes sense to follow either one of the color-coded routes or pick out the highlights that personally appeal to you. However, do not miss the Cappella Sistina (Sistine Chapel), with its frescoes by Michelangelo covering the ceiling and the altar wall, showing scenes from the Old Testament and the powerful *Last Judgment*. The Stanze di Raffaello (Raphael Rooms), one of the artist's masterpieces, were executed in 1508.

Classical sculpture, an Egyptian collection and modern religious art are among the other features at this rich venue.

MUSEO E GALLERIA BORGHESE

⊞ D4 ⊠ Villa Borghese, Piazzale Scipione
Borghese 5 ☎ 06 854 8577 🕐 Tue.–Sun. 9–7
🍴 Museum/gallery restaurant Ⓜ Spagna 🚌 5, 19,
52, 53, 56, 67, 116, 490, 495, 910 🎫 $$$ (advance
reservations necessary ☎ 06 841 7645)

The Museo e Galleria Borghese (Borghese Museum and Gallery), housed in the 17th-century summer palace of Cardinal

Rome

Scipione Borghese, is a treasure house of sculpture, mainly collected by the cardinal. He admired Giovanni Bernini, whose works dominate – the *David* is said to be a self-portrait. Look for Antonio Canova's *Paolina Borghese*; this little minx, with her come-hither look, was Napoleon's sister, married off to a later Borghese. Stunning paintings include Caravaggio's famous *Boy with a Fruit Basket.*

PANTHEON

➕ C3 ✉ Piazza della Rotonda ☎ 06 6830 0230
🕐 Mon.–Sat. 8:30–7:30, Sun. 9–6, holidays 9–1
🚇 Spagna 🚌 64, 70, 81, 86, 87, 90, 119, 170 💲 Free
The superbly engineered Pantheon, erected between AD 118 and AD 128 and still in use today, fires the imagination and gives a better idea of the splendor of ancient Rome than any other monument. Built as a temple, it became a Christian church in AD 609 and now houses Raphael's tomb and also those of two Italian kings.

PIAZZA DI SPAGNA E SCALINATA DELLA TRINITÀ DEI MONTI

➕ C3 and C4 ✉ Piazza di Spagna 26 ☎ Keats-Shelley Museum: 06 678 4235 🕐 Museum: Mon.–Fri. 9–1 and 3–6, Sat. 11–2 and 3–6 🚇 Spagna 🚌 117
💲 Museum $$
The Scalinata della Trinità dei Monti (Spanish Steps), curving gracefully up from Piazza di Spagna to the church of Trinità dei Monti, attracts myriad visitors; this is a favorite meeting place, situated at the heart of Rome's smartest shopping area. The steps, built in 1723, get their name from the piazza, which once housed the Spanish embassy. The eccentric-looking "sunken boat" fountain dates from 1627, while on the right of the steps (at No. 26) you'll find the Keats–Shelley Memorial House, in the lodgings where John Keats died in 1821.

PIAZZA NAVONA

➕ B3 ✉ Piazza Navona 🚇 Spagna 🚌 56, 60, 62, 64
Piazza Navona owes its unmistakable shape to the Roman racetrack that once

Detail from Bernini's *Il Moro* in Piazza Navona

stood here. Pope Innocent X, who commissioned Giovanni Bernini to design the focal point, the Fountain of the Four Rivers, rebuilt the piazza in 1644. The 17th-century church of Sant' Agnese is Francesco Borromini's work.

SAN CLEMENTE

➕ D2 ✉ Via di San Giovanni in Laterano ☎ 06 7045 1018 🕐 Mon.–Sat. 9–12:30 and 3–6, Sun. 10–12:30 and 3–6 🚌 15, 85, 13 💲 Church free; Temple $
No church in Rome gives a better idea of history than San Clemente, a multilayered structure whose newest part dates from the 12th century. In its dim interior, the apse mosaics glitter above the marble panels of the choir screen and pulpits. From here, descend to the fourth-century lower church, with its ghostly traces of eighth- to 11th-century frescoes, before plunging deeper to examine the fine altar of the Roman Mithraic temple.

SANTA MARIA IN ARACOELI

➕ C2–C3 ✉ Piazza d'Aracoeli ☎ 06 679 8155
🕐 Daily 7–noon and 4–6 (or dusk) 🚌 44, 56, 90
💲 Free
Santa Maria in Aracoeli (Our Lady of the Altar of Heaven) was built around 1260 to replace an older church. Approached by 124 steep steps, built in 1348 to celebrate the end of a plague epidemic, the church's plain facade hides a superb interior. The nave columns were taken from Roman buildings, while the gilded ceiling, lit by chandeliers, dates from the 1570s.

THE VATICAN

Vatican City (Città del Vaticano), an area covering about 109 acres around the Basilica of St. Peter (Basilica di San Pietro), is the world's smallest independent state. Until Italian unification in 1870, the Papacy had held territory covering a large part of central Italy, known as the Papal States. These became part of the new united Italy, and the Pope, Pius IX, retreated to the Vatican, a virtual prisoner. The supreme head of a worldwide religion clearly needed some type of sovereign territory to retain his independent spiritual authority, and in 1929 the Treaty of the Lateran was thrashed out with Benito Mussolini, bringing the Vatican State into existence.

St. Peter's Basilica (top) and the spiral staircase in the Vatican Museums (left)

The Vatican Today

The Pope, as well as being head of the Catholic church, is also Europe's only absolute monarch, ruling over the 200 plus inhabitants of the Vatican.

In April 2005, 78-year-old Cardinal Joseph Ratzinger of Germany was elected Pope following the death earlier in the month of Pope John Paul II, who had reigned for 26 years. The new Pope, who has taken the name Pope Benedict XVI, is well known for his conservative views and dislike of liberal reform. Even so, he is a popular choice among the faithful and was greeted by the cheers of tens of thousands of followers when he stepped onto the balcony of St. Peter's Basilica to give his first blessing, proclaiming that he was but "a simple, humble worker."

Defending the Pope

The Pope has been defended by the Swiss Guard since 1506. Their colorful striped red, yellow and blue dress uniform, said to have been designed by Michelangelo, is instantly recognizable. The 90 members are indeed Swiss, young men recruited between the ages of 19 and 25, from Switzerland's four Catholic cantons. They then serve tours of duty ranging from two to 20 years.

Papal Audiences

The Pope gives a weekly general audience on Wednesdays at 11 a.m. in the Papal Audience Chamber, and occasionally in the Basilica of St. Peter or in the piazza. These occasions, for up to 7,000 people, are open to everyone and tickets are free. The Pope also gives a blessing from the windows of his rooms overlooking the piazza on Sundays at midday.

Audience tickets are available by writing to Prefettura della Casa Pontificia, 00120 Città del Vaticano, or by visiting the office through the bronze doors in the right-hand colonnade of Piazza San Pietro, open daily from 9–1.

A calm retreat from the crowds – Santa Maria in Trastevere houses beautiful 12th-century mosaics

SANTA MARIA MAGGIORE

✚ D3 ✉ Piazza di Santa Maria Maggiore 42 ☎ 06
483195 🕐 Daily 7–7, Apr.–Sep.; 7–6:30, rest of year
🚇 Cavour 🚌 16, 27, 70, 71 💳 Free

As you enter Santa Maria Maggiore (St.
Mary Major), remember that Mass has
been said daily here since the fifth century,
when it was built on a site marked by an
alleged miraculous summer snowfall. The
mosaics in the nave date from the fifth
century, those in the apse from the 13th
century. The gilding on the coffered ceiling
reputedly comes from the first gold to arrive
from the New World, a gift from Spain.

SANTA MARIA IN TRASTEVERE

✚ B2 ✉ Piazza Santa Maria in Trastevere ☎ 06
589 7332 🕐 Daily 7:45 a.m.–8 p.m (may close
12:30–3:30 in winter) 🚌 44, 75, 170, 181, 280, 710, 717,
719, 774, 780

The facade of Santa Maria in Trastevere,
with its lustrous 12th-century mosaics,
overlooks an atmospheric fountained piazza.
The charming portico, added in 1702, leads
to an interior with nave columns that once
supported Roman buildings. The 12th-
century, Byzantine-style mosaics of the apse
represent the glorification of the Virgin.

VIA APPIA ANTICA

✚ D1 ✉ Catacombe di San Sebastiano: Via Appia
Antica 136 ☎ 06 785 0350 🕐 Catacombs:
Mon.–Sat. 8:30–noon and 2:30–5; closed mid-Nov. to
Feb. 🚌 78, 118, 127 💳 $$

A short bus ride from central Rome takes
you to the Via Appia Antica (Old Appian
Way), built in the fourth century BC to link
Rome with Brindisi. Here, Spartacus and
his men were executed, and St. Paul marched
to prison. This cobbled way, shaded by pine
trees, is lined with monuments and tombs;
you can visit the catacombs, with their
mementos of early Christian life.

VILLA BORGHESE

✚ C4 ✉ Porta Pinciana 🕐 Daily dawn–dusk
🚇 Flaminio, Spagna 🚌 52, 53, 116, 910

If you become sated with art and
architectural splendors and long for some
cool green grass, head for the Villa
Borghese gardens, central Rome's largest
park, an oasis of verdant lawns, umbrella
pines, lakes and fountains. The adjoining
Pincio Gardens offer wonderful views
across the rooftops to St. Peter's.

VILLA GIULIA

✚ C4 ✉ Piazzale di Villa Giulia 9 ☎ 06 322 6571 or
06 320 1951 🕐 Tue.–Sun. 8:30–7:30 🚇 Flaminio
🚌 19, 30, 52, 926 💳 $$

Visit the Villa Giulia to learn more about
the Etruscans (see page 290). The collection
is housed in a late Renaissance villa; its
architects included Michelangelo. Highlights
are the Castellani exhibits, fine Greek vases,
and gold, silver and ivory artifacts. Be sure
to see the *Sarcofago degli Sposi*, sixth-century
BC figures of a reclining married couple,
and the terracotta *Hercules* and *Apollo*.

Water is the dominant feature in the gardens of the Villa d'Este

EXCURSION TO TIVOLI

Most visitors to Rome seize the chance to escape the city's noise and heat by taking an excursion to Tivoli, a small town in a lovely wooded location some 19 miles northeast of Rome. Its main attractions are the gardens of the Villa d'Este, among the world's most beautiful, and the vast classical site of Villa Adriana (Hadrian's Villa), about 4 miles southwest of Tivoli.

It's easy to make an independent trip to Tivoli, either by train from the central railroad station, Stazione Termini, then local bus, or by bus from central Rome. There also are guided excursions from the city that take you there, while an English-speaking guide tells you all you need to know.

Villa d'Este

The Villa d'Este is famous not so much for the villa itself, built by Cardinal d'Este in 1550, but for the gardens, terraces and fountains. The main attractions are two Giovanni Bernini fountains, the elegant Fontana di Biccierone and the Fontana dei Draghi, and the breathtaking Avenue of a Hundred Fountains (Viale delle Cento Fontane). Nearby lies the Villa Gregoriana, where a pair of waterfalls cascade into a gorge.

Villa Adriana

Many prosperous Romans built retirement villas at Tivoli, and in AD 125 the Emperor Hadrian embarked on the construction of his own. The villa and its gardens grew and grew, eventually covering as much ground as Imperial Rome itself. The site is vast and romantic, and you'll need a map to make sense of it all. Don't miss the Maritime Theater (Teatro Marittimo), a palace on an island in the lake.

Villa d'Este ✚ See page 284, C3 ✉ Piazza Trento ☎ 0774 333404 ⏰ Tue.–Sun. 9–6:45, Apr.–Sep.; 9–4, rest of year 🚌 COTRAL bus from Via Tiburtina to Tivoli 🚆 Train to Tivoli 🍴 Refreshments available in gardens 💷 $$$
Villa Adriana ✉ Via di Villa Adriana 204 ☎ 0774 382733 ⏰ Daily 9 a.m.–90 minutes before dusk 🚌 COTRAL bus from Via Gaeta to Tivoli 🚆 Train to Tivoli 🍴 Refreshments available at villa site 💷 $$$

Tour Companies
Appian Line ✉ Piazza dell'Esquilino 6/7 ☎ 06 4878 6604 or 06 487 861
American Express ✉ Piazza di Spagna 38 ☎ 06 67641 or 06 6764 2413

FLORENCE

More than 3 million tourists annually visit Florence (Firenze), the capital of Tuscany, whose resident population is about 400,000. Visitors come with high expectations of beauty, stunning art, history and stylish people. Sadly, they are often so overwhelmed by heat, crowds, noise and cultural overload that the city fails to live up to expectations. When touring Florence, more so than most cities, planning pays off.

Choose the time you visit carefully. If art and architecture are the main purpose of your trip, try to come off-season, when Florence is quieter

Florence

and the heat in this largely non-air-conditioned city won't wipe you out. Be prepared for crowds, time gallery visits for early and late in the day, and check opening times for museums and churches before you visit. Book accommodations before you come, and don't plan to use Florence as a base for touring the rest of Tuscany.

Florence and Florentines

Florentines are Tuscans – restrained and rational, and less given to fiery displays than other Italians. They also are more reserved, without the easy but superficial charm of people from other regions. Accustomed to huge numbers of visitors, they do not go out of their way to befriend tourists, but are courteous and professional in their everyday dealings.

Florence is not as instantly appealing as Rome or Venice – let it grow on you and experience it as a living city, not merely as a vast treasure house of art. Get away from the major sights and explore the quieter areas, with atmospheric streets and a wealth of traditional activities. Vary the artistic glories with a bit of hedonism, and give yourself time to relax. The best way to see Florence is on foot. Most of the main attractions are clustered together in the largely pedestrian central core, making walking easier (but watch out for ebullient scooter riders).

Eating in Tuscany

There are all types of restaurants in Florence, from fast-food joints to world-class establishments. Many are specifically aimed at tourists and have prominently displayed fixed-price (but mediocre) menus. To ensure a memorable meal, eat where the Italians eat and be prepared to pay somewhat high prices. For a simple lunch, try a slice of fresh-baked pizza to go or a quick snack in a *vinaio* or *fiaschetteria*, traditional wine bars. Food markets are particularly tempting, with the makings to put together a picnic. Tuscan food is simple and excellent, with plenty of soups, superb pork dishes, grilled meats and vegetables. Bean dishes are especially popular (Tuscans are fondly nicknamed *mangiafagioli*, or "bean-eaters"). The most famous wine is

Florence

Chianti, but look for Brunello di Montalcino, a superb red from Tuscany.

Pucci, Gucci and More

Intriguing stores, markets and boutiques are scattered throughout the center of Florence. Shoes and leather goods are famous, as are fine china, exquisite bed and table linen, and gold jewelry. Designer-label fans can visit Pucci and Gucci on their home ground; other tempting gifts include brilliantly glazed majolica pottery, marbled paper, prints and antiques.

Via de'Tornabuoni and the surrounding streets house the most elegant stores; less expensive fashion is found around Piazza della Repubblica and Via dei Calzaiuoli, while jewelers line the Ponte Vecchio. There are many factory leather outlets near Santa Croce. Be sure to spend time browsing in a market; the huge Mercato San Lorenzo is probably the most enjoyable. Most stores will ship direct to the United States.

Festivals Galore

A summer visit is likely to coincide with one of the cultural festivals, the *Estate Fiesolana* or the *Maggio Musicale Fiorentino*. Together they run from May through August, with concerts, opera and ballet – often performed outdoors in an historic setting – creating an unforgettable experience.

Excursions

Even if your time in Tuscany is limited, try to fit in an excursion outside Florence, viewing the timeless landscape en route to another of the region's superb historic towns. Possibilities include Pisa, Siena, San Gimignano and the wine country of Chianti, all easily reached by tour bus or public transportation. Nearer still lies Fiesole, a picturesque hill town just above Florence, the perfect escape from noise and heat.

ESSENTIAL INFORMATION

TOURIST INFORMATION
• Via Cavour 1r ☎ 055 290 832
• Piazza Stazione 4 ☎ 055 212 245
• Borgo Santa Croce 29r
☎ 055 234 0444
www.firenze.turismo.it

URBAN TRANSPORTATION
Buses, both regular and electric, run from Sta. Maria Novella station all over town. Tickets must be purchased before boarding. They are available from machines and tobacconists and are valid for an unlimited number of trips over a period of 70 or 120 minutes; 24-hour passes also are available. Maps and timetables are available from the ATAF

office (✉ Piazza del Duomo 57r). Stamp tickets as you board, in the orange box on the bus. Taxis can be hailed at various central locations, or by calling Radio Taxi Cotafi (☎ 055 4390 or 055 4499) or Radio Taxi Socata (☎ 055 4242 or 055 4798).

AIRPORT INFORMATION
Most visitors arrive and leave from Pisa's Galileo Galilei Airport (☎ 050 849 111; 050 849 300 for flight information), connected to Florence's Sta. Maria Novella railroad station by hourly trains; journey time one hour. Florence Airport (Amerigo Vespucci Airport) is at Perètola (☎ 055 315 874; 055 306 1702 recorded information), 4 miles outside the city and easily reached by bus or taxi.

CLIMATE – average highs and lows for the month

JAN.	FEB.	MAR.	APR.	MAY	JUN.	JUL.	AUG.	SEP.	OCT.	NOV.	DEC.
4°C	8°C	13°C	18°C	23°C	26°C	28°C	27°C	23°C	17°C	10°C	6°C
39°F	46°F	55°F	64°F	73°F	79°F	82°F	81°F	73°F	63°F	50°F	43°F
0°C	2°C	5°C	9°C	13°C	17°C	20°C	19°C	16°C	11°C	5°C	2°C
32°F	36°F	41°F	48°F	55°F	63°F	68°F	66°F	61°F	52°F	41°F	36°F

Florence

CITY SIGHTS

Key to symbols

⊕ map coordinates refer to the Florence map on pages 302–303; sights below are highlighted in yellow on the map.

⊠ address or location ☎ telephone number

◉ opening times ◻ nearest bus or tram route

🍴 restaurant or café on site or nearby 💰 admission charge: $$$ more than €6, $$ €3–€6, $ less than €3

ℹ other relevant information

CAPPELLE MEDICEE

⊕ C4 ⊠ Via Madonna degli Aldobrandini 6 ☎ 055 238 8602 ◉ Daily 8:15–5 (except alternating Sun. and Mon., when it's closed) ◻ 1, 6, 10, 17 💰 $$$

Set behind San Lorenzo, the Cappelle Medicee (Medici Chapels) were built as the mausoleum for Florence's most powerful family. The *Sagrestia Nuova,* built by Michelangelo between 1520 and 1534, contains some of his most powerful sculpture. Reclining figures representing *Night* and *Day* and *Dawn* and *Dusk* decorate the tombs of Lorenzo, duke of Urbino, and Guiliano, duke of Nemours. The figures' fluid lines are a perfect foil for the austerity of the archi-tecture, and are offset by the artist's lovely *Madonna.*

DUOMO, BATTISTERO E CAMPANILE DI GIOTTO

⊕ C3–D3 ⊠ Piazza Duomo ☎ Duomo and Campanile: 055 230 2885 ◉ Duomo: Mon.–Wed. and Fri. 10–5, Thu. and Sat. 10–3:30, Sun.1:30–4:45. Cupola: Mon.–Fri. 8:30–7, Sat. 8:30–5:40 (8:30–4 on first Sat. of the month). Battistero: Mon.–Sat. noon–7, Sun. 8:30–2. Campanile: Daily 8:30–7:30 ◻ 1, 14, 17, 23 💰 Duomo free; Cupola, Battistero and Campanile: $$$ each

The Gothic Duomo (Cathedral) of Santa Maria del Fiore, the first domed structure erected in Europe since Roman times, was built between 1296 and 1436. Its austere interior, with a fine Paolo Uccello fresco, leads to the 463 steps to the top of Brunelleschi's Cupola (Dome). The chief draw of the 11th-century marble Battistero (Baptistery) is the three sets of bronze doors, with their Old Testament scenes. Andrea Pisano cast the south pair in 1326, and they inspired Lorenzo Ghiberti to design those at the north and east in the 1400s.

The Campanile (Bell Tower), designed by Giotto, was built between 1334 and 1359. Its marble walls are decorated with superb relief sculptures. The 280-foot, 414-step climb offers lovely, if vertiginous, views over Florence.

Sculptures by Michelangelo adorn the tombs of his patrons at the Medici Chapels

Galleria dell'Accademia

✚ D4 ✉ Via Ricasoli 58–60 ☎ 055 238 8612;
advance booking (advisable) 055 294 883
🕐 Tue.–Sun. 8:15–6:50 🚍 6, 14, 17, 23 💷 $$$

Founded as an art school in 1784, the
Galleria dell'Accademia (Academy
Gallery) today houses the world's most
important collection of Michelangelo
sculptures, as well as works by other
artists. The main attraction is his *David*, a
huge, anatomically precise and technically
perfect nude male figure, possibly the
most famous in the history of sculpture.
More moving by far are the other
sculptures by the artist, particularly the
four *Prisoners,* the figures struggling to
escape the stone.

Galleria degli Uffizi

✚ C2 ✉ Loggiato degli Uffizi 6 ☎ 055 238 8651
🕐 Tue.–Sun. 8:30–6:50 (occasionally stays open
later in summer) 🍽 Café in gallery 🚍 14, 23
💷 $$$

Arguably the world's greatest collection of
Renaissance paintings, the Galleria degli
Uffizi (Gallery of the Offices) is housed
in an elegant arcaded building designed
by Vasari as administrative offices – hence
the name. Here, in chronological order,
are paintings representing the greatest
names in art, among them Giotto, Paolo
Uccello, Botticelli, Piero della Francesca,
Leonardo da Vinci, Michelangelo,
Raphael and Caravaggio. Come early or
late to avoid the longest lines.

Museo di San Marco

✚ D4 ✉ Piazza San Marco ☎ 055 238 8608
🕐 Mon.–Fri. 8:30–1:50, Sat. 8:30–7, Sun. 8:30–7
(except alternating Sun. and Mon., when it's closed)
🚍 6, 14, 17, 23 💷 $$$

Rebuilt in 1437, the convent attached to
the church of San Marco, decorated by
Fra Angelico, is one of Florence's loveliest
treasures. It's a peaceful religious house,
where each monk's cell is adorned with a
tiny fresco to aid prayer. The pilgrim's
hall contains many paintings by Angelico
and his school, and additional works are
on view in the cloisters and on the stairs,
notably the radiant *Annunciation.*

Museo Nazionale del Bargello

✚ D2 ✉ Via del Proconsolo 4 ☎ 055 238 8606
🕐 Tue.–Sun. 8:15–1:50 🍽 Dino, see page 559
🚍 14, 19 💷 $$

Surrounding a courtyard, in a building
dating from 1255, the Museo Nazionale
del Bargello (National Bargello Museum)
houses Italy's finest collection of
Renaissance sculpture. The first floor has
works by Michelangelo, Benvenuto
Cellini and the flamboyant Giambologna,
but the vaulted second-floor hall contains
the museum's masterpieces. Here are
Donatello's jaunty bronze of *David*, his
exquisite *St. George,* and the superb
Baptistery door reliefs by Lorenzo
Ghiberti and Brunelleschi, made for a
competition in 1401. Upstairs are bright
enameled terracottas by the della
Robbia family.

Ponte Vecchio

✚ C1–C2 ✉ Ponte Vecchio 🚍 14, 23

Not the most beautiful Florentine bridge,
but certainly the most photographed, the
Ponte Vecchio (Old Bridge) was built in
1345 to replace an earlier one. It has been
picturesquely lined with exclusive
goldsmiths and jewelers' shops since 1593.
Above it runs a corridor used by members
of the Medici family to travel from the
Pitti Palace to the Uffizi. The sole bridge
across the Arno in Florence not destroyed
by the Germans in World War II, it also
survived the floods in 1966.

Santa Croce

✚ E1 ✉ Piazza Santa Croce 16 ☎ 055 244 619
🕐 Mon–Sat 9:30–5:30, Sun 1–5:30 🚍 14, 23
💷 $$

This huge, plain Franciscan church was
built in 1294, but was badly damaged by
the 1966 floods. Today it contains superb
early frescoes telling the story of the
Santa Croce (Holy Cross). Michelangelo
is buried here, along with Machiavelli
and Galileo Galilei. In the serene
cloisters stands the Cappella dei Pazzi
(Pazzi Chapel), among the most
beautiful of Renaissance buildings.

A
DAY IN FLORENCE

Many Florentines start working by 8 a.m., when food stores also open. Since many people live in centrally located apartments, visitors have the chance to see the neighborhoods waking up. Housewives go to market early, children walk to school and people pause for a quick bar breakfast on their way to work.

A detail from the bronze east door at the Baptistery, by Lorenzo Ghiberti (1378–1455)

For the tourist in Florence an early start makes sense. Head straight for major sights such as the Uffizi, Accademia, Duomo or Pitti Palace while you're still fresh and before the big tour groups arrive. Most of the museums open at 8:30 a.m. and the churches earlier, so it's feasible to pop into a specially noted church first thing. Pause mid-morning for a drink and a rest, but bear in mind that some attractions shut for several hours in the middle of the day, as do stores. It's a good idea to follow the siesta habit – a leisurely lunch and a quiet hour or so digesting all you've seen will leave you fresh for more touring in the late afternoon. Early evening is a popular time for Florentines to shop, and a good opportunity for you to track down that must-have leather bag, beautiful fabric, silk tie or marbled paper souvenir.

Florentines are back at work and out on the streets again some time after 4:30, looking rested, relaxed and ready for the rest of the day and evening. By 6:30 the town is thronged with well-dressed crowds, strolling, meeting friends and whole-heartedly enjoying the evening *passeggiata* through the streets of their beautiful city. Crowds thin out and shops close around 8:30, when people head home or to a restaurant for dinner, and there's a break before the evening's activities.

Florence has plenty of nightlife to choose from, with a wealth of cultural offerings such as theater, opera and classical music, movies, and numerous discos and bars with live music. The streets are busy well into the early hours – especially in summer – with locals and foreigners alike enjoying the balmy night air.

Shopping is important to the fashionable Florentines

Naples

NAPLES

Vibrant, noisy, crumbling Naples (Napoli), the capital of southern Italy and one of Europe's most beautifully located cities, is light years removed in atmosphere from the prosperous north. The city epitomizes southern Italy: confusing, passionate, dirty and charming, redolent with a rich and complicated history that has physically shaped it and emotionally shaped its residents. Naples can feel alien and intimidating, but also inspires fierce loyalty as visitors are quickly won over by its exuberance, way of life, attractions and, above all, its people.

The people of southern Italy are charming, warm and enthusiastic, and Neapolitans are no exception. They live at what appears to be a fever pitch of excitement and noise, which you'll be very aware of on the street. You'll find people genuinely eager to help, and anxious for you to enjoy Naples. In recent years authorities have encouraged citizens to welcome tourists, and have succeeded admirably. The friendliness of locals to visitors here far exceeds that of any other big Italian city.

Getting Around

Once you get your bearings, central Naples is best tackled on foot, as the traffic is so horrendous that any form of transportation can be excruciatingly slow. Much of what you'll want to see is walkable, and sights are grouped together in different areas, so take a bus or cable car to your general destination and then walk. Wandering around is an essential part of the Naples experience, as the street life is lively and beguiling – but stick to well-frequented areas.

You'll want to travel down the coast to Pompeii and the Sorrento peninsula;

Old and new – a view of Naples

both can be reached by train. The best way to appreciate the beauty of Naples' spectacular setting on the bay is from the sea; you could combine this with a boat trip to Sorrento or to the ravishing islands of Capri and Ischia.

Mediterranean Flavors

Neapolitan cooking ranks among the best in Italy, with a strong emphasis on the freshest fish and seafood, and local fruit and vegetables from the fertile volcanic soil of the hinterland. Flavors are intense, and the combination of ingredients unusual and interesting. There are pasta dishes with shellfish, grilled fish of all varieties, mozzarella cheese dripping with freshness, and numerous salamis, as well as some excellent local prosciutto.

Naples is the home of thin, tasty and crisp pizzas; they are always baked in wood-fired ovens, and can be eaten as a snack or light meal. Neapolitan cakes and pastries are famous and best enjoyed from a *pasticceria* (a specialist pastry and cake shop). Don't miss out on the ice cream – the flavors

Naples

encompass every imaginable type of fruit. Local wines to try are Lacrima Christi and Greco di Tufo. Be sure to sample *limoncello*, a lemon-flavored liqueur made all along the coast.

Shopping and Nightlife

Naples' upscale stores are clustered along the Via Toledo and the Via Chiaia, where you'll find outlets for Italy's top designers, as well as local

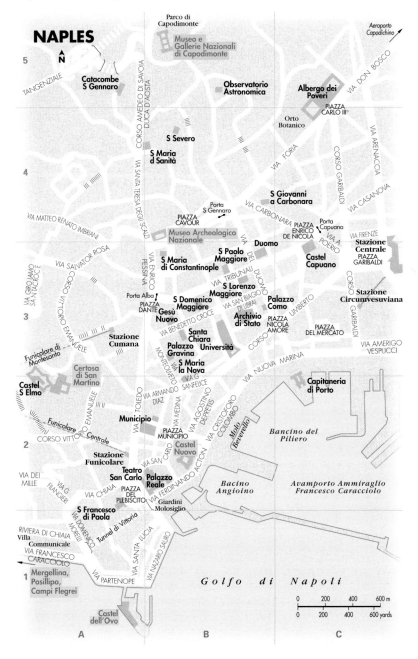

NAPLES

Parco di
Capodimonte

Museo e
Gallerie Nazionali
di Capodimonte

Aeroporto
Capodichino

Catacombe
S Gennaro

Observatorio
Astronomica

Albergo dei
Poveri

PIAZZA
CARLO III°

Orto
Botanico

S Severo

S Maria
d Sanità

S Giovanni
a Carbonara

Porta
S Gennaro

PIAZZA
CAVOUR

Museo Archeologico
Nazionale

Porta
Capuana

PIAZZA
ENRICO
DE NICOLA

Duomo

Castel
Capuano

Stazione
Centrale

PIAZZA
GARIBALDI

S Paolo
Maggiore

S Maria
di Constantinople

S Lorenzo
Maggiore

Stazione
Circumvesuviana

Porta Alba

PIAZZA
DANTE

S Domenico
Maggiore

Gesù
Nuovo

Palazzo
Como

PIAZZA
NICOLA
AMORE

PIAZZA
DEL MERCATO

Stazione
Cumana

Santa
Chiara

Palazzo
Gravina

Università

Archivio
di Stato

VIA AMERIGO
VESPUCCI

S Maria
la Nova

Certosa
di San
Martino

Capitaneria
di Porto

Castel
S Elmo

Municipio

Castel
Nuovo

PIAZZA
MUNICIPIO

*Bancino del
Piliero*

Stazione
Funicolare

Teatro
San Carlo

Palazzo
Reale

*Bacino
Angioino*

*Avamporto Ammiraglio
Francesco Caracciolo*

S Francesco
di Paola

PIAZZA
DEL
PLEBISCITO

Giardini
Molosiglio

Villa
Communicale

Mergellina,
Posillipo,
Campi Flegrei

Golfo   di   Napoli

Castel
dell'Ovo

| 0 | 200 | 400 | 600 m |
| 0 | 200 | 400 | 600 yards |

A   B   C

Naples

stores selling fine leather goods, fashion and knitwear. Jewelers abound near Via San Biagio; the traditional best buys in Naples are coral necklaces, bracelets, earrings, and cameo brooches. If you like antiques, head for Via Domenico Morelli, where stores specialize in 18th-century furniture and paintings.

Wonderful traditional nativity figurines are still made in the historic area around San Biagio, along with dolls and masks. There are shopping centers at Galleria Vanvitelli and Galleria Scartelli in the Vomero district, and you'll find a branch of the department store la Rinascente in downtown Naples.

If you like opera and classical music, a performance in the wonderful San Carlo opera house should be high on your list. Traditional Neapolitan music is easy to find, and even the least tourist-oriented restaurants have musicians serenading diners.

Safety in Naples

The city authorities have done much in recent years to clean up Naples in every way, making it a safer and more attractive city. However, it is still wise to avoid the labyrinthine back streets, the docks and, at night, the railroad station. Avoid carrying a lot of cash, and be aware of pickpockets, particularly in crowded tourist areas.

Be careful when crossing the street: Neapolitan drivers often ignore pedestrian crossings, and unless you step off the pavement you could be stranded for what seems like hours. Scooters appear to come out of nowhere, and they frequently use the sidewalks or go against the direction of traffic.

ESSENTIAL INFORMATION

TOURIST INFORMATION
• Piazza dei Martiri ☎ 081 410 7211
• Stazione Centrale ☎ 081 268 779
• Stazione Mergellina ☎ 081 761 2102
www.inaples.it

URBAN TRANSPORTATION
Neapolitan traffic makes any form of transportation slow, so it's best to walk if it's feasible. Longer distances can be covered by subway, bus and cable car (funiculari), all of which are slow. There are two types of Giranapoli transport tickets, valid for either 90 minutes or all day; they are interchangeable between buses, cable cars and the subway, and obtainable from tobacconists or newsstands. They must be validated in the special machines on board buses; before boarding cable cars; and at the entrance to subway platforms. To travel around the bay, use the Circumvesuviana railway, which leaves from

the railroad station on Corso Garibaldi every half-hour and takes an hour to reach Sorrento, its farthest point. You can also travel to Sorrento by ferry or hydrofoil from the Mergellina or Molo Beverello docks; the same companies also serve Capri, Ischia and the other islands. There are taxi stands throughout the city, or you can call Taxi Napoli (☎ 081 556 4444), Taxi Free (☎ 081 551 7070) or Taxi Partenope (☎ 081 556 0202). Taxis also will take you sightseeing outside Naples for fixed rates.

AIRPORT INFORMATION
Naples' Capodichino Airport (☎ 081 789 6259), with internal and European flights, is northwest of the city center. Airport buses run at 30-minute intervals to Piazza Municipio via Piazza Garibaldi, daily 6 a.m.–11:30 p.m. Bus 35 runs every 15 minutes as far as Piazza Garibaldi.

CLIMATE – average highs and lows for the month

JAN.	FEB.	MAR.	APR.	MAY	JUN.	JUL.	AUG.	SEP.	OCT.	NOV.	DEC.
12°C	13°C	15°C	18°C	22°C	26°C	29°C	29°C	26°C	22°C	17°C	13°C
54°F	55°F	59°F	64°F	72°F	79°F	84°F	84°F	79°F	72°F	63°F	55°F
4°C	5°C	7°C	9°C	13°C	17°C	19°C	19°C	17°C	13°C	8°C	5°C
39°F	41°F	45°F	48°F	55°F	63°F	66°F	66°F	63°F	55°F	46°F	41°F

CITY SIGHTS

Key to symbols

✚ map coordinates refer to the Naples map on page 309; sights below are highlighted in yellow on the map. ✉ address or location ☎ telephone number ⊙ opening times Ⓜ nearest subway 🚌 nearest bus or tram route 🍴 restaurant or café on site or nearby 💷 admission charge: $$$ more than €6, $$ €3–€6, $ less than €3 ⓘ other relevant information

CASTEL NUOVO

✚ B2 ✉ Piazza Municipio ☎ 081 795 5877 ⊙ Mon.–Sat. 9–7 🍴 Trattoria Medina, see page 559 🚌 R2, R3 💷 $$$

The five massive towers of the 15th-century Castel Nuovo (New Castle) dominate the Naples waterfront. A magnificent Renaissance gateway accesses the central courtyard, which is surrounded by buildings housing the Museo Civico (Civic Museum), the splendid Gothic Sala dei Baroni

(Barons' Hall) and the Cappella Palatina (Palatine Chapel), the only surviving part of a 13th-century building. Nearby is the 17th-century Palazzo Reale (Royal Palace) and the famous San Carlo opera house.

CASTEL DELL'OVO

✚ A1 ✉ Borgo Marinaro 🍴 La Cantinella, see page 559 🚌 R3; tram 1

Encircled by the sea, the Castel dell'Ovo (Egg Castle), Naples' oldest castle, was built between the ninth and 16th centuries. Run down by the 1970s, it has been fully restored and is used for cultural events.

CERTOSA DI SAN MARTINO

✚ A2–A3 ✉ Largo San Martino 5 ☎ 081 578 1769 ⊙ Certosa Tue.–Sat. 9–2, Sun. 9–1. Museum Tue.–Sat. 8:30–7:30, Sun. 9–7:30 Ⓜ Montesanto 🚌 V1 💷 $$$

Visible from all over Naples is the hilltop

Pompeii

The 20,000 inhabitants of first-century Roman Pompeii enjoyed a civilized lifestyle in their prosperous city, which boasted fine civic amenities, temples, public baths, and housing suitable for every taste and pocket. The one drawback was Pompeii's location on the slopes of Vesuvius, an active volcano. In AD 79 its worst eruption occurred, engulfing the city and many of its inhabitants in a thick layer of pumice and volcanic ash.

For nearly 1,700 years Pompeii remained buried, perfectly preserved beneath a hard layer of volcanic debris. About 1750 it was rediscovered, excavations started, and gradually the city emerged. It's a complete small city that can be explored like any other, wandering the streets and visiting the sites that appeal. It has the main features of every Roman city – the forum that was the center of public life; two theaters; an amphitheater; a sports stadium; and symmetrical rows of streets laid out in a grid pattern.

Start at the forum and make your way through the paved streets, looking into houses and shops as you go. Track down the covered market, the bakery, the laundry and the numerous taverns, some advertising bargain prices on the outside walls. The House of the Vetii, with its lovely garden and frescoed dining room, is a highlight, as is the House of the Tragic Poet, whose owners had a portrait mosaic of their dog laid by the front door with "*cave canem*," "beware of the dog," carefully inscribed.

✚ Page 284 D2–D3 ✉ Pompeii ☎ 081 857 5347 ⊙ Daily 8:30–7:30, Apr.–Sep.; 8:30–3:30, rest of year 🍴 Self-service restaurant and bar outside forum, many in modern Pompei 🚌 Circumvesuviana or FS train to Pompeii Scavi station 🚌 SITA Napoli–Salerno (stop at Piazza Esedra); CSTP No. 4 Salerno FS –Pompeii (stop at Villa dei Misteri) 💷 $$$ ⓘ Last admission 90 minutes before closing

The hilltop complex of St. Martin's Charterhouse looks down on the city of Naples

complex of the Certosa di San Martino (St. Martin's Charterhouse), constructed mainly between the 16th and 18th centuries. Highlights include the sumptuous baroque church, the arcaded Chiostro Grande (Main Cloister) and the lavishly decorated Quarto del Priore (Prior's Quarters). Don't miss the exhibition of *presepi* (crib figures), a charming collection of figures, animals and everyday objects fashioned for Christmas cribs in the 19th century, in the Museo Nazionale de San Martino (San Martino National Museum).

MERGELLINA

✚ Off the map ✉ Mergellina 🚇 Mergellina
🚌 R3, C21
This waterfront area, traditionally the fishermen's quarter, is a delightful place to stroll. Fishing boats and island ferries still leave from the harbor here.

MUSEO ARCHEOLOGICO NAZIONALE

✚ B4 ✉ Piazza Museo 19 ☎ 080 544 1494 or 081 440 166 🕐 Wed.–Sat. and Mon. 9–7, Sun. 9–8 🍴 Al 53, see page 559 🚌 1, 24, 42 💲 $$$
The Museo Archeologico Nazionale (National Archeological Museum) houses one of the world's most important collections of classical sculpture, mosaics,

gems, glass, silver and Egyptian antiquities. Finds from Pompeii are here; don't miss the graceful fresco portrayal of Flora. The *Farnese Hercules* and *Farnese Bull* are equally impressive; the *Bull* is the largest classical sculptural group to have survived, dating from 200 BC. Allow two or three hours for your visit to do the museum justice.

MUSEO E GALLERIE NAZIONALI DI CAPODIMONTE

✚ B5 ✉ Parco di Capodimonte, Via Miano 1 ☎ 081 749 9111 🕐 Tue.–Sun. 8:30–7:30 🚌 R4, 24 💲 $$$
Built in the 18th century as a palace and museum, and surrounded by a wooded park, Capodimonte has been recently restored and rearranged. Be sure to see Masaccio's *Crucifixion*, which is the star of the Renaissance painting collection, and the majolica and porcelain collection, much of it made by the Capodimonte factory.

POSILLIPO E CAMPI FLEGREI

✚ Off the map ✉ Posillipo 🚇 Mergellina or Campi Flegrei
Posillipo and the Campi Flegrei (literally "Burning Fields," named because of the area's volcanic activity) lie east of Naples on a lovely stretch of coast. Classical ruins, fishing villages, beaches, inlets and grottos dot the area, which is well worth exploring.

EXCURSION TO CAPRI

A favorite with the Roman emperors, Capri has been a tourist hot spot for more than 150 years. This tiny island, with its spectacular scenery and crystal-clear waters, now welcomes more than 2 million visitors annually.

Capri's Marina Grande is the starting point for visiting this enchanting island

Getting There

You can travel from Naples' Mergellina or Molo Beverello docks by ferry or hydrofoil, a lovely trip across the Bay of Naples that takes between 50 and 90 minutes. Spectacular views open up back to the city and across to Mount Vesuvius as you approach the steep hills of the Sorrento peninsula, with Capri lying off its tip. Boats dock at Marina Grande, the island's main harbor.

What to See

The charm of Capri lies in the combination of lovely scenery, picturesque villages and a laid-back holiday atmosphere. The two main settlements are Anacapri and Capri; their whitewashed houses and narrow, winding streets are crammed with boutiques, outdoor cafés and lively fish restaurants, and many visitors do no more than enjoy these. Most, however, take a boat trip to the Grotta Azzurra (Blue Grotto), a spectacular sea cave filled with refracted turquoise light. Another highlight is the beautiful Villa San Michele in Anacapri. Built in the late 19th century by Swedish physician Axel Munthe, this dreamlike villa is filled with classical statues. There also is a peaceful green garden, and from its shady pergola you can enjoy some of the island's loveliest views.

Walk to the ruins of Villa Jovis, Emperor Tiberius' clifftop villa, from where he allegedly threw his enemies into the sea. Or stroll to a lookout above the Faraglioni, a cluster of offshore rocks rising more than 360 feet above the water.

Capri ✚ See page 284, C2 ☎ Tourist offices: Banchina del Porto, Marina Grande ☎ 081 837 0634; Piazza Umberto I, Capri ☎ 081 837 0686; Via G. Orlandi 59, Anacapri ☎ 081 837 1524 🚢 From Marina Grande to Marina Piccola, Capri and Anacapri ⛴ Ferry operator: Caremar, from Molo Beverello, Naples (☎ 081 580 5111). Hydrofoil operators: Caremar, from Molo Beverello (☎ 081 551 3882) and from Sorrento (☎ 081 807 3077); NLG, from Molo Beverello (☎ 081 552 7209); SNAV, from Mergellina (☎ 081 761 2348)

Blue Grotto ☎ 081 837 5646 🕐 Daily 9–4 (weather permitting) 🚢 From Marina Grande 💵 $$$

Villa San Michele, Via Axel Munthe3, Anacapri ☎ 081 837 1401 🕐 Daily 9–6, May–Sep.; 9:30–5, Apr. and Oct.; 9:30–4:30, in Mar.; 10:30–3:30, rest of year 🚌 From Capri 💵 $$$

Villa Jovis 🕐 Daily 9–4 🚌 From Capri 💵 $$

VENICE

No matter how many pictures or films
you've seen, nothing can prepare you for
the real Venice (Venezia), one of the
world's most captivating cities.
Whether it's sparkling in late spring

sunshine or shrouded in winter mist, it
will enchant you in every way.

Tackling Venice

When you first arrive in Venice, don't
head straight for the main sights (which
will invariably be packed); take time to
get a feel for the city, either from the

Venice

vantage point of a ferry or by strolling the streets and squares. As for accommodations, luxury hotels lining the Grand Canal (Canale Grande) are clearly the optimum choice, but there are many with great charm elsewhere. The *sestrieri* (city areas) of Dorsoduro, San Marco, Castello and San Polo are among the nicest parts of the city to stay. Avoid the area around the train station, which is noisy and less attractive. Under no circumstances should you stay in Mestre, an industrial sprawl across the causeway on the mainland.

Accept that you will do a great deal of tiring walking around the city, and come prepared with comfortable shoes. Make a point of working out your daily itinerary; shortcuts across the city save valuable time. Main routes are clearly marked along the streets by yellow signs. There are numerous tour options; if time is short these can be helpful, and you'll have the benefit of English-speaking guides.

Venetian Glass, Velvet Slippers

The city's main fashion and leather stores cluster along the Calle dei Fabbri, the Frezzeria and the so-called Mercerie, made up of the streets connecting Piazza San Marco with the Rialto district. Glass is a true Venetian specialty, made for centuries on the island of Murano. Marbled paper is another good buy, and Venetian masks make wonderful souvenirs. Other typical products are velvet slippers in jewel-bright colors or a real gondolier's hat; you'll find one at Emilio Ceccato, near the Rialto.

Gondolas

The shiny black gondola – symbol of Venice – is a shallow-draft vessel propelled by a single oarsman, the gondolier, who stands at the back of the boat. A ride in a gondola is a great Venetian experience for many visitors, but they are expensive and normally follow a set route. Be sure to ascertain what you're getting before you set out.

Murano
Collona V

0   100   200   300   400   500 m
0   100   200   300   400   500 yards

San Michele V

Cimitero
San
Michele

Canale delle Fondamenta Nuove

Isola di
San
Michele

Gesuiti
anta Maria
Assunta)

FONDAMENTA NUOVE

V Fondamenta
Nuove

Rio dei Gesuiti

Rio dei Mendicanti

O

V Ospedale Civile

Santa Maria
dei Miracoli

Santi Giovanni
e Paolo

Tana
Celestia
V

Rio di San Giustina

Colleoni   CAMPO
SANTI GIOVANNI
E PAOLO

CAMPO
SANTA MARIA
FORMOSA

San Francesco
della Vigna

Santa Maria
Formosa

Palazzo Querini-
Stampalia
e Pinacoteca

Scuola di San
Giorgio degli
Schiavoni

Rio della Pietà

CASTELLO

San Giorgio
dei Greci

rre dell'
rologio

Basilica di
San Marco

San Zaccaria V

CAMPO
BANDIERA
E MORO

Arsenale

PIAZZA
SAN
MARCO

Palazzo
Ducale

CAMPO SAN
ZACCARIA

Santa Maria
della Pietà

San Giovanni Martino
in Brágora

ampanile

Prigioni

RIVA DEGLI SCHIAVONI

San
Martino

Museo
Storico
Navale

ocuratie
Nuove
Giardini
ex Reali

Ponte
dei Sospiri

San
Zaccaria

Riva degli
Schiavoni V

San Marco
Bacino di
San Marco

Canale di San Marco

Arsenale

San Biagio

San Pietro
di Castello

San Giorgio V

San Giorgio
Maggiore

Isola di
San
Giorgio
Maggiore

D   E

Venice

Festivals

Carnival lasts for 10 days before the start of Lent, when thousands of people wearing costumes parade the city streets. The summer sees several ancient festivals, notably the feast of *La Sensa*, when the mayor and his entourage sail out in the state barge and enact a symbolic marriage to the waters. This is followed in July by the *Festa del Redentore*, a thanksgiving festival for deliverence from a plague. During the *Regata Storica* in September, there are races of decorated craft manned by crews in period dress.

Getting Around

No cars, taxis, motorcycles or trucks are permitted within the city of Venice. If you arrive in a wheeled vehicle you must leave it in a parking lot on the city outskirts and enter Venice by boat or on foot. Every single item, from paper and pens to vegetables and vinegar, arrives at its destination by water, and so must every visitor. Take a water bus, water taxi or gondola to the landing point nearest your destination and then walk.

ESSENTIAL INFORMATION

TOURIST INFORMATION CALL CENTER
☎ 041 529 8711 (for all offices)
• Palazzina dei Santi, Giardini ex Reale
• San Marco 71f, Ascenzione ☎ 041 529 8740
• Aeroporto Marco Polo
• Stazione Santa Lucia
• Viale Santa Maria Elisabetta, Lido di Venezia
www.turismovenezia.it

URBAN TRANSPORTATION
If you arrive by car, you must leave the vehicle in one of the parking lots on the outskirts of the city. The parking at Piazzale Roma is the nearest to the city center. Venice's public transportation system is operated by ACTV (office at Piazzale Roma, ☎ 041 2424; www.actv.it) and uses two types of boats – *vaporetti* (big and slow) and *motoscafi* (small and fast). All are numbered on the front of the boat and follow set routes. *Vaporetti* boats leave from *pontile* (floating docks), which are clearly marked with service numbers and a route map. As the same numbers head in two directions, check that you are going the right way before you board; there are normally separate boarding points for each direction. Tickets can be bought at the *pontile* or at shops showing the ACTV sticker. You can save money by buying a 1-, 2- or 3-day pass. All tickets must be validated at the machine on the dock before boarding. There is a limited night service on most routes. *Vaporetti* stops are

marked on the Venice city map with a "V." *Taxi motoscafi* (water taxis) are fast and expensive; they can be hailed on various canals, but it is easier to call (☎ 041 723 112 or 041 522 2303). Gondolas can penetrate even the narrowest canals, but are very expensive.
As there are only three bridges over the Grand Canal, the seven *traghetti* (ferries) crossing at various points are useful. These ferries are old gondolas and are marked by yellow signs. Pay as you board and watch your balance, as it is customary to stand.

AIRPORT INFORMATION
Venice's Marco Polo airport (☎ 041 260 6111) is 5 miles from the city center on the northern edge of the lagoon, and handles both domestic and international flights. For city connections you can take a bus (shuttle bus ATVO or ACTV bus No. 5) from outside the terminal to the Piazzale Roma at the edge of the city, where the road ends, and then connect with your hotel by *vaporetto* (water bus). The transfer takes 15 minutes by ATVO bus and 25 minutes by ACTV bus; tickets must be purchased from the office inside the airport arrivals terminal before boarding. A *vaporetto* leaves from the dock outside the terminal for San Marco and the Lido; the transfer takes around 50 minutes. The fastest way to reach the city is by water taxi; they leave from the dock outside the terminal and take only 20 minutes to reach the center, but are expensive.

CLIMATE – average highs and lows for the month

JAN.	FEB.	MAR.	APR.	MAY	JUN.	JUL.	AUG.	SEP.	OCT.	NOV.	DEC.
5°C	8°C	12°C	17°C	21°C	24°C	27°C	26°C	23°C	18°C	12°C	8°C
41°F	46°F	54°F	63°F	70°F	75°F	81°F	79°F	73°F	64°F	54°F	46°F
0°C	2°C	5°C	9°C	13°C	17°C	19°C	18°C	16°C	12°C	7°C	3°C
32°F	36°F	41°F	48°F	55°F	63°F	66°F	64°F	61°F	54°F	45°F	37°F

Crowds converge on St. Mark's Basilica – one of the world's greatest medieval buildings

City Sights

Key to symbols

🞤 map coordinates refer to the Venice map on pages 314–315; sights below are highlighted in yellow on the map.

✉ address or location ☎ telephone number

🕐 opening times 🚤 nearest boat or ferry stop

🍴 restaurant or café on site or nearby

💶 admission charge: $$$ more than €6, $$ €3–€6, $ less than €3 ℹ other relevant information

Basilica di San Marco

🞤 D2 ✉ Piazza San Marco 1 ☎ 041 522 5205
🕐 Mon.–Sat. 9:45–4:30, Sun. 2–4, Oct.–Apr.;
Mon.–Sat. 9:45–4, Sun. 2–4, rest of year 🚤 1, 51, 82
💶 Basilica free; Loggia $, Pala d'Oro $, Tesoro $$

The Basilica di San Marco (St. Mark's Basilica), glittering with mosaics and flickering candles, is an architectural hybrid, a fusion of western and Byzantine styles. Dating from 1094, it stands on the site of the ninth-century basilica built to house the body of St. Mark. Pause before entering to admire the Romanesque carvings, then proceed inside to take in the ornate marble pavements; the gem-encrusted altar screen, the Pala d'Oro, a masterpiece of Gothic-Byzantine goldsmith art; and the third-century bronze horses, which once adorned the facade.

Ca' d'Oro

🞤 C3 ✉ Calle di Ca' d'Oro, off Strada Nova ☎ 041
523 8790 🕐 Tue.–Sun. 8:15–7:15, Mon. 8:15–2 🚤 1
💶 $$

The picture-book facade of the Ca' d'Oro (House of Gold), so called because it was once gilded, is a perfect example of the finest Venetian-Byzantine architecture. Behind the facade is a beguiling small museum with an impressive *St. Sebastian* by Andrea Mantegna and a lovely *Madonna* by Giovanni Bellini, as well as sculptural fragments, bronzes and tapestries. All pieces are arranged in rooms around the palazzo's central *portego*, or inner courtyard.

Campanile

🞤 D2 ✉ Piazza San Marco ☎ 041 522 4064
🕐 Daily 9–9, Jul.–Aug.; 9–7, Apr.–Jun. and Sep.–Oct.;
9:30–4:15, rest of year. 🚤 1, 51, 82 💶 $$$

The graceful Campanile, Venice's tallest building, is less than 100 years old. The original bell tower, reputedly built in AD 912, collapsed in 1902, killing no one and leaving St. Mark's unscathed. A cry of *"Dov'era e com'era"* ("where it was and how it was") went up, and 10 years later a perfect replica was completed. Take the elevator up for superb views – on a clear day you can see as far as the Alps.

CANAL GRANDE

⊞ B2, C1, C2, C3, D2, D3   🚤 1, 82

The allure of the Canal Grande (Grand Canal), Venice's magical highway, never seems to fade. It divides Venice in two and is crossed by three bridges. The canal is lined with a wondrous procession of palaces, built over the course of 500 years. By day numerous boats chug up and down; at night it epitomizes romance, with reflected lights twinkling on the water. Take a No. 1 or No. 82 water bus from stops on the Grand Canal.

COLLEZIONE PEGGY GUGGENHEIM

⊞ C1   ✉ Palazzo Venier dei Leoni, Calle San Cristoforo   ☎ 041 240 5411   🕐 Wed.–Mon. 10–6   🚤 1   💵 $$$

American Peggy Guggenheim's modern art collection is installed in her 18th-century *palazzo* on the Grand Canal. Here you'll find works by Pablo Picasso and Salvadore Dalí and fine examples of Jackson Pollock and Mark Rothko, all beautifully displayed. The garden makes a wonderful background for some Henry Moore sculptures and Marino Marini's *Angel of the Citadel*.

GALLERIE DELL'ACCADEMIA

⊞ C1   ✉ Campo della Carità   ☎ 041 522 2247   🕐 Tue.–Sun. 8:15–7:15, Mon. 8:15–2   🍴 Taverna San Trovaso, see page 560   🚤 1, 82   💵 $$$

Allow plenty of time for the Gallerie dell'Accademia (Academy Galleries), the finest collection of Venetian painting in the world. Arranged chronologically, the gallery's 24 rooms contain masterpieces such as Giorgio Giorgione's enigmatic *Tempest*, Giovanni Bellini's luminous *Virgins*, and superb Mantegnas. Don't miss the dramatic *Translation of the Body of St. Mark* by Jacopo Tintoretto and Paolo Veronese's sumptuous *Feast in the House of Levi*. Among other highlights are the cycles of paintings in rooms 20 and 21; *The Miracle of the True Cross* had several contributors, while the *Life of St. Ursula* is wholly by Vittore Carpaccio.

MUSEO STORICO NAVALE

⊞ E1   ✉ Campo San Biagio   ☎ 041 520 0276   🕐 Mon.–Fri. 8:45–1:30, Sat. 8:45–1   🚤 1   💵 $

Venice's Museo Storico Navale (Maritime Museum) is fittingly housed near the Arsenale, the great shipyards that once manufactured the city's fleets. It tells the story of the city's sea power through displays of every type of maritime artifact; the highlight is the collection of gondolas and other historic boats, which are housed in one of the Arsenale's old sheds.

PALAZZO DUCALE

⊞ D2   ✉ Piazzetta San Marco   ☎ 041 271 5911   🕐 Daily 9–7 (last admission at 5:30), Nov.–Mar.; 9–5 (last admission at 3:30), rest of year. Guided tours a.m. only   🚤 1, 51, 52, 82   💵 $$$

The huge Gothic complex of the Palazzo Ducale (Ducal Palace) was the seat of Venice's government, where the Council of Ten met, ambassadors were received and the Doge held councils of state. The present building dates from the 15th century, with later alterations following two fires in the 1500s. The marked route leads through a succession of sumptuous rooms to the vast Sala del Maggior Consiglio (Great Council Chamber), dominated by Jacopo Tintoretto's *Paradiso*, the world's largest oil painting. Be sure to have a look at the famous Ponte dei Sospiri (Bridge of Sighs), spanning a canal to the right of the palazzo's waterfront facade.

PIAZZA SAN MARCO

⊞ D2   ✉ Piazza San Marco   🚤 1, 51, 82

The only piazza in Venice (all the others are officially *campi*) is thronged around the clock with strolling and chattering crowds. Go early or late to avoid the worst crush, and marvel at the harmony of this wonderful open space. Highlights here are the 15th-century Torre dell'Orologio (Clock Tower) and its zodiac clock, the graceful architecture of the Libreria Sansoviniana (Sansoviniana Library), and the two columns near the waterfront, topped by the lion of St. Mark and St. Theodore with his crocodile emblem.

Time to reflect on the beauty of Venice – sample the local fare with a view of the Rialto Bridge

RIALTO

➕ C2–D2 ✉ Rialto 🚤 1, 82

Throughout the Middle Ages the Rialto was Europe's financial and banking center; the name had the same connotations as does Wall Street now. Today, you can admire the bridge and browse in Venice's food markets, one of the city's great sights. Wander through the fruit and vegetable stalls, but leave time to enjoy the scents and sights of the fish market, full of the day's catch.

SAN GIORGIO MAGGIORE

➕ E1 ✉ Campo San Giorgio, Isole San Giorgio ☎ 041 522 7827 🕐 Daily 9:30–12:30 and 2:30–5:30; Mass: Mon.–Sat. 8 a.m., Sun. 11 a.m. 🚤 82 💵 Free; $ (elevator to campanile)

To visit the superb Palladian church of San Giorgio Maggiore (St. George the Great), whose serene bulk dominates the view of St. Mark's Basin, you must take a waterbus across the canal of St. Mark's to St. George's island. Built by Andrea Palladio in 1559, the church embodies order, grace and harmony. Take the elevator up the campanile (bell tower) to enjoy fine views across to the Doge's Palace and the Campanile of San Marco.

SANTA MARIA DEI MIRACOLI

➕ D3 ✉ Campo dei Miracoli ☎ 041 275 0462 🕐 Mon.–Sat. 10–5, Sun. 1–5 🚤 1, 82 💵 $ or $$$ "Chorus Pass" for entry to Venice's minor churches

The tiny jewel-like church of Santa Maria dei Miracoli (Our Lady of the Miracles) was built around 1480 to house a miraculous image of the Virgin. Pietro Lombardo, who faced his church with colored marble and porphyry rock, created the harmonious interior as a frame for some fine sculpture and intricate carvings.

SANTA MARIA DELLA SALUTE

➕ C1 ✉ Campo della Salute ☎ 041 522 5558 🕐 Daily 9–noon and 3–6 🍽 Taverna San Trovaso, see page 560 🚤 1

During the 1630 plague, the Senate promised to build a church in honor of the Virgin if she would save the city. The pestilence passed, an architect was commissioned, and the great dome of Santa Maria della Salute (Our Lady of Health and Salvation) rose at the entrance to the Grand Canal. One of the city's outstanding skyline features, the interior has fine sculptures and paintings.

The Annunciation by Jacopo Tintoretto, in the Scuola Grande di San Rocco

SANTA MARIA GLORIOSA DEI FRARI

✚ B2 ✉ Campo dei Frari ☎ 041 275 0462 or 041 275 0494 🕐 Mon.–Sat. 9–6, Sun. 1–6 🚢 1, 82 💵 $ or $$$ with multi-church "Chorus Pass"

Santa Maria Gloriosa dei Frari (Glorious Virgin Mary of the Brothers), a lofty Franciscan church, is the resting place of Titian and the composer Claudio Monteverdi. Built as a preaching church about 1250, it contains Titian's great *Assumption*, hung over the high altar, and his *Madonna of Ca' Pesaro*. Best of all, though, is Giovanni Bellini's *Madonna and Child with Saints*, considered among the world's finest paintings. You'll find it tucked away in the right transept.

SANTI GIOVANNI E PAOLO

✚ D2, D3, E2, E3 ✉ Campo SS Giovanni e Paolo ☎ 041 523 5913 🕐 Daily 7:30–12:30 and 3:30–7:30 🚢 52

More than 20 of Venice's Doges are buried in the Gothic church of Santi Giovanni e Paolo (St. John and St. Paul), rising majestically on one side of its *campo* (square). The focal point is the great equestrian statue of Bartolomeo Colleoni, a 15th-century Venetian army officer. The 13th-century church contains many tombs, their monuments representing the best of Venetian medieval sculpture, and some lovely paintings, including Giovanni Bellini's *St. Vincent Ferrer.*

SCUOLA DI SAN GIORGIO DEGLI SCHIAVONI

✚ E2 ✉ Calle dei Furlani 3259/a ☎ 041 522 8828 🕐 Tue.–Sat. 9:30–12:30 and 3:30–6:30, Sun. 9:30–12:30, Apr.–Oct.; Tue.–Sat. 10–12:30 and 3–6, Sun. 10–12:30, rest of year 🍴 Da Franz, see page 560 🚢 1, 52, 82 💵 $

Carpaccio painted one of the city's most delightful picture cycles between 1502 and 1508 for the headquarters of Venice's Dalmatian, or Slavic, community – the Scuola di San Giorgio degli Schiavoni (School of St. George of the Slavs). He used Dalmatia's patron saints, St. George, St. Tryphon and St. Jerome, as his inspiration. Highlights are *St. George Slaying the Dragon* and *St. Augustine in his Study*, accompanied by his dog.

SCUOLA GRANDE DI SAN ROCCO

✚ B2 ✉ Campo San Rocco ☎ 041 523 4864 🕐 Daily 9–5:30, Apr.–Oct.; 10–4, rest of year 🚢 1, 82 💵 $$

In 1564, the brotherhood of St. Roche ran a competition to choose an artist to decorate the walls of their Scuola Grande di San Rocco (Grand Meeting Halls of the Confraternity of St. Roche). Tintoretto won, and spent 23 years working on a stupendous cycle of paintings. There are 54 paintings in all; including the wonderful *Crucifixion*. New Testament scenes line the walls of the main hall on the ground floor.

THE LAGOON ISLANDS

You can spend a delightful day exploring some of the islands in the lagoon. Most visitors opt for Murano, famous for its glass; Burano, with its lace-making; or Torcello, a virtually deserted island with an ancient cathedral and church. Guided excursions run to all three, but a more flexible option is to take boat number 12, which leaves from the Fondamenta Nuove and takes around 40 to 50 minutes to reach Burano and Torcello, the two farthest islands.

Colorful waterfront at Burano

Murano

Venetian glass has been made on Murano since 1291, when the furnaces were moved away from the city as a fire precaution. A visit to the fascinating Glass Museum (Museo Vetrario) will give you an idea of glass-blowers' skills through the ages. Murano also has two exquisite churches: San Pietro Martire, which contains a glowing altarpiece by Giovanni Bellini; and Santi Maria e Donato, a 12th-century structure with mosaics on its walls and floor.

Burano

Burano's colorful canal-side houses, narrow streets and sun-splashed squares are as picturesque as anything in Venice itself. This is still a fishing community, with a robust workaday atmosphere, and you'll see moored fishing boats and nets drying in the sun. Local ladies have always been skilled lace-makers, and you can admire the fragility of their exquisite work in the Lace-Making Museum (Museo del Merletto).

Torcello

Timeless Torcello is one of the most evocative and magical places in Venice. This sleepy island, with its overgrown canals and green fields, was the lagoon's first settled area, and once had fine buildings and palaces. Silt and malaria caused its 12th-century decline. Today the only remaining signs of its past importance are the Cathedral of Santa Maria Assunta and the adjacent church, Santa Fosca. The cathedral's main glories are two 12th-century mosaics, which completely cover the apse and the opposite rear wall. High above the seventh-century altar stands a lovely Byzantine *Madonna and Child*, its poignant beauty highlighted by the simple gold background, while the graphic *Judgment* scenes make a telling contrast. The nearby church of Santa Fosca, with its arcaded porch full of nesting swifts, is as lovely in its own way.

Elaborate glass candlestick produced on the Venetian island of Murano

LUXEMBOURG

"*ALL that we see is superb, the Ardennes are enchanting...*"

From a letter written by French author Victor Hugo

Opposite: Vianden Castle overlooks the valley of the Our, on the border with Germany

LUXEMBOURG

Luxembourg lies at the heart of the European landmass. It is a minuscule country, measuring 51 miles from north to south and a mere 32 miles from east to west. Belgium lies to the north and west, France to the south and Germany to the east. Because of its attractive financial laws and constitutional stability, it has become a center of European politics and finance. And despite a turbulent history, Luxembourg retains its independence and sovereignty; it is a true survivor of the Continent's stormy past.

Luxembourg Landscapes

Luxembourg is a Grand Duchy, the only one in the world, with the city of Luxembourg as its main focus, although its rural areas are remarkably varied for such a small country. They include part of the delightful Ardennes region, the hilly area that lies across the northern third of Luxembourg and extends into Belgium. The Ardennes have a distinctive landscape of forested plateaus sliced through by deep valleys that are drained by beautiful rivers. Fairy-tale castles crown wooded bluffs. At Vianden a medieval castle, one of the Grand Duchy's finest historic sites, dominates the landscape. The equally magnificent Bourscheid Castle stands above the Sûre and Wark rivers. At Clervaux, the castle is matched by the red-roofed Benedictine Clervaux Abbey, which stands amid the wooded heights above the beautiful town.

At the southern edge of the Ardennes, where the hills meet the flatter, more fertile land known as Le Bon Pays, or "The Good Land," lies the picturesque town of Diekirch. Only a short distance southwest is Ettelbrück, where there is a monument to Gen. George S. Patton Jr. and the Patton Museum containing many personal items from his life.

Southern Luxembourg is the country's economic powerhouse. Here in the "Good Land" are farms and orchards, forests and even more castles. In fact, the lovely valley of the Eisch river is known as the Vallée des Sept Châteaux (Valley of the Seven Castles).

MORE TOP DESTINATIONS IN LUXEMBOURG

- Abbaye Benédictine C3
- Abbaye St.-Maurice B4
- Château Bourscheid B3
- Diekirch B3
- Esch-sur-Sûre A3
- Grevenmacher C2 • Mondorf-les-Bains B1 • Vallée du Müllerthal C3
- Vallée des Sept Châteaux B2
- Vianden B3

View over the Old Town, city of Luxembourg

Luxembourg

Farther south and west from the city of Luxembourg is Les Terres Rouges, or "The Land of the Red Rocks" around Dudelange and Pétange, home to much of the country's industry. East of here is the delightful Mondorf-les-Bains, a fashionable spa town on the edge of the Moselle region. This area, running north to south along the border with Germany, is Luxembourg's wine-growing district.

Exploring the Country
You will find Luxembourgers are very cosmopolitan and friendly, and a large percentage of them speak English. The Grand Duchy has an excellent road system and distances are short between the many towns and villages, making independent travel a good option. There also are numerous day trips organized from the city of Luxembourg.

Luxembourg

TIMELINE

AD 963	Count Siegfried of the Ardennes builds a castle on the Bock promontory called the Lützelburg ("Little Castle").
1354	Luxembourg becomes a duchy.
1447	The Duchy of Luxembourg comes under the rule of the Habsburgs through marriage.
1542	The city of Luxembourg is captured by the French.
1554	The Spanish capture the city of Luxembourg.
1713	Under the terms of the Treaty of Utrecht, Luxembourg comes under the control of the Kingdom of the Netherlands.
1815	Congress of Vienna establishes the Grand Duchy of Luxembourg as a sovereign, neutral state.
1839	Under the terms of the Treaty of London, the western part of the Grand Duchy is ceded to Belgium.
1867	Luxembourg becomes an independent state.
1914	Germany occupies Luxembourg in World War I.
1940	Germany invades Luxembourg again in World War II.
1944	American troops liberate Luxembourg; Germany launches its "Ardennes Offensive". The Battle of the Bulge follows.
1945	Luxembourg becomes a member of the United Nations.
1948	Luxembourg joins Belgium and the Netherlands in forming BENELUX, a trading and economic union.
1949	Luxembourg abandons neutrality and joins NATO.
1957	Luxembourg joins the European Economic Community.
1992	Luxembourg ratifies the Maastricht Treaty.
1994	City of Luxembourg declared a World Heritage Site by UNESCO.

LUXEMBOURG: THE GREAT SURVIVOR

Luxembourg, with its long history at the heart of Europe, has secured a major part in the working of the European Union. The country today is a constitutional monarchy ruled by HRH Grand Duke Henri, who heads a Cabinet of 12 ministers appointed from an elected Chamber of Deputies. Consensus politics is used in Luxembourg's government, and coalitions of more than one party usually hold power. On the international front, Luxembourg is home to, among others, the General Secretariat of the European Parliament, the European Court of Justice, the European Court of Auditors, the European Bank of Investment, the Plenary Hall of the European Parliament and several General Directorates of the European Commision – all of which are based in the city of Luxembourg's Centre Européen (European Center).

Sidewalk cafés amid the downtown bustle of the city of Luxembourg

SURVIVAL GUIDE

- The *Schueberfouer*, one of Europe's largest fairs, takes place for three weeks from late August to early September.

- Most shops in the city of Luxembourg are closed on Monday mornings but often stay open until 8 p.m. on Thursdays.

- There are numerous stores in the Gare district of the city of Luxembourg, especially on avenue de la Liberté. Enjoy an evening in the Grund district. There are lovely areas, good bars and restaurants, and a different ambience to the city center, which is known as the Ville area.

- Earthenware bird whistles (*péckvillerchers*) are a popular present given on Easter Monday, when their sound fills the air.

- The city of Luxembourg has many designer shops, such as Hermès, Dolce & Gabbana, Armani, Louis Vuitton and Claudia Sträter, along Grande-Rue and rue Philippe II. There also are tempting treats in Leonidas, the renowned Belgian chocolatiers.

- Typical Luxembourg souvenirs include cast iron from the Mersch foundry, in the heart of the Grand Duchy. Designs incorporate castles and coats of arms. Authentic Luxembourg porcelain and earthenware are produced by Villeroy & Boch (330 rue du Rollingergrund, Luxembourg City ☎ 46 82 1-1; factory shop ⊙ Mon.–Fri. 9–5:45, Sat. 9–5).

- If you travel in the Moselle wine-producing region, enjoy some of Luxembourg's dry white and sparkling vintages, such as the subtle Rivaner; Pinot Blanc to go with fish dishes; or the satisfyingly strong Pinot Gris to complement a meal of *judd mat gaardebounen* (roast, smoked pork).

- Children will especially love the Exotic Butterfly Garden (route de Trèves, Grevenmacher ☎ 75 85 39 ⊙ Daily 9:30-5, Apr. 1 to mid-Oct. ⊙ $$$). They also will enjoy Parc Merveilleux (route de Mondorf, Bettembourg ☎ 51 10 48-1 ⊙ Daily 9:30–6, late Mar. to mid-Oct. ⊙ $$$), at the southern tip of Luxembourg, where there are attractions from fairy-tale tableaux and exotic birds and reptiles to children's animal enclosures and games of all types.

CITY OF LUXEMBOURG

The city of Luxembourg is known as the landlocked "Gibraltar of the North" because of its once-fortified location. It is set above the cliffs that flank the canyon-like valleys of the Alzette and Pétrusse rivers. Today, the city of Luxembourg is more fairy tale than fortress. The old city, especially, is a pleasing mix of the past and present. Its elegant towers, spires and turrets and its attractive walls of golden sandstone helped win Luxembourg the United Nations' designation of World Heritage Site in 1994.

The steep-sided plateau on which Luxembourg stands explains its origins. The Romans first set up camp here. They had one eye on military control and the other on the advantages of a strategic trading position at the crossroads of northern Europe. In AD 963, Count Siegfried of the Ardennes built a castle on the narrow Bock promontory above the Alzette river.

Over the next 900 years Luxembourg evolved into one of the mightiest fortifications in Europe. In 1867 the terms of the 1831 Treaty of London were applied, and Luxembourg became a neutral state. The military fortress was dismantled and the encircling walls were replaced by the present city's outer boulevards.

Ville and *Gare*

The main parts of the city of Luxembourg are the city center, known as *Ville*, perched on the high plateau above the Pétrusse and Alzette river valleys; and the more modern district, known as *Gare*, south of the river. The two are connected by bridges across the Pétrusse valley; the main ones are the pont Adolphe and the pont Viaduc, the latter known locally as *Passerelle*. Below the cliffs lies Grund, the main part of the city's valley settlements.

The area around the railroad station is emphatically modern and downtown. Buses leave regularly from outside the station and take you to place E.-Hamilius, on the western side of *Ville*. From here a short walk east along rue de la Poste leads to the large central square of place d'Armes.

At the east end of place d'Armes is the handsome City Hall (Palais Municipal, or Cercle Municipal), where the Luxembourg City Tourist Office is located. Ask for details on guided tours and the LuxembourgCard (available Easter through October), which is good for one, two or three days (costing 9, 16 and 22 euros respectively; two- and three-day cards must be used within two weeks), for free entry or discounts on admission fees to more than 50 museums and attractions plus free use of public transportation all over the Grand Duchy. The maze-like streets of the Old Town (Vieille Ville, see page 332) and the complex of steps and terraces that connect plateau and valley floor make Luxembourg a very walkable place.

Conversation and Music

The place d'Armes is a public space shaded by lime trees. In summer it is

A Lift in Luxembourg

You can reach the riverside Grund district in the Alzette valley by public elevator from place du St.-Esprit, near the intersection with boulevard F. D.-Roosevelt. Look for the glass-fronted elevator shelter in the corner of the place du St.-Esprit. The elevator takes you to a tunnel that emerges at montée du Grund.

filled with the chairs and tables of the surrounding restaurants and cafés, where you can enjoy the hum of relaxed conversation and the music of regular concerts on the nearby bandstand.

All around the place d'Armes are the city's pedestrian-only shopping streets.

To the north is Grande-Rue, known locally as *Groussgaass*, the city's main shopping street. Here, and in the adjoining streets of rue Phillipe II and rue des Capucins, are fashion boutiques, as well as good restaurants and cafés. Stop for coffee at Namur, on the corner

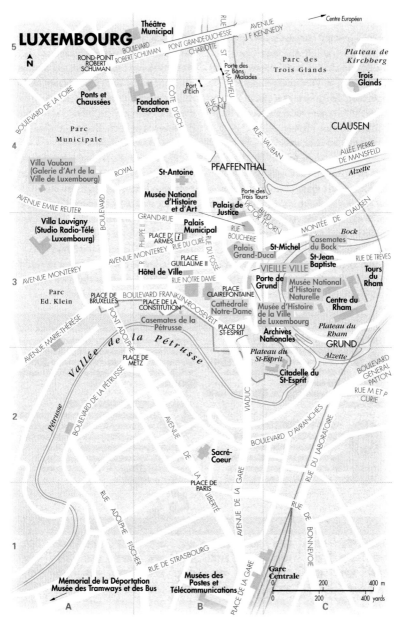

LUXEMBOURG

Théâtre Municipal
Centre Européen
RUE J F KENNEDY
AVENUE
BOULEVARD ROBERT SCHUMAN
ROND-POINT ROBERT SCHUMAN
PONT GRANDE-DUCHESSE CHARLOTTE
Plateau de Kirchberg
Parc des Trois Glands
Porte des Bons Malades
RUE ST-MATHIEU
Trois Glands
Ponts et Chaussées
BOULEVARD DE LA FOIRE
Port d'Eich
RUE DU PONT
CLAUSEN
Fondation Pescatore
CÔTE D'EICH
Parc Municipale
RUE VAUBAN
ALLÉE PIERRE DE MANSFELD
Alzette
Villa Vauban (Galerie d'Art de la Ville de Luxembourg)
ROYAL
St-Antoine
PFAFFENTHAL
AVENUE EMILE REUTER
BOULEVARD
Musée National d'Histoire et d'Art
Palais de Justice
Porte des Trois Tours
BLVD VICTOR THORN
Villa Louvigny (Studio Radio-Télé Luxembourg)
GRAND-RUE
Palais Municipal
RUE BOUCHERIE
MONTÉE DE CLAUSEN
Bock
PHILIPPE II
PLACE D'ARMES
RUE DU CURÉ
Palais Grand-Ducal
Casemates du Bock
AVENUE MONTEREY
RUE DU FOSSÉ
St-Michel
St-Jean Baptiste
RUE DE TRÈVES
AVENUE MONTEREY
PLACE GUILLAUME II
VIEILLE VILLE
Tours du Rham
Hôtel de Ville
RUE NOTRE DAME
Porte de Grund
Musée National d'Histoire Naturelle
Parc Ed. Klein
PLACE DE BRUXELLES
BOULEVARD FRANKLIN-ROOSEVELT
PLACE CLAIREFONTAINE
Centre du Rham
PLACE DE LA CONSTITUTION
Cathédrale Notre-Dame
Musée d'Histoire de la Ville de Luxembourg
Casemates de la Pétrusse
PLACE DU ST-ESPRIT
Plateau du Rham
AVENUE MARIE-THÉRÈSE
Archives Nationales
GRUND
PONT ADOLPHE
Vallée de la Pétrusse
PLACE DE METZ
Plateau du St-Esprit
Alzette
Pétrusse
BOULEVARD DE LA PÉTRUSSE
Citadelle du St-Esprit
BOULEVARD GENERAL PATTON
RUE M ET P CURIE
AVENUE DE LA
VIADUC
BOULEVARD D'AVRANCHES
RUE DU LABORATOIRE
Sacré-Coeur
RUE ADOLPHE FISCHER
PLACE DE PARIS
AVENUE DE LA GARE
LIBERTÉ
RUE DE BONNEVOIE
Mémorial de la Déportation Musée des Tramways et des Bus
RUE DE STRASBOURG
Musées des Postes et Télécommunications
PLACE DE LA GARE
Gare Centrale
RUE DE

0   200   400 m
0   200   400 yards

A   B   C

City of Luxembourg

of Grande-Rue and rue des Capucins. At the east end of Grande-Rue look for the fountain known as Hämmelsmarsch, "The March of the Sheep."

Exploring Historic Luxembourg

To reach historic Luxembourg, leave the southeast corner of place d'Armes, where a covered passage leads between bookshops and into the large place Guillaume II. A colorful flower market is held here on Wednesdays and Saturdays. From here you can quickly reach the Grand-Ducal Palace on rue du Marché-aux-Herbes.

Behind the palace lies the Old Town (Vieille Ville). Look for rue de l'Eau, with its cluster of restaurants known as Ilot Gastronomique. Then head down rue Sigefroi to the stunning viewpoint of the Bock, above the Alzette valley.

From here you can see the famous pont Grande-Duchesse Charlotte, known as the Red Bridge because of its color. It connects the city center plateau with the Kirchberg plateau and the ultramodern European Center (Centre Européen), home of numerous European Union institutions (see box, page 326). Visit the famous Bock Casemates, the maze of underground tunnels in the cliffs, and then walk the Chemin de la Corniche, the terrace that leads south above the Alzette valley.

Discover the valley district of Grund, a riverside haven of well-preserved old houses and restaurants and taverns. From here you can turn left and wander along the paths and terraced lanes of the Alzette to reach the 17th-century riverside church of St. John (Saint-Jean Baptiste), with its rich baroque altar and famous Black Madonna statue.

The city's Ville is more relaxed than the centers of other, more cosmopolitan European cities, although city life is sophisticated in its restrained way. Fine music can be enjoyed at the city's Grand Théâtre de la Ville de Luxembourg, Théâtre des Capucins and Music Conservatory. The top fashion stores of Grande-Rue speak for themselves, and Ville restaurants are excellent.

ESSENTIAL INFORMATION

TOURIST INFORMATION
Luxembourg National Tourist Office
• Gare Centrale (Central Station) ☎ 42 82 82-20; fax 42 82 82-30; www.ont.lu
Luxembourg City Tourist Office
• place d'Armes, Luxembourg City ☎ 22 28 09; fax 46 70 70; www.lcto.lu

URBAN TRANSPORTATION
Buses are the only form of public transportation in the city of Luxembourg. Visitors will probably require service only between the airport or the railroad station and the city terminus at place E.-

Hamilius. A flat fare of €1.20 is valid for 1 hour or you can buy a pack of ten tickets for €9.20. Buses run daily from 5 a.m.–midnight.. For information ☎ 47 96-29 75. Taxis are expensive, but can be hired by calling ☎ 48 00 58.

AIRPORT INFORMATION
Luxembourg's Findel Airport is located 4 miles east of the city of Luxembourg. Buses run between the airport and the city center and railroad station (fare €1.20, plus €1.20 for baggage). Taxis between airport and city are expensive (☎ 427-130). For airport information call ☎ 2456-1; www.luxair.lu

---

CLIMATE – average highs and lows for the month

JAN.	FEB.	MAR.	APR.	MAY	JUN.	JUL.	AUG.	SEP.	OCT.	NOV.	DEC.
3°C	4°C	9°C	14°C	18°C	21°C	23°C	22°C	19°C	13°C	7°C	4°C
37°F	39°F	48°F	57°F	64°F	70°F	73°F	71°F	66°F	55°F	45°F	39°F
-2°C	0°C	2°C	4°C	8°C	11°C	13°C	12°C	10°C	6°C	3°C	0°C
28°F	32°F	36°F	39°F	46°F	52°F	55°F	54°F	50°F	43°F	37°F	32°F

CITY SIGHTS

Key to symbols

🚩 map coordinates refer to the Luxembourg map on page 329; sights below are highlighted in yellow on the map.

✉ address or location ☎ telephone number
🕐 opening times 🚌 nearest bus or tram route
🍴 restaurant or café on site or nearby
🎟 admission charge: $$$ more than €4, $$ €2–€4, $ less than €2 ℹ other relevant information

CASEMATES

Casemates du Bock 🚩 C3 ✉ montée de Clausen ☎ 22 28 09 (47 96-27 09 for guided tours) 🕐 Daily 10–5, Mar.–Oct. 🚌 All city center buses 🎟 $
Casemates de la Pétrusse 🚩 B3 ✉ place de la Constitution/boulevard F. D. Roosevelt ☎ 22 28 09 (47 96-27 09 for guided tours) 🕐 Daily 11–4, Jul.–Sep. (also 11–4, Easter and Whitsunday) 🚌 All city center buses 🎟 $

The great cliffs of the Pétrusse and Alzette valleys are honeycombed with tunnels, stairways and chambers, called the Casemates, hollowed out of rock during the 17th and 18th centuries. Originally the network of Casemates measured over 14 miles and accommodated thousands of soldiers. There was room for the stabling of their horses, and for all the garrison supply services. Today about 10 miles of the Casemates survive. Two sections, the Casemates du Bock (Bock Casemates) and the Casemates de la Pétrusse (Pétrusse Casemates), are open to the public in summer (see also Fortress Luxembourg, page 333).

CATHÉDRALE NOTRE-DAME

🚩 B3 ✉ rue Notre-Dame 🕐 Mon.–Sat. 10–noon and 2–5:30, Sun 2–5:30, except during services 🚌 All city center buses 🎟 Free

The steeples of the 17th-century Cathédrale Notre-Dame (Cathedral of Our Lady) form a striking part of the city's skyline. Inside, the high altar is a shrine to Our Lady, "Comforter of the Afflicted." Stone steps lead to the crypt; at the rear, two bronze lions guard the barred entrance to the burial chamber of the Grand-Ducal family. A solitary sarcophagus lies in a dark blue marble setting.

The steeples of the Cathedral of Our Lady

MUSÉE D'HISTOIRE DE LA VILLE DE LUXEMBOURG

🚩 B3 ✉ 14 rue du St.-Esprit ☎ 47 96-45 00 🕐 Tue.–Sun. 10–6 (also Thu. 6–8 p.m.) 🚌 All city center buses 🍴 Café 🎟 $$$

A late 1990s restoration of the Musée d'Histoire de la Ville de Luxembourg (Museum of the History of the City of Luxembourg) has created a superb must-see venue. Take care in some rooms where sunken channels containing hidden lighting run around the edges of the room. The museum is located in four old 17th-, 18th- and 19th-century, six-story town houses. This is a sophisticated, interactive museum; visitors are given a card to operate audiovisual displays and touch screens that explain the city's history from the 10th century to the present day. Follow the room numbers counter-clockwise, and do not miss a trip in the big glass elevator that rises through layers of history and architecture.

MUSÉE NATIONAL D'HISTOIRE NATURELLE

🚩 C3 ✉ 25 rue Münster ☎ 46 22 33-1 🕐 Tue.–Sun. 10–6 🚌 All city center buses 🍴 Museum café 🎟 $$$

The Musée National d'Histoire Naturelle (National Museum of Natural History) is tucked away in the Grund area, below the cliffs. It is housed in the old Hospice of St. John, later a women's prison. The building's splendid entrance survives. It was refurbished in the late 1990s and

The statue of William II, Grand Duke of Luxembourg, dominates the place Guillaume II

features interactive activities of a geological and geographical nature, plus information on local flora and fauna.

PALAIS GRAND-DUCAL

✚ B3 ✉ 17 rue du Marché-aux-Herbes ◉ Guided tours run Mon.–Sat., mid-Jul. through Aug. Contact the Luxembourg City Tourist Office for details (☎ 22 28 09) 🚌 All city center buses 🎫 $$$

The Palais Grand-Ducal (Grand-Ducal Palace), the home of Grand Duke Jean of Luxembourg and his family, is in the narrow rue du Marché-aux-Herbes. The building is a much-renovated and extended replacement of a medieval town hall, which was destroyed in a fire in 1554. The 16th-century Spanish rulers of Luxembourg rebuilt it 20 years after the fire, and you can see the architectural influences of southern Spain in its Renaissance facade. The interiors are exquisite, especially the Main Hall, the King's Room and the Banqueting Hall.

VIEILLE VILLE

✚ C3

Luxembourg's Vieille Ville (Old Town) lies between the rear of the Grand-Ducal Palace and the Bock promontory. The area of the Old Town is small, lying within narrow streets and squares such as rue de l'Eau, rue de la Loge, rue du Rost and the Marché aux Poissons (Fish Market). The feeling of medieval Luxembourg is palpable here, although today's fine streets and elegantly preserved buildings hardly reflect the din and dirt of those days. The market was once the heart of the community outside the castle walls. Down rue Sigefroi from the Marché aux Poissons is Église Saint-Michel (St. Michael's Church). It is the oldest church in the city and is on the site of the 10th-century castle church, but its oldest surviving parts date from the 17th century. The church's baroque altar is superb, and there is a wonderfully vivid carved oak *pietà*.

VILLA VAUBAN (GALERIE D'ART DE LA VILLE DE LUXEMBOURG)

✚ A4 ✉ 18 avenue Emile Reuter ☎ 47 96-45 70 ◉ During temporary exhibitions only Tue.–Sun. 10–6 (also Thu. 6–8 p.m.) 🚌 All city center buses 🎫 $$

The elegant Villa Vauban (Luxembourg City Art Gallery) stands in City Park, on the foundation of the former Vauban Fortress. Today's gallery has a fine permanent collection of the works of Dutch and Flemish masters and of later European painters. There are also temporary exhibitions. The gallery is closed until 2007 for renovation.

FORTRESS LUXEMBOURG

The history of the city of Luxembourg as a medieval fortress is fascinating. Ringed by impregnable cliffs on every side but the west, it was easy to secure the western approach by building a defensive wall. The narrow and rocky Bock promontory offered the first natural fortification.

It was here on this narrow shelf, 300 feet above the Alzette valley, that prehistoric settlers may have established a camp. The Romans built their own fortifications on the Bock and called it *Castellum Lucilinburhuc*. Then, in AD 963, Count Siegfried of the Ardennes built his castle and linked it to the main plateau by a drawbridge. This *Lützelburg*, the "Little Castle," gave the city and the country its present name.

By 1050 a defensive western wall nearly 30 feet high, with numerous towers and gateways, protected the castle and the community that was growing around it to the west. In 1554 a massive explosion of stored gunpowder destroyed much of the settlement. New fortifications were built during a period of Spanish rule. They included excavation of the Pétrusse Casemates (Casemates de la Pétrusse, see page 331); the Beck Bastion; and the ramparts known today as the Corniche and dubbed the "Balcony of Europe" because of the spectacular views.

In the late 17th century Vauban, the French military engineer, reshaped and extended the ramparts. In the 18th century the Austrians extended them once more and excavated the Bock Casemates (Casemates du Bock, see page 331). Such was the strategic importance of Luxembourg as a

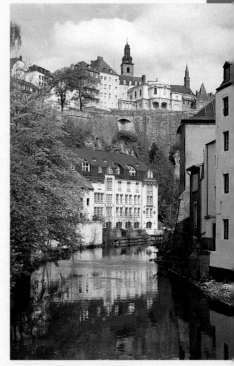

Medieval tranquility on the Alzette river below the Pétrusse Casemates

fortification that all buildings on the Bourbon Plateau, where Gare (the modern town) now stands, were built of wood so that they could be quickly destroyed before an attack on the fortress, thus robbing the enemy of cover.

On May 11, 1867, Luxembourg became an independent state. As part of the agreement, the city's fortifications were dismantled or destroyed. At that time, the fortress walls enclosed an area to the west that was larger than the city.

What remains today are the Casemates, the retaining walls of the cliffs and numerous ruins concentrated on the cliff edges, all adding drama to the city's already spectacular position. City boulevards and parkland lie where great walls and towers once protected the western approach.

THE NETHERLANDS

"I N what other country can one find such absolute freedom…"

17th-century French philosopher René Descartes

Opposite: View from the West Church tower across the rooftops and canals of Amsterdam

The Netherlands

THE NETHERLANDS

The Netherlands is a country where freedom has come with responsibility and hard work. It is a country where the word "land" means something special – a valuable resource won from the sea. For, in literal terms, when you walk on dry land in The Netherlands, your head is barely above sea level in some places, and well below it in others. Amsterdam itself is 10 feet below sea level.

Dutch Icons

To the outside world, the enduring image of The Netherlands is of a land unremittingly flat, criss-crossed by canals and dotted with windmills. Popular imagination conjures up pictures of clogs, cheese and swaths of brightly colored tulips. Then there is Amsterdam, the lively, lovely and evocative capital, seen by many as a slightly wicked city.

The Netherlands is, of course, a far more complex and fascinating entity than such assumptions imply. Although the country is often known as Holland, this name actually only relates to the country's heavily populated western

provinces of Noord (North) and Zuid (South) Holland. These provinces contain the main cities, such as Amsterdam, Rotterdam and The Hague (Den Haag), known collectively as the Randstad, or "Ring Town." Compared with this heavily urbanized area, The Netherlands' other provinces offer the visitor a remarkably diverse landscape and regional cultures that will correct any misconception that the country is homogeneous.

Land from the Sea

The Netherlands is a small country, just over 15,500 square miles in area. Its eastern neighbor, Germany, is nine times larger. To the south lies Belgium, once part of the United Provinces of The Netherlands (see page 50) but an independent nation since 1830. To the north and west of The Netherlands lies the North Sea, and it is with this near neighbor that the Dutch have their most pressing relationship. You will not be too aware of the sea in Amsterdam or The Hague. You need to go north to Noord Holland and Friesland, or south to Zeeland, to fully appreciate the astonishing control over their watery environment that the Dutch have engineered.

For the definitive story of land reclamation, visit the fascinating Zuiderzeemuseum in Enkhuizen or travel across the Afsluitdijk, a 20-mile dam that seals the great inland lake of IJsselmeer and connects Noord Holland to Friesland. You could go south to Zeeland, a glittering mosaic of water within a vast web of land. There you'll want to visit the Delta Expo at Neeltje Jans in Zeeland to learn about the Delta Plan. This system of huge dams and movable barriers was built after the

---

MORE TOP DESTINATIONS IN THE NETHERLANDS

- Arnhem B2 ● De Hoge Veluwe B2
- Delta Expo A2 ● Edam B3
- Enkhuizen B3 ● Haarlem B3
- Het Loo B2 ● Heusden B2
- Keukenhof B2 ● Maastricht B1
- Orvelte C3 ● Scheveningen A2
- Utrecht B2 ● Zwolle C3

storm-driven North Sea breached the existing dykes in 1953, killed more than 1,800 people and devastated the countryside.

Exploring Inland

Beyond these water lands – beyond the great dunes and beaches of the North Sea coast, and the red, white and neon-bright lights of Amsterdam – lie the delights of the landlocked Netherlands. In the south, Limburg is known as the Dutch "hill country." In the province of Noord Brabant, the De Kempen

region's landscape of sandy heath and woodland is a very different image from that of the "flat" Holland most people envision. You can explore Gelderland meadows and orchards; the serene villages and waterways of Overijssel; and the moorlands and flower-filled bogs of Drenthe, so beloved by Vincent van Gogh. They all add to the variety of rural Netherlands. In the north country, in Groningen, the quintessential Dutch images of windmills, clogs and flat green landscapes reassert themselves. In

The Netherlands

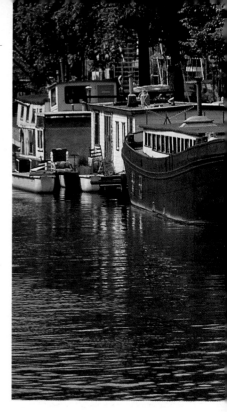

neighboring Friesland you will find another country altogether, a province with its own language and distinctive cultural heritage.

Reaching these fascinating districts is not difficult. Public transportation in The Netherlands is efficient and generally inexpensive. Virtually every place is within a three-hour train ride from Amsterdam. Excellent bus services run between cities, and there is an extensive bus network linking towns and villages in the provinces. Driving in rural areas is convenient and reasonably straightforward, but in urban areas it can be stressful.

The Dutch

The Dutch people are self-confident and accomplished, qualities that have evolved from their history and surroundings. Although they could easily boast of the way in which their environment has been mastered, they are refreshingly modest and restrained. Once the ice is broken, however, people are enthusiastic and friendly, and show tolerance and mutual respect for others.

Pancakes and Beer

Contemporary Dutch cuisine, especially fish dishes, is fast reversing the view that Dutch food is dull. In larger cities – especially in Amsterdam – Holland's colonial past has left a fine tradition of Indonesian cooking. Most hotels have plentiful buffet breakfasts, including smoked meats, pickled herring and a variety of cheeses. For a traditional lunch try *erwtensoep*, a satisfying soup of peas and pork; or *uitsmijter*, an open sandwich of meat or ham with cheese, topped with a fried egg. For dinner have a *hutspot* stew of vegetables, smoked bacon and meat; or *stampott*, mashed potatoes and vegetables with smoked sausage or bacon. For more exotic experiences, eat Indonesian specialties, especially *rijsttafel* ("rice table"), or any of several dozen other spiced, sauced, tangy, exquisite dishes. For sweets try *pannekoek*, pancakes with *stroop* (molasses) or *poedersuiker* (powdered sugar). If you're on the move, street stalls also serve a smaller type of pancake, *poffertjes*.

As in Belgium, beer is the most popular drink. Dutch beers tend to be lighter, although you will know that you are drinking something substantial when you sample lager in a Dutch "brown café" – a traditional bar. An excellent light beer is Grölsch, often drunk with meals instead of wine. Heavier Belgian beers also are available, as is *jenever*, a grain spirit. *Oude jenever* is the sweetest; *jonge* is for the stronger palate. These and vintage gins and liqueurs can be enjoyed in a *proeflokaal*, or "tasting house."

Canal homes – Amsterdammers have traditionally lived on houseboats and barges

Porcelain and Jewelry

Some stores in Holland are closed all day Sunday and on Monday morning, but many are open every day, and stores in the larger cities usually stay open late one night a week. Cities such as Amsterdam and The Hague have a variety of international clothing stores, but the real shopping experience is in the antique and craft districts, looking for such specialties as jewelry and porcelain. In the provinces, search around and you will find some excellent regional buys.

Take a break in Amsterdam's largest and oldest municipal park, the Vondelpark

The Netherlands

TIMELINE

AD 50 Iron Age Frisian and Batavi tribes settle in present-day Netherlands; they build settlements above the tide line on artificial mounds called *terpen*.

751 Charlemagne, the Holy Roman Emperor, rules the Low Countries, the lands alongside the North Sea.

12th century Herring fishermen settle at the mouth of the Amstel river, later site of Amsterdam.

1519 Charles V of Spain is crowned Holy Roman Emperor; the Low Countries come under Spanish rule.

1566–67 Repression by Spain leads to lengthy struggle against Spanish control.

1579 Formation of Republic of the United Provinces of The Netherlands.

1602 Formation of Dutch East India Company; "Golden Age" of Amsterdam as a world trading center lasts for most of the 17th century.

1814 Northern and southern Netherlands become a united kingdom after fall of Napoleon.

1831 Southern Netherlands becomes independent Belgium.

1914–18 The Netherlands remains neutral during World War I.

1940 Germany invades The Netherlands; Amsterdam finally liberated in 1945.

1947 Formation of Benelux Trade Treaty between Belgium, The Netherlands and Luxembourg.

1957 The Netherlands signs up as a founding member of the European Community.

1980 Queen Beatrix is crowned.

1999 The Netherlands adopts the euro as its official currency.

TULIPS

Tulips are a universal symbol of the country. They also are part of the Dutch flower trade, which accounts for 60 percent of the world market in exported flowers. In the 17th century the importation of tulip bulbs from Turkey led to "tulip mania"; during the 1630s, single bulbs sold for thousands of dollars. The tulip has been a major focus of Dutch flower growing since, although carnations, roses and chrysanthemums outsell tulips today. The great floral explosion is in late April, when the fields just inland from the east coast are vibrant with color. Visit the Keukenhof Gardens at Lisse, north of Leiden, for floral extravaganzas from about mid-March to late May.

SURVIVAL GUIDE

- Large cities have regulated routes for pedestrians, cyclists, trams and automobiles. Next to the sidewalk there may be a bicycle lane. Always remember that bicycles approach silently, and always check to your left. Beyond the cycle lane you may find a second sidewalk, then a tram track, then the main thoroughfare for buses and automobiles. This sequence is the same on each side of the road. Remember that trams also approach quietly from the left.
- There are few public restrooms, and those that exist are not known for their cleanliness. Railroad and bus stations, restaurants and the bigger cafés have public bathrooms with attendants. You are expected to pay about 10 or 20 cents to use them.
- Eating out in The Netherlands is considered a fashion event as much as an eating experience. The Dutch tend to dress their best when going out for a meal, although attitudes are relaxing.
- You may tip for good restaurant service. Always tell the waiter or waitress that you're tipping them, and the amount; don't leave a cash tip on the table when you leave.
- You may be tempted to sample raw herring. Follow local custom: Dip the herring in a bowl of diced onions, hold it by its tail, tip your head back, and savor.
- For tasty snacks, try the always-available *patat* (french fries) with mayonnaise or spicy sauce dips; *kroketten*, small

Great way to get around; there are over half a million bicycles in Amsterdam

rolls of meat filling covered in bread crumbs and fried; and pickled herring or smoked eel. *Broodjes*, like their Belgian counterparts, are baguettes filled with smoked sausage, spicy meat and cheeses.

- If you buy a present in a shop, especially chocolates, tell the assistant that it is a present and it will be carefully wrapped in gift paper.
- If you buy Delftware porcelain, make sure the trade name has a D, and buy from reputable outlets only.

Not always the traditional blue and white, Delft pottery comes in a variety of styles and colors

AMSTERDAM

Amsterdam is a city whose dramatic past, remarkable canals and decorative buildings have all combined to make it one of the most exciting and seductive capitals in western Europe.

The city, like so much of the

Netherlands, has triumphed over water. It began life in the 12th century, when fishermen built a dam across the mouth of the Amstel river and settled nearby in rough wooden houses. The city developed on reclaimed land around a network of canals. By the end of the 17th century the city was the leading commercial port of the post-medieval

Amsterdam

world. Its success was based on seamanship and entrepreneurial skills.

For most of the 18th century Amsterdam prospered – until its ships lost command of the seas to England. The city became the capital of the Netherlands in 1813. During World War II, Amsterdam was occupied by the Germans. Since then its history has been characterized by consolidation, urban maturity and social liberalism – influences that have produced the vigorous and tolerant city of today.

First Impressions

Most visitors arrive by train at Amsterdam's Centraal Station, a smoothly run modern complex within a handsome 1880s neoclassic building. A helpful tourist information office is on platform (*spoor*) 2b; the main tourist office (see page 344) is just outside the railroad station. In front of the station is the busy Stationsplein, a mix of tram line, bus track, bicycle lane and pedestrian concourse with street entertainers and crowds of people. Straight ahead lies the Damrak thoroughfare; watch out for traffic here, and always wait patiently for the green light at pedestrian crossings.

A Cultural and Liberal City

Amsterdam's liberal traditions are apparent in the notorious Red Light District (Walletjes), located mainly between Warmoesstraat and Oudezijds Achterburgwal. Be advised – do not take photographs of prostitutes' booths. Be on the lookout for pickpockets.

Amsterdam also is notorious for its "coffee shops," where hashish and marijuana sold for personal use is tolerated by the authorities. *Eetcafes*, on the other hand, are conventional cafés where coffee is served. "Brown Cafés" (*Bruine Cafés*) are traditional bars where liquor is sold.

All this alternative culture is a minor aspect of the larger Amsterdam, a sophisticated city and a working community. There are peaceful canals and tree-shaded, cobbled streets lined with narrow gabled houses. It's a flower-filled city of exhilarating art museums, glorious civic buildings, medieval churches, quality stores, superb restaurants and an entertaining street life.

Amsterdam

Getting to Know Amsterdam

Get the I Amsterdam Card (valid for one, two or three days), for free admission to more than 20 museums, the Holland Casino, use of the tram, bus and subway system and a canal tour, a guided tour of a diamond factory, a 25 percent reduction on city attractions and restaurants, plus other benefits. For a taste of the city's canal culture, take a trip on the Museumboat. It makes seven stops, all near major museums, and you get up to a 50 per cent discount on entry to the museums. Walking tours show you the city's architecture, history, art and special neighborhoods.

Amsterdam also is a rewarding city to explore by foot on your own. Enjoy street theater in Leidseplein, or walk in the footsteps of Rembrandt through the Jewish Quarter. The major shopping street of Kalverstraat leads to the busy open space of Spui, or try wandering down to the daily Bloemenmarkt (Flower Market) along the Singel canal.

Supporting the City

Amsterdam is built on hundreds of thousands of pilings that have been driven through the surface layers of soft peat to rest soundly on hard sand. The 17th-century Royal Palace (Koninklijk Paleis, see page 346) on the Dam rests on 13,659 wooden pilings. Concrete pilings sunk to 65 feet have replaced the original ones.

ESSENTIAL INFORMATION

TOURIST INFORMATION
VVV Amsterdam Tourist Office
• Centraal Station, spoor (platform) 2b
• Stationsplein 10 (opposite Centraal Station entrance)
• Leidsestraat 1, corner of Leidseplein
• Gedempte Gracht 76, Zaandam, northern outskirts of Amsterdam
• Holland Tourist Information (HTI), Amsterdam Airport Schiphol (arrival hall 2)
• Koestraat 11, Purmerend, 12 miles north of Amsterdam

For general tourist information telephone ☎ 0900 400 4040; fax 020 625 2869; www.visitamsterdam.nl

URBAN TRANSPORTATION
Trains run from Centraal Station (central railroad station), Stationsplein. The city public transportation authority is Gemeentevervoerbedrijf Amsterdam-Spoorwegen (GVB). For information and tickets there is a GVB office opposite Centraal Station; open Mon.–Fri. 7 a.m.– 9 p.m., Sat.–Sun. 8 a.m.–9

p.m. Amsterdam's subway (metro) mainly serves suburban areas. Subway stations are marked with an "M" on the city map. There is a station and information desk at Centraal Station. For information on all public transportation within the Netherlands ☎ 0900 9292 (Mon.–Fri. 6 a.m.–midnight, Sun. 7 a.m.–midnight). Taxis are expensive, but can be picked up at the stands at Amsterdam Airport Schiphol, Centraal Station, Dam and Leidseplein. You also can call Taxicentrale (☎ 020 777 7777, 24-hour service).

AIRPORT INFORMATION
Amsterdam Airport Schiphol, 11 miles southwest of the city, is one of the most modern facilities in Europe. Fast, efficient trains run from a station just south of the airport complex to Amsterdam's Centraal Station; the journey takes 20 minutes. They depart every 15 minutes daily 4 a.m.–12:30 a.m., on the hour 1 a.m.–5:40 a.m. Buses run regularly to Amsterdam and leave from Schiphol Plaza. There are post offices, banks, shops and a Holland Tourist Information office in arrival hall 2. For airport information ☎ 0900 7244 746 (toll call).

CLIMATE – average highs and lows for the month

JAN.	FEB.	MAR.	APR.	MAY	JUN.	JUL.	AUG.	SEP.	OCT.	NOV.	DEC.
5°C	5°C	9°C	11°C	15°C	18°C	20°C	21°C	18°C	13°C	9°C	7°C
41°F	41°F	48°F	52°F	59°F	64°F	68°F	70°F	64°F	55°F	48°F	45°F
1°C	0°C	3°C	5°C	8°C	11°C	13°C	13°C	10°C	8°C	4°C	2°C
34°F	32°F	37°F	41°F	46°F	52°F	55°F	55°F	50°F	46°F	39°F	36°F

City Sights

Key to symbols

⊞ map coordinates refer to the Amsterdam map on pages 342–343; sights below are highlighted in yellow on the map.

✉ address or location ☎ telephone number ⏰ opening times Ⓜ nearest subway 🚌 nearest bus or tram route 🚤 Museum Boat stop 🍴 restaurant or café on site or nearby 💲 admission charge: $$$ more than €6, $$ €3–€6, $ less than €3 ⓘ other relevant information

Amsterdams Historisch Museum

⊞ C3 ✉ Entrances: Kalverstraat 92 or Nieuwezijds Voorburgwal 357 ☎ 020 523 1822 ⏰ Mon.–Fri. 10–5, Sat.–Sun. 11–5 🍴 Museum café 🚌 Tram 1, 2, 4, 5, 9, 14, 16, 24, 25 💲 $$

Amsterdam's story is well told in the enjoyable Amsterdams Historisch Museum (Amsterdam Historical Museum). Once a monastery, and then a city orphanage for four centuries, the museum is now an elegant complex of bright and airy rooms. Highlights include a superb model of a Dutch East India sailing ship and the silver drinking horn of the medieval Guild of St. George. To the right of the entrance is the glass doorway into Schuttersgalerij. This was once an open street and is now the Civic Guards Gallery, with splendid group portraits of 17th-century city militiamen.

Anne Frankhuis

⊞ B3 ✉ Prinsengracht 267 ☎ 020 556 7100 ⏰ Daily 9–9, Apr.–Aug.; 9–7, rest of year. Closed Yom Kippur 🍴 Museum café 🚌 21, 170, 171, 172; tram 13, 17 🚤 Museum Boat stop 💲 $$$ ⓘ Last admission 30 minutes before closing

No matter how often you have heard the Anne Frank story, a visit to Het Achterhuis, "The Secret Annexe," is unforgettable. Here, in the Anne Frankhuis (Anne Frank House), the Frank family and their friends lived secretly in Nazi-occupied Amsterdam until their arrest only months before the Liberation. The only one to survive the concentration camps was Anne's father, Otto. The lively, passionate diary kept by

Visitors pay homage at Anne Frank House, preserved exactly as it was in 1944

Anne during her years in hiding was later published to worldwide acclaim. The museum has absorbing displays and multimedia installations, but the secret annex is the heart of it all. The stark emptiness intensifies the experience, and the atmospheric rooms throng with ghosts. From every corner Anne Frank bears witness on behalf of millions of Nazi victims. After your visit, a quiet walk through the peaceful, reflective Jordaan district, just across the canal, is recommended.

Begijnhof

⊞ C2–C3 ✉ Access via a gateway at Gedempte Begijnensloot (9–5); via the gate at the Spui (after 5 p.m.) ☎ 020 622 1918 ⏰ Chapel: Tue.–Fri. 9–6:30, Sat.–Sun. 9–6, Mon. 1–6:30 🚌 Tram 1, 2, 5 💲 Free

Amsterdam's secluded Begijnhof (Béguinage) is an outstanding example of a medieval almshouse community. It was built in the 14th century to accommodate Béguines, pious single women of the Catholic faith, who lived a religious and charitable life without the stricture of holy vows. The Béguines were later ostracized because of their

Tomb of Admiral du Ruyter, the country's most valiant naval hero, honored in the Gothic New Church

faith, and today the discreet facade of the Beguinage's once clandestine Catholic church masks a haunting little Italianate chapel. Opposite is the original church that was transferred to the city's Protestant community in the late 16th century. In the south corner of the Begijnhof is the 15th-century Houten Huys, one of Amsterdam's oldest houses, wooden-fronted and steeply gabled. Today's Begijnhof still accommodates single women of modest means.

NIEUWE KERK

✚ C3 ✉ Dam 34–38 ☎ 020 638 6909 ◷ During exhibitions: daily 10–6 (also Thu. 6–10 p.m.); opening hours may vary depending on the event 🍴 Church café 🚊 Tram 1, 2, 4, 5, 9, 16, 24, 25 💵 $$$

The 17th-century Nieuwe Kerk (New Church) was new only in its original form, as compared with the more venerable Oude Kerk (Old Church). The New Church is a fine counterpoint to Dam square's Koninklijk Paleis (Royal Palace), with its beautifully decorated rooms. Today the church is used for major art exhibitions. There are a dozen or so side chapels and a magnificent vaulted roof. The church's baroque pulpit and its splendid organ are permanent highlights. Dutch monarchs have been crowned here, including the present Queen Beatrix.

OUDE KERK

✚ C3 ✉ Oudekerksplein 23 ☎ 020 625 8284 ◷ Mon.–Sat. 11–5, Sun. 1–5 🚉 Centraal Station or Nieuwmarkt 🚊 Tram 4, 9, 14, 16, 20, 24, 25 💵 $$ (may be more expensive for concerts and exhibitions) ℹ Art exhibitions and music recitals at various times

The Oude Kerk (Old Church) is the oldest building in Amsterdam. It has been much restored, but retains an authentic medieval atmosphere. The church stands on the banks of the Oudezijds Voorburgwal canal in the heart of the Red Light District. Its glorious stained-glass windows, featuring Lambert van Noorts' *Annunciation* and *The Visit of Mary to Elizabeth*, look down on prostitutes' booths in the narrow Enge Kerk Straat, much as they might have done in medieval times. A triple nave and high-vaulted roof give added spaciousness to the dramatically bare interior of the Old Church. A poignant feature is the gravestone of Rembrandt's wife Saskia van Uylenburgh, set among slabs below the choir organ.

RIJKSMUSEUM

✚ B1 ✉ Jan Luijkenstraat 1 ☎ 020 674 7047 ◷ Daily 9–6 🍴 Museum café/restaurant 🚊 Tram 2, 5, 6, 7, 10 ⛴ Museum Boat stop 💵 $$$ ℹ Audio tour available

The Rijksmuseum (National Museum) contains some of the world's greatest works of Dutch art. The building dates from

1885 and was designed by Pierre Cuypers. Its neo-Gothic facade is something of a mirror image to Cuypers' Centraal Station.

From December 2003 until summer 2008, the museum's main building is undergoing extensive renovation. During that period its finest works will continue to be on display in the redesigned Philips Wing, under the title *The Masterpieces*. Featuring more than 400 17th-century Dutch paintings, there are numerous highlights, including Johannes Vermeer's *The*

Entrance to the Rijksmuseum, Amsterdam's national collection

Kitchenmaid, a masterpiece of complementary colors, and Rembrandt's *The Nightwatch*. These are shown in conjunction with dazzling displays of sculpture, Delftware, silverware, furniture and dolls' houses, together with historical artifacts from the Dutch Golden Age.

VAN GOGH MUSEUM

➕ B1　✉ Paulus Potterstraat 7　☎ 020 570 5200; 020 570 5252 (recorded information)　🕐 Daily 10–6 (also Fri. 6–10 p.m.)　🍴 Museum restaurant
🚋 Tram 2, 3, 5, 12　⛴ Museum Boat stop　💲 $$$ (more for special exhibitions)　ℹ Audio tour ($)

To view the finest and largest collection of Vincent van Gogh's paintings, visit the Van Gogh Museum, where the artist's works (200 paintings and nearly 500 drawings) chart his intense and ultimately tragic life. The collection takes you through his early period, when he was a missionary in the Dutch coal fields; pieces include such dark social commentary as *The Potato Eaters*. His later Parisian work reflects the influence of the Impressionists, but it is the paintings inspired by his life at Arles, in sunny Provence (France), that exhilarate with their fiery yellows and oranges. The most famous works are the iconic *Sunflowers* series. Conversely, *The Garden of St. Paul's Hospital,* painted at St.-Rémy mental asylum the year before van Gogh's death, is a heartrending evocation

of a dejected figure. The trees are as rigid as the bars of a cell. But the sum of the Van Gogh Museum, the painter's legacy of outstanding work, is uplifting. There are other works by such contemporaries of Van Gogh as Toulouse-Lautrec, Gauguin and Redon. The adjacent Stedelijk Museum is one of the finest and most exuberant collections of modern art in the world.

VONDELPARK

➕ A1　✉ Stadhouderskade　🕐 Daily dawn–dusk
🍴 t'Blauwe Theehuis ("The Blue Teahouse"), by the lake　🚋 Tram 1, 2, 3, 5, 6, 12　⛴ Museum Boat stop
ℹ Excellent open-air theater and concerts during summer

The Vondelpark, Amsterdam's principal park, is named after 17th-century playwright Joost van den Vondel. The park starts modestly enough as a green avenue that leads southwest from a busy corner on Stadhouderskade, a short distance south of Leidseplein. Soon it opens invitingly into a broad green space peppered with trees and interspersed with ornamental lakes and linked waterways. There are children's playgrounds, a sweetly scented rose garden, teahouses, a bandstand and the Nederlands Filmmuseum (Netherlands Film Museum), which shows a regular program of arthouse films. During the summer, music, theater and entertainment in the sun enliven the park even more.

Amsterdam

AMSTERDAM'S CANALS

So many northern European capitals claim the title "Venice of the North" that the sobriquet has become devalued. Some say there is no substitute for the real thing, but perhaps Amsterdam has the strongest claim to the title. The city lacks the romantic splendor of Venice, but there is a cool, restrained beauty about Amsterdam's canals (*grachten*) and their attendant buildings.

The finest canals are west of the city center, beyond the bustling main streets of Damrak and Nieuwezijds Voorburgwal, both of which were canals at one time. A stroll along narrow side streets from Nieuwezijds Voorburgwal and across the busy Spuistraat brings you suddenly to the great waterways of Singel, Herengracht, Keizersgracht and Prinsengracht.

Flower stalls are an essential part of the Amsterdam scene

Herengracht

Herengracht is the finest canal of the *grachtengordel*, the ring or girdle of canals that were built in the early 17th century to defend the city. The name Herengracht translates into English as the "Gentlemen's Canal," a sign of contemporary male ascendancy. This was the district where the wealthiest Amsterdam merchant families built themselves handsome canal-side mansions notable for their superb ornate gables. The houses were designed to be tall and narrow because of limited space.

Take a stroll down Herengracht to appreciate it all. You can start from the canal's northern end at its junction with Brouwersgracht. The Brouwersgracht is the short stretch of canal that links Herengracht to the Singel canal at the Haarlemmer Sluis, one of the 40 or so sluices that are opened each night to flush clean water through the canal system. Haarlemmer Sluis can be reached from Centraal Station by walking northwest along Prins Hendrikkade for about 300 yards and then turning left. Cross the wide sluice bridge. (There is a superb cheese shop on the opposite corner.) Go left, then turn right along Brouwersgracht to reach the tree-shaded bridges at the junction with Herengracht.

Walk south, then east for a mile of scenic history to where the Herengracht meets the Amstel river. You can stroll down either side of the great canal and cross over bridges to get the best views of canal-side houses. Visit the Theatermuseum and garden at Herengracht 168, and the exquisite Bartolotti House next door. The latter is a 17th-century Renaissance mansion built by the head of the Bartolotti Bank. Enjoy the *Gouden Bocht*, which translates as "Golden Bay" or "Bend," between

Houseboats and barges line the picturesque Prinsengracht, in Amsterdam's Jordaan district

Leidsestraat and Vijzelstraat – note the decorative double-fronted houses along the elegant curve of the canal.

The curve is an engaging motif amid Amsterdam's general flatness – in the decorativeness of house gables, the elegant bridges, the sweep of railings, even in the curved handlebars of the wonderful old upright bicycles still favored by Amsterdammers. There are said to be 600,000 bicycles in the city, and it seems that everybody cycles in Amsterdam. Elderly *dames* and *heren* (ladies and gentlemen) cruise past to the tinkling of bells like songbirds. Stylishly dressed young people skim along with their backs straight and a wary eye on the tourists' uncertain bid to run across the street in front of them.

Connections

Explore the Prinsengracht (Princes' Canal) and the Keizersgracht (Emperors' Canal), as well as the main canals, and don't neglect the connecting waterways.

There's the Leidsegracht on the Golden Bend, or the peaceful, leafy Egelantiersgracht near the Anne Frank House (Anne Frankhuis, see page 345) that takes you into the quiet heart of the Jordaan district. Sidestep between Herengracht and the Singel canal into enchanting streets such as Gasthuismolensteeg or Oude Spiegelstraat, where craft and antiques shops and boutiques rub shoulders with delightful little cafés and restaurants. And try a nighttime walk along the great canals, when many of the finest houses are floodlit and the numerous bridges twinkle with lights.

In summer the canals become venues for concerts by the water, rowing regattas, Chinese dragon boat races and various other events. Amsterdam is many things to many people, but the city's fascinating network of canals will always be the enduring motif of this very special city. For the walking route, see the city map on pages 342–343.

The Hague

THE HAGUE

The Hague (Den Haag), third-largest city in The Netherlands, is justly proud of its status as the political and royal capital of the country and as a focus of international affairs. It lacks the fast pace and excitement of Amsterdam, yet a sense of well-being and security underpins the rich cultural and political heritage.

The city's name derives from *Gravenhage,* which means "the Count's hedge." In the 13th century the Count of Holland built a hunting lodge among sand dunes – this is where The Hague's historic center, the Binnenhof (Inner Court), now stands. The settlement that developed around the lodge was the Count's "hedge" sheltering him against the outside world.

In the 16th century the States General of the United Netherlands met at The Hague, and since then the city has been the seat of Dutch government. The Hague Convention of 1907, which formulated laws governing warfare worldwide, gave this city international status. The 1913 opening of the Peace

THE HAGUE

SCHEVENINGEN

Palace (Vredespaleis, see page 354) further enhanced The Hague's standing, and it is today considered a center of international diplomacy and business. The Permanent Court of Arbitration and the International Court of Justice are located at the Peace Palace; numerous embassies, ministries and headquarters of international organizations also are based here. In 1980, after the Dutch queen, Juliana, abdicated in favor of her daughter Beatrix, the royal residency was relocated from Utrecht to The Hague.

Arrival

The Hague's main railroad station, Den Haag Centraal Station, is plain but functional. Local tram and bus stations stand next to it, and the tourist information center is located by the railroad station's main entrance. From here you can see the skyline of modern buildings that lies between the station and the city itself. A short walk southwest leads to the elegant heart of The Hague, where the Binnenhof and several fine museums cluster around a graceful little lake, Hofvijver.

Guided bus, cycling and walking tours of the city are offered during the summer. A "Royal Tour" (Thu.–Sat. 1–4, early April to late September), part by bus and part walking, takes in the main sights, including the seaside resort of Scheveningen and outside views of four royal palaces (closed to the public), a visit to Panorama Mesdag and (except September), a tour of the Knights' Hall in the Binnenhof. Tours can be booked through the tourist information centers in The Hague and Scheveningen, the two tour departure points.

On Your Own

Exploring The Hague on your own can be a very satisfying experience. The oldest section centers on the Hofvijver,

the "Court Pond." On its south side the Hofvijver laps against the walls of the Binnenhof and the Mauritshuis (see page 354), which houses The Hague's outstanding art collection. Its northern side is lined with trees and is backed by the elegant 18th-century street Lange Vijverberg.

From the Hofvijver you can stroll north beneath the lime trees on the wide avenue Lange Voorhout. A colorful arts and antiques market is held here on Thursdays and Sundays from early May to late September. Continue past the grand facade of the Hotel des Indes to reach Denneweg, a charming street with a Parisian flavor and a host of interesting antiques and craft galleries, delicatessens, restaurants, cafés and distinctive fashion boutiques.

Quickening Pace

West of the Hofvijver and the Binnenhof lies the bustling open area of

Gate at the Binnenhof – the complex where The Hague had its beginnings

The Hague

the Buitenhof, where the pace quickens to that of a busy city. Beyond the Buitenhof is The Hague's commercial and shopping district and the pedestrian-only streets that lead to the Kerk Plein (Church Square) and the hexagonal-towered Grote Kerk (Great Church), beside which operates a lively market Wednesdays from 11 until 6.

North of the church is the Hofkwartier, one of the oldest areas of The Hague. There are many specialty shops, small restaurants and cafés here. Be sure to stroll along the Hoogstraat (Palace Promenade) and on into Noordeinde, one of The Hague's most attractive streets. Here you will find a marvelous selection of art galleries, antiques shops, craft shops and fashion boutiques, restaurants and the Paleis Noordeinde (Royal Palace).

Enjoy this fine city by filling your day with activities involving the arts and history and then seek out the numerous musical and cultural events that take place in the summer.

A short journey on tram 1, 8 or 9, or bus 14, 22 or 23 will take you to the coast and the popular resort of Scheveningen (proper pronunciation of the name Scheveningen is the sign of a true local; try "Shravin-eeng-e" and you might get by). You can break the journey halfway at the miniature "town" of Madurodam, a favorite with children. In addition to Scheveningen's superb beach and promenade, the numerous attractions include the Holland Casino, the muZee Scheveningen and a pier.

Hooigracht

Several ring canals were built around The Hague during the 17th century. Although many of them have been filled in, you can walk east from Denneweg to reach the serene little stretch of surviving canal, the Hooigracht, its leafy banks lined with elegant and attractive old buildings.

ESSENTIAL INFORMATION

TOURIST INFORMATION
Tourist information centers are known as **VVV (Vereniging Voor Vreemdelingenverkeer)**
• VVV, Koningin Julianaplein 30, near Centraal Station ☎ 0900 340 3505 (toll call); fax 00900 352 0426; www.denhaag.com
• VVV, Wagenstraat 193, near Station Hollands Spoor ☎ (0)70 402 3336 (toll call); fax (0)70 365 0400
• VVV, Gevers Deynootweg 1134, Palace Promenade shopping center, Scheveningen ☎ 0900 340 3505 (toll call); fax 070 352 0426

URBAN TRANSPORTATION
Den Haag has an excellent transportation system with tram lines serving The Hague, Scheveningen,

Kijkduin and neighboring Voorburg, Rijswijk, Wassenaar, Wateringen, Leidschendam, Delft and Nootdorp. For information and tickets for buses and trams inquire at the tourist information centers or ☎ 070 384 8666. Taxi stands are at the railroad stations and throughout the city. To call a taxi try HTMC, ☎ 070 390 7722.

AIRPORT INFORMATION
Amsterdam Airport Schiphol (see page 344) serves The Hague. Trains for The Hague leave the airport at regular intervals (journey time 30 minutes). Trains from the airport stop first at Station Hollands Spoor, south of the city center. If you are going to the city center, stay on the train until Centraal Station.

CLIMATE – average highs and lows for the month

	JAN.	FEB.	MAR.	APR.	MAY	JUN.	JUL.	AUG.	SEP.	OCT.	NOV.	DEC.
	5°C	5°C	9°C	11°C	15°C	18°C	20°C	21°C	18°C	14°C	9°C	7°C
	41°F	41°F	48°F	52°F	59°F	64°F	68°F	70°F	64°F	57°F	48°F	45°F
	1°C	0°C	3°C	5°C	8°C	12°C	14°C	13°C	11°C	9°C	4°C	3°C
	34°F	32°F	37°F	41°F	46°F	54°F	57°F	55°F	52°F	48°F	39°F	37°F

The picturesque Hofvijver, lined with an impressive ensemble of public buildings

CITY SIGHTS

BINNENHOF

➕ C1 ✉ Binnenhof 8a ☎ 070 364 6144
🕐 Mon.–Sat. 10–4; closed holidays (except Good Friday) and 2 days in mid-Sep. for the opening of parliament 🚌 4, 5, 22; tram 1, 16, 17 💳 $$ (exhibition free) ➕ Last tour at 3:45. Reservations recommended. May be closed to the public on other occasions

The Binnenhof (Inner Court) of the original lodge of the Counts of Holland is the oldest part of The Hague. The turreted Ridderzaal (Knights' Hall), where medieval guests were received, stands at the heart of a central square; behind it is the parliament building. The complex retains a timeless atmosphere; the main room is the Knights' Hall, an impressive grand hall, restored in 1900 to its medieval glory, with coats of arms, Dutch provincial flags, stained glass and artifacts. Ceremonies, including *Prinsjesdag*, the day of the Queen's speech to the Dutch parliament, are held here. There are guided tours of the Knights' Hall and the two chambers of parliament when they are not in use. Below the knights' hall a reception room houses an exhibition containing a scale model of the Binnenhof.

GEMEENTEMUSEUM DEN HAAG

➕ A2 ✉ Stadhouderslaan 41 ☎ 070 338 1111
🕐 Tue.–Sun. 11–5 🍴 Museum café 🚌 4, 14; tram 17 💳 $$$

Renovations have added to the attractions of the Gemeentemuseum Den Haag (The Hague Municipal Museum), which is located northwest of the city center. The museum has collections of musical instruments and ceramics, including Delftware and The Hague silverware. The modern art collection includes works by Vincent van Gogh and Claude Monet, and there is a large collection of paintings and drawings by the 20th-century Dutch painter Piet Mondrian. The fashion department features temporary exhibitions of Dutch and international fashion.

HAAGS HISTORISCH MUSEUM

➕ C1 ✉ Korte Vijverberg 7 ☎ 070 364 6940
🕐 Tue.–Fri. 11–5, Sat.–Sun. noon–5 🚌 4, 5, 22; tram 1, 16, 17 💳 $$

Haags Historisch Museum (The Hague Historical Museum) is very much a Dutch institution; there are no English translations to supplement the almost exclusively Dutch labeling of the paintings. A visit is nonetheless rewarding, especially to see such big paintings as Jan van Goyen's *View of The Hague*. In the attic there is a permanent exhibition illustrating the history of The Hague; look for the explanatory panels that are translated in English.

The Peace Palace – seat of the International Court of Justice

MAURITSHUIS

➕ C1 ✉ Korte Vijverberg 8 ☎ 070 302 3435
🕐 Mon.–Sat. 10–5, Sun and holidays 11–5, Apr.–Aug.; closed Mon. rest of year 🚌 4, 5, 22; tram 1, 16, 17
🎧 $$$ ℹ Includes admission to Galerij Prins Willem V (Prince William V Gallery), 35 Buitenhof

The original Mauritshuis (Maurits' House) was built as a private home in the 17th century by Johan Maurits van Nassau-Siegen and was reconstructed after a disastrous fire in 1704. Today it contains the Royal Cabinet of Paintings, an outstanding collection of Dutch art. As well as temporary exhibitions, highlights include Johannes Vermeer's *Girl with a Pearl Earring* and the crowning glory, Rembrandt's famous *The Anatomy Lesson of Doctor Nicolaes Tulp*.

MUSEUM DE GEVANGENPOORT

➕ B1 ✉ Buitenhof 33 ☎ 070 346 0861 🕐 Tue.–Fri. 11–5, Sat.–Sun. noon–5 (guided tour only) 🚌 4, 5, 22; tram 1, 16, 17 🎧 $$ ℹ Tours on the hour (last tour at 4), extra tours Jul.–Aug.

A guided tour of the Museum de Gevangenpoort (Prisoner's Gate Museum) is great fun, but is not for the fainthearted.

The Prisoner's Gate Museum was The Hague's notorious prison for hundreds of years. Interrogation rooms and a debtors' chamber give a gruesome picture of medieval justice. The final visit to the torture room in the basement should finish you off nicely. The Dutch treat the whole thing with a commendable black humor. The tour commentary is mostly in Dutch, but information sheets in other languages are available and the guide will answer questions in English.

MUSEUM MESDAG

➕ B2 ✉ Laan van Meerdervoort 7f ☎ 070 362 1434
🕐 Tue.–Sun. noon–5 🚌 4; tram 1 🎧 $$

Hendrik Willem Mesdag was a leading figure in the art world of The Hague during the 19th century. Famous for his *Panorama Mesdag* (a cylinder-shaped painting of nearby coastal resort Scheveningen in 1881), Mesdag was himself a painter and an avid collector of works, especially of the Barbizon School of French painters, including Jean-François Millet, Jean Baptiste Camille Corot and Gustave Courbet. Their works – along with Mesdag's and those of other members of The Hague School – grace the Mesdag Museum. Mesdag built the museum as an annex to his house, and the carpets and artifacts are all original.

VREDESPALEIS

➕ B2 ✉ Carnegieplein 2 ☎ 070 302 4137
🕐 Mon.–Fri. 10–4, Jun.–Sep.; 10–3 rest of year. Visit by guided tour (on the hour except 1 p.m.) only 🚌 4, 13; tram 1 🎧 $$ ℹ Tour times are subject to change. Contact the tourist information office for details

The Vredespaleis (Peace Palace) is an awe-inspiring building symbolizing the power of statehood. Scottish philanthropist Andrew Carnegie, who made his fortune in America, paid for its Gothic splendor in the early 20th century. Its exquisite furnishings and artifacts were donated by nations around the world. A guided tour of the building includes a visit to the International Court of Justice. Due to security control, you must wait in the open at the palace gates for the hourly tour to begin.

The Hague

DELFT

Fine ceramics and architecture are the main features of Delft. The ceramics have been exported worldwide, but Delft's buildings remain much as they were when immortalized on canvas by Johannes Vermeer, a native of the town.

There are organized coach trips to Delft from The Hague, and seats can be reserved through tourist information centers (see page 352). The town is only 20 minutes from The Hague via tram 1, and takes even less time by train. Tram and train both arrive at a two-lane highway, but a few steps along cobbled lanes transport you into a delightful medieval world enclosed by tranquil canals. Delft centers on an imposing main square, the Markt, where there are numerous stores, cafés and restaurants.

Delft is a popular tourist destination, and in summer the Markt can be especially crowded. Explore farther afield; follow the canal-side street of Oosteinde from behind the New Church (Nieuwe Kerk) to reach the medieval city gate of Oostport.

Visit the Old Church (Oude Kerk) west of the Markt, at the head of the lovely street of Oude Delft. The Old Church is a splendid Gothic building full of interest and charm. View it from the Peperstraat Bridge, three bridges to the south on Oude Delft, to fully appreciate its remarkable leaning tower. Close to the Old Church is the Prinsenhof Museum, with a fine collection of paintings. Stop for coffee and crêpes at Stads Pannekoeckhuys, Oude Delft 113–115.

Many stores on the Markt sell Delft china. The Lambert van Meerten Museum at Oude Delft 199 (☎ 015 260 2358) has a superb collection of Delft earthenware and tiles from around the world. The Koninklijke Porceleyne Fles, a factory involved in producing delftware since the 17th century, is located a short distance out of town at 196 Rotterdamsweg (☎ 015 251 2030) and offers guided tours.

Tourist Information Point (Toeristen Informatie Punt)
✉ Hippolytusbuurt 4 ☎ 015 215 4051; www.delft.nl

Take a break from a spring shopping expedition and relax with coffee by one of Delft's canals

NORWAY

Norway

" ***N****OVEMBER always seemed to me the Norway of the year. "*

American poet Emily Dickinson, from a letter to friends, 1864

Opposite: Clean air, clear water and majestic mountains at Sognefjord, in Norway's dramatic fjord region

NORWAY

Norway is the edge of Europe's most northerly land mass, where sea and mountains have merged to produce one of the world's most breathtaking landscapes. This is a country whose ancient peoples, the Vikings, helped shape the history of northern Europe. The Vikings once controlled half of Britain, and sent mariners as far west as Newfoundland and as far south as the Strait of Gibraltar.

It is this vigorous and resourceful national character, reflected in Viking tradition, that still exemplifies modern Norway. This is a nation that has mastered an inhospitable landscape without despoiling it, even becoming a leading oil producer in the hostile environment of the North Sea.

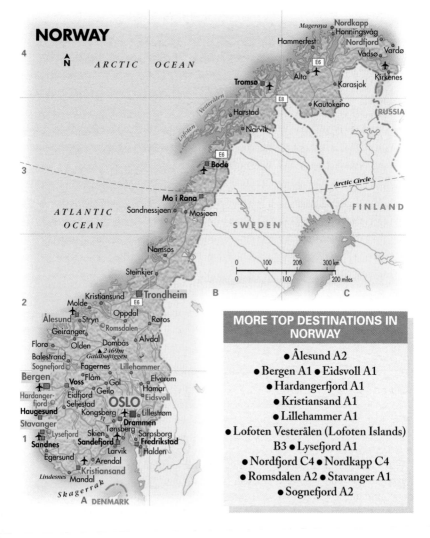

NORWAY

ARCTIC OCEAN

N

Magerøya · Nordkapp
Honningsvåg
Hammerfest · Nordfjord
Vadsø · Vardø
E6
Alta · Karasjok · Kirkenes
Tromsø
E8
Kautokeino
RUSSIA
Vesterålen
Harstad
Lofoten
Narvik
E6
Bodø
Arctic Circle
FINLAND
ATLANTIC
OCEAN
Sandnessjøen · Mosjøen
Mo i Rana
Namsos
SWEDEN
Steinkjer

0   100   200   300 km
0   100   200 miles

B   C

Kristiansund · Trondheim
Molde · E6
Oppdal · Røros
Ålesund · Stryn
Geiranger · Romsdalen
Floro · Olden · Dombås · Alvdal
Balestrand · Galdhøpiggen 2469m
Sognefjord · Fagernes · Lillehammer
Bergen · Flåm · Gol · Elverum
Voss · Geilo · Hamar
Hardanger- · Eidfjord · Eidsvoll
fjord · Seljestad · OSLO
Haugesund · Kongsberg · Lillestrøm
Stavanger · Tønsberg · Drammen
Lysefjord · Skien · Sarpsborg
Sandnes · Sandefjord · Fredrikstad
Larvik · Halden
Egersund · Arendal
Lindesnes · Kristiansand
Mandal
Skagerrak
A DENMARK

Landscape

Norway's landscape is dominated by intervening seas – the Barents Sea to the north, the Norwegian Sea to the west and the North Sea to the southwest. The corrugated coastline measures nearly 13,600 miles, including fjords and the country's 150,000 offshore islands. This scattered mosaic of islands – the "Skerry Guard" – is Norway's natural sea defense. The islands break the onslaught of the ocean, creating the country's sheltered seaways to north and south and protecting the gateways to the fjords.

Norway is shaped like a Viking club, narrowing in the north and with a broad base in the south. The country's mountain system runs from northeast to southwest and reaches its greatest height at Galdhøppigen, at 8,100 feet. The mountains separate the rugged western seaboard, the Vestlandet, from the gentler eastern region, the Øslandet.

The broad southwestern half of the country is known as Sørlandet, the South Country. Here, on the coastal fringe and around Oslo, is lowland Norway, where the sheltered coast is a favorite vacation destination for Norwegian families – a landscape of mellow woods and fields and tranquil blue waters. On the southern tip of Sørlandet is the sunny town of Kristiansand, with its flock of offshore islands. Southwest along the coast is Mandal, where attractive beaches catch the best of the summer sun; nearby is the promontory of Lindesnes, where a *fyr* (lighthouse) marks Norway's southernmost point.

Then the coast turns to the northwest, twisting through a rugged landscape of rocky headlands and deeply indented fjords, past the pleasant town of Egersund and finally through rich farming country to Stavanger and the open west.

Fjordland

Norway's famous Fjordland begins at Stavanger. Stretching for more than 375 miles is one of the most spectacular landscapes and seascapes in the world. In the Ryfylke area, northeast of Stavanger, lies the stunning Lysefjord, with its flat-topped and sheer-sided Pulpit Rock. Farther north is the mighty Hardangerfjord, with its massive cliffs, and the silver-white waterfalls of Skykkjedalsfoss and Vøringfoss, set off by snowcapped mountains.

Farther north into Hordaland lies fascinating Bergen, against a setting of islands and mountains. Bergen is the starting point for boat journeys to the north along the coastal islands and into the 127-mile-long and 4,291-foot-deep Sognefjord, the deepest and longest fjord in the world. Its side fjords twist between towering cliffs and penetrate as far as Flåm and Gudvangen, at the head of Nærøyfjord (the narrowest fjord in Europe), and to Fjærland, below the southernmost edge of the great Jostedalsbreen glacier (the largest glacier in continental Europe).

Along Sognefjord are lovely villages such as Balestrand. Throughout the area, ancient pagoda-like stave churches survive at settlements such as Vik, Kaupanger and Urnes. Inland to the east lies the mighty mountain range of Jotunheimen, known as the "Land of the Giants."

The Northern Fjords

Beyond the Sognefjord lies Nordfjord and then the county, or *fylke*, of Møre og Romsdal. The coastal town of Ålesund is renowned for its art nouveau architecture of turrets, towers and medieval motifs. Inland is the Geirangerfjord and its magnificent waterfalls. From Ålesund, spectacular roads lead over the mountains to the town of Åndalsnes and the

Traditional embroidered costume, worn at festivals

land you should be selective about how and where to explore. Roads are well maintained throughout. Good driving skills are required, however, where roads are narrow and twisting and where they pass through long tunnels. Norway's public transportation system is excellent.

This is a country that copes impressively with some of the most difficult winter conditions in Europe. Only in severe conditions are train services to the northwest likely to be curtailed. Buses serve more remote villages throughout the north and west. Travel by boat is a way of life in Norway, especially on the western seaboard. There is no finer way of touring Fjordland than by boat.

Most of Norway has a comparatively mild, wet, maritime climate. The west coast and mountains have high rainfall even in midsummer. But there can be long spells of fair weather, when Fjordland is glorious. In eastern and southeastern Norway, summers can be warm and dry. Winter in the higher elevations is cold and extremely snowy, creating excellent skiing conditions at Norway's winter resorts. The Norwegians are philosophical about their weather, preferring to think of it as invigorating.

The Norwegians

Norway, as a constitutional monarchy, is extremely well run. The moderate Labor Party has dominated government since the 1930s. The Norwegians are a level-headed, open and generous people. They are unfailingly courteous, and only in busy Oslo does an occasional impatience with visitors emerge.

The people share the Scandinavian tendency toward self-effacement, but they are understandably proud of their success at shaping a modern nation out of such a wild landscape.

Romsdalsfjord. Along the coast farther north is the Atlantic Road, a highway linking a chain of islands. Northeast from here lies Trollheimen, the mountainous "Home of the Trolls," and then comes the great expanse of Trondheimsfjorden and Trondheim itself – once called Nidaros – the ancient capital of Norway.

Beyond Trondheim is the narrowing edge of Norway's northwestern seaboard, fertile coastal lands backed by barren mountains that reach into Nordland and to the Arctic Circle. At Narvik, you look out across the waters of Vestfjorden to the spectacular Lofoten Islands before continuing north to Tromsø, known as "The Paris of the North." You then go on through Finnmark, the land of the Saami people and of the midnight sun, to the Arctic island of Honningsvåg and Nordkapp (North Cape), the symbolic northern end of Europe.

Traveling in Norway

Norway is a pleasant country in which to travel, but to enjoy this magnificent

Stunning mountain pass at Stalheim

Norway

TIMELINE

2000–1000 BC	Early neolithic and Bronze Age people leave numerous rock carvings throughout Scandinavia.
AD 787	Viking expansion begins with increased expeditions to Britain and northern Europe.
870	Vikings settle in Iceland.
1000	Christianity is introduced to Norway; Lief Eriksson reaches the coast of Labrador.
circa 1300	Oslo becomes capital of Norway.
1350	The Black Death kills over half of Norway's population.
1397	Union of the Three Crowns of Denmark, Sweden and Norway signed at Kalmar.
1536	Norway is reduced to a "province" of Denmark and remains so for nearly 300 years.
1814	The country is forced into union with Sweden.
1905	Prince Carl of Denmark is invited to become king of an independent Norway.
1914–18	Norway remains neutral during World War I.
1925	City of Christiana reverts to its original name of Oslo.
1940	Invasion of Norway by Germany, in spite of Norway's declaration of neutrality.
1945	German troops surrender; Norway becomes one of the founders of the United Nations.
1949	Norway becomes a founding member of NATO.
1970s	Oil and gas extraction from Norwegian sector of North Sea boosts Norway's economy.
1994	In a referendum, Norwegians reject membership of the European Union.
2000	Oslo celebrates its 1,000th anniversary.

THE VIKING SETTLERS

History has painted the Vikings as aggressive, anarchic sea raiders, but this view has changed somewhat in recent times. The restless voyaging that took the Vikings around the coasts of Britain and into the deep estuaries of northern France led to bloody conflict. There seems no question that the Vikings plundered and destroyed. But modern theory argues that a desire for new territory made them settlers in foreign lands more often than just violent raiders. In later, more stable times, the Vikings' commercial success was just as powerful as their military ferocity had been.

Norway

SURVIVAL GUIDE

- Mid-June to mid-August is the national vacation period, and many Norwegians depart cities and towns for the fjords, mountains and countryside. This can be a good time to visit Oslo.

- During the peak summer vacation season, North Cape (Nordkapp) and its approaches are very busy with traffic and visitors.

- When driving in Norway, dimmed headlights must be kept on even during daylight hours.

- Because of Norway's strict control on the sale of alcohol, you will have difficulty buying your own wines and spirits outside larger towns. You cannot buy alcohol (except beer) from supermarkets. Special state-controlled Vinmonopolet are the only liquor stores, and they are very expensive. Most restaurants are licensed, and you may be able to buy beer in some grocery stores.

- Norwegians are catching up on international fashion, but there is more interest in good outdoor clothing. For something truly Norwegian try the Oslo Sweater Shop AS, at the Radisson SAS Scandinavia Hotel (✉ Tullins gate 5, ☎ 22 11 29 22), the Clarion Royal Christiania Hotel or (✉ Skippergaten/ Biskop Gunnerus gate 3, ☎ 22 42 42 25). Other souvenirs include ceramics, pewter, glass, wooden troll figures, enamel jewelry and woven wall hangings.

- You can eat very well in Norway, especially in Oslo and the larger towns. Norwegians are experts at buffet preparation, the ideal lunch experience, often with elaborate fish specialties. Smoked salmon and trout, and lamb dishes such as *fenalår* (smoked leg of lamb) are delicious, or try reindeer or elk for a real taste of mountain Norway.

- As in Sweden and Finland, some things are about 30 percent more expensive in Norway than in the rest of Europe. Several passes and discount schemes offer reduced prices at hotels (contact your local travel agent for information). Overall, prices are higher than elsewhere in Europe. If you're on a budget, watch for Lavpris (low-price) food stores.

A troll statue greets visitors to Lillehammer

Oslo

OSLO

Oslo is a small, modern city of great character, but without the grandeur of many larger European capitals. Its spacious suburbs, forests and parks, all within sight and sound of the sea, give the city great vistas. It has outstanding art galleries and maritime museums, music venues, cafés, restaurants and fashionable boutiques. Yet there is always that inescapable feeling that wide-open spaces are not too far away.

Oslo Through History

Oslo was founded in 1000 (it celebrated its 1,000th anniversary in 2000) but its progress to capital city was checkered. It was significant only as a fjord settlement during the Viking age. In the 11th century, the Norwegian King Harald Hardråde chose to make Oslo a rival to the northern capital of Trondheim. Oslo's fortunes rose and fell thereafter, and in the 17th century, following a devastating fire and while under Danish rule, the settlement was rebuilt to the west of its original site and renamed Christiana, after the Danish King Christian IV.

Christiana became the capital of Norway in 1814. Throughout the 19th century the profitable timber trade and the economic advantages of union with Sweden increased its prosperity. By 1905, when Norway broke with the union, Christiana was a mature city economically and politically, and by 1925 the country was confident enough to reinstate the traditional name of Oslo.

The story of Oslo in the final decades of the 20th century was one of rapid modernization, as much on cultural as on social, political and economic terms. Wealth from the oil industry, the internationalization of Norwegian culture and a growing Norwegian self-confidence transformed the city into the cosmopolitan, vibrant capital of today.

The City's Stage

The most impressive way to arrive in Oslo is by sea. Viewed from the narrow neck of the Oslofjorden, the city's buildings are set against a backdrop of serene peninsulas and wooded hills. The hills are dotted with houses and accented by the great white view tower at the famous Holmenkollen ski jump.

Arrival by train, however, lands you at Jernbanetorget, the big open space in front of Oslo's central railroad station. This is not the most attractive part of the city, but a short walk along Karl Johans gate takes you quickly to Oslo Cathedral (Oslo Domkirke) and the busy open space of Stortorget, with its colorful flower market.

A few steps farther on is the Parliament (Stortinget). Before it lies the open space of Eidsvollsplass, the

The hub of the city; try Karl Johans gate for shopping, relaxing and eating out

Oslo

busy city center, alive with action and entertainment in summer, its pond a skating rink in winter.

To the northwest of Eidsvollsplass is the neoclassic Nationaltheatret (National Theater), where statues of Norwegian dramatists Bjørnstjerne Bjørnson and Henrik Ibsen stand guard. Farther northwest is tree-lined Slottsparken, which encompasses the unfenced and accessible Royal Park and the Kongelige Slott (Royal Palace) within its bounds.

To the south of the National Theater, down busy Olav V's gate and Roald Amundsen gate (passing Oslo's main tourist information office on Fridtjok Nansens plass on the way), lies Oslo *rådhus* (Oslo City Hall) and the open space of Rådhusplassen. Adjoining this square is Rådhusbrygge (City Hall Pier) and the local ferryboat dock on Pipervika inlet. The ferry to the Bygdøy peninsula operates here from April to September.

Exploring Oslo

Central Oslo is easily explored on foot, but you should become familiar with the transportation system so you can take one of the many day trips within easy reach. Public transportation is very efficient and easily understood; travel on city trams is a relaxing experience in itself. Visit the outlying Bygdøy peninsula, with its clutch of outstanding museums, or Frogner Park and Vigelandsparken (Vigeland Park), Norway's most visited attraction (see page 368).

Oslo's main street, Karl Johans gate, is full of stores of all kinds, including David-Andersen AS at No. 20 (☎ 24 14 88 00), Scandinavia's largest jewelry store. The Paléet shopping mall has a mix of fashion boutiques and restaurants. Stop for coffee and pastries at the Grand Café at the Grand Hotel, one of Henrik Ibsen's former haunts.

A short distance north of the Royal Palace is the busy shopping street of Hegdehaugsveien and its continuation,

Oslo

Bogstadveien. Down at the harbor, on the western side of Pipervika inlet in the converted shipyard buildings, is Aker Brygge, a modern complex with numerous stores, restaurants, cafés and entertainment venues. The area's attractive waterside setting adds to the character.

Eating out in Oslo offers a variety of local and international cuisine. Try traditional restaurants such as Blom-Kunsterernes Restaurant (see page 563) on Karl Johans gate, where you can enjoy seasoned or smoked Norwegian specialties. Feast on excellent music too, in the Oslo Konserthus on Munkedamsveien, to the west of Aker Brygge.

The Oslo experience is a relaxed one, because of the compactness of the city center and because of the ease with which you can reach the outlying attractions and surrounding countryside. The openness of the city

Nobel Peace Prize

The Nobel Peace Prize has been awarded in Oslo *rådhus* (Oslo City Hall) since 1990. The award was founded at the end of the 19th century by Swedish inventor and industrialist Alfred Bernhard Nobel. The Peace Prize winner is decided on criteria in Nobel's will citing "the person(s) who shall have done the most or the best work for brother-hood between nations,...." The ceremony takes place each year on Dec. 10, the anniversary of Nobel's death.

is reflected in the people, who are brisk but friendly in their attitude. English is a second language, especially to younger Norwegians, and you are never far away from advice and guidance to help you make the most of your stay.

ESSENTIAL INFORMATION

TOURIST INFORMATION
Oslo Promotion (Oslo Visitors and Convention Bureau)
• Fridtjof Nansens plass 5 ☎ 24 14 77 00; fax 22 42 92 22 ; www.visitoslo.com
• Oslo Sentralstasjon (Oslo Central Station), Jernbanetorget 1

URBAN TRANSPORTATION
Oslo's main railroad station is Sentralstasjon (Central Station), known as Oslo S; it has modern facilities and is on Jernbanetorget, only minutes from the city center. Oslo has an efficient bus and tram network. The bus terminal is next to Oslo Sentralstasjon. Seven tram lines run east to west. The city also has a subway system, called the bane, with five lines identified by a "T" sign. Its main junction is at Stortinget Station. For information on local trains, bane, buses, trams and ferries contact Trafikanten at Jerbanetorget, by Oslo S (Mon.–Fri. 7 a.m.–8 p.m., Sat.–Sun. 8–6), ☎ 177 or 81 50 01 76 (Mon.–Fri. 7 a.m.–11 p.m., Sat.–Sun. 8 a.m.– 11 p.m.). Taxis are available from Oslo Taxi (☎ 02323).

AIRPORT INFORMATION
Oslo Airport is located at Gardermoen, 19 miles north of the city (☎ 81 55 02 50). An Airport Express Train (FlyToget, ☎ 81 50 07 77) runs between the airport and Oslo S (Central Station) every 10 minutes; the trip takes 19 minutes. Regular train services also stop at the airport and take less than 30 minutes to Oslo S. SAS airport buses (☎ 81 50 01 76) run every 20 minutes between the airport and the Oslo Bussterminal, located alongside Sentralstasjon (Central Station); journey time 40 minutes.

CLIMATE – average highs and lows for the month

	JAN.	FEB.	MAR.	APR.	MAY	JUN.	JUL.	AUG.	SEP.	OCT.	NOV.	DEC.
	0°C	0°C	4°C	9°C	16°C	19°C	22°C	20°C	16°C	9°C	4°C	0°C
	32°F	32°F	39°F	48°F	61°F	66°F	72°F	68°F	61°F	48°F	39°F	32°F
	-7°C	-7°C	-3°C	1°C	7°C	10°C	12°C	12°C	7°C	3°C	-2°C	-5°C
	19°F	19°F	27°F	34°F	45°F	50°F	54°F	54°F	45°F	37°F	28°F	23°F

Oslo

CITY SIGHTS

Key to symbols

➕ map coordinates refer to the Oslo map on page 365;
sights below are highlighted in yellow on the map.

✉ address or location ☎ telephone number
🕐 opening times Ⓜ nearest subway 🚌 nearest
bus or tram route 🚢 Bygdøynes Boat 🍴 restaurant
or café on site or nearby 🎟 admission charge: $$$
more than KR50, $$ KR15–KR50, $ less than KR15
ℹ other relevant information

AKERSHUS SLOTT OG FESTNING

Slott ➕ B1 ✉ Oslo Mil./Akershus ☎ 23 09 35 53
🕐 Mon.–Sat. 10–4 (guided tours at 11, 1 and 3), Sun.
12:30–4 (guided tours), early May to mid-Sep. (closed
during official engagements) 🍴 Engebret Café, see
page 563 Ⓜ Stortinget 🚌 60; tram 10, 12, 13, 15, 19
🎟 $$
Festning ✉ Oslo Mil./Akershus ☎ 23 09 39 17
🕐 Outdoor area: daily 6 a.m.–9 p.m. Information
center: Mon.–Fri. 9–5, Sat.–Sun. 11–5), mid-Jun. to
mid-Aug.; Mon.–Fri. 9–4, Sat.–Sun. 11–4, rest of year;
guided tours available (times change seasonally; call
for times) 🍴 Engebret Café, see page 563
Ⓜ Stortinget 🚌 60; tram 10, 12, 13, 15, 19 🎟 Free
Norges Hjemmefrontmuseum ✉ Oslo Mil./Akershus
☎ 23 09 31 38 🕐 Mon.–Sat. 10–5 (also Tue. and Thu.
5–6 p.m.), Sun. 11–5, mid-Jun. to Aug. 31; Mon.–Sat.
10–4, Sun. 11–4, mid-Apr. to mid-Jun. and Sep.;
Mon.–Fri. 10–3, Sat.– Sun. 11–4, rest of year
🍴 Engebret Café, see page 563 Ⓜ Stortinget
🚌 60; tram 10, 12, 13, 15, 19 🎟 $$

Akershus slott (Akershus castle) stands on
a rocky height on the eastern side of the
harbor inlet of Pipervika. It was founded
in 1299 as a royal residence, but by the
end of the 17th century it had been
transformed into the powerful *festning*
(fortress) by the addition of ramparts.
Guided tours take you into the castle's halls
and subterranean passages. The Norges
Hjemmefrontmuseum (Norway's
Resistance Museum) here is a compelling
record of Norway's experiences in World
War II, when, for five years, the Nazi
occupation headquarters were at Akershus.

FRAMMUSEET

➕ A1 ✉ Bygdøynesveien 36, Bygdøynes ☎ 23 28
29 50 🕐 Daily 9–6:45, mid-Jun. to Aug. 31; daily

9–5:45, mid-May to mid-Jun. and Sep.; daily 10–5:45,
May 1 to mid-Jun.; daily 10–3:45, rest of year 🚌 30
🚢 Bygdøynes Boat 91, from Rådhusbrygge 3
(Apr.–Sep.) 🎟 $$

The centerpiece of the Frammuseet (Fram
Museum) is the preserved Arctic
exploration vessel *Fram*, with a bow like a
battering ram and a hull as solid as a castle
wall. The *Fram* was built in 1892 and was
used by Norwegian explorers Fridtjof
Nansen, Otto Sverdrup and Roald
Amundsen in polar expeditions. Go aboard
the *Fram* to see its sturdiness and get a
sense of the tough, determined life that its
crew led.

KON-TIKI MUSEET

➕ A1 ✉ Bygdøynesveien 36, Bygdøynes ☎ 23 08
67 67 🕐 Daily 9:30–5:30, Jun.–Aug.; 10:30–5,
Apr.–May and Sep.; 10:30–4, rest of year 🚌 30
🚢 Bygdøynes Boat 91, from Rådhusbrygge 3
(Apr.–Sep.) 🎟 $$

The Kon-Tiki museet (Kon-Tiki
Museum) is a colorful celebration of Thor
Heyerdahl's voyages. It complements the
general maritime themes of the adjacent
Fram Museum and the Norwegian
Maritime Museum. Heyerdahl's ethos of
adventure, linked to environmentalism
and international cooperation, is vividly
expressed. The original *Kon-Tiki* balsa
wood raft of his 1947 Pacific crossing and
the papyrus vessel *Ra II* of his 1970 Atlantic
crossing both reflect the Norwegian
genius for maritime exploration.

MUNCH-MUSEET

➕ C2 ✉ Tøyengata 53 ☎ 23 49 35 00 🕐 Daily
10–6, Jun.–Aug.; Tue.–Fri. 10–4, Sat.–Sun. 11–5, rest
of year 🍴 Museum café Ⓜ Tøyen/ Munchmuséet
🚌 60 🎟 $$$

The Munch-museet (Munch Museum) is
a fitting celebration of Norway's most
famous artist. Edvard Munch's (Moonk)
The Scream, is a world-famous cultural
icon; several versions are on display,
including the famous one stolen from this
museum in 2004. Munch produced a
huge body of work, however, and the
Munch Museum provides an insight into
the complex personality of this intense
and fascinating artist.

Gustav Vigeland's *Monolitten* at Vigeland Park

NASJONALGALLERIET

🔲 B2 ✉ Universitetsgaten 13 ☎ 22 20 04 04
🕐 Tue.– Fri. 10–6 (also Thu. 6–8 p.m.), Sat.–Sun. 10–5
🍴 Gallery Restaurant 🚇 Nationaltheatret 🚌 Buses
to Nationaltheatret; tram 10, 11, 17, 18 💵 Free, except
during special exhibitions

Oslo's Nasjonalgalleriet (National Gallery)
has works by painters such as Georges
Braque and Pablo Picasso, but its main
collection is of work from 1800 up to 1945
by Norwegian masters such as Christian
Krohg, Johan Christian Dahl, Thomas
Fearnley and Edvard Munch. Highlights
include Krohg's lively portrait *Oda Krohg,
the Painter,* a charming rendition of artist
Oda Krohg in vivid red and blue clothes.
The Romantic Fjordland paintings of
Johan Christian Dahl and Thomas
Fearnley will entice you to visit the fjords.
Look on the top floor for Ernst Josephson's
The Spanish Blacksmiths. The room devoted
to Munch shows some classic masterpieces,
including a version of *The Scream,* the
powerful *Dance of Life,* the sensual *Day
After* and the ravishing *Madonna.*

NORSK FOLKEMUSEUM

🔲 A1 ✉ Museumsveien 10, Bygdøy ☎ 22 12 37 00
🕐 Daily 10–6, mid-May to mid-Sep.; 11–3 (also
Sat.–Sun. 3–4), rest of year. Park: Mon.–Fri. 9–8,
Sat.–Sun. 9:30–8, mid-May to mid-Sep.; daily 9–6, rest

of year 🍴 Museum restaurant and café 🚌 30
⛴ Bygdøynes Boat 91, from Rådhusbrygge 3
(Apr.–Sep.) 💵 $$$

The Norsk Folkemuseum (Norwegian Folk
Museum) gives an excellent view of
Norway's folk culture. Located on the
Bygdøy peninsula, it includes a parklike area
with more than 150 traditional buildings
and reconstructed 19th-century village
streets. The main buildings display crafts,
folk costumes and rural interiors. There is an
exhibition on the culture of the Sami, the
indigenous people of northern Scandinavia.

NORSK SJØFARTSMUSEUM

🔲 A1 ✉ Bygdøynesveien 37, Bygdøynes ☎ 24 11
41 50 🕐 Daily 10–6, mid-May to Aug. 31; 10:30–4
(also Thu. 4–6), rest of year 🍴 Museum restaurant
and café 🚌 30 ⛴ Bygdøynes Boat 91, from
Rådhusbrygge 3 (Apr.–Sep.) 💵 $$

The Norsk Sjøfartsmuseum (Norwegian
Maritime Museum), on the tip of the
Bygdøy peninsula, overlooks the waters of
the Oslofjorden. In the main hall,
Christian Krogh's great marine painting,
Leiv Eriksson's Discovery of America, sets
the scene for exhibits on shipping and the
sea. The basement theater shows a video
on Norway's maritime history. On the
main floor is the escape boat, secretly
made from rough planking by Norwegian
sailors while they were imprisoned aboard
their ships in West Africa by the Germans
during World War II.

VIGELANDSPARKEN

🔲 A2 ✉ Kirkeveien ☎ 22 13 54 90 🕐 Daily 24
hours (visitor center: daily 9–8:30, mid-May to mid-
Sep.; 10–6, rest of year) 🍴 Café Vigeland
🚇 Majorstuen 🚌 20; tram 12 💵 Free; Vigeland-
museet $$

Vigelandsparken (Vigeland Park) is a
memorial to Norwegian sculptor Gustav
Vigeland (1869–1943), and a celebration of
the human body. The centerpiece of around
200 life-size sculptures is the famous
Monolitten (Monolith), a tall granite column
composed of writhing human figures
struggling upward. The park lies within the
larger Frogner Park, near to central Oslo.
The Vigeland-museet (Vigeland
Museum) lies just south of Frogner Park.

Oslo

FJORD AND MOUNTAIN LINE

Most visitors to Norway go to the western fjords at some time during their stay. Even if your time is limited you can still make the famous "Norway in a nutshell" journey by train, bus and boat (year-round). The trip takes you from Oslo to the Sognefjord via the well-known Flåmsbana (Flåm Railway). Some people make the round trip from Oslo in a day, but an alternative is to take an early train from Oslo to Bergen, from where you can catch the fast coastal ferry into the Sognefjord.

Try to stay in the delightful city of Bergen. The ferry from Bergen races under high bridges, skims past scores of islands and rugged peninsulas, and slows only at narrow channels with feet to spare. You travel deep into the mighty Sognefjord to Balestrand. Here fruit trees flourish in the fjordland summer, yet glaciers are only a few miles away in the mountains. It is possible to stay overnight here.

From Balestrand, a final boat trip takes you to the very end of Sognefjord. Flåm (pronounced Flum) is not a traditional fjord village, but it caters to bus and car parking, and the many traveling tourists. The famous Flåm to Myrdal railroad is the reason for it all. The stylish train, with its comfortable quarters, takes 50 minutes to travel 12$\frac{1}{2}$ miles along the valley floor behind Flåm. It climbs steadily through spectacular scenery to the head of the valley, where the track rises through a series of S-bends, protected in places by snow shelters. Finally, the train reaches the plateau and the Myrdal railroad station, where you connect with the Oslo train for the last leg (5 hours) of one of the world's great round trips.

You can arrange this tour yourself through Norwegian State Railways, NSB (☎ 81 50 08 88, then dial 4 for an English-speaking operator; www.nsb.no), or in the United States. through Rail Europe (☎ 800 438-7245), or contact Fjord Tours (☎ 81 56 82 22; www.fjordtours.no) for details about organized tours.

Within easy reach of Bergen is the spectacular Hardangerfjord, looking towards the Folgefonn glacier

PORTUGAL

"THERE is something very extraordinary in the nature of the people of the Peninsula, the most loyal and best-disposed..."

The Duke of Wellington, in an early 19th-century dispatch

Opposite: Spectacular display of color at the fishing village of Sesimbra, south of Lisbon

PORTUGAL

Portugal, lying on the western edge of the Continent and overshadowed by Spain, its powerful neighbor to the east, is sometimes considered the poor relation of southwestern Europe. Political turmoil and poverty have long hindered development, but after joining the European Union in 1986, billions of dollars have poured into the country, helping to modernize its economy.

The Land

For travelers who knew Portugal a couple of decades ago, some things have changed beyond recognition; others remain stubbornly the same. In many ways Portugal is still old-fashioned and underdeveloped, a real bonus for visitors seeking something a little different from mainstream European travel. The country is small, diverse and beautiful. Stretching 350 miles from north to south, it is packed with mountains, plateaus, river valleys, flat dry plains, rolling forested hills and a truly beautiful coastline. Portugal

---

MORE TOP DESTINATIONS IN PORTUGAL

- Alcobaça B3 ● Batalha B3
- Braga B4 ● Bragança C4
- Castelo de Vide C3 ● Chaves C4
- Coimbra B3 ● Douro B4
- Évora B2 ● Fátima B3
- Guimarães B4 ● Monsanto C3
- Óbidos B3 ● Parque Nacional da Peneda-Gerês B4 ● Sagres B1
- Serra de Monchique B1
- Silves B1 ● Tomar B3
- Torres Vedras A2

---

borders the Atlantic, and weather conditions can range from hot and sunny to stormy and wet. In the northern Douro region, winter temperatures drop well below freezing; in summer, it is not uncommon for the thermometer to top 100 degrees.

The Algarve, a popular vacation area on the southern coast that's often visited by northern Europeans, enjoys a Mediterranean climate, and the vegetation is subtropical. On the whole, summers are warm and dry, winters mild and wet, although it can be cold in the mountains. Portugal's highest mountain is Torre, in the Serra da Estrela, which rises above 6,500 feet. The Tagus (Tejo) river roughly divides the country in half. The Tagus and two other important rivers, the Douro and the Guadiana, rise in Spain, and Portugal must share their waters with its bigger neighbor, a factor leading increasingly to difficulties in supply and environmental problems.

Portuguese Empire

It's easy to forget that Portugal was once at the head of a powerful empire. From the early 15th century, Portuguese explorers pushed far into the unknown, challenging the traditional view that the world ended somewhere west of Gibraltar. Madeira and the Azores were the first to be discovered, and these islands remain part of Portugal. Portuguese ships rounded the Cape of Good Hope in 1488, and in 1497 Vasco da Gama reached Calicut, India. By 1560, Portugal had claimed Brazil and had an empire stretching east as far as Japan, with missionary and trading posts in Africa, India, Malaysia, Macao and Timor.

Despite strong rivalry between Portugal and Spain over discoveries in the Americas, the 16th century was a Golden Age, with spices, slaves and

Portugal

gold making Portugal hugely rich. But the voyages and maintenance of an overseas empire were extremely costly, and the home economy was worsening. By 1580, Philip II of Spain had claimed the throne, becoming Philip I of Portugal the following year. Within 100 years, many of the overseas possessions had fallen to the English and Dutch.

The legacy of the empire still exists, however. Portugal extricated itself from Africa in the 1970s, when Angola, Mozambique and Guinea became independent; East Timor in Indonesia

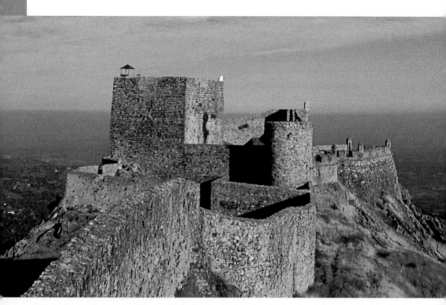

Perched on a ridge overlooking the Alentejo valley and the Spanish border, the 13th-century castle of Marvao dominates the surrounding landscape

was relinquished at the same time. Today there are buildings, churches and monuments wherever the Portuguese held power, but language became the country's most important legacy. Portuguese is the seventh most widely spoken language in the world. Brazil retains strong ties with Portugal and, unlike many other former colonies, there is genuine respect between the two countries.

The People

Geographical isolation from most of Europe has kept Portuguese bloodlines pure, and you'll notice a definite racial type – most people are short, with dark eyes, skin and hair. They are conservative people who are generally courteous and respectful. Northerners, with a harsher climate and historically poorer living conditions, tend to be less easygoing than people in the south, and more religious. Even so, the Catholic church continues to hold great sway everywhere.

Most of the population still lives in rural areas, although there was a large urban increase in the 1970s, when people came home from former African colonies following independence. In Lisbon in particular, many Afro-Portuguese have integrated into Portuguese life; there's a good level of interracial harmony.

The country still has one of Europe's highest emigration rates, with around 3 million people living and working abroad. With few natural resources, many people in northern Portugal are forced to seek work overseas; you can see the results of their labors in the new houses and cars found in even the poorest villages.

Society and Language

Being polite and friendly will smooth your path as you travel through Portugal. The Portuguese tend to be welcoming and unhurried, so be prepared for things to take a long time. There are traditional ideas and attitudes toward women, and the farther away from major towns you travel the more obvious this becomes. It's considered disrespectful to wear skimpy clothing, and it is customary to speak formally and politely until you get to know the people you are talking to.

One of the major hurdles in getting to know the Portuguese is the language barrier. Don't try your Spanish in Portugal. Despite – or because of – proximity to Spain, the Portuguese don't appreciate being addressed in Spanish. However, if you can read Spanish you'll have no problem reading Portuguese. It's a romance language with Latin roots, similar to Spanish and Italian. Pronunciation is a different matter altogether, however, and spoken Portuguese, with its sibilants, nasal vowels and guttural consonants, reminds some people of Russian and Slavic languages.

The narrow, picturesque streets of Porto cluster together on the hillsides of the city

The Portuguese are very aware that they speak a difficult language and are excellent linguists; you'll find English spoken in major tourist areas, although rarely in the deep countryside. Do try and tackle one or two words; your efforts will be appreciated and faces will light up when you try to communicate.

Changing Portugal

Since the watershed year of 1986, huge changes have occurred in Portugal. From being one of the poorest nations in Europe, the country now has one of the highest economic growth rates, while unemployment has plummeted. Despite a recession in the early 1990s, things still look good for the country as the economy continues to expand. But

this has been achieved at the cost of a widening gap between the rich and poor, noticeable wherever you travel. Education levels are low, with an embarrassing percentage of the population having few if any literacy skills. Agriculture still lags far behind the rest of Europe, and a high proportion of national earnings comes from money earned overseas or spent by tourists within Portugal.

For visitors, the blend of old and new is alluring and adds an extra dimension to the travel experience. Recent investment has improved the infrastructure to the visitor's benefit, while the uneven wealth distribution means that a rustic way of life is still evident throughout the country.

Portugal

TIMELINE

1000 BC to AD 400	Occupation by Phoenicians, Carthaginians, Iberians, Celts, Romans and Visigoths.
AD 713	Moors control most of the country and remain in power for 400 years.
1179	Pope recognizes Kingdom of Portugal.
1255	Afonso III makes Lisbon the capital of Portugal.
1480–1500s	Age of Discovery.
1488	Bartolomeu Dias rounds Cape of Good Hope.
1580	End of Golden Age with invasion by Philip II of Spain, who declares himself Philip I of Portugal.
1668	Treaty of Lisbon recognizes Portuguese independence.
1755	Lisbon earthquake.
1910	Portuguese monarchy overthrown and replaced by republic.
1916–18	Portugal joins Allies in World War I.
1933	*Estado Novo* (New State) established.
1939–45	Portugal neutral throughout World War II.
1960s	Portuguese colony of Goa occupied by India; local nationalist uprisings in Angola, Guinea and Mozambique.
1976	New constitution drawn up after the fall of the *Estado Novo* in 1974.
1986	Portugal admitted to European Union; start of period of huge economic growth and social reform.
1999	Portugal joins European Monetary System.
2001	Porto is named European Capital of Culture for 2001.
2004	Portugal hosts the European Football (soccer) Championship.

PRINCE HENRY THE NAVIGATOR

The impetus for the great Portuguese "Age of Discovery" of the late 15th century came from the son of João I, Prince Henry, who was born in 1394. He can be credited with transforming Portugal into a great maritime power whose success was based on a scientific approach to exploration, navigation and cartography. At his base in the Algarve, Henry collected accomplished shipbuilders, sailors, instrument makers and astronomers, encouraging them to prepare for long voyages into the unknown. The highly successful caravel was designed, a speedy ship that made the great voyages possible. Motivated by religion as well as commerce, Henry's ships sailed ever farther south, rounding Cape Bojador in West Africa, then thought to be the end of the world, in 1434. By Henry's death in 1460 the Portuguese had reached Sierra Leone, and the known world had become a bigger place.

Portugal

Survival Guide

- The Portuguese are committed wine drinkers. Generally, when you order house wine in restaurants you'll get something very drinkable, even if it appears in an earthenware jug.

- Water everywhere is safe to drink, although sometimes less than delicious. Avoid tap water in the Algarve during the summer and drink bottled water instead, to be on the safe side.

- The modest Portuguese are shocked by scanty clothes worn anywhere except at the beach. If you are wearing a sleeveless top, take along a scarf to wrap around your shoulders as needed.

- Portuguese drivers are among Europe's worst, and the country also has the Continent's highest accident rate.

- Portugal's telephone system is improving, but is still not up to the standards of other European countries. If you call from your hotel room, you'll pay a high surcharge. Use an on-street "Credifone," which accepts plastic phone cards available from street kiosks.

- Be prepared for Portugal to be different in many ways from its neighbor, particularly if you've already visited Spain. Despite their proximity, the two countries are very different.

- Public restrooms are few and far between, but it's acceptable – even if you're not a customer – to ask to use hotel or restaurant facilities. Men's toilets are marked "H" and women's are marked "S."

- Try not to let grime and shabbiness in Portuguese cities affect you; look for the positive qualities, such as daily clean sheets in many hotels.

- Don't be surprised by the sometimes startling amount of garbage in public places. In Portuguese bars and cafés, it's acceptable to throw paper wrappings on the floor.

- You probably won't find luxury accommodations or excellent service if you're away from the major tourist centers; Portugal is still considered a poor country.

- Portuguese food can be monotonous, and some dishes are unappealing to foreigners. If you are not feeling adventurous, stick to grilled fish and chicken.

- Leave small change in a bar; otherwise about 10 percent is an adequate tip.

- *Pousadas* are by far the nicest places to stay when traveling in Portugal. These are state owned but privately run, deluxe establishments located in historic or beautiful places such as former monasteries, palaces and castles. Advance reservations are recommended.

Strong ties with Brazil – a restaurant entrance in Rua Garret, Lisbon

LISBON

Lisbon (Lisboa) is a beguiling city. It has a great past and a promising future. It may easily strike the visitor as old-fashioned and crumbling – but these elements also are an essential part of its charm. Look for the positive: the port city's vigor and life; its great colonial past; the atmospheric old trams; and the evocative sights and scents – laundry flapping in the wind, shoeshine men hawking their trade, the smell of roasting coffee and chestnuts. Most sights of interest are within walking distance of downtown, with the exception of the glorious attractions of suburban Belém, an easy train, bus or tram ride away.

Lisbon Flavors and *Bacalhau*

Lisbon has a wide range of restaurants at every price level, with the emphasis on traditional Portuguese cooking, although fast-food outlets are easy to find as well. Breakfast consists of small cakes and pastries, but hotels can usually prepare meals tailored to foreign tastes. Lunch is more substantial than in other European cities.

Heavy soups are popular, salads are surprisingly hard to find, and fresh fruit juice is virtually non-existent. Lisbon inhabitants eat a lot of fish and seafood, including *bacalhau* (a dried, salted codfish), and the warming winter stews can be good.

You may be surprised at the number of pastry and cake shops; the Portuguese are notoriously sweet-toothed, and Lisbon has many old-fashioned shops selling traditional specialties like the delicious *pastéis de Belém* (pastries filled with custard). Portugal makes good red and white wine, national and foreign beers are everywhere, and all the usual spirits and aperitifs are available.

Souvenirs from Lisbon

Shopping is great fun in Lisbon, and there are many stores selling lovely Portuguese crafts. The area known as the Chiado, in downtown Lisbon, is the

Lisbon

smartest shopping district, with streets lined with numerous classy clothing and jewelry boutiques.

Carpets from the village of Arraiolos are a superb buy, as is the exquisite porcelain manufactured by Vista Alegre. Linen and cotton sheets and tablecloths are another Portuguese specialty. You can even have the lovely glazed tiles, *azulejos*, made to order, or

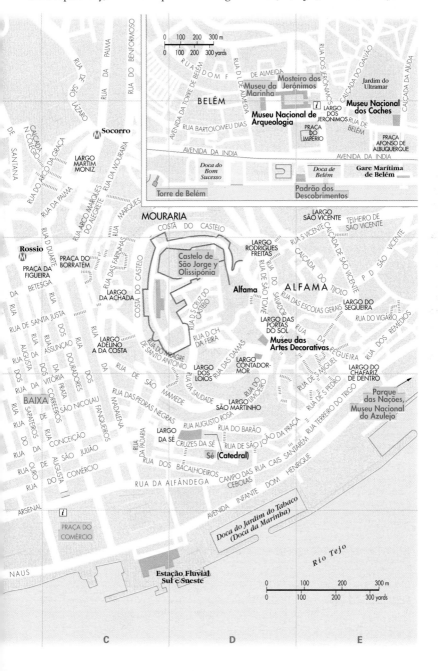

Lisbon

track down something made from cork, one of Portugal's biggest exports.

Film, Music and *Fado*

As befits its capital status, Lisbon offers a variety of music, theater and ballet. Moviegoing is a particular pleasure, as films are all shown in their original language with subtitles, rather than dubbed, so you can catch the latest releases from home.

Fado, a unique style of Portuguese music, is heard at its best in Lisbon and should at least be experienced. This melancholy and passionate music is traditionally sung by a woman, accompanied by guitar. Its origins lie deep in history, a mix of Moorish and African elements, and can be described as a kind of light operetta. The best place to hear it is at one of the *fado* houses in the Upper Town of Lisbon (Bairro Alto, see page 381), or in the Alfama district.

The Lisbon Earthquake

On All Saints Day (November 1), 1755, the Lisbon earthquake struck. Churches were packed for this major feast day, and thousands of lighted candles toppled during the tremors, starting fires that were as destructive as the quake itself. A massive tidal wave followed, swallowing Lisbon's fleet and flooding the already-destroyed lower city.

During the aftermath, corpses were sent to sea on barges and sunk in order to avert the plague. Hospitals opened, prices were fixed and a tax was levied to cover rebuilding costs, including the renovation of the lower city, today known as the Baixa district. Although Lisbon largely recovered, 1755 marked the end of its role as Europe's leading port city.

ESSENTIAL INFORMATION

TOURIST INFORMATION
Turismo de Lisboa (Lisbon Tourist Office)
• Welcome Center, Praça do Comércio
☎ 21 031 2810
• Santa Apolónia (railway station) ☎ 21 882 1606
• Lisbon International Airport (arrivals) ☎ 21 845 0660
Tourist information helpline ☎ 0800 296 296 (toll-free); www.visitlisboa.com or www.askmelisboa.com

URBAN TRANSPORTATION
Lisbon has a subway system, buses, trams, funiculars and even ferries. Subway stations are marked with an "M" on the city map. For visitors, the Lisboa Card, valid for 24, 48 or 72 hours, gives free unlimited travel and free entry into 26 museums, monuments and other tourist attractions. Cards are available from tourist offices (see above). Otherwise you can buy

bus and tram tickets when boarding, and subway tickets from a machine or office at the subway station. The trams and funiculars are one of Lisbon's glories, so make a point of traveling on them; the modern tram 15 is a particularly useful line. Ferry tickets are available from offices at the ferry stations; again, a ferry trip is recommended as part of your sightseeing. Taxis are beige, or occasionally green and black. There are taxi stands on the open squares of the Rossio and the Praça da Figueira, or you can call a cab (☎ 218 119 000 and 21 812 5060).

AIRPORT INFORMATION
Lisbon Airport (☎ 21 841 3500 for flight information) is about 4 miles (a 20-minute drive) north of the downtown area. The Aero-Bus shuttle service leaves every 20 minutes daily 7 a.m.–9 p.m. from outside the terminal to downtown Lisbon.

CLIMATE – average highs and lows for the month

JAN.	FEB.	MAR.	APR.	MAY	JUN.	JUL.	AUG.	SEP.	OCT.	NOV.	DEC.
13°C	15°C	17°C	19°C	21°C	25°C	28°C	29°C	27°C	21°C	18°C	14°C
55°F	59°F	63°F	66°F	70°F	77°F	82°F	84°F	81°F	70°F	64°F	57°F
8°C	9°C	10°C	12°C	12°C	15°C	18°C	18°C	17°C	14°C	10°C	9°C
46°F	48°F	50°F	54°F	54°F	59°F	64°F	64°F	63°F	57°F	50°F	48°F

CITY SIGHTS

Key to symbols

✚ map coordinates refer to the Lisbon map on pages 378–379; sights below are highlighted in yellow on the map.

✉ address or location ☎ telephone number ⏰ opening times ⓡ nearest overground train or subway 🚌 nearest bus or tram route ⛴ nearest ferry 🍴 restaurant or café on site or nearby 🎟 admission charge: $$$ more than €4, $$ €2–€4, $ less than €2 ℹ other relevant information

BAIRRO ALTO

✚ A3 ✉ Area on slopes to west of Baixa ⓡ Restauradores 🚌 Tram 28

The Bairro Alto (Upper Town) is one of the five areas that constitute Lisbon's historic center. It was virtually untouched by the 1755 earthquake, and the atmospheric jumble of streets and squares tumble down steep slopes to the Baixa (the Lower Town) below. At night it's one of the city's liveliest quarters, where in *fado* houses you can hear melancholy, evocative Portuguese songs. The Elevador de Santa Justa, a wonderfully clanky funicular built in 1902, runs up the hill.

BAIXA AND ROSSIO

✚ B2–B3 ✉ Praça Dom Pedro IV and streets between it and Praça do Comércio ⓡ Rossio 🚌 All services to Rossio and Praça do Comércio

Rossio Square, properly known as Praça Dom Pedro IV, and the grid of streets forming the Baixa district will repeatedly draw you back. The Teatro Nacional (National Theater) and a soaring column topped by a statue of Dom Pedro IV dominate the spacious Rossio, which is lined with stores and cafés. The square has an ancient history and was the scene of Inquisition burnings in the 16th century. Between Rossio and the waterfront lies Baixa, a perfect example of rational 18th-century planning, erected at the Marquês de Pombal's instigation after the 1755 earthquake. The orderly streets are lined with lovely old stores, gracious buildings and tiled facades.

CASTELO DE SÃO JORGE Y OLISIPÓNIA

✚ C3–D3 ✉ Rua do Chão da Feira ☎ 21 810 0620 ⏰ Daily 9–5 🚌 37; tram 12, 28 🎟 $$$

Visible from many parts of Lisbon, the Castelo de São Jorge (St. George's Castle) stands on the site of the earliest settlement. Fortified by the Romans, Visigoths and Moors, it was besieged in 1147 by Afonso Enriques and his Christian army and finally fell after 17 weeks – a turning point in the struggle to evict the Moors from Portugal. The Moorish battlements still stand, offering superb views over the rooftops to the river. Today, extensive restoration within the main structure has made a verdant, cool oasis, with terraces, pools and fountains. A

Shady cloisters of the 16th-century Jerónimos Monastery enclose formal gardens

multimedia exhibition (Centro de Interpretação da Cidade de Lisboa – Olisipónia) gives insight into the history of Lisbon. The Alfama district around the palace is worth exploring.

MOSTEIRO DOS JERÓNIMOS

🞣 See map inset ✉ Praça do Império ☎ 21 362 0034 🕐 Tue.–Sun. 10–5 🍴 São Jerónimo, see page 564 🚆 Train: Belém 🚌 27, 28, 29, 43, 49, 51; tram 15 ⛴ Belém 💲 $$$

The stunning architectural ensemble of the Mosteiro dos Jerónimos (Jerónimos Monastery), a UNESCO World Heritage Site, stands on the site of an earlier chapel, visited by Portuguese explorers before their great voyages. Building began on the present church in 1501 to celebrate Vasco da Gama's successful voyage to the Indies. It took almost 100 years to complete, by which time various architectural fashions had come and gone. The church and adjoining cloisters are a glorious mix of Gothic, Renaissance and Manueline styles. Pause first at the great south door. Its intricate carving includes the figure of Henry the Navigator; the west door, equally splendid, features Manuel I, who originally started the construction. The soaring interior contains the simple tomb of Vasco da Gama, a contrast to the surrounding riot of stonework. The two-story cloisters are equally elaborately carved, a wonderful combination of delicacy and weighty strength.

MUSEU CALOUSTE GULBENKIAN

🞣 A5 ✉ Avenida de Berna 45A ☎ 21 782 3000 🕐 Tue.–Sun. 10–5:45 🍴 Restaurant and café in museum 🚇 S. Sebastião or Praça de Espanha 🚌 16, 26, 31, 46, 56 💲 $$$; free to all Sun.

Portugal's greatest museum, the Museu Calouste Gulbenkian (Calouste Gulbenkian Museum) was financed by a bequest from the Armenian magnate, whose private collection makes up the bulk of the exhibits. It comprises two sections: European art and artifacts, and Oriental and ancient pieces. The museum is not vast, but everything it contains is of the highest quality. Most visitors are particularly enthralled by the

Lalique jewelry and glass, distinctive art deco pieces displayed in a darkened room.

MUSEU DA MARINHA

🞣 See map inset ✉ Praça do Império ☎ 21 362 0010 🕐 Tue.–Sun. 10–6, Apr.–Sep.; 10–5, rest of year 🚆 Train: Belém 🚌 27, 28, 29, 43, 49, 51; tram 15 💲 $$; free to all Sun.

The Museu da Marinha (Maritime Museum), located at Belém, is one of the best of its kind in Europe. It's a huge collection, with full-size boats and royal barges, paintings, uniforms and archaic navigational instruments. Most evocative, perhaps, is the polychrome wooden statue of the Archangel Raphael, said to have accompanied Vasco da Gama on his epic voyage to the Indies in 1497.

MUSEU NACIONAL DO AZULEJO

🞣 E2 ✉ Rua da Madre de Deus 4 ☎ 21 810 0340 🕐 Wed.–Sun. 10–6, Tue. 2–6 🍴 Café in museum 🚌 18, 42, 104, 105 💲 $$

Throughout Lisbon and Portugal, you'll notice the exquisite tiles, or *azulejos*, adorning the walls of countless buildings. The Museu Nacional do Azulejo (National Tile Museum) traces the history of the painted glazed tile, which has been used in Portugal since the 15th century. You can see how the art developed from simple early tiles to complex, multicolored modern examples. Blue and white has predominated since Chinese porcelain arrived in Europe; the wonderful tiled view of Lisbon, made in 1738, is a fine example.

PADRÃO DOS DESCOBRIMENTOS

🞣 See map inset ✉ Avenida de Brasília ☎ 21 303 1950 🕐 Tue.–Sun. 9–6:30, Jul.–Aug.; 9–5, rest of year 🍴 São Jerónimo, see page 564 🚆 Train: Belém 🚌 27, 28, 43, 49; tram 15 💲 $$ (temporary exhibitions free)

The eye-catching white mass of the Padrão dos Descobrimentos (Monument to the Discoveries) soars up from the water's edge at Belém, serving as a reminder of Portugal's great maritime past. It was erected in 1960 to mark the 500th anniversary of the death

Topiary gardens on the Italianate grounds of the Fronteira Palace, in north Lisbon

LISBON LIFE

Everyday life in Lisbon, a relatively small city, is far more relaxed than in other capitals. The day starts around 7:30, when commuters are on the move and children make their way to school. Trams, the subway and buses all are crowded. Some people travel to town on the ferries that crisscross the Tagus. Many grab breakfast in a bar before work. Breakfast is usually tea or coffee, with one of the cloyingly sweet pastries so loved by the Portuguese.

Lunch in Lisbon is taken seriously, and many people eat a full meal rather than a snack, although they eat it fast, often standing at a bar counter. Workers also use the lunch hour to shop for food or browse in stores. At the end of the afternoon, commuters head home but will often re-emerge later to meet friends for a drink or more tea and cakes. Midweek evenings are often spent at home, although in summer the streets will be thronged

for a few hours as people stroll and chat outside.

Weekends are a different matter; people head for the Upper Town to eat and drink before going to concerts, movies or the theater, while young Portuguese enjoy the old district's waterfront clubs.

Saturday and Sunday are popular shopping days when crowds flock to huge malls on the outskirts of the city, which stay open late. Sundays, too, are high points for soccer fans, with the big matches attracting large crowds. Lisbon is blessed by its proximity to a beautiful coastline, and it's easy in summer to drive or catch a train to the coast for a day at the beach and dinner in an excellent fish restaurant. In midsummer, an outing to the cool green countryside around Sintra (see page 385), some 15 miles away, is another weekend option.

Statue in the Praça Sao Roque

Lisbon

of Henry the Navigator, and has an angular front and curving form that represents a ship's prow and sails. Figures crowd the prow, led by Henry, who holds a ship. An elevator rises more than 435 feet to the top, offering panoramic views. Below, a mosaic map traces the Portuguese voyages of exploration.

PARQUE DAS NAÇÕES

✚ E1 ✉ Parque das Nações ☎ 21 891 9333 ◷ Park: Sun.–Thu. 9:30 a.m.–1 a.m., Fri.–Sat. 9:30 a.m.–3 a.m. Oceanarium: Daily 10–8, May–Sep.; 10–7, rest of year Ⓜ Oriente 🚌 28, 81 💵 Park free; Oceanarium $$$

The Parque das Nações (Park of the Nations) is used for trade fairs and exhibitions. Striking buildings, moorings, landscaped gardens, street cafés and restaurants front the Tagus. From the water rises Oceanário (Oceanarium), a state-of-the-art aquarium. Europe's largest aquarium features a vast central tank, surrounded by four others representing the main oceans. Marine mammals and seabirds thrive, as well as fish, underwater creatures and vegetation, making this one of Lisbon's most impressive new attractions.

Belém Tower, rising beside the Tagus, an enduring symbol of Portugal's maritime past

PRAÇA DO COMÉRCIO

✚ C1 ✉ Praça do Comércio Ⓜ Rossio 🚌 All buses to Praça do Comércio; tram 15 ⛴ Terreiro do Paço for ferries to Cacilhas

One side of the spacious Praça do Comércio (Commercial Square) opens on the water, emphasizing its original purpose as an imposing gateway to the city from the sea. To experience its original perspective, take the five-minute ferry trip from nearby Terreiro do Paço (Palace Square) across the Tagus to the suburb of Cacilhas. The vista of the square and the triumphal arch leading to the streets of the Baixa opens up to buildings, churches and monuments, an excellent chance to feel the city's past.

SÉ

✚ D2 ✉ Largo da Sé ☎ 21 886 6752 ◷ Tue.–Sat. 9–7, Sun.–Mon. 9–5 Ⓜ Rossio 🚌 37; tram 12, 28 💵 $

Construction of the Sé (Cathedral) started in 1150, soon after the expulsion of the Moors. It was the city's first church, a solid and harmonious Romanesque edifice. Its two massive towers are a city landmark. It largely escaped damage in the 1755 earthquake, making it a superb symbol of Lisbon's history. Inside, be sure to see the font where Lisbon-born St. Anthony of Padua was baptized.

TORRE DE BELÉM

✚ See map inset ✉ Avenida de Brasília ☎ 21 362 0034 ◷ Tue.–Sun. 10–5 🍴 São Jerónimo, see page 564 Ⓜ Train: Belém 🚌 27, 28, 29, 43, 49, 51; tram 15 💵 $$

In the nearby suburb of Belém, the Torre de Belém (Belém Tower) rises beside the Tagus river. This exquisite honey-colored stone tower is a symbol of Portugal's maritime past. Built between 1515 and 1520, it was designed by Francisco de Arruda, a Portuguese architect whose earlier Moroccan travels influenced his style. His work shows delightful Moorish elements – little domes topping the battlements, corner towers, and arcaded windows and loggias. Built as a bastion against pirate attack, it later served as a prison and has been designated a World Heritage Site by UNESCO.

Sintra

By far the most popular day trip from Lisbon is to beautiful Sintra, a small town packed with delights, set in lush and mountainous country some 15 miles northwest of Lisbon. Once there, the attractions are scattered over a wide area, so unless you have plenty of time, it makes sense to take a tour or rent a car and drive from the city. As a bonus, most tour operators include a detour to Cabo da Roca, the Continent's westernmost point.

Palaces

For more than 500 years Sintra was the summer resort of Portuguese kings – a legacy that is apparent in the town's two astounding palaces. The Queluz National Palace (Palácio Nacional de Queluz) was first built by João I in the 15th century and remained in use until the end of the 19th century.

Ornate stonework at Sintra's Queluz National Palace

Architecturally imposing, it's nevertheless a muddle of mainly Gothic and Manueline styles. The interior is worth exploring. Note the superb ceramic tiles, as well as the elaborately decorated ceilings: one is painted with gold-collared swans and another with magpies.

The other main palace is the Pena National Palace (Palácio Nacional da Pena), built in the 1840s by Ferdinand of Saxe-Coburg-Gotha, husband of Queen Maria II. It's a creation rivaling the best of Disney, complete with towers, turrets and battlements. Inside is a riot of flamboyant furniture, wall hangings and paintings, including a whole room of nudes.

Nearby is the eighth-century Castelo dos Mouros, a ruined Moorish stronghold with superb views.

Gardens

The other outstanding attractions in Sintra are its gardens and parks. The warm, damp climate is ideal for a profusion of exotic trees, shrubs and roses, and you'll see everything from rhododendrons and camellias to tree ferns and palms. The Pena Gardens, below the Pena National Palace, are lovely, with lakes and mock temples. But the highlight is the Monserrate Gardens, west of Sintra. Two Englishmen laid out the gardens between 1790 and 1860, and they ramble over 74 acres.

Around Sintra lies the Sintra-Cascais Natural Park (Parque Natural Sintra-Cascais), a wonderful area stretching from the tree-clad mountains of Sintra down to the dramatic Atlantic coastline at Guincho.

Tour Operators

Cityrama ✉ Avenida Praia da Vitória 12-B
☎ 21 319 1090; fax 21 353 3291

Cityline ✉ Avenida Praia da Vitória
☎ 21 319 1090; fax 21 356 0868

Portugal Tours ✉ Avenida Praia de Vitoria 14
☎ /fax 21 352 2902

Porto

PORTO

Porto, Portugal's second-largest city with about 300,000 residents, stands on the steep and rocky north bank of the Douro river, just a couple of miles from its outlet on the Atlantic. The suburbs sprawl to the coast. Many visitors encounter Porto on their way up the beautiful Douro valley. The city also is known for its long association with port wine, which has been shipped from Vila Nova de Gaia, a suburb of Porto, since the 17th century. It has long been referred to as "Oporto," a name never used by the Portuguese and now declining in use elsewhere.

Development of Porto

Founded in pre-Roman times, the city gave its name to the country, and was the birthplace of Prince Henry the Navigator in 1394. Traditionally liberal, its residents have always had a strong rebellious streak, which goes well with the city's industrious and down-to-earth image.

Porto is a refreshing antidote to the faded elegance of Lisbon – a bustling city lying at the center of Portugal's most important economic area, its layout inextricably entwined with the history of the port trade. Grandiose buildings testify to 18th- and 19th-century wealth, but the true spirit of the city lies in the maze of narrow streets below the cathedral, the old docks and the waterfront houses. Pockets throughout the city are endowed with *azulejo* decoration (glazed ceramic tiles).

Suggested Itineraries

Two or three days is sufficient to see Porto. Nearly everything of interest is within a short walk or bus ride from the city center. The streets are steep and hilly, so wear comfortable shoes. If you're just passing through on your way up the Douro valley, visit the port lodges in Vila Nova de Gaia, Porto's main tourist attraction. If you've got more time, the city can be neatly divided into cultural itineraries, focusing on medieval, baroque and neoclassic monuments and churches. And for a state-of-the-art attraction, Porto now boasts a world-class arts center, the Casa da Musica, opened in 2005.

The heart of modern Porto centers around Avenida dos Aliados, a broad avenue with the monumental town hall at one end and the Praça da Liberdade, a transportation hub, at the other. Seething with people, this stretch is a good place to observe locals going about their daily business. The main shopping areas are east and north of this avenue. You can use the river to help orient yourself to the city.

Porto Flavors

The people of Porto have traditionally been known as *tripeiros*, or "tripe-eaters," allegedly because they sacrificed all their meat except the tripe to their army during a legendary battle – an historic indicator that refined cooking doesn't top the priority list here. Expect hearty, tasty meals, plenty of fish, the much-beloved *bacalhau* (dried, salted cod) and super-sweet desserts on every menu.

On the other hand, a glass of smooth, unctuous and subtle port – drunk on its native soil – may convert even the most inveterate port-hater. An especially atmospheric place to dine is beside the river at Ribeira, in the heart of the oldest part of Porto. Until recently it was run-down and decayed, but most of the area has now been given a face-lift, and it is filled with good, lively restaurants with tremendous tourist appeal.

Crafts and Shopping

Porto is the place to track down northern handicraft specialties, fine port, locally made shoes and the village of Minho's traditional gold filigree jewelry. The city's wonderfully old-fashioned stores, many of which still retain their early 20th-century facades and details, are worth a visit even if you're not buying. Highlights include the Lello and Irmão bookstore on Rua do Carmelitas, with its superb double staircase and somber wooden paneling, and Cardoso Cabeleiro on Rua do Bonjardim, a shop specializing in wigs and toupees. Similar stores cluster together in Porto, so you'll find streets packed with hardware stores, seed merchants, jewelers and linen stores. Marques Soares, a chic department store on Rua do Carmelitas, carries exquisite leather goods.

Porto

The Igreja e Torre dos Clérigos overlooks Porto

Excursions and Entertainment

Operators run cruises on the Douro river, ranging from a week-long trip up the river on a luxury cruiser to a couple of hours puttering around the lower reaches in a reproduction of a *rabelo*, the glorious old boats once used to carry barrels of port downstream from the vineyards. Sections of the 19th-century narrow-gauge railway still operate in the Douro valley – a fun way to do a little exploring. Tour operators also run bus trips in, around and out of Porto; Diana Tours (☎ 22 377 1230, or toll-free 800 203 983) is a reliable operator with English-speaking guides. Alternatively, tickets may be bought at the tourist office. Be sure to visit the port lodges in Vila Nova de Gaia (see page 390), an essential stop on any Porto visit.

For evening entertainment, locals attend theaters, concerts and the movies, although many people prefer to while away the hours at one of the terrace cafés or simply strolling along the riverbank.

ESSENTIAL INFORMATION

TOURIST INFORMATION
Turismo do Porto (Porto Tourism)
• Rua Clube dos Fenianos 25
☎ 22 339 3472; fax 22 332 3303;
www.portoturismo.pt
• Rua do Infante D Henrique 63 ☎ 22 200 9770

URBAN TRANSPORTATION
The Sociedade de Transportes Colectivos do Porto (STCP) issue a Mapa de Transportes showing both day and nighttime bus, tram and metro routes (available from Tourist Offices). Pay as you get on the bus or the tram. You can buy a 1-, 4- or 7-day travel pass from kiosks in the city center, a considerable saving on single tickets. Porto

Tourism issues a Porto Tour Pass, valid for 1 or 2 days which offers free public transportation around the city as well as free entrance to many attractions. Taxis are inexpensive; there is an additional charge to cross the river to Gaia.

AIRPORT INFORMATION
Francisco Sá Carneiro International Airport (☎ 22 943 2400) is about 12 miles northwest of central Porto. Bus 56 runs daily every 20 minutes from 6 a.m. until midnight, with a journey time of 30–60 minutes. It terminates at Jardins da Cordoaria, next to Torre dos Clérigos. The faster Aero-Bus service to downtown Porto is an alternative; for information ☎ 808 200 166 (toll-free).

CLIMATE – average highs and lows for the month

JAN.	FEB.	MAR.	APR.	MAY	JUN.	JUL.	AUG.	SEP.	OCT.	NOV.	DEC.
13°C	13°C	15°C	17°C	18°C	22°C	23°C	23°C	23°C	19°C	17°C	14°C
55°F	55°F	59°F	63°F	64°F	72°F	73°F	73°F	73°F	66°F	63°F	57°F
6°C	7°C	7°C	9°C	10°C	13°C	14°C	14°C	14°C	12°C	8°C	7°C
43°F	45°F	45°F	48°F	50°F	55°F	57°F	57°F	57°F	54°F	46°F	45°F

Porto

CITY SIGHTS

Key to symbols

⊞ map coordinates refer to the Porto map on page 387; sights below are highlighted in yellow on the map.

⊠ address or location ☎ telephone number

◉ opening times ▣ nearest bus or tram route

🍴 restaurant or café on site or nearby ⓦ admission charge: $$$ more than €4, $$ €2–€4, $ less than €2

🅘 other relevant information

IGREJA E TORRE DOS CLÉRIGOS

⊞ B2 ⊠ Rua dos Clérigos ☎ 22 200 1729
◉ Church: Mon.–Sat. 9–noon and 3:30–7:30, Sun. 10–1 and 9–10 p.m., in summer; Mon.–Sat. 9–noon and 3:30–5:30, Sun. 10–1 and 8:30–10:30 p.m., in winter. Tower: Daily 9:30–5, in Aug.; 9:30–1 and 2–5, Apr.–Jun. and Sep.; 10–noon and 2–5, rest of year
▣ 6, 20, 35 ⓦ Church free; Tower $$

The soaring Torre dos Clérigos (Tower of Clérigos), attached to an 18th-century granite church (Igreja dos Clérigos), is a Porto landmark, and most visitors climb it to admire the views. Nicolau Nasoni designed the oval church, with its elaborately festooned facade of swags and garlands, in the 1730s in Italian baroque style.

JARDINS DO PALÁCIO DE CRISTAL

⊞ A2–A3 ⊠ Rua de Dom Manuel II ☎ 22 608 1000
◉ Tue.–Sat. 10–6, Sun. 2–6 🍴 Cafeteria in gardens
▣ 3, 20, 52, 78

The Jardins do Palácio de Cristal (Crystal Palace Gardens), close to Porto's center, offer one of the best vantage points in the city. A lime-tree lined avenue leads from pools and fountains past rhododendrons, magnolias and camellias to rose gardens and terraces high above the river. Summer concerts are held in the park's pavilion.

MUSEU NACIONAL SOARES DOS REIS

⊞ A3 ⊠ Rua Dom Manuel II ☎ 22 339 3770
◉ Wed.– Sun. 10–6, Tue. 2–6. Frequently closed for restoration or rearrangement ▣ 3, 6, 20, 35, 36, 37, 41, 44, 50, 52, 78 ⓦ $$$

The Museu Nacional Soares dos Reis (Soares dos Reis National Museum), named after the 19th-century sculptor Soares dos Reis, is Porto's most important museum. It's housed in an impressive 1795 neoclassic edifice, occupied in the early 1800s during the Peninsular War by first the French and then the English. The museum emphasizes works by dos Reis, with fine exhibits of glass and porcelain; look for pieces from the famous Vista Alegre factory.

MUSEU ROMÂNTICO

⊞ A2 ⊠ Rua de Entre-Quintas 220 ☎ 22 605 7033
◉ Tue.–Sat. 10–12:30 and 2–5:30, Sun. 2–5:30
▣ 3, 20, 35, 37, 52,78 ⓦ $

For an insight into how the prosperous bourgeois of Porto lived in the 19th century, visit the Museu Romântico (Romantic Museum), housed in a pretty villa overlooking the river. Admire the furniture and paintings; many of the furnishings have connections with the last king of Piedmont, who lived here in exile. The basement houses the Solar do Vinho do Porto (Port Wine Rooms), where you can sample a wide selection of ports.

PONTE DO DOM LUÍS I

⊞ B1–C1 ⊠ Ponte do Dom Luís I ▣ 32, 57, 91
Five bridges span the Douro river, all built dramatically high above the water to span the gorge cut by the lower reaches of the river. Perhaps the most impressive is the Ponte do Dom Luís I (Luis I Bridge), a striking bi-level iron construction designed by Théophile Seyring (one of Gustave Eiffel's collaborators) and dating from 1886. The bridge effectively links four city areas and is currently undergoing extensive renovation to take the new metro line.

PRAÇA DA RIBEIRA

Casa do Infante ⊞ B1 ⊠ Rua da Alfândega 10, Ribeira ☎ 22 608 1000 ◉ Tue.–Sat. 10–12:30 and 2–5:30, Sun 2–5:30 ▣ 1, 32, 57, 88, 91 ⓦ Free
Centro Regional de Artes Tradicionais ⊠ Rua de Reboleira 37, Ribeira ☎ 22 332 0201 ◉ Tue.–Fri. 10–noon and 1–6 ▣ 88

The waterfront Praça da Ribeira (Ribeira Square) is the focal point of the Ribeira district, by far the most atmospheric area of Porto and designated a UNESCO World

Porto

Heritage Site. Many of the buildings – arcaded neoclassic constructions – were erected between 1776 and 1782. Although you can approach the area by descending the steep Rua de Alfândega past Casa do Infante (House of the Prince), Prince Henry the Navigator's reputed birthplace, the easiest way is to walk through the warren of canyon-like streets tumbling down to the river from the cathedral.

There's no better place to experience historic Porto than in this district, which has plenty of bars and restaurants. While you're here, visit the Centro Regional de Artes Tradicionais (Regional Center for Arts and Crafts), selling a wonderful range of traditional northern handicrafts.

SÉ

⊞ B2   ✉ Terreiro da Sé   ☎ 22 205 9028
🕐 Church: Mon.–Sat. 8:45–12:30 and 2:30–7, Sun. 8:30–12:30 and 2:30–7, Apr.–Oct.; Mon.–Sat. 8:45–12:30 and 2:30–6, Sun. 8:30–12:30 and 2:30–6, rest of year. Cloisters: Mon.–Sat. 9–12:15 and 2:30–6, Sun. 2:30–6, Apr.–Oct.; Mon.–Sat. 9–12:15 and 2:30–5:15, Sun. 2:30–5:15, rest of year   🚌 3, 6, 71, 78
🎫 Church free; Cloisters $$

Porto's Sé (Cathedral) stands high above the steep slopes leading to the river. Built in the 12th century as a fortress church, it was extensively altered in the 1700s in the baroque style, although the vast silver altarpiece in the north transept dates from the mid-16th century. The two-story cloisters are more appealing than the cathedral itself; the solid granite lines are enlivened with beautiful tiles, and there are good views over the town. A museum in the treasury houses archeological finds from pre-Roman to Gothic times, plus liturgical objects from the 15th to 19th centuries.

VILA NOVA DE GAIA

⊞ C1   ✉ Vila Nova de Gaia   🕐 Most lodges open Mon.–Fri. 10–noon and 2–6 (also Sat. in summer)
🍴 Porto Ibérico, see page 565   🚌 57, 91
Officially a separate municipality, Vila Nova de Gaia lies across the Douro river from Porto itself. Its name is synonymous with port, for until 1987 all port had to be matured here to be so named. The riverside slopes are dominated by the solid granite buildings of the port warehouses, or lodges. There are many oportunities for free tours and tastings. This is *the* place to buy port; the white aperitif variety – subtly sweet yet dry – is hard to find overseas. The huge complex high above the river is the old monastery of Serra do Pilar, now a military installation and closed to the public.

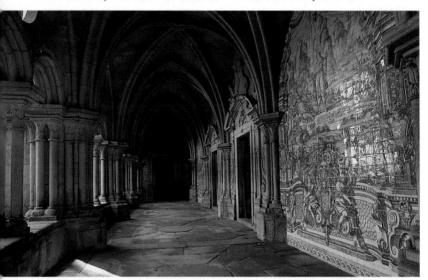

The cathedral cloisters are beautifully lined with 18th-century *azulejos* (glazed ceramic tiles). This form of tile is Arabic in origin, but the large designs of blue-on-white tiles are characteristically Portuguese

PORT WINE

Port is drunk all over the world, as an aperitif and a digestive aid. In the 18th century, its production area was the world's first demarcated wine zone, helping to make port one of the few wines with a flavor that has remained untouched for centuries. Be sure to try it in Porto, a city more associated with port than any other.

No longer used commercially to transport barrels of port along the Douro valley, *barcos rabelos* (flat-bottomed boats) now decorate the waterfront

The Wine

Port is a fortified wine, which means that brandy is added to the grapes during the production process. This both "fortifies" the wine, making it stronger, and halts the fermentation process, leaving half the natural grape sugar in the wine. These two factors give port its strength, sweetness and smoothness; its complex flavors come from the soil and climate where the grapes are grown.

To people accustomed to the lush vineyards of other countries, those in the upper Douro valley, which produce port, are a revelation. It's a stony, barren area, a micro-climatic zone where temperatures reach extremes of heat and cold. The soil is a thin layer on top of schist, and the vine roots must force their way through the rock as much as 20 feet to find water. The Portuguese insist, probably rightly, that these conditions are what gives port its unique character.

The vineyards grow on steep terraces, so much of the harvest is done by hand, and until recently the grapes were still trodden by foot. Today more than 90 percent are crushed and fermented at a controlled temperature, sometime between mid-September and mid-October. The new wine is stored

up-river to clear until the following spring. In March it's ready for transportation. Following strict tradition, until 1987 it could not be called port unless the maturation had taken place in Vila Nova de Gaia, across the Douro from Porto. Now it can mature on site, although much is still stored and bottled down-river.

Drinking Port

Port comes in several varieties: white, a semi-sweet light wine; ruby, a clear, intense red; tawny, which is older and more complex; and late bottled vintage and vintage port. Vintage port is aged in the bottle and comes from grapes from a single year; late bottled is matured for up to four years before further maturing after bottling. White port is delicious chilled before a meal; ruby goes down well with a cup of coffee after lunch or in the early evening. Tawny and vintage port are best after dinner, savored slowly to appreciate the depth of flavor.

SPAIN

"*MEN have no idea of time in any country that is or has been connected with Spain.*"

From *The West Indies and the Spanish Main* by English novelist Anthony Trollope

Opposite: Exploring the enchanting streets of the Barrio de Santa Cruz, Seville

Spain

Spain

Spain is a country of diverse landscapes, climates, peoples and cultures, forged over the centuries into a political unity. Physically separated from the rest of Europe by the Pyrenees mountain chain, Spain also found itself isolated internationally during General Francisco Franco's dictatorship (1939–75). Since Franco's death, however, and with the restoration of its monarchy, Spain has

Spain

regained its place politically, economically and culturally within mainstream Europe. But despite the rate of progress, many aspects of life remain untouched, and Spain still retains much of its traditional character.

Spain Today

Spain's long and checkered history peaked in the Golden Age of the 16th century, when it was one of the most influential nations of the world. It had immense power across Europe and possessed many overseas colonies. The following centuries saw a gradual decline and increasing isolation from the rest of Europe, culminating in the bitter Civil War (1936–39) and Franco's long dictatorship.

In Spain today, political, cultural and artistic life flourishes, along with national confidence. In 1992 Madrid was chosen as the Cultural Capital of Europe, the same year that dynamic Barcelona hosted the Olympic Games and Seville the World Fair.

From Pyrenees to Portugal

One of Europe's most mountainous countries, Spain occupies most of the Iberian peninsula, stretching southwest from the Pyrenees. Much of the land area is covered by the Meseta, a huge plateau surrounded by long mountain ranges. These stretch from the Sierra Nevada in the south to the Cordillera Cantábrica in the north, and give Spain an average altitude of 2,100 feet. The highest mainland peak is 11,424-foot Mulhacen in the Sierra Nevada, although Mount Teide on the island of Tenerife is nearly 1,000 feet higher.

MORE TOP DESTINATIONS IN SPAIN

● Burgos C4 ● Córdoba B2 ● Costa Brava E4 ● Costa de la Luz A1
● Costa Verde B4 ● Granada C1
● León B4 ● Monestir de Poblet E3
● Pamplona D4 ● Parque Nacional de los Picos de Europa B4
● Peñíscola D3 ● Ronda B1
● Salamanca B3 ● Segovia C3 ● Sierra de Montserrat E3 ● Zaragoza D3

D

Africa. Such diversity is echoed in
Spain's climate, which varies from the
mild, wet weather of the northern
Atlantic coast to the typical
Mediterranean hot, dry summers and
mild, wet winters in the south. Winter
inland can be very cold. The island
groups of the Balearics and the
Canaries have their own geographical
and climatic characteristics.

Diversities of Spain

Regional differences are reflected in the
Spanish people, their looks, their
character, their attitudes and above all,
their cuisine. The 800 years of Moorish
occupation, the eventual unification of
a number of small kingdoms, and the
power and wealth of 16th-century
colonial Spain have all played their
part in the evolution of diverse
provincial characteristics.

The concept of centralized power is
alien to many Spaniards, and regionalism
is still strong in Spain. It has its base in
the peninsula's linguistic groups:
Galician, spoken in the northwest;
Basque, another northern language;
Castilian, or pure, central Spanish; and
Catalan, based in the northeast, with
Valencian a variation of this. These
different languages are still spoken daily.

In 1977, when the present
constitution was established, various
regional groups were provided for
through the establishment of 17
autonomous governments. The Basque
Country and Catalonia are the two
regions in Spain having the most
autonomy, although Basque extremists
have pushed for independence.

Spanish Characters

There are physical differences between
Spaniards from different parts of the
peninsula. With a population of 40
million, there's room for diversity;
contrary to popular belief, not all

Originally from southern Spain, flamenco music is
now heard all over the country

The mild, moist Atlantic coast of
the Costa Verde in the north contrasts
with the sun-baked Mediterranean
beaches of the southern Costa del Sol.
The grandeur of the Pyrenees is more
than rivaled by the dramatic peaks of
the Asturian mountains on Spain's
northern coast, probably the most
beautiful region in Spain. East of
Asturia the Ebro valley slashes
southeast toward the Mediterranean,
where it bisects the coastal plain
southwest of Barcelona.

The fertile gardens of Murcia and
the agricultural flatlands of the
Guadalquivir yield harvests rivaled
only by the tourist crop drawn from
the golden sands of the Mediterranean
beaches. The Mediterranean coast
ends on the northern shore of the
Straits of Gibraltar, only 9 miles from

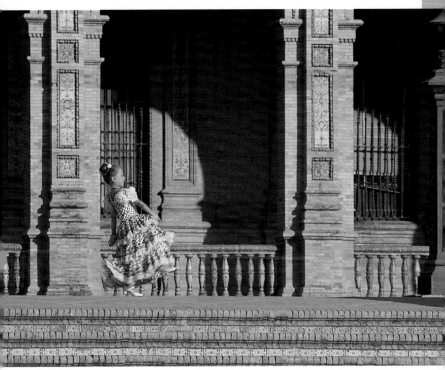

Exuberant, spontaneous and passionate – dancing the flamenco outside the Plaza de España, Seville

Spaniards are dark-eyed and olive-skinned. The Moorish genetic legacy is strongest in Andalucia, where many are delicate-featured and dark, personifying the Spanish stereotype.

Spaniards are sometimes thought of as an exuberant, passionate and light-hearted people, much like the Italians, but nothing could be further from the truth. They are certainly passionate, but there's a strong streak of self-control and melancholy in the national character. History has given them loyalty and tolerance. Kindness to children and respect for the elderly are the norm. You will find a tendency to delay until tomorrow (*mañana*) anything that can wait.

Young Spaniards enjoy a freedom and lifestyle their grandparents could never have imagined, yet society is still in a state of flux, and there are huge contrasts between different regions, towns and rural areas. But wherever you go you'll find the same level of hospitality and friendliness, particularly if you speak a little Spanish. English is widely spoken along the Mediterranean coast and by hotel staff in big cities, but very rarely elsewhere.

Cities, Towns and Villages

For visitors the three great cities are Madrid, Barcelona and Seville, but in Spanish eyes the industrial centers of Zaragoza and Bilbao are of equal importance, and the inhabitants of each region claim their capital as the most beautiful in Spain. Andalucia, with the architectural treasures of Granada and Córdoba, is rich in Moorish history. The region of Castille has Christian castles built during the struggle to oust the Moors.

Spain

The Mediterranean coast has many remains from centuries of Roman occupation, while the Atlantic port of Cádiz boasts 2,000 years of maritime history. Rural Spain continues largely unchanged; agriculture is more mechanized, but the way and pace of life are still deeply rooted in the past.

Spanish Lifestyle

Daily life in Spain differs in one major way from other southern European countries; mealtimes are very late. Breakfast in hotels is served from around 7:30 until 9:30 or 10. Most Spaniards rise early and eat very little first thing, so they are ready for a snack around 11. This delays lunch until 2 at the earliest, and therefore dinner is often around 10:30 p.m. or later.

An early start means you can take advantage of the cool mornings, vital in a country where air-conditioning is not universal. Virtually everything – stores, offices, churches and museums – closes from 1:30 until 5, and most people sleep after lunch for a couple of hours, during the fabled siesta.

This bypasses the worst heat and leaves people ready to stay up late and enjoy the comparatively fresh evening air. It's a pleasure to sit at a café or restaurant table until 1 or 2 in the morning, as long as you've had a midday rest.

You'll find that most entertainment begins very late, around 10 p.m., and clubs don't get going until the early hours of the morning. Along the Mediterranean coast things are more geared toward foreigners, and you should be able to have dinner soon after 8:30 p.m.

Spain is a deeply Catholic country. When you visit churches, cover the tops of your arms and shoulders and avoid wearing shorts. The many local fiestas held in every town and village are always in honor of the Virgin or some favorite local saint, and if you get the chance to watch one, you will see how religion plays an integral part in everyday life.

Traveling in Spain

The economic boom of the last two decades has resulted in a sound infrastructure. Spain has an excellent network of well-signed toll roads and highways. Spaniards drive fast but safely, and you should have no problems if you rent a car. Public transportation is good, with a choice of internal flights, inexpensive and punctual trains, and long-distance buses going to even the most remote corners.

Hotels are graded and inspected by the government, so you are guaranteed a clean and adequate room no matter how little you pay. Try to spend at least a few nights at one of the *paradores*. These are state-owned hotels housed in historic buildings such as castles and monasteries, often furnished with antiques and offering a high standard of comfort and service.

Spanish Passions

Spaniards throw themselves wholeheartedly into eating out, shopping, going to a soccer match or spending a day on the beach. Their most famous and controversial passion is bullfighting (see page 429), but soccer has more supporters. Huge crowds follow the fortunes of teams such as Real Madrid and Barcelona.

Spain has some of Europe's finest golf courses, chiefly along the Mediterranean coast, where you'll also find excellent marinas and water-sports facilities, as well as untouched wilderness areas. Young people travel from all over Europe to experience Spain's club scene, at its most frenetic on the Balearic island of Ibiza.

The Moorish legacy of color and decoration is boldly kept alive in Alicante

Spain

TIMELINE

15,000–12,000 BC Caves at Altamira painted; earliest sign of habitation.

218–210 BC Rome begins conquest of Iberian peninsula.

AD 411 Visigoths invade and establish powerful kingdom at Toledo.

711 Moors defeat Visigoths and begin period of occupation.

1478–79 Spanish Inquisition against Jews, Moors and Protestants.

1492 Christopher Columbus discovers New World.

1519 Spanish conquistadores move across America.

1588 Spanish Armada is sent against Protestant England; fleet destroyed and maritime pre-eminence lost.

1808–14 Peninsular War (War of Independence) sees expulsion of French and defeat of Napoleon.

1898 Philippines and Cuba rebel against Spanish rule; the United States occupies Puerto Rico; end of Spanish Empire.

1914–18 Spain remains neutral in World War I.

1936–39 Spanish Civil War; General Francisco Franco leads Nationalist troops from Morocco against Republicans.

1939 Franco becomes head of state; Spain enters period of isolation and remains neutral throughout World War II.

1955 Spain joins United Nations.

1975 Death of Franco; Juan Carlos becomes king.

1986 Spain joins the European Union.

1992 Barcelona hosts Olympic Games; Madrid declared Cultural Capital of Europe; Seville is the venue for Expo 92.

THE MOORISH OCCUPATION

In AD 711 a faction of the ruling Visigoth tribe in Spain went to Islamic Africa to seek help with some domestic political problems. They returned with an army of 7,000; after victory at Cádiz, the Moors encountered little resistance in taking over all but a small strip of northern Spain over the next 30 years. Their tactics were a blend of intelligent strategy and diplomacy; they never demanded religious subordination, as long as Christians paid taxes. Beginning in AD 744, however, resistance against the invaders spread south from the small, unoccupied northern territory, fueled by the legend of St. James the Moorslayer. El Cid succeeded in capturing Toledo from the Moors in 1085, and despite some setbacks a coalition of Christian armies was finally victorious at the Battle of Navas de Tolosa in 1212, the last great battle between Moors and Christians. The Moorish occupation left important legacies, however – they brought mathematics, papermaking, oranges, spices and rice to Spain, which were then introduced to the rest of Europe.

SURVIVAL GUIDE

- English is not widely spoken, even in large cities. Keep in mind that the Spanish you may have learned in high school differs in accent, pronounciation and some vocabulary from that spoken in Spain.
- It's best not to discuss politics, since Spaniards are very proud and the subject could be sensitive.
- Beachwear, shorts and revealing necklines are not acceptable away from coastal resorts.
- Public restrooms are few except in museums, but it's acceptable to use the facilities in a bar; leave a small tip on the counter or stop and have a cup of coffee while you're there.
- Inebriation is frowned on in Spain; the Spanish drink alcohol every day, but in moderation.
- The Spanish are formal and polite; it is best to ask, in Spanish, if the person you're addressing speaks English before you start to speak, and shake hands at the end of casual conversations.
- Water is precious in many parts of Spain; you may find that hotel bathrooms have a shower rather than a tub. Shower pressure is generally low.
- You can safely drink the water throughout Spain, although you may prefer to drink bottled mineral water, which is inexpensive and served chilled. Ice is not generally served in drinks unless you ask.
- Throughout Spain, especially along the Mediterranean, bars specialize in *tapas*, delicious selections of hot or cold savory mouthfuls served with drinks. Be sure to try some of

Colorful flower market in La Rambla, Barcelona

the dozens available: fish, smoked ham, stewed peppers, salads, local almonds, olives. Two or three little dishes will make a delicious lunch.
- All large cities have malls, usually away from the town center; downtown department stores; and a range of antiques stores, designer boutiques, local craft and souvenir shops, gourmet food stores, and clothing and bric-a-brac markets.
- Prices in Spain are comparable to the rest of Europe; meals are a little cheaper.
- Try to arrange your trip so that it coincides with a major local festival. Spain has some of the most colorful and exotic celebrations in Europe.

Profile of a bullfighter – the *matador*

Madrid

MADRID

Unlike most European capital cities, Madrid did not evolve as the nation's capital. It was chosen. In 1561, Philip II settled the court permanently in Madrid, as much for its position in the center of Spain as for political reasons.

Today Madrid is noisy, vibrant and chaotic – a city of great wealth and grueling poverty, but one with a booming economy.

Like so much of Spain, Madrid's spirit is elusive and diffused, and will surprise you repeatedly. Plan to stay in the city center, so you can easily reach your hotel in the middle of the day,

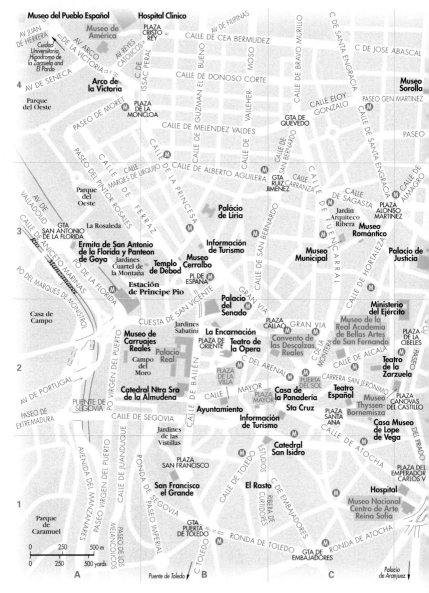

Madrid

when many museums and monuments are closed for the siesta. The best way to tackle sightseeing is to concentrate on one section at a time. There are three historical areas of interest in the vicinity of the city's main plaza, Sun's Gate (Puerta del Sol) – Old Madrid (Viejo Madrid), centering on the Plaza Mayor; the Eastern Quarter (Barrio de Oriente), by the Palacio Real; and Bourbon Madrid, the heart of which is the sweeping avenues and sparkling fountains around the Prado Museum.

A convenient tourist bus, Madrid Vision (☎ 91 779 1888), links all three, allowing passengers to get on and off when they want to. Tickets are valid for one or two days, and there's English commentary. The city also has an efficient subway system. Plan your day in advance and also take along a good English-Spanish dictionary, because English is not widely spoken here.

Dining Out

Eating is a real pleasure in Madrid, and there is much to choose from. Local specialties such as offal, blood sausage and pig's ear are usually unpopular with visitors, but there are many regional restaurants featuring traditional dishes from all over Spain. The cuisine of the Basque country and Galicia is particularly good, or you could try a Latin-American restaurant, where even the meat is imported from Argentina. Fast-food outlets are everywhere; take your pick of hamburgers, tortillas or even paella to go.

By law, all restaurants have to offer a fixed-price lunch menu from Monday to Friday, , which is usually good value and includes a choice of first and second courses, a dessert and drink. Madrid has innumerable bars, where you'll find everything from tea and coffee to beer, champagne and exotic cocktails. In summer, bar life moves onto the sidewalks, with hundreds of outdoor venues (*terrazas)* crowded until 4 or 5 in the morning.

Malls and Markets

The central department stores, such as the nationwide chain El Corte Inglés, are clustered in the commercial area around the Puerta del Sol. If you're looking for

MADRID

Museo de Ciencas Naturales
PLAZA DOCTOR MARAÑON
CALLE DE MARIA DE MOLINA
CALLE SERRANO
CALLE DE VELAZQUEZ
CALLE DE FRANCISCO SILVELA
AV DE AMERICA
PLAZA MIGUEL ANGEL
GTA DE EMILIO CASTELAR
CAMPOS
Museo Lázaro Galdiano
CALLE DE
CALLE DE
CALLE DIEGO DE LEON
EDUARDO DATO
CALLE DE JUAN BRAVO
CALLE DE LA CASTELLANA
PASEO DE LA CASTELLANA
CALLE DE JOSE
SALAMANCA
ORTEGA Y GASSET
CALLE DE VELAZQUEZ
CALLE
DE
CALLE DE PRINCIPE DE VERGARA
AYALA
Plaza Monumental de Toros de las Ventas
PL DE COLON
Museo de Cera
CALLE DE SERRANO
CALLE DE GOYA
CALLE DE VELAZQUEZ
CALLE DE NARVAEZ
Biblioteca Nacional
RECUETOS
Museo Arqueológico Nacional
CALLE DE ALCALA
CALLE DE O'DONNELL
Puerta de Alcalá
PLAZA DE LA INDEPENDENCIA
Museo Naval
Museo Nacional de Artes Decorativas
Estanque
AVENIDA DE MENENDEZ Y PELAYO
CALLE
C DE IBIZA
Parque
del
Museo del Ejército
Retiro
C DEL ALCALDE
Casón del Buen Retiro
Iglesia de los Jerónimos
Palacio de Velázquez
Hospital del Niño Jesus
Museo del Prado
CALLE DE ALFONSO
Palacio de Cristal
PASEO DEL URUGUAY
Jardin Botánico
PASEO DEL DUQUE DE FERNAN NUÑEZ
AV DE MENENDEZ PELAYO
Museo Etnológico
AV DE LA
Observatorio Astronómico
XII
Inst Ramon y Cajal
AV DEL MEDITERRANEO
Estación de Atocha
CIUDAD DE BARCELONA
PASEO REINA CRISTINA
Real Fabrica de Tapices
C DE MENDEZ
D
E

malls, the large Vaguada is in northern Madrid; the ABC Serrano, between Serrano and Castellana in the center of Madrid, is smaller and more upscale. The smartest shopping area is the Salamanca district around the streets of Calle de Serrano and Goya, where you'll find a range of expensive stores. Madrid is a good place to find Spanish souvenirs, and there are many antiques stores; the Salamanca district alone has more than 50. Visit the Rastro flea market on a Saturday or Sunday morning and browse in some of the tiny boutiques.

Evening Entertainment

Classical music, opera and theater thrive in Madrid, and the tourist office publishes a monthly guide, *Qué hacer en Madrid*, with excellent listings. You might enjoy a *zarzuela* performance, a traditional form of musical combining elements of opera, vaudeville and melodrama. Jazz is very popular, with nightly performances at some of Europe's best venues. If you're looking for flamenco, there are several clubs (*tablaos*) where it is staged. Madrid has an exceptional nightclub scene. A number of movie theaters show movies in their original language.

Late, Late Nights

People eat late and go to bed late all over Spain, especially in the capital. Locals do not eat dinner much before 10 or 11 at night, even in winter; in summer the "night" is still young at 3:30 in the morning. In recent years the siesta has become threatened, as Spanish business practices come in line with the rest of Europe. One result of this is that *Madrileños* are functioning on less and less sleep – a fact beginning to worry Spanish health watchdogs.

ESSENTIAL INFORMATION

TOURIST INFORMATION
Oficinas de Información Turística de la Comunidad de Madrid (Madrid Community Tourist Information Offices)
• Calle Duque de Medinaceli 2 ☎ 91 429 4951; fax 91 429 3705
• Plaza Mayor 3 ☎ 91 588 1636
• Mercado Puerta de Toledo (market), Glorieta Puerta de Toledo ☎ 91 364 1876
• Aeropuerto de Madrid-Barajas (airport), international arrivals terminal ☎ and fax 91 305 8656
• Estación de Chamartín (railroad station), central hall (gate 16) ☎ and fax 91 315 9976; www.munimadrid.es; www.comadrid.es/turismo

URBAN TRANSPORTATION
Getting around Madrid is simple on the subway (metro) and bus systems. Subway stations are marked on the Madrid city map as the letter "M" on a blue background inside a red diamond. The subway has 11 lines and runs daily

6 a.m.–1:30 a.m. Purchase tickets from machines or ticket offices in the stations. The Metrobus ticket, valid for 10 trips on the subway and bus systems, is available from metro stations, tobacconists (*estancos*) and Municipal Transport Company (EMT) booths at some bus stops. Buses run daily 6 a.m.–midnight, with a limited all-night service. Pay the driver or stamp your pass in the machine when you board. Taxis are cheap and can be hailed on the street. To call a taxi dial Tele-Taxi (☎ 91 371 2131).

AIRPORT INFORMATION
Madrid's Barajas Airport (☎ 90 235 3570) is 8 miles northeast of the city center, about a 30-minute drive. Buses run every 12 minutes into Madrid, where they terminate beneath the Plaza de Colón, near to the subway station of the same name. There is a subway (metro) line from the airport to Nuevos Ministerios (metro station of the same name).

CLIMATE – average highs and lows for the month

JAN.	FEB.	MAR.	APR.	MAY	JUN.	JUL.	AUG.	SEP.	OCT.	NOV.	DEC.
9°C	12°C	15°C	18°C	21°C	27°C	32°C	31°C	26°C	19°C	13°C	10°C
48°F	54°F	59°F	64°F	70°F	81°F	90°F	88°F	79°F	66°F	55°F	50°F
1°C	2°C	4°C	6°C	9°C	14°C	17°C	17°C	13°C	9°C	4°C	2°C
34°F	36°F	39°F	43°F	48°F	57°F	63°F	63°F	55°F	48°F	39°F	36°F

CITY SIGHTS

Key to symbols

✚ map coordinates refer to the Madrid map on pages 402–403; sights below are highlighted in yellow on the map.

✉ address or location ☎ telephone number
🕐 opening times Ⓜ nearest subway 🍴 restaurant or café on site or nearby 🎟 admission charge: $$$ more than €6, $$ €3–€6, $ less than €3 ℹ other relevant information

CONVENTO DE LAS DESCALZAS REALES

✚ C2 ✉ Plaza de las Descalzas Reales 3 ☎ 91 454 8800 🕐 Tue.–Sat. 10:30–12:45 (also Tue.–Thu. and Sat. 4–5:45), Sun. and holidays 11–1:45 Ⓜ Sol, Callao or Opera 🎟 $$

The oddly named Convento de las Descalzas Reales (Convent of the Royal Barefoot Nuns) was founded in 1560 as a convent for aristocratic ladies seeking the religious life. They and their families endowed and decorated 33 chapels with treasures by mainly Spanish artists.

IGLESIA DE LOS JERÓNIMOS

✚ D2 ✉ Calle Moreto 4 ☎ 91 420 3078
🕐 Mon.–Sat. 10–1 and 5–8:30, Sun. and holidays 9:30–2:30 and 5:30–8:30 Ⓜ Atocha

Iglesia de los Jerónimos (St. Jerome's Church) is the royal church where princes were consecrated and monarchs married until King Alfonso XIII married Queen Victoria in 1878. Rebuilt in 1505 by King Ferdinand for his queen, Isabella, this simple Gothic church is far less flamboyant than many other churches in the country.

MUSEO DE AMÉRICA

✚ A4 ✉ Avenida Reyes Católicos 6 ☎ 91 549 2641 🕐 Mon.–Sat. 9:30–3, Sun. 10–3; closed Mon., Jan.–May Ⓜ Moncloa or Islas Filipinas 🎟 $$

The Museo de América (America Museum), an archeological and ethnological museum, is devoted to pre-Columbian and Hispanic artifacts telling the story of European ties with America. The information is in Spanish, but anyone can appreciate the powerful Quimbayas Treasure and the collection's high point, the Cortesiano Codex, which

An allegorical statue outside the America Museum

records in Mayan runes the arrival of the Spaniards in the New World.

MUSEO NACIONAL CENTRO DE ARTE REINA SOFÍA

✚ D1 ✉ Calle Santa Isabel 52 ☎ 91 467 5062
🕐 Mon. and Wed.–Sat. 10–9, Sun. 10–2:30 🍴 Café
Ⓜ Atocha 🎟 $$ (senior citizens and under 18 free; free to all Sat. after 2:30 p.m. and Sun.)

The Museo Nacional Centro de Arte Reina Sofía (Queen Sofía National Art Center),

Golden altar inside the Descalzas Convent

The Royal Palace viewed from the Campo del Moro

Olivareo by Velázquez, in the Prado

the city's modern art museum, is housed in the former Hospital de San Carlos. Exterior glass elevators whisk you up to the permanent exhibitions. Visitors flock to Pablo Picasso's *Guernica*. When it was commissioned for the 1937 World Fair, his only instruction was to paint a big picture; this black-and-white composition has become the icon of 20th-century antiwar symbolism. Other highlights include paintings by Salvador Dalí and Joan Miró.

MUSEO DEL PRADO

✚ D2 ✉ Paseo del Prado ☎ 91 330 2800 🕐 Tue.–Sat. 9–7, Sun. 9–2 🍴 Café in museum 🚇 Banco de España or Atocha 🎫 $$ (free to all on Sun.)

Since its opening in 1819 the Museo del Prado (Prado Museum), with its unrivaled

collection of Spanish paintings, has been among the world's finest. Once the royal collection, the Prado represents the personal taste of the Spanish monarchs, with a noticeable emphasis on religious and courtly paintings. Because of space limitations only about 1,500 of the 7,000 works are on display. Paintings are frequently moved around or loaned to other museums, but the most famous are normally on view; get an up-to-date floor plan as you arrive. Some works, particularly those by Diego Velázquez and Francisco Goya, attract huge crowds.

Highlights include Velázquez' *Las Meninas*, often described as "the finest painting in the world." Goya's work occupies many rooms; look for his *Majas*, two paintings thought to be of the Duchess of Alba, one demure and clothed, the other sensuously naked. His *pinturas negras*, the dark pictures, stand in stark contrast; disturbing and pessimistic, they represent the apocalyptic vision of a man on the edge of madness. The Spanish monarchs were fascinated by the surreal work of Hiëronymous Bosch; his *Garden of Earthly Delights*, with its wealth of weird detail, is one of his finest works.

MUSEO DE LA REAL ACADEMIA DE BELLAS ARTES DE SAN FERNANDO

✚ C2 ✉ Calle Alcalá 13 ☎ 91 524 0864 🕐 Tue.–Fri. 9–7, Sat.–Mon. 9–2:30 🚇 Sol or Sevilla 🎫 $ (senior citizens and under 18 free; free to all on Wed.)

Art lovers will enjoy the peaceful Real Academia de Bellas Artes de San Fernando

Madrid's Plaza Mayor, constructed in the early 17th century and still a focus for social activities

(Royal Academy of Fine Arts), founded in the 18th century to emulate art venues in Paris and London. The academy has some fine paintings by Francisco Goya and a good Diego Velázquez portrait of Philip IV. The highlight is *Spring* by Italian artist Giuseppe Arcimboldo, a portrait in which the sitter's features are entirely composed of fruit and vegetables.

MUSEO THYSSEN-BORNEMISZA

➕ C2–D2 ✉ Paseo del Prado 8 ☎ 91 420 3944
🕐 Tue.–Sun. 10–7 🍴 Café and restaurant in museum 🚇 Banco de España 💶 $$
Acquired in 1993 for about $350 million, the art collection of the Museo Thyssen-Bornemisza (Thyssen-Bornemisza Museum) includes much of the best of Western art produced throughout the last 800 years. It contains more than 700 works, all acquired since the 1920s by Baron Heinrich and his son, Baron Hans-Heinrich Thyssen-Bornemisza.

Western paintings from the 13th to 20th centuries are arranged chronologically, so start on the top floor and work down. Early portraits and Renaissance works are grouped together, followed by Dutch interiors. Nineteenth-century American paintings feature a portrait of George Washington's cook by Gilbert Stuart and a sea scene by Winslow Homer. The 20th century is well represented by Joan Miró, Salvador Dalí and Mark Rothko, and German expressionists on view include Edvard Munch and Otto Kirchner.

PALACIO REAL

➕ B2 ✉ Calle Bailén ☎ 91 454 8800
🕐 Mon.–Sat. 9–6, Sun. 9–3, Apr.–Sep.; Mon.–Sat. 9–5, Sun. 9–2, rest of year. Closed when official events are held 🚇 Opera 💶 $$$
The vast white bulk of the Palacio Real (Royal Palace) looks particularly striking from the Campo del Moro, a peaceful garden behind the palace where you'll also find the Museo de Carruajes Reales (Royal Carriage Museum). After a fire destroyed the Moorish original, the palace was planned to be three times its existing size. Funds ran out, and the present structure was finally completed in 1764. In use until 1931, it is now occasionally used for state receptions. Everything is opulent and awesomely large. Madrid's 1993 Cathedral of the Almudena stands nearby; the Plaza de Oriente is a pleasant square across the road.

PARQUE DEL RETIRO

➕ D2 ✉ Main entrance: Plaza de la Independencia
🕐 Daily dawn–midnight 🚇 Retiro, Ibiza 💶 Free
The Parque del Retiro (Retreat Park) was laid out in the 1630s as part of the French-style pleasure gardens surrounding the Buen Retiro Palace. The building itself was destroyed during the Napoleonic Wars. Today the park is bright with flowers and scattered with statues and fountains. Many people head for the lake, with its ornate statue of Alfonso XII, but other attractions include the Palacio de Cristal (Crystal Palace), a 19th-century glass palace.

The Alcalá Gate – Madrid's finest example of neoclassic architecture

PLAZA MAYOR

➕ B2 ✉ Plaza Mayor 🚇 Sol

One of Europe's most dazzling squares, the present Plaza Mayor (Main Square) stands on the site of the medieval market, the Plaza del Arrabal. When Madrid became Spain's capital, Philip III ordered it to be rebuilt as the focal point, and it was completed in 1620. Harmonious brick facades are punctuated with elegant stonework and arcades. The plaza was used for fiestas, bullfights and royal proclamations, and was the scene of many executions during the later days of the Inquisition.

PLAZA MONUMENTAL DE TOROS DE LAS VENTAS

➕ E3 ✉ Alcalá, 237 Plata de las Ventas ☎ 91 356 2200 (Museo Taurino: 91 725 1857) 🕐 Museo Taurino: Tue.–Fri. 9:30–2:30, Sun. 10–1 🚇 Ventas 🎟 Museum free; tickets for fights $$$

Madrid's Plaza Monumental de Toros de las Ventas (Las Ventas Bullring) was opened in 1934, and for aficionados is the most important bullring in the world. The Museo Taurino (Bullfight Museum), devoted to some of bullfighting's famous names, features the "suit of lights" worn by Manolete during his fateful fight in 1947.

PLAZA DE LA VILLA

➕ B2 ✉ Plaza de la Villa 🕐 Buildings: Guided tour Mon. at 5 🚇 Sol or Opera

Despite their different dates, the three main stone buildings around this little plaza (Town Square) coexist harmoniously. The Gothic Torre de los Lujanes (Lujanes Tower), one of Madrid's few surviving 15th-century structures, is balanced by the Casa de Cisneros, a restored 1537 Plateresque-style palace. The Casa del Ayuntamiento was designed as the meeting place for the town council in 1640, a function it still serves today.

PUERTA DE ALCALÁ

➕ D2 ✉ Plaza de la Independencia 🚇 Retiro

Surrounded by roaring traffic, the Puerta de Alcalá (Alcalá Gate) is a symbol of Madrid, along with the equally splendid Plaza de la Cibeles, a street away. Designed in 1778 as the main entrance to the Spanish court, it's a gateway on a monumental scale, with five grandiose arches topped by lion heads, cherubim and coats of arms.

PUERTA DEL SOL

➕ C2 ✉ Puerta del Sol 🚇 Sol

Puerta del Sol (Sun's Gate) has been a plaza since 1570, when the original gate was demolished. This is the heart of Madrid. The headquarters of the regional government are housed on the south side, where a stone in the sidewalk marks Kilometer Zero, from which all distances in Spain are measured.

MONASTERIO DE EL ESCORIAL

Twenty-five miles northwest of Madrid, on the southern slopes of the Sierra da Guadarrama mountain range, stands the massive religious complex known as El Escorial. One of the most impressive monuments in Spain, it's easily accessible from Madrid and gives true insight into the extraordinary wealth and power of the 16th-century Spanish monarchy.

Harmonious facade of the Monastery of El Escorial

The Story of El Escorial

In 1557 the Spanish forces of Philip II defeated the French at St. Quentin. To give thanks to God, Philip conceived the idea of building a monastery dedicated to St. Lawrence (San Lorenzo), which would also serve as a royal palace and burial place.

The vast complex was principally designed in 1584 by Juan de Herrera, and it required 1,500 laborers to complete the work. It has more than 1,200 doors, 2,600 windows and 16 courtyards, and measures nearly 670 feet long. The granite stone accentuates the severe lines of the building, which is built on a grid plan, and the clear air has kept the stone and tiles pristine. Later Bourbon monarchs also left their stamp on the palace by means of decoration, furnishings and pictures.

El Escorial Today

Philip II's modest private apartments are in marked contrast to his grand throne room. He lived in a suite of relatively small rooms with direct access to the chapel.

Later Bourbon monarchs extended these royal Habsburg apartments near the church to the third floor. You will find sumptuously painted ceilings, frescoes and a wonderful tapestry collection. A frescoed courtyard gives access to the marbled staircase leading down to the Royal Pantheon (Pantéon de los Reyes), where many Spanish kings from the time of Charles V onward are buried.

The church itself, in the heart of the monastery, is on a monumental scale. Its 100-foot-high altarpiece with onyx, marble and jasper columns is punctuated by bronze sculptures. Move on to the equally opulent library, with its rare wood shelves, marble tables and ornate ceiling.

One of the highlights is the art museum. Among numerous paintings by Peter Paul Rubens, Titian and Jacopo Tintoretto are Rogíer van der Weyden's thought-provoking *Calvary* and the acidic angularity of El Greco's *Martyrdom of St. Maurice*.

🕀 C3 ✉ El Escorial ☎ 91 890 5902 🕓 Tue.–Sun. 10–6, Apr.–Sep.; 10–5, rest of year 🚆 Trains from Atocha and Chamartín (☎ 91 328 9020) 🚌 Autobuses Herranz (☎ 91 890 4122); buses leave from the terminus at Moncloa subway station in Madrid 🎟 $$$

BARCELONA

Barcelona, the capital of the autonomous Spanish region of Catalonia (Catalunya), is one of the Mediterranean's most vibrant cities. Catalonia is Spain's leading economic region, the most innovative and prosperous area of the country, with a proud history, an independent spirit and a strong sense of identity.

In 1975 King Juan Carlos restored Catalonia's status as an autonomous region, which marked the beginning of Barcelona's renaissance. The pride and self-confidence engendered by a thriving economy and urban renewal culminated in the Barcelona Olympic Games of 1992. Since then, the city has continued to forge ahead. With its 2,000-year-old history, exhilarating atmosphere and superb architecture from nearly every age, it can't fail to please.

The City and Its People

Wherever you stay, the excellent public transportation system gives easy access to the entire city. For atmosphere, you might want to be somewhere near the street La Rambla or in the old town, and thus within easy walking distance of many of the main sights and the waterfront. The architecturally interesting Eixample area is more spacious, with excellent shopping and restaurants; other hotels are relatively far out of the city center. Barcelonans are exceptionally helpful and polite, with an ability to combine efficiency with a relaxed Mediterranean attitude.

English is not widely spoken, although most hotel staff speak it adequately. All signs are in Catalan and Spanish. Both are official languages in Barcelona; like Spanish, Catalan is a romance language with Latin roots.

Barcelonan Themes

Since there's so much to see in Barcelona, concentrate on specific areas and themes. Spend a day on the waterfront taking in the Old Port district, Little Barcelona and the ultra-modern Olympic Port. There's a choice of boat tours around the harbor and up the coast, which is the best way to admire the port.

Head for l'Eixample, the Passeig de Gràcia and the Sagrada Família to enjoy the Modernista architecture for which the city is so well known. Barcelona is blessed with two hills, the Montjuïc and Tibidabo; each offers a refuge from the summer noise and heat and has magnificent views over the city and sea.

Barcelona has more than 50 museums and galleries. The Maritime Museum, the Pedralbes Monastery, the Football Museum, the City History Museum and the Comic Book and Illustrations Museum cater to a wide range of interests, and are all fascinating. Modern art lovers shouldn't

Gaudí

Antoni Gaudí was born in Barcelona in 1852, and lived and worked in the city throughout his life. His architectural vision was flamboyant and unique, and he designed some of Barcelona's most outstanding Modernist buildings. Curved lines, pinnacles, organically inspired stone and towers are his trademarks, seen at their best in the remarkable Holy Family Temple (Temple Expiatori de la Sagrada Família). He was run over by a tram in 1926 and died, unrecognized, in a hospital. When his body was identified, the people of Barcelona lined the streets for his funeral.

Barcelona

miss the Contemporary Art Museum and the Modern Art Museum. If time is short, there are plenty of English-language guided tours and excursions that take in the main city sights by day and night, and also offer a chance to explore other parts of Catalonia.

Parks and Pools

Barcelona is rich in parks offering a welcome contrast to the bustle and noise of city streets. The Parc de la Ciutadella, near the Old Town and waterfront, is particularly nice. It has shady trees, a lake and Spain's best zoo, with more than 7,000 animals. Other parks in the city include the Parc Joan

Miró, with its flamboyant ceramic sculpture, and the Parc Espanya Industrial, laid out in the early 1980s. Good beaches are within easy reach, and Barcelona also has excellent swimming pools.

Where to Shop

Prosperous Barcelona is a great shopping center. You'll find serious shopping along the Passeig de Gràcia and on its surrounding streets, which have all the big fashion names, expensive antiques stores and some enticing interior design outlets. The wide avenue of Diagonal is lined with good stores, while the Plaça de

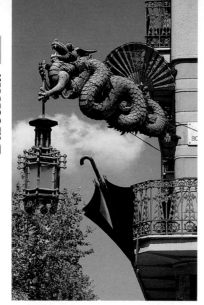

Quirky decoration on a corner of La Rambla

Barcelona

Catalunya has a large branch of the department store El Corte Inglés.

For Spanish souvenirs, porcelain, fans and items made of wood, try the stores on Portal de l'Angel and around La Rambla. Mercat de les Encants is a second-hand market held on the Plaça de les Glòries on Monday, Wednesday, Friday and Saturday (7 to 7).

Nightlife

Classical music, jazz, rock, dance, theater and movies are popular forms of entertainment; there are comprehensive listings in the *Guía del Ocio*, available from newsstands. Dancing is very popular, and the club scene is one of the best in Spain, ranging from the elegant to the avant-garde. As everywhere in the country, nightlife reaches its peak around 3 a.m. and continues until dawn.

Barcelona has some superb festivals throughout the year, often featuring decorated floats, fireworks and processions of the huge dragon and demon figures known as *capgrossos*, or "big heads."

ESSENTIAL INFORMATION

TOURIST INFORMATION
Barcelona Turisme (Barcelona Tourism)
• Plaça de Catalunya 17-S
• Plaça Sant Jaume
• Estació Barcelona-Sants (railroad station)
• Barcelona Airport (arrivals hall)
☎ For all inquiries: 807 117 222 (to call within Spain)
www.barcelonaturisme.com

URBAN TRANSPORTATION
Getting around is easy on the subway and bus systems. Subway stations are marked on the Barcelona city map by the letter "M" in a red circle. There are five color-coded lines on the subway; trains run Mon.–Thu. 5 a.m.–midnight, Fri.– Sat. 5 a.m.– 2 a.m., Sun. 6 a.m.–midnight. Combination tickets valid for 1, 2, 3 or 5 days give unlimited use of the bus, tram, subway and urban trains; tickets and maps are available from subway stations. Don't forget to validate tickets by stamping them at the turnstile before boarding trains, or when you get on the bus or tram. Bus Turístic operates daily 9–7:45 all year and has two routes that cover Barcelona's main attractions, taking you closer to the sights than the regular city service. A cable car links La Barceloneta and Montjuïc, and there are two funiculars, serving Montjuïc and Tibidabo; the latter also is served by tram. You can pick up a black-and-yellow taxi at a stand, hail one on the street, or call Radio Taxi (☎ 93 303 3033).

AIRPORT INFORMATION
Barcelona International Airport (☎ 93 298 3838) connects to most major European cities and is 7 miles southwest of the city center, about a 30-minute drive. A train connects to Estació Barcelona-Sants and Plaça Catalunya, daily 5:38 a.m.–10:11 p.m. (to 11:40 p.m. from the airport); journey time 20 minutes. The Aerobus runs to and from Plaça de Catalunya every 12 minutes daily 5:30 a.m.–midnight. (journey time 30 minutes). The last bus from the airport leaves at midnight.

CLIMATE – average highs and lows for the month

JAN.	FEB.	MAR.	APR.	MAY	JUN.	JUL.	AUG.	SEP.	OCT.	NOV.	DEC.
13°C	14°C	15°C	17°C	21°C	24°C	28°C	28°C	25°C	21°C	17°C	14°C
55°F	57°F	59°F	63°F	70°F	75°F	82°F	82°F	77°F	70°F	63°F	57°F
5°C	6°C	8°C	10°C	12°C	17°C	20°C	20°C	19°C	13°C	9°C	8°C
41°F	43°F	46°F	50°F	54°F	63°F	68°F	68°F	66°F	55°F	48°F	46°F

CITY SIGHTS

Key to symbols

⊞ map coordinates refer to the Barcelona map on page 411; sights below are highlighted in yellow on the map.
✉ address or location ☎ telephone number
🕐 opening times 🚇 nearest subway 🚌 nearest bus or tram route 🍴 restaurant or café on site or nearby 💷 admission charge: $$$ more than €6, $$ €3–€6, $ less than €3 ℹ other relevant information

ANELLA OLÍMPICA

⊞ A1 ✉ Montjuïc ☎ 93 426 2089 🕐 Olympic Stadium: daily 10–8, Jun.–Sep.; 10–6, rest of year. Closed during events 🚇 Espanya 🚌 61, 50 💷 $. Guided tours by arrangement

The 1992 Olympic complex, the Anella Olímpica (Olympic Ring), centers around the Estadi Olímpic (Olympic Stadium), which can seat 70,000 people. Its basement now houses the Olympic Gallery, recalling the 1992 games with videos and souvenirs. Nearby are Barcelona's sports university; the steel-and-glass Sant Jordi Stadium; and the pools, all dominated by the silhouette of the communications tower, one of the city's modern landmarks.

LA BARCELONETA

⊞ C2 ✉ La Barceloneta 🚇 Barceloneta 🚌 14, 17, 51, 64

The district of La Barceloneta (Little Barcelona) occupies a triangle of reclaimed land between the harbor and the sea. Developed in the 18th century to house seamen, fishermen and dock workers, this delightful neighborhood retains its maritime atmosphere. It's a great place to eat; many seafood restaurants (*chiringuitos*) line the seafront, where you'll find local fresh fish specialties.

CATEDRAL

⊞ C2 ✉ Plaça de la Seu ☎ 93 315 1554 (museum: 93 310 2580) 🕐 Daily 8–7:30; Museum: Mon.–Fri. 10–1 and 4–6:30, Sat.–Sun. 10–1 🍴 Nou Celler, see page 566 🚇 Jaume I 🚌 17, 19, 40, 45 💷 Cathedral free (Clock tower $; Museum $). Guided tour $ $ (1–5)

Nothing more strongly represents Barcelona's historic past than the great

Barcelona's fortress-like Cathedral

Catedral (Cathedral). It was built between the 13th and 15th centuries (with a 19th-century neo-Gothic facade), and the soaring space beneath the Catalan Gothic arches and numerous side chapels houses a wealth of treasures. The tranquil 14th-century cloister, with its fountains, magnolias and palms, is particularly beautiful.

CIUTAT VELLA

⊞ B2 ✉ Bounded by Rambla, Universitat, Laietana and Ferran 🍴 Nou Celler, see page 566 🚇 Jaume I 🚌 14, 17, 19

A maze of narrow streets and squares comprises the Ciutat Vella (Old City). It was built within the old Roman walls when Barcelona was one of the richest and most important Mediterranean trading cities. At its heart lies the Barri Gòtic (Gothic Quarter), centered around the Catedral and Plaça Sant Jaume. This plaza, once the power center of Catalonia's kings, is still the site of city hall and the administrative buildings of the government of Catalonia.

The Plaça del Rei, formerly the medieval marketplace, is said to be where King Ferdinand and Queen Isabella welcomed Christopher Columbus home from America in 1493. Nearby is the Plaça Reial, a fine arcaded square built in 1848. Gothic mansions line the streets, and you'll find museums, historic churches, bars and restaurants.

Gaudí's exuberant Casa Batlló

L'EIXAMPLE

✚ A3 🚇 Diagonal, Catalunya or Paseo de Gracia

Between 1860 and 1920 Barcelona expanded into a grid of uniform streets parallel to the sea, an area known as l'Eixample (the Extension). Today this is a residential, commercial and business district, divided in half by the Diagonal, a grand avenue cutting through the grid at a 45-degree angle. An interesting example of innovative town planning, it contains Barcelona's finest Modernist buildings. Some of the best are in the Passeig de Gràcia; look for No. 43, Casa Batlló, with a mosaic facade and wavy roofline that represent St. George's dragon. The block at No. 92 is known as La Pedrera, Gaudí's last secular work, built with no single straight line or sharp corner.

FUNDACIÓ JOAN MIRÓ

✚ B1 ✉ Avenida Miramar, Parc de Montjuïc ☎ 93 443 9470 🕐 Tue.–Sat. 10–7 (also Thu. 7–9:30 p.m.), Sun. 10–2:30 🍴 Café in museum 🚇 Espanya 🚌 50, 55, 61; Montjuïc funicular to Miramar 💵 $$$

More than 200 instantly recognizable and vibrantly colored paintings, along with sculptures, tapestries and drawings, are displayed in the white, bright space of the Fundació Joan Miró (Joan Miró Foundation).

Born in Barcelona in 1893, Miró spent most of his life in the city before retiring to Mallorca in 1956. In 1971 he established the foundation to house the world's largest collection of his works and to promote contemporary art.

MERCAT DE LA BOQUERÍA

✚ B2 ✉ Plaça de la Boquería 🕐 Mon.–Sat. 8 a.m.–8:30 p.m. 🚇 Liceu 🚌 14, 38, 59

Make time to visit the glorious Mercat de la Boquería (Boquería Market), housed since the 1830s in a covered hall just off La Rambla. If you arrive at lunchtime, take advantage of the snack bars here. The scents and colors of the fish, hams and sausages, freshly picked fruit and vegetables, and the babble of noise from the area will be one of the most enduring memories of your visit to Barcelona.

MONTJUÏC

✚ A1–B1 ✉ Montjuïc 🕐 Font Màgica displays: Thu.–Sun. evenings, late Jun.–late Sep; Fri.–Sat. rest of year 🚇 Take the subway to Parallel station, then the funicular to Parc de Montjuïc and the *telefèric* cable car to Mirador and Castell 🚌 13, 50, 55, 61

The green hill of Montjuïc, 698 feet high, dominates Barcelona's southern suburbs. Once known as the "Mountain of the Jews," Montjuïc today is a pleasant recreational area, dotted with gardens, museums, galleries and sports facilities. The most impressive approach is through the monumental Plaça de Espanya to the Font Màgica (Magic Fountain). The fountain stands below the pavilions built for the 1929 International Exhibition, many of which now house galleries.

MUSEU D'HISTÒRIA DE CATALUNYA

✚ C2 ✉ Plaça Pau de Vila 3 ☎ 93 225 4700 🕐 Tue.–Sat. 10 –7 (also Wed. 10 a.m.–8 p.m.), Sun. 10–2:30 🍴 Café in museum 🚇 Barceloneta or Drassanes 🚌 14, 17, 36, 39, 40, 45, 57, 59, 64 💵 $$ (free first Sun. of the month)

The Museu d'Història de Catalunya (Catalonian History Museum), Barcelona's newest museum, helps explain Catalonia, a "nation within a nation." It is located in a converted 19th-century warehouse, and exhibits depict the political, historical, cultural and everyday life of this vibrant region. The museum uses state-of-the-art and hands-on displays, interactive screens and special effects to convey its story.

MUSEU NACIONAL D'ART DE CATALUNYA (MNAC)

A1 ✉ Palau Nacional, Parc de Montjuïc ☎ 93 622 0360 🕑 Tue.–Sat. 10–7, Sun. 10–2:30 🍴 Café-restaurant in museum 🚇 Espanya 🚌 9, 13, 38, 50, 55, 56, 57, 61, 65, 109, 157 💰 $$ (free first Thu. of the month); guided tours by appointment

Still in the middle of ongoing renovations, the Museu Nacional d'Art de Catalunya (National Museum of Catalonian Art) is among the world's finest medieval art museums. Catalan Romanesque art, with its solid rounded forms and stunning simplicity, is represented by sculpture and carving, gold, enamel and textiles. The outstanding treasures are the 11th- and 12th-century murals, removed from isolated country churches and reassembled in the museum in order to preserve them. The ornate forms of the Gothic sculptures and altarpieces, which form the other major part of the museum, make a perfect contrast.

MUSEU PICASSO

C2 ✉ Calle Montcada 15–23 ☎ 93 319 6310 🕑 Tue.–Sat. 10–8, Sun. 10–3 🍴 Café-restaurant in museum 🚇 Jaume I 🚌 14, 17, 19, 39, 40, 45, 51, 59 💰 $$ (free first Sun. of the month)

Pablo Picasso, born in Andalucia in 1881, lived in Barcelona from 1895 until 1904, and he held his first exhibition in the city in 1900. The Museu Picasso (Picasso Museum), Barcelona's top attraction, is the most important collection of his works in Spain. It contains examples from each of his stylistic periods, from early street scenes to the major cubist works and ceramics he produced in later years.

PARC GÜELL

A3 ✉ Calle Olot ☎ 93 424 3809 🕑 Daily 10–9, May–Aug.; 10–8, Apr. and Sep.; 10–7, Mar. and Oct.; 10–6, rest of year 🚇 Vallcarca, Lesseps 🚌 25, 31, 32, 74

With its lovely views and wide green

Mosaic fountain by Gaudí on Güell Park steps

spaces, Parc Güell (Güell Park) would be worth visiting even without the interesting architectural elements by Antoni Gaudí scattered throughout its 50 acres. Originally planned as a residential landscaped area by Gaudí's main patrons, the Güell family, only the grand entrance, the plaza, the paths and the steps were completed. These are interspersed with colorful and weirdly shaped sculptures, fountains and columns, many intricately decorated with thousands of tiny pieces of broken ceramics (*trencadís*).

POBLE ESPANYOL

A1 ✉ Avenida de Marquès de Comillas ☎ 93 508 6330 🕑 Tue.–Sat. 9 a.m.–2 a.m. (also Fri.–Sat. 2–4 a.m.), Sun. 9 a.m.–midnight, Mon. 9–8 🚇 Espanya 🚌 13, 23, 50, 55, 61, 91 💰 $$$

The streets and squares of the Poble Espanyol (Spanish Village), built for the 1929 World Exhibition, give a glimpse of the country's many architectural styles. Reproductions range from the gleaming white houses of Andalucia to the flat granite facades of Galicia, all blended to form one "village." The buildings house workshops where you'll find crafts and artifacts from all over Spain, while evening brings live music and flamenco.

The soaring interior of the Gothic church of Santa Maria del Mar

PORT VELL

✠ C1–C2 🚇 Port Vell 🚋 Drassanes or Barceloneta 🚌 17, 19, 36, 64

The Port Vell (Old Port) district, once decayed and run-down, was transformed for the 1992 Olympics. An integral part of the city again, it is a busy recreation area, with a new marina and elegant new bridges and walkways connecting its various attractions. The centerpiece is Maremagnum, a shopping, eating and leisure center, complete with IMAX movie theater and Europe's largest aquarium.

LA RAMBLA

✠ B2–C2 🚇 La Rambla 🚋 Catalunya, Drassanes or Liceu 🚌 14, 38, 59, 91

La Rambla, Barcelona's most famous street, runs from Plaça de Catalunya to the waterfront. It's an exuberant tree-lined promenade effectively joining the old and new parts of the city, divided into seven distinctive sections. Here is Liceu, Barcelona's opera house, restored after a fire in 1994. The name Rambla is Arabic, from *ramla,* "a torrent," a reminder that the street follows an old watercourse. From here head to the statue of Christopher Columbus on a 164-foot iron plinth near the waterfront; take the elevator to an observation deck near the top for views of the city and port.

SANTA MARIA DEL MAR

✠ C2 🚇 Plaça de Santa Maria ☎ 93 310 2390 🕐 Daily 9–1:30 and 4:30–8 🚋 Jaume I 🚌 14, 17, 51

Built between 1329 and 1384 at the height of Barcelona's medieval prestige, the beautiful Gothic church of Santa Maria del Mar (Our Lady of the Sea) is tucked away in the Gothic streets of the Ribera district. Its stark, serene interior allows the elegant architecture to speak for itself.

TEMPLE EXPIATORI DE LA SAGRADA FAMÍLIA

✠ C3 🚇 Plaça de la Sagrada Família ☎ 93 207 3031 🕐 Daily 9–8, Apr.–Sep.; 9–6, rest of year 🚋 Sagrada Família 🚌 19, 33, 34, 43, 44, 50, 51 🎟 $$$; guided tours $$

The famous Catalan Modernist architect, Antoni Gaudí, worked on the Temple de la Sagrada Família (Expiatory Temple to the Holy Family) for over 40 years. He envisioned a vast cathedral, with facades to show the birth, death and resurrection of Christ, and 18 towers to represent the Twelve Apostles, the Four Evangelists, the Virgin and Christ. At his death in 1926 only the nativity facade, the crypt and one of the towers was complete, and it seems unlikely the project will ever be completed.

CATALAN FARE

You can eat as well in Barcelona as anywhere in Spain, sampling local Catalan dishes, fresh fish and seafood, and specialties from other parts of Spain and abroad. Since restaurants here cater to foreigners, dinner is served much earlier than elsewhere in Spain.

Fish and Seafood

Be sure to eat fish during your visit, preferably in one of Little Barcelona's restaurants where it is a specialty. Appetizers often include a selection of shellfish, tiny grilled sardines or giant prawns. Local main fish dishes are often a type of *sarsuela,* fish stew, or *suquet de peix,* a soupy fish and potato casserole. Although not the home of paella (that's Valencia), there are wonderful *arròs* dishes, where rice, subtly flavored with vegetables and spices, is combined with fish and its stock. Try *fideuà,* cooked like paella but using fine pasta in place of rice.

Above: Spain's national dish – paella
Below: Catalan mussels served in a marine sauce

Mar i Muntanya

Mar i muntanya (sea and mountain), or surf 'n' turf, has inspired some of Catalonia's best recipes. Using local ingredients, cooks have created combination dishes featuring rabbit, shrimp, prawns, chicken and meat. Look for *mar i cel* (sea and sky) on local menus, or try some of the excellent pork products. Main dishes are usually accompanied by intensely flavored vegetables, a saffron sauce, a garlic mayonnaise or a crisp salad. The local bread, baked several times a day, is crisp and light, a reminder of Barcelona's proximity to the French border. Cured ham, spicy sausages and garlic snails are often part of a *tapas* lunch, a good time to try a variety of tastes.

Thirst-quenchers

Bars serve tea, coffee, soda and fruit juice as well as every conceivable form of alcohol. You'll find many familiar drinks, and a range of Spanish beers and wines.

Beer comes in bottles or on tap, and you can buy wine by the glass. Local red, white and rosé wines come from the Penedès area; Torres and Masia Bach are reliable labels. Cava makes a great aperitif; a light sparkling dry wine, it's made the same way as champagne.

Santiago

SANTIAGO

Tucked away in the green fringes of Galicia, in northwest Spain, is Santiago de Compostela – one of the great shrines of medieval Christendom. Millions of pilgrims braved hazardous travel to worship at the shrine of St. James, the patron saint of Spain. People still come here on pilgrimages today, especially during holy years, which occur when St. James' Day (July 25) falls on a Sunday.

Santiago is one of Europe's most perfect medieval cities – a mix of religious and secular buildings, with an ancient and thriving university and a unique spiritual atmosphere. It is also home to the parliament of Galicia, which is an autonomous region, and there is a lively and prosperous modern town surrounding the central core.

Old Santiago

The historic heart is pedestrian-only and can be traversed on foot in less than a half-hour; everything you'll want to see lies within this small area. Santiago offers quality, not quantity, so most visitors find a stay of a few days ample.

The two main streets, Rúa do Franco and Rúa do Vilar, lead south from the cathedral square and are lined with stores, bars and restaurants. Pick up a map at the tourist office; it's easy to lose your bearings in the maze of streets and squares behind the cathedral.

Santiago Flavors

Galician cooking is delicious, robust and tasty, and relies on the excellent quality of local ingredients. Seafood and shellfish are extensively farmed in the *rias*, deeply indented coastal inlets, and are of superb quality. Regional specialties include *pulpo* (octopus) cooked in various ways; blood puddings and sausages; and *empanadas*, a flat pie with a meat or fish filling.

This is one of the few Spanish regions where lamb is eaten, and local beef also is particularly good. Santiago

Stone carvings adorn the medieval buildings in the old quarter of the city

has many pastry shops, where you'll find wonderful cakes and cookies. Local wine varieties include Ribeiro and Albaríno, straightforward whites, and the excellent red Amandi and Condado. If the weather's cold try a cup of hot chocolate; thick enough to eat, it's some of the best in Spain.

Souvenirs and Entertainment

Santiago's streets are lined with stores selling pilgrim souvenirs – medals, rosaries, key rings, holy pictures and statues, all decorated with the image of St. James and his scallop shell emblem. The traditional material for pilgrimage souvenirs is jet, polished and cut, or fashioned into the *figa*, a clenched-fist amulet. The guild of silversmiths, hugely important in the past, is still active and makes some fine pieces.

This is a university town with a thriving cultural life, and there are year-round classical concerts, as well as clubs frequented by students. You'll

Santiago Festivals

Santiago's biggest festival is July 25, the feast of St. James, when the city is packed with pilgrims, tourists and local people. The night before sees the Apostle's Fire (Fuego del Apóstol), a spectacular fireworks display in front of the cathedral. The feast itself represents a solemn Mass, with music, choirs and Galician bagpipes. The huge incense burner, the *botafumeiro*, is swung in the cathedral. The feast falls in the middle of Santiago's folklore festival, a two-week celebration of Galician culture, with street music, parades, concerts and markets. An international music festival is held in August and September.

hear bagpipes, Galicia's national instrument, played on the streets; this is a favorite way for students to make extra cash.

ESSENTIAL INFORMATION

TOURIST INFORMATION
• Rúa do Vilar 63, ☎ 981 584 081
• Plaza de Galicia, ☎ 981 573 990;
www.santiagoturismo.com

URBAN TRANSPORTATION
Santiago's historic center is pedestrian-only; the only vehicular access is for taxis and delivery vehicles. It takes around 15 to 20 minutes to walk from one end of the center to the other, and everything you'll want to see is within this area, even most of the hotels. If you are staying outside the historic center, take a taxi to the edge of the

old town and then walk. Taxis can be found at stands outside the old city, or you can call them (☎ 981 598 488, or 981 561 028 or 981 595 964 for night service).

AIRPORT INFORMATION
Santiago-Lavacolla International Airport (☎ 981 547 500), with services to many European cities, is 7 miles east of the city, about a 15- to 30-minute drive. Buses into Santiago run hourly from the terminal, Mon.–Fri. 6:40 a.m.–11:30 p.m., Sat. 7:15 a.m.–10 p.m.,Sun. 9:30 a.m.–11:30 p.m. (journey time 30 minutes). Taxis also leave from the terminal.

CLIMATE – average highs and lows for the month

JAN.	FEB.	MAR.	APR.	MAY	JUN.	JUL.	AUG.	SEP.	OCT.	NOV.	DEC.
13°C	14°C	15°C	17°C	19°C	22°C	25°C	25°C	24°C	20°C	17°C	14°C
55°F	57°F	59°F	63°F	66°F	72°F	77°F	77°F	75°F	68°F	63°F	57°F
5°C	6°C	7°C	8°C	10°C	14°C	16°C	16°C	14°C	12°C	9°C	7°C
41°F	43°F	45°F	46°F	50°F	57°F	61°F	61°F	57°F	54°F	48°F	45°F

The baroque facade of the Cathedral

CITY SIGHTS

Key to symbols

🔲 map coordinates refer to the Santiago map on page 418; sights below are highlighted in yellow on the map.

🖂 address or location   ☎ telephone number
🕐 opening times   🍴 restaurant or café on site or nearby   🎟 admission charge: $$$ more than €6, $$ €3–€6, $ less than €3   🛈 other relevant information

BARRIO ANTIGUO

🔲 B2   🖂 Barrio Antiguo

The Barrio Antiguo (Old Quarter) of Santiago is packed with beautiful, historic buildings. The main streets are lined with arcaded old granite houses in the traditional Galician style. East of the cathedral, the spacious Plaza da Quintana is surrounded by notable buildings, including the arcaded Casa de la Canónica (Canon's Residence). This faces a gracious flight of steps leading up to the 17th-century Casa de la Parra (House of the Bunch of Grapes). On the third side is the austere facade of San Paio de Antealtares Monastery, founded in the ninth century. Opposite, the Puerta del Perdón (Door of Pardon) opens onto the east end of the cathedral – this is only

used during holy years. On the cathedral's north side stands the huge complex of the Monasterio de San Martín Pinario, with its church and three cloisters. Behind the monastery lies the 17th-century Convento de San Francisco, commemorating a pilgrimage by St. Francis of Assisi in 1213. It is now a museum devoted to the Holy Land and incorporates a hotel.

CATEDRAL

🔲 A2   🖂 Plaza do Obradoiro   ☎ 981 560 527
🕐 Daily 7 a.m.–9 p.m.; hours sometimes vary
🍴 Botafumeiro, see page 567

The present Catedral (Cathedral) dates from the 11th to 13th centuries. The simple Romanesque lines of the interior provide a superb contrast to the ornate facade, added in 1750, at the cathedral's main entrance. Here stands the 12th-century triple doorway known as the Pórtico de la Glória (Doorway of Glory), one of the sculptural marvels of Spain. Prophets and Apostles surround Christ the Savior and the Four Evangelists, all carved with exceptional imagination and fluidity. Behind the worn entrance pillar and the figure of St. James is a figure said to be Maestro Mateo, the cathedral's designer. It's customary to bump your head against his in the hope some of his artistic genius may rub off.

You'll notice a pulley system high above the transept; this operates the *botafumeiro*, a monster incense burner used during major feasts, which requires eight men to swing it through a huge arc above the transept. The silverwork and gilded figures of the High Altar glitter under the lights of the candelabra.

MUSEO DAS PEREGRINACIÓNS

🔲 B2   🖂 Rúa San Miguel 4   ☎ 981 581 558
🕐 Tue.–Fri. 10–8, Sat. 10:30–1:30 and 5–8, Sun. 10:30–1:30   🎟 $ (senior citizens and under 18 free; free to all Sat. afternoon and Sun.)

The Museo das Peregrinacións (Pilgrimage Museum) tells the story of pilgrimage in general, and the Santiago pilgrimage in particular. Exhibits show how the cathedral and town grew around the apostle's tomb,

St. James and Santiago

To medieval Europeans, a pilgrimage (*peregrinación*) was a means of earning extra grace and thus attaining heaven faster. Pilgrimages were made to many holy places, but the great goals were Jerusalem, Rome and Santiago de Compostela. The apostle St. James is known as "Sant Iago" in Spanish. The city which bears his name also is the site of his shrine and burial place. According to legend, he had preached in Spain before returning to martyrdom in Judea in AD 44. His disciples brought his body back to Spain, where it lay hidden until AD 844.

Legend tells that he appeared in a vision to Christian leaders and led them to victory against the Muslim invaders, earning him the title of *Matamoros*, the Moorslayer. His body and relics were rediscovered at Compostela, which soon became the center of devotion for Spain's new patron saint. By the 11th century, pilgrims were traveling from all over Europe to pray at Santiago.

The pilgrims' well-trodden route into Santiago

The *Camino de Santiago*

Pilgrims traveled from France, Britain, Germany, Italy and Scandinavia, as well as Spain and Portugal, many of them taking years to complete their journey. By the mid-12th century, between 500,000 and 2 million people were on the move annually, a vast number in relation to the total population.

Roads to Spain threaded their way across the Continent, but once across the Pyrenees converged into a well-organized route across northern Spain. This became known as the *Camino de Santiago*, the Way of St. James. Administered by a religious military order, the *camino* was policed and marked along its length, with hostels, inns and churches offering practical and spiritual sustenance to travelers. Towns grew up around the stopping points, with their own churches, hospitals and hospices.

Dressed in sandals and heavy capes and armed with stout staffs, pilgrims also wore the scallop shell emblem of the saint in their broad-brimmed hats. On arrival in Santiago, the custom was to enter the cathedral and embrace the golden effigy of the saint placed high above his tomb, while giving alms and thanks in gratitude for the safe completion of the pilgrimage.

The *Camino* Today

The custom of walking the *camino* died out during the 16th century, but was revived around 1880. Today thousands of people make the journey to Santiago, by car, train, plane and on foot.

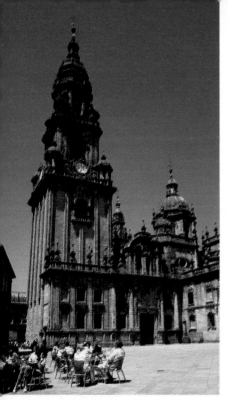

Relax amid the grandeur of Obradoiro Square

Museo y Tesoro de la Catedral

✚ A2 ✉ Plaza Platerías ☎ 981 560 527 ⊙ Daily
10–2 and 4–8, Jun.–Sep.; Mon.–Sat. 10–1:30 and
4–6:30, Sun. 10–1:30, rest of year ⋔ Botafumeiro,
see page 567 ✋ $$

The Museo y Tesoro de la Catedral
(Cathedral Museum and Treasury) is
housed around the magnificent 16th-
century cloisters adjoining the cathedral.
It also includes the Romanesque Old
Cathedral (a crypt beneath the Pórtico de
la Glória) and the Chapel of San
Fernando, which opens off the interior of
the cathedral. In the latter you can see
gem-encrusted gold crucifixes and statues
still used for important feasts. The museum
includes a fine collection of tapestries from
the most prestigious workshops.

The cloisters, a lovely blend of
Castilian-Gothic and Renaissance
architecture, are some of the largest in
Spain. Stairs lead up to the gallery,
completed in 1590, which offers a good
vantage point over the cathedral square.
The building adjoining the left of the
cathedral is the old Bishop's Palace.

Plaza do Obradoiro

✚ A2 ✉ Plaza do Obradoiro ⋔ Botafumeiro, see
page 567

The sweeping expanse of Plaza do
Obradoiro (Obradoiro Square), in front of
the cathedral, is surrounded on its other
sides by three harmonious buildings. These
are the Hostal de los Reyes Católicos
(Hostel of the Catholic Monarchs), the
Colegio de San Jerónimo (College of St.
Jerome) and the Pazo de Raxoi, or
Ayuntamiento (City Hall). The oldest
building is the hostel (now a hotel),
originally founded by Ferdinand and
Isabella as a pilgrims' lodging house. It has
an elegantly plain facade centered by a
superb Plateresque doorway. Inside, the
building is laid out around four lovely patios.

Across from the hostel is the college
and its charming balcony, which dates
mainly from the 17th century – although
its doorway is 200 years younger. Facing
the cathedral, the 18th-century City Hall,
seems to unite the whole ensemble.

how the routes west across Europe
developed, what the pilgrims wore and
how they traveled. There's a copy of the
fascinating *Codex Calixtinus*, a 13th-century
guide to the route, full of tips about travel
and information about Santiago. Look for
the collection of souvenirs 14th-century
pilgrims took home.

Museo do Pobo Galego

✚ B2 ✉ Monistero de San Domingos de Bonaval
☎ 981 583 620 ⊙ Tue.–Sat. 10–2 and 4–8, Sun. 11–2
✋ free

Santiago is more than a noted shrine, it's
also one of the main towns in Galicia. The
Museo do Pobo Galego (Museum of the
Galician People), set in the old convent of
San Domingo, explains Galicia and the
traditional way of life in this part of Spain.
There are displays of tools, pottery,
costumes, handicrafts and musical
instruments, as well as exhibits on Galicia's
dolmens, stone circles and hill forts. The
museum's galleries encircle the 17th-
century cloister; in one corner a superb
staircase, with three intertwining flights of
steps, rises through the building.

The Cathedral of St. James dominates the city skyline

A Day in Santiago

A Spiritual Morning

Your first stop should be a visit to the excellent Pilgrimage Museum (Museo das Peregrinacións, see page 420), where you can learn about the history of pilgrimage. This will give you a sense of perspective and will pave the way for a visit to the cathedral, next on the list. As you go in, place your hand on the worn stones of the entrance pillar, the first gesture of arriving pilgrims.

Spend time admiring the architecture and artistic treasures, then join the line and mount the steps behind the altar to embrace the effigy of St. James, as pilgrims have done for more than 1,000 years. You could time your visit to coincide with the daily noontime Pilgrims' Mass.

A Secular Afternoon

Head up Rúa do Franco or Rúa do Vilar, the main streets, and choose one of the many restaurants for lunch – shellfish or octopus are both traditional Galician specialties. After lunch, you could head back toward the cathedral and visit the Cathedral Museum and Treasury (Museo y Tesoro de la Catedral) before walking back across town to the Museum of the Galician People (Museo do Pobo Galego). At about 6 p.m. the streets begin to fill with shoppers and university students, and the bars become busy.

A Peaceful Evening

There's no problem finding an excellent restaurant for dinner; try some fish or one of the flavorful Galician meat dishes, often pork-based, with potatoes and turnip tops. Be sure to order some of the local dome-shaped cheese, and finish with a slice of *tarta de Santiago*, a special almond pastry made only here. As you wander through the ancient streets after dinner, you'll probably hear the strains of bagpipes echoing through some hidden courtyard. For the walking route, see the city map on page 418.

SEVILLE

Some of Spain's quintessential images are of whitewashed streets, Moorish architecture, flamenco dresses, orange trees and proud horsemen. This mental picture actually reflects Andalucia and its capital, Seville (Sevilla). It is the fourth-largest city in Spain, the seat of a university, an important industrial city and the center of a rich agricultural region. Renowned for architectural treasures, great festivals and a relaxed lifestyle, Seville has attracted visitors for many years, and cares for them far better than many other Spanish cities.

Seville on Foot

In Seville, every building, garden and street is designed as an escape from the sun. If you're visiting in summer, take lengthy siestas during the hottest hours. The central old core is relatively small, and you'll be able to walk to many of the main sights. The narrow, twisting streets can be confusing, so always take a city map with you; maps are free and available at the tourist office and many hotels. Blue-and-white signs direct visitors to the main sights. There's plenty of information in English, and helpful multilingual guides – often university students – offer assistance at the main attractions.

There's plenty to see in Seville besides the main attractions. The range of museums, fine churches and civic buildings attracts many visitors: the Casa de Pilatos, an elegant private palace, is a favorite. Also look for the Tobacco Factory (Fabrica de Tabacos), now part of the university but also where Carmen (of opera fame) worked.

Walking is only one option. Visitors can take an open-carriage drive from outside the cathedral that takes in many of the sights. Alternatively, 30-minute cruises run from the Torre del Oro on the Guadalquivir river, one of Spain's greatest waterways, and this is a relaxing way to admire Seville.

Festivals in Seville

Seville has two major festivals: the *Semana Santa* (Holy Week), the last week of Lent, and the *Feria de Abril*

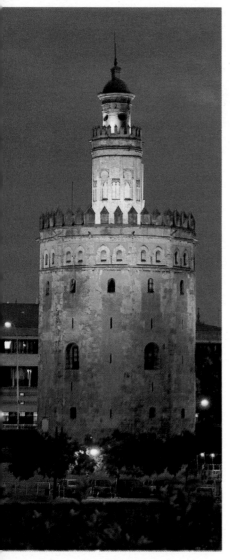

Bathed in light – the Moorish "Tower of Gold"

Seville

(April Festival), held the last week in April. If you plan to visit the city during either of these, reserve a room far in advance. Holy Week is a deeply religious time, celebrated by *pasos* processions held by rival brotherhoods in Seville's different districts. *Pasos* are huge carriers supporting religious statues, sumptuously decorated and carried by up to 60 men. The April Festival is completely secular, a

weeklong celebration of Andalucia's love affair with horses, music and beautiful women. Carriages filled with laughing girls in flounced dresses, accompanied by horseback riders in traditional dress, parade the streets, and the graceful *sevillana* is danced all night.

Eating Southern Style

Eating is a pleasure in Seville, with a wide range of restaurants and *tapas*

Seville

bars. More than almost anywhere else in Spain, *tapas* has a special place here. There's a fabulous choice of dishes, traditionally eaten with a glass of *copa*, or sherry, the fortified wine from Jerez – a lovely city south of Seville.

Mealtimes are late, particularly in summer, with lunch often finishing around 4 or 5 and dinner starting at midnight. The more cosmopolitan restaurants are geared to foreigners' dining habits. Andalucian coffee is very strong, so it's best to ask for a *café con agua* (coffee with water) if you like it weaker.

Mantillas and Castanets

Shoppers throng Sierpes – "the Serpent" – the winding pedestrian-only street running north from near the cathedral. Stroll around and enjoy the traditional storefronts; it's a good place to find Sevillian fans, mantillas, shawls, flamenco dresses, castanets and

gourmet candies. You'll find attractive pottery at tiny stores in Santa Cruz or across the river in the Triana district, where they also make fine wrought-iron goods, saddles and guitars.

Flamenco

Flamenco is a synthesis of dance and music, ideally performed spontaneously to express joy and sorrow about everyday life, religion and work. Its heartland lies in Andalucia, but its origins stretch as far afield as Egypt and India. It reaches its zenith in the songs known as *cante jondo* (deep song), expressions of deep feelings. The profound meaning of flamenco is hard for foreigners to grasp, but the music and dance, the distinctive costume and the click of castanets can be enjoyed by all.

ESSENTIAL INFORMATION

TOURIST INFORMATION
Oficinas Municipales de Turismo (Municipal Tourist Offices)
• Paseo de la Delicias 9
☎ 95 423 4465/902 194 897
• Naves del Barranco, Calle Arjona 28
☎ 95 422 1714; www.turismo.sevilla.org

URBAN TRANSPORTATION
Seville has an efficient bus system that mainly services the sprawling residential suburbs, with only a few buses going into the heart of the old city. Some city-center routes run past the cathedral to the Plaza Nueva, and other lines terminate at Plaza de la Incarnación. Maria Luisa Park and the surrounding area also is well served from the center. Buy single tickets when you board, or show your 3- or 7-day tourist pass, available at

newsstands or from the Tussam bus office. There's also a special tourist bus, run by Sevirama (☎ 95 456 0693). This hop-on-and-off service covers the main sights, with an English commentary, and runs all year; tickets are valid all day. White-and-yellow taxis can be hailed on the street or at a stand, or you can call Radio Taxi (☎ 95 458 0000), Radio Taxi Giralda (☎ 95 467 5555), or Tele-Taxi (954 622 222).

AIRPORT INFORMATION
Seville International Airport (☎ 95 444 9000), with connections to major European cities, is about 5 miles northeast of the city, a 15- to 30-minute drive. An airport bus runs hourly from the terminal to Puerta Jerez, Mon.–Fri. 6:45 a.m.–11:30 p.m, with less frequent service on weekends. Taxis are available outside the airport terminal.

CLIMATE – average highs and lows for the month

JAN.	FEB.	MAR.	APR.	MAY	JUN.	JUL.	AUG.	SEP.	OCT.	NOV.	DEC.
15°C	16°C	18°C	22°C	27°C	32°C	35°C	35°C	32°C	25°C	20°C	16°C
59°F	61°F	64°F	72°F	81°F	90°F	95°F	95°F	90°F	77°F	68°F	61°F
5°C	7°C	8°C	10°C	13°C	17°C	18°C	19°C	18°C	14°C	10°C	4°C
41°F	45°F	46°F	50°F	55°F	63°F	64°F	66°F	64°F	57°F	50°F	40°F

City Sights

Key to symbols

⬛ map coordinates refer to the Seville map on page 425; sights below are highlighted in yellow on the map. ✉ address or location ☎ telephone number 🕐 opening times 🚌 nearest bus route 🍴 restaurant or café on site or nearby 💺 admission charge: $$$ more than €6, $$ €3–€6, $ less than €3 ⓘ other relevant information

Barrio de Santa Cruz

⬛ A3–B3 ✉ Santa Cruz 🚌 21, 22, 23, 24, 25, 26, 30, 31, 33, 34, 40, 41, 42, C3, C4

The Barrio de Santa Cruz (Santa Cruz Quarter), with its narrow white streets, ironwork grilles and sun-splashed squares shaded by orange trees, typifies Seville and draws visitors night and day. Originally the Jewish quarter, it was popular with 17th-century nobility, who added mansions along its alleyways.

Catedral

⬛ B2 ✉ Plaza Virgen de los Reyes ☎ 95 421 4971 🕐 Mon.–Sat. 11–5, Sun. 2:30–6 🍴 El Giraldillo, see page 567 🚌 21, 22, 23, 24, 25, 26, 30, 31, 33, 34, 40, 41, 42, C3, C4 💺 $$$ (free to all Sun.). Combined ticket for Cathedral and Giralda

Seville's magnificent Catedral (Cathedral), built on the site of the Moorish mosque, is the third largest in Europe; only St. Peter's in Rome and St. Paul's in London are larger. Vast, rich and harmoniously balanced, it was built between 1401 and 1507, a blend of Gothic austerity and Spanish flamboyance. Almost as wide as it is long, the interior is dominated by the chancel, the *Capilla Mayor*, its splendidly carved Flemish altarpiece glistening with gold leaf behind immense grilles. Opposite lie the choir stalls. Stand between the two and look up at the transept roof, 184 feet above your head; this riot of stone filigree is supported by massive arches and columns, but even these are dwarfed by the scale of the cathedral. Other highlights include Christopher Columbus' tomb in the south transept; the treasury and sacristy, packed with paintings and precious altar vessels; and the domed Royal Chapel, the burial place of Alfonso X of Castille.

Dine beneath the beautiful 12th-century Giralda

Giralda

⬛ B3 ✉ Plaza Virgen de los Reyes ☎ 95 421 4971 🕐 Mon.–Sat. 11–5, Sun. 2:30–6 🍴 El Giraldillo, see page 567 🚌 21, 22, 23, 24, 25, 26, 30, 31, 33, 34, 40, 41, 42, C3, C4 💺 $$$ (free to all Sun.). Combined ticket for Cathedral and Giralda

When Christians destroyed the mosque to build the cathedral, they kept the minaret and transformed it into the new cathedral's bell tower. Nicknamed the *Giralda,* the "weather-vane," the 322-foot-tall tower was built in the 12th century. Instead of stairs, you climb a series of interior ramps; 17 levels lead to the top, from where there are views over Seville. Below the tower lies the lovely Patio de los Naranjos (Courtyard of the Orange Trees), once part of the mosque.

Isla Mágica

⬛ A4 ✉ Pabellón de España, Isla de la Cartuja ☎ 902 16 17 16 or 902 16 00 00 🕐 Daily 11 a.m.–midnight, mid-Jul. to mid-Sep.; days and times vary,

Apr. 1 to mid-Jul. and mid-Sep. to early Nov. 🚇 C1, C2 🚌 $$$ (reduction for evening)

Seville hosted Expo '92 on the Isla de la Cartuja, an island between two branches of the Quadalquivir river. This is now the site of Isla Mágica, a theme park devoted to the Spanish discovery of the New World in the 15th and 16th centuries.

MUSEO DE ARTES Y COSTUMBRES POPULARES

✚ B1 ✉ Plaza de América, Parque de María Luisa ☎ 95 423 2576 🕐 Tue. 2:30–8:30, Wed.–Sat. 9–8:30, Sun. 9–2:30 🚇 6, 34, 35 🚌 $

The Museo de Artes y Costumbres Populares (Museum of Arts and Popular Traditions), located in one of the 1929 International Exhibition pavilions, the Mudéjar Pabellón (Mudéjar Pavilion), is devoted to everyday life in Andalucia. There are reconstructions of workshops where you can see how guitars and castanets are made, old agricultural implements, pottery, furniture and much more. Upstairs are intricately embroidered costumes, painted fans and delicate lace. You also can learn about the history of Seville's great Spring Festival, the *Fiesta Primaverales*.

MUSEO DE BELLAS ARTES

✚ A3 ✉ Plaza del Museo 9 ☎ 95 422 0790 🕐 Tue. 2:30–8:30, Wed.–Sat. 9–8:30, Sun. 9–2:30 🚇 43, C1, C2, C3, C4 🚌 $

Seville's Museo de Bellas Artes (Fine Arts Museum), housed in an 18th-century convent, concentrates on the Golden Age of Spanish painting. The former church is devoted to the Spanish religious painter Bartolome Murillo, and pride of place is given to his *Immaculate Conception*. Francisco de Zurbarán, another great master, also is represented, his masterpiece being the sculptural *Christ on the Cross*.

PLAZA DE ESPAÑA AND PARQUE DE MARÍA LUISA

✚ B1–B2 ✉ Plaza de España 🚇 6, 34, C1, C2

Built as the centerpiece for the 1929 International Exhibition, the Plaza de España overlooks Parque de María Luisa

(María Luisa Park). Traditionally styled and lavishly decorated with thousands of colored tiles, the 650-foot-wide plaza is framed by a semicircular range of buildings and encircled by a canal. The park, laid out in the 19th century, is a tranquil area with pools and fountains. It plays a central part in Seville's Spring Festival, when hundreds of horsemen accompany carriages of smiling, silk-robed girls around the park.

PLAZA DE TOROS DE LA REAL MAESTRANZA

✚ A2–A3 ✉ Paseo Colón 12 ☎ 95 421 0315 🕐 Daily 9:30–7 (9:30–3 on bullfight days); Museum: daily 10:30–2 and 4–6 (on bullfight days 10–3) 🚇 5, 41, C3, C4 🚌 $$

Seville's Plaza de Toros (Bullring) is one of the oldest and most prestigious in Spain. Once built of wood, the present 14,000-seat ring was designed around the Prince's Balcony and is oval rather than round. Tours, in Spanish only, include the Museo Taurino (Bullfighting Museum), stables, chapel and modern operating theater.

REALES ALCÁZARES

✚ B2 ✉ Patio de Banderas ☎ 95 450 2323 🕐 Tue.–Sat. 9:30–7, Sun. 9:30–5, Apr.–Sep.; Tue.–Sat. 9:30–5, Sun. 9:30–1:30, rest of year 🍴 El Giraldillo, see page 567 🚇 21, 22, 23, 24, 25, 26, 30, 31, 33, 34, 40, 41, 42, C3, C4 🚌 $$

The unforgettable Reales Alcázares (Royal Palace) epitomizes the elegance and charm of Mudéjar secular architecture. Little remains of the original Moorish Alcaza; most of the palace you see today was built by Pedro the Cruel in the 1360s, long after the Moors left Spain. But the builders were Christianized Moors, the inventors of Mudéjar style, and this "Arabian Nights" complex is one of the purest examples of their art remaining today. It's a labyrinth of courtyards, delicate stucco and tile rooms, terraces and coffered chambers, fountains and arched patios. From here you pass into the 16th-century Palace of Charles V, with its tapestries and lavish rooms. Outside are gardens with terraces, pools and shady magnolia and orange trees. Labeling and information are poor, so your best option is to rent the English-language audio guide.

Spectators fill the Plaza Monumental de Toros de las Ventas in Madrid, Spain's premier bullring

BULLFIGHTING

Bullfighting is the least understood of all Spanish traditions. Performed on horseback until the 18th century, bullfighting had attained its present form by the 19th century, with established rules and a strict pattern to the *corrida,* or fight.

The *Corrida*

Six four-year-old bulls are killed during a *corrida,* which starts at 5 p.m. Bred on huge estates on the rolling grasslands of Andalucia and Castille, the 1,000-pound bulls have never seen an unmounted man until the moment they enter the ring. The afternoon starts with a parade, the *paseo* – three *matadors,* bright figures in their "suits of light" who will each kill two bulls. The *matadors* are accompanied by their teams, known as *cuadrillas.*

Each fight falls into three parts, marked by a trumpet call. First the *matador* must appraise the bull, using a cape to make the animal turn so he can judge its speed and dexterity. Bred for aggression, it will charge at the two mounted team members, the *picadores,* who attack its flanks with pikes.

The next act allows the bull to regain its wind while it is further enraged by the *banderillas,* who pierce the neck muscles with ribboned darts. The pikes and darts gradually weaken the bull's immensely strong neck and cause its head to drop, allowing the matador access to the heart.

The final stage of the drama belongs to the matador alone. Working with the *muleta,* a small red cloth, he draws the bull in a series of passes across his body, which can be as elegant as they are fearless. Finally, the bull will stand still, tired but still mesmerized by the *muleta.* This is the moment for the matador to take his sword and, reaching over the horns and shoulder blades, strike the bull cleanly through the heart.

Bullfighting can be seen throughout Spain at all the major summer festivals. Not all Spaniards enjoy bullfighting, but they are tolerant of it. Those upset by the spectacle's inherent cruelty, however, should definitely not attend.

SWEDEN

"THE further I came north, the more like New England everything grew to look..."

American historian Henry Adams

Opposite: Houses on stilts at the waterfront town of Orust

SWEDEN

Sweden is the largest of the Scandinavian countries, famed for the perceived efficiency of its people and the pragmatism of its government. This is a land of wide-open spaces, where even a large city like Stockholm seems to merge urban and rural elements in a way that benefits the people.

Swedish Landscapes

Southern Sweden is an area of forests and farmland punctuated by a vast number of lakes, of which two – Vänern and Vättern – dominate the landscape. The south also is the center of Sweden's industrial powerhouse. The main cities are Gothenburg (Göteborg) and Malmö on the southwest coast.

The southernmost province, Skåne, is a rich farming area where you will find a hint of Danish features, both in the people and in the landscape. This is Sweden's vacation land. Off the east coast, the islands of Gotland and Öland have superb beaches that benefit from calm waters and warm summer sunshine.

Stockholm lies on the east coast of Sweden, within a beautiful mosaic of inland lakes and offshore islands. In the surrounding provinces there is a richly varied countryside centered on mighty Lake Mälaren. North of Stockholm is

Sweden's ancient capital, the lively university town of Uppsala. This entire area is accessible by ferries and cruise boats that ply a network of waterways and lakes.

Northern Sweden is known as Norrland, with similarities to northern Finland, and it enjoys the same "Land of the Midnight Sun" tag. It is a country of vast forests and tumbling rivers that are fed by icy, crystal waters from the mountains. Lapland, or Sápme (see page 434), is a vast and magnificent wilderness of mountains, moorland, birch forest and tundra.

Travel and Climate

Sweden has an extensive road network, but public transportation throughout the country also is a very efficient and convenient way to get around. Trains are modern and comfortable, and buses serve even the most remote northern parts of the country.

Sweden's climate is similar to that of its neighbors, but the country is generally much drier than Norway's western regions. Summers can be as warm and sunny as anywhere else in northern Europe, and along the southern coast you may even find yourself enjoying a Scandinavian heat wave. Conversely, visitors need to be prepared for wet weather in Sweden's maritime climate.

A remarkable number of Swedes are fluent in English, and most people in the cities have at least some command of English. The people are generally very helpful, and have a great awareness of the world in general; they are politely curious about visitors and are lively conversationalists, once their initial reserve is overcome.

Swedes are conservative by nature, and on first impression may seem overly serious about life. They are very aware that their society operates on the basis

---

MORE TOP DESTINATIONS IN SWEDEN

- Göteborg A2 • Gotland B2
- Kalmar A1 • Lund A1 • Malmö A1
- Siljan A3 • Skokloster B2
- Uppsala B2

Sweden

of co-operation and willingness to accept the norm. You may mistake Swedish directness for impatience, especially in Stockholm, but this simply reflects a national confidence about how things work.

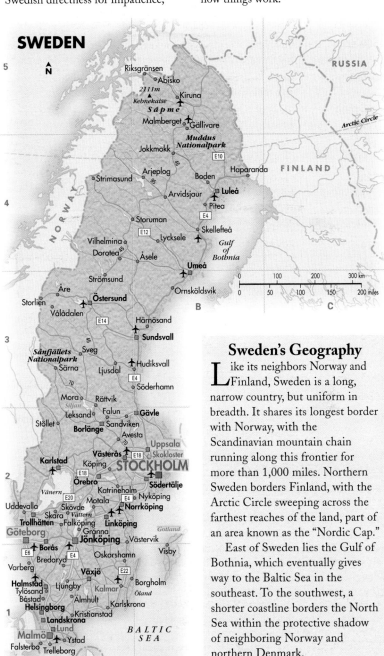

SWEDEN

Sweden's Geography

Like its neighbors Norway and Finland, Sweden is a long, narrow country, but uniform in breadth. It shares its longest border with Norway, with the Scandinavian mountain chain running along this frontier for more than 1,000 miles. Northern Sweden borders Finland, with the Arctic Circle sweeping across the farthest reaches of the land, part of an area known as the "Nordic Cap."

East of Sweden lies the Gulf of Bothnia, which eventually gives way to the Baltic Sea in the southeast. To the southwest, a shorter coastline borders the North Sea within the protective shadow of neighboring Norway and northern Denmark.

Sweden

TIMELINE

8000 BC	Hunter-gatherers move throughout Scandinavia in the wake of retreating ice sheets; the Sami (Lapp) people are thought to descend from these early settlers.
1500 BC	Germanic tribes in southern Sweden develop trading links with the European lands to the south, from which they came.
AD 750	Battle of Bråvalla; the Svear emerge as the dominant tribe and give their name to the country (Sverige).
800–1000	Swedish "Vikings" travel east via the great rivers of eastern Europe, as far as Constantinople.
1397	Union of Kalmar unites Denmark, Sweden and Norway under Queen Margaret of Denmark.
1523	Gustav Vasa establishes Sweden's independence; becomes King Gustav I; Lutheran Protestantism becomes the country's main religion.
1658	Treaty of Roskilde secures all of southern Swedish mainland from Danish control.
1814	Sweden wins control of Norway from Denmark.
1905	Norway achieves independence from Sweden.
1914–18	Sweden remains neutral during World War I.
1939–45	Sweden again remains neutral during World War II.
1946	Sweden maintains neutrality but joins the United Nations.
1989	The Sami people are granted their own parliament, known as the Sametinget.
1995	Sweden joins the European Union.
1998	Stockholm is named Cultural Capital of Europe.
2000	The 10-mile Öresund tunnel and bridge linking Malmö and Copenhagen opens.

THE SAMI

The Sami are the indigenous people of Sápme, the area popularly called Lapland. They are known historically as Lapps, but this is not a native name and is one that the Sami themselves feel is derogatory. The ancient name Sápme, a form of Sami which is said to mean "the people of the interior," is now considered accepted usage. Sápme covers the Scandinavian Arctic region from the Russian Kola peninsula to the northwest coast of Norway, and extends down either side of the Norwegian-Swedish border to the central area of both countries. There are about 60,000 Sami people today, of which about 17,000 live in Sweden. A minority of Sami are reindeer herders, but the Sami also are developing alternative lifestyles while strengthening their self-awareness and political position within Scandinavia. Tourism is increasing in Scandinavian Lapland, but some Sami people are concerned about what they believe is too much intrusion on their fragile environment and culture.

Sweden

SURVIVAL GUIDE

- For lunch you must experience *smörgåsbord*, a Scandinavian institution, although less common these days. The name translates as *smörgås* for "bread," *bord* for "table." The reality of a true *smörgåsbord* means much more than this simple image implies. There may be more than 100 different dishes in a true *smörgåsbord*, with items ranging from *gravad lax* (salmon slices in herbs) to *köttbullar* (tasty meatballs), *sillbullar* (herring rissoles) or *kåldolmar* (stuffed cabbage rolls).

- Sweden has the same tight control over alcohol sales as does Norway and Finland, and alcohol is expensive. The government-controlled liquor monopoly, *Systembolaget*, has branches throughout the country, which are open Mon.–Fri. 10–6 (some until 7 or 8 p.m.), Sat. 10–1 (some until 2 or 3). They sell spirits, wines and strong beers; the minimum age to purchase is 20. Light beers can be purchased at grocery stores and super-markets. Try some *aquavit* with your food. The beverage is distilled from grain or potatoes and is then given added taste with spices or herbs. Drink small quantities, consumed in one gulp.

- July is a popular month for vacations in Sweden. You will find the countryside and coast very busy, and especially populated with Swedes.

- Swedish design is world famous, especially in silver, ceramics, glassware and stainless steel. The Småland area in southeast Sweden is particularly noted for its fine glassware. Stores such as NK in Stockholm's Hamngatan have good selections of glassware, as does Nordiska Kristall, a store in Österlånggatan.

- Home furnishings are a Swedish specialty. Visit the world's biggest IKEA store at Kungens Kurva, outside Stockholm. A free bus leaves Mon.–Fri. every hour between 11 and 5 from Regeringsgatan, the street leading north from Hamngatan, a short distance east of the NK department store. Or try the very stylish Nordiska Galleriet, in Nybrogatan.

- Don't miss the lively Stockholm Jazz Festival, a five-day event held in mid-July. People flock to Skeppsholmen, Stockholm to listen to world-famous Swedish and international artists and groups playing jazz, blues, soul and Latin American music.

- In big cities you'll find public restrooms along some main streets, in main subway stations and in some department stores. Signs are *Damer* for ladies and *Herrar* for men. If there is an attendant the charge is normally between 1SKr and 5SKr.

Replica of the *Hand of God* by Swedish-American sculptor Carl Milles

STOCKHOLM

Stockholm is probably the only city in the world where you can catch a salmon at a busy road intersection under the walls of a royal palace, and where the city's subway stations double as eye-catching art galleries. The salmon thrive in Stockholm's clean waters at the very heart of the city, and local anglers fish from the Strömbron bridge. And the artwork that enlivens the subway stations is just one expression of the vigorous cultural life that makes Stockholm one of the world's most civilized cities.

City of Islands

Modern Stockholm is a large, exhilarating city. The scale of its public buildings is monumental, the bustle of its streets all-embracing; yet the city is given a uniquely open character by the thousands of islands in its archipelago and by the mirror images of lakes that pepper its hinterland. Stockholm stands on 14 interlocking islands; the city is a mosaic of land, lake and waterway stitched together by 57 bridges, making it a vibrant urban environment.

Gamla Stan is the heart of old Stockholm, a dramatic and fascinating expression of heritage and tradition. It stands on an island in the middle of the narrow bottleneck channel between the salty Baltic Sea and the inland freshwater lake of Mälaren. To the south is the hilly island of Södermalm, a suburban area with generous expanses of grass and trees. North of Gamla Stan and the buildings of state (the Royal Palace and the Parliament House) is Norrmalm, the business and commercial district. This is the heart of the modern city – glass, steel, concrete and good Swedish design – a cityscape of towering buildings, stylish shopping

Subway Art

Subway art in Stockholm is not freelance graffiti but spectacular and eclectic art. When the Stockolm *Tunnelbana* was built in the late 1940s an inspired decision was made to decorate each station with individual artworks. T-Centralen, the hub of the system, has the most, with examples ranging from terrazzo sofas to wrought-iron gates and ceramic figures on a white-stone background. Visit the Blue Line's amazing Kungsträdgården station; not only is it enormously deep, but it has outstanding sculptures. A guide to subway art is available from transport and tourist offices, and guided tours are regularly arranged.

malls, busy streets and traffic-free concourses that satisfy the demands of both vehicles and pedestrians. East of Norrmalm is the residential district of Östermalm and the city's island park, Djurgården, the world's first National City Park. To the west, the island mosaic spreads across the waters of Lake Mälaren, Stockholm's magnificent "inland" sea.

Compass Bearings

Most visitors arrive at the city's big, bustling central railroad station in Norrmalm, and the experience can be disorientating at first. Just east of the railroad station along Klarabergsgatan is the big sunken square of Sergels Torg, with its landmark *Kristall* tower of glass and steel and a huge glass facade on the south side. This is Stockholm's contemporary hub. You can orient yourself here and, within the pedestrian concourse, even relax in spite of the surrounding traffic and the bustle. Running north and south of Sergels

Torg are busy shopping streets, such as the pedestrian-only Drottninggatan. The northern section of Drottninggatan runs past many additional stores.

Continuing east from Sergels Torg into the street of Hamngatan takes you past elegant NK, the best name in Swedish shopping. This massive department store has floor after floor of fine shops and such fashionable restaurants as Bobergs Matsal, where Greta Garbo is said to have whiled away the time. Also in Hamngatan is Gallerian, a big shopping mall. Farther along are the offices of the Stockholm Visitors Board and the great open

swath of the Old Royal Gardens (Kungsträdgården). They sweep south to the waters of Strömmen, the magnificent Royal Palace and enchanting Gamla Stan.

Seeing Stockholm

For all its size Stockholm is a city that can be enjoyed on a human scale. You can see it by tour bus, or you can book a knowledgeable personal guide or a taxi tour, although the latter is expensive. Try a boat trip for the wider view of Stockholm's islands, and visit some attractions, such as Djurgården and Drottningholm Palace, by ferry boat.

to around 75 museums and attractions; a free boat trip; free public transportation in Stockholm and the surrounding area; free city-center parking for one, two or three days; and other benefits.

Stockholm is neatly packaged into separate entities because of its island nature, so you can plan your visit one day at a time. At night the city becomes even more majestic when it is lit up and vibrant with music and lively entertainment.

Stockholmers

Stockholm's confidence is infectious. Listen closely to advice and don't be afraid to ask for clarification or guidance. Then let the magic of the city take over; relax. Stockholmers have created one of the most endearing and enchanting cities in the world, and know how to enjoy it.

View over Stockholm's Old Town, with Riddarholm in the foreground

Ask at the tourist center about the Stockholmskortet (Stockholm Card). Once purchased, it offers free admission

ESSENTIAL INFORMATION

TOURIST INFORMATION
Stockholm Visitors Board
• Sverigehuset (Sweden House), Hamngatan 27, Kungsträdgården
☎ 08 789 24 90; fax 08 789 24 91; www.stockholmtown.com

URBAN TRANSPORTATION
Stockholm Centralstationen (Central Station) ☒ Klarabergsviadukten, ☎ 0771 75 75 75, is the main train station. The subway (*Tunnelbana*) is known as T-Bana. Subway stations are indicated by signs bearing a blue "T" on a white background. On the Stockholm city map subway stations are marked with the letter "T" in a red circle. An efficient bus system serves Stockholm and its environs. Public transportation in Stockholm has a unified ticket system, allowing you to transfer between systems. There is a Transit Authority information center in the T-Centralen subway station. For information ☎ 08 600 10 00. For buses ☎ 08 762 59 97.

For information on taxis and rates, ☎ 08 30 00 00, 08 15 00 00 or 020 20 20 20.

AIRPORT INFORMATION
Stockholm-Arlanda Airport is 28 miles north of the city and is Stockholm's main air terminal (information: ☎ 08 797 60 00). The Arlanda Express train links the airport and Central Station at 15-minute intervals daily 5:05 a.m.–12:05 a.m. (information: ☎ 08 588 890 00). The journey takes about 20 minutes. Airport buses (Flygbussana) run at 5- to 10-minute intervals (less frequently at night) and take 35 minutes to reach the Cityterminalen (City Terminal) at Klarabergsviadukten, near the Central Station (information: ☎ 08 600 10 00). Bromma Airport is 5 miles west of Stockholm and handles domestic and some international flights. For information ☎ 08 797 68 00. Buses run between the airport and the City Terminal; journey time 20 minutes. For information ☎ 08 600 10 00.

CLIMATE – average highs and lows for the month

JAN.	FEB.	MAR.	APR.	MAY	JUN.	JUL.	AUG.	SEP.	OCT.	NOV.	DEC.
-1°C	-1°C	3°C	8°C	15°C	19°C	21°C	20°C	15°C	9°C	4°C	0°C
30°F	30°F	37°F	46°F	59°F	66°F	70°F	68°F	59°F	48°F	39°F	32°F
-5°C	-6°C	-3°C	0°C	5°C	11°C	13°C	13°C	9°C	4°C	1°C	-2°C
23°F	21°F	27°F	32°F	41°F	52°F	55°F	55°F	48°F	39°F	34°F	28°F

CITY SIGHTS

Key to symbols

⊞ map coordinates refer to the Stockholm map on page 437; sights below are highlighted in yellow on the map.

✉ address or location ☎ telephone number
Ⓣ opening times Ⓢ nearest subway Ⓑ nearest bus or tram route ⛴ nearest ferry stop ⛽ restaurant or café on site or nearby 🖐 admission charge: $$$ more than 35SKr, $$ 15SKr–35SKr, $ less than 15SKr ⓘ other relevant information

DROTTNINGHOLMS SLOTT

Drottningholms Slott ⊞ A2, off the map
✉ Drottningholm ☎ 08 402 62 80 Ⓣ Daily 10–4:30, May–Aug.; daily noon–3:30, Sep.; Sat.–Sun. noon–3:30, early Jan.–Apr. 30 and Oct. 1 to mid-Dec.
Kina Slott ✉ Drottningholm ☎ 08 402 62 70
Ⓣ Daily 11–4:30, May–Aug.; noon–3:30, in Sep.
Slottsteater ✉ Drottningholm ☎ 08 759 04 06 (May–Sep.), 08 556 931 00 (rest of year) Ⓣ Guided tours daily 11–4:30, Jun.–Aug.; noon–4:30, in May; 1–3:30, in Sep.
Drottningholms Slott, Kina Slott and Slottsteater:
🍴 Café Ⓣ T-Brommaplan; then bus 301 or 323 Ⓑ 177, 178 ⛴ Stadshuskajen (in summer) 🖐 $$$ ⓘ Guided tours

Drottningholms Slott (Drottningholm Palace) is located on Lovön island, west of the city center. The palace, home of Sweden's royal family since 1981, is a superb 17th-century baroque building in the style of Versailles. It overlooks Lake Mälaren amid its own gardens, a mix of French and English styles. On the grounds is the 18th-century Kina Slott (Chinese Pavilion), where Asian meets rococo. Nearby is the 18th-century baroque Slottsteater (Palace Theater), which is a venue for opera and ballet from May through September. There also is a museum.

KUNGLIGA SLOTTET

Representationsvåningarna, Tre Kronor Museum, Skattkammaren and Gustav III's Antikmuseum ⊞ B2
✉ Slottsbacken ☎ 08 402 61 30
Ⓣ Daily 10–5, late Jun. to mid-Aug.; 10–4, mid-May to late Jun.

and mid-Aug. to Aug. 31; Tue.–Sun. noon–3, Feb. 1 to mid-May and Sep. 1 to early Jan. (Gustav III's Antikmuseum closed Sep. 1 to mid-May) Ⓢ Gamla Stan Ⓑ 43, 46, 55, 59, 76 🖐 $$$ (combination ticket available) ⓘ Guided tours
Livrustkammaren ✉ Slottsbacken 3 ☎ 08 10 24 88 Ⓣ Daily 10–5, Jun.–Aug.; Tue.–Sun. 11–5 (also Thu. 5–8), rest of year Ⓢ Gamla Stan Ⓑ 43, 46, 55, 59, 76 🖐 $$$ (combination ticket available) ⓘ Guided tours

The northern corner of Old Town is dominated by the monumental Kungliga Slottet (Royal Palace), the official residence of the king and queen, a stunning mix of classical styles developed throughout the 18th century on the site of the original Castle of Three Crowns. The palace's Representationsvåningarna (Royal Apartments) are a fine expression of French baroque, rococo and imperial styles. There are several museums within the palace, including the Tre Kronor Museum, with remnants of the Tre Kronor Castle; the Skattkammaren (Treasury), where state regalia are on display; Gustav III's Antikmuseum (Gustav III's Museum of Antiquities), with a collection of classical sculptures; and the Livrustkammaren (Royal Armory), where Sweden's 500-year military history is depicted in a colorful way. Time your visit to observe the changing of the guard in the palace's courtyard in summer (call for times).

MEDELTIDSMUSEET

⊞ B2 ✉ Strömparterren ☎ 08 508 318 90
Ⓣ Daily 11–4 (also Tue.–Thu. 4–6), Jul.–Aug.; Tue.–Sun. 11–4 (also Wed. 4–6), rest of year Ⓢ Gamla Stan; Kungsträdgården Ⓑ 43, 62
🍴 Museum café in summer 🖐 $$$

The Medeltidsmuseet (Museum of Medieval Stockholm) is a fascinating attraction, not least because of its underground location below the Riksdagshuset (Parliament House) on the tiny island of

Thespian pose – statue outside Drottningholm Palace Theater

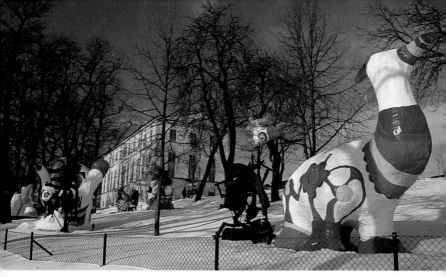

Colorful sculptures in the snow outside the Modern Museum

Helgeandsholmen, between Gamla Stan and the main city. Here, in the late 1970s, layers of medieval remains, including sections of old city wall, were uncovered during excavations for an underground parking lot. Admirably, the parking plan was abandoned in favor of preservation. Depicting the history of Stockholm from the 1250s to the 1520s, the museum is entered via steps leading down from Norrbro, the bridge between Gustav Adolfs Torg and Gamla Stan.

MODERNA MUSEET

🕂 C2 ✉ Skeppsholmen ☎ 08 519 552 00
🕐 Tue.–Sun. 10–6 (also Tue. and Wed. 6–8 p.m.)
🍴 Museum restaurant and café
🚇 Kungsträdgården 🚌 65 🚢 Slussen 💶 Free, except some exhibitions

The collection of contemporary art at Stockholm's Moderna Museet (Modern Museum) includes works by Roy Lichtenstein, Willem de Kooning, René Magritte and Pablo Picasso. Don't miss Salvador Dalí's startling *The Enigma of William Tell* and Marcel Duchamp's *Fountain*. There also are compelling works by Viking Eggeling and Isaac Grünewald.

NATIONALMUSEUM

🕂 C3 ✉ Södra Blasieholmshamnen ☎ 08 519 543 00
🕐 Tue.–Sun. 11–5 (also Tue. 5–8 all year and Thu. 5–8, Sep.–May) 🍴 Museum restaurant and café
🚇 T-Kungsträdgården 🚌 46, 55, 59, 62, 65, 76
💶 Free; special exhibitions $$$

The Nationalmuseum (National Museum of Fine Arts) is a dignified Italianate building on little Blasieholmen peninsula, across the water east of Gamla Stan and facing the Royal Palace. The museum has a superb collection of Swedish, international and applied art from the Middle Ages to the early 20th century. Among the paintings are works by Rembrandt, Goya and Paul Gauguin. Swedish art includes superb watercolors by Carl Larsson and fine works by Anders Zorn. The applied art section is a feast of furnishings and artifacts, and there are additional displays of sculpture and Russian icons.

NORDISKA MUSEET

🕂 C3 ✉ Djurgårdsvägen 6–16, Djurgården ☎ 08 519 546 00 🕐 Mon.–Fri. 10–4, Sat.–Sun. 11–5
🍴 Museum restaurant 🚇 T-Karlaplan 🚌 44, 47; tram from Nybroplan and Norrmalmstorg 🚢 From Slussen to Allmänna Gränd 💶 Free

The building housing the Nordiska Museet (Northern Museum) is a splendid work in its own right. Standing at the entrance to Djurgården, its gabled facade of brick and stone has elegant turrets and a handsome central steeple. The exhibits illustrate Swedish and general Nordic cultural life from the medieval period onward. There is an excellent section depicting the life of the Sami (Lapp) people and exhibits of Swedish traditional dress. Note as you enter the oak statue of Gustav Vasa, the 16th-century warrior who established the Swedish state.

SKANSEN

⊞ C2, off the map ✉ Djurgårdsslätten 49,
Djurgården ☎ 08 442 80 00 ⏰ Park and zoo: daily
10–10, Jun.–Aug.; 10–8, in May; 10–5, in Sep.; 10–4,
rest of year. Traditional buildings: daily 11–5,
May–Sep. (some houses also 5–7, Jun.–Aug.); 11–3,
rest of year (only a few houses open) 🍴 Museum
restaurant and café 🚌 44, 47; tram 7 from
Norrmalmstorg some weekends and holidays
⛴ From Slussen Nybroviken 💳 $$$

The Skansen open-air museum is located
on Djurgården, Stockholm's island park.
This area was the old hunting domain of
Swedish royalty and is now preserved as
an urban escape zone for Stockholmers
and visitors. Individual attractions on
Djurgården include the Vasamuseet (Vasa
Museum, see below) and the Nordiska
Museet (Northern Museum, see
opposite), but the island offers numerous
other diversions. Make a day of it,
enjoying delightful woodland walks or a
stroll alongside the quiet waters of the
Djurgårdsbrunnsviken. At the heart of
Djurgården, Skansen features more than
150 traditional buildings from the 18th to
20th centuries, and is a lively working
environment in summer for artisans. You
can sample traditional Swedish delicacies
here, such as *smörgåsbord* and waffles with
cream and cloudberries. Skansen's other
attraction is its zoo, which boasts elk,
bear, lynx and reindeer as well as an
aquarium. There are several smaller
museums and art galleries scattered
around Djurgården, and fun for everyone
at Gröna Lunds Tivoli amusement park.

STADSHUSET

⊞ B2 ✉ Ragnar Österbergs plan 1 ☎ 08 508 290
59 (City Hall); 08 508 290 00 (Tower) ⏰ Guided tours
daily at 10, 11, noon, 2 and 3, Jun.–Aug.; at 10 and
noon, rest of year. Tower: daily 10–4:30, May–Sep.
🍴 Restaurant in City Hall Ⓣ T-Centralen, Rådhuset
🚌 3, 62 💳 City Hall $$$, Tower $$

Stockholm's Stadshuset (City Hall) is
perhaps the city's finest example of early
20th-century Scandinavian Romantic
Nationalist style. This was the same style
that produced the *Jugend* buildings of
Helsinki (see page 163). Built of red brick
and with a magnificent Italianate tower, it

The steeple and façade of the Northern Museum

stands on the shore of Lake Mälaren. The
City Hall Tower (Stadshustornet) tapers
gently to an upper platform and lantern
that supports the gleaming *Tre Kronor*, the
three crowns symbol of the city. Interiors
are no less striking, the highlight being
the Golden Hall with its mosaic walls and
gleaming marble floor.

Admission to City Hall is by guided
tour only. From May to September you can
climb the 450-foot tower – or take the
elevator – for fine views over the city.

VASAMUSEET

⊞ C2 ✉ Galärvarvsvägen 14, Djurgården ☎ 08
519 548 00 ⏰ Daily 9:30–7, mid-Jun. to mid-Aug.;
10–5 (also Wed. 5–8), rest of year 🍴 Museum
restaurant and café 🚌 44, 47, 69 ⛴ Slussen (all
year); Nybroplan (summer) 💳 $$$ ℹ Guided tours in
English

The Vasamuseet (Vasa Museum) is a
great celebration of a unique historical
event. The focus of the museum is the
sailing ship *Vasa*, which sank
spectacularly in Stockholm harbor within
minutes of starting its maiden voyage in
1628. At 230 feet long and fully restored
and rigged, the *Vasa* is breathtaking. The
ship was ornamental as well as
functional, and the vessel's finest features
were preserved in the muddy waters of
the Baltic for more than 330 years. The
museum also tells the story of the people
who salvaged the *Vasa* in 1961, and there
are exhibits showing some of the 12,000
artifacts recovered.

A STROLL AROUND GAMLA STAN

Stockholm's Gamla Stan (Old Town) – or *staden mellan broarna,* "the city among the bridges," as it is more lyrically known to Swedes – is not a perfectly preserved medieval townscape by any means. Disastrous fires in 1407 and 1640 destroyed the original wooden buildings of medieval Gamla Stan. But the island nature of the settlement, its small area and its crowded layout have spared Gamla Stan from too much modernization. What remains today is a superb enclave of old stone buildings dating from the 15th to the 18th centuries.

You can wander at will through the Old Town without getting lost. On this tiny island you are never far from the waterside or a bridge to re-orient yourself. Pick up an enlarged Gamla Stan map, widely available in stores, restaurants and tourist venues, to help you find specific places.

There are many easily missed treasures hidden away from the busy main streets of Västerlånggatan and Österlånggatan. Pay a visit to the Great Church (Storkyrkan), Stockholm's 13th-century cathedral, which lies just south of the courtyard of the Royal Palace. The church's finest artifact is the oak- and elkhorn-gilded sculpture of *St. George and the Dragon,* a 15th-century Gothic masterpiece of thorny carving. You may be lucky and catch a lunchtime organ recital or other musical performance in the church.

From the church, go into the narrow street of Trångsund and then turn left past a charming old phone booth to reach Great Square (Stortorget). This was the scene in 1520 of the notorious Stockholm "Blood Bath," when Christian II of Denmark slaughtered 82 Swedish nobles and citizens in a bid to seal with blood his overlordship of Sweden. This brutal act inspired Gustav Vasa, son of a murdered nobleman, to rebel successfully against Denmark and to secure Sweden's independence. On the west side of Great Square is a row of splendid gabled houses with little cafés and restaurants on their ground floors. The 18th-century Bourse, or Stock Exchange, commands the north side of the square. The Swedish Academy, the body that selects Nobel prize winners, meets at the Bourse.

Leave the square via the east side and walk down Köpmangatan, "Street of the Merchants," the oldest street in the Old Town and home to several fine antiques shops with attractively painted ceilings. At the end of Köpmangatan, in the little square of Köpmantorget, is a dramatic reprise of the Great Church's statue of *St. George and the Dragon,* this time in bronze but just as powerful. Farther east is Österlånggatan, a long, winding street that was once the Old Town's shoreline.

Bear right, down the short slope of Köpmanbrinken street, and then keep right along Österlånggatan, past stylish restaurants, antiques and craft stores, and fashion salons. There are lots of gift possibilities here, especially for children, in shops such as Textilarna, Kalikå and Tomtar & Troll, which has a wonderful array of painted wooden handicrafts. The narrow streets running east to the sea, such as Drakens Gränd, Ferkens Gränd and Packhusgränd, mark the old piers of the early medieval era. Near the end of Österlånggatan is the well-known restaurant Den Gyldene Freden (see page 568).

Soon you reach Iron Square (Järntorget), a name probably derived from the days when the Old Town's

A rest from sightseeing – sample the delights of Swedish food in the Old Town

fortunes were built on its status as the main outlet for the Swedish iron and copper trade. Here, against the wall of the old Central Bank, is the remarkably lifelike statue of Stockholm poet Evart Taube, a popular performer who died in 1976. Take a break at the nearby Sundbergs Konditori, a long-established institution (established 1785 and the oldest bakery in the city), selling coffee and delicious pastries.

From Järntorget, turn right onto Västerlånggatan, the busiest street in the Old Town, crammed with stores and tempting restaurants and cafés. On the right, just past the Mårten Trotzig restaurant, you'll pass the narrow entrance to Mårten Trotzigs Gränd,

reputed to be the narrowest alleyway in Stockholm and named after a German medieval copper trader who had a business here.

All the way along Västerlånggatan you will be tempted by souvenir stores; Swedish craft stores, such as Handkraft Swea at No. 24 and a host of specialty shops. Note the glass-paneled ceilings of many of the stores. Wandering along the delightful side streets is equally rewarding.

To end your Old Town excursion, stroll to where the bridge over the canal Stallkanalen leads through the arched passage to the gate at Riksgatan. Follow this back into Stockholm via the shopping street of Drottninggatan.

SWITZERLAND

"SWITZERLAND is simply a large, humpy, solid rock, with a thin skin of grass stretched over it."

From *A Tramp Abroad* by Mark Twain

Opposite: Mountains, green pastures and picture-postcard villages – all ingredients for a Swiss landscape

Switzerland

SWITZERLAND

With stunning Alpine scenery, lush meadows, a medley of beautiful lakes and attractive cities and towns, Switzerland has a wonderful variety of natural and man-made attractions.

Neutral Territory

The Swiss Constitution, modeled on that of the United States, was drawn up in 1848 and revised in 1874; it is still in force today. Modern Switzerland is a federation of democracies (cantons), and neutrality has traditionally been the cornerstone of state policy. Switzerland has interfered in no foreign conflicts and has made no alliances, although it became a member of the United Nations in 2002.

Remaining neutral through both world wars, Switzerland emerged in 1945 as a powerful commercial player. Banking has long thrived here due to the political stability of the country and because of Swiss financial acumen. The superb infrastructure of railroads, tunnels and roads has overcome the mountainous terrain and allows the country to exploit a trading position at the center of Europe.

MORE TOP DESTINATIONS IN SWITZERLAND

- Ascona D1 ● Baden C3
- Basel B3 ● Bern B2 ● Brienz C2
- Château de Chillon B2
- Engelberg C2 ● Fribourg B2
- Grindelwald C2 ● Gstaad B2
- Interlaken C2 ● Lausanne A2
- Montreux B2 ● St.-Moritz E2
- Schaffhausen C3 ● Wilderswil C2
- Villars B1 ● Zermatt C1

The Swiss Landscape

Europe's continental watershed runs through Switzerland, a landlocked nation, with a central lowland sandwiched between the Jura mountains to the north and the mighty Alps. The mountain glaciers and peaks of the Swiss Alps occupy 60 percent of the country. Forests cover another quarter of the land and the rest is a delightful mix of lakes and meadow pasture. Switzerland's weather is typical of central Europe; Ticino canton, south of the Alps, has a Mediterranean climate, and some days the *föhn* – a warm, dry wind – blows from the northern slopes of the Alps.

Language and Manners

Reflecting Switzerland's location in central Europe, the Swiss speak four different languages: Schwyzerdütsch, a Swiss-German dialect (although German is used for reading and writing); French; Italian; and Romansch, an ancient Latin tongue. This linguistic diversity results in very different types of people, and you'll notice this as you travel.

On the whole, the Swiss are extremely law-abiding, and consider punctuality very important. Manners are formal, with hand-shaking and serious toasts in all social circumstances. Efficient, civic-minded and polite, they make Switzerland one of Europe's best-run countries.

Vacationing in Switzerland

The fabled Swiss efficiency has positive benefits for visitors: trains run punctually, hotels are clean and comfortable, opening times for attractions are reliable, and everyone connected with tourism speaks English. You'll also discover that Switzerland is expensive, so if you're watching your budget, don't plan on staying too long. There's something to enjoy throughout the year – skiing in the mountains during the winter, walking, sailing and other outdoor pursuits all summer. Late spring sees the countryside at its best, with carpets of mountain and meadow wildflowers; autumn, when the leaves turn and the first snow whitens the lower peaks, also is magnificent.

Switzerland

TIMELINE

3,000 BC	Evidence of earliest neolithic settlers by Lake Neuchâtel.
circa 100 BC	Romans invade from the south, incorporating Helvetic tribes.
circa AD 400	Romans expelled southward; Burgundians occupy western areas (modern French-speaking Switzerland) and Alemans the north and east (German-speaking Switzerland).
1032	Existing country incorporated into Holy Roman Empire, followed by gradual emergence of powerful independent nobles.
1515	Defeat at Battle of Marignano inaugurates neutrality.
1526	Zwingli's Reformation takes hold in Zurich, continued by John Calvin in Geneva beginning in 1532.
1648	Treaty of Westphalia recognizes Swiss neutrality and independence of 13 cantons.
1798	French invasion and rule under Napoleon, who establishes Helvetic Republic.
1815	Congress of Vienna guarantees Swiss independence.
1848	Adoption of Swiss Constitution, which defines political organization of the country.
1864	First Convention of Geneva is accepted and signed by 16 nations; the Red Cross is founded.
1914–18	Switzerland remains neutral during World War I.
1919	President Woodrow Wilson chooses Geneva as headquarters of the League of Nations.
1939–45	Switzerland remains neutral during World War II, but image is tarnished by pro-Nazi activities.
1946	United Nations takes over role of League of Nations; Geneva retained as European headquarters.
1990	Population votes to freeze nuclear power development.
1999	Ruth Dreifuss becomes Switzerland's first woman president.
2002	Switzerland becomes the 190th member of the United Nations.

THE SWISS ARMY PENKNIFE

The Swiss army penknife was first manufactured more than 100 years ago to equip the Swiss army. Over 200 models of this versatile penknife now exist, each with a distinctive white cross in a shield on a red background. Its blades and attachments, ranging from tweezers, corkscrews and magnifying glasses to tiny hacksaws and nail files, can perform a wide range of tasks; it has justifiably been called the "smallest toolbox in the world."

Switzerland

SURVIVAL GUIDE

- Keep more money available than you think you will need; cash seems to be spent alarmingly fast throughout Switzerland. Credit cards are widely accepted.
- Although most Swiss are excellent linguists, it's polite to ask if they speak English before starting a conversation or asking a question.
- Be polite to everyone – *bitte, prego* or *je vous en prie* is the equivalent of "you're welcome," and it's important to use one of these expressions when you're thanked. When you use public transportation, it's customary to give up your seat for elderly people, pregnant women and people with disabilities.
- Be punctual; if you're likely to be arriving later than planned at your hotel, let them know you've been held up.
- It is considered rude to eat or drink on the street. If you purchase food to go, find somewhere to sit down and eat it.
- Don't drop litter; it is a finable offense. When getting rid of trash, make sure you put it in the compartment designated for that particular type of waste.
- Although informality is the norm in active, health-conscious Switzerland, very casual clothing – such as beachwear – isn't usually seen in cities.
- There is no state medical health service in Switzerland; treatment must be paid for on the spot. Therefore, it is very important to carry medical travel insurance valid in Switzerland. Many drugs can be bought over the counter. If you need a prescription drug, the prescription must be written by a Swiss doctor.
- In large towns and cities, stores are often closed on Monday mornings. Museums are usually closed on Mondays.
- Always cross the street at designated crossings, and wait for the green man symbol.
- Each canton and community is responsible for its own laws and law enforcement. The police uniform differs widely from place to place, as do local bylaws. Respect authority at all times, even if you see no point in what you are being requested to do.
- Use the superbly efficient public transportation system rather than the inordinately expensive taxis.
- You'll save money by eating and drinking in smaller establishments away from the more upscale areas.
- There is no need to tip in Switzerland; a service charge is automatically added to all bills.

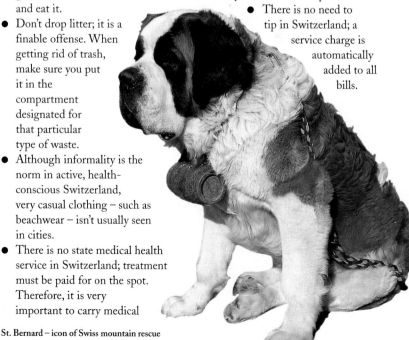

St. Bernard – icon of Swiss mountain rescue

GENEVA

Sparkling Geneva (Genève), beautifully situated by the shores of Lake Geneva (Lac Léman) and backed by the Jura mountains and Alps, is indeed an elegant city. With its key role as an important international meeting place, many visitors are here on business, but others come to enjoy the scenic location, excellent museums, stores, restaurants and lively cultural life.

The Modern City

Strategically positioned at the head of the Rhône river, Geneva joined the Swiss Confederation in 1815, after Napoleon's downfall. Since then the city has grown, prospered and become increasingly cosmopolitan.

Today Geneva hosts meetings, exhibitions, conventions and many organizations involved with humanitarian and social causes. It plays a major part in Swiss industry, finance and commerce, but has succeeded in retaining much of its French style and attitude, resulting in a pleasing blend of charm and efficiency.

An important university and scientific center, Geneva also is home to CERN, the European Center of Nuclear Research. The city is ringed with attractive countryside – the ski slopes of the French Alps are less than an hour away, and Lake Geneva offers superb water sports facilities.

Old Town and Beyond

Geneva is used to foreign visitors, and it's an easy city with which to become familiar. Getting around by public transportation is simple, and the center of the city is small enough to cover on foot, with much of the Old Town pedestrian-only. It's worth spending a couple of hours getting your bearings by walking around the town center, which lies on either side of the Rhône river.

Much of what you'll want to see is in or around the Old Town and is well signed, although with more than 30 museums to choose from, you are likely to take a bus at some point. Tourist trams run through the Old Town, leaving from the place Neuve every half-hour; they're a relaxing way to enjoy the city, although guided walking tours are available.

Tour buses travel to Lausanne and Château de Chillon, and into the Alps to Mont Blanc and Gstaad. Many lake cruises are offered, most lasting from one to three hours and many with an English commentary.

The steeple of St. Peter's Cathedral

Gourmet Geneva

Like all Swiss cities, Geneva has a large range of restaurants offering cuisine from around the world. It also has its own specialties, many of which have more in common with France than the rest of Switzerland. Eating out can be expensive, although away from the city center you'll find friendly and atmospheric neighborhood restaurants where prices are considerably lower.

Many places serve Swiss specialties such as fondue and *rösti*, but you can choose from French, Italian, Thai, Japanese, Korean, Chinese, Russian, Spanish, Australian, Moroccan and many more. You'll find all the usual fast-food outlets in the center, and it's fun to shop for a picnic to eat in one of the lakeside parks. There's a plethora of bars throughout the city; the nicest are in the Old Town and along the lakeside.

Festivals and Fun

Geneva's biggest traditional festival is the *Escalade*, a December commemoration of a 1602 battle. A wonderful costumed parade marches through the Old Town, and the whole city is out in the streets. The *Bol d'Or* annual sailing regatta is held in June, when more than 600 boats and their crew take over the lakeshore, and at the beginning of August the city is lit up by musical fireworks displays during the renowned *Fêtes de Genève*.

The globe of unity outside the Palace of Nations

Designer Style and Souvenirs

Geneva stores do not close at lunchtime and are open until 8 p.m. on Thursdays. There are vast malls on the city outskirts, but it's likely you'll be shopping in the downtown area, where the most attractive and elegant stores are located. Many of them are along the rue du Rhône, the rue du Mont Blanc and neighboring streets.

Don't miss Globus in the Grand Passage, a large department store that's a Geneva institution. You'll find watches, jewelry, high fashion and superb leather goods from outlets such as Boucheron and Piaget, Christian Dior, Giorgio Armani, Gucci, Hermes and Chanel.

If you're looking for souvenirs to take home, try the tourist boutique in Globus in the Grand Passage, Swiss Corner on the rue des Alpes, or l'Ours de Berne on the place du Port.

ESSENTIAL INFORMATION

 TOURIST INFORMATION
Genève Tourisme (Geneva Tourism)
• Rue du Mont Blanc 18
   Mon. 10–6, Tue.–Sat. 9–6
☎ 022 909 7000; fax 022 909 7011;
www.geneva-tourism.ch

 URBAN TRANSPORTATION
Geneva is efficiently served by swift and punctual trolley buses and buses that cover the city's various areas; it's likely you'll be traveling mainly inside Zone 10, which covers the city center. You buy and validate your ticket from the machines at each bus stop, which also have route maps and clear instructions about using the system. A ticket for one zone is valid 30 minutes; two zones, 60 minutes. The best ticket for visitors is a day pass, which provides unlimited travel in two zones (SF6) or all zones (SF12). To board or leave the bus, press the red button near the door;

the doors will open and close automatically. You can get more information from the Transports Publics Genevois (TPG) head office, route de la Chapelle 1, or call the Mobility Call Center (☎ 022 308 344). Taxis can be found at stands in the city center and also can be hailed on the street or called from your hotel. Call Taxiphone SA Genève (☎ 022 331 4133).

 AIRPORT INFORMATION
The Aéroport Internationale de Genève-Cointrin (Geneva International Airport, ☎ 022 717 7111) is 3 miles north of the city center. It is linked to the central railroad station by trains departing every 10 minutes, daily 6:30 a.m.– 12:30 a.m., with a 7-minute journey time. Bus No. 10 runs approximately every 10 minutes between the airport and the city center; the trip takes around 20–25 minutes. Taxis are available outside the airport terminal.

CLIMATE – average highs and lows for the month

JAN.	FEB.	MAR.	APR.	MAY	JUN.	JUL.	AUG.	SEP.	OCT.	NOV.	DEC.
4°C	5°C	10°C	13°C	18°C	22°C	25°C	25°C	20°C	13°C	8°C	4°C
39°F	41°F	50°F	55°F	64°F	72°F	77°F	77°F	68°F	55°F	46°F	39°F
-2°C	0°C	2°C	3°C	7°C	12°C	14°C	14°C	11°C	6°C	2°C	0°C
28°F	32°F	36°F	37°F	45°F	54°F	57°F	57°F	52°F	43°F	36°F	32°F

CITY SIGHTS

Key to symbols

➕ map coordinates refer to the Geneva map on page 451; sights below are highlighted in yellow on the map.

✉ address or location ☎ telephone number
🕐 opening times 🚌 nearest bus or tram route
🍴 restaurant or café on site or nearby 💲 admission charge: $$$ more than SF10, $$ SF7–SF10, $ less than SF7 ℹ other relevant information

CATHÉDRALE ST-PIERRE

➕ B2 ✉ cour St.-Pierre ☎ 022 311 7575; tours 022 310 2929 🕐 Cathédrale: Mon.–Sat. 9:30–6:30, Sun. noon–6:30, Jun.–Sep.; Mon.–Sat. 10–5:30, Sun. noon–5:30, rest of year. Site archéologique: Tue.–Fri. 11–5, Sat.–Sun. 11–5:30, Jun.–Sep.; Tue.–Fri. 2–5, Sat.–Sun. 1:30–5:30, rest of year 🚌 3, 5, 17; tram 12 💲 Cathedral free

The vast and austere Cathédrale St-Pierre has been a Protestant church since 1536. It was built in the 12th and 13th centuries, and its current neoclassic facade was added in the 18th century. This is where John Calvin preached; his seat is still in the north aisle. Climb the 157 steps up the tower for fine views over Geneva and the lake. The cathedral has a long-standing musical tradition; the Clémence, the largest bell in the tower, weighs over 6 tons and was placed there in 1407. The carillon changes monthly, and there are organ recitals at 6 p.m. on Saturdays from June through September.

COLLECTIONS BAUR

➕ C1 ✉ rue Munier-Romilly 8 ☎ 022 704 3282 🕐 Tue.–Sun. 2–6 🚌 1, 8 💲 $

An elegant 19th-century mansion houses the Collections Baur (Baur Collection), the Asian art collection of connoisseur Alfred Baur. Among the exhibits on show you'll find exquisite Chinese ceramics and jade, snuff bottles, prints and *netsuke* (Japanese carved toggles), and intricate Japanese and Chinese lacquerwork dating from the eighth to the 18th century. Spend some time lingering over the porcelain and marveling at the depth and translucency of the yellow and celadon-green glazes.

JARDIN ANGLAIS

➕ B2–C2 ✉ promenade du Lac 🕐 Daily dawn–dusk 🍴 Cafés and restaurants 🚌 6, 8, 10

Statues, trees and colorful flowers help make the lakeside Jardin Anglais (English Garden) and its mountain views the perfect place to escape the city's bustle. Admire the 1862 fountain, complete with numerous reclining nymphs, before spending a few minutes at the Floral Clock. This huge timepiece, made entirely of 6,500 flowers and plants, was installed in 1955 as a symbol of the Geneva watch industry. A short walk along the lake will bring you to Parc de la Grange, a lovely rose garden seen at its best in mid-June.

MUSÉE ARIANA

➕ A3 ✉ avenue de la Paix 10 ☎ 022 418 5450 🕐 Wed.–Mon. 10–5 🚌 5, 8, 11, 14, 18 💲 Free; temporary exhibitions $

The Musée Ariana is Switzerland's only public museum dedicated entirely to ceramics and glass. With some 18,000 objects, this collection is one of Europe's largest, covering seven centuries of European, Middle Eastern and Asian ceramic and glass manufacture. The main techniques represented are pottery, stoneware, faïence and porcelain.

MUSÉE D'ART ET D'HISTOIRE

➕ B1 ✉ rue Charles-Galland 2 ☎ 022 418 2600 🕐 Tue.–Sun. 10–5 🍴 Restaurant 🚌 1, 2, 3, 5, 8, 36 💲 Free; temporary exhibitions $

Behind the grandiose facade of Geneva's Musée d'Art et d'Histoire (Museum of Art and History) lies a dauntingly large collection of paintings, archeological finds and objets d'art. Ancient history fans will enjoy the Egyptian, Greek, Roman and Etruscan rooms. The galleries cover the full range of European painting but concentrate on Swiss specialties, such as Ferdinand Hodler's powerful work *The Drinkers* or Konrad Witz's 1444 altarpiece; its background is one of Europe's first accurate landscape representations. Other rooms contain applied arts collections, fine furniture, silver and porcelain.

Place du Bourg-de-Four – the heart of old Geneva

MUSÉE D'HISTOIRE NATURELLE

✚ C1 ✉ route de Malagnou 1 ☎ 022 418 6300
🕐 Tue.–Sun. 9:30–5 🍴 Café and snack bar
🚌 1, 8, 20, 27; tram 12, 16 🎟 Free, except some temporary exhibitions

The splendid Musée d'Histoire Naturelle (Natural History Museum) is immensely popular, so get there early. The exhibits cover everything from the history of the Earth through the dinosaur age to comprehensive displays of animals, birds, reptiles and fish from all over the world. It's all excellently displayed, with some very realistic sound effects to help your imagination. Don't miss the relief map of Switzerland on the fifth floor.

MUSÉE INTERNATIONAL DE L'AUTOMOBILE

✚ B3 ✉ Voie-des-Traz 40, 1218 Grand-Saconnex ☎ 022 788 8484 🕐 Wed.–Fri. 3–8, Sat.–Sun. 10–6
🍴 Cafeteria 🚌 5, 10, 18 🎟 $$$

A short trip out of town is Palexpo, Geneva's impressive exhibition complex, housing the Musée International de l'Automobile (International Automobile Museum), a must for automobile fans. Four hundred vehicles are grouped in chronological order, from early speedsters to General George Patton's jeep and Elvis Presley's Cadillac. Space is devoted to cars of the future, rally and Formula 1 models, and there are numerous movie clips, posters, models and hands-on games.

MUSÉE INTERNATIONAL DE LA CROIX-ROUGE ET DU CROISSANT-ROUGE

✚ A3 ✉ avenue de la Paix 17 ☎ 022 748 9525
🕐 Wed.–Mon. 10–5 🍴 Restaurant 🚌 8, F, V, Z
🎟 $$ ℹ Guided tours by appointment (☎ 022 748 9506)

It's well worth visiting the state-of-the-art Musée International de la Croix-Rouge et du Croissant-Rouge (International Red Cross and Red Crescent Museum), which explains the principles and history of the organization during some of the most serious crises of the 20th century.

PALAIS DES NATIONS

✚ A3 ✉ avenue de la Paix (Porte 39) ☎ 022 917 4896 or 022 917 4539 🕐 Daily 10–5, Jul.–Aug.; 10–noon and 2–4, Apr.–Jun. and Sep.–Oct.; Mon.–Fri. 10–noon and 2–4, rest of year 🍴 Café 🚌 5, 8, 11, 14, 18, F, V, Z 🎟 $$

Built between 1929 and 1936 to house the League of Nations, the Palais des Nations (Palace of Nations) is now the European seat of the United Nations. The vast marble and travertine-stone complex is beautifully situated on the slopes above the lake, with views of Mont Blanc. You can tour some of the interior and see the Salle des Pas-Perdus, a room decorated with marble donated by United Nations member countries, and the 2,000-seat Salle des Assemblées, one of the world's most active conference centers. After the tour, learn more through the multilingual interactive games.

PLACE DU BOURG-DE-FOUR

✚ B1 ✉ place du Bourg-de-Four 🍴 Cafés and restaurants nearby 🚌 8, 17

Bourg-de-Four square is the heart of Old Geneva, historically the site of the Roman market, medieval trade fairs, and political and religious meetings. Today the square and its surrounding streets are a lovely place to enjoy a drink at one of the bars and cafés. Many of the fine buildings date from the 16th century; note their extra floors, added later to accommodate the flood of Protestant religious exiles.

Headquarters of the International Red Cross, in Geneva

THE RED CROSS

In 1859 Henri Dunant, son of a prominent Genevan family, set off to appeal to Napoleon III of France on a personal matter. Dunant caught up with Napoleon the day after the Battle of Solferino, where he saw more than 40,000 wounded men desperately in need of care and attention.

Dunant returned to Geneva and wrote a moving book, *Souvenir of Solferino*, in which he proposed the establishment of a body of volunteer male nurses to impartially care for the wounded in wartime. He further suggested that these men be recognized through an international agreement. Three friends added their support, the book was published and the International Committee of Help for the Wounded in Case of War (Comité Internationale de Secours aux Blessées en Cas de Guerre) was set up.

In 1864, the First Convention of Geneva was accepted and signed by 16 nations; a revised version of its standards of treatment for prisoners of war is still in effect today. An easily recognizable logo for the new movement was needed, and a reverse version of the Swiss flag was used; a red cross on a white background, rather than a white cross on a red background, and a symbol known the world over.

The Red Cross, present in more than 50 countries throughout the world, works hand in hand with the Red Crescent, an identical body functioning in Muslim and other non-Christian countries. Henri Dunant was awarded the Nobel Peace Prize in 1901.

The Red Cross functions at both international and national levels. The international headquarters are in Geneva, and it is from here that major humanitarian relief work is coordinated. Each participating country has its own national committee that deals with day-to-day work in that particular country. The Red Cross is still manned largely by volunteers, who cover everything from terrorist attacks and natural disasters to organizing collections for war victims and refugees, as well as training the public in emergency aid procedures.

ZURICH

Zurich

Primarily a business center, with an emphasis on international finance and banking, this prosperous and clean city has plenty for visitors to enjoy. It is dotted with fine buildings, museums, historic churches and green spaces, the perfect background for affluent stores, elegant cafés and well-dressed citizens.

Lakeside City

Zurich surrounds the northern end of Zürichsee (Lake Zurich), from which the Limmat river flows to bisect the city. The oldest part lies on either side of the river, with the 19th-century

Swiss precision watch

Peaceful St. Peter's

ZURICH

| 0 | 200 | 400 m |
| 0 | 200 | 400 yards |

N

Museum für Gestaltung

Liebfrauenkirche

Musee Suisse

Hauptbahnhof

Kantonale Verwaltung

Zurich HB

Universitätsspital

Sihlpost

Seillbahn

Polytechnicum

Sihl

Amtshäuser

Universtät

Zooh!

Zentralbibliothek

Predigerkirche

Konservatorium

ALTSTADT

Lindenhof

SIHLPORTE

Kantonales Gerichtsgebäude

Rathaus

Zinnfiguren Museum

Alter Botanischer Garten

PELIKANPLATZ

St Peterskirche

HEIMPLATZ

Kunsthaus

Zunfthaus zur Meisen

MÜNSTERHOF

PARADEPLATZ Fraumünster

Grossmünster

Schau-spielhaus

Stadthaus

Helmhaus

Börse

Wasserkirche

Stiftung Sammlung E G Bührle

Nationalbank

Stadelhofen

BÜRKLIPLATZ

Sechseläutenplatz

Kongresshaus

Opernhaus

Zürichsee

Arboretum

Zurich

grandeur of the Bahnhofstrasse area on the west. East of the river, gentle hills rise to the impressive university complex, while wide boulevards, parks and gardens run along the lake.

A tram ride is an essential experience; these efficient vehicles ensure that city streets are virtually traffic-free. If you feel in need of exercise, you can borrow a free bike from four places in the city, including the main railroad station (daily 7:30 a.m. to 9:30 p.m., May through October; ID and deposit of SF20 required).

Evenings Out

There's a wide range of excellent restaurants in Zurich, most of them expensive. It is possible to eat well and relatively cheaply on the east side of the river. You'll find the usual fast-food outlets, excellent cafés and tearooms, and cozy taverns and wine cellars.

Notice boards all over the city list movie theaters (often showing American films in English), concerts, theater and opera. For a relaxed evening with the locals, you'll find plenty of packed bars, open late, in and around the Limmatquai; on summer nights there is an array of street performers. Zurich also has a number of cabarets and discos.

Chocolates and Watches

Bahnhofstrasse, running from the main railroad station to the lake, is one of Europe's great shopping streets. Lined with expensive stores, it is where you'll find luxury items, including fashion, jewelry, watches, porcelain, furs and accessories. It's also home to Schweizer Heimatwerk, a lovely store specializing in every type of Swiss handicraft.

Don't miss Sprüngli, one of the most mouthwatering chocolate shops you'll ever visit. And the narrow old streets on each side of the river are packed with antiques stores, clock and watch outlets, and fun places for picking up souvenirs.

ESSENTIAL INFORMATION

TOURIST INFORMATION
Zürich Tourism
• Hauptbahnhof ☎ 01 215 4000; fax 01 215 4044; www.zuerich.com

URBAN TRANSPORTATION
Zurich's efficient tram and bus system runs daily 4:30 a.m.–12:30 a.m. It is easy to use, fast and never late. Tickets must be purchased and validated before boarding; all bus stops have ticket machines with detailed transportation maps and instructions for buying and validating your ticket. If you are in Zurich for a couple of days or more, you can buy a "Zurich Day Ticket" (24-hour pass) or the "9 O'Clock Pass" (travel after 9 a.m.) for unlimited travel in the city. Like standard single tickets, these also are valid for trams, buses, local trains and some boats. Numbers and stops (which are all named) are displayed on the front of the vehicles as well as inside. You must press the red

button on the door to open the door before getting off; it will close automatically. For general information about public transportation ☎ 848 988 988; www.zvv.ch. Taxis are an expensive option; call Alpha Taxi (☎ 01 777 7777), or Taxi 44 AG (☎ 01 444 4444). Boats run on Lake Zurich April through October. Their timetables are listed at departure points; call Wassertaxi (☎ 01 928 1811).

AIRPORT INFORMATION
Zurich-Kloten Airport, ☎ 043 816 2211, or for flight information ☎ 0900 300 313 (toll call), is about 6 miles north of the city center. Trains run every 5–15 minutes from the Hauptbahnhof, daily 5:30 a.m.–12:30 a.m., with a ride time of around 10 minutes. There are two terminals, arrivals terminals 1 and 2, which are interconnected. Taxis are available from outside the terminals; the journey from the airport to downtown costs around CHF50.

CLIMATE – average highs and lows for the month

JAN.	FEB.	MAR.	APR.	MAY	JUN.	JUL.	AUG.	SEP.	OCT.	NOV.	DEC.
2°C	3°C	8°C	12°C	16°C	19°C	22°C	22°C	18°C	12°C	6°C	3°C
36°F	37°F	46°F	54°F	61°F	66°F	72°F	72°F	64°F	54°F	43°F	37°F
-2°C	-2°C	2°C	4°C	8°C	11°C	14°C	14°C	11°C	7°C	2°C	0°C
28°F	28°F	36°F	39°F	46°F	52°F	57°F	57°F	52°F	45°F	36°F	32°F

The twin towers of Grossmünster overlook the Limmat river and the Old Town

City Sights

Key to symbols

✚ map coordinates refer to the Zurich map on page 456; sights below are highlighted in yellow on the map.
✉ address or location ☎ telephone number
🕐 opening times 🚌 nearest bus or tram route
🍴 restaurant or café on site or nearby ✋ admission charge: $$$ more than SF10, $$ SF7–SF10, $ less than SF7 ℹ other relevant information

Altstadt

✚ A3–B3 ✉ Altstadt ☎ (Tours) 044 215 4088 🚌 4, 6, 7, 15 🕐 Two-hour guided tours (German and English): Mon.–Fri. at 3, Sat.–Sun. at 11 and 3, May–Oct.; Wed.–Sat. at 11 a.m. rest of year (information: tourist office, see page 457) ✋ Tours: $$$

The narrow streets and peaceful squares on either side of the Limmat river make up the Altstadt (Old Town) with its well-preserved old buildings. Take in the Lindenhof, a square planted with lime trees on the site of the original Roman settlement, then cross the river to amble down the east side's lively Niederdorfstrasse and Hirschengasse.

Fraumünster

✚ A2 ✉ Am Münsterhofplatz ☎ 01 211 4100
🕐 Daily 9–6, May–Sep.; 10–5, Mar.–Apr. and in Oct.; 10–4, rest of year. Sun. service at 10 a.m. 🚌 2, 4, 6, 7, 8, 9, 11, 13 ✋ Free

The graceful spire of the Fraumünster (Our Lady's Minster Church), founded in the ninth century by two German princesses, rises near the west riverbank in the Old Town. The interior dates from 1250 and earlier; against its gray stone serenity, Marc Chagall's stained-glass choir windows vibrate with green, blue and yellow. Alberto Giacometti designed the transept glass.

Grossmünster

✚ B2 ✉ Zwingliplatz ☎ 01 252 5949
🕐 Mon.–Sat. 9–6, Sun. noon–6, mid-Mar. to Oct. 31; daily 10–5, rest of year. Open Sun. for services 🚌 4, 15 ✋ $

Grossmünster (Great Cathedral) played a major part in Zurich's Reformation (a 16th-century movement which aimed at reforming the Roman Catholic Church and resulted in the establishment of Protestant churches). It was here that Ulrich Zwingli, the father of Swiss Protestantism, preached and taught. He transformed this Catholic foundation into a theological college that became the focal point of the University of Zurich. The church, galleries and three naves were built between 1100 and 1260, a superb Romanesque basilica with some outstanding sculpture on the capitals of its columns. Be sure to visit the tranquil cloister, which has exhibits telling the story of the Reformation, and save energy to climb up the tower, which has lovely views over Zurich and the lake.

KUNSTHAUS

✚ B2 ✉ Heimplatz 1 ☎ 01 253 8484 ◷ Tue.–Thu. 10–9, Fri.–Sun. 10–5 🍴 Café and restaurant 🚃 Tram 3, 5, 8, 9. 31, N8 💷 $$

Zurich's Kunsthaus (Art Gallery), a lively museum that often mounts important temporary exhibitions, is mainly devoted to 19th- and 20th-century paintings and artworks. Earlier times are represented by a clutch of Venetian paintings, as well as some splendid Dutch works. The exhibits of modern art are housed in the newer wing. Here you'll find the largest collection of Edvard Munch outside Scandinavia, paintings by Marc Chagall, and a good cross-section of modern work by Mark Rothko, Francis Bacon and Roy Lichtenstein, whose contribution is a baked potato oozing with butter.

MUSEE SUISSE

✚ A4 ✉ Museumstrasse 2 ☎ 01 218 6511 ◷ Tue.–Sun. 10–5 🍴 Café and restaurant 🚃 3, 10, 14, 31 💷 $

Housed in a bizarre-looking castle complete with towers and turrets, the Musee Suisse (Swiss National Museum) should top your sightseeing list. This is the place to learn about Switzerland's history and development, and it is one of Europe's best organized museums. From prehistoric times, you can follow the flowering of Swiss civilization through frescoes, religious woodcarvings and exquisite jewelry, wood-paneled interiors, and furniture and costumes from every corner of the land. The 16th-century globes, showing all that had so far been discovered, and the reconstruction of rooms from different eras are fascinating.

ST. PETERSKIRCHE

✚ A2 ✉ St. Peter-Hofstatt ☎ 01 211 2588 ◷ Mon.–Fri. 8–6, Sat. 9–4, Sun. noon–5 and service at 10 a.m. 🚃 Tram 2, 4, 8, 9, 11, 13, 15 💷 Free

The oldest church foundation in Zurich, St. Peterskirche (St. Peter's Church), stands in a tranquil square at the heart of the Old Town, its delightfully restrained baroque interior perfectly typifying the city's God-fearing prosperity. Four churches predated the existing one, which preserves the late Romanesque choir and 13th-century tower. All is harmony and balance, from the richly carved choir stalls to the superb plasterwork. The clock in the tower is Europe's largest clock-face, measuring an impressive 28½ feet across.

STIFTUNG SAMMLUNG E. G. BÜHRLE

✚ B2 ✉ Zollikerstrasse 172 ☎ 01 422 0086 ◷ Tue.,Fri. and Sun. 2–5, Wed. 5–8 🚃 77; tram 2, 4 💷 $$

A lovely suburban villa houses the Stiftung Sammlung E. G. Bührle (E. G. Bührle Collection), a wonderful range of Impressionist and post-Impressionist works of art collected by a German industrialist between 1934 and 1956. The exhibits are outstanding and the building a delight, so allow plenty of time.

There are delicate Jean Honoré Fragonards and François Bouchers – all flowery pinks and blues, sun-filled Camille Pissarros, the dazzling *Poppies near Vétheuil* by Claude Monet and the stunning *Chestnut Tree* by Vincent van Gogh. Upstairs you'll find Pablo Picasso, Henri Matisse and Georges Braque, among others. Linger in the room devoted to Pierre Renoir, where there's also a lovely painting by Monet of his garden at Giverny. The 22 Degas bronzes of *The Dancer* are another highlight.

ZOOH!

✚ B3 ✉ Zürichbergstrasse 221 ☎ 01 254 2505 ◷ Daily 9–6, Mar.–Oct.; 9–5, rest of year 🍴 Cafés and restaurant on zoo grounds 🚃 39 💷 $$$

Zurich's zoo enjoys a parkland setting on a hill overlooking Zurich. More than 2,000 animals are exhibited, with emphasis on species from South America, Africa and Asia. If you're traveling with kids, arrange to be here at 10 a.m. when the elephants and monkeys enjoy their daily bath. The zoo has a successful breeding program; a board near the entrance gives information about any new arrivals.

A tasty shared experience – fondue, the Swiss national dish

SWISS FLAVORS

Switzerland has a range of regional dishes – German, French and Italian – rather than a national cuisine. With many foreigners working in the country, there's plenty of choice, and in the cities you'll find everything from Japanese to Tex-Mex. The Swiss call a restaurant menu the *Karte* or *carte*; *menu* means the "dish of the day."

Swiss Cheese Specials

The country's best-known specialty, fondue, is made by melting a selection of Swiss hard cheeses, such as Gruyère, Emmental and Vacherin, in white wine spiked with garlic and then adding spices and kirsch. The bubbling pot sits in the middle of the table on a little brazier, and you help yourself by dipping forkfuls of bread into the unctuous mixture. Be careful not to drop the bread in the pot – traditionally the culprit has to buy the next bottle of wine. Fondues also are made by cooking cubed beef in either hot oil (*fondue bourguignonne*) or beef stock (*fondue chinoise*); these are served with a variety of tasty dips. The traditionally French *raclette* is undergoing a revival and is popular throughout Switzerland, particularly with large groups. A whole block of cheese is cut into slices and melted under a grill and then draped over boiled potatoes to be eaten with gherkins, smoked ham and sausage. It's delicious!

Main Dishes

Bündnerfleisch – raw, dried smoked beef – is well worth sampling, as are the many kinds of *wurst*, sausages eaten raw, grilled or boiled. The traditional accompaniment is *rösti*, a crisp potato cake studded with onions and bacon. Hungry diners might enjoy the *Berner Platte*, a groaning plate of sausage, beef and ham served with potatoes and sauerkraut. The Swiss also are fond of liver, pork and veal. Traditional fish recipes in this landlocked country feature lake trout, carp and perch.

A Little Something Sweet

Chocolate and cream feature heavily in Swiss desserts; in addition to the ubiquitous Nestlé and Cailler, Lindt, Sprüngli, Teuscher and Tobler are varieties worth sampling. There are some splendid local cakes; try *leckerli* (spiced bread with honey), meringues, and delicious kirsch-flavored cakes and fruit breads. Start the day with a breakfast bowl of muesli, a tasty mixture of grains, fruit and nuts.

ESSENTIAL
INFORMATION

" ***L****ET your boat of life be light, packed only with what you need...* *"*

From *Three Men in a Boat*
by English author Jerome K. Jerome

The information in this guide has been compiled for U.S. citizens traveling as tourists.

Travelers who are not U.S. citizens, or who are traveling on business, should check with their embassies and tourist offices for information on the countries they wish to visit.

Entry requirements are subject to change at short notice, and travelers are advised to check the current situation before they travel.

Austria – Essential Information

PRE-TRIP ESSENTIALS...

WHAT YOU NEED

ESSENTIAL FOR TRAVELERS

● Required ● Recommended ● Not required

Passport	●
Visa	●
Travel, medical insurance	●
Round-trip or onward airline ticket	●
Local currency	●
Traveler's checks	●
Credit cards	●
First-aid kit and medicines	●
Inoculations*	●

*see also HEALTH section

ESSENTIAL FOR DRIVERS*

Driver's license	●
International Driving Permit	●
Car insurance (for nonrental cars)	●
Car registration (for nonrental cars)	●

*see also DRIVING section

IMPORTANT ADDRESSES

Austrian National Tourist Office
PO Box 1142
New York, NY 10018-1142
☎ (212) 944-6880
Fax (212) 730-4568
www.austria-tourism.at/us

Österreich Werbung
Österreich (Austrian National Tourist Office)
Margaretenstrasse 1
A-1040 Vienna, Austria
☎ 01 588 66-0
Fax 01 588 66-20
www.austria.info

American Citizen Services
Parkring 12
A-1010 Vienna, Austria
☎ 01 31 339-7535
Fax 01 512 5835
Mon.–Sat. 8–11:30 a.m. (until 5 p.m. for emergency services only)

COUNTRY ESSENTIALS...

CUSTOMS

YES
Duty-free limits on goods brought in from non-European Union countries: 200 cigarettes, 100 cigarillos, 50 cigars or 250 g. tobacco; 1 L alcohol over 22% volume; or 2 L alcohol under 22% volume or 2 L sparkling wine; 2 L wine; 50 ml. perfume or toilet water; plus any other duty-free goods (including gifts) to the value of €175. Personal allowance from Czech Republic, Slovakia, Hungary or Slovenia: €125 (unless you arrive by air, when it is €175, as above). This information applies to visitors aged 17 and over. There are no currency regulations. There is no limit on the importation of tax-paid goods purchased within the European Union, provided they are for your own personal use.

NO
No unlicensed drugs, weapons, ammunition, obscene material, pets or other animals, counterfeit money or copied goods, meat or poultry.
For customs limits for returning U.S. citizens see page 16.

MONEY

Austria's currency is the euro (€), a currency shared by 11 other European Union countries. The euro is divided into 100 cents (¢). The denominations of euro bills are 5, 10, 20, 50, 100, 200 and 500. There are coins of 1, 2, 5, 10, 20 and 50¢ and €1 and €2. You can exchange dollars or traveler's checks *(Reiseschecks)* at a bank *(Bank)*, exchange office *(Wechselbüro)*, post office *(Postamt)* and at hotels. Credit cards are widely accepted.
Exchange rate at press time: $1 = €0.82

TIPS AND GRATUITIES

Tips *(Trinkgeld)* are welcomed and expected in restaurants and cafés.

Restaurants (even when service is included)	10%
Cafés/bars	10%
Taxis	10%
Porters	at your discretion
Chambermaids	at your discretion
Hairdressers	5% (and change to shampooer)

TIME ZONES

VIENNA	NEW YORK	CHICAGO	DENVER	SAN FRANCISCO
12:00 noon	6 hours behind Austria	7 hours behind Austria	8 hours behind Austria	9 hours behind Austria

463

COMMUNICATIONS

POST OFFICES

Buy stamps *(Briefmarken)* at a post office *(Postamt)* or newsstand/tobacconist *(Tabak Trafik)* or from a hotel.

Post offices can be recognized by a golden trumpet symbol and can often be found close to the main square or railroad station. Hours for out-of-town post offices may vary. Mailboxes are yellow or orange.

TELEPHONES

You can use cash or a prepaid phone card *(Wertkarte)* to make a call in Austria. Telephones have direct dialing for national and international calls. Phone cards can be bought from newsstands, gas stations, post offices and hotels. Some city phone booths take credit cards.

Phoning inside Austria

All Austrian telephone numbers in this book include an area code: dial the number that is listed.

To call the operator dial 11 88 77.

Phoning Austria from abroad

The country code for Austria is 43. Note that Austrian numbers in this book do not include the country code; you will need to prefix this number if you are phoning from another country. To phone Austria from the United States or Canada, omit the first zero from the Austrian number, and add the prefix 011 43. (Note that the number of digits in Austrian area codes varies.)
Example: 01 12 23 34-4 becomes 011 43 1 12 23 34-4.

Phoning from Austria

To phone the United States or Canada from Austria, prefix the area code and number with 00 1.
Example: (111) 222-3333 becomes 00 1 111 222-3333.

To call National and European information dial 11 88 77. To call overseas information dial 0900 11 88 77.

EMERGENCY TELEPHONE NUMBERS

Police *(Polizei)*	133
Fire *(Feuerwehr)*	122
Ambulance *(Krankenwagen)*	144
Mountain rescue service *(Bergrettung)*	140

Emergency calls are free from phone booths.

HOURS OF OPERATION

- ● Stores Mon.–Sat.
- ● Museums/monuments
- ● Offices Mon.–Fri.
- ● Pharmacies Mon.–Fri.
- ● Banks Mon.–Fri.
- ● Post offices Mon.–Fri.

Saturday is early closing day; shops close between noon and 5 p.m. Thursday or Friday is late night shopping (until 7 or 8).

Banks stay open until 5:30 p.m. on Thursday. Post offices may also open 8–10 on Saturday. In cities, main post offices are open 24 hours a day.

Main and station post offices in larger cities are open 24 hours, including weekends and public holidays.

Pharmacies usually follow store opening hours with a 2-hour lunch break. There is always one pharmacy open late in each city: details are displayed in pharmacy windows.

Facilities at tourist resorts may have special hours of operation.

NATIONAL HOLIDAYS

Banks, businesses and most stores close on these days. Also, some museums may be closed or have restricted hours.

Jan. 1	New Year's Day
Jan. 6	Epiphany
Mar./Apr.	Easter Monday
May 1	Labor Day
May	Ascension Day
May/Jun.	Pentecost Monday
May/Jun.	Corpus Christi
Aug. 15	Assumption of the Virgin
Oct. 26	National Day
Nov. 1	All Saints' Day
Dec. 8	Immaculate Conception
Dec. 25	Christmas Day
Dec. 26	St. Stephen's Day

PHOTOGRAPHY

Magnificent and varied subject matter awaits the photographer in Austria. Make sure you choose a perspective that will do justice to the architectural masterpieces and narrow city lanes. Away from the city, the Alpine peaks give enormous scope for landscape photography, and the light is generally very good.

Austria – Essential Information

Austria – Essential Information

HEALTH

MEDICAL INSURANCE

The cost of medical treatment in Austria is high, and private medical insurance is recommended. The Austrian Medical Society can suggest a doctor *(Arzt)* or hospital *(Krankenhaus):* Lazarettgasse 13, Vienna, ☎ 01 405 45 68. The south and east are home to *Zecken* – a kind of tick that can transmit encephalitis. This disease is potentially lethal, and it is essential you seek medical advice if you are bitten. An inoculation is available.

DENTAL SERVICES

Dentists *(Zahnarzt)* will charge for any treatment given. Dental work is expensive, so check that it is covered by your medical insurance. Dentists are listed in the telephone directory, or ask for English-speaking dentists at your embassy, a tourist office or hotel.

SUN ADVICE

Austria has strong sun during the summer months so sun protection is needed. Wear a hat, cover shoulders, drink plenty of fluids and use sunblock.

DRUGS

Pharmacies *(Apotheken)* can dispense prescriptions. Many assistants speak English, and a schedule displayed on the door enables you to find a late-opening or 24-hour pharmacy in every town.

SAFE WATER

Tap water is safe to drink throughout Austria. Mineral water *(Mineralwasser)* is widely available.

RESTROOMS

Public restrooms *(Toiletten/WC)* are generally easy to find and immaculately clean. A small charge is levied.

ELECTRICITY

Austria has a 220-volt power supply. Electrical sockets take plugs with two round pins; American appliances will need a plug adapter and will require a transformer if they do not have a dual-voltage facility.

NATIONAL TRANSPORTATION

TRAIN *(Zug)*

The Austrian Federal Railways (Österreichische Bundesbahnen or ÖBB) runs a comfortable and efficient service, with connections to all European countries. If you like a slower pace try a steam train journey through valleys and along lakesides, or a cable-car trip; local tourist offices can give details. For rail information ☎ 051 717.

BUS *(Bus)*

Austria has a good network of local, federal and private bus companies. Bus travel is slower but less expensive than the train; for information contact Austria Info ☎ 0810 10 18 18, Mon.–Fri. 9–5:30.

FERRY *(Fähre)*

From Easter to the end of October you can enjoy steamer services on the Danube; some continue into neighboring countries. Steamers ply the larger Austrian lakes from May to September. WienTourismus can supply details on steamer companies: ☎ 01 24-555.

DRIVING

 DRIVE ON THE RIGHT

SPEED LIMITS

Police impose on-the-spot fines (for which receipts are issued), although a foreign motorist may refuse and instead be asked to make a surety payment.

 Limited-access highways *(Autobahnen)* **130 k.p.h. (80 m.p.h.)**

 Main roads **100 k.p.h. (62 m.p.h.)**

 Urban areas **50 k.p.h. (31 m.p.h.)**

SEAT BELTS

Must be worn in front and back seats at all times. Children under 14 are not allowed to use a front seat, unless in a child safety seat.

BLOOD ALCOHOL

The legal blood alcohol limit is 0.05%. Random breath tests on drivers are carried out frequently, especially late at night, and the penalties for offenders are severe.

DRIVING continued

TOLLS
To use toll highways, purchase a windshield sticker *(Vignette)* at automobile clubs in Austria or abroad, or at a border crossing, gas station, post office or tobacconist. There also are charges for several other major roads. Nonpayment of tolls results in a fine.

CAR RENTAL
The leading rental firms have offices at airports and train stations. Hertz offers discounted rates for AAA members (see page 15). For reservations:

	UNITED STATES	AUSTRIA
Alamo	(800) 462-5266	174050 (Europcar)
Avis	(800) 230-4898	0800 0800 8757
Budget	(800) 527-0700	07242 77774
Hertz	(800) 654-3080	0800 20 11 11

FUEL
Many gas stations *(Tankstelle)* are self-service, and 24-hour facilities are common. Unleaded gas *(Bleifrei)* is available at 91 and 95 octane. Diesel is available and credit cards are accepted in most garages.

AAA AFFILIATED MOTORING CLUB
Österreichischer Automobil-,
Motorrad-und Touring Club (ÖAMTC)
Schubertring 1-3, A-1010 Vienna
☎ 01 711 99-0, fax 01 713 18 07
If you break down while driving, phone ☎ 120 (ÖAMTC breakdown service). Not all automobile clubs offer full services to AAA members.

BREAKDOWNS AND ACCIDENTS
There are 24-hour emergency phones at regular intervals on highways.
All accidents involving personal injury must be reported to the police (☎ 133).
Most car rental firms provide their own free rescue service; if your car is rented, follow the instructions given in the documentation. Use of a car repair service other than those authorized by your rental company may violate your agreement.

OTHER INFORMATION

The minimum age for driving a car is 17 (may be higher for some car rental firms).
An International Driving Permit (IDP) is recommended; some rental firms require them, and they can speed up formalities if you are involved in an accident. A Green Card (international motor insurance certificate) is recommended if you are driving a private car (see page 15).
Only hands-free phone use is permitted while driving. Cars must carry a first-aid kit and warning triangle.
In winter, snow tires or chains are essential, and are legal from Nov. 15 to the first Monday after Easter. Rent chains at automobile clubs and border crossings.

USEFUL WORDS AND PHRASES

The official language in Austria is German, although Austrians are very proud of their brand of the language *(Österreichisch)*, and are offended if it is treated as a mere dialect of "standard" German *(Hochdeutsch)*. On paper, the differences between the two varieties are not obvious, but the Austrian accent is distinctive, and especially strong in rural regions.

There are numerous words that are peculiar to Austria and the south of Germany. The Austrian diminutive is *-el* or *-lein* compared with the German *-chen*, so *Mädchen* (girl) in German becomes *Mädel* in Austrian. A small number of Austrian words, such as *Fauteuil* (armchair) and *Plafond* (ceiling), are in fact of French origin.

See page 493 for a pronunciation and basic vocabulary guide to the German language; the following list is an eclectic sample of words peculiar to Austrian German.

Everyday life

a girl's dress	*Dirndl*
masked ball	*Fetzenball*
hello	*Grüss Gott*
policeman	*Gendarm*
friend, guy	*Haberer*
legs	*Haxen*
funny	*Hetzig*
work	*Hockn*
guitar	*Klampfe*
goodbye	*Pfiat di*
slippers	*Schlapfen*

Food and drink

blood sausage	*Blunzn*
potato	*Erdäpfel*
green beans	*Fisole*
green salad	*Häuplsalat*
carrot	*Karotte*
croissant	*Kipferl*
lemonade	*Kracherl*
doughnut	*Krapfen*
corn	*Kukuruz*
milky coffee	*Melange*
mushroom	*Schwammerl*

Common words and phrases

how much?	*wieviel kostet es?*
excuse me	*entschuldigen*
I don't understand	*Ich verstehe nicht*
I'd like	*Ich möchte*
where is…?	*wo ist…?*
no smoking	*nicht rauchen*
closed	*geschlossen*
open	*geöffnet*
please	*bitte*
thank you	*danke*
key	*schlussel*
room	*zimmer*
shower	*dusche*
breakfast	*frühstück*

Austria – Essential Information

BELGIUM – ESSENTIAL INFORMATION

Belgium – Essential Information

PRE-TRIP ESSENTIALS...

WHAT YOU NEED

ESSENTIAL FOR TRAVELERS

● Required ● Recommended ● Not required

Passport	●
Visa (check regulations before you travel)	●
Travel, medical insurance	●
Round-trip or onward airline ticket	●
Local currency	●
Traveler's checks	●
Credit cards	●
First-aid kit and medicines	●
Inoculations	●

ESSENTIAL FOR DRIVERS*

Driver's license	●
International Driving Permit	●
Car insurance (for nonrental cars)	●
Car registration (for nonrental cars)	●

*see also DRIVING section

IMPORTANT ADDRESSES

Belgian Tourist Office
220 East 42nd Street, Suite 3402
New York, NY 10017
☎ (212) 758-8130
Fax (212) 355-7675

Belgian Tourist Office Information Office
rue du Marché-aux-Herbes 63/Grasmarkt 63
1000 Brussels, Belgium
☎ 02 504 0390
Fax 02 504 0270
www.visitbelgium.com

American Embassy
boulevard du Régent 27/Regentlaan 27
1000 Brussels,
Belgium
☎ 02 508 2111
Fax 02 511 2725
www.usembassy.be

Open Mon.–Fri. 9–6

COUNTRY ESSENTIALS...

CUSTOMS

YES
Duty-free limits on goods brought in from non-European Union countries:
200 cigarettes or 100 cigarillos or 50 cigars or 250 g. tobacco; 1 L. alcohol over 22% volume or 2 L. alcohol under 22% volume; 2 L. wine; 50 ml. perfume; 250 ml. toilet water; plus any other duty-free goods (including gifts) to the value of €90. There is no limit on the importation of tax-paid goods purchased within the European Union, provided the goods are for personal use. There are no currency regulations.

NO
No unlicensed drugs, weapons, ammunition, obscene material, pets or other animals, counterfeit money or copied goods, meat or poultry.

For customs limits for returning U.S. citizens see page 16.

MONEY

Belgium's currency is the euro (€), a currency shared by 11 other European Union countries. The euro is divided into 100 cents (¢). The denominations of euro bills are 5, 10, 20, 50, 100, 200 and 500. There are coins of 1, 2, 5, 10, 20 and 50¢ and €1 and €2. Credit cards are widely accepted but can be unwelcome for small amounts.

Exchange rate at press time: $1 = €0.82

TIPS AND GRATUITIES

Tips are not obligatory; a service charge is usually included for restaurants, cafés and taxis.

Restaurants (where service is not included)	10%
Cafés/bars	change
Taxis	change
Porters	€1 per item
Chambermaids	change
Cloakroom attendants	€1–€2

TIME ZONES

BRUSSELS	NEW YORK	CHICAGO	DENVER	SAN FRANCISCO
12:00 noon	6 hours behind Belgium	7 hours behind Belgium	8 hours behind Belgium	9 hours behind Belgium

467

COMMUNICATIONS

POST OFFICES

Buy stamps *(timbres/postzegels)* at a post office *(bureau de poste/postkantoor)*, a tobacconist or

newsstand *(tabac/tabaksverkoper)*, or from a vending machine.
Allow a week for mail to reach the United States.
Mailboxes are painted red.

Hours for out-of-town post offices may vary.

TELEPHONES

Coin-operated public phones exist, but phone card booths are more common. Phone cards *(télécartes/kaarttelefoon)* are available from Belgacom Teleboutiques, post offices, train stations, bookstores and some newsstands for €5 or

€10. Phones accepting credit cards are available at certain tourist sites. Dialing instructions in English are often displayed in public booths.

Phoning in Belgium
All Belgian telephone numbers in this book include an area code: always dial the entire number. To call the operator dial 1307 (French-speaking areas) or 1207 (Flemish-speaking areas).

Phoning Belgium from abroad
The country code for Belgium is 32.
Note that Belgian numbers in this book do not include the country code; you will need to prefix this number if you are phoning from another country. To phone Belgium from the United States or Canada, omit the first zero from the Belgian number and add the prefix 011 32. (Note that Belgian area codes are two or three digits.)
Example: 01 122 3344 becomes 011 32 1 122 3344.

Phoning from Belgium
To phone the United States or Canada from Belgium, prefix the area code and number with 00 1.
Example: (111) 222-3333 becomes 00 1 111 222-3333.

To call international information dial 1204 (French-speaking areas) or 1304 (Flemish-speaking areas).

EMERGENCY TELEPHONE NUMBERS
Police *(police)*	101
Fire service *(pompiers)*	100
Ambulance *(ambulance)*	100
Red Cross ambulance	105

HOURS OF OPERATION

● Stores Mon.–Sat.   ● Museums/monuments
● Offices Mon.–Fri.   ● Pharmacies Mon.–Sat.
● Banks Mon.–Fri.
● Post offices Mon.–Fri.

7 8 9 10 11 12 1 2 3 4 5 6 7

While Sunday is the official closing day, souvenir shops in many towns stay open, usually 10–4.

Many bakeries and *patisseries* open at 7:30 or 8 a.m. and also open on Sunday morning.

Department and other major stores often stay open until 7 p.m. on weekdays and 8 or 9 p.m. on Friday.

Smaller stores and out-of-town post offices and banks may close for lunch.

Some city post offices and banks open on Saturday morning. Post offices and banks outside cities and large towns may close for 2 hours at lunch.

It is common for museums to close on Monday (except for some small museums) and open later one evening a week. Many close for 2 hours at lunch.

NATIONAL HOLIDAYS

Banks, businesses and most stores close on these days. Most cities, towns and villages celebrate their patron saint's day, but most places stay open.

Jan. 1	**New Year's Day**
Mar./Apr.	**Easter Monday**
May 1	**Labor Day**
May	**Ascension Day**
May/Jun.	**Pentecost Monday**
Jul. 21	**National Day**
Aug. 15	**Assumption of the Virgin**
Nov. 1	**All Saints' Day**
Nov. 11	**Armistice Day**
Dec. 25	**Christmas Day**

PHOTOGRAPHY

Belgium is not renowned for bright sunshine, so pack plenty of 200 ASA-speed film. Check that flash photography is permitted before taking pictures in museums. Film and camera batteries are readily available from tourist stores. Rapid-developing services are also widely available.

Belgium – Essential Information

Belgium – Essential Information

HEALTH

 MEDICAL INSURANCE
Private medical insurance is recommended. Visitors from non-European Union countries can receive treatment in a hospital emergency room but are charged if admitted to a hospital *(hôpital/ziekenhuis)*.

 DENTAL SERVICES
Dental treatment is not available free of charge; all dentists practice privately. A list of dentists *(dentiste/tandarts)* can be found in the yellow pages *(pages jaunes/Gouden Gids)*. Check that dental treatment is covered by your private medical insurance.

 SUN ADVICE
The warmest months are July and August, with average daytime temperatures of 60°F. Belgian weather can be unpredictable and although the sun is not often very fierce, protection is still required.

 DRUGS
Prescription and nonprescription medicines are available from a pharmacy *(pharmacie/apotheek)*. If you need a medicine outside regular hours, the addresses of 24-hour facilities are posted on the door of all pharmacies.

 SAFE WATER
Tap water is safe to drink and mineral water *(eau minérale/mineraalwater)* is widely available. The origin of the English word "spa" is in fact the Belgian town of Spa, especially popular during the 19th century for its mineral springs.

RESTROOMS

 Public restrooms *(toilettes/toilets)* are not always easy to find, but are usually clean. If you need to use the facilities at a restaurant or café purchase a drink first. Restrooms in the larger restaurants and cafés sometimes have attendants; you should tip them 25–50¢, which goes toward their wages.

ELECTRICITY

 Belgium has a 220-volt power supply. Electrical sockets take plugs with two round pins; American appliances will need a plug adapter and will require a transformer if they do not have a dual-voltage facility.

NATIONAL TRANSPORTATION

 TRAIN *(train/trein)*
The national rail network is the SNCB/NMBS (Société Nationale des Chemins de Fer Belges in French, and Nationale Maatschappij der Belgische Spoorwegen in Flemish). For national and international reservations and information ☎ 02 528 28 28. The Eurostar trains from London arrive in the Gare du Midi (☎ 02 528 28 28; www.raileurope.com). Brussels has good connections with the Thalys network that operates high-speed trains to Paris, Amsterdam, Cologne and Geneva (☎ 02 528 28 28).

 BUS *(bus/bus)*
Local bus service is good, although there are few international long-distance buses. Details are available at tourist offices. Open the door yourself on buses and trams; where there is no handle, press the black strip or button. International Eurolines buses also operate from Belgium (☎ 02 274 1350).

DRIVING

 DRIVE ON THE RIGHT

SPEED LIMITS
Police impose on-the-spot fines (for which receipts are issued), although a foreign motorist may refuse and instead be asked to make a surety payment.

 Limited-access highways *(autoroutes/ autoweg)* **120 k.p.h. (74 m.p.h.)** Minimum speed on straight, level stretches **70 k.p.h. (43 m.p.h.)**

 Main roads **90 k.p.h. (56 m.p.h.)**

 Urban areas **50 k.p.h. (31 m.p.h.)**

 SEAT BELTS
Must be worn in front and back seats at all times; children under 10 must travel in the rear. If a child is sitting in the front, a seat belt/child restraint appropriate to his or her size/weight must be used.

 BLOOD ALCOHOL
The legal blood alcohol limit is 0.05%. Random breath tests on drivers are carried out frequently, especially late at night, and the penalties for offenders are severe.

Belgium – Essential Information

DRIVING continued

TOLLS
There are no tolls on Belgian highways.

CAR RENTAL
The leading rental firms have offices at airports, train stations and ferry terminals. Hertz offers discounted rates for AAA members (see page 15). For reservations:

	UNITED STATES	BELGIUM
Alamo	(800) 327-9633	02 753 2060
Avis	(800) 331-1212	02 720 0944
Budget	(800) 527- 0700	02 753 2170
Hertz	(800) 654-3080	02 720 6044

FUEL
Gasoline *(essence/benzine)* and diesel are priced in liters and are expensive. There are two grades of unleaded gas *(sans plomb/loodvrij)*: normal (92 octane) and super (97 octane). Most gas stations are self-service, and 24-hour facilities are common.

AAA AFFILIATED MOTORING CLUB
Touring Club Belgium (TCB)
44 rue de la Loi, 1040 Brussels
☎ 02 233 2202, fax 02 286 3323; www.touring.be. If you break down while driving, phone ☎ 070 344 777 (TCB breakdown service) or, on a limited-access highway, use one of the emergency telephones located every 1.2 miles. Ask for *"Touring-Secours."* Not all automobile clubs offer full services to AAA members.

BREAKDOWNS AND ACCIDENTS
Most car rental firms have their own free rescue service; if your car is rented, follow the instructions given in the documentation. Use of a car repair service other than those authorized by your rental company may violate your rental agreement.

If you are involved in an accident phone 101 for police assistance.

OTHER INFORMATION
The minimum age for driving a car is 18 (may be higher for some car rental firms).

An International Driving Permit (IDP) is recommended; some rental firms require them, and they can speed up formalities if you are involved in an accident.

A Green Card (international motor insurance certificate) is recommended if you are driving a private car; see page 15 for more information.

Drivers must yield the right of way to vehicles approaching from the right (except on major roads) and to vehicles on rails and public transport buses.

Beware of cobbled roads, in both cities and rural areas, which can be slippery in wet weather.

USEFUL WORDS AND PHRASES

A linguistic battle has existed in Belgium for many centuries; settlers have long entered from neighboring countries, and as a result there are three distinct language communities: French, Dutch and German.

The two dominant languages are Walloon (a form of French, spoken in the south) and Flemish (related to Dutch, spoken in the north). Passions run deep between the two groups; prosperity has moved back and forth between them over the centuries, and their relationship is still difficult to this day. The Flemish fear their language is being diminished, aware of the strength that French has as a world language.

Both Walloon and Flemish hold equal status as official languages, and although the bilingual signs can be confusing to the visitor, English is widely spoken.

In Brussels, where Flemish and French are both spoken, the street signs also are in both languages. Place names are not usually a problem, since the Flemish and French proper names have similarities, but there can be differences. Following is a selection of locations:

English	Flemish	French
Aalst	*Aalst*	Alost
Antwerp	*Antwerpen*	Anvers
Bruges	*Brugge*	Bruges
Brussels	*Brussel*	Bruxelles
Ghent	*Gent*	Gand
Jodoigne	*Geldenaken*	Jodoigne
Kortrijk	*Kortrijk*	Courtrai
Liège	*Luik*	Liège
Louvain	*Leuven*	Louvain
Mechelen	*Mechelen*	Malines
Mons	*Bergen*	Mons
Mouscron	*Moeskroen*	Mouscron
Nivelles	*Nijvel*	Nivelles
Ostend	*Oostende*	Ostende
Roeselare	*Roeselare*	Roulers
Ronse	*Ronse*	Renaix
Scheldt	*Scheede*	Escaut
Tongeren	*Tongeren*	Tongres
Tournai	*Doornik*	Tournai
Veurne	*Veurne*	Furnes
Ypres	*Ieper*	Ypres

For useful phrases in French, see page 489; for phrases in German, see page 493; for phrases in Dutch, see page 517.

PRE-TRIP ESSENTIALS...

WHAT YOU NEED

ESSENTIAL FOR TRAVELERS

● Required   ● Recommended   ● Not required

Passport	●
Visa	●
Travel, medical insurance	●
Round-trip or onward airline ticket	●
Local currency	●
Traveler's checks	●
Credit cards	●
First-aid kit and medicines	●
Inoculations	●

ESSENTIAL FOR DRIVERS*

Driver's license	●
International Driving Permit	●
Car insurance (for nonrental cars)	●
Car registration (for nonrental cars)	●

*see also DRIVING section

IMPORTANT ADDRESSES

VisitBritain
551 Fifth Avenue
Suite 701
New York, NY 10176-0799
☎ (212) 986-2200 or (800) 462-2748
Fax (212) 986-1188
www.visitbritain.com

British and London Visitor Centre (walk-in only)
1 Regent Street, Piccadilly Circus,
London SW1Y 4XT, U.K.
www.visitbritain.com
Mon. 9:30–6:30, Tue.–Fri. 9–6:30, Sat.–Sun. 10–4
(Sat 9–5, Jun.–Oct.)

American Embassy
24 Grosvenor Square
London W1A 1AE, U.K.
☎ 020 7499 9000; fax 020 7495 5012
www.usembassy.org/uk

COUNTRY ESSENTIALS...

CUSTOMS

YES
Duty-free limits on goods brought in from non-European Union countries:
200 cigarettes or 100 cigarillos or 50 cigars or 250 g. tobacco; 2 L. wine; 1 L. of alcohol over 22% volume or 2 L. of alcohol under 22% volume; 60 ml. perfume; 250 ml. toilet water; plus any other duty-free goods (including gifts) to the value of £145.

There is no limit on the importation of tax-paid goods purchased within the European Union, provided the goods are for your own personal use.

NO
No unlicensed drugs, weapons, obscene material, counterfeit and copied goods, meat or poultry.
For customs limits for returning U.S. citizens see page 16.

MONEY

Britain's currency is the pound sterling (£), which is divided into 100 pence (p). The denominations of pound bills are 5, 10, 20 and 50. There are coins of 1, 2, 5, 10, 20 and 50p and £1 and £2. You can exchange dollars or traveler's checks at banks, main post offices, exchange offices and some travel agencies. Buy traveler's checks in pounds sterling, so you do not lose money every time you change them. Credit cards are widely accepted throughout Britain, and ATMs are very common in shopping areas. When sightseeing, it is a good idea to carry a mix of large and small denominations.
Exchange rate at press time: $1 = £0.55

TIPS AND GRATUITIES

Restaurants (where service is not included)	10–15%
Cafés/bars	change
Taxis	10%
Porters	50p–75p per item
Hairdressers	10%
Tour guides	£2
Chambermaids	change
Cloakroom attendants	10p–20p

TIME ZONES

LONDON	NEW YORK	CHICAGO	DENVER	SAN FRANCISCO	471
12:00 noon	5 hours behind Britain	6 hours behind Britain	7 hours behind Britain	8 hours behind Britain	

Britain – Essential Information

COMMUNICATIONS

POST OFFICES

Buy stamps at post offices, gas stations, tobacconists and supermarkets. Out-of-town post offices often close 1–2 p.m. and Wednesday afternoon. Mailboxes ("pillar-boxes") are red, and are usually free-standing. Pillar-boxes show who was monarch at the time of their installation (ER II, for instance, stands for Elizabeth *Regina* II).

TELEPHONES

Public telephones are easy to find, although the traditional red booths are now rare in towns and cities. Use cash, a credit card or a country card (available at many outlets worldwide). Public telephones accept 10p, 20p, 50p, £1 and £2 coins, but only unused coins are returned. There is a minimum

charge of 30p, which allows 15 minutes for a local or national call. If using a credit card there is a £1 connection charge.

Phoning in Britain
All British numbers in this book include an area code: dial the number listed. To call the operator dial 100.

Phoning Britain from abroad
The country code for Britain is 44. British numbers in this book do not include the country code; you need to prefix it if you are phoning from another country. To phone Britain from the United States or Canada, omit the first zero from the British number, and add the prefix 011 44.
Example: 011 2233 4455 becomes 011 44 11 2233 4455.

Phoning from Britain
To phone the United States or Canada from Britain, prefix the area code and number with 00 1.
Example: (111) 222-3333 becomes 00 1 111 222-3333.

To call the international operator dial 155.

EMERGENCY TELEPHONE NUMBERS
Police	999 or 112
Fire service	999 or 112
Ambulance	999 or 112

Emergency calls are free from phone booths.

HOURS OF OPERATION

○ Stores Mon.–Sat.	● Museums/monuments
● Offices Mon.–Fri.	● Pharmacies Mon.–Sat.
● Banks Mon.–Fri.	
● Post offices Mon.–Fri.	

7 8 9 10 11 12 1 2 3 4 5 6 7

The times above are traditional hours of operation. Many malls and city-center stores open for longer hours and also on Sunday. Convenience grocery stores stay open until late in the evening.

Main town banks and post offices open on Saturday mornings.

Museum opening times vary. Some major sights close on Monday and open later one evening a week; more modest sights of interest may close off season, so it is advisable to check with the local tourist office.

Note that many restaurants do not open for dinner until around 6 or 7 p.m. Up to this time chain restaurants and fast-food outlets are usually the only places serving meals.

NATIONAL HOLIDAYS

Banks, businesses and smaller stores close on these days, although larger stores may remain open.

Jan. 1	New Year's Day
Jan. 2	Bank Holiday (Scotland only)
Mar./Apr.	Good Friday
Mar./Apr.	Easter Monday
1st Mon. of May	May Day
Last Mon. of May	Spring Bank Holiday
First Mon. in Aug.	Summer Bank Holiday (Scotland only)
Last Mon. of Aug.	Summer Bank Holiday
Dec. 25	Christmas Day
Dec. 26	Boxing Day

When Dec. 25 and 26 fall on a weekend, the following Monday and Tuesday are public holidays. If Jan. 1 falls on a weekend, usually the first Monday in January is a public holiday.

PHOTOGRAPHY

British skies are unpredictable, so pack a range of film speeds. The countryside is very green, however, so landscape shots work well if the weather is good. Most museums will not allow you to take pictures; check first. Film and camera batteries are available from grocery stores, pharmacies and camera stores. Rapid-developing services are common and reasonably priced.

Britain – Essential Information

HEALTH

MEDICAL INSURANCE
Private insurance is recommended. Visitors can receive treatment in emergency rooms but are charged if admitted to a hospital. You can seek advice from a doctor at a surgery or health center; you must make an appointment, and a charge will be made. Doctors are listed in the yellow pages, or ask at your hotel or a tourist office.

DENTAL SERVICES
Dentists charge for consultations or treatment. Emergency treatment is available out of hours in towns and cities (see the yellow pages). Check if it is covered by your medical insurance.

SUN ADVICE
Although not renowned for warm weather, Britain does have its moments, and it is not unheard of for July and August to be as hot as the Mediterranean. Visiting historic sights can involve being outside for prolonged periods, so cover up, apply sunscreen and drink plenty of water.

DRUGS
Prescription and nonprescription medicines are available from pharmacies (chemists). Pharmacists can advise on medication for common ailments. Notices in all pharmacy windows give details of emergency facilities open outside regular hours.

SAFE WATER
Tap water is safe to drink, even in remote areas. Mineral water is widely available but is usually quite expensive, particularly in restaurants.

RESTROOMS

Public restrooms (toilets, lavatories, WCs or, in everyday parlance, "loos") are generally easy to find and maintained to a high standard. Most are free, but a charge is made for those at major rail stations (about 20p).

ELECTRICITY

Britain has a 240-volt power supply. Electrical sockets take plugs with three square pins, so an adapter is needed for American appliances. A transformer is also required for appliances operating on 110 or 120 volts.

NATIONAL TRANSPORTATION

TRAIN
Rail services are good in Britain. First class is comfortable but more expensive than standard. Intercity (high-speed) trains connect cities. If you plan to use trains frequently, rail cards offer discounts: contact Rail Europe Group, ☎ (800) 361-7245. Once you are in Britain, Rail Rover passes are good value for regional rail travel: ☎ 08457 484950.

BUS
It is cheaper to travel by bus than by rail. The main operator for local (bus) and long-distance (coach) travel in Britain is National Express. For details ☎ 08705 808080. Euroline's coaches operate from Britain to the rest of Europe: ☎ 08705 143219.

FERRY
The busiest ferries run between south-east England and France (a high-speed train also shuttles passengers and cars through the Channel Tunnel). Service is frequent, especially in summer. Ferries serve the smaller British islands, Ireland, Spain, Belgium, The Netherlands, Germany, Denmark, Sweden and Norway.

DRIVING

DRIVE ON THE LEFT

SPEED LIMITS
British speed limits are stringently enforced by police patrols and also by strategically positioned cameras that detect speeding motorists.

Limited-access highways (motorways); divided highways (dual carriageways)
70 m.p.h.

Main roads
50 or 60 m.p.h.

Urban areas
30 or 40 m.p.h.

SEAT BELTS
Must be worn in front and rear seats at all times.

BLOOD ALCOHOL
The legal blood alcohol limit is 0.08%. Random breath tests on drivers are carried out frequently, especially late at night, and the penalties for offenders are severe.

DRIVING continued

TOLLS
Most limited-access highways are free. Some bridges levy a toll. In central London there is a weekday congestion charge (see page 16). Phone 020 7649 9122 or visit www.cclondon.com for payment information.

CAR RENTAL
The leading rental firms have offices at airports, train stations and ferry terminals. Hertz offers discounted rates for AAA members (see page 15). For reservations:

	UNITED STATES	BRITAIN
Alamo	(800) 327-9633	08705 994000
Avis	(800) 331-1212	08700 100287
Budget	(800) 527-0700	08701 565656
Hertz	(800) 654-3080	08708 448844

FUEL
Gasoline (petrol) and diesel are priced in liters and are expensive. There are two grades of unleaded gas: super (98 octane) and premium (97 octane). Most gas stations are self-service, and 24-hour facilities are common.

AAA AFFILIATED MOTORING CLUB
The Automobile Association
(AA) Ltd, Fanum House, Basing View Basingstoke, Hampshire RG21 4EA
☎ 08705 448866,
www.theAA.com (administration).
AAA members staying in the UK for up to 3 months get free AA Breakdown Service. If you break down while driving a privately owned car in the U.K. call ☎ 0800 028 90 18 (AA Breakdown Service). If you're driving a rental car, contact the rental company's assistance service. If you're staying for longer than 3 months, call the AA on 0800 587 7150 when you arrive in the U.K. to obtain AA Breakdown Service. You also can purchase the service online: www.theAA.com

BREAKDOWNS AND ACCIDENTS
There are emergency telephones at regular intervals on limited-access and divided highways.
If you are involved in an accident ☎ 999 or 112 for police, fire and ambulance assistance. Most car rental firms provide their own free rescue service; if your car is rented, follow the instructions in the documentation. Use of a car repair service other than those authorized by your rental firm may violate your rental agreement.

OTHER INFORMATION
The minimum age for driving a car is 17. An International Driving Permit (IDP) is recommended. A Green Card (international motor insurance certificate) is recommended if you are driving a private car; see page 15 for more information.

USEFUL WORDS AND PHRASES

Spotting the differences between American and British English is fun, especially as some regional accents are almost incomprehensible to the untrained ear! Britons have become familiar with Americanisms through imported American television shows, but it is still possible to make a blunder. Below are some illustrations of the "Atlantic divide."

American	British
ATM	cashpoint
ball-point pen	biro
to call collect	to reverse the charges
check	cheque
check (in a restaurant)	bill
elevator	lift
first/second floor (etc.)	ground/first floor (etc.)
movie theater	cinema
phone booth	phone box
reserve (reservation)	book (reservation)
restroom	toilet/loo (colloquial)
Scotch™ tape	sticky tape/Sellotape™
trash or garbage can	dustbin or rubbish bin

food and drink

(soft hamburger) bun	bap
beer	bitter (dark), lager (light)
candy	sweets
(potato) chips	crisps
cookies	biscuits
corn	maize
cotton candy	candyfloss
eggplant	aubergine
french fries	chips
grocery store	supermarket
Jell-O™	jelly
jelly	jam
liquor store	off-licence
oatmeal	porridge
Saranwrap™	cling film
zucchini	courgette

fashion

bangs	fringe
pants	trousers
pantyhose	tights
suspenders	braces
undershirt	vest
vest	waistcoat

getting around

hood (of a car)	bonnet
one-way trip	single
parking lot	car park
paved shoulder	lay-by
rotary/traffic circle	roundabout
round trip	return ticket
sidewalk	pavement
stick shift	manual
subway	tube/underground
truck	lorry
trunk (of a car)	boot

Britain – Essential Information

PRE-TRIP ESSENTIALS...

WHAT YOU NEED

ESSENTIAL FOR TRAVELERS

● Required   ● Recommended   ● Not required

Passport	●
Visa*	●
Travel, medical insurance	●
Round-trip or onward airline ticket	●
Local currency	●
Traveler's checks	●
Credit cards	●
First-aid kit and medicines	●
Inoculations	●

*U.S. citizens can stay in the Czech Republic for up to 90 days without a visa. For stays of longer than 90 days, visas must be obtained from an embassy outside the Czech Republic.

ESSENTIAL FOR DRIVERS*

Driver's license	●
International Driving Permit	●
Car insurance (for nonrental cars)	●
Car registration (for nonrental cars)	●

*see also DRIVING section

IMPORTANT ADDRESSES

CzechTourism
1109 Madison Avenue,
New York, NY 10028
☎ (212) 288-0830
Fax (212) 288-0971; www.czechtourism.com

**Česká centrála cestovního ruchu
(Czech Tourist Authority)**
Vinohradská 46, PO Box 32,
120 41, Praha (Prague) 2, Czech Republic
☎ 221 580 111
Fax 222 514 421; www.czechtourism.com

American Embassy
Tržiště 15, Malá Strana,
118 01 Praha (Prague) 1, Czech Republic
☎ 257 530 663
Fax 257 534 028
Telephone inquiries Mon.–Fri. 8–4:30
Personal inquiries Mon.–Fri. 9–noon

COUNTRY ESSENTIALS...

CUSTOMS

→ **YES**
Duty-free limits on goods brought in from non-European Union countries:
200 cigarettes or 100 cigarillos or 50 cigars or 250 g. tobacco; 1 L. alcohol other than non-sparkling wine; 2 L. non-sparkling wine; 50 ml. perfume or 250 ml. toilet water; plus any other duty-free goods (including gifts) to the value of 175 euros, (90 euros for those under 15). Persons importing alcohol must be 18 and over, for cigarettes and tobacco products 16 and over. There is no restriction on the import or export of Czech or foreign currencies, but amounts in excess of 350,000Kč must be declared.

⊖ **NO**
No unlicensed drugs, firearms, ammunition, offensive weapons, obscene material, unlicensed animals, counterfeit or copied goods, meat and poultry.

For customs limits for returning U.S. citizens see page 16.

MONEY

The Czech Republic's currency is the Koruna česká (Kč) – or Czech crown – which is divided into 100 haléřů (h) – or hellers – although you won't find many of the latter around. The denominations of bills are 20, 50, 100, 200, 500, 1,000, 2,000 and 5,000. There are coins of 50h and 1, 2, 5, 10, 20 and 50Kč. You can exchange dollars or traveler's checks *(cestovní šek)* at a bank *(banka)*, exchange office *(směnárna)*, post office *(pošta)* or hotel; you will need ID. It is an offense to change money through black-market money dealers; in any case, they rarely offer an attractive rate.

Exchange rate at press time: $1 = 25Kč

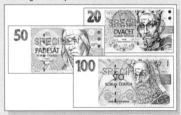

TIPS AND GRATUITIES

Tips are welcomed in restaurants and cafés, although service is normally included.

Restaurants (even when service is included)	5–10%
Cafés/bars	5–10%
Taxis	10%
Porters	40Kč
Hairdressers	10%
Tour guides	20Kč

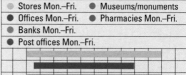

| TIME ZONES | PRAGUE 12:00 noon | NEW YORK 6 hours behind Czech Republic | CHICAGO 7 hours behind Czech Republic | DENVER 8 hours behind Czech Republic | SAN FRANCISCO 9 hours behind Czech Republic | 475 |

Czech Republic – Essential Information

COMMUNICATIONS

POST OFFICES

Buy stamps *(známky)* at a post office *(pošta)*, a newsstand/kiosk *(trafika/tabák)* or from a hotel.

The postal service is slow and erratic but not expensive. Mailboxes are orange. Hours for out-of-town post offices may vary.

TELEPHONES

City booths take telephone cards *(telefonní karta)* worth 175 or 320Kč, which can be bought from newsstands, tobacconists, post offices, shops, hotels and travel agencies. Coin-operated telephones use 1, 2, 5 and 10Kč. There are often instructions in English inside the booth.

Phoning inside the Czech Republic
All Czech telephone numbers in this book include an area code: dial the number that is listed. For

national directory inquiries dial 1180.

Phoning the Czech Republic from abroad
The country code for the Czech Republic is 420. You will need to prefix this number to the numbers in this book if you are phoning from another country. To phone the Czech Republic from the United States or Canada dial the prefix 011 420. Example: 112 233 445 becomes 011 420 112 233 445.

Phoning from the Czech Republic
To phone the United States or Canada from the Czech Republic, prefix the number with 00 1. Example: (111) 222-3333 becomes 00 1 111 222-3333. To call international information dial 1181. For an English-speaking international operator dial 133004. Beginning September 2002, all Czech Republic area codes dropped the initial zero "0"; for instance, Prague became 2 instead of 02. All domestic numbers are now a uniform nine digits. Other numbers are no longer valid.

EMERGENCY TELEPHONE NUMBERS

General Emergencies	112
Police *(policie)*	158
Fire *(požár)*	150
Ambulance *(ambulance)*	155

Emergency calls are free from phone booths.

HOURS OF OPERATION

● Stores Mon.–Fri.	● Museums/monuments
● Offices Mon.–Fri.	● Pharmacies Mon.–Fri.
● Banks Mon.–Fri.	
● Post offices Mon.–Fri.	

Saturday afternoon is early closing; many stores close at noon or 1. Some stores, especially in the country, close noon–1 for lunch.

Food stores in the large cities open at 6 a.m., and large stores and shopping centers stay open until 8 p.m. (4 p.m. on Saturday). In the centre of Prague, most stores are open all day Saturday and Sunday.

Some post offices open on Saturday morning. Some tourist resorts may have special opening times.

Museums often close on Monday and days following public holidays, and opening times may be reduced during the winter.

NATIONAL HOLIDAYS

Banks, businesses and most stores close on these days. Monuments, museums and galleries usually open on public holidays (except Jan. 1, Easter, and Dec. 25 and 26) but are closed the following day.

Jan. 1	New Year's Day and Day of Restoration of Independent Czech State
Mar./Apr.	Easter Monday
May 1	Labor Day
May 8	Liberation Day
Jul. 5	SS Cyril and Methodius' Day
Jul. 6	Jan Hus Day
Sep. 28	Czech Statehood Day
Oct. 28	Independence Day
Nov. 17	Day of Fight for Freedom and Democracy
Dec. 24	Christmas Eve
Dec. 25	Christmas Day
Dec. 26	St. Stephen's Day

PHOTOGRAPHY

The Czech Republic is an amateur photographer's dream: the picturesque vistas make almost every photo postcard-perfect. You can buy film in the small shops at Staré Město (Old Town) and Malá Strana (Lesser Quarter). Avoid Czech brands of color film – you may not be able to get them processed outside the country. Many stores in tourist areas offer developing services.

EMERGENCY PHONE NUMBERS

 GENERAL EMERGENCIES 112

POLICE 158 *(Policie)*

Czech Republic – Essential Information

HEALTH

MEDICAL INSURANCE
Private medical insurance is recommended. U.S. and Canadian visitors can receive treatment in a hospital emergency and accident unit, but you will be charged if you are admitted to a hospital *(nemocnice)*. You may be asked to show your passport when seeking hospital treatment. The following clinics in Prague have English-speaking doctors: the Unicare Medical Center, ☎ 235 356 553, and Canadian Medical Center ☎ 235 360 133.

DENTAL SERVICES
A dentist *(zubař)* will charge for any treatment given, so check if it is covered by your medical insurance. For an English-speaking dentist, ask at your hotel or embassy or at a tourist office.

SUN ADVICE
June through August is the sunniest period, when adequate sun protection should be applied.

DRUGS
A pharmacy *(lékárna)* is the only place you can buy over-the-counter medicines. Pharmacies also dispense many drugs normally available only on prescription in other Western countries. However, it is advisable to bring supplies of your own medicines with you. If you need a pharmacy outside regular hours, information about the nearest all-night facility is posted at some pharmacies.

SAFE WATER
Tap water is safe but may have an unpleasant taste. Bottled water is available everywhere; still table water *(Stolní pitní voda)* is the most common.

RESTROOMS

Public restrooms *(toaleta)* are not easy to find, and you may be charged for toilet tissue. It may be best to use a café or restaurant facility after buying a drink. Attendants appreciate small change – 2Kč or thereabouts; attendants in public restrooms are state employees.

ELECTRICITY

The Czech Republic has a 220-volt power supply. Electrical sockets take plugs with two round pins; American appliances will need a plug adapter, and will require a transformer if they do not have a dual-voltage facility.

NATIONAL TRANSPORTATION

TRAIN *(vlak)*
The Czech national rail company, České dráhy (CD), is extensive and inexpensive, but often crowded. The fast trains stop at major cities; local trains stop everywhere; but usually provide only second-class service. All long-distance trains have two classes; some have dining carriages and overnight services. Reserve seats on express trains; don't rely on international trains having air conditioning: ☎ 221 111 122.

BUS *(autobus)*
Inexpensive and popular with the Czechs. Reserve for weekends, national holidays or early morning. Tickets are purchased from the bus station kiosk or the driver. For information ☎ 900 144 444 (daily 24-hours). Large items of luggage will be stowed for a small charge. Euroline's buses connect to other countries: ☎ 224 239 318.

FERRY *(prévos)*
From April to September boats cruise the Vltava river as far as Troja Château to the north of Prague and Slapy Dam to the south: ☎ 224 810 030 or 224 931 013.

DRIVING

DRIVE ON THE RIGHT

SPEED LIMITS
Police can give on-the-spot fines of up to 5,000Kčs. If this should happen to you, ask for a receipt.

Limited-access highways *(dalnice)*
130 k.p.h. (80 m.p.h.)

Main roads
90 k.p.h. (55 m.p.h.)

Urban areas
50 k.p.h. (31 m.p.h.)

SEAT BELTS
Must be worn in front and back seats at all times. Children under 12 (or under 4 feet 10 inches) must not travel in the front seat.

BLOOD ALCOHOL
The legal blood alcohol limit is zero. Random breath tests on drivers are carried out frequently, especially late at night, and the penalties for offenders are severe.

Czech Republic – Essential Information

DRIVING continued

TOLLS
A tax is levied for use of highways and express roads. A sticker must be purchased and displayed, and failure to do so will result in a fine. The sticker can be bought at the Czech border, ÚAMK offices (see below), gas stations or post offices.

CAR RENTAL
The leading rental firms have offices at airports and train stations. Hertz offers discounted rates for AAA members (see page 15). For reservations:

	UNITED STATES	CZECH REPUBLIC
Alamo	(800) 462-5266	224 826 825
Avis	(800) 230 4898	221 851 225
Budget	(800) 527-0700	235 325 713
Hertz	(800) 654-3080	220 102 424

FUEL
Gas, sold in liters, is leaded (*special:* 90 octane and *super:* 96 octane), unleaded (*natural:* 91 octane and *super plus* 95 octane) or diesel (*nafta*). Some out-of-town stations *(benzinová pumpa)* close for lunch and after 6 p.m. There are 24-hour gas stations in cities and along highways.

AAA AFFILIATED MOTORING CLUB
Ústřední automotoklub České republiky (ÚAMK; CR)
Na Strži 9, CZ-140 02 Prague 4
☎ 261 104 242, fax 261 104 235
If you break down while driving phone ☎ 1230 (ÚAMK breakdown service). Not all automobile clubs offer full services to AAA members.

BREAKDOWNS AND ACCIDENTS
There are 24-hour emergency phones at regular intervals on highways. Most car rental firms provide their own free rescue service; if your car is rented, follow the instructions given in the documentation. Use of a car repair service other than those authorized by your rental company may violate your agreement. ☎ 158 for police assistance.

OTHER INFORMATION
The minimum age for driving a car is 18 (may be higher for some car rental firms). An International Driving Permit (IDP) is required; some rental firms require them, and they can speed up formalities if you are involved in an accident. A Green Card (international motor insurance certificate) is required for a private car; see page 15 for more information. Visible damage to a car entering the country must be certified by border authorities. If damage occurs inside the country, a police report must be obtained at the scene of the accident. Damaged vehicles are allowed out of the country only upon presentation of this document.

USEFUL WORDS AND PHRASES

The official language of the Czech Republic is Czech *(česky)* – a highly complex Slav tongue. Czech sounds and looks daunting, but apart from a few special letters, each letter and sound is pronounced as it is written – the key is to stress the first syllable of a word. If you have any knowledge of Polish or Russian you will be able to understand many written words.

Any attempt to speak Czech will be heartily appreciated, although English is spoken by many involved in the tourist trade. Below are a few words that may be helpful.

Do you speak English?	*Mluvíte anglicky?*
What is your name?	*Jak se jmenujete?*
hello, goodbye (casual)	*ahoj*
good morning	*dobré ráno*
goodbye	*na shledanou*
good night	*dobrou noc*
How much?	*Kolik?*
excuse me	*promiňte*
I am American	*Jsem Američan(ka)*
I would like	*Chtěl(a) bych*
I don't understand	*Nerozumím*
no smoking	*kouření zakazano*
okay	*dobře*
open	*otevřeno*
closed	*zavřeno*
please	*prosím*
thank you	*děkuji*
ticket	*lístek*
(one-way/round trip)	*(jednosměrnou/zpáteční)*
Where is...?	*Kde je...?*
yes/no	*ano/ne*
you're welcome	*prosím*

the hotel	*hotel*
breakfast	*snídaně*
reservation	*reservaci*
key	*klíč*
single/double room	*jednolužkový dvoulužkový pokoj*
room	*pokoj*
Where is the toilet?	*Kde je toalet?*
shower	*sprcha*
bathroom	*koupelna*

the restaurant	*restaurace*
beef	*hovězí*
beer	*pivo*
bread	*chleb*
chicken	*kuře*
the check	*účet*
coffee	*káva*
dish of the day	*nabídka dne*
dessert	*moučnik*
fish	*ryba*
lamb	*jehněcí*
meat	*maso*
pork	*vepřové maso*
seafood	*mořské ryby*
starter	*předkrm*
wine	*víno*

Denmark – Essential Information

PRE-TRIP ESSENTIALS...

WHAT YOU NEED

ESSENTIAL FOR TRAVELERS

● Required　● Recommended　● Not required

Passport	●
Visa (check regulations before you travel)	●
Travel, medical insurance	●
Round-trip or onward airline ticket	●
Local currency	●
Traveler's checks	●
Credit cards	●
First-aid kit and medicines*	●
Inoculations	●

*see also HEALTH section

ESSENTIAL FOR DRIVERS*

Driver's license	●
International Driving Permit	●
Car insurance (for nonrental cars)	●
Car registration (for nonrental cars)	●

*see also DRIVING section

IMPORTANT ADDRESSES

VisitDenmark
PO Box 4649
Grand Central Station
New York, NY 10163-4649
☎ (212) 885-9700
Fax (212) 885-9710
www.visitdenmark.com

Danmarks Turtistråd (Danish Tourist Board)
Islands Brugge 43, 3rd Floor
DK-2300 Copenhagen S, Denmark
☎ 32 88 99 00
Fax 32 88 99 01
www.visitdenmark.com

American Embassy
Dag Hammarskjölds Allé 24
DK-2100 Copenhagen Ø, Denmark
☎ 33 41 71 00
Fax 35 43 02 23
Personal visits require an appointment.

COUNTRY ESSENTIALS...

CUSTOMS

YES
Duty-free limits on goods brought in from non-European Union countries:
200 cigarettes or 100 cigarillos or 50 cigars or 250 g. tobacco; 2 L. wine; 1 L. alcohol over 22% volume; 2 L. alcohol under 22% volume; 50 ml. perfume; 250 ml. toilet water; plus any other duty-free goods (including gifts) to the value of DKr1,350. There is no limit on the importation of tax-paid goods purchased within the European Union, provided they are for your own personal use. Limits for alcohol and tobacco products apply to visitors aged 17 or over. There are no currency regulations.

NO
No unlicensed drugs, weapons, ammunition, obscene material, pets or other animals, counterfeit money or copied goods, meat or poultry.

For customs limits for returning U.S. citizens see page 16.

MONEY

Denmark's currency is the krone (DKr), which is divided into 100 øre. The denominations of krone bills are 50, 100, 200, 500 and 1,000. There are coins of 25 and 50 øre and 1, 2, 5, 10 and 20DKr. Banks may not exchange foreign bank notes of high denominations. Denmark was one of the two Scandinavian countries that chose not to adopt the euro as its official currency on Jan. 1, 1999. However, tourists coming from the euro zone may still use a euro credit card; the exchange rate does not fluctuate.
Senior citizens and holders of International Student Identity Cards (ISIC) can often obtain discounts on travel and entrance fees.
Exchange rate at press time: $1 = DKr6.15

TIPS AND GRATUITIES

Tips are not expected, but may be given for outstanding service.

Restaurants (service is always included)	change
Cafés/bars	change
Taxis (tips included in fare)	change
Porters	change
Chambermaids	change
Cloakroom attendants	change

| TIME ZONES | COPENHAGEN 12:00 noon | NEW YORK 6 hours behind Denmark | CHICAGO 7 hours behind Denmark | DENVER 8 hours behind Denmark | SAN FRANCISCO 9 hours behind Denmark | 479 |

COMMUNICATIONS

POST OFFICES

Stamps *(frimerker)* can be bought at a post office *(postkontoret)*, newsstand *(aviskiosk)* or stationer *(papirhandel)*.

Mailboxes *(postkasse)* are red with a yellow horn and crown. Hours for out-of-town post offices may vary. For postal service inquiries telephone Post Danmark ☎ 80 20 70 30; www.postdanmark.dk

TELEPHONES

Danish public telephones *(telefon)* work efficiently for national and international calls, but do not refund your money if the call is not answered. Some phones require coins to be inserted after dialing, when you hear ringing. Use DKr1, DKr2, DKr5, DKr10 and DKr20 coins. Phone card booths are

also available; buy the cards (DKr30, DKr50 or DKr100) from a post office, railroad station or newsstand.

Phoning inside Denmark

All telephone numbers are 8 digits and include the regional code. Dial all digits when making a call. To call the operator dial 110; to call collect dial 115; for the long-distance operator dial 114.

Phoning Denmark from abroad

The country code for Denmark is 45. Note that Danish numbers in this book do not include the country code; you will need to prefix this number if you are phoning from another country. To phone Denmark from the United States or Canada add the prefix 011 45.
Example: 11 22 33 44 becomes 011 45 11 22 33 44.

Phoning from Denmark

To phone the United States or Canada from Denmark, prefix the area code and number with 00 1. Example: (111) 222-3333 becomes 00 1 111 222-3333. To call directory inquiries in Denmark dial 118. To call international information dial 113.

EMERGENCY TELEPHONE NUMBERS

Police *(politi)*	112
Fire *(brandvæsen)*	112
Ambulance *(sygevogn)*	112

Emergency calls are free from phone booths.

HOURS OF OPERATION

● Stores Mon.–Sat.	● Museums/monuments
● Offices Mon.–Fri.	● Pharmacies Mon.–Fri.
● Banks Mon.–Fri.	
● Post offices Mon.–Fri.	

7 8 9 10 11 12 1 2 3 4 5 6 7

Although Sunday is the official closing day, souvenir shops in many towns, supermarkets and grocery stores in summer vacation areas stay open during the high season.

Many bakeries and *patisseries* also open on Sunday morning.

On Friday stores open until 7 or 8 p.m. Most shops close at 1 or 2 p.m. on Saturday afternoon, but many shops in Copenhagen are open until 5 p.m.

Department stores and supermarkets often stay open later than 5:30/6 p.m.

Large gas stations sell convenience foods 7 days a week.

Banks in Copenhagen are open until 5 p.m. On Thursday all banks are open until 6 p.m. Post offices open at 9 or 10 and close at 5 or 6; some post offices open Saturday 9–noon.

NATIONAL HOLIDAYS

Banks, businesses and most stores close on these days.

Jan. 1	New Year's Day
Mar./Apr.	Maundy Thursday
Mar./Apr.	Good Friday
Mar./Apr.	Easter Monday
Apr./May	Great Prayer Day
May/Jun.	Ascension Day
May/Jun.	Pentecost Monday
Jun. 5	Constitution Day
Dec. 24	Christmas Eve
Dec. 25	Christmas Day
Dec. 26	St. Stephen's Day
Dec. 31	New Year's Eve

PHOTOGRAPHY

Denmark is not renowned for bright sunshine and the winter months have short daylight hours, so pack plenty of 200 ASA-speed film. Check that photography is permitted before taking pictures in museums. Film and camera batteries are sold in tourist stores, and rapid-developing services are widely available.

Denmark – Essential Information

EMERGENCY PHONE NUMBERS

 POLICE 112 *(Politi)*

Denmark – Essential Information

HEALTH

 MEDICAL INSURANCE
Private medical insurance is recommended. In an emergency, visitors from the U.S. and Canada can receive free temporary treatment in a hospital *(hospitalet)*. You will be charged for more extensive treatment. Health offices *(kommunes social og sundhedforvaltning)* have lists of hospitals and doctors, or ask at your hotel.

 DENTAL SERVICES
Dentists *(tandlægen)* will charge for any treatment given. They are listed in the telephone directory, and off-hours treatment is available in some clinics. Advice can be sought at tourist and health offices. Check that treatment is covered by your medical insurance.

 SUN ADVICE
The warmest months are July and August. The sun in Denmark is not particularly fierce, but sun protection is still advised, especially on boats or near the water.

 DRUGS
To obtain a prescription medicine at a pharmacy *(apotek)* it must be prescribed by a Scandinavian doctor, so make sure that your supply of prescribed medicines will last your stay. Additionally, some preparations available over the counter in the U.S. may be obtained in Denmark only with a prescription. Outside regular hours, the nearest all-night facility is posted at all pharmacies.

 SAFE WATER
Tap water is safe to drink, and mineral water *(mineralvand)* is widely available.

RESTROOMS

 Public restrooms *(toiletterne)* are easy to find, clean, well equipped and usually free. They are often indicated by a symbol, or marked WC or *Damer* (women) and *Herrer* (men).

ELECTRICITY

 Denmark has a 220-volt power supply. Electrical sockets take plugs with two round pins; American appliances will need a plug adapter and will require a transformer if they do not have a dual-voltage facility.

NATIONAL TRANSPORTATION

 TRAIN *(tog)*
Copenhagen is an important meeting point for trains between Europe and the rest of Scandinavia. Danish State Railways, Danske Statsbaner (DSB), runs an efficient service with trains linking to Germany and via the Øresund Link to Sweden. Most domestic trains have refreshment facilities; seat reservations are recommended. For information 70 13 14 15 (national routes) or 70 13 14 16 (international routes).

 BUS *(bus)*
The domestic bus service is good; ask for details at local tourist offices. Eurolines services run between other European countries (33 88 70 00).

 FERRY *(færge)*
There are numerous ferry services from Denmark, with year-round connections to many northern European countries. DFDS Seaways has an office in Denmark, 33 42 30 00, and in Florida, 1 800 533 3755 ext.114.

DRIVING

 DRIVE ON THE RIGHT

SPEED LIMITS
Police can impose on-the-spot fines.

 Limited-access highways *(motorvej)*
110 k.p.h. (68 m.p.h.)

 Main roads
80 k.p.h. (49 m.p.h.)
Minimum speed **40 k.p.h. (24 m.p.h.)**

 Urban areas
50 k.p.h. (31 m.p.h.) but **40 k.p.h. (24 m.p.h.)** in central Copenhagen

 SEAT BELTS
Must be worn in front and back seats at all times.

BLOOD ALCOHOL
The legal blood alcohol limit is 0.05%. Random breath tests on drivers are carried out frequently, especially late at night, and the penalties for offenders are severe.

DRIVING continued

TOLLS
There are no tolls on highways. However, the Great Belt *(Store Bælt)* tunnel and bridge from Korsør to Nyborg and the impressive 10-mile Øresund tunnel and bridge from Copenhagen to Malmö (Sweden) both levy a toll.

CAR RENTAL
The leading car rental companies have offices at airports, principal railroad stations and ferry terminals. Hertz offers discounted rates for AAA members (see page 15). For reservations:

	UNITED STATES	DENMARK
Alamo	(800) 327-9633	89 33 11 33 (Europcar)
Avis	(800) 331-2112	33 15 22 99
Budget	(800) 527-0700	33 55 70 00
Hertz	(800) 654-3080	33 17 90 00

FUEL
Gas *(benzin)* is sold in liters; unleaded gas *(blyfri)* comes in 95 and 98 octane ratings. Self-service gas stations *(tank selv* or *selvbetjening)* are common, except on limited-access highways. Most gas stations take credit cards, and some have automatic pumps for DKr100 and DKr50 bills.

AAA AFFILIATED MOTORING CLUB
Forenede Danske Motorejere (FDM)
Firskovvej 32, P.O. Box 500, 2800 Kgs.Lyngby ☎ 45 27 07 07, fax 45 27 09 93
Not all automobile clubs offer full services to AAA members.

BREAKDOWNS AND ACCIDENTS
Report accidents to the Dansk Forening for International Motorkoretojsforsikring, Amaliegade 10, 1256 Copenhagen (☎ 33 13 75 55). Most car rental firms provide their own free rescue service; if your car is rented, follow the instructions given in the documentation. Use of a car repair service other than those authorized by your rental company may violate your agreement.

OTHER INFORMATION
The minimum legal age for driving a car is 18 (may be 20 to 25 for some car rental firms).

An International Driving Permit (IDP) is recommended; some rental firms require them, and they can speed up formalities if you are involved in an accident.

A Green Card (international motor insurance certificate) is recommended if you are driving a private car; see page 15 for more information.

Use dimmed headlights at all times.

USEFUL WORDS AND PHRASES
Danish is a Germanic language, close to Swedish and Norwegian, but it is tricky to pronounce because some letters *(d, g)* are silent in the middle or at the end of words, *h* before a *v* becomes silent, and some specifically Scandinavian vowels *(å, ø,* and *æ)* are awkward to say correctly. But Danes are aware of this, and most of them speak very good English. In addition, menus are often in English or German.

In the Danish alphabet, the following letters come after *z*: *å, ø* and *æ.* (Århus, for example, comes at the end of the alphabet.) *Å* is used in place of *aa,* although the city of Aalborg prefers to write the two vowels out in full.

The following words and phrases should help you:

Do you speak English?	*Taler de Engelsk?*
excuse me	*undskyld*
hello/goodbye	*hej/farvel*
how much is...?	*hvor meget koster det?*
I am American	*Jeg er Amerikaner*
I'd like...	*jeg vil gerne have...*
I don't understand	*jeg forstår det ikke*
open/closed	*åben/lukket*
please/thank you	*værså venlig/tak*
ticket (one-way/	*billet (enkeltbillet/*
round trip)	*en tur-retur)*
where is/are...?	*hvor er...?*
yes/no	*ja/nej*
the hotel	***hotel***
breakfast	*morgenmad*
key	*nøgle*
for one/two nights	*en nat/to nætter*
for one person/	*enkeltværelse/*
two people	*dobbeltværelse*
room	*værelse*
shower	*brusebad*
the restaurant	***restaurant***
beef	*bøf*
bread	*brød*
butter	*smør*
cheese	*ost*
chicken	*kylling*
the check	*regningen*
coffee/tea	*kaffe/the*
Danish pastry	*Wienerbrød*
dessert	*dessert*
fish	*fisk*
shellfish	*skaldyr*
herring	*sild*
trout	*ørred*
cod	*torsk*
shrimps	*rejer*
fruit salad	*frugtsalat*
pork	*svinkød*
potatoes	*kartofler*
starter	*forret*
vegetables	*grøntsager*
wine	*vin*

Finland – Essential Information

PRE-TRIP ESSENTIALS...

WHAT YOU NEED

ESSENTIAL FOR TRAVELERS

● Required   ● Recommended   ● Not required

Passport	●
Visa	●
Travel, medical insurance	●
Round-trip or onward airline ticket	●
Local currency	●
Traveler's checks	●
Credit cards	●
First-aid kit and medicines	●
Inoculations	●

ESSENTIAL FOR DRIVERS*

Driver's license	●
International Driving Permit	●
Car insurance (for nonrental cars)	●
Car registration (for nonrental cars)	●

*see also DRIVING section

IMPORTANT ADDRESSES

Finnish Tourist Board (MEK)
PO Box 4649
Grand Central Station
New York, NY 10163-4649
☎ (212) 885 9700 or (800) FIN-INFO
Fax (212) 885 9710
www.gofinland.org

Finnish Tourist Board (MEK)
P O Box 625
Töölönkatu 11
FIN-00101 Helsinki, Finland
☎ 09 417 6911
Fax 09 4176 9399
www.visitfinland.com

American Embassy
Itäinen Puistotie 14B
FIN-00140 Helsinki, Finland
☎ 09 616 250
Fax 09 616 2 5800
Personal appointments Mon.–Fri. 9–noon
Telephone inquiries Mon.–Fri. 2–4

COUNTRY ESSENTIALS...

CUSTOMS

YES
Duty-free limits on goods brought in from non-European Union countries:
200 cigarettes or 100 cigarillos or 50 cigars or 250 g. tobacco; 1 L. alcohol over 22% volume or 2 L. alcohol under 22% volume; 2 L. wine; 16 L. beer; 50 ml. perfume; 250 ml. toilet water; plus any other duty-free goods (including gifts) to the value of €175. **Tax-free allowances for goods purchased within the European Union**: 300 cigarettes or 150 cigarillos or 75 cigars or 400 g. tobacco; 1 L. alcohol over 22% volume; 3 L. alcohol under 22% volume; 5L. wine; 64 L. beer. There are no currency regulations. Pets are allowed if vaccinated against rabies between one and 12 months prior to date of arrival.

NO
No unlicensed drugs, weapons, ammunition, obscene material, counterfeit money or copied goods.

For customs limits for returning U.S. citizens see page 16.

MONEY

Finland's currency is the euro (€), a currency shared by 11 other European Union countries. The euro is divided into 100 cents (¢). The denominations of euro bills are 5, 10, 20, 50, 100, 200 and 500. There are coins of 5, 10, 20 and 50¢ and €1 and €2. Exchange dollars and traveler's checks at a bank *(pankki)* or an exchange office, as the exchange rate in city hotels may be poor.

Exchange rate at press time: $1 = €0.82

TIPS AND GRATUITIES

Tips are welcomed, but not expected.

Restaurants	change
Cafés/bars	change
Taxis; hairdressers	none
Porters; restroom attendants	change
Chambermaids	change
Cloakroom attendants; hotel/restaurant doormen	€1

| TIME ZONES | HELSINKI 12:00 noon | NEW YORK 7 hours behind Finland | CHICAGO 8 hours behind Finland | DENVER 9 hours behind Finland | SAN FRANCISCO 10 hours behind Finland | 483 |

COMMUNICATIONS

POST OFFICES

Most post offices are open Mon.–Fri. 9–6.

Hours for out-of-town post offices may vary. Stamps *(postimerkki)* can be bought at post offices, bookstores, newsstands (R-kiosks), railroad and bus stations, and some hotels. Mailboxes are usually yellow and set into walls.

TELEPHONES

The Finnish public telephone system is efficient and accepts mostly credit cards and prepaid telephone cards. Phone cards are available from R-kiosks, telephone company (Sonera) shops and some post offices. Most people have cell phones, and you can rent one for the length of your stay.

Phoning inside Finland

All Finnish telephone numbers in this book include an area code: dial the number listed.

To call the operator dial 115; for directory inquiry information dial 118.

Phoning Finland from abroad

The country code for Finland is 358; to phone Finland from the United States or Canada, omit the first zero from the Finnish number and prefix with 011 358. (Finnish area codes have two or three digits including the first zero.) Example: 01 122 3344 becomes 011 358 1 122 3344.

Phoning from Finland

To phone the United States or Canada from Finland, prefix the area code and number with 00 1. (There are other numbers to dial out of the country depending on what telephone system you are using: 990, 994 or 999, followed by 1.) Example: (111) 222-3333 becomes 00 1 111 222-3333. To make a long distance call, dial 02 0222. For national information, dial 02 0208.

EMERGENCY TELEPHONE NUMBERS

Police *(poliisi)*	112 (also 10022)
Fire *(palokunta)*	112
Ambulance *(ambulanssi)*	112

Emergency calls are free from phone booths.

HOURS OF OPERATION

- Stores Mon.–Sat. ● Pharmacies Mon.–Sat.
- Offices Mon.–Fri.
- Banks Mon.–Fri.
- Post offices Mon.–Fri.

| 7 | 8 | 9 | 10 | 11 | 12 | 1 | 2 | 3 | 4 | 5 | 6 | 7 |

Many stores close at 2 or 3 on Saturday, but department stores and shopping malls stay open until 5 or 6. During the week, large stores extend their hours to 8 or 9, and open on Sunday from June through August and during December. Grocery stores stay open until 8 or 9. Some supermarkets and convenience stores open on Sunday.

Some gas stations close on Sunday.

Out-of-town post offices and banks may have shorter hours, and some city post offices and banks stay open into the evening.

Museum and monument opening times vary according to the season. Check opening times with the local tourist office.

Some pharmacies *(apteekki)* close early on Saturday. In Helsinki, the Apteekki Yliopiston, Mannerheimintie 96, ☎ 09 4178 0300, is open 24 hours.

NATIONAL HOLIDAYS

Banks, businesses and most stores close on these days.

Jan. 1	New Year's Day
Jan. 6	Epiphany
Mar./Apr.	Good Friday
Mar./Apr.	Easter Monday
Apr. 30	May Day Eve
May 1	May Day
May	Ascension
Jun. 21–22	Midsummer's Day Eve and Midsummer's Day
Nov. 1	All Saints' Day
Dec. 6	Independence Day
Dec. 24	Christmas Eve
Dec. 25	Christmas Day
Dec. 26	St. Stephen's Day

PHOTOGRAPHY

There is a contrast in seasonal light conditions: subarctic winter nights are long, while in the north the midnight sun shines throughout the summer. Bring a tripod if you hope to photograph the northern lights *(aurora borealis)*. Check whether photography is permitted in museums. Film and batteries can be purchased at tourist-oriented stores, and rapid-developing services are widely available.

Finland – Essential Information

Finland – Essential Information

HEALTH

 MEDICAL INSURANCE
Private medical insurance is recommended. All treatment in a hospital *(sairaala)* has to be paid for. Foreign visitors can receive good service at a private hospital or health center *(lääkäriasema)*; for 24-hour medical advice ☎ 10023. For private medical care contact **Mehiläinen**, Runeberginkatu 47A, Helsinki ☎ 010 414 4444 (24 hours).

 DENTAL SERVICES
Dentists *(hammaslääkäri)* charge for treatment and can be expensive, so check that treatment is covered by your medical insurance. 24-hour clinics are available in city hospitals.

 SUN ADVICE
Southeast Finland has the highest summer temperature in Scandinavia, so precautions are necessary. Use a suitable sunscreen and cover up sensitive skin.

 DRUGS
Prescription and nonprescription medicines are available from pharmacies *(apteekki)*. If you need a pharmacy outside regular hours, information about the nearest all-night facility is posted at all pharmacies. Note that drugstores *(kemikaalikaupa)* sell only cosmetics.

 SAFE WATER
Tap water is safe to drink, and mineral water *(kivennäisvesi)* is widely available.

RESTROOMS

Public restrooms are easy to find, immaculately clean and modern, and are designated by *Miehille/Miehet* (men) and *Naisille/Naiset* (women). There may be a small charge, but many are free. Attendants welcome loose change as a tip.

ELECTRICITY

 Finland has a 220-volt power supply. Electrical sockets take plugs with two round pins; American appliances will need a plug adapter and will require a transformer if they do not have a dual-voltage facility.

NATIONAL TRANSPORTATION

 TRAIN *(juna)*
The Finnish Railway *(Valtion Rautatiet, or VR)* extends north to southern Lapland. For timetable *(Suomen kulkuneuvot)* information ☎ 0600 41 902. If you are planning extensive rail travel, buy a FinnRailpass, which can be bought at main railroad stations or Finnish travel agencies. For information ☎ 0600 41 902. In the US, you can buy a FinnRailpass from Rail Europe ☎ 1 877 257 2887.

 BUS *(bussi)*
Bus lines run to even the most remote corners of Finland. Bus Holiday Tickets (discount cards) are available for those traveling long distances (valid 2 weeks). For information, phone ☎ 0200 4000.

 FERRY *(laiva)*
There are many excursions exploring Finland's eastern lake system and the country's canal network. Trips into Russia, Estonia, Latvia and Lithuania are possible; check with the tour operator whether a short-term visa is required. These can be obtained through the country's embassy or a travel agent. Contact Silja Line: ☎ 09 18041; Tallink: ☎ 09 228 311; and Viking Line: ☎ 09 12 351.

DRIVING

 DRIVE ON THE RIGHT

SPEED LIMITS
Minor fines can be imposed on the spot, but not collected. Payment can be made at banks.

 Limited-access highways *(moottoritie)*
120 k.p.h. (74 m.p.h.) in summer
100 k.p.h. (62 m.p.h.) in winter
Divided highways
100 k.p.h. (62 m.p.h.)

 Main roads
80 k.p.h. (49 m.p.h.)

 Urban areas
40–60 k.p.h. (24–37 m.p.h.)

 SEAT BELTS
Must be worn in front and back seats at all times.

 BLOOD ALCOHOL
The legal blood alcohol limit is 0.05%. Random breath tests on drivers are carried out frequently, especially late at night, and the penalties for offenders are severe.

DRIVING continued

TOLLS
There are no highway tolls in Finland.

CAR RENTAL
The leading rental firms have offices at airports and train stations. Hertz offers discounted rates for AAA members (see page 15). For reservations:

	UNITED STATES	FINLAND
Alamo	(800) 327-9633	0800 121 54 (Europcar)
Avis	(800) 331-2112	09 441 155
Budget	(800) 527-0700	0800 124 424
Hertz	(800) 654-3080	0800 112 233

FUEL
There is no leaded gas in Finland. Unleaded Super (98 and 99 octane) gas is suitable for cars not yet converted to unleaded fuel. For cars fitted with a catalytic converter, use regular (95 octane) gas. Diesel is available. Gas stations are open Mon.–Sat. 7 a.m.–9 p.m., shorter hours on Sunday.

AAA AFFILIATED MOTORING CLUB
Autoliitto (AL)
Hämeentie 105A, FIN-00550 Helsinki
☎ 09 7258 4400, fax 09 7258 4460
If you break down while driving, phone ☎ 09 7747 6400 (24 hours) for the AL breakdown service. Not all automobile clubs offer full services to AAA members.

BREAKDOWNS AND ACCIDENTS
There are 24-hour emergency phones at regular intervals on highways. If you are involved in an accident, phone ☎ 112 for police, fire or ambulance. Accidents should be reported without delay to: Finnish Motor Insurance Center (Liikenne-vakuutuskeskus), Bulevardi 28, FIN-00120 Helsinki ☎ 09 680 401, fax 09 6804 0474. Most car rental firms provide their own free rescue service. Use of a car repair service other than those authorized by your rental company may violate your agreement.

OTHER INFORMATION
The minimum age for driving a car is 18 (19–25 for car rental firms). An International Driving Permit (IDP) is recommended; some rental firms require them, and they can speed up formalities if you are involved in an accident. A Green Card (international motor insurance certificate) is recommended if you are driving a private car; see page 15 for more information. Dimmed headlights must be used at all times. In winter, snow tires or chains are essential. From December through February, winter tires (with or without studs) or tires intended for year-round use are compulsory. You can buy or rent winter driving equipment from Autoliitto. Watch out for signs warning of elk and reindeer crossing roads, indicating the approximate length of danger zones – these animals are more active at dusk.

USEFUL WORDS AND PHRASES

Finnish is a complex and difficult language to learn, and bears little or no resemblance to neighboring languages. However, Swedish is Finland's second, more accessible language, and most people speak some English.

Finnish uses compound words, which are pronounced exactly as they are written. The first syllable of a word is always stressed, and each letter is pronounced individually.

Do you speak English?	*Puhutteko englantia?*
excuse me	*anteeksi*
hello	*terve*
goodbye	*näkemiin*
how much?	*kuinka paljon?*
how are you?	*kuinka voitte?*
Is it near?	*Onko se lähellä?*
I'd like…	*Haluaisin…*
I don't understand	*en ymmärrä*
non-smoking	*tupakointi kielletty*
okay	*ja lyh*
open/closed	*avoinna/suljettu*
please/thank you	*olkaa hyvä/kiitos*
ticket (one-way/	*menolippu*
round trip)	*meno-paluulippu*
where is…?	*missä on…?*
yes/no	*kyllä or joo/ei*

the hotel	***hotelli***
breakfast	*aamiainen*
key	*avain*
room	*huone*
shower	*suihku*
it's too expensive	*se on liian kallis*

the restaurant	***ravintola***
beef	*nauta*
bread	*leipä*
chicken	*kana*
steak	*pihvl*
coffee	*kahvi*
milk	*maito*
dessert	*jälkiruoka*
main course	*pääruoka*
fish	*kala*
lamb	*karitsa*
pork	*sianliha*
seafood	*äyrläisiä*
soup	*keitto*
wine	*vini*

Finland – Essential Information

France – Essential Information

PRE-TRIP ESSENTIALS...

WHAT YOU NEED

ESSENTIAL FOR TRAVELERS

● Required ● Recommended ● Not required

Passport	●
Visa	●
Travel, medical insurance	●
Round-trip or onward airline ticket	●
Local currency	●
Traveler's checks	●
Credit cards	●
First-aid kit and medicines	●
Inoculations	●

ESSENTIAL FOR DRIVERS*

Driver's license	●
International Driving Permit	●
Car insurance (for nonrental cars)	●
Car registration (for nonrental cars)	●

*see also DRIVING section

IMPORTANT ADDRESSES

French Government Tourist Office
16th Floor, 444 Madison Avenue
New York, NY 10022-6903
☎ 410 268 3810
Fax (212) 838-7800
www.franceguide.com

Maison de la France
(French Government Tourist Office)
20 avenue de l'Opéra
75041 Paris Cedex 01, France
☎ 01 42 96 70 00
Fax 01 42 96 70 11
www.franceguide.com

American Embassy
2 avenue Gabriel
75008 Paris, France
☎ 01 43 12 22 22
Fax 01 42 66 97 83

American Consulate
2 rue St.-Florentin
75382 Paris, France
☎ 01 43 12 22 22; fax 01 42 66 97 83
Open Mon.–Fri. 9–12:30 and 1–3

COUNTRY ESSENTIALS...

CUSTOMS

YES
Duty-free limits on goods brought in from non-European Union countries:
200 cigarettes or 100 cigarillos or 50 cigars or 250 g. tobacco; 2 L. wine; 1 L. alcohol over 22% volume; 2 L. alcohol under 22%; 60 ml. perfume; 250 ml. toilet water; plus any other duty-free goods (including gifts) to the value of €45. There is no limit on the importation of tax-paid goods purchased within the European Union, provided they are for your own personal use. Unlimited currency may be taken into France, but large amounts must be declared if it is to be re-exported.

NO
No unlicensed drugs, weapons, ammunition, obscene material, pets or other animals, counterfeit money or copied goods, meat or poultry.

For customs limits for returning U.S. citizens see page 16.

MONEY

France's currency is the euro (€), a currency shared by 11 other European Union countries. The euro is divided into 100 cents (¢). The denominations of euro bills are 5, 10, 20, 50, 100, 200 and 500. There are coins of 1, 2, 5, 10, 20 and 50¢ and €1 and €2. You can exchange dollars or traveler's checks (chèques de voyage) at a bank (banque) or an exchange office (bureau de change).

Exchange rate at press time: $1 = €0.82

TIPS AND GRATUITIES

Tips (pourboires) are welcomed, but not expected.

Restaurants (service is almost always included)	change
Cafés/bars (service is almost always included)	change
Taxis	€1–€2
Porters	€1–€2
Chambermaids	€2–€10
Hairdressers	€1–€2
Cloakroom attendants	50¢–€1

TIME ZONES

487

PARIS	NEW YORK	CHICAGO	DENVER	SAN FRANCISCO
12:00 noon	6 hours behind France	7 hours behind France	8 hours behind France	9 hours behind France

France – Essential Information

COMMUNICATIONS

POST OFFICES

Buy stamps *(timbres-poste)* at a post office *(poste)*, newsstand *(marchand de journaux)* or tobacconist *(tabac)*.

Hours of out-of-town post offices may vary. Mailboxes are yellow and wall mounted or free-standing; there are separate compartments for local mail *(départemental)*, for elsewhere in France, and abroad *(autres départements/ destinations)*.

TELEPHONES

The telephone system in France is efficient, and phone booths with instructions in English are easy to find. Most phones are operated solely with a phone card *(télécarte),* which can be bought for 50 or 120 units from post offices, France Telecom offices, newsstands, tobacconists *(tabacs)*, and SNCF (railway) counters. Some booths accept credit cards.

Phoning inside France

All telephone numbers are 10 digits, and include the regional code. Paris and Ile de France numbers begin with 01; the rest of France is divided into four zones (02, 03, 04 and 05). Dial all digits when making a call.

Phoning France from abroad

The country code for France is 33. Note that French numbers in this book do not include the country code; you need to prefix this number if you are phoning from another country. To phone France from the United States or Canada, omit the first zero from the French number, and add the prefix 011 33.
Example: 01 22 33 44 55 becomes 011 33 1 22 33 44 55.

Phoning from France

To phone the United States or Canada from France, prefix the area code and number with 00 1.
Example: (111) 222-3333 becomes 00 1 111 222-3333.

For directory inquiries dial 12.
For the operator dial 3123.
For international directory inquiries dial 3213.

EMERGENCY TELEPHONE NUMBERS

Police *(police)*	17
Fire *(pompiers)*	18
Ambulance *(ambulance)*	15

Emergency calls are free from phone booths.

HOURS OF OPERATION

○ Stores Tue.–Sat.	● Museums/monuments
● Offices Mon.–Fri.	Tue.–Sun.
● Banks Mon.–Fri.	● Pharmacies Mon.–Sat.
● Post offices Mon.–Sat.	

Many stores close on Sunday and all day or a half-day Monday, although some food establishments, especially bakeries, open Sunday mornings. Hypermarkets (large all-purpose stores) are open Mon.–Sat. 9 a.m.– 9 or 10 p.m., although many close Monday morning. Opening hours are longer in resort areas and major towns and cities.

Out-of-town banks may stay closed on Monday, while city banks may open on Saturday morning. Post offices close at noon on Saturday.

Museum times vary considerably, and it is best to check before a visit. Municipal museums close on Monday, while national museums close on Tuesday (except Versailles, Trianon Palace and Musée d'Orsay, which close on Monday). Many museums close on national holidays.

NATIONAL HOLIDAYS

Banks, businesses and most stores close on these days.

Jan. 1	New Year's Day
Mar./Apr.	Easter Monday
May 1	May Day
May 8	VE Day
May	Ascension Day
May/Jun.	Pentecost Monday
Jul. 14	Bastille Day
Aug. 15	Assumption of the Virgin
Nov. 1	All Saints' Day
Nov. 11	Armistice Day
Dec. 25	Christmas Day

PHOTOGRAPHY

The range of subjects to photograph in France is enormous, and the light is usually favorable in the summer months. Film is readily available from stores and photo labs, although development is rather expensive. Some museums and churches will allow you to photograph inside, but permission for flash photography is usually required.

France – Essential Information

HEALTH

 MEDICAL INSURANCE
Private medical insurance is recommended. Visitors from non-E.U. countries have to pay for all medical treatment; keep all receipts and medicine labels to claim on your travel insurance. If you wish to see an English-speaking doctor *(médecin)* ask at your consulate or hotel.

 DENTAL SERVICES
A dentist *(dentiste)* charges for treatment. Emergency help is available from dentists listed in the yellow pages *(pages jaunes)*. Check that your private medical insurance covers dental treatment.

 SUN ADVICE
The yearly average for sunshine is high: 2,500 hours (3,000 hours along the coast). Summers, particularly July and August, can be dry and hot, especially in the south. When outside wear a hat and drink plenty of fluids. On the beach a high factor sunscreen is essential.

 DRUGS
Prescription medicines and medical advice can be obtained from a pharmacy *(pharmacie)*, designated by a green cross sign. If you need medicines outside regular hours, information about the nearest 24-hour facility is posted on the door of all pharmacies.

 SAFE WATER
It is safe to drink tap water, but never drink from a fountain marked *"eau non potable"* ("not drinking water"). Many French people prefer the taste of bottled mineral water *(eau minérale en bouteille)*, which is widely available. A less expensive alternative is *eau de source*, which is spring water.

RESTROOMS

 It is not difficult to find a restroom *(toilettes* or *WC*, pronounced *vay-say* in French), although you may still find the old-fashioned "squat" variety. Hygiene is usually of a reasonable standard. There is a small fee to use facilities in train stations. If you need to use the restroom in a café or bar, buy a drink first.

ELECTRICITY

France has a 220-volt power supply. Electrical sockets take plugs with two round pins (occasionally with three round pins); American appliances will need a plug adapter and will require a transformer if they do not have a dual-voltage facility.

NATIONAL TRANSPORTATION

 TRAIN *(train)*
The state rail company is the Société Nationale des Chemins de Fer Français (SNCF): ☎ 08 36 35 35 35. Trains are fast, reliable and comfortable, with numerous discounts available. A "turn-up-and-go" car-carrying service from Calais (Le Shuttle) to Folkstone, England, and a Paris–London passenger train (Eurostar – call ☎ 08 92 35 35 39) both run through the tunnel under the English Channel.

 BUS *(bus)*
Bus services in cities are excellent, but rural areas may be less well served. Long-distance bus stations are usually close to railroad stations, and major train and bus services usually co-ordinate (a long-distance bus is called a *car*). Bus services shown on train timetables are run by the SNCF, and rail tickets are often valid for them. The Eurolines international bus network operates in France: ☎ 08 92 89 90 91.

 FERRY *(ferry)*
There are frequent traditional and fast ferry sailings to Britain from ports along the English Channel. A car-carrying train service also operates – see TRAIN above. Some Mediterranean ferries operate in summer only and may need reservations in advance.

DRIVING

 DRIVE ON THE RIGHT

SPEED LIMITS
Traffic police can impose severe on-the-spot fines.

 Limited-access toll highways *(autoroutes à peage)* **130 k.p.h. (80 m.p.h.)** Outer lane minimum **80 k.p.h. (49 m.p.h.)** On wet roads **110 k.p.h. (68 m.p.h.)** In fog with visibility less than 50 m (55 yards) **50 k.p.h. (31 m.p.h.)** Toll-free highways *(autoroutes)* and divided highways **110 k.p.h. (68 m.p.h.)**

 Main roads **90 k.p.h. (55 m.p.h.)** On wet roads **80 k.p.h. (49 m.p.h.)**

 Urban areas **50 k.p.h. (31 m.p.h.)**

 SEAT BELTS
Must be worn in front and back seats at all times.

BLOOD ALCOHOL
The legal blood alcohol limit is 0.05%. Random breath tests on drivers are carried out frequently, and the penalties for offenders are severe.

France – Essential Information

DRIVING continued

TOLLS
There are tolls on many limited-access highways *(autoroutes à péage)*.
Collect a ticket on entry and keep it in a safe place: you must show the ticket and pay when exiting. Cash and credit cards are accepted.

CAR RENTAL
The leading rental firms have offices at airports and train stations. Hertz offers discounted rates for AAA members (see page 15). For reservations:

	UNITED STATES	FRANCE
Alamo	(800) 462-5266	08 25 35 23 52 (Europcar)
Avis	(800) 230-4898	0820 05 05 05
Budget	(800) 527-0700	08 25 00 35 64 (toll call)
Hertz	(800) 654-3080	08 25 03 00 40 (toll call)

FUEL
Gas stations are generally easy to find, and highway service areas are open 24 hours. Gas *(essence)* is unleaded *(sans plomb)* and sold in liters. Credit cards (though not all international credit cards) are widely accepted; many pumps read cards directly, so the customer does not have to pay at the counter. Gas stations are less common in rural areas, and some close on Sunday.

AAA AFFILIATED MOTORING CLUB
Automobile Club de L'Ile de France (FFAC)
14 Avenue de la Grand Armee, Paris
☎ 01 40 55 43 00, fax 01 43 80 90 51
Not all automobile clubs offer full services to AAA members.

BREAKDOWNS AND ACCIDENTS
If you are involved in an accident, phone ☎ 17 for police assistance.
There are orange emergency telephones every 2 km (1.2 miles) on highways. Most car rental firms provide their own free rescue service; if your car is rented, follow the instructions given in the documentation. Use of a car repair service other than those authorized by your rental company may violate your agreement.

OTHER INFORMATION
The minimum age for driving a car is 18 (may be higher, usually between 21 and 25, for some car rental firms).
An International Driving Permit (IDP) is recommended; some rental firms require them, and they can speed up formalities if you are involved in an accident.
A Green Card (international motor insurance certificate) is recommended if you are driving a private car; see page 15 for more information.
In built-up areas you must yield the right-of-way to vehicles coming from a side street on the right.

USEFUL WORDS AND PHRASES

You'll be well received if you try to pronounce words correctly. Don't worry too much about rolling your r's, though; the French realize how difficult it can be.

Final consonants are seldom pronounced. For instance, the masculine adjective *ouvert* (open) is pronounced [oo-ver]; the feminine *ouverte* [oo-vert]. The final consonant in a word like *vin, bon* or *grand* alters the last vowel, making it nasal.

h is silent	*hôtel* [o-tel]
th is *t* (but *ch* is *sh*)	*thé* [tay]; *chaud* [show]
ou is full	*tout* [too]
u is tight, as in cupola	*tu* [tu], *menu* [meuh-nu]
c and g hard before a, o, u	*car* [car], *guide* [geed]
c and g soft before i or e	*cigarette, age* [arzh]
ç is soft (before an a)	*français* [frahn-say]
gn as in union	*agneau* [an-yo]

Do you speak English?	*Parlez-vous anglais?*
excuse me	*excusez-moi*
hello/goodbye	*bonjour/au revoir*
How much is this?	*C'est combien?*
I am American	*Je suis Américain/e*
I'd like…	*je voudrais…*
I don't understand	*Je ne comprends pas*
non-smoking	*non-fumeurs*
okay	*OK (informal)*
open/closed	*ouvert/fermé*
please/thank you	*s'il vous plaît/merci*
ticket	*billet*
(one-way/round trip)	*(simple/aller-retour)*
where is…?	*où est…?*
yes/no	*oui/non*
you're welcome	*de rien*

the hotel	***l'hôtel***
breakfast	*petit déjeuner*
I have a reservation	*j'ai réservé*
key	*clé*
for one/two nights	*pour une/deux nuit(s)*
one/two people	*une/deux personne(s)*
room	*une chambre*
shower	*une douche*
with en-suite bathroom	*avec salle de bains*

the restaurant	***le restaurant***
beef	*boeuf*
bread	*pain*
the check	*l'addition*
chicken	*poulet*
coffee	*café*
dessert	*dessert*
dish of the day	*plat du jour*
fish	*poisson*
lamb	*agneau*
main course	*plat principal*
pork	*porc*
seafood	*fruits de mer*
starter	*entrée*
wine	*vin*

Germany – Essential Information

PRE-TRIP ESSENTIALS...

WHAT YOU NEED

ESSENTIAL FOR TRAVELERS

● Required ● Recommended ● Not required

Passport	●
Visa	●
Travel, medical insurance	●
Round-trip or onward airline ticket	●
Local currency	●
Traveler's checks	●
Credit cards	●
First-aid kit and medicines	●
Inoculations	●

ESSENTIAL FOR DRIVERS*

Driver's license	●
International Driving Permit	●
Car insurance (for nonrental cars)	●
Car registration (for nonrental cars)	●

*see also DRIVING section

IMPORTANT ADDRESSES

German National Tourist Office
122 East 42nd Street, 52nd floor
New York, NY 10168-0072
☎ (212) 661-7200
Fax (212) 661-7174
www.visits-to-germany.com

**Deutsche Zentrale für Tourismus e.V
(German National Tourist Office)**
Beethovenstrasse 69
60325 Frankfurt am Main, Germany
☎ 069 974 64-0
Fax 069 751 903
www.deutschland-tourismus.de

American Embassy
Neustädtische Kirchstrasse 4–5
10117 Berlin, Germany
☎ 030 832-9233 (Mon.–Fri. 2–4) or 030 8305-0
(emergencies only)
Fax 030 8305-1215
American Citizen Services
Mon.–Fri. 8:30–noon
www.usembassy.de

COUNTRY ESSENTIALS...

CUSTOMS

YES
**Duty-free limits on goods brought in
from non-European Union countries:**
200 cigarettes or 100 cigarillos or 50 cigars
or 250 g. tobacco; 1 L alcohol over 22% volume and
2 L alcohol under 22% or 2 L sparkling or fortified wine
and 2 L still wine; 50 ml. perfume; 250 ml. toilet water;
plus any other duty-free goods (including gifts) to the
value of €178.95. There is no limit on the importation of
tax-paid goods purchased within the European Union,
provided they are for your own personal use. There are
no currency regulations.

NO
No unlicensed drugs, weapons,
ammunition, obscene material, pets
or other animals, counterfeit money
or copied goods, meat or poultry.

**For customs limits for returning U.S. citizens
see page 16.**

MONEY

Germany's currency is the euro (€), a currency
shared by 11 other European Union countries. The
euro is divided into 100 cents (¢). The denominations of
euro bills are 5, 10, 20, 50, 100, 200 and 500. There are
coins of 1, 2, 5, 10, 20 and 50¢ and €1 and €2.

You can exchange dollars or traveler's checks
(Reiseschecks) at a bank *(Bank)* or an exchange
office *(Wechselbüro).*

Exchange rate at press time: $1 = €0.82

TIPS AND GRATUITIES

Restaurants (where service is not included)	10%
Cafés/bars (where service is not included)	10%
Taxis	10%
Porters	change
Chambermaids	change
Hairdressers	change
Restroom attendants	change
Cloakroom attendants	change

TIME ZONES

BERLIN	NEW YORK	CHICAGO	DENVER	SAN FRANCISCO
12:00 noon	6 hours behind Germany	7 hours behind Germany	8 hours behind Germany	9 hours behind Germany

491

COMMUNICATIONS

POST OFFICES

Buy stamps *(Briefmarken)* at a post office *(Postamt)*.

Hours for out-of-town post offices may vary. Mailboxes are bright yellow.

TELEPHONES

Black telephones have instructions in English, and most operators are bilingual. Increasingly fewer phones accept coins; most are operated by telephone cards *(Telefonkarten)*, which can be bought at any post office. International calls can be made from any booth.

Phoning inside Germany
German telephone numbers in this book include an area code: dial the number listed.

Operator: ☎ 0180 200 10 33 (extra cost)

Phoning Germany from abroad
The country code for Germany is 49. Note that German numbers in this book do not include the country code; you will need to prefix this number if you are phoning from another country. To phone Germany from the United States or Canada, omit the first zero from the German number, and add the prefix 011 49. (Note that the number of digits in German area codes varies.)
Example: 011 22 33 44 becomes 011 49 11 22 33 44.

Phoning from Germany
To phone the United States or Canada from Germany, prefix the area code and number with 00 1.
Example: 111 222-3333 becomes 00 1 111 222-3333.
National information for Germany: dial 11833
To call international information dial 11834.

EMERGENCY TELEPHONE NUMBERS

Police *(Polizei)*	110
Fire *(Feuerwehr)*	112
Ambulance *(Krankenwagen)*	112

Emergency calls are free from phone booths.

HOURS OF OPERATION

- ● Stores Mon.–Sat.
- ● Offices Mon.–Fri.
- ● Banks Mon.–Fri.
- ● Post offices Mon.–Sat.
- ● Museums/monuments Tue.–Sat.
- ● Pharmacies Mon.–Sat.

7 8 9 10 11 12 1 2 3 4 5 6 7

Store opening hours vary considerably, so even within cities there is no standard rule. Stores are open until 8 p.m. latest Mon.–Fri. and are open until 10:30 p.m. on Thursday.
Pharmacies tend to close earlier during the week and at 4 on Saturday.

Banks stay open until 6 on Thursday. Post offices open 8–noon on Saturday. Post offices at airports and railway stations operate longer hours.

Government offices close promptly at 4, or at 2 on Friday.

Museums often close on Monday and open late on Thursday; some outside cities close for lunch.

NATIONAL HOLIDAYS

Banks, businesses and most stores close on these days.

Jan. 1	New Year's Day
Jan. 6	Epiphany (Bavaria, Baden Württemberg and Saxony only)
Mar./Apr.	Good Friday
Mar./Apr.	Easter Monday
May 1	Labor Day
May	Ascension Day
May/Jun.	Pentecost Monday
Aug. 15	Assumption of the Virgin (Bavaria and Saarland only)
Oct. 3	Day of German Unity
Nov. 1	All Saints' Day (Baden-Württemberg, Bavaria, North Rhine-Westphalia, Rhineland-Palatinate and Saarland only)
Dec. 25	Christmas Day
Dec. 26	St. Stephen's Day

PHOTOGRAPHY

In addition to the glorious architecture of the big cities, there are many colorful, quaint street scenes to be snapped in provincial Germany, and the landscapes are equally appealing.
Photography is generally forbidden in museums and churches or needs special permission.
Quality brand film and batteries are easy to find, and there are many rapid-developing facilities.

Germany – Essential Information

Germany – Essential Information

HEALTH

MEDICAL INSURANCE
U.S. and Canadian visitors must pay for medical treatment from a doctor or at a hospital *(Krankenhaus)*. Keep all receipts to claim on your travel insurance. For details on emergency, weekend or English-speaking doctors, ask your hotel or consulate.

DENTAL SERVICES
A dentist *(Zahnarzt)* always charges for treatment. Emergency help is available from dentists listed in the local telephone directory. Check that your private medical insurance covers dental treatment.

SUN ADVICE
Germany's Continental climate brings cold, clear winters and warm summers, when sun protection is needed. Use sunscreen; children and those with fair skin should be vigilant.

DRUGS
Prescription medicines and advice can be obtained from a pharmacy *(Apotheke);* cosmetics and toiletries at a *Drogerie.* If you need medicine outside regular hours, information about the nearest 24-hour facility is posted on the door of all pharmacies.

SAFE WATER
Water is safe to drink in Germany, but you may prefer to drink bottled mineral water *(Mineralwasser),* which is widely available.

RESTROOMS

Finding a restroom *(Toilette)* is not difficult; they are usually identified by symbols, or are designated *Herren* (men) and *Damen* or *Frauen* (women). Most are free, although some are operated by a 20¢ coin. If there is an attendant, small change is appreciated as a tip.

ELECTRICITY

Germany has a 220-volt power supply. Electrical sockets take plugs with two round pins or sometimes three pins in a vertical row; American appliances will need a plug adapter and will require a transformer if they do not have a dual-voltage facility.

NATIONAL TRANSPORTATION

TRAIN *(Zug)*
Germany's fast, efficient rail network is operated by Deutsche Bahn (DB). ICE is a modern service of long-distance, high-speed trains. IC and EC trains operate between major towns and cities. Regional (IR) trains are modern and comfortable, and connect with long-distance services. Local services are called SE or S-Bahn. There are many fare reductions available; for bookings and information, phone ☎ 01805 99 6633 (24 hours; toll call).

BUS *(Bus)*
Towns and villages not served by the rail network usually have bus links, with timetables and routes co-ordinating with trains. German towns have their own buses, and one ticket is often good for other types of city transportation. The Eurolines international bus service operates in Germany: ☎ 089 54 58 70-11.

FERRY *(Fähre)*
Ferries from the ports of Lübeck and Kiel in the north connect to Denmark and Sweden. Boats also offer a service on many German lakes, rivers and canals. Ask for details at your travel agency or a local tourist office, where reservations can often be made.

DRIVING

DRIVE ON THE RIGHT

SPEED LIMITS
Traffic police can impose severe on-the-spot fines.

Limited-access highways *(Autobahn):* unless signposted there is no speed limit but the **suggested limit** is **130 k.p.h. (80 m.p.h.)**

Main roads
100 k.p.h. (62 m.p.h.)

Urban areas
50 k.p.h. (31 m.p.h.)

SEAT BELTS
Must be worn in front and back seats at all times. Children under 12 must sit on child seat cushions to enable seat belts to fit properly.

BLOOD ALCOHOL
The legal blood alcohol limit is 0.05%. Random breath tests on drivers are carried out frequently, especially late at night, and the penalties for offenders are severe.

Germany – Essential Information

DRIVING continued

TOLLS
There are no highway tolls.

CAR RENTAL
The leading rental firms have offices at airports and train stations. Hertz offers discounted rates for AAA members (see page 15). For reservations:

	UNITED STATES	GERMANY
Alamo	(800) 462-5266	0405 075 23 01
Avis	(800) 230-4898	0180 5 55 77 55
Budget	(800) 527-0700	0180 5 24 43 88
Hertz	(800) 654-3080	0180 5 33 35 35

FUEL
Gas *(Benzin)* and diesel fuel are sold in liters. Gas stations are easy to find, and most highway services are open 24 hours. Self-service stations are called *Selbstbedienung* or *SB-Tanken,* and credit cards are widely accepted.

AAA AFFILIATED MOTORING CLUB
Allgemeiner Deutscher Automobil-Club E.V. (ADAC)
Am Westpark 8, 81373 Munich
☎ 089 76 76-0, fax 089 76 76-25 00
If you break down while driving, phone ☎ 01802 22 22 22 (ADAC breakdown service).
Not all automobile clubs offer full services to AAA members.

BREAKDOWNS AND ACCIDENTS
Most car rental firms provide their own free rescue service; if your car is rented, follow the instructions given in the documentation. Use of a car repair service other than those authorized by your rental company may violate your agreement.

If you are involved in an accident, ☎ 110 for police.

OTHER INFORMATION
The minimum age for driving a car is 18 (may be higher for some car rental firms).

You must keep an official translation with your driver's license; your embassy or a tourist office can help. An International Driving Permit (IDP) is recommended; some rental firms require them, and they can speed up formalities if you are involved in an accident.

A Green Card (international motor insurance certificate) is recommended if you are driving a private car; see page 15 for more information.

On-the-spot fines can be imposed if you run out of gas on a highway.

Using a cellular phone while driving is not permitted.

USEFUL WORDS AND PHRASES

German has many dialects. Language in the north descended from Old Saxon, and in the south from Old High German. Their differences were resolved by Standard German *(Schriftdeutsch)*, created by Martin Luther when he translated the Bible in the 16th century.

Germans are helpful to visitors who attempt to communicate in German, although English is widely spoken.

ü is like the *u* in cupola	*über* (over)
ie sounds like heat	*Sie* (you)
ei sounds like height	*Eingang* (entrance)
ch is a harsh rasp…	*J. S. Bach*
j is like the English *y*	*ja* (yes)
r is rolled, as in French	*Fräulein* (Miss)
w sounds like English *v*	*wo* (where)
z is like English *ts*	*Zeit* (time)

Do you speak English?	*Sprechen Sie Englisch?*
excuse me	*Verzeihung*
hello	*Guten Tag*
goodbye	*Auf Wiedersehen*
How much is…?	*Wieviel kostet…?*
I am American	*Ich bin Amerikaner (in)*
I'd like…	*Ich hätte gerne*
I don't understand	*Ich verstehe nicht*
non-smoking	*Nichtraucher*
open/closed	*offen/geschlossen*
please/thank you	*bitte/danke*
one-way ticket	*einfache Fahrkarte*
round trip ticket	*Rückfahrkarte*
where is…?	*wo ist…?*
yes/no	*ja/nein*
you're welcome	*bitte*

the hotel	***das Hotel***
breakfast	*Frühstück*
reservation	*Reservieren/ Reservierung*
key	*Schlüssel*
for one/two nights	*für eine Nacht/ zwei Nächte*
for one/two people	*für eine Person/ zwei Personen*
room	*Zimmer*
shower	*Dusche*

the restaurant	***das Restaurant***
beefsteak	*Steak*
bread	*Brot*
chicken	*Hähnchen*
the check	*Rechnung*
coffee	*Kaffee*
dish of the day	*Tagesgericht*
dessert	*Dessert*
entree	*Hauptgericht*
first courses	*Vorspeisen*
fish	*Fisch*
lamb	*Lamm*
pork	*Schweinefleisch*
seafood	*Meeresfrüchte*
wine	*Wein*

Greece – Essential Information

PRE-TRIP ESSENTIALS...

WHAT YOU NEED

ESSENTIAL FOR TRAVELERS

● Required   ● Recommended   ● Not required

Passport	●
Visa	●
Travel, medical insurance	●
Round-trip or onward airline ticket	●
Local currency	●
Traveler's checks	●
Credit cards	●
First-aid kit and medicines*	●
Inoculations	●

*see also HEALTH section

ESSENTIAL FOR DRIVERS*

Driver's license	●
International Driving Permit	●
Car insurance (for nonrental cars)	●
Car registration (for nonrental cars)	●

*see also DRIVING section

IMPORTANT ADDRESSES

Greek National Tourism Organization
Olympic Tower
645 Fifth Avenue
New York, NY 10022
☎ (212) 421-5777
Fax (212) 826-6940
www.gnto.gr

**Hellenic Tourism Organization
(Greek National Tourism Organization)**
Ødos Amerikis 2
10564 Athens, Greece
☎ 01 331 0565 or 01 327 1300
Fax 01 325 2895
www.gnto.gr

American Embassy
91 Vassilissis Sophias Avenue
10160 Athens, Greece
☎ 210 721 2951
Mon.–Fri. 8:30–5

COUNTRY ESSENTIALS...

CUSTOMS

→ **YES**
Duty-free limits on goods brought in from non-European Union countries:
200 cigarettes or 100 cigarillos or 50 cigars or 250 g. tobacco; 2 L. wine; 1 L. alcohol over 22% volume; 2 L. alcohol under 22% volume; 50 ml. perfume; 250 ml. toilet water; plus any other duty-free goods (including gifts) to the value of €150. There is no importation limit for tax-paid goods purchased within the European Union for personal use. Foreign currency over $200 (U.S.) or the equivalent must by law be declared at the customs entry point. Up to $1,000 in foreign currency may be exported by visitors.

⊖ **NO**
No unlicensed drugs, weapons, ammunition, obscene material, pets or other animals, counterfeit money or copied goods, meat or poultry.

For customs limits for returning U.S. citizens see page 16.

MONEY

The Greek currency is the euro (€), a currency shared by 11 other European Union countries. The euro is divided into 100 cents (¢). The denominations of euro bills are 5, 10, 20, 50, 100, 200 and 500. There are coins of 1, 2, 5, 10, 20 and 50¢ and €1 and €2.
Traveler's checks are widely accepted, and some gift stores accept dollars. Exchange dollars or traveler's checks *(taxithiotiki epitayi)* at a bank *(trapeza)* or an exchange office *(sarafiko)*. You can get cash at a bank with a credit card, but there is usually a charge.

Exchange rate at press time: $1 = €0.82

TIPS AND GRATUITIES

Tips *(poorbwáar)* are welcomed, but not expected or obligatory.

Restaurants (where service is not included)	10–15%
Cafés/bars	change
Taxis	change
Porters	€1.50
Chambermaids	€1 per day
Cloakroom attendants	change

ATHENS	NEW YORK	CHICAGO	DENVER	SAN FRANCISCO
12:00 noon	6 hours behind Greece	7 hours behind Greece	8 hours behind Greece	9 hours behind Greece

Greece – Essential Information

COMMUNICATIONS

POST OFFICES
Buy stamps (*ghramatósima*) at a post office (*takhithromio*), distinguished by a yellow "OTE" sign. City and town post offices often cash traveler's checks. Lines can be long at post office counters; if you simply need stamps, try a corner kiosk (*periptero*) selling postcards.

Hours for out-of-town post offices may vary.

TELEPHONES
Most public telephones take phone cards available from kiosks, local stores and OTE (Organismos Tilepikoinonion Ellados, pronounced O-tay) offices. If your calls are short and local, use a street kiosk (*periptero*) where you pay after the call. For an international call, you can also use a coin-operated telephone in a restaurant, bar or hotel lobby. You can be called back on these telephones, and they have instructions in English.

Phoning inside Greece
All Greek telephone numbers in this book include an area code: dial the number that is listed.

To call the operator dial 132 (or 131 in Athens).

Phoning Greece from abroad
The country code for Greece is 302. Note that Greek numbers in this book do not include the country code; you will need to prefix this number if you are phoning from another country. To call a Greek number from the United States or Canada, omit the first zero and add the prefix 011 302. (Note that Greek phone numbers vary in the number of digits.)
Example: 01 122 3344 becomes 011 302 1 122 3344.

Phoning from Greece
To phone the United States or Canada from Greece, prefix the area code and number with 00 1.
Example: (111) 222-3333 becomes 00 1 111 222-3333.
To call international information dial 161.

EMERGENCY TELEPHONE NUMBERS
Police (*astínomia*), general emergencies	100
Tourist police (Athens only)	171
Fire (*fotyá*)	199
Ambulance (*asthenoforo*)	166

Emergency calls are free from phone booths.

HOURS OF OPERATION

- Stores Mon.–Sat.
- Offices Mon.–Fri.
- Banks Mon.–Fri.
- Post offices Mon.–Sat.
- Museums/monuments
- Architectural sites
- Pharmacies Mon.–Fri.

| 7 | 8 | 9 | 10 | 11 | 12 | 1 | 2 | 3 | 4 | 5 | 6 | 7 |

In tourist areas stores open at 8 a.m. and close late; they have shorter hours off-season, and some close completely in winter.

Banks close at 1:30 Fridays. They may stay open longer hours at peak season in resort areas.

Post offices close at noon on Saturday.

Architectural sites usually close in the afternoon; some reopen in the evening in the summer, but all sites vary their hours depending on the time of year. It is best to check locally. Many architectural sites, museums and monuments close on Monday.

Restaurants open all day in resort areas but may close off-season.

NATIONAL HOLIDAYS

Banks, businesses and most stores and museums close on these days, but restaurants and some stores in tourist areas may stay open.

Jan. 1	New Year's Day
Jan. 6	Epiphany
Feb./Mar.	Shrove Monday
Mar. 25	Independence Day
*Apr./May	Good Friday
*Apr./May	Easter Monday
May 1	Labor Day
May/Jun.	Pentecost Monday
Aug. 15	Assumption of the Virgin
Oct. 28	Óchi Day
Dec. 25	Christmas Day
Dec. 26	St. Stephen's Day

* Greece observes the Orthodox calendar, and the date on which Easter falls may differ from that observed by Western nations.

PHOTOGRAPHY

The sun in Greece is strong, and slow film is ideal. Photograph the sights early in the morning, before the crowds mass and when the light is at its best. In rural areas deep blue seas and rustic villages make interesting subjects. **Never** take shots near military bases, and ask first in museums and churches. Brand names of film and camera batteries are widely available.

Greece – Essential Information

HEALTH

 MEDICAL INSURANCE
Private medical insurance is recommended. Visitors from non-E.U. countries can receive basic treatment at hospital emergency rooms. Admittance to a hospital *(nosokomío)* or consultation with a doctor *(iatrós)* will entail a fee. Ask your hotel, consulate or the tourist police for information on English-speaking doctors.

 DENTAL SERVICES
Dentists *(odhondoyatrós)* always charge for treatment, so check that your medical insurance covers it; keep all receipts for insurance purposes. Treatment is available from English-speaking dentists listed in the telephone directory, or ask at your hotel.

 SUN ADVICE
Summer, particularly July and August, can be oppressively hot and humid. Seek shelter inside a museum, or cover up, apply a sunscreen and drink plenty of fluids. Be especially careful on boats or near the water.

 DRUGS
A pharmacy *(farmakío)*, distinguished by a green cross, has staff qualified to offer medical advice and provide a wide range of prescription medicines. Information about the nearest all-night facility is usually posted at pharmacies. Note that codeine is banned and you can be fined for carrying it.

 SAFE WATER
Tap water is safe to drink but because of the high level of minerals it can cause upsets. Bottled water *(metaliko nero)* is available everywhere at a reasonable cost.

RESTROOMS

 Finding a clean restroom *(toualéta)* away from tourist areas can be difficult. It is advisable to use facilities in cafés and restaurants after buying a drink. Restrooms are free. The Greek sewage system does not take toilet tissue, even in café and restaurant facilities; use the wastebin provided.

ELECTRICITY

 Greece has a 220-volt power supply. Electrical sockets take plugs with two round pins; American appliances will need a plug adapter and will require a transformer if they do not have a dual-voltage facility.

NATIONAL TRANSPORTATION

 TRAIN *(tréno)*
Greek trains are run by Organismos Sidirodromon Ellados (OSE), a service predominantly for the mainland. The network is limited, and a reservation is essential on most express trains. For rail information in Athens: 145 (domestic services) or 147 (international services).

 BUS *(leoforío)*
Buses are popular and frequent; few villages or ferry ports are without a bus link. Buy city-to-city tickets from the bus station; in rural areas tickets *(isitirio)* are issued by a conductor on the bus. For bus information in Athens: 185.

 FERRY *(féribot)*
Ferries serve all of the Greek islands, and boat excursions run from May to October. You can take a boat from the port of Piréas to most islands, but check the length of the trip on the timetable – some ferries stop at every island. You can usually buy a ticket on the day of travel unless you are reserving a cabin or taking a car. You may need to reserve in advance in mid-August and over the Easter period; ask at a travel agency or tourist office.

DRIVING

 DRIVE ON THE RIGHT

SPEED LIMITS
Police can impose on-the-spot fines but they cannot collect them.

 Limited-access highways
120 k.p.h. (74 m.p.h.)
Divided highways
110 k.p.h. (68 m.p.h.)

 Main roads
90 k.p.h. (56 m.p.h.)

 Urban areas
50 k.p.h. (31 m.p.h.)

 SEAT BELTS
Must be worn in the front seat at all times and in the rear seat where fitted. Children under 12 are not allowed to travel in the front seat.

 BLOOD ALCOHOL
The legal blood alcohol limit is 0.05%. Random breath tests on drivers are carried out frequently, especially late at night, and the penalties for offenders are severe.

Greece – Essential Information

DRIVING continued

TOLLS
There are some highway tolls in Greece.

CAR RENTAL
The leading rental firms have offices at airports, train stations and principal ferry terminals. Hertz offers discounted rates for AAA members (see page 15). For reservations:

	UNITED STATES	GREECE
Alamo	(800) 462-5266	210 353 3323 (Inter-Rent/Europcar)
Avis	(800) 230-4898	210 322 4951
Budget	(800) 527-0700	(800) 472 3325
Hertz	(800) 654-3080	210 626 4444

FUEL
Gas *(venzini)* is sold in liters and usually comes in five grades: super *(sooper)*, regular *(apli)*, unleaded *(amolyvdhi)*, super unleaded *(sooper amolyvdhi)* and diesel *(petrelaio)*. There are few stations in remote areas; they are less likely to be open on weekends and may not take credit cards.

AAA AFFILIATED MOTORING CLUB
Automobile and Touring Club of Greece (ELPA)
395 Messogion Street, 153 43 Agia Paraskevi, Athens ☎ 01 606 8800, fax 01 606 8981
If you break down while driving, phone ☎ 104 (ELPA breakdown service).
Not all automobile clubs offer full services to AAA members.

BREAKDOWNS AND ACCIDENTS
There are emergency telephones at regular intervals on highways. If you are involved in an accident, phone ☎ 100 for police.
Most car rental firms provide their own free rescue service; if your car is rented, follow the instructions given in the documentation. Use of a car repair service other than those authorized by your rental company may violate your agreement.

OTHER INFORMATION
The minimum age for driving a car is 18 (may be higher for some car rental firms).

An International Driving Permit (IDP) is recommended; some rental firms require them, and they can speed up formalities if you are involved in an accident. A Green Card (international motor insurance certificate) is recommended if you are driving a private car; see page 15 for more information.

You can be fined for unnecessary use of the horn.

USEFUL WORDS AND PHRASES

The Greek language can be daunting to the visitor; it uses a different alphabet and is spoken with staccato rapidity. The way words and place names are converted into English varies considerably according to which transliteration system a translator happens to prefer.

With patience and a keen ear, you should be able to recognize what sounds these unfamiliar letters stand for. Learning the Greek alphabet may enable you to deduce the meaning of signs and notices. The easiest thing to do, however, is to learn a few basic courtesy phrases.

The Greeks realize how difficult their language appears to foreigners, and they appreciate visitors' attempts to speak it.

Do you speak English?	*milate angliká?*
excuse me	*signomi*
hello/goodbye	*yásou/chérete*
how much?	*póso?*
I'd like	*tha íthela*
I do not understand	*dhen katalavéno*
non-smoking	*khoros ya mi kapnízondes*
okay	*endáysi*
open/closed	*aniktos/klistos*
please/you're welcome	*parakaló*
thank you	*efharistó*
ticket	*isitíro*
one-way/round trip	*apló/isitiro met epistrofís*
where is…?	*poo íne?*
yes/no	*né/óhi*
the hotel	***xenodochio***
breakfast	*proino*
key	*klidhí*
for one/two nights	*ya mía/dhýo vradhiés*
for one/two people	*yiá éna/dhýo átoma*
room	*éna dhomátio*
shower	*doos*
the restaurant	***estiatorio***
food	*fagitó*
starter	*proto piato*
olives	*eliés*
stuffed vine leaves	*dolmadakia*
beans	*fasólia*
bread	*psomi*
water	*neró*
beer	*bira*
wine	*krasí*
coffee	*kafé*
meat balls	*kefthédes*
chicken	*kotópoulo*
lamb	*arnáki*
pork	*hirino*
cod's roe paté	*taramasalata*
lobster	*astakós*
red mullet	*barboúnia*
squid	*kalamarákia*
dessert	*glikisma*
the check	*logariasmós*

Hungary – Essential Information

PRE-TRIP ESSENTIALS...

WHAT YOU NEED

ESSENTIAL FOR TRAVELERS

● Required   ● Recommended   ● Not required

Passport	●
Visa	●
Travel, medical insurance	●
Round-trip or onward airline ticket	●
Local currency	●
Traveler's checks	●
Credit cards	●
First-aid kit and medicines	●
Inoculations	●

ESSENTIAL FOR DRIVERS*

Driver's license	●
International Driving Permit	●
Car insurance (for nonrental cars)	●
Car registration (for nonrental cars)	●

*see also DRIVING section

IMPORTANT ADDRESSES

Hungarian National Tourist Office
150 East 58th Street, 33rd Floor
New York, NY 10155-3398
☎ (212) 355-0240
Fax (212) 207-4103
www.gotohungary.com

Tourinform (Hungarian National Tourist Office)
v. Sütő utca 2
H3 Budapest
Hungary
☎ 1 438 8080 (24 hrs) or 06 80 66 00 44 (24 hrs, toll free) within Hungary, or (011 36 30) 30 30 600 (24 hrs) from United States
www.hungarytourism.hu

American Embassy
H-1054 Budapest
Szabadság tér 12
Hungary
☎ 1 475 4400 (8 a.m.–5 p.m.); 1 475 4703 or 1 475 4924 (5 p.m.–8 a.m.)
Fax 1 475 4764

COUNTRY ESSENTIALS...

CUSTOMS

YES
Duty-free limits on goods brought in from non-European Union countries:
200 cigarettes or 100 cigarillos or 50 cigars or 250 g. tobacco; 2 L. wine; 1 L. spirits or strong liqueurs over 22% volume or 2 L. fortified wine, sparkling wine or other liqueurs; 60 ml. perfume; 250 ml. toilet water; plus any other duty-free goods (including gifts) to the value of Ft 54,000. There is no limit on the importation of tax-paid goods purchased within the European Union, provided the goods are for your own personal use. If you are bringing in cash or traveler's checks to the value $10,000, customs must be notified and proof of ownership will be required.

NO
No unlicensed drugs, weapons, ammunition, obscene material, pets or other animals, counterfeit money and copied goods, meat or poultry. **For customs limits for returning U.S. citizens see page 16.**

MONEY

Hungary's currency is the forint (Ft or HUF), which is divided into 100 fillérs, although fillérs are no longer legal tender. The denominations of forint bills are 200, 500, 1,000, 2,000, 5,000, 10,000 and 20,000. There are coins of 1, 2, 5, 10, 20, 50 and 100 forints. You can exchange dollars or traveler's checks (utazasi csekket) at a bank (bank), exchange office (penzvalto), post office (posta) and some hotels. Credit card acceptance is limited; although they are increasingly common, they are not accepted everywhere. Exchange rate at press time: $1 = Ft206

TIPS AND GRATUITIES

Tips (borravaló) are welcomed, but not expected, where service is not included.

Restaurants	10–20%
Cafés/bars	10–20%
Taxis	10%
Porters	to reflect quality of service
Chambermaids	ro reflect quality of service
Hairdressers	10%
Gas station attendants	change
Cloakroom attendants	change

TIME ZONES

BUDAPEST	NEW YORK	CHICAGO	DENVER	SAN FRANCISCO
12:00 noon	6 hours behind Hungary	7 hours behind Hungary	8 hours behind Hungary	9 hours behind Hungary

499

COMMUNICATIONS

POST OFFICES

Buy stamps *(bélyeg)* at a post office *(posta)*, newsstand/tobacconist *(dohanyaruda)* or from a hotel.

Hours for out-of-town post offices may vary. Mail boxes are wall-mounted and red with a calling-horn emblem.

TELEPHONES

You can use cash and prepaid phone cards to make a call in Hungary. For direct dialing for national and international calls, use Ft20, Ft50 and Ft100 coins (minimum Ft20). International calls can be made from red phone booths. Phone cards of 50 and 100 units can be bought from newsstands/

tobacconists, gas stations, post offices and hotels.

Phoning inside Hungary
Hungarian telephone numbers include an area code of one or two digits (there is no initial zero). For long-distance calls within Hungary precede the number with 06.

Numbers in Budapest are seven digits, not including the area code; the area code is 1. To call the operator dial 191.

Phoning Hungary from abroad
The country code for Hungary is 36. Note that Hungarian numbers in this book do not include the Hungarian country code; you will need to prefix this number if you are phoning from another country. To phone Hungary from the United States or Canada, add the prefix 011 36 before the area code and number. Example: 1 122 3344 becomes 011 36 1 122 3344.

Phoning from Hungary
To phone the United States or Canada from Hungary, prefix the area code and number with 00 1. Example: (111) 222-3333 becomes 00 1 111 222-3333. To call the international operator dial 190; for international directory inquiries dial 199.

EMERGENCY TELEPHONE NUMBERS

Police *(rendörség)*	107
Fire *(tüzoltóság)*	105
Ambulance *(mentök)*	104

HOURS OF OPERATION

- ○ Stores Mon.–Fri.
- ● Offices Mon.–Fri.
- ● Banks Mon.–Fri.
- ● Post offices Mon.–Sat.
- ● Museums/monuments
- ● Pharmacies Mon.–Sat.

7 8 9 10 11 12 1 2 3 4 5 6 7

Department stores are open Mon.–Fri. 10–6, Sat. 9–1. Saturday afternoon is early closing, and few stores remain open after 1 or 2 p.m. Thursday is late-night shopping until 7 or 8 p.m. Grocery stores and other food stores have longer hours and also open on Sunday morning. In large cities, some stores stay open 24 hours. In smaller towns, stores close over lunchtime. Large shopping centers in cities are open Mon.–Sat. 10–9, Sun. 10–6.

The National Bank of Hungary is open Mon.–Fri. 10:30–2. Most other banks close at 1 p.m. on Friday.

Post offices close at 1 p.m. on Saturday.

Many museums close on Monday.

NATIONAL HOLIDAYS

Banks, businesses and most stores are closed on these days; if a public holiday falls on a Tuesday or a Thursday, the day between it and the weekend also becomes a holiday.

Jan. 1	**New Year's Day**
Mar. 15	**Day of the Nation (anniversary of 1848 revolution)**
Mar./Apr.	**Easter Monday**
May 1	**Labor Day**
May/Jun.	**Pentecost Monday**
Aug. 20	**Constitution Day**
Oct. 23	**Day of the Proclamation of the Republic**
Nov. 1	**All Saints' Day**
Dec. 25	**Christmas Day**
Dec. 26	**St. Stephen's Day**

PHOTOGRAPHY

Hungary has spectacular landscapes, including the Danube bend north of Budapest, one of the most beautiful stretches of this great river, and romantic Lake Balaton, framed by vineyards. Vendors near historic sights sell overpriced 35mm color film; it is widely available, so buy it elsewhere. Batteries and developing services are available in towns and cities.

Hungary – Essential Information

Hungary – Essential Information

HEALTH

MEDICAL INSURANCE
Private medical insurance is recommended. U.S. and Canadian visitors can receive free essential first-aid and emergency treatment. All further treatment and care has to be paid for. Fees for medical care are set by the individual hospital or practice. There is a 24-hour private medical care service with English-speaking doctors in Budapest: Falck SOS Hungary. It also has its own ambulance service ✉ Kapy utca 49B, Budapest II ☎ 1 200 0100.

DENTAL SERVICES
Dentists *(forgovos)* charge for treatment, but quality dental work is relatively inexpensive. Check that it is covered by your medical insurance. Dentists are listed in the yellow pages; ask for English-speaking dentists at your embassy or hotel, or at a tourist office. There is a 24-hour dental service in Budapest: SOS Dental Service ✉ Király utca 14, Budapest VI ☎ 1 267 9602.

SUN ADVICE
Hungary has up to 2,500 hours of sun annually, one of the highest levels in Europe. In summer, 9 or 10 hours a day can be expected, so protection is essential.

DRUGS
A pharmacy *(gyógyszetár* or *patica)* sells both prescription and nonprescription medicines (bring your own medication if you need a specific product). Most are cheaper than similar U.S. products. Information about the nearest 24-hour facility is posted at all pharmacies.

SAFE WATER
Although tap water is safe, you may find it causes mild upsets. Bottled mineral water *(ásvány víz)* and soda water *(szoda víz)* are widely available and advised.

RESTROOMS

Public restrooms *(mosdó)* are fairly easy to find, and are usually indicated by a symbol or marked WC, and designated by *férfi* for men and *nöi* for women. There may be a charge of between Ft50 and Ft200.

ELECTRICITY

Hungary has a 220/230-volt power supply. Electrical sockets take plugs with two round pins; American appliances will need a plug adapter and will require a transformer if they do not have a dual-voltage facility.

NATIONAL TRANSPORTATION

TRAIN *(vonat)*
The state railroad, Magyar Államvasutak (MÁV), serves most towns. Express trains link Budapest with provincial centers; when journeying cross-country it may be quicker to go via the capital. Fares are low, and MÁV offers many discounted fares and passes including rail cards for unlimited travel; ☎ 1 461 5400 (national); 1 461 5500 (international).

BUS *(busz)*
Long-distance buses are expensive, but sometimes quicker than trains. The main Budapest terminal is at Erzsébet tér. The main operator is state-owned Volánbusz, whose yellow buses serve even very small communities. Volánbusz is a member of Eurolines, who operate an international bus service; ☎ 1 219 8080 (for domestic and international services).

FERRY *(komp)*
Ferries run from spring to late autumn on Lake Balaton, the Danube between Budapest and Esztergom, and the Tisza river (serving Sárospatak, Tokaj, Szolnok, Csongrád and Szeged). Service information available from the Vigadó tér landing stage; ☎ 1 318 1223.

DRIVING

DRIVE ON THE RIGHT

SPEED LIMITS
On-the-spot fines of up to Ft10,000 can be imposed by the police. Receipts must be issued.

Limited-access highways *(autópályára)*
130 k.p.h. (80 m.p.h.)
Divided highways **110 k.p.h. (68 m.p.h.)**

Main roads
90 k.p.h. (55 m.p.h.)

Urban areas
50 k.p.h. (31 m.p.h.)
Some resorts and residential zones
30 k.p.h. (18 m.p.h.)

SEAT BELTS
Must be worn in front and rear seats at all times.

BLOOD ALCOHOL
The legal blood alcohol limit is zero. Random breath tests on drivers are carried out frequently, especially at night.

TOLLS
There are tolls on the M1, M3, M5 and M15 highways. Toll stickers (valid for 9 days, one month or a year), must be purchased for the M1, M3, M5 and M7 at toll booths or at fuel stations.

DRIVING continued

CAR RENTAL
The leading rental firms have offices at airports and railroad stations. Hertz offers discounted rates for AAA members (see page 15). For reservations:

	UNITED STATES	HUNGARY
Alamo	(800) 327-9633	1 4218 370 (Europcar)
Avis	(800) 331-2112	06 80 203 777
Budget	(800) 527-0700	1 214 0420
Hertz	(800) 654-3080	1 296 0999

FUEL
Fuel *(benzin)* is sold in liters: unleaded *(ólommentes benzine)* is graded 91, 95 and 98 octane. Diesel can be bought along major routes and in cities. Many gas stations *(benzinkút)* are self-service, although you may not be able to use a credit card in smaller stations. A map of rural gas stations is available from MAK (see below).

AAA AFFILIATED MOTORING CLUB
Magyar Autóklub (MAK)
H-1024 Budapest, Rómer Flóris u 4/1
☎ 1 345 1800, fax 1 345 1801
If you break down while driving, phone ☎ 188 or 1 345 1755 (MAK breakdown service). Not all automobile clubs offer full services to AAA members.

BREAKDOWNS AND ACCIDENTS
If you have an accident, phone ☎ 107 for police, and ask for an interpreter at the scene. You are legally required to report personal injury. Most car rental firms provide their own free rescue service;
if your car is rented, follow the instructions given in the documentation. Use of a car repair service other than those authorized by your rental company may violate your agreement.
Vehicles with damaged bodywork may only leave the country with an official certificate.

OTHER INFORMATION

The minimum age for driving a car is 18 (may be higher for some car rental firms).

An International Driving Permit (IDP) is recommended; some rental firms require them, and they can speed up formalities if you are involved in an accident. A Green Card (international motor insurance certificate) is needed if you are driving a private car; see page 15 for more information.

Dimmed headlights must be used by cars at all times outside built-up areas.

USEFUL WORDS AND PHRASES

Hungarian, called Magyar by its speakers, is a difficult language, related to Finnish and Estonian. German is traditionally the second language, but English is gradually replacing it, especially among the younger generation.

Apart from a few international words *(posta, telefon)*, Hungarian offers few clues as to its meaning. However, pronunciation is regular – letters consistently stand for the same sounds.

By learning basic words, street signs, notices and labels will begin to make sense.

Do you speak English?	*Beszél angolul?*
What is your name?	*Hogy hívnak?*
excuse me	*elnézést*
hello	*jó napot kivanok*
goodbye	*viszontlátásra*
yes/no	*igen/nem*
how much?	*mennyibe kerul?*
I am American	*Amerikai vagyok*
I don't understand	*nem értem*
non-smoking	*nem domanyzo*
open	*nyitva*
closed	*zárva*
please	*kérem*
thank you	*köszönöm*
ticket	*jegy*
(one-way/round trip)	*(egyiranyu/retur)*
where is...?	*hol van...?*

the hotel	***szálloda***
you're welcome	*szívesen*
Where is the restroom?	*Hol a mosdó?*
breakfast	*reggeli*
reservation	*foglalás*
key	*kulcs*
room	*szoba*
shower	*zuhany*

the restaurant	***étterem/vendeglo/***
	etkezde
beef	*marha*
beer	*sör*
bread	*kenyer*
the check	*szamla*
coffee/tea	*kávé/tea*
dessert	*édesség*
fish	*hal*
fruit	*gyümölcs*
ice cream	*fagylalt*
meat	*hús*
pork	*sertés*
potato	*burgonya*
poultry	*csirke*
starter	*elöételek*
vegetable	*zöldség*
wine	*bor*

PRE-TRIP ESSENTIALS...

WHAT YOU NEED

ESSENTIAL FOR TRAVELERS

● Required ● Recommended ● Not required

Passport	●
Visa	●
Travel, medical insurance	●
Round-trip or onward airline ticket	●
Local currency	●
Traveler's checks	●
Credit cards	●
First-aid kit and medicines	●
Inoculations	●

ESSENTIAL FOR DRIVERS*

Driver's license	●
International Driving Permit	●
Car insurance (for nonrental cars)	●
Car registration (for nonrental cars)	●

*see also DRIVING section

IMPORTANT ADDRESSES

Tourism Ireland (Republic of Ireland and Northern Ireland)
345 Park Avenue, New York, NY 10154
☎ (800) 223-6470, fax (212) 371-9052
www.tourismireland.com

Bord Fáilte – Irish Tourist Board
Baggot Street Bridge, Dublin 2, Republic of Ireland
☎ 01 602 4000, fax 01 855 6821
www.ireland.travel.ie

American Embassy (Republic of Ireland)
42 Elgin Road, Ballsbridge
Dublin 4, Republic of Ireland
☎ 01 668 8777, fax 01 668 9946,
www.dublinusembassy.gov
American Citizens Services: Mon.–Tue. and
Thu.–Fri. 8:30–noon and 1–4

Belfast Welcome Centre
47 Donegall Place, Belfast BT1 5AD,
Northern Ireland
☎ 028 9024 6609, fax 028 9031 2424
www.gotobelfast.com

American Consulate (Northern Ireland)
Danesfort House, 223 Stranmillis Road
Belfast BT9 5GR
☎ 028 9038 6100; fax 028 9068 1301
Open Mon.–Fri. 8:30–5

COUNTRY ESSENTIALS...

CUSTOMS

YES
Duty-free limits on goods brought in from non-European Union countries:
200 cigarettes or 100 cigarillos or 50 cigars or 250 g. tobacco; 2 L. wine; 1 L. spirits or strong liqueurs over 22% volume or 2 L. fortified wine, sparkling wine or other liqueur; 60 ml. perfume; 250 ml. toilet water; plus any other duty-free goods (including gifts) to the value of €175. There is no limit on the importation of tax-paid goods bought within the EU, if they are for your own personal use. There are no currency regulations.

NO
No unlicensed drugs, weapons, ammunition, obscene material, pets or other animals, counterfeit money or copied goods, meat or poultry.

For customs limits for returning U.S. citizens see page 16.

MONEY

The Republic of Ireland's currency is the euro (€), a currency shared by 11 other European Union countries. The euro is divided into 100 cents (¢). The denominations of euro bills are 5, 10, 20, 50, 100, 200 and 500. There are coins of 1, 2, 5, 10, 20 and 50c and €1 and €2. Credit cards are accepted in hotels, large stores and upscale restaurants; check first in small or rural establishments. Exchange dollars or traveler's checks at a bank, exchange office, post office or a large hotel. Exchange rate at press time: $1 = €0.82
For information about currency in Northern Ireland, see page 470.

TIPS AND GRATUITIES

Restaurants (if service is not included)	10–15%
Cafés/bars (if service is not included)	10%
Taxis	10%
Porters	75¢ (IR) or 50p (NI) per bag
Hairdressers	75¢–€1.50 (IR) or 50p–£1 (NI)
Tour guides	€1.50 (IR) or £1 (NI)
Cloakroom attendants	75¢ (IR) or 50p (NI)

TIME ZONES

| DUBLIN | NEW YORK | CHICAGO | DENVER | SAN FRANCISCO | 503 |
| 12:00 noon | 5 hours behind Ireland | 6 hours behind Ireland | 7 hours behind Ireland | 8 hours behind Ireland | |

Ireland – Essential Information

OMMUNICATIONS

POST OFFICES

Buy stamps at post offices, newsstands/tobacconists, large grocery stores and hotels.

Hours for out-of-town post offices may vary. Mailboxes are green in the Republic of Ireland and red in Northern Ireland (as in Britain).

TELEPHONES

Public phone booths are blue and cream, although many are now glass and metal. Take cash or prepaid phone cards bought from newsstands, post offices and local stores. Some city phones take credit cards.

For calls made to or from Northern Ireland, except calling Northern Ireland from the Republic (see below), follow the instructions for Britain on page 471.

Phoning inside Ireland
All Irish phone numbers in this book include the area code; dial the number listed.

To call the operator dial 10.

Phoning the Republic of Ireland from abroad
The country code for the Republic of Ireland is 353. To phone the Republic from another country, prefix 353 to the number given. To phone the Republic from the United States or Canada, omit the first zero from the Irish number, and add the prefix 011 353. (The number of digits in Irish area codes varies.) Example: 01 122 3344 becomes 011 353 1 122 3344.

Phoning from Ireland
To phone the United States or Canada from Ireland, prefix the area code and number with 00 1. Example: (111) 222-3333 becomes 00 1 111 222-3333. To phone Northern Ireland from the Republic of Ireland, replace the code 028 with 048. Example: 028 1122 3344 becomes 048 1122 3344. To call international information dial 11818.

EMERGENCY TELEPHONE NUMBERS

Police *(gardaí)*	999
Fire	999
Ambulance	999

Emergency calls are free from phone booths.

HOURS OF OPERATION

- ● Stores Mon.–Sat.
- ● Museums/monuments
- ● Offices Mon.–Fri.
- ● Pharmacies Mon.–Sat.
- ● Banks Mon.–Fri.
- ● Post offices Mon.–Sat.

7 8 9 10 11 12 1 2 3 4 5 6 7

Hours in chart refer to the Republic of Ireland; hours for Northern Ireland may differ slightly.

Some stores stay open until 8 or 9 on Thursday or Friday. On Sunday some bigger stores and many supermarkets open from noon until 5 or 6. In smaller towns and rural areas stores close in the afternoon on one day of the week. Pharmacies may close earlier on Saturday.

Some banks in small towns close 12:30–1:30. Banks open until 5 p.m. one day a week (Thursdays in Dublin). Nearly all banks are closed on Saturday.

Post offices close for lunch (1–2:15) and open until 5 p.m. on Saturdays.

Hours for museums and tourist sights vary; always check with the local tourist office. Some places close from October to March, although most major sights are open all year.

NATIONAL HOLIDAYS

Banks, businesses and most stores close on these days. Museums also may have restricted hours.

Jan. 1	New Year's Day
Mar. 17	St. Patrick's Day
Mar./Apr.	Good Friday
Mar./Apr.	Easter Monday (also day after in NI)
1st Mon. in May	May Bank Holiday
Last Mon. in May	Spring Bank Holiday (NI)
1st Mon. in Jun.	June Bank Holiday (Republic)
Jul. 14	Orangeman's Day (NI)
1st Mon. in Aug.	August Bank Holiday (Republic)
Last Mon. in Aug.	Summer Bank Holiday (NI)
Last Mon. in Oct.	October Bank Holiday (Republic)
Dec. 25	Christmas Day
Dec. 26	St. Stephen's Day

PHOTOGRAPHY

Irish skies are unpredictable and the light frequently poor, so you may need fast film. Bring a tripod for landscape work, and possibly black-and-white film. Film and camera batteries are widely available in many stores and drugstores.

Ireland – Essential Information

HEALTH

 MEDICAL INSURANCE
Private medical insurance is recommended. U.S. and Canadian visitors can receive treatment in emergency rooms, but are charged if admitted to a hospital bed. A general practitioner also will charge for services.

 DENTAL SERVICES
Dental work is expensive, so check to see if it is covered by your medical insurance. Dentists are listed in the yellow pages, or ask at your hotel or embassy. For the Irish Dental Association call ☎ 01 283 0499.

 SUN ADVICE
The sunniest months are May and June, with 5–6½ hours of sun a day (the extreme southwest is the sunniest). July and August are the warmest. During these months you should take sensible precautions against the sun.

 DRUGS
Pharmacies (also called chemists) sell a range of prescription and non-prescription medicines. If you need medicine outside regular hours, information about the nearest 24-hour facility should be posted on the door of all pharmacies.

 SAFE WATER
Tap water is safe to drink throughout Ireland. If, however, you prefer mineral water you will find it widely available.

RESTROOMS

 Identify restrooms by *Fir* (men) and *Mná* (women). A small charge is levied in restrooms at some railroad stations, but most other facilities are free. The standards of hygiene are moderate. You will be welcomed into any local pub if you need to use their facilities, but stop for a drink and a talk while you are there.

ELECTRICITY

The Republic of Ireland has a 230-volt and Northern Ireland a 240-volt power supply. Electrical sockets either take plugs with two round pins or three square pins; American appliances will need a plug adapter and will require a transformer if they do not have a dual-voltage facility.

NATIONAL TRANSPORTATION

 TRAIN
The Republic of Ireland's rail company is Iarnród Éireann (IÉ or Irish Rail). Trains are the fastest way of covering long distances and are generally reliable and comfortable, but the network is limited and one-way tickets cost almost as much as round-trip tickets. Midweek is less expensive than weekends, and there are many special offers on fares. For information: ☎ 01 850 366 222; www.irishrail.ie. For Northern Ireland call Translink ☎ 028 9066 6630 for rail schedules and fares; www.translink.co.uk

 BUS
Bus Éireann (Irish Bus) operates a network of express bus routes serving most of the country (some run summer only). For information: ☎ 01 836 6111; www.buseireann.ie. For Northern Ireland call Translink ☎ 028 9066 6630 for schedules and fares.

 FERRY
A car ferry runs between Ballyhack (County Wexford) and Passage East (County Waterford); ☎ 051 382 480, saving 60 miles on the road trip. Another serves Killimer (County Clare) and Tarbert (County Kerry); ☎ 065 905 3124. There also are ferries to several islands; ask for details at a local tourist office. There are regular ferries from Belfast, Larne, Dublin, Dun Laoghaire, Cork and Rosslare to ports on the mainland of Britain, and from Cork and Rosslare to France.

DRIVING

 DRIVE ON THE LEFT

SPEED LIMITS
Traffic police can impose on-the-spot fines.

 Limited-access highways (motorways)
110 k.p.h. (68 m.p.h.)

 Main roads
100 k.p.h. (62 m.p.h.)

 Urban areas
50 k.p.h. (31 m.p.h.)
In Northern Ireland:
50–60 k.p.h (30–40 m.p.h.)

 SEAT BELTS
Must be worn in front and back seats at all times.

 BLOOD ALCOHOL
The legal blood alcohol limit is 0.08%. Random breath tests on drivers are carried out frequently, especially late at night, and the penalties for offenders are severe.

DRIVING continued

 TOLLS
Tolls are charged at three locations in the Dublin area: the M50 between the N4 and N3 interchanges, the M1 near Drogheda and on the R131 East Link Bridge. There are no tolls on other highway or national routes.

 CAR RENTAL
The leading rental firms have offices at airports, railroad stations and large ferry terminals. Hertz offers discounted rates for AAA members (see page 15). Advise the car rental company if you plan on traveling between the Republic and Northern Ireland
For reservations:

	UNITED STATES	REPUBLIC OF IRELAND
Alamo	(800) 462-5266	021 432 0755
Avis	(800) 230 4898	021 428 111
Budget	(800) 527-0700	0906 627 711
Hertz	(800) 654-3080	01 676 7476

 FUEL
Gas is unleaded and sold in liters; diesel also is easily purchased. Gas stations in villages stay open until 8 or 9 p.m. and usually open after Mass on Sunday.

 AAA AFFILIATED MOTORING CLUB
AA Ireland
23 Suffolk Street, Dublin 2
☎ 01 617 9999, fax 01 617 9900
If you break down while driving, phone ☎ 1800 66 77 88 (AAI breakdown service). Not all automobile clubs offer full services to AAA members. Northern Ireland: see BRITAIN section (page 473).

 BREAKDOWNS AND ACCIDENTS
There are 24-hour emergency phones at regular intervals on highways:
☎ 999 if involved in an accident.
Most car rental firms provide their own free rescue service; if your car is rented, follow the instructions given in the documentation. Use of a car repair service other than those authorized by your rental company may violate your agreement.

OTHER INFORMATION
The minimum age for driving a car is 17 (may be higher for some car rental firms).

An International Driving Permit is recommended; some rental firms require it, and it can speed up formalities if you are involved in an accident.

A Green Card (international motor insurance certificate) is recommended if you are driving a private car; see page 15 for more information.

In the Republic of Ireland road signs are marked in kilometers, but you may find old signs in miles. In Northern Ireland all road signs are in miles.

In some urban areas, parking is limited to certain times and periods. Where this is signed, buy a disk from a newsstand and display it on the dashboard of your car.

USEFUL WORDS AND PHRASES

Although the Republic of Ireland is officially bilingual, and the Irish language (Gaelic or *Gaeilge*) is learned by all schoolchildren, English is more commonly spoken. There are around 80,000 native speakers of Irish, making it Europe's least widespread official language.

Because it often reflects expressions in Gaelic, Irish English is famed for its picturesque turns of phrase, much more poetic than American or British English.

The Gaelic language is enjoying a revival: radio, television and the Internet all stir up interest in the old language. There are Gaelic-speaking clubs as far away as the U.S. West Coast.

You are not likely to pick up very much Irish on a brief trip to Ireland; it is not related to English, and to an English speaker the spelling does not appear to reflect the pronunciation.

Following are pronunciations of words you may come across:

Bord Fáilte (Irish Tourist Board)	bord fawlty
Ceilidh (traditional dance night)	kaylee
Gaeilge (the Irish language)	gale-geh
Gaeltacht (Irish-speaking country)	gale-tackt
Garda (policeman)	gawrdah
Fleadh (traditional music evening)	flah
Taoiseach (prime minister)	teeschock

Numbers:

1	*a haon*	a hay-on
2	*a dó*	a doe
3	*a trí*	a tree
4	*a ceathair*	a ca-hir
5	*a cuíg*	a koo-ig
6	*a sé*	a shay
7	*a seacht*	a shocked
8	*a hocht*	a huct
9	*a naoi*	a neigh
10	*a deich*	a de

Other words:

good day	*lá maith*	law mah
goodbye	*slán*	slawn
goodnight	*oíche mhaith*	ee-ha vah
How are you?	*Conas taio?*	co-nus tee?
please	*más é do thoil é*	maws eh duh hull eh
thanks	*gura maith agat*	gurrah mah a-gut
pub	*tábhairne*	taw-er nay
water	*uisce*	ishkek
whiskey	*fuisci*	fwishgee
yes	*sea*	shah

PRE-TRIP ESSENTIALS...

WHAT YOU NEED

ESSENTIAL FOR TRAVELERS

● Required ● Recommended ● Not required

Passport	●
Visa (check regulations before you travel)	●
Travel, medical insurance	●
Round-trip or onward airline ticket	●
Local currency	●
Traveler's checks	●
Credit cards	●
First-aid kit and medicines	●
Health innoculations	●

ESSENTIAL FOR DRIVERS*

Driver's license	●
International Driving Permit	●
Car insurance (for private cars)	●
Car registration (for private cars)	●

*see also DRIVING section

IMPORTANT ADDRESSES

Italian Government Tourist Board
630 Fifth Avenue
Suite 1565, Rockefeller Center
New York, NY 10111
☎ (212) 245-5618 or (212) 245-4822
Fax (212) 586-9249
www.italiantourism.com

**Ente Nazionale Italiano per il Turismo
(Italian State Tourist Board)**
Via Marghera 2
00185 Rome, Italy
☎ 06 49711
Fax 06 446 3379
www.enit.it

American Embassy
Via Vittorio Veneto 119a
00187 Rome, Italy
☎ 06 46741 or 06 4674 2214
Fax 06 488 2672
Open Mon.– Fri. 8:30–1 and 2–5:30
www.usembassy.it

COUNTRY ESSENTIALS...

CUSTOMS

YES

Goods brought into Italy from non-European Union countries limited to:
200 cigarettes or 100 cigarillos or 50 cigars or 250 g. tobacco; 2 L. wine; 1 L. alcohol over 22% volume or 2 L. alcohol under 22% volume; 50 ml. perfume; 250 ml. toilet water; plus any other duty-free goods (including gifts) to the value of €15. There is no limit on the importation of tax-paid goods purchased within the European Union, provided they are for your own personal use. Foreign or local currency in excess of €10,300 must be declared on arrival.

NO

No unlicensed drugs, weapons, ammunition, obscene material, pets or other animals, counterfeit money or copied goods, meat or poultry.

For customs limits for returning U.S. citizens see page 16.

MONEY

Italy's currency is the euro (€), a currency shared by 11 other European Union countries. The euro is divided into 100 cents (¢). The denominations of euro bills are 5, 10, 20, 50, 100, 200 and 500. There are coins of 1, 2, 5, 10, 20 and 50¢ and €1 and €2. Exchange dollars or traveler's checks *(assegni touristici)* at a bank *(banca)* or exchange office *(ufficio di cambio)*. Hotels may exchange traveler's checks, but stores do not. ATMs *(sportello automatico)* are fairly common and accept major credit cards.

Exchange rate at press time: $1 = €0.82

TIPS AND GRATUITIES

Restaurants (service usually included but add 50¢ per person)	
Cafés/bars	20¢
Taxis	15%
Porters	€1
Chambermaids	€2 weekly
Restrooms	minimum
Cloakroom attendants	50¢

TIME ZONES

ROME	NEW YORK	CHICAGO	DENVER	SAN FRANCISCO	507
12:00 noon	6 hours behind Italy	7 hours behind Italy	8 hours behind Italy	9 hours behind Italy	

COMMUNICATIONS

POST OFFICES

Buy stamps *(francobolli)* at a post office *(ufficio postale)* or at a tobacconist *(tabaccaio)*. Mailboxes

(red or blue) often have two slots, one for local mail *(per la città)*, the other for out-of-town mail *(tutte le altre destinazioni)*. Mail can take up to three weeks; to speed delivery send it priority post *(posta priorità)* or recorded *(raccomandata)*.

TELEPHONES

Pay phones are usually found in bars and other public places. Prepaid cards *(carta telefonica)* for card-operated phones are available from tobacconists, bars, post offices, newsstands, railroad stations and dispensers showing a Telecom Italia (TI) logo. When making international calls use a prepaid

card; tear the corner off before using it. Calls from hotel rooms always incur a surcharge.

Phoning inside Italy
All telephone numbers in Italy include an area code that must always be dialed.

To call the operator dial 10.

Phoning Italy from abroad
The country code for Italy is 39. Note that Italian numbers in this book do not include the country code; you will need to prefix this number if you are phoning from another country. To call Italy from the United States or Canada dial the prefix 011 39. Include the first zero of the regional code. There is no standard number of digits in Italian numbers. Example: 01 122 3344 becomes 011 39 01 122 3344.

Phoning from Italy
To phone the United States or Canada from Italy, prefix the area code and number with 00 1. Example: (111) 222-3333 becomes 00 1 111 222-3333.

To call international information dial 4176.

EMERGENCY TELEPHONE NUMBERS
Police *(policia)* 113 (local), 112 (national)
Fire service *(pompieri)* 115
Ambulance *(ambulanza)* 118
Emergency calls are free from phone booths.

HOURS OF OPERATION

● Stores Mon.–Sat.	● Museums/monuments
● Offices Mon.–Fri.	● Architectural sites
● Banks Mon.–Fri.	● Churches/pharmacies
● Post offices Mon.–Fri.	

Time scale: 7 8 9 10 11 12 1 2 3 4 5 6 7

Department stores, some grocery stores and stores in tourist areas may not close at lunchtime, and sometimes stay open until later in the evening. Some stores close on Monday morning and may close on Saturday afternoon in summer; most stores close on Sunday.

Some banks close at 2 and do not reopen later in the afternoon.

Post office times may vary slightly; some may close at 2 p.m. and not reopen later in the afternoon, and they may be open Saturday 8:30–noon.

Many museums are open in the late afternoon (usually 5–7), others are open all day, and a few stay open late into the evening. Many museums close early on Sunday (around 1), and most are closed Monday.

NATIONAL HOLIDAYS

Banks, businesses and most stores and museums close on these days. Most cities, towns and villages celebrate their patron saint's day, but generally most establishments remain open.

Jan. 1	New Year's Day
Jan. 6	Epiphany
Mar./Apr.	Easter Monday
Apr. 25	Liberation Day 1945
May 1	Labor Day
Jun. 2	Anniversary of the Republic
Aug. 15	Assumption of the Virgin
Nov. 1	All Saints' Day
Dec. 8	Immaculate Conception
Dec. 25	Christmas Day
Dec. 26	St. Stephen's Day

PHOTOGRAPHY

The light in Italy is usually very good, so you will probably be using film with a low ASA rating. Avoid taking shots around noon, when the shadows are harsh. Photography is banned in most museums and churches, but you may be allowed to shoot without a flash. Film *(pellicola)* and developing *(sviluppo)* are expensive, especially near popular tourist sights.

Italy – Essential Information

Italy – Essential Information

HEALTH

 MEDICAL INSURANCE
Private medical insurance is strongly recommended. Visitors from non-European Union countries can receive treatment in a hospital accident and emergency room, but you will be charged if you are admitted to a bed. A general practitioner *(medico)* can deal with less urgent cases, but also will charge.

 DENTAL SERVICES
Emergency dental treatment is available from English-speaking dentists listed in the yellow pages *(pagine gialle)*. A fee will be charged, so check that you are covered for treatment on your private medical insurance.

 SUN ADVICE
In summer, particularly in July and August, it can be oppressively hot and humid in cities. On sunny days cover head and shoulders and use a sunscreen. Cathedrals and other stone buildings can be refreshingly cool. Take frequent breaks in the shade and drink plenty of fluids.

 DRUGS
A pharmacy *(farmacia)* displays a green cross symbol and has staff who can provide prescription medicines and offer advice on minor ailments. Information about the address of the nearest 24-hour facility is normally posted at every pharmacy.

 SAFE WATER
In isolated rural areas it is not advisable to drink tap water. However, across most of the country tap water is perfectly safe, although most Italians prefer to drink bottled mineral water *(acqua minerale)*, which is inexpensive and widely available.

RESTROOMS

 Finding a restroom *(gabinetto/bagno)* can be difficult away from airports, rail and bus stations, highway service areas and museums. Leave a small tip (about 50¢) for the attendant. If using the facilities in a bar you will be expected to buy a drink. Some bars have separate restrooms for men *(signori)* and women *(signore)*.

ELECTRICITY

 Italy has a 220-volt power supply (in some areas, 125 volts). Electrical sockets take plugs with two round pins or sometimes three pins in a vertical row. American appliances will need a plug adapter and will require a transformer if they do not have a dual-voltage facility.

NATIONAL TRANSPORTATION

 TRAIN *(treno)*
Italian State Railways (*Trenitalia* ☎ 89 2021) provide an efficient range of services. Regionale, Diretto and Espresso trains are slow for long journeys; InterCity trains, which do not make stops at each station *(stazione)*, cost more but are faster; the Pendolino is the fastest and most expensive.

 BUS *(autobus)*
There is no national bus company, but each major city has its own company for short-, medium- and some long-distance bus travel. International Eurolines buses run from the main Italian cities: ☎ 055 357 110.

 FERRY *(traghetto)*
Genoa and Naples are the main Mediterranean ports, with regular services to Sicily and Sardinia. Naples also has services to Capri and other islands. Many services are reduced off-season, and some are cut altogether. Reserve well in advance for car ferries.

DRIVING

 DRIVE ON THE RIGHT

SPEED LIMITS
Police can demand up to a quarter of an imposed fine to be paid on the spot.

 Limited-access highways *(autostrada)* **130 k.p.h. (80 m.p.h.)** Some designated stretches of autostrada have a 150 k.p.h. (93 m.p.h.) limit.

 Main roads **90–110 k.p.h. (55–68 m.p.h.)**

 Urban areas **50 k.p.h. (31 m.p.h.)**

 SEAT BELTS
Must be worn in front and back seats at all times.

BLOOD ALCOHOL
The legal blood alcohol limit is 0.08%. Random breath tests are carried out frequently, especially late at night.

Italy – Essential Information

DRIVING continued

TOLLS
You will be issued a ticket on entering nearly every limited-access highway *(autostrada)*: pay on leaving. You can buy a prepaid card *(viacard)* at tollbooths, service areas, tourist offices and tobacconists.

CAR RENTAL
The leading rental firms have offices at airports, railroad stations and ferry terminals. Hertz offers discounted rates for AAA members. Also see page 15 for general information about renting a car in Europe. For reservations:

	UNITED STATES	ITALY
Avis	(800) 230-4898	199 100 133
Budget	(800) 467-9337	06 659 65203
Europcar	(800) 252-897	06 6501 0879
Hertz	(800) 654-3080	199 117 711

FUEL
Gas *(benzina)* is unleaded *(senza piombo)* and sold in liters. Outside urban areas, stations are open daily 7–12:30 and 3–7:30. Highway services are open 24 hours. Credit cards are not widely accepted away from highways.

AAA AFFILIATED MOTORING CLUB
Automobile Club D'Italia (ACI)
Via Marsala 8, 00185 Rome
☎ 06 49 981 or 06 491 716, fax 06 445 2702. If you break down while driving, phone ☎ 803116, or 800 116 800 from a mobile phone. Not all automobile clubs offer full services to AAA members.

BREAKDOWNS AND ACCIDENTS
There are emergency phones at regular intervals on all highways. If you are involved in an accident, phone ☎ 113 for emergency medical help and police.
Most car rental firms provide their own free rescue service; if your car is rented, follow the instructions given in the documentation. Use of a car repair service other than those authorized by your rental company may violate your agreement. In the event of a breakdown, you must put on a fluorescent vest when you are outside your vehicle.

OTHER INFORMATION
The minimum age for driving a car is 18 (may be higher for some car rental firms).
An International Driving Permit (IDP) is recommended; some rental firms require it, and it can speed up formalities if you are involved in an accident. A Green Card (international motor insurance certificate) is recommended if you are driving a private car; see page 15 for more information.
Dimmed headlights are required by law at all times outside built-up areas. They must be used inside built-up areas once street lights are lit.

USEFUL WORDS AND PHRASES

Italian pronunciation is consistent with spelling, and vowels are always pronounced. The letter *h* is always silent, but can modify the sound of letters *c* and *g*. As a general rule, accentuate the next-to-last syllable.

c is hard before a, o, u, h	*medico; Chianti*
c is soft before i or e	*ciao* [chow]
g is hard before a, o, u, h	*Gucci, Lamborghini*
g is soft before i or e	*gelati* [jel-ah-tee]
gl as in Amelia	*figlia* [fee-lyah]
gn as in union	*gnocchi* [nyee-ok-kee]
sc before i or e is soft	*prosciutto* [pro-shoot-toh]

Where two consonants appear together, each belongs to a different syllable.

Do you speak English?	*Parla inglese?*
excuse me	*mi scusi*
goodbye	*arrivederci*
hello	*buongiorno*
How much is…?	*Quanto costa…?*
I am American	*sono Americano/-a*
I'd like…	*vorrei…*
I don't understand	*non capisco*
non-smoking	*per non fumatori*
okay	*va bene*
open/closed	*aperto/chiuso*
please/thank you	*per favore/grazie*
ticket (one-way/round trip)	*biglietto (andata sola/andata ritorno)*
where is…?	*dov'è…?*
yes/no	*si/no*
you're welcome	*prego*

the hotel	***l'albergo***
breakfast	*prima colazione*
I have a reservation	*ho prenotato*
key	*una chiave*
for one/two nights	*per una/due notte/-i*
one/two people	*una/due persona/-e*
room	*una camera*
shower	*una doccia*
with en-suite bathroom	*con bagno privato*

the restaurant	***il ristorante***
starter	*l'antipasto*
entrée	*il secondo*
beef	*il manzo*
bread	*il pane*
chicken	*il pollo*
coffee	*il caffè*
dish of the day	*il piatto del giorno*
seafood	*i frutti di mare*
fish	*il pesce*
lamb	*l'agnello*
pork	*il maiale*
wine	*il vino*
dessert	*il dolce*
the check	*il conto*

Luxembourg – Essential Information

PRE-TRIP ESSENTIALS...

WHAT YOU NEED

ESSENTIAL FOR TRAVELERS

● Required   ● Recommended   ● Not required

Passport	●
Visa	●
Travel, medical insurance	●
Round-trip or onward airline ticket	●
Local currency	●
Traveler's checks	●
Credit cards	●
First-aid kit and medicines	●
Inoculations	●

ESSENTIAL FOR DRIVERS*

Driver's license	●
International Driving Permit	●
Car insurance (for nonrental cars)	●
Car registration (for nonrental cars)	●

*see also DRIVING section

IMPORTANT ADDRESSES

Luxembourg National Tourist Office
17 Beekman Place
New York, NY 10022
☎ (212) 935-8888
Fax (212) 935-5896
www.visitluxembourg.com

**Office National du Tourisme
(Luxembourg National Tourist Office)**
Gare Centrale
Boîte Postale 1001
L-1010 Luxembourg
☎ 42 82 82-20
Fax 42 82 82-30
www.ont.lu

American Embassy
22 boulevard Emmanuel Servais
L-2535 Luxembourg
☎ 46 01 23
Fax 46 14 01

COUNTRY ESSENTIALS...

CUSTOMS

YES
Duty-free limits on goods brought in from non-European Union countries:
200 cigarettes or 100 cigarillos or 50 cigars or 250 g. tobacco; 2 L wine; 1 L alcohol over 22% volume or 2 L alcohol under 22% volume; 50 ml. perfume; 250 ml. toilet water; plus any other duty-free goods (including gifts) to the value of €175 (€90 for children under 15). There is no limit on the importation of tax-paid goods purchased within the European Union, provided they are for your own personal use. There are no restrictions on the import or export of cash or traveler's checks in euros or foreign currency.

NO
No unlicensed drugs, weapons, ammunition, obscene material, pets or other animals, counterfeit money or copied goods, meat or poultry.

For customs limits for returning U.S. citizens see page 16.

MONEY

Luxembourg's currency is the euro (€), a currency shared by 11 other European Union countries. The euro is divided into 100 cents (¢). The denominations of euro bills are 5, 10, 20, 50, 100, 200 and 500. There are coins of 1, 2, 5, 10, 20 and 50¢ and €1 and €2.

Exchange dollars and traveler's checks *(cheques de voyage)* at a bank *(banque)* or an exchange office *(bureau de change)*.

Exchange rate at press time: $1 = €0.82

TIPS AND GRATUITIES

Restaurants, cafés and bars (service usually included) round up to nearest €1 or €2	
Taxis	15%
Porters, chambermaids	€1–€2
Hairdressers	€2
Restroom attendants	20¢
Cloakroom attendants	50¢ per coat

TIME ZONES

LUXEMBOURG	NEW YORK	CHICAGO	DENVER	SAN FRANCISCO
12:00 noon	6 hours behind Luxembourg	7 hours behind Luxembourg	8 hours behind Luxembourg	9 hours behind Luxembourg

511

COMMUNICATIONS

POST OFFICES

Buy stamps *(timbres-poste)* at a post office *(poste)*, newsstand/tobacconist *(tabac-journaux)*, or at a bookstore.

Mailboxes are yellow, and are attached to walls and post offices. Luxembourg City's main post office is ✉ 25 rue Aldringen ☎ 4765-1 🕐 Mon.–Fri. 7–7, Sat.7– 5. Another is opposite the railroad station 🕐 Mon.–Fri. 6 a.m.–7 p.m., Sat. 6–noon. Hours for out-of-town post offices may vary.

TELEPHONES

Finding a public telephone *(cabine téléphonique)* is easy. Phone booths usually have pictorial instructions, with French and German text. You can use most denominations of coins, or buy a prepaid phone card *(télécarte)* from a post office or railroad station. International phone booths display a

yellow sign showing a telephone dial with a receiver in the center.

Phoning inside Luxembourg
There are no area codes in Luxembourg; dial the number that is listed.

To call the operator dial 017.
To call the international operator dial 0010.

Phoning Luxembourg from abroad
The country code for Luxembourg is 352. Note that Luxembourg numbers in this book do not include the country code; you will need to prefix this number if you are phoning from another country. To phone Luxembourg from the United States or Canada, add the prefix 011 352.
Example: 11 22 33 becomes 011 352 11 22 33.

Phoning from Luxembourg
To phone the United States or Canada from Luxembourg, prefix the area code and number with 00 1.
Example: (111) 222-3333 becomes 00 1 111 222-3333.

EMERGENCY TELEPHONE NUMBERS
Police *(police)*	112 or 113
Fire *(pompiers)*	112
Ambulance *(ambulance)*	112

Emergency calls are free from phone booths.

HOURS OF OPERATION

- ⬤ Stores Mon.–Sat.
- ⬤ Pharmacies Mon.–Sat.
- ⬤ Offices Mon.–Fri.
- ⬤ Museums/monuments
- ⬤ Banks Mon.–Fri.
- ⬤ Post offices Mon.–Fri.

7 8 9 10 11 12 1 2 3 4 5 6 7

Many stores and pharmacies do not open until 2 on Monday afternoon, and most are closed on Sunday. Many establishments have long lunch breaks.

Provincial post offices and banks may have shorter hours, but some stay open at lunchtime and Saturday morning. Some post offices open earlier and stay open in the evening.

Opening times for museums and monuments vary; they are frequently closed on Monday – check with the local tourist office.

NATIONAL HOLIDAYS

Banks, businesses and most stores close on these days.

Jan. 1	New Year's Day
Feb./Mar.	Carnival Day
Mar./Apr.	Easter Monday
May 1	Labor Day
May/Jun.	Ascension Day
May/Jun.	Pentecost Monday
Jun. 23	National Day
Aug. 15	Assumption of the Virgin
First Mon. in Sep.	Luxembourg City Fete (city of Luxembourg only)
Nov. 1	All Saints' Day
Dec. 25	Christmas Day
Dec. 26	St. Stephen's Day

PHOTOGRAPHY

Luxembourg enjoys a temperate climate, and the light is good. Check that photography is permitted before taking pictures in museums. Film and camera batteries can be bought from tourist stores, and rapid-developing services are widely available.

Luxembourg – Essential Information

Luxembourg – Essential Information

HEALTH

MEDICAL INSURANCE
Private medical insurance is recommended; U.S. and Canadian visitors can be treated in emergency rooms, but are charged if admitted to a hospital *(hôpital)*. Phone ☎ 112 for 24-hour information on hospitals and English-speaking doctors.

DENTAL SERVICES
A dentist *(dentiste)* will charge a fee for treatment, so check whether this is covered by your medical insurance. Emergency clinics are available in city hospitals. To find a dentist look in the yellow pages *(pages jaunes)* or ask at your hotel.

SUN ADVICE
You will not experience extremes of temperature in Luxembourg, but the sunshine during summer months can burn, so good sun protection is essential.

DRUGS
Prescription medicines and advice can be obtained from a pharmacy *(pharmacie)*, identified by a green cross. Information about the nearest 24-hour facility is posted at all pharmacies.

SAFE WATER
Tap water is safe to drink, and bottled mineral water *(eau minérale)* is widely available.

RESTROOMS

Restrooms *(toilettes)* are usually clean, modern and easy to find. They may also be called *"WC"* (pronounced vay-say). Coin-operated facilities exist; those with an attendant usually charge 20¢.

ELECTRICITY

Luxembourg has a 220-volt power supply. Electrical sockets take plugs with two round pins; American appliances will need a plug adapter and will require a transformer if they do not have a dual-voltage facility.

NATIONAL TRANSPORTATION

TRAIN *(train)*
The national rail company is Chemins de Fer Luxembourgeois (CFL). Most services run through the city of Luxembourg. Combined train and bus one-day network cards (the "Oeko-Pass") are good value and are valid until 8 a.m. the following day. "Short distance" train and bus tickets are available and are valid for 1 hour (€1.20 each or €9.20 for 10). For information: ☎ 49 90-49 90 (daily 6 a.m.–8 p.m.); www.cfl.lu

BUS *(bus)*
Long-distance, CFL-operated buses complement the rail network. The Eurolines European bus network serves Brussels; from there you must catch a train to Luxembourg.

RIVER BOAT *(bateau-mouche)*
There are many excursions (mostly Easter to October) exploring Luxembourg's magnificent Moselle river. For details, contact Entente Touristique de la Moselle Luxembourgeoise, P.O. Box 33, 10 route du Vin, L-6701 Grevenmacher ☎ 75 82 75; fax 75 86 66; www.moselle-tourist.lu

DRIVING

DRIVE ON THE RIGHT

SPEED LIMITS
Police impose minor on-the-spot fines varying from €24 to €145 depending on the seriousness of the offense.

Limited access highways *(autoroutes)*
130 k.p.h. (80 m.p.h.)
minimum speed **40 k.p.h. (24 m.p.h.)**

Main roads
90 k.p.h. (55 m.p.h.)

Urban areas
50 k.p.h. (31 m.p.h.)

SEAT BELTS
Must be worn in front and back seats at all times. Children under 12 and/or under 59 inches in height are not permitted to sit in the front seat.

BLOOD ALCOHOL
The legal blood alcohol limit is 0.08%. Random breath tests on drivers are carried out frequently, especially late at night, and the penalties for offenders are severe.

Luxembourg – Essential Information

DRIVING continued

TOLLS
There are no highway tolls in Luxembourg.

CAR RENTAL
The leading rental firms have offices at airports and train stations. Hertz offers discounted rates for AAA members (see page 15). For reservations:

	UNITED STATES	LUXEMBOURG
Alamo	(800) 327-9633	40 42 28 (Europcar)
Avis	(800) 331-2112	48 95 95
Budget	(800) 527-0700	44 19 38
Hertz	(800) 654-3080	43 46 45

FUEL
Many gas stations *(station de service)* are self-service, and 24-hour facilities are common. Stations on highways often have café facilities. The price of gas is fixed by the government, but self-service stations often offer discounts. Major credit cards are accepted.

AAA AFFILIATED MOTORING CLUB
Automobile Club du Grand-Duché de Luxembourg (ACL)
54 route de Longwy, L-8007 Bertrange,
☎ 45 00 45-1, fax 45 04 55; www.acl.lu
If you break down while driving, phone ☎ 45 00 45-1 (ACL 24-hour breakdown service).
Not all automobile clubs offer full services to AAA members.

BREAKDOWNS AND ACCIDENTS
There are emegency phones at regular intervals on highways. If you are involved in an accident, phone for emergency assistance (☎ 112 or 113 for police or ☎ 112 for fire or ambulance).
Most car rental firms provide their own free rescue service; if your car is rented, follow the instructions given in the documentation. Use of a car repair service other than those authorized by your rental company may violate your agreement.

OTHER INFORMATION
The minimum age for driving a car is 17 (may be higher for some car rental firms).

An International Driving Permit (IDP) is recommended; some rental firms require them, and they can speed up formalities if you are involved in an accident.

A Green Card (international motor insurance certificate) is recommended if you are driving a private car; see page 15 for more information.

USEFUL WORDS AND PHRASES

Because the Grand Duchy of Luxembourg is tucked between Belgium, France and Germany, Luxembourgers often slip unconsciously between different languages.

The official language (and, unofficially, the language of the elite) is French, but German is used for many situations. In addition to this, there is a third, everyday language: Lëtzebuergesch, a symbol of both national identity and Luxembourg's ability to assimilate other cultures.

The roots of Luxembourg's own language are Germanic, but it has evolved into a dialect that Germans no longer understand. The use of Lëtzebuergesch is primarily an oral tradition. It was only in 1984 that its spelling was decreed by law; up until then Luxembourgers spelled words more or less as they pleased.

French, German and Lëtzebuergesch are taught in schools, and English also is widely spoken, especially among the young and those working in the tourist trade. Don't expect Luxembourgers in rural areas to have mastered a fourth language, however!

Lëtzebuergesch is resilient enough to exist side-by-side with such widely spoken languages as French and German; but as the patois of a tiny, landlocked duchy it's evidently not very exportable. So if you have the opportunity to speak a word or two of this country's uniting language you'll raise a smile and a welcome.

good morning/hello	*moien*
goodbye	*addi*
thank you (very much)	*merci (villmols)*
sorry	*pardon*
excuse me	*entschellest*
please	*wanneschglift*
I don't understand	*ech verstin*

Food and drink

coffee	*Kaffi*
green bean soup	*Bou'neschlupp*
nettle soup	*Brennesselszopp*
potato soup	*Gromperenzopp*
potato dumplings	*Grompereknïddeln*
trout in Riesling sauce	*F'rell am Rèisleck*
pike in green liquor	*Hiecht mat Kraïderzooss*
crayfish	*Kriibsen*
blood sausage	*Trèipen*
pork in aspic	*Jhelli*
chicken in Riesling sauce	*Hong am Rèisleck*
tripe	*Kuddelfleck*
cheesecake	*Kéiskuch*
apple cake	*Äppelkuch*

For useful phrases in French, see page 489; for phrases in German see page 493.

PRE-TRIP ESSENTIALS...

WHAT YOU NEED

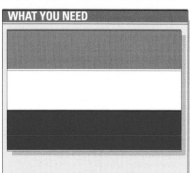

ESSENTIAL FOR TRAVELERS

● Required ● Recommended ● Not required

Passport	●
Visa	●
Travel, medical insurance	●
Round-trip or onward airline ticket	●
Local currency	●
Traveler's checks	●
Credit cards	●
First-aid kit and medicines	●
Inoculations	●

ESSENTIAL FOR DRIVERS

Driver's license	●
International Driving Permit	●
Car insurance (for nonrental cars)	●
Car registration (for nonrental cars)	●

IMPORTANT ADDRESSES

Netherlands Board of Tourism
355 Lexington Avenue, 19th floor
New York, NY 10017
☎ (212) 370 7360
Fax (212) 370-9507
www.goholland.com

**Nederlands Bureau voor Toerisme & Congressen
– NBTC (Netherlands Board of Tourism &
Conventions – NBTC)**
Vlietweg 15, 2260 MG Leidschendam
The Netherlands
☎ 070 370 5705
Fax 070 320 1654
www.holland.com

American Embassy
Lange Voorhout 102
2514 EJ The Hague, The Netherlands
☎ 070 310 9209
Fax 070 361 4688

COUNTRY ESSENTIALS...

CUSTOMS

 YES
**Duty-free limits on goods brought in
from non-European Union countries:**
200 cigarettes or 100 cigarillos or 50 cigars
or 250 g. tobacco; 2 L wine; 1 L alcohol over 22%
volume or 2 L alcohol under 22% volume; 50 ml.
perfume; 250 ml. toilet water; plus any other duty-free
goods (including gifts) to the value of €45. There is no
limit on the importation of tax-paid goods purchased
within the European Union, provided they are for your
own personal use. There are no currency regulations.

 NO
No unlicensed drugs, weapons,
ammunition, obscene material, pets
or other animals, counterfeit money
or copied goods, meat or poultry.

**For customs limits for returning U.S. citizens
see page 16.**

MONEY

The Dutch currency is the euro (€), a currency
shared by 11 other European Union countries. The
euro is divided into 100 cents (c). The denominations of
euro bills are 5, 10, 20, 50, 100, 200 and 500. There are
coins of 1, 2, 5, 10, 20 and 50c and €1 and €2. You can
change dollars and traveler's checks *(reischeques)*
at a bank, a GWK exchange office or other
exchange office or the larger VVV (tourist
information center) bureaus.

Exchange rate at press time: $1 = €0.82

TIPS AND GRATUITIES

Restaurants (service is always included)	change
Cafés/bars (service is always included)	change
Taxis (service is always included)	change
Porters	change
Hairdressers	change
Chambermaids	change
Restroom attendants	10c–20c
Cloakroom attendants	none

TIME ZONES

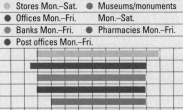

THE HAGUE	NEW YORK	CHICAGO	DENVER	SAN FRANCISCO
12:00 noon	6 hours behind Netherlands	7 hours behind Netherlands	8 hours behind Netherlands	9 hours behind Netherlands

515

COMMUNICATIONS

 ### POST OFFICES

Buy stamps *(postzegels)* at a post office *(postkantoor* or *PTT),* tobacco shop, newsstand or souvenir shop.

There are stamp vending machines in post offices, but if you are buying from a counter make sure you are in a line for stamps. Mailboxes have two slots; foreign mail should be dropped into the slot marked *Overige.* Hours for out-of-town post offices may vary.

 ### TELEPHONES

You can use cash (uncommon), credit cards and prepaid phone cards *(kaarttelephoon)* to make a call in The Netherlands. Phone cards can be bought from GWK – Holland Welcome Service offices, post offices, VVV tourist offices and shops displaying the PTT-phone card symbol. Orange-and-gray colored booths, located at most railroad stations, require a different phone card, available from GWK–Holland Welcome Service offices, Wizzl shops and railroad ticket offices. Calls also can be

made from post offices and *Telehouse* booths.

Phoning inside The Netherlands
All Dutch telephone numbers in this book include an area code; dial the number listed. To call the operator dial 0800 0410.

Phoning The Netherlands from abroad
The country code for The Netherlands is 31. Dutch numbers in this book do not include the country code; prefix this number if you are phoning from another country. To phone The Netherlands from the United States or Canada, omit the first zero from the Dutch number and dial the prefix 011 31. Example: 011 223 3445 becomes 011 31 11 223 3445.

Phoning from The Netherlands
To phone the United States or Canada, prefix the area code and number with 00 1. Example: (111) 222-3333 becomes 00 1 111 222-3333.
To call international information dial 0900 8418 (toll call).
For directory inquiries dial 0900 8008 (toll call).

EMERGENCY TELEPHONE NUMBERS

Police *(politie)*	112
Fire *(brandweer)*	112
Ambulance *(ziegenwagen)*	112

Emergency calls are free from phone booths.

HOURS OF OPERATION

● Stores Mon.–Sat.	● Museums/monuments
● Offices Mon.–Fri.	Mon.–Sat.
● Banks Mon.–Fri.	● Pharmacies Mon.–Fri.
● Post offices Mon.–Fri.	

7 8 9 10 11 12 1 2 3 4 5 6 7

Stores open from 11 a.m. on Monday and close at 5 on Saturday. In Amsterdam many stores open Sunday noon–7 and in The Hague and Rotterdam noon–5. In other Dutch cities stores open one Sunday a month. Larger city stores stay open until 9 p.m. on Thursday or Friday. In rural areas many stores close for lunch.
Banks generally open at 1 p.m. Monday.
Post offices also are open 9–noon or 12:30 on Saturday. Some city post offices stay open into the evening (Thursday or Friday). There is an all-night post office in Nieuwezijds Voorburgwal, Amsterdam. Out-of-town post offices and banks may have shorter hours.
Museums and monuments usually are open 1–5 on Sunday; some may close on Monday. In rural areas they may be closed October through March.

NATIONAL HOLIDAYS

Banks, businesses and most stores close on these days, except for Good Friday, when most shops remain open.

Jan. 1	New Year's Day
Mar./Apr.	Good Friday
Mar./Apr.	Easter Monday
Apr. 30	Queen's Birthday
May 5	Liberation Day (occurs every 5 years; next in 2009)
May/Jun.	Ascension Day
May/Jun.	Pentecost Monday
Dec. 25	Christmas Day
Dec. 26	St. Stephen's Day

PHOTOGRAPHY

 The Dutch climate is essentially maritime; conditions for outdoor photography are gentle but changeable. Some museums do not allow photography; check before taking pictures. Film and camera batteries are readily available from stores catering to tourists; rapid-developing services also are widely available.

The Netherlands – Essential Information

HEALTH

MEDICAL INSURANCE
Private medical insurance is recommended. U.S. and Canadian visitors can receive emergency treatment, but are charged if admitted to a hospital *(ziekenhuis)*. Doctors *(dokter)* are listed at the beginning of the telephone directory; English is widely spoken throughout the medical profession.
Tourist Medical Service: doctor, ☎ 020 592 3355.

DENTAL SERVICES
Dentists charge for treatment and can be expensive. Look in the telephone directory, or ask about local dentists at your hotel or embassy.
Tourist Medical Service: dentist ☎ 020 570 9595.

SUN ADVICE
The Netherlands' maritime climate is not one of extremes, but precautions against sunburn should be taken from June through August.

DRUGS
For nonprescription medicines go to a pharmacy *(drogisterij)*. If you need prescription medicines you will have to go to an *apotheek*, where staff also are trained to treat minor ailments. If you need medicine outside regular hours, information about all-night facilities is posted at all pharmacies.

SAFE WATER
Tap water is safe to drink throughout the Netherlands. Mineral water is widely available.

RESTROOMS

There are not many public restrooms, although you will usually find adequate and clean facilities in museums, department stores and roadside service areas. A small charge of 10 or 20 cents is usually made. Cafés provide restrooms for the use of customers; buy a drink if you need to use them.

ELECTRICITY

The Netherlands has a 220-volt power supply. Electrical sockets take plugs with two round pins; American appliances will need a plug adapter and will require a transformer if they do not have a dual-voltage facility.

NATIONAL TRANSPORTATION

TRAIN *(trein)*
Netherlands Railways, or Nederlandse Spoorwegen (NS), network is fast, clean, modern, punctual and fairly inexpensive. Information in English is widely available from stations; ☎ 0900 9296 (toll call) for international train service, ☎ 0900 9292 (toll call) for all domestic transportation services.

BUS *(bus)*
Bus travel is well-organized, with many connections to trains (bus and railroad stations are usually next to each other). If you're planning several trips ask for the Nationale Buswijer, which provides maps and full route details; ☎ 0900 9292 (toll call) for information. The Eurolines European bus network operates in The Netherlands; ☎ 020 560 8788.

FERRY *(veerboot)*
There are ferry services from the mainland across the Waddenzee to the Wadden Island (from Den Helder for Texel; Harlingen for Vlieland and Terschelling; Holwerd for Ameland; and Lauwersoog for Schiermonnikoog), and in summer services between the islands. For details about canal trips, contact VVV tourist information centers.

DRIVING

DRIVE ON THE RIGHT

SPEED LIMITS
Police can impose on-the-spot fines.

Limited-access highways *(autoweg)*
100 k.p.h. (62 m.p.h.) or **120 k.p.h. (74 m.p.h.)**

Main roads
80 k.p.h. (49 m.p.h.)

Urban areas
50 k.p.h. (31 m.p.h.)

SEAT BELTS
Must be worn in front and back seats at all times. Children under 12 years should not travel in the front seat.

BLOOD ALCOHOL
The legal blood alcohol limit is 0.05%. Random breath tests on drivers are carried out frequently, especially late at night, and the penalties for offenders are severe.

The Netherlands – Essential Information

DRIVING continued

 TOLLS
There are no highway tolls in The Netherlands, but there is a toll for the Dordse Kil tunnel near Dordrecht.

CAR RENTAL
The leading rental firms have offices at airports and train stations. Hertz offers discounted rates for AAA members (see page 15). For reservations:

	UNITED STATES	NETHERLANDS
Alamo	(800) 327-9633	070 381 1891 (Europcar)
Avis	(800) 331-2112	0800 235 2847 (toll free)
Budget	(800) 527-0700	0900 1576
Hertz	(800) 654-3080	020 201 3521

 FUEL
Many gas stations are self-service and 24-hour facilities are common. Unleaded gas *(Super-Plus* and *Euro-Super)*, lead-replacement fuel and diesel are available, and credit cards are accepted at most garages.

 AAA AFFILIATED MOTORING CLUB
Koninklijke Nederlandse Toeristenbond (ANWB)
Wassenaarseweg 220, 2596 The Hague ☎ 070 314 7147, fax 070 314 6969; www.anwb.nl
If you break down while driving, telephone ☎ 0800 0888 (ANWB breakdown service, toll free). Not all automobile clubs offer full services to AAA members.

BREAKDOWNS AND ACCIDENTS
There are yellow 24-hour emergency phones at regular intervals on highways. All accidents involving personal injury must be reported to the police; ☎ 112.
Most car rental firms provide their own free rescue service; if your car is rented, follow the instructions given in the documentation. Use of a car repair service other than those authorized by your rental company may violate your agreement.

OTHER INFORMATION
The minimum age for driving a car is 18 (usually between 21 and 25 for car rental firms).

An International Driving Permit (IDP) is recommended; some rental firms require them, and they can speed up formalities if you are involved in an accident.

A Green Card (international motor insurance certificate) is recommended if you are driving a private car; see page 15 for more information.

Drivers should yield to vehicles approaching from the right. In built-up areas, trams and buses have the right of way when leaving bus stops. Also beware of cyclists and skaters.

USEFUL WORDS AND PHRASES

It is not easy to reproduce the guttural sounds that make up the Dutch language. There are many similarities between German and Dutch, although the Dutch go to great lengths to point out the differences.

English is spoken fluently by a large proportion of the population, who learn foreign languages from an early age.

Dutch pronunciation is similar to English, with some variations:

> *j* as in *y*ellow
> *v* like an *f* as in *f*ar
> *w* like a *v* as in *v*at
> *ng* as in bri*ng*
> *nj* as in o*ni*on

Double consonants keep their separate sounds: for instance, *k* and *n* together are never pronounced as in the English "know."

Some letters and diphthongs are tricky. If the letter is doubled, the vowel sound is lengthened. For example:

> a as in sap, aa as in art
> e as in let, ee as in fate
> o as in mop, oo as in mope
> oe as in food
> au, ou and ui as in how
> ei and ij as in line
> ch as in Bach
> tje as in church
> tie as in tee

Do you speak English?	*Spreekt u Engels?*
excuse me	*pardon*
hello	*hallo* or *dag*
goodbye	*tot ziens*
yes/no	*ja/nee*
how much is?	*wat kost?*
I want…	*ik wil…*
I don't understand	*Ik begrijp het niet*
open/closed	*open/gesloten*
please	*alstublieft*
thank you	*bedankt*
ticket (one-way/	*enkele reis*
round trip)	*retour*
where's the…?	*waar is het…?*
airport	*vliegveld*
room	*kamer*
breakfast	*ontbijt*
dinner	*diner*
May I order?	*Mag ik even bestellen?*
steak	*biefstuk*
bread	*brood*
chicken	*kip*
coffee/tea	*koffie/thee*
sandwich	*broodje*
dish of the day	*daschotel*
lamb	*lamsvlees*
pork	*fricandeau*
wine	*wijn*

PRE-TRIP ESSENTIALS...

WHAT YOU NEED

ESSENTIAL FOR TRAVELERS

● Required   ● Recommended   ● Not required

Passport	●
Visa	●
Travel, medical insurance	●
Round-trip or onward airline ticket	●
Local currency	●
Traveler's checks	●
Credit cards	●
First-aid kit and medicines	●
Inoculations	●

ESSENTIAL FOR DRIVERS*

Driver's license	●
International Driving Permit	●
Car insurance (for nonrental cars)	●
Car registration (for nonrental cars)	●

*see also DRIVING section

IMPORTANT ADDRESSES

Innovation Norway
655 Third Avenue, Suite 1810,
New York, NY 10017
☎ (212) 885-9700; fax (212) 885-9710
www.visitnorway.com

Oslo Promotion (Oslo Visitors and Convention Bureau)
Grev Wedels plass 4
N-0151 Oslo, Norway
☎ 23 10 62 00; fax 23 10 62 01
www.visitoslo.com

Norges Turistråd (Norwegian Tourist Board)
Postboks 722 Sentrum
Stortorvet 10
N-0105 Oslo, Norway
☎ 24 14 46 00; fax 24 14 46 01
www.visitnorway.com

American Embassy
Drammensveien 18
N-0244 Oslo, Norway
☎ 22 44 85 50; fax 22 56 27 51
Mon.–Fri. 9–5
www.usa.no

COUNTRY ESSENTIALS...

CUSTOMS

YES
Duty-free limits on goods brought in from non-European countries:
400 cigarettes or 500g. tobacco and 200 cigarette papers; 1 L. alcohol 23–60%; 1 L. alcohol up to 22%; 2 L. beer. If you have no alcohol 23–60% you are allowed one extra liter of alcohol up to 22% or 2L. beer, or 4L. beer if no other alcohol. Also 50g. perfume and 50cl. toilet water, 10kg of foodstuffs and goods to the value of KR6,000. You must be 20 and over to bring in spirits and 18 and over to bring in wine, beer and tobacco products. You may bring in or take out local currency to the value of KR25,000.

NO
No unlicensed drugs, weapons, ammunition, obscene material, pets or other animals, counterfeit money or copied goods, alcohol over 60%, meat or poultry.
For customs limits for returning U.S. citizens see page 16.

MONEY

Norway's currency is the krone (KR), which is divided into 100 øre. The denominations of krone bills are 50, 100, 200, 500 and 1,000. There are coins of 50 øre and KR1, KR5, KR10 and KR20. You can exchange dollars or traveler's checks *(reisesjekk)* at a bank *(bank)*, exchange office *(vekslekontor)*, post office *(posten)* or hotel; you will need ID. Credit cards *(kredittkort)* are widely accepted in hotels, main stores and more expensive restaurants.
Exchange rate at press time: $1 = KR6.5

TIPS AND GRATUITIES

Restaurants (service is included)	5–10%
Cafés/bars (service is included)	5–10%
Taxis (service is included)	10% (optional)
Porters	KR5 per bag
Hairdressers	change
Chambermaids	KR5
Restroom attendants	KR3
Cloakroom attendants	change

TIME ZONES

OSLO	NEW YORK	CHICAGO	DENVER	SAN FRANCISCO
12:00 noon	6 hours behind Norway	7 hours behind Norway	8 hours behind Norway	9 hours behind Norway

COMMUNICATIONS

POST OFFICES

Buy stamps *(frimerker)* at a post office *(posten)*, a newsstand/tobacconist such as Narvesen or MIX or from a hotel.

Hours for out-of-town post offices may vary. Mailboxes are red.

TELEPHONES

You can use cash or a telephone card *(telekort)* to make a call in Norway. Most phone booths have direct dialing for international calls. Use KR1, KR5, KR10 and KR20 coins (there is a minimum charge of KR2). Greencard phones accept phone cards (KR40, KR90 and KR140), available from Narvesen and MIX kiosks and from post offices. Some card phones accept

credit cards. In cities and large towns, phone company offices are open late and have English-speaking operators.

Phoning inside Norway

There are no area codes in Norway; all numbers are eight digits: dial the number that is listed. To call the operator

dial 117; for directory inquiry information (Norway, Sweden and Denmark) dial 1881.

Phoning Norway from abroad

The country code for Norway is 47. Note that Norwegian numbers in this book do not include the country code; you will need to prefix this number if you are phoning from another country. To phone Norway from the United States or Canada, simply add the prefix 011 47. Example: 11 22 33 44 becomes 011 47 11 22 33 44.

Phoning from Norway

To phone the United States or Canada from Norway, prefix the area code and number with 00 1. Example: (111) 222-3333 becomes 00 1 111 222-3333.

To call international information dial 1882. For the international operator dial 115.

EMERGENCY TELEPHONE NUMBERS

Police *(politi)*	112
Fire *(brannvesen)*	110
Ambulance *(ambulanse)*	113

Emergency calls are free from phone booths.

.HOURS OF OPERATION

○ Stores Mon.–Fri.	● Museums/monuments
● Offices Mon.–Fri.	● Pharmacies Mon.–Fri.
● Banks Mon.–Fri.	
● Post offices Mon.–Fri.	

7 8 9 10 11 12 1 2 3 4 5 6 7

On Thursday most stores open at 9 and remain open until between 6 and 8 p.m. On Saturday most stores close between 1 and 3. Supermarkets are generally open Mon.–Fri. 9–8, Sat. 9–6. Many shopping complexes are open until 8. Kiosks are open daily and stay open until 10 or 11 p.m. Most stores are closed on Sunday. Stores around tourist attractions may have special hours.

Offices usually close at 3 p.m. in summer. Banks generally close half an hour earlier from mid-May to mid-September, but stay open until 5 on Thursday all year and are closed weekends. Some post offices may only be open Mon.–Fri. 8:30–4. They are open 8–1 on Saturday. Museums often close on Monday, and hours of operation may be reduced during the winter. Pharmacies are open the same hours as stores.

NATIONAL HOLIDAYS

Banks, businesses and most stores close on these days.

Jan. 1	New Year's Day
Mar./Apr.	Maundy Thursday
Mar./Apr.	Good Friday
Mar./Apr.	Easter Monday
May 1	Labor Day
May 17	National Day
May	Ascension Day
May/Jun.	Pentecost Monday
Dec. 25	Christmas Day
Dec. 26	St. Stephen's Day

PHOTOGRAPHY

Spectacular shots are possible in fjord country if the weather is right (bear in mind that Norway is susceptible to poor light, especially during the winter). Photography is not permitted in some museums and places of historic interest – check before taking pictures. Film and camera batteries are readily available in towns.

Norway – Essential Information

Norway – Essential Information

HEALTH

MEDICAL INSURANCE
U.S. and Canadian visitors will be charged for medical assistance, including treatment in a hospital *(sykehus)* emergency room. For medical emergency service in Oslo contact Oslo Kommunale legevakt, ☎ 23 48 70 00. For general practitioners, see *Lege* in the phone directory.

DENTAL SERVICES
A dentist *(tannlege)* will charge you for treatment, so check your medical insurance coverage. Many dentists speak English; ask a tourist office or your hotel to find one for you. For after-hours emergency treatment *(tannlegevakten)* in Oslo contact Oslo Kommunale Tannlegevakt, (☎ 22 67 30 00).

SUN ADVICE
Despite its northerly location, Norway has warm weather during the summer months. Use an appropriate sunscreen.

DRUGS
A pharmacy *(apotek)* sells prescription medicines; many pharmacists speak English. Information about the nearest late-night or 24-hour facility is posted at all pharmacies. For a 24-hour pharmacy in Oslo go to Jernbanetorgets Apotek, Jernbanetorget 4B, near Sentralstasjon/Oslo Central Station (☎ 23 35 81 00).

SAFE WATER
Tap water is safe to drink throughout Norway. Mineral water *(mineralvann)* is widely available.

RESTROOMS

Public restrooms *(toaletter)* are easy to find. Facilities are separate for men *(herrer)* and women *(damer),* and are identified by symbols or a "WC" sign. They are invariably clean and modern, and a small charge (usually KR3) may be made.

ELECTRICITY

Norway has a 220-volt power supply. Electrical sockets take plugs with two round pins; American appliances will need a plug adapter and will require a transformer if they do not have a dual-voltage facility.

NATIONAL TRANSPORTATION

TRAIN *(tog)*
The Norges Statsbaner (NSB) network operates as far north as the Arctic Circle. Travel is comfortable but not cheap. Reservations are recommended on train journeys and a must on long distance and overnight trains; inquire about discounts when booking (☎ 81 50 08 88, then dial 4 for an English-speaking operator, or www.nsb.no).

BUS *(buss)*
Buses are an excellent, inexpensive way to explore regions that are less well-served by train. NOR-WAY Bussekspress (☎ 81 54 44 44; www.nor-way.no) is the national operator. Buy your ticket on board; it is not usually necessary to book in advance.

FERRY *(ferje)*
Norway relies heavily on ferries and express boats/catamarans, which connect with trains and buses. Car ferries operate on a first-come, first-served system; payment is made on board. Some waterways have ferry services. *Hurtigruten,* a grand coastal steamer, links Bergen with Kirkenes, in far northern Norway, and calls at 34 ports en route.

DRIVING

DRIVE ON THE RIGHT

SPEED LIMITS
Speed controls are stringent. Police can impose on-the-spot fines.

Limited-access highways *(motorvei)*
90 k.p.h. (55 m.p.h.)

Main roads
80 k.p.h. (49 m.p.h.)

Urban areas
50 k.p.h. (31 m.p.h.); usually **30 k.p.h. (18 m.p.h.)** in residential areas

SEAT BELTS
Must be worn in front and back seats at all times. Children under four must use child safety equipment. Failure to comply may result in a KR750 fine.

BLOOD ALCOHOL
The legal blood alcohol limit is 0.02%. Random breath tests on drivers are carried out frequently, especially late at night, and the penalties for offenders are extremely severe.

Norway – Essential Information

DRIVING continued

 TOLLS
There are tolls to enter Bergen, Oslo, Stavanger and Trondheim. There also are tolls for some highways, bridges and tunnels.

 CAR RENTAL
The leading rental firms *(bilutleie)* have offices at airports and train stations. Hertz offers discounted rates for AAA members (see page 15). For reservations:

	UNITED STATES	NORWAY
Alamo	(800) 462-5266	67 16 58 20 (Europcar)
Avis	(800) 230-4898	66 77 11 11
Budget	(800) 527-0700	81 56 06 00
Hertz	(800) 654-3080	0800 32 000 (toll free)

 FUEL *(olje)*
Lead replacement fuel is available instead of leaded gas; diesel is available. Unleaded gas is 95 and 98 octane. Gas stations *(bensinstasjon)* are few in remote areas; credit cards might not be accepted.

 AAA AFFILIATED MOTORING CLUB
Norges Automobil-Forbund (NAF)
PO Box 6682 Etterstadt, NO. 0609; www.naf.no ☎ 22 34 14 00 or 81 00 06 06, fax 22 33 13 72
If you break down while driving, phone ☎ 81 00 05 05 (24-hour NAF breakdown service). A fee is charged for breakdown service. Not all automobile clubs offer full services to AAA members.

BREAKDOWNS AND ACCIDENTS
NAF patrols main roads and mountain passes mid-June to mid-August.There are 24-hour emergency phones at regular intervals on highways and along mountain passes. All accidents involving personal injury must be reported to the police (☎ 112).
Most car rental firms provide their own free rescue service; if your car is rented, follow the instructions given in the documentation. Use of a car repair service other than those authorized by your rental company may violate your agreement.

OTHER INFORMATION
The minimum age for driving a car is 18 (may be higher for some car rental firms).

An International Driving Permit (IDP) is recommended; some rental firms require them, and they can speed up formalities if you are involved in an accident. A Green Card (international motor insurance certificate) is highly recommended if you are driving a private car; see page 15 for more information.

You are required by law to use dimmed headlights at all times when driving. Snow tires and chains are advised from Nov. 1 until Easter (Oct. 16 until Apr. 30 in northern Norway); rent tires and chains from NAF or at border crossings.

USEFUL WORDS AND PHRASES

There are two official, and similar forms of Norwegian. Riksmal, or Bokmal ("book language"), is an old form of Norwegian. Athough many bureaucrats speak in Bokmal, it is mostly used in its written form. Landsmal, or Nynorsk, has its roots in Old Norse dialects but developed out of the wave of Norwegian nationalism in the 19th century. You will encounter both forms during your stay; it is not uncommon for speakers to use a combination of both, but writing rarely mixes styles.

Most people, especially the young, speak some English; alternatively, a knowledge of German will help. The phrases below are translated into Bokmal.

Do you speak English?	*Snakker du engelsk?*
excuse me	*unnskyld*
hello	*god dag*
goodbye	*ha det bra*
how much?	*hvor mye?*
I would like	*Jeg vil gjerne*
I don't understand	*Jeg forstår ikke*
non-smoking	*røyking forbudt*
open/closed	*åpen/stengt*
please	*vaer så snill*
thank you	*takk*
ticket (one-way/ round trip)	*enkeltbillett/ tur-returbillett*
Where is...?	*Hvor er...?*
yes/no	*ja/nei*
early/late	*tidlig/sent*
hot/cold	*varm/kald*
big/small	*stor/liten*
good/bad	*god/dårlig*
airport	*flyplass*
you're welcome	*vaer så god*
the restaurant	***restaurant***
beef	*oksekjøtt*
bread	*brød*
breakfast	*frokost*
biscuits	*kjeks*
chicken	*kylling*
coffee/tea	*kaffe/te*
salad	*salat*
dessert	*dessert*
entree	*hovedrett*
fish	*fisk*
lamb	*lammekjøtt*
pork	*svinekjøtt*
sandwich	*smørbrød*
hot-dog	*pølse*
seafood	*sjømat*
lobster	*hummer*
herring	*sild*
starter	*forrett*
waffles	*vafler*
cranberries	*tranebær*
ice cream	*is*
wine	*vin*
the check	*regningen*

Portugal – Essential Information

PRE-TRIP ESSENTIALS...

WHAT YOU NEED

ESSENTIAL FOR TRAVELERS

● Required   ● Recommended   ● Not required

Passport	●
Visa	●
Travel, medical insurance	●
Return or onward ticket	●
Local currency	●
Traveler's checks	●
Credit cards	●
First-aid kit and medicines	●
Inoculations	●

ESSENTIAL FOR DRIVERS*

Driver's license	●
International Driving Permit	●
Car insurance (for nonrental cars)	●
Car registration (for nonrental cars)	●

*see also DRIVING section

IMPORTANT ADDRESSES

Portuguese Trade Commission
590 Fifth Avenue, 3rd Floor
New York, NY 10036-4702
☏ (212) 354 4403
Fax (212) 764 6137
www.portugal.org

Icep Portugal,
Investimento, Comércio e Turismo
(Investment, Trade and Tourism)
rua Ivone Silva, lote 6
1050–124 Lisbon, Portugal
☏ (351) 217 810 000
Fax (351) 217 937 537
www.portugalinsite.pt

American Embassy
Avenida Forças Armadas
1600 Lisbon, Portugal
☏ 21 727 3300
Fax 21 726 9109
Mon.–Fri. 8–5

COUNTRY ESSENTIALS...

CUSTOMS

YES
Duty-free limits on goods brought in
from non-European Union countries:
200 cigarettes or 100 cigarillos or 50
cigars or 250 g. tobacco; 2 L. wine; 1 L. alcohol over
22% volume or 2 L. alcohol under 22% volume; 50 ml.
perfume; 250 ml. toilet water; plus any other duty-free
goods (including gifts) to the value of €37.41. Local or
foreign currency exceeding €12,470 must be
declared on arrival. Foreign currency may be
exported if it was declared on entry, but no more than
€4,988 may be exported. There is no limit on the
importation of tax-paid goods purchased within the
European Union if they are for personal use.

NO
No unlicensed drugs, weapons,
ammunition, obscene material, pets
or other animals, counterfeit money
or copied goods, meat or poultry.
For customs limits for returning U.S. citizens
see page 16.

MONEY

Portugal's currency is the euro (€), a currency
shared by 11 other European Union countries. The
euro is divided into 100 cents (¢). The denominations of
euro bills are 5, 10, 20, 50, 100, 200 and 500. There are
coins of 1, 2, 5, 10, 20 and 50¢ and €1 and €2. You can
change dollars or traveler's checks *(cheques de
viagem)* at a bank *(banco)* or an exchange office
(casa de cambio).

Exchange rate at press time: $1 = €0.82

TIPS AND GRATUITIES

Restaurants (where service is not included)	10%
Cafés/bars (where service is not included)	change
Taxis	10%
Porters	50¢–€1
Hairdressers	€1
Chambermaids	€2
Restroom attendants	50¢
Cloakroom attendants	50¢

TIME ZONES

LISBON	NEW YORK	CHICAGO	DENVER	SAN FRANCISCO
12:00 noon	5 hours behind Portugal	6 hours behind Portugal	7 hours behind Portugal	8 hours behind Portugal

523

COMMUNICATIONS

POST OFFICES

Buy stamps *(selos)* at a post office *(correios)*, identified by a sign showing a white horse on a red background.

You may also see the words "Correios."

Hours for out-of-town post offices may vary.

TELEPHONES

You can use coins or a phone card, available from post offices, in a phone booth *(telefonar)*. Public phones are easily found on the street and in cafés, main post offices, and at some newsstands and tourist offices. Most public phones also take international credit cards.

Phoning inside Portugal
All Portuguese telephone numbers in this book include an area code; dial the number listed.

To call the operator dial 099. To call information dial 118.

Phoning Portugal from abroad
The country code for Portugal is 351. Note that Portuguese numbers in this book do not include the country code; you will need to prefix this number if you are phoning from another country. To phone Portugal from the United States or Canada dial the prefix 011 351.
Example: 11 122 3344 becomes 011 351 11 122 3344.

Phoning from Portugal
To phone the United States or Canada from Portugal, prefix the area code and number with 00 1.
Example: (111) 222-3333 becomes 00 1 111 222-3333.
For international operator outside Europe dial 098.
To call international information dial 179.

EMERGENCY TELEPHONE NUMBERS

Police *(polícia)*	112
Fire *(serviço do fogo)*	112
Ambulance *(ambulância)*	112

Emergency calls are free from phone booths.

HOURS OF OPERATION

- ○ Stores Mon.–Sat.
- ● Offices Mon.–Fri.
- ● Banks Mon.–Fri.
- ● Post offices Mon.–Fri.
- ● Museums/monuments
- ● Pharmacies Mon.–Sat.

7	8	9	10	11	12	1	2	3	4	5	6	7

Most stores and pharmacies close at 1 on Saturday and are not open on Sunday. Stores in large towns or tourist areas are open Mon.–Sat. until midnight; some also open on Sunday. Grocery stores are usually open until 9 p.m.

Post offices and banks in rural areas often close for lunch. Some banks in Lisbon stay open until 6.

Museums generally close on Monday (some also close on Wednesday), and the smaller sights may have shorter hours of operation off-season.

NATIONAL HOLIDAYS

Banks, businesses and most stores close on these days. Additionally, there are many local festivals when everything comes to a halt and a whole town takes part in events.

Jan. 1	New Year's Day
Feb./Mar.	Shrove Tuesday
Mar./Apr.	Good Friday
Apr. 25	Liberty Day
May 1	Labor Day
May/Jun.	Corpus Christi
Jun. 10	Portugal Day
Aug. 15	Assumption of the Virgin
Oct. 5	Republic Day
Nov. 1	All Saints' Day
Dec. 1	Independence Day
Dec. 8	Immaculate Conception
Dec. 25	Christmas Day

PHOTOGRAPHY

Finding adequate light is rarely a problem in Portugal; rise early for atmospheric shots of fishing ports, villages, castles and the mountains. You will not be permitted to photograph at airports or military areas, and ask permission before taking pictures in museums and churches. Popular brands of film and batteries are widely available.

Portugal – Essential Information

Portugal – Essential Information

HEALTH

MEDICAL INSURANCE
U.S. and Canadian visitors will be charged for emergency medical treatment, consultation with a doctor and/or admittance to a hospital *(hospital)*. Ask at a tourist office or your hotel to find an English-speaking doctor.

DENTAL SERVICES
Dental treatment is charged for in Portugal. Ask at a tourist office or your hotel for a list of English-speaking dentists. Check that dental treatment is covered by your medical insurance.

SUN ADVICE
The sun is strong during summer, particularly in the south. Do not be deceived by the cooling breeze off the Atlantic. Avoid prolonged exposure and protect yourself with a sunscreen or cover up.

DRUGS
Prescription medicines are available from a pharmacy *(fármacia)*, distinguished by a large green cross. Pharmacists can prescribe remedies for minor ailments, and many speak English. Information about the nearest late-night or 24-hour facility is posted at all pharmacies.

SAFE WATER
Tap water is generally safe, but does not always taste too pleasant. It is advisable to drink bottled water *(agua mineral)*, especially in rural areas; *sem gas* means noncarbonated, *com gas* means carbonated.

RESTROOMS

Public restrooms *(retretes* or *lavabos)* are easy to find. Ladies' *(senhoras)* restrooms usually have a minimal charge and are generally clean. Men's *(homens)* restrooms are usually free.

ELECTRICITY

Almost all of Portugal has a 220-volt power supply. Electrical sockets take plugs with two round pins; American appliances will need a plug adapter and a transformer if they do not have a dual-voltage facility.

NATIONAL TRANSPORTATION

TRAIN *(comboios)*
The Caminhos de Ferro Portugueses (CP) operates three types of service: *Inter-regional* and *Intercidade* (which both stop at most stations) and *Rapido* (express between Lisbon and Porto). For information ☎ 808 208 208 (national toll number).

BUS *(autocarros)*
Bus services have been privatized and several companies now cover Portugal. Eva runs services in the Algarve and the south with services into Spain(☎ 289 89 97 40); Rede Expressos covers much of the country (☎ 21 358 1460); Rodest covers Lisbon to Fátima (☎ 21 751 1600); and Rodonorte covers north into Lisbon (☎ 25 934 0710).

FERRY *(barcos)*
Ferries cross the Rio Tejo from Lisbon to the suburb of Cacilhas from Cais da Alfândega (Terreiro do Paço) or from Cais de Sodré. From Setúbal ferries cross the Rio Sado to the Tróia peninsula. Tickets can be bought at the boat stations' ticket offices.

DRIVING

DRIVE ON THE RIGHT

SPEED LIMITS
Police can impose on-the-spot fines.

Limited-access highways *(autoestrada)*
120 k.p.h. (74 m.p.h.), minimum speed 40 k.p.h. (25 m.p.h.)
Divided highways
100 k.p.h. (62 m.p.h.)

Main roads
90 k.p.h. (55 m.p.h.)

Urban areas
50 k.p.h. (31 m.p.h.)

SEAT BELTS
Must be worn in front and back seats at all times.

BLOOD ALCOHOL
The legal blood alcohol limit is 0.05%. Random breath tests on drivers are carried out frequently, especially late at night, and the penalties for offenders are severe.

Portugal – Essential Information

DRIVING continued

TOLLS
There are tolls on highways *(auto-estradas)* in Portugal. Highway numbers are prefixed by IP, A and E.

CAR RENTAL
The leading rental firms have offices at airports and train stations. Hertz offers discounted rates for AAA members (see page 15). For reservations:

	UNITED STATES	PORTUGAL
Alamo	(800) 462 5266	21 848 6191
Avis	(800) 230 4898	800 20 1002
Budget	(800) 527-0700	808 25 26 27
Hertz	(800) 654-3080	21 942 6300

FUEL *(gasolina)*
Gas and diesel are sold in liters, and many stations *(posto de gasolina)* are self-service. Gas stations, generally open daily 7 a.m.–8 p.m. (some 24 hours), are not as common in the more remote northern areas, and credit cards are not always accepted or incur an additional charge.

AAA AFFILIATED MOTORING CLUB
Automóvel Club de Portugal (ACP)
Rua Rosa Araújo 24–26, 1250–195 Lisbon ☎ 21 318 0100, fax 21 318 0237. Not all automobile clubs offer full services to AAA members.

BREAKDOWNS AND ACCIDENTS
There are 24-hour emergency phones at regular intervals on highways. If you are involved in an accident ☎ 112 or 115 for police assistance.
Most car rental firms provide their own free rescue service; if your car is rented, follow the instructions given in the documentation. Use of a car repair service other than those authorized by your rental company may violate your agreement.

OTHER INFORMATION
The minimum age for car rental is 21 (some rental firms stipulate 23).

An International Driving Permit (IDP) is essential; some rental firms require them, and they can speed up formalities if you are involved in an accident.

A Green Card (international motor insurance certificate) is essential if you are driving a private car; see page 15 for more information.

You are required by law to carry ID at all times.

USEFUL WORDS AND PHRASES

Portuguese is a Latin language, so an acquaintance with French, Spanish or Italian makes written Portuguese quite easy to understand. Understanding spoken Portuguese, however, is more difficult. Although on paper Portuguese words look similar to Spanish, they actually sound very different. Consonants are slurred, and vowels are flat and truncated, nasal or sometimes disregarded completely.

Although English is widely spoken in tourist areas, knowing a few Portuguese words will make your trip more rewarding.

Do you speak English?	*Fala Inglês?*
I'm sorry	*desculpe*
hello/goodbye	*olá/adeus*
yes/no	*sim/não*
how much?	*quanto?*
I am American	*sou Americano*
I would like	*queria um*
I don't understand	*não entendo*
non-smoking	*não fumadores*
okay	*está bem*
today/tomorrow	*hoje/amanhã*
open/closed	*aberto/fechado*
right/left	*direita/esquerda*
near/far	*perto/longe*
big/little	*grande/pequeno*
cheap/expensive	*barato/caro*
please	*se faz favor*
thank you	*obrigado (m.)/obrigada (f.)*
ticket	*bilhete*
one way/return	*ida/ida e volta*
where is…?	*onde é…?*
the hotel	***hotel***
breakfast	*pequeno almoço*
lunch	*almoço*
dinner	*jantar*
I have a reservation	*tenho uma marcacao*
key	*chave*
for one night	*para uma noite*
room	*quarto*
shower	*duche*
with bathroom	*com casa de banho*
the restaurant	***restaurante***
beef	*bife*
bread	*pão*
cheese	*queijo*
chicken	*frango*
the check	*a conta*
coffee/tea	*café/chà*
dish of the day	*prato do dia*
dessert	*sobremesa*
fish	*peixe*
ham	*fiambre*
lamb	*carneiro*
pork	*porco*
starter	*entrada*
veal	*vitela*
wine	*vinho*
Is the service included?	*O serviço está incluido?*

Spain – Essential Information

PRE-TRIP ESSENTIALS...

WHAT YOU NEED

ESSENTIAL FOR TRAVELERS

● Required　● Recommended　● Not required

Passport	●
Visa (check regulations before you travel)	●
Travel, medical insurance	●
Round-trip or onward airline ticket	●
Local currency	●
Traveler's checks	●
Credit cards	●
First-aid kit and medicines	●
Inoculations	●

ESSENTIAL FOR DRIVERS*

Driver's license	●
International Driving Permit	●
Car insurance (for nonrental cars)	●
Car registration (for nonrental cars)	●

*see also DRIVING section

IMPORTANT ADDRESSES

Tourist Office of Spain
666 Fifth Avenue, 35th floor
New York, NY 10103
☎ (212) 265-8822
Fax (212) 265-8864
www.okspain.org
Visitors by appointment only

Turespaña (Tourist Office of Spain)
Calle José Lázaro Galdiano 6
28036 Madrid, Spain
☎ 901 300 600
Fax 91 343 3446
www.tourspain.es

American Embassy
Serrano 75
28006 Madrid, Spain
☎ 91 587 2200
Fax 91 587 2303
Personal inquiries: Mon.–Fri. 9–6

COUNTRY ESSENTIALS...

CUSTOMS

YES
Duty-free limits on goods brought in from non-European Union countries:
200 cigarettes or 100 cigarillos or 50 cigars or 250 g. tobacco; 2 L wine; 1 L alcohol over 22% volume; 2 L alcohol under 22% volume; 60 ml. perfume; 250 ml. toilet water; plus any other duty-free goods (including gifts) to the value of €200. The import of currency of any denomination exceeding €6,010 must be declared on arrival in Spain. There is no limit on the importation of tax-paid goods purchased within the European Union if they are for personal use.

NO
No unlicensed drugs, weapons, ammunition, obscene material, pets or other animals, counterfeit money or copied goods, meat or poultry.

For customs limits for returning U.S. citizens see page 16.

MONEY

Spain's currency is the euro (€), a currency shared by 11 other European Union countries. The euro is divided into 100 cents (¢). The denominations of euro bills are 5, 10, 20, 50, 100, 200 and 500. There are coins of 1, 2, 5, 10, 20 and 50¢ and €1 and €2. Exchange dollars or traveler's checks *(cheques de viaje)* at a bank *(banco)* or exchange office *(oficina de canvi)*.

Exchange rate at press time: $1 = €0.82

TIPS AND GRATUITIES

Tips are welcomed as a sign of good service. Most hotel, restaurant and café checks will include a service charge.

Restaurants (service is normally included)	5–10%
Cafés/bars (service is normally included)	change
Taxis	10%
Porters, chambermaids	50¢
Cloakroom attendants	change

TIME ZONES

MADRID	NEW YORK	CHICAGO	DENVER	SAN FRANCISCO
12:00 noon	6 hours behind Spain	7 hours behind Spain	8 hours behind Spain	9 hours behind Spain

527

COMMUNICATIONS

POST OFFICES

Buy stamps *(sellos)* at a post office *(correos)*, a tobacconist *(estancos)* denoted by a "T" or at some hotels. Hours for out-of-town post offices may vary.

TELEPHONES

A public telephone *(teléfono)* takes 5, 10, 20 and 50 cent and 1 and 2 euro coins. A phone card *(teletarjeta)* issued by Telefónica is available from post offices, tobacconists, newsstands and authorized retailers for 6 and 12 euros. Many public phone booths are thoroughly modern, with instructions in English and lists of national and international

dialing codes posted inside them. In major cities, telecommunications stores offer facilities such as faxing and e-mail.

Phoning inside Spain
All Spanish phone numbers in this book include an area code; dial the number that is listed.

To call the operator dial 11818.

Phoning Spain from abroad
The country code for Spain is 34. Note that Spanish numbers in this book do not include the Spanish country code; you will need to prefix this number if you are phoning from another country. To phone Spain from the United States or Canada dial the prefix 011 34. (Note that the number of digits in Spanish area codes varies.)
Example: 11 122 3344 becomes 011 34 11 122 3344.

Phoning from Spain
To phone the United States or Canada from Spain, prefix the area code and number with 00 1.
Example: (111) 222-3333 becomes 00 1 111 222-3333.
To call international information dial 11825.

EMERGENCY TELEPHONE NUMBERS

Police *(policía)*	091
Fire *(bomberos)*	080
Ambulance *(ambulancia)*	061
General emergencies	112

Emergency calls are free from phone booths.

HOURS OF OPERATION

- Stores Mon.–Sat.
- Offices Mon.–Fri.
- Banks Mon.–Fri.
- Post offices Mon.–Sat.
- Museums/monuments Tue.–Sat.
- Pharmacies Mon.–Sat.

Department stores and grocery stores may operate the hours shown, especially in summer. Department stores are open Mon.–Sat. 10–10, and in Madrid also open the first Sun. of each month.

Business hours vary depending on season; many companies work *horas intensivas* (shorter, more intensive hours) from 8–3 in summer.

Some banks are open Saturdays 9–1 in winter.

Most museums and monuments are closed on Monday, but many are open 9–2 on Sunday.

NATIONAL HOLIDAYS

Banks, businesses and most stores close on these days. Days marked (*) are not national holidays but are celebrated in Catalonia, when shops and offices may close.

Jan. 1	New Year's Day
Jan. 6	Epiphany
Mar. 19	St. Joseph's Day (not Catalonia)
Mar./Apr.	Good Friday
*Mar./Apr.	Easter Monday
May 1	Labor Day
*May/Jun.	Pentecost Monday
*Jun. 24	St. John's Day
Aug. 15	Assumption of the Virgin
*Sep. 11	National Day (Catalonia)
*Sep. 24	Our Lady of Mercy Day
Oct. 12	National Day
Nov. 1	All Saints' Day
Dec. 6	Constitution Day
Dec. 8	Immaculate Conception
Dec. 25	Christmas Day
*Dec. 26	St. Stephen's Day
Dec 31	New Year's Eve

PHOTOGRAPHY

The Spanish summer sun can be powerful at noon, making photos appear flat; take your pictures early in the morning or late in the evening. Ask permission before taking pictures in museums and churches. Film and camera batteries are readily available from specialist stores and department stores.

Spain – Essential Information

Spain – Essential Information

HEALTH

MEDICAL INSURANCE
U.S. and Canadian visitors can receive treatment in a hospital emergency room, but are charged if admitted to a bed. There is an Anglo-American clinic in Madrid: ☎ 91 435 1823.

DENTAL SERVICES
You will be charged for dental treatment, so check whether it is covered by your medical insurance. Dentists *(dentista)* are listed in the yellow pages.

SUN ADVICE
The sun is strong during summer, particularly in the south. Dress sensibly, avoid prolonged exposure and protect yourself with a sunscreen.

DRUGS
Prescription medicines are available from pharmacies *(farmacias)*, designated by a red or green cross. Information about the nearest late-night or 24-hour facility is posted at all pharmacies.

SAFE WATER
Tap water is generally safe, although it can be heavily chlorinated. Mineral water *(agua mineral)* is inexpensive and is sold *con gas* (carbonated) and *sin gas* (noncarbonated). Drink plenty of water during hot weather.

RESTROOMS

Public restrooms *(servicios)* can usually be found in large department stores, museums and other places of interest to visitors. Elsewhere, restrooms may not be easy to find, but there is no charge. If you use the facilities in a bar you will be expected to buy a drink. Spanish words are *señores* for men and *señoras* for women.

ELECTRICITY

Most of Spain has a 220-volt power supply, but in some rural areas the supply is 110 or 125 volts. Electrical sockets take plugs with two round pins; American appliances will need a plug adapter, and either a dual voltage facility or a transformer.

NATIONAL TRANSPORTATION

TRAIN *(tren)*
The Red Nacional de los Ferrocarriles Españoles (RENFE) rail network is inexpensive to use. There are express services for long-distance travel: Alaris, Talgo 200 and AVE (reservations required/advisable for all three). Information and reservations: ☎ 902 24 02 02 (24 hours).

BUS *(autobus)*
Spain has a good bus system, and the Spanish Tourist Board publishes a guide to domestic services. Ask at a tourist office for details. The Eurolines international bus service operates in Spain: ☎ 91 506 3360.

FERRY *(transbordador)*
Barcelona is the Mediterranean's biggest port and offers regular ferry service to the Balearic islands. One of the largest ferry operators is Trasmediterránea. ☎ 902 45 46 45. "Mini-cruises" of two or three days operate from northern Spain to and from Britain; obtain details from a travel agent.

DRIVING

 DRIVE ON THE RIGHT

SPEED LIMITS
Police can impose on-the-spot fines.

Limited-access highways *(autopistas)*
120 k.p.h. (75 m.p.h.)
Divided highways
100 k.p.h. (62 m.p.h.)

Main roads
90 k.p.h. (56 m.p.h.)

Urban areas
40 k.p.h. (25 m.p.h.)

SEAT BELTS
Must be worn in front and back seats at all times.

BLOOD ALCOHOL
The legal blood alcohol limit is 0.05%. Random breath tests on drivers are carried out frequently, especially late at night, and the penalties for offenders are severe.

FIRE SERVICE 080
(Bomberos)

 AMBULANCE 061
(Ambulancia)

529

Spain – Essential Information

DRIVING continued

TOLLS
A toll *(autopista de peaje)* is levied on limited-access highways. Take a ticket when you enter and pay when exiting.

CAR RENTAL
The leading rental firms have offices at airports and train stations. Hertz offers discounted rates for AAA members (see page 15). For reservations:

	UNITED STATES	SPAIN
Alamo	(800) 327-9633	91 323 7232
Avis	(800) 331-2112	902 13 55 31
Budget	(800) 527-0700	902 18 08 54
Hertz	(800) 654-3080	902 402 405

FUEL
Gas *(gasolina)* and diesel are sold in liters. Many gas stations *(gasolineras)* in towns and cities and on highways are open 24 hours.

AAA AFFILIATED MOTORING CLUB
Real Automóvil Club de España (RACE)
Parque Tecnológico de Madrid
☎ 91 594 7275 or 91 594 9347, fax 91 594 7276
If you break down while driving, phone ☎ 91 594 9347 or 902 30 05 05 (RACE breakdown service). Not all automobile clubs offer full services to AAA members.

BREAKDOWNS AND ACCIDENTS
There are 24-hour emergency phones at regular intervals on highways. If you are involved in an accident, phone ☎ 091 for police.
Most car rental firms provide their own free rescue service; if your car is rented, follow the instructions given in the documentation. Use of a car repair service other than those authorized by your rental company may violate your agreement.

OTHER INFORMATION
The minimum age for driving a car is 18 (may be higher for some car rental firms).
An International Driving Permit (IDP) is recommended; some rental firms require them, and they can speed up formalities if you are involved in an accident.

A Green Card (international motor insurance certificate) is recommended if you are driving a private car. See page 15 for more information. The police may impound your car if you fail to produce a Green Card after an accident.

It is advisable to obtain a bail bond from your automobile insurer. This will facilitate your release if you commit a traffic offense or are involved in an accident. A bail bond is usually included when you rent a car in Spain; if you rent a car in another country and intend to drive to Spain, advise your rental company.

USEFUL WORDS AND PHRASES

Castilian is the main language in Spain, with three important regional languages: Catalan, spoken in Catalonia and Valencia; Basque, the official language of the Basque north; and Galician, spoken in the northwest.

Catalan is closely related to Occitan (or Provençal), and Galician has noticeable links with Portuguese. The Basque tongue is unique, having no connection with any language in Europe.

The following words and phrases are in Castilian:

Do you speak English?	*¿Habla usted inglés?*
excuse me	*perdone*
hello	*hola*
goodbye	*adiós*
yes/no	*si/no*
how much?	*¿cuánto?*
I would like	*me gustaría*
I don't understand	*no entiendo*
no smoking	*no fumadores*
okay	*vale*
open/closed	*abierto/cerrado*
today/tomorrow	*hoy/mañana*
here/there	*aquí/allí*
more/less	*más/menos*
please	*por favor*
thank you	*gracias*
you're welcome	*de nada*
how/what	*cómo/qué*
left/right	*izquierda/derecha*
What time is it?	*¿Qué hora es?*
travel ticket	*el billete*
one way/return	*ida/ida y vuelta*
where is…?	*¿donde está…?*
the hotel	***el hotel***
breakfast	*desayuno*
lunch	*la comida*
dinner	*la cena*
I have a reservation	*Tengo una reserva*
key	*llave*
room	*habitación*
shower	*ducha*
the restaurant	***restaurante***
beef	*la carne de vaca*
bread	*el pan*
cheese	*queso*
chicken	*el pollo*
coffee	*el café*
dish of the day	*el plato del día*
dessert	*el postre*
fish	*el pescado*
pork	*la carne de cerdo*
starter	*primer plato*
wine, red/white	*el vino tinto/blanco*
the check	*la cuenta*

Sweden – Essential Information

PRE-TRIP ESSENTIALS...

WHAT YOU NEED

ESSENTIAL FOR TRAVELERS

● Required ● Recommended ● Not required

Passport	●
Visa	●
Travel, medical insurance	●
Round-trip or onward airline ticket	●
Local currency	●
Traveler's checks	●
Credit cards	●
First-aid kit and medicines	●
Inoculations	●

ESSENTIAL FOR DRIVERS*

Driver's license	●
International Driving Permit	●
Car insurance (for nonrental cars)	●
Car registration (for nonrental cars)	●

*see also DRIVING section

IMPORTANT ADDRESSES

Swedish Travel & Tourism Council
PO Box 4649, Grand Central Station
New York, NY 10163-4649
☎ (212) 885-9700
Fax (212) 885-9710
www.visit-sweden.com
(not open to personal callers)

**Sveriges Rese- och Turistråd
(Swedish Travel & Tourism Council)**
P.O.Box 3030, Kungsgatan 36
SE-103 61 Stockholm, Sweden
☎ 08 789 10 00
Fax 08 789 10 31
www.visit-sweden.com

American Embassy
Dag Hammarskjölds väg 31
SE-112 89 Stockholm, Sweden
☎ 08 783 53 00
Fax 08 661 1964 (general) or
08 660 58 79 (consular)
http://www.stockholm.usembassy.gov

COUNTRY ESSENTIALS...

CUSTOMS

YES
Duty-free limits on goods brought in from non-European Union countries:
200 cigarettes or 100 cigarillos or 50 cigars or 250 g. tobacco; 1 L alcohol over 22% volume or 2 L. alcohol under 22% volume; 2 L. wine; 32 L. beer; 60 ml. perfume; 250 ml. toilet water; plus any other duty-free goods (including gifts) to the value of 1,000SKr. There are no currency regulations. Allowances for the importation of tax-paid goods purchased within the European Union are: 400 cigarettes or 200 cigarillos or 100 cigars or 550g. tobacco; 5L. alcohol over 22% volume or 6L. alcohol 15–22% volume or 52L. alcohol under 15% volume; 64L. beer.

NO
No unlicensed drugs, weapons, ammunition, obscene material, pets or other animals, counterfeit money or copied goods, meat or poultry.
For customs limits for returning U.S. citizens see page 16.

MONEY

Sweden's currency is the krona (SEK, SKr or Kr; plural kronor), which is divided into 100 öre. The denominations of krona bills are 20, 50, 100, 500, 1,000 and 10,000. There are coins of 50 öre, and 1, 5 and 10SKr. Exchange dollars and traveler's checks *(resechecker)* at a bank or an exchange office. "Forex" exchange offices have distinctive yellow signs and offer favorable exchange rates. Although a member of the European Union, Sweden chose not to adopt the euro as its official currency on Jan. 1, 1999. However, it is possible for tourists coming from the euro zone to pay with a euro credit card.
Exchange rate at press time: $1 = 7.5SKr

TIPS AND GRATUITIES

Tips are welcomed but not expected or obligatory. In restaurants it is usual to round off the check to the nearest 10SKr; service is usually included.

Restaurants, cafés/bars (service is included)	change
Taxis	10%
Hairdressers, chambermaids	none
Porters, restroom attendants	change
Cloakroom attendants	5SKr

COMMUNICATIONS

POST OFFICES

Buy stamps *(frimarken)* at a post office *(postkontoret)*, supermarket, newsstand *(nyhetsbyra)*, stationer *(handel)*

or kiosk displaying a blue-and-yellow post sign. Hours for out-of-town post offices may vary.

TELEPHONES

You can use cash, credit cards and phone cards to make a phone call in Sweden. A public phone *(telefon)* takes 1SKr or 5SKr coins. Phone cards can be bought from newsstands, stores, hotels or magazine kiosks *(Pressbyrån)*. Credit card phones are indicated by a "CCC" or "Tele2" sign. Operators speak English. You can make a half-price call from a Turist Telefon (only found in cities) from mid-June to mid-August; these

phones are clearly marked.

Phoning inside Sweden
All Swedish numbers in this book include an area code; dial the number that is listed. To call the operator dial 90130.

Phoning Sweden from abroad
The country code for Sweden is 46. Note that Swedish numbers in this book do not include the Swedish country code; you will need to prefix this number if you are phoning from another country. To phone Sweden from the United States or Canada, omit the first zero from the Swedish number and add the prefix 011 46.
Example: 01 122 33 44 becomes 011 46 1 122 33 44.

Phoning from Sweden
To phone the United States or Canada from Sweden, prefix the area code and number with 00 1.
Example: (111) 222-3333 becomes 00 1 111 222-3333.

To call international information dial 07977.

EMERGENCY TELEPHONE NUMBERS

Police *(polis)*	112
Fire *(brandkår)*	112
Ambulance *(ambulans)*	112

Emergency calls are free from phone booths.

HOURS OF OPERATION

● Stores Mon.–Fri.	● Museums/monuments
● Offices Mon.–Fri.	● Pharmacies Mon.–Fri.
● Banks Mon.–Fri.	
● Post offices Mon.–Fri.	

7 8 9 10 11 12 1 2 3 4 5 6 7

In large towns, department stores stay open until 8 or 10 p.m., and some also are open Sunday 10–4. Stores often close on Saturday afternoon between 1 and 4 p.m., and usually close early the day before a public holiday. Some smaller stores may close for lunch.

Banks also are open on Thursday between 4 and 5:30 and in some cities until 5:30 or 6 Mon.–Fri. All banks are closed on weekends.

Post offices may stay open later in main cities. They also are open Sat. 10–1. The post office at Centralstationen (Central Station) in Stockholm is open Mon.–Fri. 7 a.m.–10 p.m., Sat.–Sun. 10–7. Some museums close on Monday and stay open late one or two nights a week.

Some pharmacies *(apotek)* in major cities are open 24 hours.

NATIONAL HOLIDAYS

Banks, businesses and most stores close on these days; they may also be closed or close earlier the day before a holiday.

Jan. 1	New Year's Day
Jan. 6	Epiphany
Mar./Apr.	Good Friday
Mar./Apr.	Easter Monday
May 1	Labor Day
May	Ascension Day
May/Jun.	Pentecost Monday
Jun. (Sat. nearest Jun. 21)	Midsummer's Day
Nov. 1	All Saints' Day
Dec. 25	Christmas Day
Dec. 26	St. Stephen's Day

PHOTOGRAPHY

Pack film for poor light at certain times in the winter. With the right equipment, photographs of the Northern Lights *(Aurora Borealis)* are possible. Check before taking photographs in museums; it may be forbidden or you may have to ask permission. Film and camera batteries are readily available from tourist stores. Rapid-developing services also are widely available.

Sweden – Essential Information

HEALTH

MEDICAL INSURANCE
Private medical insurance is recommended. There are no general practitioners; go straight to a hospital clinic *(akutmottagning* or *vårdcentral)*, taking your passport with you. You will be charged for treatment (free for under16). For information contact Stockholm Care, ☎ 08 672 24 00.

DENTAL SERVICES
Dentists *(tandläkeren)* always charge for treatment. Emergency treatment is available after hours in major cities. Clinics are indicated by *"Tandläkare"* or *"Folktandvård"* signs.

SUN ADVICE
The Gulf Stream dictates Sweden's temperate climate of warm sunshine during July and August. Although the sun is not fierce, good sun protection is necessary. Take precautions near the water.

DRUGS
Prescription and nonprescription drugs and medicines are available from a pharmacy *(apotek)*. If you need a pharmacy outside regular hours, information about the nearest all-night facility is posted at all pharmacies. A 24-hour service is available in most cities.

SAFE WATER
Tap water is safe to drink, and mineral water *(mineralvatten)* is widely available.

RESTROOMS

Public restrooms *(toalett)* are easy to find. There is a charge of around 5SKr to use some restrooms. Separate facilities for men *(Herrar)* and women *(Damer)* are always clean and modern.

ELECTRICITY

Sweden has a 220-volt power supply. Electrical sockets take plugs with two round pins; American appliances will need a plug adapter and will require a transformer if they do not have a dual-voltage facility.

NATIONAL TRANSPORTATION

TRAIN *(tåg)*
The Swedish State Railways (Statens Järnvägar or SJ), ☎ 0771 75 75 75, runs an efficient and extensive system, extending above the Arctic Circle. On some trains reservations are necessary. Obtain tickets from travel agents or Sweden Booking, ☎ 0498 20 33 80. Timetables are available from any station *(järnvägsstation)*.

BUS *(buss)*
Swedish bus travel is inexpensive. Express services run between 300 towns and cities and into Norway, Finland and Denmark. The domestic service runs to northern Sweden. The largest bus operator is Swebus Express. For long-distance bus service information, ☎ 0200 218 218. International Euroline buses operate in Sweden, ☎ 031 10 02 40.

FERRY *(farja)*
There are ferry services in Sweden, and you can get various island-hopping boat passes or coupons. Most depart from Stockholm. Passes are available from Waxholmsbolaget, on Stromkajen in Stockholm; ☎ 08 679 58 30.

DRIVING

DRIVE ON THE RIGHT

SPEED LIMITS
Police can impose on-the-spot fines, but cannot collect them.

Limited-access highways
110 k.p.h. (68 m.p.h.)
Divided highways
90 k.p.h. (55 m.p.h.)

Main roads
70 k.p.h. (43 m.p.h.)

Urban areas
50 k.p.h. (31 m.p.h.)

SEAT BELTS
Must be worn in front and rear seats at all times.

BLOOD ALCOHOL
The legal blood alcohol limit is 0.02% so alcohol should be avoided completely. Random breath tests on drivers are carried out frequently, especially late at night, and the penalties for offenders are severe.

Sweden – Essential Information

DRIVING continued

TOLLS
There are no highway tolls in Sweden except when crossing the Öresund tunnel and bridge.

CAR RENTAL
The leading rental firms have offices at airports and train stations. Hertz offers discounted rates for AAA members (see page 15). For reservations:

	UNITED STATES	SWEDEN
Alamo	(800) 462-5266	084 62 48 48 (Europcar, toll-free)
Avis	(800) 230-4898	020 78 82 00 (toll-free)
Budget	(800) 527-0700	020 78 77 87 (toll-free)
Hertz	(800) 654-3080	020 21 12 11 (toll-free)

FUEL
Gas *(bensin)* is sold in liters. Major credit cards are usually accepted. Self-service *(tanka själv)* stations require 20SKr, 50Skr or 100SKr bills in their automated machines *(sedel automat)*; service not available for diesel. Many gas stations on highways and in main towns are open 24 hours.

AAA AFFILIATED MOTORING CLUB
Motormännens Riksförbund (M)
Sveavägen 159, Stockholm
☎ 08 690 38 00, fax 08 690 38 24
Not all automobile clubs offer full services to AAA members.

BREAKDOWNS AND ACCIDENTS
There are 24-hour emergency phones at regular intervals on highways. If you are involved in an accident, phone ☎ 112 for police.
If you break down while driving, contact the Larmtjänst service: ☎ 020 91 00 40 (toll-free). Most car rental firms provide their own free rescue service; if your car is rented, follow the instructions given in the documentation. Use of a car repair service other than those authorized by your rental company may violate your agreement.

OTHER INFORMATION
The minimum age for driving a car is 18 (may be higher for some car rental firms).

An International Driving Permit (IDP) is recommended; some rental firms require them, and they can speed up formalities if you are involved in an accident.
A Green Card (international motor insurance certificate) is recommended if you are driving a private car; see page 15 for more information.

Dimmed headlights must be turned on year-round, even during daylight hours. Be aware of moose, roe deer and reindeer appearing on road surfaces, especially at dawn or dusk.

USEFUL WORDS & PHRASES

Swedes are not used to foreigners speaking their language, although efforts to speak Swedish are appreciated; most Swedes also speak English. German, Danish and Norwegian are often understood.

In Swedish, a vowel sound is usually long when it is the final syllable, and verbs are the same regardless of person. Definite articles are determined by the ending of the noun: -en and -et for singular nouns and -na or -n for plural. There are an additional three letters in the Swedish alphabet - å, ä and ö - which always appear at the end in alphabetical lists.

There are two words for "you": *du* and *ni. Ni* is the polite form, *du* is the familiar form. Unlike some other European countries, it is not necessarily impolite to address a complete stranger with the familiar form. In fact, many Swedes consider the polite form to be old-fashioned.

Do you speak English?	*Talar ni Engelska?*
excuse me	*ursäkta mig*
hello	*hej*
goodbye	*adjö/hej då*
yes/no	*ja/nej*
how much is it?	*hur mycket kostar den?*
I am American	*Jag är från U.S.A.*
I'd like	*Jag skulle vilja ha*
I don't understand	*Jag förstår inte*
non-smoking	*rökning förbjuden*
open	*öppen/öppet*
closed	*stängt*
please	*snälla, vänligen*
thank you	*tack*
(one-way) ticket	*en enkelbiljett*
What is your name?	*Vad heter du?*

the hotel	**hotell**
breakfast	*frukost*
lunch	*lunch*
dinner	*middag*
key	*nyckel*
room	*rum*
shower	*dusch*

the restaurant	**restaurang**
bread	*bröd*
coffee/tea	*kaffe/te*
beef	*nötkött, oxkött*
chicken	*kyckling*
fish	*fisk*
lamb	*lammkött*
pork	*fläsk*
poultry	*fågel*
beer	*öl*
wine	*vin*
dessert	*efterrätt*
ice cream	*glass*
please bring the check	*notan tack*

PRE-TRIP ESSENTIALS...

WHAT YOU NEED

ESSENTIAL FOR TRAVELERS

● Required   ● Recommended   ● Not required

Passport	●
Visa (check regulations before you travel)	●
Travel, medical insurance	●
Round-trip or onward airline ticket	●
Local currency	●
Traveler's checks	●
Credit cards	●
First-aid kit and medicines	●
Inoculations	●

ESSENTIAL FOR DRIVERS*

Driver's license	●
International Driving Permit	●
Car insurance (for nonrental cars)	●
Car registration (for nonrental cars)	●

*see also DRIVING section

IMPORTANT ADDRESSES

Switzerland Tourism
Swiss Center, 608 Fifth Avenue
New York, NY 10020
☎ (877) 794-8037 (toll free), 011800 100 200 30
(international toll free), 1 (877) 794 8037 (U.S.)
Fax (212) 262-6116
www.myswitzerland.com

Schweiz Tourismus (Switzerland Tourism)
Postfach 695
8027 Zürich, Switzerland
☎ 00800 100 200 30
Fax 00800 100 200 31
www.switzerlandtourism.com

American Embassy
Jubiläumsstrasse 93
CH-3005 Bern, Switzerland
☎ 031 357 7011
Fax 031 357 7344
Open Mon.–Fri. 9–12:30 and 1:30–5:30

COUNTRY ESSENTIALS...

CUSTOMS

YES
Duty-free limits on goods brought in from non-European countries:
400 cigarettes or 100 cigarillos or cigars or 500 g. tobacco; 2 L. alcohol under 15% volume or 1 L. alcohol over 15% volume; plus any other duty-free goods (including gifts) to the value of SF100. These limits apply to visitors aged 17 and over. There are no currency regulations. There is no limit on the importation of tax-paid goods purchased within the European Union if they are for personal use.

NO
No unlicensed drugs, weapons, ammunition, obscene material, pets or other animals, counterfeit money or copied goods, meat or poultry.

For customs limits for returning U.S. citizens see page 16.

MONEY

Switzerland's currency is the Swiss franc (SF), which is divided into 100 centimes or "Rappen." The denominations of franc bills are 10, 20, 50, 100, 200, 500 and 1,000. There are coins of 5, 10, 20 and 50 centimes and 1, 2 and 5SF. Exchange dollars or traveler's checks *(Reiseschecks)* at a bank *(Bank)*, exchange office *(Wechselbüro)*, post office *(Postamt)* or hotel. Swiss Bankers traveler's checks (in Swiss francs) can be obtained from various overseas branches of most Swiss banks as well as branches of American Express, and are accepted in Switzerland at their face value and without a commission fee. Exchange rate at press time: $1 = 1.25SF

TIPS AND GRATUITIES

Tips are welcomed but not expected, as a service charge is always included. A small tip is accepted for exceptional service.

Restaurants, cafés/bars (service included)	change
Taxis (usually includes service)	change
Porters, chambermaids	change
Hairdressers	change
Restroom/cloakroom attendants	change

TIME ZONES	ZÜRICH 12:00 noon	NEW YORK 6 hours behind Switzerland	CHICAGO 7 hours behind Switzerland	DENVER 8 hours behind Switzerland	SAN FRANCISCO 9 hours behind Switzerland	535

Switzerland – Essential Information

COMMUNICATIONS

POST OFFICES

Buy stamps *(Briefmarken)* at a post office *(Postamt)*, newsstand *(Informationsstand)* or from a hotel.

Hours for out-of-town post offices may vary.

TELEPHONES

You can use cash or a prepaid phone card *(Kartentelefon)* to make a call in Switzerland. Most telephones have direct dialing for international calls; if you need to go through an operator dial 114. A Taxcard (phone card) can be bought from newsstands, gas stations, railroad stations and post offices for 5, 10 and 20SF. Check that the phone booth is equipped with a Taxcard reader. You can also make a call with 1 and 5SF coins.

Phoning inside Switzerland
All Swiss telephone numbers in this book include an area code; dial the number that is listed. To call national information dial 111.

Phoning Switzerland from abroad
The country code for Switzerland is 41. Note that Swiss numbers in this book do not include the country code; you will need to prefix this number if you are phoning from another country. To phone Switzerland from the United States or Canada, omit the first zero from the Swiss number and add the prefix 011 41. (Note that Swiss area codes are either one or two digits.) Example: 01 122 33 44 becomes 011 41 1 122 33 44.

Phoning from Switzerland
To phone the United States or Canada from Switzerland, prefix the area code and number with 00 1.
Example: (111) 222-3333 becomes 00 1 111 222-3333.
To call the international operator dial 114.
To call international information dial 1159.

EMERGENCY PHONE NUMBERS

Police *(Polizei)*	117
Fire *(Feuerwehr)*	118
Ambulance *(Krankenwagen)*	117 or 144

Emergency calls are free from phone booths.

HOURS OF OPERATION

- Stores Mon.–Sat.
- Offices Mon.–Fri.
- Banks Mon.–Fri.
- Post offices Mon.–Fri.
- Museums/monuments
- Pharmacies Mon.–Sat.

7 8 9 10 11 12 1 2 3 4 5 6 7

Stores close on Saturday afternoon at 4 or 5. In large towns stores may close on Monday morning, while out-of-town stores often close on a Wednesday or Thursday afternoon; some also may close for lunch (noon–1:30).

The hours of operation for banks are varied and complicated depending on the town; inquire at your hotel or a tourist office.

Post offices close at 11 on Saturday morning except for some major offices in cities, which close later; small offices have briefer hours of operation.

Museums often close on Monday and hours vary, so check locally.

NATIONAL HOLIDAYS

Banks, businesses and most stores close on these days. Various cantons observe other national holidays such as Jan. 2, May 1, Corpus Christi and All Saints' Day.

Jan. 1	New Year
Mar./Apr.	Good Friday
Mar./Apr.	Easter Monday
May	Ascension Day
May/Jun.	Pentecost Monday
Aug. 1	National Day
Dec. 25	Christmas Day
Dec. 26	St. Stephen's Day

PHOTOGRAPHY

Check first before taking photographs in churches and museums; it may be forbidden or you may have to ask for permission. Film and camera batteries are readily available around tourist areas, but prices may be high. Photography is prohibited in some military areas, which includes some public footpaths, parks and forest areas. It is quite common to come across the Swiss army when you are walking, hiking or mountain biking. Some footpaths are closed during maneuvers, and temporary barriers set up by the army should be observed at all times.

Switzerland – Essential Information

HEALTH

 MEDICAL INSURANCE
Private medical insurance is recommended. U.S. and Canadian visitors will have to pay for all medical treatment, including emergency assistance, consultation or admittance to a hospital *(Krankenhaus)*. If you are planning to take part in winter sports, special sports policies are widely available. For information on medical issues dial Anglo-Phone, 157 5014 (toll call), from anywhere in Switzerland.

 DENTAL SERVICES
A dentist *(zahnarzt)* will charge for any treatment; dental work is expensive, so check whether it is covered by your medical insurance. Dentists are listed in the telephone directory. You also can ask for English-speaking dentists at your embassy or hotel, or at a tourist office.

 SUN ADVICE
Conditions vary considerably; no country in Europe combines within so small an area such marked climatic contrasts. The sun can be deceptively strong in the mountains; protection is essential. The warmest part of Switzerland is south of the Alps, which is under the influence of the Mediterranean. Sun protection is needed; it is advisable to wear a hat and apply a sunscreen.

 DRUGS
Pharmacies sell a range of medicines and drugs and dispense prescriptions. Many pharmacists speak English. At least one pharmacy in every town stays open late; information is displayed on store doors.

 SAFE WATER
Tap water is safe to drink throughout Switzerland. Mineral water *(sprudelwasser)* is widely available.

RESTROOMS

 Most toilets *(Toiletten)* are clean and well maintained. They are indicated by a variety of signs, such as "WC" or Toiletten. Women's restrooms are designated *Damen, Frauen, Femmes, Dames, Signore* or *Donne;* men's as *Herren, Männer, Hommes, Messieurs, Signori* or *Uomini.*

ELECTRICITY

 Switzerland has a 220-volt power supply. Electrical sockets take plugs with two round pins; American appliances will need a plug adapter and will require a transformer if they do not have a dual-voltage facility.

NATIONAL TRANSPORTATION

 TRAIN *(Zug)*
Swiss Federal Railways is Chemins de Fer Fédéreaux (CFF) in French, Schweizerische Bundesbahnen (SBB) in German, and Ferrovie Federali Svizzere (FFS) in Italian. It runs a fast, clean and efficient service. Express trains only stop at major cities. Regionalzuge are slow trains usually running the same routes. To reach an English-speaking operator, ☎ 0900 300300 (toll call). There are various good-value rail passes available. Inquire at tourist offices or any large railroad station.

 BUS *(Bus)*
The bus service takes passengers to mountainous regions where railroads are unable to go. Mail bus routes encounter magnificent scenery joining villages and towns, occasionally even delivering the mail. There are many special offers; passes and cards that combine train, bus and boat travel are available at reduced rates. Eurolines operates in Switzerland; ☎ 0900 573747 (toll call).

 FERRY *(Fähre)*
There are many excursions on Switzerland's lakes. Regional tourist offices in different cantons can offer information, and some take reservations.

DRIVING

 DRIVE ON THE RIGHT

SPEED LIMITS
Police can impose on-the-spot fines, for which a receipt is issued.

 Limited-access highways *(Autobahn)*
120 k.p.h. (74 m.p.h.)
Divided highways
100 k.p.h. (62 m.p.h.)

 Main roads
80 k.p.h. (49 m.p.h.)

 Urban areas
50 k.p.h. (31 m.p.h.) or 30 k.p.h. (18 m.p.h.)

 SEAT BELTS
Must be worn in front and back seats at all times. Children under 7 are not allowed in a front seat.

BLOOD ALCOHOL
The legal blood alcohol limit is 0.08%. Random breath tests on drivers are carried out frequently, especially late at night, and the penalties for offenders are severe.

Switzerland – Essential Information

DRIVING continued

TOLLS
An annual road tax of SF40 is levied on all cars and motorcycles using Swiss highways. Permits *(Vignettes)* are available at border crossings, post offices and service areas in Switzerland and are valid for multiple re-entry into Switzerland within the duration of the license period. To avoid delay at the border it is advisable to buy the permit in advance from a Swiss tourist office.

CAR RENTAL
The leading rental firms have offices at airports and train stations. Hertz offers discounted rates for AAA members (see page 15). For reservations:

	UNITED STATES	SWITZERLAND
Alamo	(800) 327-9633	022 717 8430
Avis	(800) 331-1212	08700 100 287
Hertz	(800) 654-3080	0848 822 020

FUEL
Gas and diesel are sold in liters. There are 24-hour gas stations on highways and in cities; many have refreshment facilities and stores. Credit cards are accepted for payment.

AAA AFFILIATED MOTORING CLUB
Touring Club Suisse (TCS)
Chemin de Blandonnet 4, CH-1214 Vernier/Geneva, Switzerland
☎ 022 417 2727, fax 022 417 2020
If you break down while driving ☎ 140 (TCS breakdown service). Not all automobile clubs offer full services to AAA members.

BREAKDOWNS AND ACCIDENTS
There are 24-hour emergency phones at regular intervals on highways. If you are involved in an accident ☎ 117 for police. Most car rental firms provide their own free rescue service; if your car is rented, follow the instructions given in the documentation. Use of a car repair service other than those authorized by your rental company may violate your agreement.

OTHER INFORMATION
The minimum age for driving a car is 18 (may be higher for some car rental firms). An International Driving Permit (IDP) is recommended; some rental firms require them, and they can speed up formalities if you are involved in an accident. A Green Card (international motor insurance certificate) is recommended if you are driving a private car; see page 15 for more information. Dimmed headlights must be used when passing through tunnels. Yellow mail buses have priority at all times, as do vehicles ascending mountain roads. Many mountain pass roads are closed from October through June. For road conditions ☎ 163. For general information ☎ 111.

USEFUL WORDS AND PHRASES

There are four official languages spoken in Switzerland: German, French, Italian and Romansch. About 18% of the population in southwest Switzerland speak French. South of the Alps, Italian (12%) is predominant throughout Ticino and parts of the Grisons (also known as the Graubunden). Most Swiss (65%) speak German. A Swiss-German dialect with a variety of local variations is used in everyday conversation; traditional German is used for business purposes.

The fourth language is Romansch, an ancient hybrid of Celtic and Latin tongues spoken by about 40,000 people in the Surselva region of southeastern Switzerland.

This coexistence of distinct languages results in a true "European" nation. The Romansch area is probably the most "Swiss" part of the country. French influence is evident in Lausanne, while Lugano exhibits both Italian and Swiss influences.

Every Swiss child learns two or three languages. English is spoken throughout the country, but an attempt to say a few words in any of Switzerland's languages will always be appreciated.

See page 489 for French words, page 493 for German and page 509 for Italian.

The hotels and restaurants in this book were selected by on-site contributing authors and include establishments in several price ranges. Since price is often the best indication of the level of facilities and quality of service guests can expect, a three-tiered price guide appears at the beginning of the listings for each featured city. Keep in mind, however, that prices vary widely depending on the country; dinner in Helsinki, for example, can cost much more than a similar dinner in Athens or Prague. Because variable rates will affect the amount of foreign currency that can be exchanged for dollars (and thus affect the cost of a room or a meal), price ranges are given in the local currency.

Although price ranges and any given days/times restaurants are closed were accurate at press time, this information is always subject to change without notice. If there is a certain establishment in which you're interested, it is always advisable to call ahead and verify specific amenities or hours of operation. The larger and more expensive hotels, and the better-known restaurants, are more likely to have someone who speaks English on staff; smaller establishments, particularly in southern Europe, may not. In such cases it may be more productive to inquire by fax rather than phone.

Map coordinates given in each listing relate to the city maps and give an idea of the approximate area in which each establishment is located. Although you may be able to find some of the street locations on these maps, pick up a more detailed city map from the local tourist office to help you find places.

Facilities suitable for travelers with disabilities vary greatly, and you are strongly advised to contact an establishment directly to determine whether it will be able to meet your needs. Buildings in the old sections of city centers may not be adequately designed or equipped for visitors with limited or impaired mobility.

Accommodations

Accommodations have been selected with two considerations in mind: a particularly attractive character or sense of local flavor, or a central location that is convenient for sightseeing. Establishments in different price ranges are included for each city.

Centrally located hotels fill up quickly, especially during busy summer vacation periods; make reservations well in advance. Many international hotel chains have Internet sites that either

HOTELS AND RESTAURANTS

"NOTHING helps scenery like ham and eggs."

From *A Tramp Abroad*,
by Mark Twain

allow you to make online reservations or provide a central reservation phone number. In-room bathrooms (usually referred to as "en-suite facilities") may not be available in smaller budget hotels.

European hotels normally provide a light breakfast of rolls or croissants and coffee (where this is not the case, the listing description notes that the rate is for "room only"). Breakfast in British and Irish hotels, however, is likely to be a full meal of bacon, sausage, eggs, fried potatoes and toast that should leave you feeling well-fed most of the day.

Some hotels offer a price for overnight accommodations that includes an evening meal (known as "half-board" in Great Britain and Ireland and *demi-pension* in French-speaking countries).

Eating Out

Listed restaurants range from upscale places suitable for an elegant evening out to small cafés where you can stop and take a leisurely break from a busy day of sightseeing. Some are close to attractions; where this is the case, there is a cross-reference under the attraction listing. Other possibilities for getting a bite to eat are the cafeterias and restaurants on the premises of museums and galleries.

For the homesick, many U.S. fast-food chains have found their way to Europe. But be sure to sample the amazing variety of indigenous European fast food: *crêpes* (filled pancakes) in France; tasty hot *Wurst* (sausages) in Germany and Austria; fish and chips (fish fillets and french fries) in Britain; the savory *tapas* appetizers served in Spanish bars; and the wonderful pizzas in Italy – served crusty and piping hot from charcoal ovens or *al taglio* (sliced to go) on street corners.

For a more civilized break, many European hotels, especially the larger ones in big cities, are not only options for an overnight stay but also for a meal. Their lounges and bars often are comfortable, quiet places to stop and relax over morning coffee, afternoon tea with cakes and sandwiches, or an evening drink. A stop also provides an opportunity to use the hotel's restroom. Top-flight hotels often serve fairly reasonably priced snacks, but inquire about prices before ordering if you're traveling on a budget.

Alcoholic beverages have a rich European heritage. France, Germany and Spain produce memorable wines; beers in the Czech Republic, Belgium and Britain are justly famed; and Guinness, of course, is an Irish institution. And the nonalcoholic fruit juices (*portokalada freska*) served in Greece – orange, lemon, watermelon, peach – are wonderfully fresh and a perfect antidote to the hot Greek summer sun.

Austria

KEY TO SYMBOLS

- ✚ map page number and coordinates
- ✉ address
- ☎ telephone number
- ⊙ days/times closed
- Ⓢ nearest subway station
- 🚍 nearest bus/trolley bus/tram/funicular route
- ⛴ ferry
- $$$ expensive
- $$ moderate
- $ inexpensive
- AX American Express
- DC Diners Club
- MC MasterCard
- VI VISA

Eating in Innsbruck

Most of Innsbruck's best – and most expensive – restaurants are located in a tiny area of Old Town, along with some excellent cafés and coffeehouses. Many serve meals all day, so you can eat when you feel like it, a bonus if you've been skiing or hiking. Maria-Theresien-Strasse has a number of self-service and fast-food restaurants if you're looking for a quick lunchtime snack. For lunch with a view, take the Hungerburgbahn to Hoch-Innsbruck, where there are several restaurants with pretty terraces, or ride the cable car up to Seegrube mountain and eat on the terrace while enjoying a superb mountain panorama. The daily market, held in the Markthalle building beside the river, is an excellent place to buy provisions for a picnic.

VIENNA HOTELS

Price guide: (double room with breakfast for two people)
$ €50–€70
$$ €70–€150
$$$ over €150

ANA Grand Hotel Wien $$$

This is the ultimate in luxury, combining the style and service of a majestic old European hotel with modern comforts. Ask about the Grand Opera package, which includes a champagne buffet break-fast, the best seats at the opera (book 2 weeks in advance) and a two-course menu afterward in the hotel's restaurant, Le Ciel.
✚ 26 D2　✉ Kärntner Ring 9
☎ 01 51 58 00; fax 01 51 51 313
🚍 Tram 1, 2, D, J　AX, DC, MC, VI

Kärntnerhof $$

The Kärntnerhof, situated in the city center, is convenient for sight-seeing. It occupies a 19th-century building with a roof garden and sits quietly on a cul-de-sac, where a gate leads to the beautiful courtyard of Heiligenkreuzerhof.
✚ 26 D3　✉ Grashofgasse 4
☎ 01 51 21 923; fax 01 51 32 22 833
Ⓢ Stephansplatz, Schwedenplatz
AX, DC, MC, VI

König von Ungarn $$$

A hotel since 1815, this building has rooms set around a covered central courtyard, which has been converted into an elegant bar/sitting room. The restaurant serves traditional Viennese meals in the vaulted dining rooms. It's very close to St. Stephen's Cathedral and next to the Figarohaus (Figaro House), so named because Mozart composed his opera *The Marriage of Figaro* while living in an apartment there.
✚ 27 D2　✉ Schulerstrasse 10
☎ 01 51 58 40; fax 01 51 58 40
Ⓢ Stephansplatz　🚍 1A
AX, DC, MC, VI

Pension Felicitas $

Hidden away on a quiet side street in Josefstadt, just behind the parlia-ment building, this accommodation is for those who like a personal hotel touch: it feels a little as if you're staying in somebody's home, perfect after a day's sightseeing.
✚ 27 C3　✉ Josefsgasse 7
☎ 01 40 57 21 20　Ⓢ Rathaus
No credit cards

Römischer Kaiser $$–$$$

Originally a small baroque palace in the Old City, this is now an exotically furnished hotel with crimson fabrics and sparkling chandeliers. A generous buffet breakfast is served. The hotel makes special arrangements such as a casino package, called "Fortuna in Vienna." There's no restaurant on the premises.
✚ 27 D2　✉ Annagasse 16　☎ 01 51 27 75 10; fax 01 51 27 75 113
Ⓢ Stephansplatz　🚍 1, 71, D
AX, DC, MC, VI

VIENNA RESTAURANTS

Price guide: (dinner per person, excluding drinks)
$ €10–€15
$$ €15–€22
$$$ over €22

Augustinerkeller $$

Delicious Austrian- and Viennese-style dishes are complemented by good, locally produced wines. It's popular with foreign visitors.
✚ 27 D2　✉ Augustinerstrasse 1
☎ 01 53 31 026　Ⓢ U1, U2, U4 to Oper　AX, DC, MC, VI

Café Drechsler $$

This café opens at 3 a.m. and thus has an interesting mix of customers, including people on their way home from a night out and stall owners on their way to the market. Expect a quiet, smoky atmosphere and billiard tables. Hot dishes are served throughout the day.
✚ 27 C2　✉ Linke Wienzeile 22
☎ 01 587 8580　⊙ Closed Sun.
Ⓢ U1, U2, U4　🚍 4A, 59A; trams 62, 65　No credit cards

Do & Co Im Haas-Haus $$$

Shellfish, Thai and Japanese dishes are specialties at this trendy top-floor restaurant in the glass-fronted Haas-Haus building. You'll have good views of the cathedral.
✚ 27 D3　✉ 7th floor, Haas-Haus, Stephansplatz 12　☎ 01 53 53 969
Ⓢ U1, U3　VI

Im Palais Schwarzenberg $$$

For excellent views of the Belvedere gardens come to this classy restaurant, which specializes in the Austrian-Italian style of cooking.
✚ 27 D2　✉ Schwarzenbergplatz 9
☎ 01 79 84 515 600　🚍 Trams D, 1, 2　AX, DC, MC, VI

Plachutta $$–$$$

This is one of the best restaurants for original Viennese dishes in the Old Town. Typical items include *Wiener Tafelspitz* (boiled rump of beef with apple and horseradish sauce), delicious sautéed pike or perch with garlic butter, and pork with dumplings and cabbage. Reservations are advisable.

🏠 27 D2 ✉ Wollzeile 38
☎ 0152 15 77 🚇 U3 Stubentor AX DC MC VI

Steirereck am Stadtpark $$$

This intimate (22 tables) restaurant is ideal for a special occasion or a relaxing lunch. The food is a mix of traditional, new, regional and international, and there is an outstanding wine list from the richly stocked, vaulted cellars. Reservations are necessary.

🏠 27 D2 ✉ Am Heumarkt 2
☎ 01 71 33 168 🕐 Closed Sat.–Sun. and holidays 🚇 U4 to Stadtpark AX, DC, MC, VI

INNSBRUCK HOTELS
Price guide: (double room with breakfast for two people)
$ €50–€70
$$ €70–€150
$$$ over €150

Best Western Goldener Adler $$–$$$

A charming hotel in the heart of old Innsbruck, where modern comfort combines with Tyrolean character. The hotel also has two excellent restaurants.

🏠 35 A2 ✉ Herzog-Friedrichstrasse 6 ☎ 0512 571111; fax 0512 584409 🚌 A, O; tram 1, 3 AX, DC, MC, VI

Central $$

This centrally located hotel is big on comfort and service and has a wide range of facilities, including a sunning terrace.

🏠 35 A1 ✉ Gilmstrasse 5
☎ 0512 5920; fax 0512 580310 🚌 4, O AX, DC, MC, VI

Europa Tyrol $$$

Innsbruck's top hotel has a wide range of rooms at varying prices, some elegant public areas, and a friendly and welcoming staff.

🏠 35 B1 ✉ Südtirolerplatz 2
☎ 0512 5931; fax 0512 587800 🚌 O, 1, 3, 6 AX, DC, MC, VI

Maximilian $$–$$$

On the edge of Old Town, this modern hotel combines comfort with traditional service and atmosphere.

🏠 35 A2 ✉ Marktgraben 7–9
☎ 0512 59967; fax 0512 577450 🚌 A, C, D, E, J, O; tram 1, 3 AX, DC, MC, VI

Weisses Kreuz $–$$

Mozart and his father once stayed at this 15th-century Old Town hotel, which combines Tyrolean charm with modern comfort. Restaurants are on the premises.

🏠 35 A2 ✉ Herzog-Friedrichstrasse 31 ☎ 0512 59479; fax 0512 59479-90 🚌 A, C, J, O; tram 1, 3, 6 AX, MC, VI

INNSBRUCK RESTAURANTS
Price guide: (dinner per person, excluding drinks)
$ €10–€15
$$ €15–€22
$$$ over €22

Altstadtstüberl $$

Known for its international cooking, this Old Town restaurant offers good vegetarian dishes.

🏠 35 A2 ✉ Riesengasse 13
☎ 0512 582347 🕐 Closed Sun. 🚌 A, O; tram 1 AX, DC, MC, VI

Hirschenstuben $$

This Old Town restaurant offers fish and international dishes, as well as traditional favorites.

🏠 35 A2 ✉ Kiebachgasse 5
☎ 0512 582979 🕐 Closed Sun. 🚌 A, O; tram 1 AX, DC, MC, VI

Ottoburg $

This historic restaurant was established around 1745 in a building that some historians say is the oldest in Innsbruck.

🏠 35 A2 ✉ Herzog-Friedrichstrasse 1 ☎ 0512 584338 🕐 Closed Mon. 🚌 Tram 1, 3 AX, DC, MC, VI

Restaurant Goldener Adler $$

Its decor and friendly staff make this traditional restaurant popular with locals and tourists alike.

🏠 35 A2 ✉ Herzog-Friedrichstrasse 6 ☎ 0512 571111 🚌 Tram 1, 3 AX, DC, MC, VI

Stiftskeller $$

In the heart of the Old Town, this restaurant serves Tyrolean and Austrian specialties.

🏠 35 A2 ✉ Burggraben 31
☎ 0512 583490 🚌 A, O AX, DC, MC, VI

SALZBURG HOTELS
Price guide: (double room with breakfast for two people)
$ €50–€70
$$ €70–€150
$$$ over €150

Altstadthotel Wolf-Dietrich $$–$$$

This family-run hotel near the city's historic center has a good restaurant and an indoor swimming pool.

🏠 40 C4 ✉ Wolf-Dietrich-Strasse 7 ☎ 0662 871 275; fax 0662 871 275-9 🚌 29 AX, DC, MC, VI

Altstadt Radisson $$$

This renovated luxury hotel, in one of Salzburg's oldest buildings in the heart of the Old Town, has lovely rooms and an excellent restaurant.

🏠 40 C2 ✉ Rudolfskai 28/Judengasse 15 ☎ 0662 848 571-0; fax 0662 848 571-6 🚌 5, 6, 49, 51, 55, 95 AX, DC, MC, VI

Am Dom $$

Reserve ahead to ensure a room at this good, reasonably priced choice in the heart of Salzburg's historic center.

🏠 40 C2 ✉ Goldgasse 17
☎ 0662 842 765; fax 0662 842 765-55 🕐 Closed Feb. 🚌 5, 6, 51, 55, 95 AX, DC, MC, VI

Goldener Hirsch $$$

This luxurious, baronial-style hotel is one of Salzburg's oldest and most famous accommodations, and provides service to match.

🏠 40 B3 ✉ Getreidegasse 37
☎ 0662 80 84-0; fax 0662 843 349 🚌 1, 2, 15, 27, 29 AX, DC, MC, VI

Schloss Mönchstein $$$

This luxury-class hotel is beautifully situated in wooded grounds high above the old center of Salzburg.

🏠 40 A3 ✉ Mönchsberg Park 26
☎ 0662 848 555-0; fax 0662 848 559 🚌 1, 2, 15, 27, 29, 49, 60, 80, 95 AX, DC, MC, VI

SALZBURG RESTAURANTS
Price guide: (dinner per person, excluding drinks)
$ €10–€15
$$ €15–€22
$$$ over €22

Austria

Austria, Belgium

KEY TO SYMBOLS

- ✚ map page number and coordinates
- ✉ address
- ☎ telephone number
- 🕐 days/times closed
- 🚇 nearest subway station
- 🚌 nearest bus/trolley
  bus/tram/funicular route
- ⛴ ferry
- **$$$** expensive
- **$$** moderate
- **$** inexpensive
- AX American Express
- DC Diners Club
- MC MasterCard
- VI VISA

Chocolates Galore

Bruges' best chocolate shop is Spehelaere at Ezelstraat 92. Here you can see the daily production of fresh chocolate in a workshop where traditional methods are used – from the preparation of the chocolate in melting cauldrons to the hand-making process, in which white, milk and dark chocolate is fashioned into a variety of forms. A fascinating chocolate museum, Choco-Story, recently opened in Bruges at Sint-Jansstraat 7B (☎ 050 612 237, daily 10–5). The museum explains the origins of chocolate and the production process. The Museum for Cacao and Chocolate in Brussels is at Grand' Place 13 (☎ 02 514 20481).

Augustiner Bräu $

This huge restaurant and summer beer garden serves beer, wurst and simple Austrian fare in wood-paneled halls and is very popular with tourists.
✚ 40 A4 ✉ Augustinergasse 4 ☎ 0662 431 246 🚌 27, 60, 80, No credit cards

Bei Bruno $$$

This smart restaurant features dishes from the Tyrol, along with local specialties and a good wine list.
✚ 40 B2 ✉ Sigmund-Haffner-Gasse 4 ☎ 0662 878 417 🕐 Closed Sun. 🚌 2, 6 AX, DC, MC, VI

Festungsrestaurant $$

Located in the Hohensalzburg Fortress (see page 43), this restaurant has panoramic views of the Salzburg area and serves old-fashioned Austrian cooking (reservations required for dinner Jul.–Aug.).
✚ 40 C1 ✉ Hohensalzburg, Mönchsberg 34 ☎ 0662 841 780 🕐 Closed mid-Jan. to end of Feb. and in Nov. 🚌 Festungbahn funicular AX, DC, MC, VI

Stiftskeller St. Peter $$

Said to be Europe's oldest restaurant, Stiftskeller is a popular beer cellar serving reasonably priced beer, wine and local dishes.
✚ 40 B2 ✉ Stiftsbezirk 1/4 ☎ 0662 841 268-0 🚌 1, 2, 5, 6, 15, 29, 49, 51, 55, 95 MC, VI

BRUSSELS HOTELS

Price guide: (double room with breakfast for two people)
$ up to €75
$$ €75–€175
$$$ over €175

Amigo $$$

This charming hotel is located near the heart of old Brussels, behind Grand-Place. It has modern amenities, but with luxurious style and elegance; frequented by media stars.
✚ 56 B2 ✉ rue de l'Amigo 1–3 ☎ 02 547 4747; fax 02 513 5277 🚇 Gare Centrale 🚌 34, 48, 94; tram 23, 52, 55, 56 AX, DC, MC, VI

Le Dixseptième $$$

Seventeenth-century ambience and quality service typify this very stylish central hotel, not far from Grand-Place.

✚ 56 B2 ✉ rue de la Madeleine 25 ☎ 02 517 1717; fax 02 502 6424 🚇 Gare Centrale AX, DC, MC, VI

Hyatt Regency Brussels-Barsey $$$

This is one of Brussels' very few boutique hotels, having 99 ultra chic rooms and suites, all furnished with beautiful furniture and objets d'art. The restaurant, Le Barsey, is a favorite with celebrities and artists.
✚ 56 off B3 ✉ avenue Louise 381–383 ☎ 02 649 9800 🚇 Louise then tram 93, 94 AX, DC, MC, VI

Métropole $$$

Built in 1895, the Métropole Hotel's glorious and flamboyant façade and ground floor are now a protected monument. The hotel has a fine restaurant, L'Alban Chambon, a beautiful bar, "Le 19ième," and a year-round heated terrace.
✚ 56 B3 ✉ place De Brouckère 31 ☎ 02 217 2300; fax 02 218 0220 🚇 De Brouckère 🚌 Tram 23, 52, 55, 81 AX, DC, MC, VI

Welcome $$

A charming hotel where each of the 15 spacious rooms is decorated in the style of a different country. The buffet breakfast is served in a lovely room.
✚ 56 B3 ✉ 5 rue du Peuplier ☎ 02 219 9546 🚇 St.-Catherine DC, MC, VI

BRUSSELS RESTAURANTS

Price guide: (dinner per person, excluding drinks)
$ up to €20
$$ €20–€40
$$$ over €40

Belgaqueen $$–$$$

The superb Hôtel de la Poste, with its grand entrance hall and late 19th-century stained-glass windows, is now a trendy dining complex, all in true époque style.
✚ 56 B3 ✉ rue Fosse aux Loups 32 ☎ 02 217 2187 🚇 Gare Centrale, De Brouckère AX, DC, MC, VI

Bonsoir Clara $$

Trendy brasserie on Brussels' hippest shopping street. The menu includes mainly light Mediterranean-style dishes, but you can also get an excellent Belgian *steak frites* or delicious caramelized duck.

🚫 56 A3 ✉ rue Antoine Dansaert 26 ☎ 02 502 0990 🚇 Bourse 🚃 Tram 23, 52, 55, 56, 81 AX, MC, VI

Comme Chez Soi $$$

Brussels' top gastronomic experience can be savored at this celebrated restaurant. New Belgian cuisine with traditional specialties is featured; reserve well in advance.

🚫 56 A2 ✉ place Rouppe 23 ☎ 02 512 2921 🔵 Closed Sun. and Mon., Jan. 1, Jul. and Dec. 25 🚃 Tram 23, 52, 55, 56 AX, DC, MC, VI

In 'tSpinnekopke $

In the Spider's Head is one of Brussels' most traditional restaurants. The menu lists the dishes by their name in Bruxellois dialect, so order blindfolded, or have the traditional *Stoemp mi sossisse* (hotch-potch with sausage). The bar stocks a vast selection of traditional beers.

🚫 56 A3 ✉ place Jardin-aux-Fleurs 1 ☎ 02 511 8695 🔵 Closed Sat. and Sun. lunch 🚇 Bourse AX, DC, MC, VI

La Maison du Cygne $$$

This restaurant, in one of the guild houses in Grand-Place, was originally a medieval tavern. Karl Marx wrote part of the *Communist Manifesto* here.

🚫 56 B2 ✉ Grand-Place 9 ☎ 02 511 8244 🔵 Closed Sat. lunch and Sun. 🚇 Gare Centrale 🚃 Tram 23, 52, 56, 81 AX, DC, MC, VI

Taverne du Passage $$

This hugely popular and staunchly Belgian brasserie, founded in 1928, serves all the key Belgian dishes in style. Specialties include *croquettes au crevettes* (shrimp croquettes).

🚫 56 Off the map ✉ Galerie de la Reine 30 ☎ 02 512 3731 🚇 Gare Centrale

Price guide: (double room with breakfast for two people)
$ up to €75
$$ €75–€175
$$$ over €175

tBourgoensch-Hof $$

This small, comfortable, quality hotel sits within a courtyard and its rooms overlook the canal. The Markt

and the Dijver walkway are nearby.

🚫 62 B2 ✉ Wollestraat 41–43 ☎ 050 331 645; fax 050 346 378 🚃 1, 6, 11, 16 AX, MC, VI

De Orangerie $$$

One of Bruges' most lauded hotels is within this 15th-century building, with a canal-side location and views of the tree-lined Dijver walkway. Guests can breakfast in the paneled dining room or on the canal-side terrace; they also can use the pool and sauna of the De Tuilerieën Hotel.

🚫 62 B2 ✉ Kartuizerinnensstraat 10 ☎ 050 341 649; fax 050 333 016 🚃 1, 6, 11, 16 AX, DC, MC, VI

Marie Paul $

There are three rooms in this spacious ivy-clad house set in a courtyard with views over a windmill. Breakfasts are excellent.

🚫 62 C3 ✉ Oostproosse 14 ☎ 050 339 246 🚃 114 No credit cards

Relais Ravenstein $$$

The Relais Ravenstein is a stylish hotel with contemporary décor. Some of its 15 spacious suites overlook the canal. Service is good, and there is a restaurant and a terrace.

🚫 62 C2 ✉ Molenmeers 11 ☎ 050 476 947 🚃 6, 16 AX, DC, MC, VI

Romantik Pandhotel $$

The Romantik Pandhotel is in one of Bruges' most beautiful and tranquil corners. The 18th-century carriage house is tastefully decorated and the rooms are spacious. Guests can relax in the library or lovely lounge.

🚫 62 B2 ✉ Pandreitje 16 ☎ 050 340 666 🚃 All buses to Markt DC, MC, VI

Price guide: (dinner per person, excluding drinks)
$ up to €20
$$ €20–€40
$$$ over €40

Breydel-De Coninck $$

This traditional mussel restaurant is favored by locals. The mussels arrive in big, steaming pots and served with *frites*.

🚫 62 Off the map ✉ Breydelstraat 24 ☎ 050 339 746 🔵 Closed on Wed. in June 🚃 1, 3, 4, 6, 8, 11, 13, 16 AX, MC, VI

Den Gouden Harynck $$$

This popular and costly restaurant serves fine Belgian and international cuisine. Seafood dishes from caviar to lobster are the specialty. Reserve well ahead.

🚫 62 B1–B2 ✉ Groeninge 25 ☎ 050 337 637 🔵 Closed Sun. and Mon., the week after Easter, mid-Jul. to the first week of Aug. and last week of Dec. 🚃 1 MC, VI

De Karmeliet $$$

Three-Michelin-starred chef Geert van Hecke creates inspired Belgian cuisine. The stylish interior is as well thought out as the superb food. Reserve well in advance.

🚫 C2 ✉ Langestraat 19 ☎ 050 338 259 🔵 Closed Sun. evening, Mon. and Tue. lunch 🚃 4, 6 AX, DC, MC, VI

Rock Fort $$

The Rock Fort is run by two friends who cook well prepared and beautifully presented dishes with seasonal produce. This means a bit of Belgian, a bit of fusion, but mainly sunny Mediterranean food. Save space for the dessert selection. Next door is a lounge-bar.

🚫 62 C2 ✉ Langestraat 15 ☎ 050 334 113 🔵 Closed Sun. and Mon. 🚃 4, 6 AX, MC, VI

T'Zonneke $$

Lovely, friendly family-run restaurant, popular with locals who come for the set menu lunch. Traditional Flemish dishes are seved in an airy but rustic décor.

🚫 62 B3 ✉ Genthof 5 ☎ 050 330 781 🔵 Closed Sun. dinner; closed all day Sun. in Jul. and Aug. 🚃 All buses to Markt MC, VI

Price guide: (double room with breakfast for two people)
$ up to €75
$$ €75–€175
$$$ over €175

The Boatel $$

This converted canal barge with seven rooms, moored on a canal a 10-minute walk away from the city center, offers an unusual Ghent hotel experience. A hearty breakfast is served on deck, weather permitting.

🚫 70 Off the map ✉ Voorhoutkaai 29A ☎ 09 267 1030; fax 09 267 1039

Belgium

KEY TO SYMBOLS

⊕ map page number and coordinates
✉ address
☎ telephone number
🕐 days/times closed
Ⓜ nearest subway station
🚌 nearest bus/trolley
bus/tram/funicular route
⛴ ferry
$$$ expensive
$$ moderate
$ inexpensive
AX American Express
DC Diners Club
MC Mastercard
VI VISA

Banquets for All

You can go back through history while enjoying a hearty meal in Ghent. Various traditional banquets are staged in such fascinating venues as a 13th-century monastery, a medieval crypt or the hall of a castle. The Medieval Banquet is accompanied by troubadours, dancers and a court jester. The Belle Époque Cabaret Banquet features song and dance, tap dancers, a ventriloquist and other acts with themes from the 1870s to the 1930s. The Renaissance Banquet features court dances by dancers in period costume. The Mississipi Jazz Evening features Cajun food and an accompaniment of Dixieland and blues music. For information and reservations, ☎ 09 222 4904.

Erasmus $$

This cozy, old-fashioned hotel with personal touches and antique furnishings is located near historic Kornlei; breakfasts are ample and very good.

⊕ 70 A3　✉ Poel 25　☎ 09 224 2195; fax 09 233 4241　🕐 Closed mid-Dec. to mid-Jan.　🚌 16, 18, 38 AX, MC, VI

Gravensteen $$

Housed in a 19th-century mansion, this comfortable hotel is conveniently located close to the Castle of the Counts and other city attractions. Try to get a reservation in the tower room, which has one of the best views over Ghent.

⊕ 70 A4　✉ Jan Breydelstraat 35　☎ 09 225 1150; fax 09 225 1850　🚌 Tram 1, 10, 11, 13 AX, DC, MC, VI

Novotel Gent Centrum $$

With an outdoor swimming pool, restaurant and good location, this large, comfortable hotel in the center of Ghent has quiet rooms overlooking a central courtyard.

⊕ 70 B3　✉ Goudenleeuwplein 5　☎ 09 224 2230; fax 09 224 3295　🚌 16, 17, 18, 19, 38; tram 12, 41 AX, DC, MC, VI

Sofitel Gent Belfort $$$

This is a large luxury hotel in the historic heart of the city, opposite the Town Hall. Its many amenities, including a restaurant and fitness room, make it a decent value.

⊕ 70 B3　✉ Hoogpoort 63　☎ 09 233 3331; fax 09 233 1102　🚌 16, 17, 18, 19, 38; tram 12, 41 AX, DC, MC, VI

GHENT RESTAURANTS

Price guide: (dinner per person, excluding drinks)
$ €10–€12
$$ €12–€25
$$$ over €25

Belgaqueen $$–$$$

Set in a converted 13th-century grain storehouse, which now also houses a restaurant, a beer bar, an oyster bar and a cigar lounge. The food is good and the atmosphere is lively. Sister restaurant to the Belgaqueen in Brussels (see page 542).

⊕ 70 A3　✉ Graslei 10　☎ 09 280 0100　🕐 Closed Sun.　🚌 1, 11, 12 AX, DC, MC, VI

De Blauwe Zalm $$

Charming restaurant with a contemporary feel, with tables set up in an impressive courtyard. Specialties of the house are fresh seafood and fish.

⊕ 70 off the map　✉ Vrouwebroerstraat 2　☎ 09 224 0852　🕐 Closed Sun. and for lunch Mon. and Sat.　🚌 Tram 1, 11, 12, 40, 42 AX, DC, MC, VI

De Hel $$$

This is a small restaurant in one of the Kraanlei's most delightful buildings, "The Flying Deer." French and Belgian cuisine is at its best in the candlelit dining room. Reservations are advised.

⊕ 70 A4–B4　✉ Kraanlei 81　☎ 09 224 3240　🕐 Closed Tue.–Wed. and for lunch Sat. and Thu.　🚌 Tram 1, 11, 12, 40, 42 AX, DC, VI

T'Buikske Vol $$–$$$

Near the castle of Gravensteen and on a beautiful canal, this charming brasserie offers local and regional specialties. The menu includes waterzooi of North Sea fish. There is a good wine list and beer selection.

⊕ 70 A4　✉ Kraanlei 17　☎ 09 224 4446　🕐 Closed Mon., Wed. and for lunch Tue. and Thu.–Sun.　🚌 Tram 1, 11, 12, 40 AX, DC, MC, VI

Tête à Tête $$$

Refined and stylish French restaurant serving traditional dishes with an inventive twist. The decor is sumptuous – the perfect setting for a romantic dinner. The garden overlooks t'Gravensteen.

⊕ 70 Off the map　✉ Jan Breydelstraat 32　☎ 09 233 9500　🕐 Closed Mon.–Thu. lunch　🚌 Tram 1, 11, 12 AX, DC, MC, VI

LONDON HOTELS

Price guide: (double room with breakfast for two people)
$ £50–£100
$$ £100–£150
$$$ over £150

The Delmere Hotel $

Friendly, close to Hyde Park and within walking distance of Oxford Street. Italian restaurant.

⊕ 86 A3　✉ 130 Sussex Gardens　☎ 020 7706 3344; fax 020 7262 1863　Ⓜ Paddington AX, DC, MC, VI

Britain

The Dorchester $$$

This world-class hotel offers guests the very best in luxury accommodations.

🏥 86 B2 ✉ Park Lane ☎ 020 7629 8888; fax 020 7409 0114 🚇 Hyde Park Corner or Green Park AX, DC, MC, VI

London Marriott Hotel, County Hall $$$

The large London Marriott occupies a prime South Bank riverside location. Many rooms have superb views.

🏥 86 D2 ✉ County Hall, Westminster Bridge Road ☎ 020 7928 5200; fax 020 7928 5300 🚇 Waterloo AX, DC, MC, VI

The Mandeville Hotel $$

This quiet hotel, popular with foreign visitors, is a short walk from Oxford Street.

🏥 86 B3 ✉ Mandeville Place ☎ 020 7935 5599; fax 020 7935 9588 🚇 Bond Street AX, DC, MC, VI

The Ritz $$$

Luxurious Louis XVI interiors and all the expense and style that goes with the name are the details you can expect at this top hotel.

🏥 86 C2 ✉ 150 Piccadilly ☎ 020 7493 8181; fax 020 7493 2687 🚇 Green Park AX, DC, MC, VI

LONDON RESTAURANTS

Price guide: (dinner per person, excluding drinks)
$ £10–£15
$$ £15–£30
$$$ over £30

Alastair Little Restaurant $$$

Cream walls hung with modern art, light wood flooring and white tablecloths create a minimalist setting for a menu that changes daily. Cooking is modern British. Reserve ahead.

🏥 86 C3 ✉ 49 Frith Street ☎ 020 7734 5183 🚇 Closed Sat. lunch, Sun. and public holidays 🚇 Tottenham Court Road AX, DC, MC, VI

Bank Aldwych Restaurant $$–$$$

Lively urban brasserie serving fresh, robust and creative food with a modern twist on the classics.

🏥 86 D3 ✉ 1 Kingsway ☎ 020 7379 9797 🚇 Closed Jan. 1, Dec. 25, public holidays 🚇 Holborn, Charing Cross AX, DC, MC, VI

The Connaught Hotel $$–$$$

The hotel's Menu restaurant serves classic and contemporary dishes with an Italian influence.

🏥 86 B3 ✉ Carlos Place ☎ 020 7592 1222 🚇 Bond Street or Green Park AX, DC, MC, VI

Pied à Terre $$$

This restaurant's stylish yet simple ambience conbines with highly refined Frezch cuisine.

🏥 86 B3 ✉ 34 Charlotte Street ☎ 020 7636 1178 🚇 Closed Sat. lunch, Sun.–Mon. and 2 weeks in late Dec. and early Jan. 🚇 Knightsbridge AX, DC, MC, VI

Quaglino's $$–$$$

Superbly designed and stylish Quaglino's is one of London's most glamorous eateries. British cuisine and contemporary dishes are served; reservations are advised.

🏥 86 C3 ✉ 16 Bury Street, St. James ☎ 020 7930 6767 🚇 Green Park AX, DC, MC, VI

Red Lion $$–$$$

Dating from 1752, this historic, friendly pub is likely to be frequented by Mayfair's rich and famous. You can eat in the bar or the restaurant.

🏥 86 B3 ✉ 1 Waverton Street, Mayfair ☎ 020 7499 1307 🚇 Green Park AX, MC, VI

EDINBURGH HOTELS

Price guide: (double room with breakfast for two people)
$ £50–100
$$ £100–150
$$$ over £150

Balmoral Hotel $$$

This classic Edwardian building dominates the east end of Princes Street. Traditional afternoon tea is served in the Palm Court.

🏥 98 B2 ✉ 1 Princes Street ☎ 0131 556 2414; fax 0131 3747 8740 🚌 City center buses AX, DC, MC, VI

Greenside Hotel $

Quietly situated on the north side of Calton Hill, this pleasant, small hotel offers good views to the Firth of Forth from the top floors and has an in-house bar.

🏥 99 E3 ✉ 9 Royal Terrace ☎ 0131 557 0022; fax 0131 557 0022 🚌 1, 5, 19, 26, 34, 44 AX, MC, VI

Ivy Guest House $

This friendly guesthouse occupies an elegant Victorian townhouse just a short distance from the city center.

🏥 99 Off the map ✉ 7 Mayfield Gardens ☎ 0131 667 3411; fax 0131 620 1422 🚌 3, 29, 31, 49 No credit cards

Old Waverley Hotel $–$$$

This long-established hotel, a landmark building in the heart of the city on Princes Street, enjoys fine views of Edinburgh Castle and the Scott Monument.

🏥 98 B2 ✉ 43 Princes Street ☎ 0131 556 4648; fax 0131 557 6316 🚌 City center buses AX, DC, MC, VI

The Roxburghe Hotel $$–$$$

Traditional Scottish hospitality prevails at this upscale hotel in the heart of Georgian Edinburgh, with amenities and extras to match its status.

🏥 98 B2 ✉ 38 Charlotte Square ☎ 0131 240 5500; fax 0131 240 5555 🚌 City center buses AX, DC, MC, VI

EDINBURGH RESTAURANTS

Price guide: (dinner per person, excluding drinks)
$ £10–£15
$$ £15–£30
$$$ over £30

Le Café St. Honore $–$$

French-style café on a delightful cobbled back lane. Buzzing at lunchtime, cozy and candlelit at night. The food is built on Scottish foundations.

🏥 99 C2 ✉ 34 NW Thistle Street Lane ☎ 0131 226 2211 🚇 Closed 3 days around Jan. 1 and Dec. 24–26 🚌 City center buses AX, DC, MC, VI

Duck's at Le Marche Noir $$

The unusual name of this restaurant is derived from the proprietor's last name. Expect excellent contemporary cuisine – from quail eggs to haggis – and some exquisite desserts. This restaurant also has an excellent wine list and a wide range of malt whiskeys.

🏥 98 Off the map ✉ 2–4 Eyre Place 🚇 Closed Sat.–Mon. lunch and Dec. 25–26 ☎ 0131 558 1608 🚌 8, 13, 17, 23, 27, 36 AX, DC, MC, VI

Britain

KEY TO SYMBOLS

- ✚ map page number and coordinates
- ✉ address
- ☎ telephone number
- ⓓ days/times closed
- Ⓜ nearest subway station
- Ⓑ nearest bus/trolley bus/tram/funicular route
- ⛴ ferry
- **$$$** expensive
- **$$** moderate
- **$** inexpensive
- AX American Express
- DC Diners Club
- MC MasterCard
- VI VISA

English Pubs

The traditional English pub, from the term "public house," is another of those treasured institutions by which an entire culture is measured. The great thing about traditional pubs is their spirit of easygoing informality. Pubs were always the focus of local life, places where people exchanged views and took their hard-earned leisure. It is no coincidence that village pub and village church often stand cheek by jowl. In medieval times, churches and monasteries often owned the local pub, or "hostelry."

In and around Oxford you will find traditional pubs that have not compromised with modern fashion, while still maintaining the highest standards of comfort and service. Try The Chequers, off High Street; the King's Arms, on Holywell Street; the Turf Tavern, in Bath Place; the Isis Tavern on the towpath at Iffley Lock; or The Rose and Crown on North Parade Avenue.

The Restaurant at the Bonham $$

Contemporary-style decor provides the backdrop to the traditional Scottish cuisine served in this hotel restaurant, which makes good use of seasonal organic produce. Located at the west end of Princes Street.
✚ 98 B2 ✉ 35 Drumsheugh Gardens ☎ 0131 623 9319 Ⓑ 19, 35, 37, 37A, 41 AX, DC, MC, VI

Stac Polly $$–$$$

City-center eatery with the charm and atmosphere of a country restaurant. The traditional Scottish and British cuisine features global touches. It is advisable to make reservations.
✚ 98 B1 ✉ 8–10 Grindlay Street ☎ 0131 229 5405 ⓓ Closed Sat.–Sun. lunch Ⓑ 4, 8, 10, 11, 12, 15, 15A, 16, 17, 26, 44 AX, DC, MC, VI

The Witchery by the Castle $$

This restaurant is located by the gates of Edinburgh Castle and is made even more atmospheric by hundreds of candles reflected off Gothic furnishings, tapestries and hand-painted timber ceilings. The French menu features Scottish produce. Reservations are advised.
✚ 98 C1 ✉ 352 Castlehill ☎ 0131 225 5613 ⓓ Closed Dec 25–26 Ⓑ 23, 27, 28, 41, 42, 45 AX, DC, MC, VI

OXFORD HOTELS

Price guide: (double room with breakfast for two people)
$ £50–£100
$$ £100–£150
$$$ over £150

The Balkan Lodge Hotel $$

Located east of Oxford but with easy access to the city center. One of the bright, attractive bedrooms is furnished with a four-poster bed and Jacuzzi.
✚ 107 C1 ✉ 315 Iffley Road ☎ 01865 244524; fax 01865 251090 Ⓑ 3, 4, 4A 4C MC, VI

The Eastgate Hotel $$

A charming mid-size hotel occupying the site of the medieval East Gate of the city. Very convenient to the city center and historic university buildings.
✚ 107 C1 ✉ 73 High Street ☎ 0870 400 8201; fax 01865 791681 Ⓑ All city center buses AX, DC, MC, VI

The Manor House Hotel $

A small family-run hotel 1 mile from the city center. There is a comfortable lounge, as well as a bar and dining facilities.
✚ 107 C1 ✉ 250 Iffley Road ☎ 01865 727627; fax 01865 200478 Ⓑ 3, 4, 4A, 4C AX, DC, MC, VI

The Old Bank Hotel $$$

This skillfully restored former bank is a place of tranquility away from the bustle of High Street.
✚ 107 C1 ✉ 92–94 High Street ☎ 01865 799599; fax 01865 799598 Ⓑ All city center buses AX, DC, MC, VI

The Randolph $$–$$$

Top-of-the-line hotel with neo-Gothic architectural features and elegant interiors, extremely comfortable rooms and luxury service. Located near the Ashmolean Museum and close to the city center.
✚ 107 A2 ✉ Beaumont Street ☎ 0870 400 8200; fax 01865 791678 Ⓑ 2A, 2B, 2C, 7B, 7D, 7(Kiddlington) AX, DC, MC, VI

OXFORD RESTAURANTS

Price guide: (dinner per person, excluding drinks)
$ £10–£15
$$ £15–£30
$$$ over £30

Gee's Restaurant $$

This conservatory restaurant (a former florist and greengrocer business dating from 1900) is a 20-minute walk from the city center. The modern British food also shows French influences.
✚ 107 Off the map ✉ 61 Banbury Road ☎ 01865 553540 ⓓ Closed Dec. 25–26 Ⓑ 6A AX, MC, VI

Le Petit Blanc Brasserie $$

This popular, stylish yet friendly brasserie is owned by renowned French chef Raymond Blanc.
✚ 107 Off the map ✉ 71–72 Walton Street ☎ 01865 510999 ⓓ Closed Dec. 25 Ⓑ All city center buses AX, DC, MC, VI

Quod Restaurant and Bar $–$$

A trendy all-day bar and grill serving a choice of meat and pasta dishes with a distinctly Italian accent.
✚ 107 C1 ✉ 92–94 High Street ☎ 01865 202505 ⓓ Closed Dec.

25–26 🚌 All city center buses AX, MC, VI

Turf Tavern $
At this very traditional English pub-restaurant, in the heart of the university area near Radcliffe Square, you can experience British dishes like pork in cider, beef and beer pie or minted lamb, all at reasonable prices.
➕ 107 B2 ✉ 4 Bath Place
☎ 01865 243235 🚌 All city center buses AX, DC, MC, VI

The Whitehouse $$
A former tollhouse where people crossed the river to enter Oxford is now a popular and spacious pub restaurant.
➕ 107 Off the map ✉ 2 Botley Road ☎ 01865 242823; fax 01865 793331 🚌 4A, 4B, 4C, 400 Park and Ride, X3, 5, 14 MC, VI

YORK HOTELS
Price guide: (double room with breakfast for two people)
$ £50–£100
$$ £100–£150
$$$ over £150

The Alhambra Court Hotel $
This attractive Georgian building is on a quiet side road within walking distance of central York. Pleasantly furnished, with home-style cooking.
➕ 113 Off the map ✉ 31 St. Mary's, Bootham ☎ 01904 628474; fax 01904 610690 🚌 14 MC, VI

Dean Court Hotel $$–$$$
A handsome Victorian building in an unsurpassed location close to York Minster, with views of the Minster from upper front rooms. Very stylish, first-class facilities, including an award-winning restaurant.
➕ 113 B3 ✉ Duncombe Place
☎ 01904 625082; fax 01904 620305 🚶 Pedestrian area, no buses AX, DC, MC, VI

The Groves Hotel $
The Groves, a few minutes' walk from central York, is in a quiet tree-lined area. It offers a good standard of accommodation and service as well as excellent home-style cooking.
➕ 113 Off the map ✉ 8 St. Peter's Grove, Clifton ☎ 01904 559777; fax 01904 627729 🚌 14 MC, VI

Lady Anne Middleton's Hotel $$$
This well-furnished, city-center hotel, created from several buildings of historic importance, features an adjoining leisure club.
➕ 113 B1 ✉ Skeldergate
☎ 01904 611570; fax 01904 613043
🚶 Pedestrian area, no buses AX, MC, VI

The Royal York $–$$
Magnificent, top-quality Victorian hotel near the railroad station offers easy access to the city center and provides excellent service.
➕ 113 A2 ✉ Station Road
☎ 01904 653681; fax 01904 623503 🚶 Pedestrian area, no buses AX, DC, MC, VI

YORK RESTAURANTS
Price guide: (dinner per person, excluding drinks)
$ £10–£15
$$ £15–£30
$$$ over £30

The Grange Hotel $$
The Ivy restaurant here has beautifully set tables and serves a mix of contemporary and classic dishes, with a strong emphasis on seasonal seafood.
➕ 113 B3 ✉ 1 Clifton ☎ 01904 644744 🕒 Closed Mon.–Fri. lunch and Sun. dinner 🚌 15 AX, DC, MC, VI

Knavesmire Manor Hotel $$
A bistro-style restaurant in an attractive Georgian house. The unfussy, European-based menu includes classic meat dishes and vegetarian options.
➕ 113 Off the map ✉ 302 Tadcaster Road ☎ 01904 702941
🕒 Closed Mon.–Sat. lunch 🚌 4, 12, 13 AX, DC, MC, VI

Melton's Restaurant $$
This long-established, family-run restaurant features modern British cooking. There is an appealing *prix-fixe* lunch and a lower-price early evening menu.
➕ 113 Off the map ✉ 7 Scarcroft Road ☎ 01904 634341 🕒 Closed Mon. lunch, Sun., 1 week in Aug. and 3 weeks in Dec. 🚌 21 MC, VI

Middlethorpe Hall Hotel $$$
Traditional English fare is served in an oak-paneled restaurant in this restored William III house, only 1.5 miles from the center of York.

➕ 113 Off the map ✉ Bishopthorpe Road, Middlethorpe ☎ 01904 641241 🕒 Closed Dec. 25 lunch and Dec. 31 lunch 🚌 11 MC, VI

Sous le Mont $–$$
Georgian elegance prevails in this formal restaurant overlooking a delightful garden.
➕ 113 Off the map ✉ 119 The Mount ☎ 01904 619444
🕒 Closed Jan 1–6 🚌 4, 12, 13 AX, DC, MC, VI

PRAGUE HOTELS
Price guide: (double room with breakfast for two people)
$ 1,000Kč–2,500Kč
$$ 2,500Kč–4,500Kč
$$$ over 4,500Kč

Evropa $–$$
This landmark art nouveau hotel on Wenceslas Square, rebuilt between 1903 and 1905, features sculptures, wrought-iron balconies and a glass mosaic and offers good value accommodations. The restaurant has even more art nouveau embell-ishments to admire.
➕ 124 E2 ✉ Václavské náměstí 25 ☎ 224 228 117; fax 224 224 544 🚇 Mrstek AX, DC, MC, VI

Penzion U Medvídků $$
The name of this 15th-century former brewery tavern means "The Little Bears." There are 33 rooms in two categories: all have bathrooms, but those with extra facilities are double the price. There's a break-fast buffet.
➕ 124 C3 ✉ Na Perštýně 7
☎ 224 211 916; fax 224 220 930
🚇 Národní trída AX, DC, MC, VI

Savoy $$$
A relaxed atmosphere prevails at this top Prague hotel, located behind Prague Castle. Rooms are well designed and modernized, making it a perfect vacation base.
➕ 124 Off the map ✉ Keplerova 6 ☎ 224 302 430; fax 224 302 128 🚊 Tram 22, 23 AX, DC, MC, VI

Sax $$
On the steep hill leading to Prague Castle (just off Nerudova, near Charles Bridge), this hotel has an attractive interior and well-equipped, comfortable rooms.
➕ 124 A4 ✉ Jánský vršek 328/3

KEY TO SYMBOLS

🔳 map page number and coordinates

⊠ address

☎ telephone number

🕐 days/times closed

Ⓜ nearest subway station

🚌 nearest bus/trolley bus/tram/funicular route

⛴ ferry

$$$ expensive

$$ moderate

$ inexpensive

AX American Express

DC Diners Club

MC MasterCard

VI VISA

☎ 257 531 268; fax 257 534 101
Ⓜ Malostranská 🚌 Tram 12, 22
AX, MC, VI

U tří pštrosů $$$

"The House of the Three Ostriches" was built in 1606 by a man who sold ostrich feathers to nobles. The painted Renaissance ceilings survive, and the hotel is just a step from Charles Bridge.

🔳 124 B3 ⊠ Dražického náměstí 12/76 ☎ 257 532 410; fax 257 533 217 🚌 Tram 12, 22 AX, DC, MC, VI

PRAGUE RESTAURANTS

Price guide: (dinner per person, excluding drinks)
$ 100Kč–200Kč
$$ 200Kč–600Kč
$$$ over 600Kč

Kampa Park $$$

This is the restaurant that invented casual haute cuisine in post-revolution Prague. It's a see-and-be-seen kind of place with a million-dollar view of the Charles Bridge and an ambitious menu of seafood and continental specialties. Reservations are essential.

🔳 124 B3 ⊠ Na Kampě 8B
☎ 257 532 685 Ⓜ Malestranské náměstí 🚌 Tram 12, 20, 22, 23 AX, MC, VI

Kogo $$–$$$

Popular with local politicians, celebrities and foreign residents, this Italian restaurant serves a variety of fresh seafood and a smattering of Balkan specialties.

🔳 124 D3 ⊠ Havelská 27, Staré Město ☎ 224 214 543 Ⓜ Můstek AX, MC, VI

Plzenska Restaurace $$

This stylish art-nouveau, Czech-style pub, located in the cellar of the landmark Obecní dům (Municipal House), offers traditional specialties including roast duck. Live music every night.

🔳 124 E3 ⊠ Náměstí Republiky 5, Staré Město ☎ 222 002 780 Ⓜ Náměstí Republiky AX, MC, VI

U Ševce Matouše $$

The name means "Matthew the Cobbler," and this is indeed a former cobbler's workshop under the arcades in Loreta Square. Generous portions of steak, ham, duck and beef stroganoff are served.

🔳 124 Off the map ⊠ Loretánské náměstí 4 ☎ 220 514 536
🚌 Tram 22 MC, VI

U Zlaté Hrušky $$$

Excellent Czech specialties, including pâté, duck and venison, and good wines are served in an attractive house with rustic furniture. The name means "The Golden Pears."

🔳 124 Off the map ⊠ Nový svět 3/77, Hradčany ☎ 220 514 778 🚌 Tram 22 AX, DC, MC, VI

COPENHAGEN HOTELS

Price guide: (double room with breakfast for two people)
$ DKr400–DK700
$$ DKr700–DK1,200
$$$ over DKr1,200

Copenhagen Admiral Hotel $$$

This waterfront hotel, in a superbly renovated, 18th-century redbrick granary warehouse, is located close to Amalienborg Plads (square). Regular rooms and family suites are available; a restaurant (breakfast is extra) and sauna are on the premises.

🔳 140 D3 ⊠ Toldbodgade 24–28 ☎ 33 74 14 14; fax 33 74 14 16 Ⓜ Kongens Nytorv 🚌 28 AX, MC, VI

Hotel d'Angleterre $$$

Famous, and famously expensive, this luxury hotel is on Kongens Nytorv square. An 18th-century building, reconstructed from the 1630 original, features sumptuous furnishings, an indoor pool and luxury fitness facilities, making it a favorite with visiting celebrities.

🔳 140 C2–C3 Ⓜ Kongens Nytorv 34 ☎ 33 12 00 95; fax 33 12 11 18 Ⓜ Kongens Nytorv 🚌 10, 28 AX, MC, VI

Hotel City $$

This attractive, comfortable, modernized hotel in an old Copenhagen town house is near the center of things, but in a quiet location. Only breakfast is served.

🔳 140 D2 ⊠ Peder Skrams Gade 24 ☎ 33 13 06 66; fax 33 13 06 67 Ⓜ Kongens Nytorv 🚌 27 AX, MC, VI

Sofitel Plaza Copenhagen $$$

Located in the heart of the city across from Tivoli, the luxurious, modern Plaza has superbly furnished rooms. The Library Bar encourages

---

Danish *Smørrebrød*

Like their fellow Scandinavians, Danes are great believers in hearty lunches – and nothing is more filling or mouthwatering than *smørrebrød*, which translates simply as "buttered bread." If it sounds like "smothering," then that's exactly what happens to the large slice of rye bread that is the basis of *smørrebrød* when it is piled high with a tasty mix of salads and garnishes, shrimps and chunks of fish, beef or pork. You can accompany this mini-banquet with a Danish lager and a small glass of chilled *akvavit* (aquavit). You also can enjoy the Danish *kolt bord*, or cold table, a fantastic array of meat and fish dishes, salads and savory dips, hot dishes, and a selection of bread and rolls.

literary browsing over drinks, and there's a good restaurant.
⊞ 140 B1 ✉ Bernstorffsgade 4 ☎ 33 14 92 62; fax 33 93 93 62 Ⓢ S-train København H 🚌 8, 250S AX, MC, VI

Top Hotel Hebron $$
This is a friendly family hotel close to the railroad station and Tivoli. Comfortable rooms have many amenities, and breakfast is available.
⊞ 140 A1 ✉ Helgolandsgade 4 ☎ 33 31 69 06; fax 33 31 90 67 Ⓢ S-train København H 🚌 6, 10, 16, 27, 28 AX, MC, VI

COPENHAGEN RESTAURANTS
Price guide: (dinner per person, excluding drinks)
$ DKr100–DK250
$$ DKr250–DK300
$$$ over DKr300

Nyhavns Færgekro $
One of the best restaurants on canal-side Nyhavn is this one, with a nautical theme that includes model boats hanging from the ceiling. Superb lunchtime buffets featuring a variety of herring dishes are a great deal; the Danish and French cuisine offered at dinner is more expensive.
⊞ 140 D2 ✉ Nyhavn 5 ☎ 33 15 15 88 Ⓠ Kongens Nytorv MC, VI

Peder Oxe $$
Built on the foundation of an old monastery, this noted restaurant/cellar bar is on Grey Brothers Square. Traditional Danish cuisine emphasizes hearty helpings of meat; the lunchtime *smørrebrød* is very good.
⊞ 140 C2 ✉ Gråbrødretorv 11 ☎ 33 11 00 77 Ⓠ Kongens Nytorv DC, MC, VI

Restaurant Els $$$
Original painted wall panels from the 1850s add style to this popular Nyhavn restaurant, situated on a street leading off Kongens Nytorv square. Excellent fish specialties and fine wines are served. Reservations are advised.
⊞ 140 D2–D3 ✉ Store Strandstræde 3 ☎ 33 14 13 41 Ⓠ Kongens Nytorv AX, DC, MC, VI

Riz Raz $
This popular buffet restaurant serves Mediterranean-style hot and cold vegetarian dishes and salads, as

well as Greek lamb and fish dishes. In good weather the garden is open.
⊞ 140 C2 ✉ Kompagnistræde 20 Ⓠ Kongens Nytorv or Nørreport ☎ 33 15 05 75 DC, MC, VI

Skt. Gertruds Kloster $$$
Housed in an old monastery building, this smart, candlelit restaurant has a vaulted cellar and atmospheric dining rooms. Fish dishes are the specialty, with everything from mussels to lobster, and there's a big selection of wines. Reservations are advised.
⊞ 140 C3 ✉ Hauser Plads 32 Ⓠ Closed for lunch Ⓠ Nørreport ☎ 33 14 66 30 AX, DC, MC, VI

ODENSE HOTELS
Price guide: (double room with breakfast for two people)
$ DKr400–DK700
$$ DKr700–DK1,200
$$$ over DKr1,200

City Hotel Odense $$
This is a comfortable, modern hotel near the Hans Christian Andersen House in the heart of the Old Town.
⊞ 146 C2 ✉ Hans Mulesgade 5 ☎ 66 12 12 58; fax 66 12 93 64 AX, MC, VI

Hotel Domir $
This friendly, medium-size hotel with comfortable rooms and plenty of amenities is located in the city center, within minutes of the railroad station and within easy walking distance of the Town Hall.
⊞ 146 Off the map ✉ Hans Tausensgade 19 ☎ 66 12 14 27; fax 66 12 14 13 AX, MC, VI

First Hotel Grand $$–$$$
One of Odense's most expensive hotels is situated in a handsome old building across from the Fyns Kunstmuseum (Funen Art Museum), close to the city center.
⊞ 146 B2–B3 ✉ Jernbanegade 18 ☎ 66 11 71 71; fax 66 14 11 71 AX, MC, VI

Pjentehus $
Just outside the city center, Pjentehus is a small, reasonably priced and comfortable bed and breakfast in a pleasant villa near the Hans Christian Andersen House.
⊞ 146 C2 ✉ Pjentedamsgade 14 ☎ 66 12 15 55; fax 66 17 82 08 No credit cards

Radisson SAS Hans Christian Andersen Hotel $$$
A very luxurious, modern hotel, located close to Hans Christian Andersen House and next door to the Concert Hall and the Carl Nielsen Museum, the Radisson has its own restaurant, sauna, solarium, billiards room and casino.
⊞ 146 C2 ✉ Claus Bergs Gade 7 ☎ 66 14 78 00; fax 66 14 78 90 AX, MC, VI

ODENSE RESTAURANTS
Price guide: (dinner per person, excluding drinks)
$ DKr100–DK250
$$ DKr250–DK300
$$$ over DKr300

Den Gamle Kro $$$
This restaurant occupies a magnificent old building dating from 1683. Meals are served in several rooms, including the brick-vaulted cellar. Expect excellent Danish cuisine and other dishes.
⊞ 146 B2–C2 ✉ Overgade 23 ☎ 66 12 14 33 AX, MC, VI

Den Grimme Ælling $
A charming little restaurant on a cobbled lane, just across the main road from the Hans Christian Andersen House. It is known for its extravagant buffets.
⊞ 146 B2 ✉ Hans Jensens Stræde 1 ☎ 65 91 70 30 AX, MC, VI

Jensens Bøfhus $
This popular lunchtime grill and evening favorite serves steaks with lavish salads.
⊞ 146 A2 ✉ Kongensgade 10 ☎ 66 14 59 59 AX, MC, VI

Marie Louise $$$
A very stylish French restaurant located in a charming courtyard complex. It is surrounded by old houses.
⊞ 146 B2 ✉ Lottrupsgård 9 ☎ 66 17 92 95 AX, MC, VI

Restaurant Air Pub $$
This pub and restaurant has a good atmosphere to go along with hearty Danish cooking and a decent selection of beers.
⊞ 146 A2 ✉ Kongensgade 41 ☎ 66 14 66 08 Ⓞ Closed Sun. AX, MC, VI

Denmark

Finland, France

KEY TO SYMBOLS

✚ map page number and coordinates
✉ address
☎ telephone number
🕐 days/times closed
Ⓜ nearest subway station
🚌 nearest bus/trolley
bus/tram/funicular route
⛴ ferry
$$$ expensive
$$ moderate
$ inexpensive
AX American Express
DC Diners Club
MC MasterCard
VI VISA

Russian Restaurants

You can sample authentic Russian cuisine in Helsinki at one of the city's several Russian restaurants. Russian food is not noted for its lightness of touch, but it can be adventurous and is extremely filling. You can even start with caviar and sour cream if you want, before plunging into hearty meat dishes – lamb is a specialty – with cakes, fruit pies and ice cream for dessert. Two notable choices to try are Kasakka at Meritullinkatu 13, (☎ 06 135 6288), and Galleria Hariton at Kasarmikatu 44, (☎ 09 622 1717).

HELSINKI HOTELS

Price guide: (double room with breakfast for two people)
$ €50–€100
$$ €100–€150
$$$ over €150

Hotel Anna $$–$$$

This comfortable hotel is conveniently located on one of the quiet streets of the city center, within walking distance of the Esplanade. Its moderate size contributes to a friendly and relaxed atmosphere.
✚ 158 C3 ✉ Annankatu 1 ☎ 09 616 621; fax 09 602 664 🚌 14, 14B, 17; tram 3B, 10 AX, MC, VI

Helka $–$$

Located in the heart of the city, this recently renovated hotel offers good service, good value and a sauna. Special weekend rates.
✚ 158 B4 ✉ Pohjoinen Rautatiekatu 23 ☎ 09 613 580; fax 09 441 087 🚌 14, 14B, 32, 39, 45, 47 AX, MC, VI

Palace Hotel & Restaurant Linna $$–$$$

Formerly known as the Hotel Lord, this 48-room, Jugend-style hotel is part of the upscale Palace group of hotels and restaurants.
✚ 158 C4 ✉ Lönnrotinkatu 29 ☎ 010 344 4100; fax 010 344 4101 🚌 20, 20N; tram 10 AX, MC, VI

Scandic Hotel Grand Marina $$$

Step from ferry to foyer, if you travel by Viking Line, and stay in this large hotel on the western side of the harbor. Rooms are elegant and there are bars, a bistro and the Grand Café.
✚ 158 D4 ✉ Katajanokanlaituri 7 ☎ 09 16661; fax 09 664 764 🚌 52; tram 4 AX, MC, VI

Scandic Hotel Marski $$$

This large hotel is conveniently located right at the heart of things on Mannerheimintie street.
✚ 158 C4 ✉ Mannerheimintie 10 ☎ 09 68061; fax 09 642 377 🚌 20N, 24, 42; tram 10 AX, MC, VI

HELSINKI RESTAURANTS

Price guide: (dinner per person, excluding drinks)
$ €10–€25
$$ €25–€35
$$$ over €35

G W Sondmans $$$

Located in the 19th-century house of a naval captain, this restaurant serves modern Finnish dishes such as roasted arctic char and fillet of reindeer.
✚ 159 D3 ✉ Eteläranta 16 ☎ 09 622 6410 🚌 Tram 36 AX, DC, MC, VI

George $$

Try pigeon stuffed with spinach in herb sauce at this small restaurant, where Finnish cuisine is tempered with French and Italian flair.
✚ 158 C4 ✉ Kalevankatu 17 ☎ 09 647 662 🕐 Closed Sat. lunch and Sun. 🚌 20N, 24, 42 AX, MC, VI

Kappeli $$

This is a stylish restaurant and café, with outside terraces on the Esplanade, in a pavilion of cast iron and glass dating from 1867. Good Finnish and Scandinavian dishes are offered, with an emphasis on fresh seasonal produce. In summer there are concerts at the nearby bandstand.
✚ 158 C4 ✉ Eteläesplanadi 1 ☎ 09 681 2440 🚌 13, 64S, 77S; tram 1, 1A AX, MC, VI

Lyon $$

Good-quality French cuisine is presented in this unassuming and friendly restaurant opposite the Helsinki Opera House. The roasted breast of goose is a favorite.
✚ 158 C5 ✉ Mannerheimintie 56 ☎ 09 408 131 🕐 Closed Mon. lunch, Sat. lunch and Sun. 🚌 16, 13, 21v; tram 4, 10 AX, DC, MC, VI

Nuevo $$$

This top-quality restaurant in the "Street Museum" serves Finnish cuisine; fish specialties are offered when in season.
✚ 158 C4 ✉ Sofiankatu 4 ☎ 09 626 6676 🕐 Closed Sun. 🚌 Tram 1, 2, 4, 7, 3B, 3T AX, DC, MC, VI

PARIS HOTELS

Price guide: (double room with breakfast for two people)
$ under €120
$$ €120–€180
$$$ over €180

Bristol Paris $$$

The Louis XV-style rooms affirm the elegance of this hotel, which has a

rooftop pool and superb restaurant.
✚ 174 B3 ✉ 112 rue du Faubourg-
St.-Honoré ☎ 01 53 43 43 00;
fax 01 53 43 43 01 🚇 Miromesnil
AX, DC, MC, VI

Hôtel des Deux-Îles $$$

A peaceful hotel, beautifully housed
in a 17th-century dwelling, with
understated charm and elegance.
✚ 174 D2 ✉ 59 rue St.-Louis-en-
l'Île ☎ 01 43 26 13 35; fax 01 43 29
60 25 🚇 Pont-Marie AX, MC, VI

Hôtel des Grandes Écoles $

This typically French hotel has pretty
bedrooms and is set in a garden on a
narrow street in the Latin Quarter.
It's an excellent value.
✚ 174 D2 ✉ 75 rue Cardinal-
Lemoine ☎ 01 43 26 79 23; fax 01
43 25 28 15 🚇 Cardinal-Lemoine
MC, VI

Istria $

Set in the heart of Montparnasse,
this small and comfortable hotel
once hosted Ernest Hemingway.
✚ 174 C1 ✉ 29 rue Campagne-
Première ☎ 01 43 20 91 82;
fax 01 43 22 48 45 🚇 Raspail
AX, DC, MC, VI

Pavillon de la Reine $$$

A romantic and luxurious hotel,
complete with four-poster beds, set
in a garden on the beautiful place
des Vosges.
✚ 174 E2 ✉ 28 place des Vosges
☎ 01 40 29 19 19; fax 01 40 29 19 20
🚇 Saint-Paul AX, DC, MC, VI

PARIS RESTAURANTS
Price guide: (dinner per person,
excluding drinks)
$ €20–€30
$$ €30–€45
$$$ over €45

La Coupole $$

This sprawling art-deco brasserie,
renowned in the 1920s, serves
seafood, fish and steaks.
✚ 174 C1 ✉ 102 boulevard du
Montparnasse ☎ 01 43 20 14 20
🚇 Vavin AX, DC, MC, VI

Le Dôme $$$

The specialties at this famous
Montparnasse brasserie are seafood
and fish. Service is efficient.
✚ 174 C1 ✉ 108 boulevard du
Montparnasse ☎ 01 43 35 25 81
🚇 Vavin AX, DC, MC, VI

Le Grizzli $$

In the heart of the Marais, this old-
fashioned bistro serves dishes from
central and southwest France.
✚ 174 D3 ✉ 7 rue St.-Martin
☎ 01 48 87 77 56 🚇 Hôtel-de-
Ville AX, MC, VI

Nos Ancêtres les Gaulois $$

This picturesque island restaurant
offers a prix-fixe menu in convivial
17th-century surroundings.
✚ 174 D2 ✉ 39 rue St.-Louis-en-
l'Île ☎ 01 46 33 66 07 🚇 Closed
Mon.–Sat. lunch 🚇 Pont-Marie
AX, DC, MC, VI

Le Poulbot Gourmet $$

This cozy restaurant is decorated
with pictures of Montmartre. The
owner-chef's cuisine is refined (veal
kidneys in wine sauce are a
specialty). Prix-fixe menu available.
✚ 174 Off the map ✉ 39 rue
Lamarck ☎ 01 46 06 86 00
🚇 Closed Sun. dinner 🚇 Lamarck-
Caulaincourt VI

Saint Amarante $

Hearty country cooking is the
specialty at this friendly and relaxed
bistro near the Bastille.
✚ 174 E2 ✉ 4 rue Biscornet
☎ 01 43 43 00 08 🚇 Closed Sat.
lunch, Sun., Mon. and Aug.
🚇 Bastille MC, VI

LYON HOTELS
Price guide: (double room with
breakfast for two people)
$ under €120
$$ €120–€180
$$$ over €180

Grand Hôtel des Terreaux $–$$

This comfortable, medium-size hotel
is beautifully situated just behind a
lovely central square.
✚ 186 B3 ✉ 16 rue Lanterne
☎ 04 78 27 04 10; fax 04 78 27 97
75 🚇 Hôtel de Ville AX, DC, MC, VI

Hotel Sofitel Lyon Bellecour $$$

This deluxe hotel, centrally located
on the Rhône river, is a good choice.
✚ 186 B2 ✉ 20 quai Gailleton
☎ 04 72 41 20 20; fax 04 72 40 05 50
🚇 Bellecour AX, DC, MC, VI

Libertel Beaux-Arts Tradition $–$$

An early 20th-century building
houses this comfortable hotel in the
center of the Presqu'Île.

✚ 186 B3 ✉ 75 rue Président
Édouard-Hérriot ☎ 04 78 38 09 50;
fax 04 78 42 19 19 🚇 Cordeliers or
Bellecour AX, DC, MC, VI

St.-Paul $

Consider staying at this excellent
budget choice in the middle of the Old
Town. It has simple and airy rooms.
✚ 186 A3 ✉ 6 rue Lainerie
☎ 04 78 28 13 29; fax 04 72 00 97 27
AX, DC, MC, VI

La Villa Florentine $$$

A former convent, this deluxe hotel
with many amenities – including a
pretty garden – stands above the
Old Town, on the slopes of Fourvière.
✚ 186 A2 ✉ 25–27 montée
St.-Barthélémy ☎ 04 72 56 56 56;
fax 04 72 40 90 56 🚇 Hôtel de Ville
or Vieux Lyon AX, DC, MC, VI

LYON RESTAURANTS
Price guide: (dinner per person,
excluding drinks)
$ €20–€30
$$ €30–€45
$$$ over €45

Brasserie Lyon Plage $$$

This wonderful restaurant uses fine
ingredients, such as lobster and foie
gras, in balanced dishes.
Reservations are advised.
✚ 186 Off the map ✉ Hôtel
Métropole Concorde, 85 quai
Joseph-Gillet ☎ 04 72 10 44 34
🚇 Closed first 3 weeks of Aug.
🚌 40, 43, 90E AX, DC, MC, VI

Le Café du Soleil $

One of the oldest bouchons in
Lyon serves huge portions of French
and Lyonnaise fare in a friendly
atmosphere.
✚ 186 A2 ✉ 2 rue St.-Georges,
place de la Trinité ☎ 04 78 37 60 02
🚇 Closed Sun. 🚇 Vieux Lyon
AX, DC, MC, VI

Chabert et Fils $

Sophisticated Lyonnais specialties
served here include a chicken-liver
gateau and delicate soups.
✚ 186 B2 ✉ 11 rue des
Marronniers ☎ 04 78 37 01 94
🚇 Bellecour AX, DC, MC, VI

Le Comptoir du Bœuf $

You can try Lyonnais specialties in
this cozy, late-night restaurant next
to the cathedral.
✚ 186 A2 ✉ rue Boeuf 22

France

France

KEY TO SYMBOLS

- ➕ map page number and coordinates
- ✉ address
- ☎ telephone number
- ⊘ days/times closed
- Ⓜ nearest subway station
- 🚌 nearest bus/trolley
- bus/tram/funicular route
- ⛴ ferry
- **$$$** expensive
- **$$** moderate
- **$** inexpensive
- AX American Express
- DC Diners Club
- MC MasterCard
- VI VISA

☎ 04 78 92 69 27   Ⓜ Vieux Lyon AX, DC, MC, VI

Têtedoie $$–$$$
Rich but light specialties are on the menu at this elegant and professionally staffed restaurant.
➕ 186 A3   ✉ 54 quai Pierre-Scize   ☎ 04 78 29 40 10   ⊘ Closed Sat. lunch, Sun. and Aug.   Ⓜ Hôtel de Ville   AX, DC, MC, VI

NICE HOTELS
Price guide: (double room with breakfast for two people)
$ under €120
$$ €120–€180
$$$ over €180

Four Points Sheraton Elysée Palace $$$
There are excellent facilities, including a rooftop pool, at this modern luxury hotel.
➕ 194 B1   ✉ 59 promenade des Anglais   ☎ 04 93 97 90 90; fax 04 93 44 50 40   🚌 6, 9, 10, 12 AX, DC, MC, VI

Gounod $$
This moderately priced *belle époque* choice is in a quiet location, and is a 10-minute walk from the sea.
➕ 194 C2   ✉ 3 rue Gounod   ☎ 04 93 16 42 00; fax 04 93 88 23 84   ⊘ Closed late Nov.–late Dec.   🚌 9, 10, 12 AX, DC, MC, VI

Négresco $$$
This is one of the world's great hotels in the flamboyant *belle époque* style; superb comfort, service and facilities.
➕ 194 B1   ✉ 37 promenade des Anglais   ☎ 04 93 16 64 00; fax 04 93 88 35 68   🚌 6, 9, 10, 12 AX, DC, MC, VI

Villa Eden $
Converted mansion built for a Russian countess, half a block inland from the seafront. Some rooms have sea views.
➕ 194 B1   ✉ 99bis Promenade des Anglais   ☎ 04 93 86 53 70; fax 04 93 97 67 97   🚌 6, 9, 10, 12 AX, DC, MC, VI

Windsor $$
This famous hotel is centrally located and has a garden pool and beautifully frescoed rooms.
➕ 194 B1   ✉ 11 rue Dalpozzo   ☎ 04 93 88 59 35; fax 04 93 88 94 57   🚌 6, 9, 10, 12 AX, DC, MC, VI

NICE RESTAURANTS
Price guide: (dinner per person, excluding drinks)
$ €20–€30
$$ €30–€45
$$$ over €45

Boccaccio $$–$$$
Located in the city center, this restaurant offers mouthwatering seafood specialties; in summer you can dine on the terrace.
➕ 194 C1   ✉ 7 rue Masséna   ☎ 04 93 87 71 76   🚌 3, 7, 10 AX, DC, MC, VI

Le Chantecler $$$
Nice's finest restaurant, and one of the best in France, is housed in the opulent Hôtel Négresco and serves traditional French food. Reservations are advised.
➕ 194 B1   ✉ Hôtel Négresco, 37 promenade des Anglais   ☎ 04 93 16 64 00   ⊘ Closed Jan.   🚌 6, 12 AX, DC, MC, VI

Flo Nice $–$$
The food in this lively open-kitchen brasserie, housed in an old theater, is fine, but the decor and ambience are what make it worth a visit. It's also open late.
➕ 194 D1   ✉ 2–4 rue Sacha Guitry   ☎ 04 93 13 38 38   🚌 1, 4, 10, 22 AX, DC, VI

Nissa La Bella $
Locals flock to this Old Town restaurant, which serves a good range of Niçoise specialties including *socca*, a chickpea pancake.
➕ 194 D1   ✉ 6 rue Ste.-Réparate   ☎ 04 93 62 10 20   ⊘ Closed Tue. in winter   🚌 6, 9, 10 AX, DC, MC, VI

La Petite Maison $–$$$
Join the regulars who enjoy good home cooking from a menu that features seasonal specialties and a fantastic range of hors d'oeuvres. Reservations are advised.
➕ 194 D1   ✉ 11 rue St.-François-de-Paule   ☎ 04 93 92 59 59   ⊘ Closed Sat. lunch   🚌 9, 10, 12, 22 AX, DC, MC, VI

STRASBOURG HOTELS
Price guide: (double room with breakfast for two people)
$ €50–€100
$$ €100–€150
$$$ over €150

France, Germany

Baumann $–$$
Situated opposite the cathedral, this comfortable, traditional hotel has a lovely terrace and good restaurant. It's an excellent vacation choice.
➕ 200 B1–B2 ✉ 16 place de la Cathédrale ☎ 03 88 32 42 14; fax 03 88 23 03 92 🚌 10, 11, 21, 24; tram A, D AX, DC, MC, VI

Cardinal de Rohan $$
This pretty hotel on one of Strasbourg's most picturesque and historic streets is an easy stroll from the main sights.
➕ 200 B1 ✉ 17–19 rue du Maroquin ☎ 03 88 22 12 12; fax 03 88 75 65 37 🚌 10, 11, 14, 21, 24; tram A, D AX, DC, VI

Cathédrale $–$$
This excellent cathedral square hotel is close to Strasbourg's main sights and some of the city's best restaurants.
➕ 200 B1–B2 ✉ 12–13 place de la Cathédrale ☎ 03 88 22 12 12; fax 03 88 23 28 00 🚌 11, 14, 21, 24; tram A D AX, DC, MC, VI

Comfort Hotel Center $
This good-value budget hotel, built in the 19th century, overlooks the water on the northern side of the old city center.
➕ 200 A2 ✉ 1 quai de Paris ☎ 03 88 15 17 17; fax 03 88 15 17 15 🚌 4, 6; tram A, B, C, D AX, VI

Mercure Strasbourg Centre $$
This convenient and comfortable hotel, located in the historic center, has large, soundproof rooms and offers very good facilities.
➕ 200 B2 ✉ 25 rue Thomann ☎ 03 90 22 70 70; fax 03 90 22 70 71 🚌 4, 6; tram A, B, C, D AX, DC, MC, VI

STRASBOURG RESTAURANTS
Price guide: (dinner per person, excluding drinks)
$ €20–€30
$$ €30–€45
$$$ over €45

Aux Armes de Strasbourg $
Interesting local dishes and a huge variety of beers are served at this wonderfully atmospheric, wood-paneled restaurant.
➕ 200 B1 ✉ 9 place Gutenberg ☎ 03 88 32 85 62 🚌 11, 14, 21, 24; tram A, D AX, DC, MC, VI

Au Bon Vivant $
One of the few remaining traditional family-run restaurants in the city center is this winner, serving local specialties in a relaxed atmosphere.
➕ 200 B1 ✉ 7 rue du Maroquin ☎ 03 88 32 77 81 🕐 Closed Thu. dinner and Fri. 🚌 11, 14, 21, 24; tram A, D AX, MC, VI

Le Bæckeoffe d'Alsace $
An old timbered building in the loveliest part of the Old Town is the setting for this traditional, family-run *winstub* (there is another at 24 rue des Hallebardes).
➕ 200 A1 ✉ 14 rue des Moulins ☎ 03 88 23 05 40 🚌 11, 14, 21, 24; tram A, D AX, MC, VI

La Cloche à Fromage $$
This renowned restaurant concentrates on cheese-based cuisine, with over 200 French varieties to sample in addition to *raclettes* and fondues. Meat and fish dishes also are available.
➕ 200 B1 ✉ 27 rue des Tonneliers ☎ 03 88 23 13 19 🕐 Closed Tue. lunch 🚌 11, 14, 21, 24; tram A, D MC, VI

Au Petit Tonnelier $
This family-run restaurant, on one of the Old Town's prettiest streets, serves seasonal and regional dishes.
➕ 200 B1 ✉ 16 rue des Tonneliers ☎ 03 88 32 53 54 🕐 Closed Sun. lunch 🚌 11, 14, 21, 24; tram A, D AX, MC, VI

BERLIN HOTELS
Price guide: (double room with breakfast for two people)
$ up to €75
$$ €75–€150
$$$ over €150

Alsterhof $$–$$$
This is a small 1960s hotel located behind the KaDeWe department store. Despite the plain exterior, it is stylish inside, with 200 rooms, a smart restaurant and an annex conservatory.
➕ 216 B2 ✉ Augsburger Strasse 5 ☎ 030 212 420; fax 030 212 42 73 🚇 U-Bahn to Augsburger Strasse, or Wittenbergplatz; S-Bahn to Zoologischer Garten AX, DC, MC, VI

Golden Tulip Kronprinz $$–$$$
This elegant hotel, in a 70-room late 19th-century house surrounded

by chestnut trees, is only a few steps from the Ku'damm and has an attractive terraced beer garden.
➕ 216 A2 ✉ Kronprinzendamm 1 ☎ 030 896 030; fax 030 893 1215 🚇 U-Bahn to Adenauerplatz; S-Bahn to Halensee AX, DC, MC, VI

Kempinski Hotel Bristol $$$
This hotel, once on Unter den Linden but now in the Ku'damm, has a famous name and a traditional style, with formal furnishings, chandeliers and deep-pile carpets. There are 301 rooms and 44 suites, and an elaborate menu in the restaurant.
➕ 216 B2 ✉ Kurfürstendamm 27 ☎ 030 884 340; fax 030 883 6075 🚇 U-Bahn to Uhlandstrasse; U-Bahn/S-Bahn to Zoologischer Garten AX, DC, MC, VI

Transit $
Once a factory, this hotel has been converted into pleasant, airy accommodations. It's basic but clean, in an attractive part of the Kreuzberg quarter, and the English-speaking staff are welcoming.
➕ 217 D1 ✉ Hagelberger Strasse 53–54 ☎ 030 789 0470; fax 030 78 90 47 77 🚇 U-Bahn to Mehringdamm; S-Bahn to Yorckstrasse AX, MC, VI

Hotel-Pension Wittelsbach $$
The Wittelsbach caters to children, with a family floor including fully equipped playhouses, strollers and highchairs.
➕ 216 B1 ✉ Wittelsbacherstrasse 22 ☎ 030 864 9840; fax 030 862 1532 🚇 U-Bahn to Konstanzer Strasse; S-Bahn to Charlottenburg AX, MC, VI

BERLIN RESTAURANTS
Price guide: (dinner per person, excluding drinks)
$ up to €15
$$ €15–€30
$$$ over €30

Alt Luxemburg $$$
What you get at one of the city's best restaurants is German food by chef Karl Wannemacher, some of the country's best.
➕ 216 A2 ✉ Windscheidstrasse 31 ☎ 030 323 8730 🕐 Closed for lunch and Sun. 🚇 U-Bahn to Sophie-Charlotten-Platz AX, DC, VI

Germany

KEY TO SYMBOLS

- ✚ map page number and coordinates
- ✉ address
- ☎ telephone number
- 🕐 days/times closed
- Ⓜ nearest subway station
- 🚌 nearest bus/trolley bus/tram/funicular route
- ⛴ ferry
- **$$$** expensive
- **$$** moderate
- **$** inexpensive
- AX American Express
- DC Diners Club
- MC MasterCard
- VI VISA

Strasbourg Specials

Visualize French flair and imagination combined with high-quality ingredients and German influences, and you'll begin to understand the gastronomic delights that await you in Strasbourg. This is the home of foie gras, fatted goose liver eaten whole or made into pâté; *choucroute* (sauerkraut), assorted meats and spicy sausages served with mounds of pickled cabbage; and *kougelhupf*, yeast cake traditionally eaten for breakfast. There are other, less well-known regional dishes; look for *bæckeoffe*, a slow-cooked casserole featuring three different meats, and *tarte flambée*, an unctuous hot onion tart. The smooth, pungently aromatic Munster is Strasbourg's local cheese.

Berliner Stube $$

Berliner Leber (liver) is the specialty at this restaurant near the Ku'damm; international dishes are served, too.
✚ 216 B2 ✉ Los Angeles Platz 1
☎ 030 212 7750
Ⓜ Kurfürstendamm AX, DC, MC, VI

Borchardt $$$

Discerning Berliners love this attractive, 1920s-style bistro, a lunch spot where "new" and international cuisine is featured.
✚ 216 D2 ✉ Französische Strasse 47 ☎ 030 8188 6262
Ⓜ Französische Strasse AX, DC, MC, VI

Dressler $$–$$$

Fine German or French cuisine can be enjoyed inside this sophisticated Art Deco restaurant or outside on the sun terrace. Seasonal cuisine includes game and young herring.
✚ 216 B2 ✉ Kurfürstendamm 207–208 ☎ 030 883 35 30
Ⓜ Kurfürstendamm AX, DC, MC, VI

Lutter & Wegner $$$

Austrian and German dishes are served in a historic 19th-century restaurant/wine bar on the Gendarmenmarkt, where the very popular Berlin Symphony Orchestra has its home.
✚ 217 D/E2 ✉ Charlottenstrasse 56 ☎ 030 20 29 54 10 Ⓜ U-Bahn Stadtmitte AX, MC, VI

Zum Nussbaum $

The name of this pub-style restaurant, or *Gasthaus*, in the Nikolaiviertel area means "The Nut Tree."
✚ 216 E3 ✉ Am Nussbaum 3
☎ 030 242 3095 Alexanderplatz MC, VI

COLOGNE HOTELS

Price guide: (double room with breakfast for two people)
$ up to €75
$$ €75–€150
$$$ over €150

Buchholz $$–$$$

This privately owned, family-run hotel with a friendly staff has 19 bedrooms. The central but quiet location is an added bonus. A shuttle service to the airport can be provided for customers on request.
✚ 225 C4 ✉ Kunibertsgasse 5
☎ 0221 16083-0; fax 0221 16083-41
Ⓜ Dom/Hbf AX, DC, MC, VI

CM City Class Hotel Europa am Dom $$–$$$

Conveniently located directly opposite the cathedral, this hotel is close to most museums. Nonsmoking rooms are available.
✚ 225 B3 ✉ Am Hof 38–46
☎ 0221 2058-0; fax 0221 258 2032
Ⓜ Dom/Hbf AX, DC, MC, VI

Das Kleine Stapelhäuschen $$

Two adjacent town houses, in historically interesting buildings on the Rhine promenade, house a friendly hotel with a comfortable wine bar that's just a short walk from the cathedral.
✚ 225 C3 ✉ Fischmarkt 1–3
☎ 0221 272 7777; fax 0221 257 4232 🚌 Tram 1, 7, 9 AX, MC, VI

Sofitel Mondial am Dom $$–$$$

Despite its dull exterior, this is a comfortable, stylish hotel, situated between the cathedral and the river – ideal for exploring the Old Town. There's also a restaurant serving international and regional cuisine.
✚ 225 B3 ✉ Kurt-Hackenberg-Platz 1 ☎ 0221 20630; fax 0221 206 3522 Ⓜ Dom/Hbf AX, DC, MC, VI

Viktoria $$

This turn-of-the-20th-century *Jugendstil* building by the Rhine offers some rooms with river views and a generous breakfast buffet.
✚ 225 Off the map ✉ Worringer Strasse 23 ☎ 0221 973 1720; fax 0221 727 067 Ⓜ Reichensperger Platz AX, DC, MC, VI

COLOGNE RESTAURANTS

Price guide: (dinner per person, excluding drinks)
$ up to €15
$$ €15–€30
$$$ over €30

Bosporus $$$

Located in the multicultural quarter of Weidengasse, Bosporus has four set menus offering a wide range of Turkish dishes. The nearby Eigelstein quarter is equally lively.
✚ 225 B4 ✉ Weidengasse 36
☎ 0221 125 265 🚌 Tram 6, 15, 17 AX, DC, MC, VI

Brauhaus Sion $$

This busy side-street brewery-tavern, near the cathedral, is especially popular for lunch and coffee, and for strong *Kölsch* beer.

Traditionally dressed waiters roll out the barrels.

➕ 225 B3   ✉ Unter Taschenmacher 5–7   ☎ 0221 257 8540   🚋 Tram 1, 7, 9 MC, VI

Kintaro $$–$$$
Japanese dishes are served in this popular sushi restaurant, where particularly good entrées include seaweed *(hijiki)* and octopus, and cucumber and seaweed in vinegar *(tako su)*. Reservations are advised.

➕ 225 A3   ✉ Friesenstrasse 16   ☎ 0221 135 255   🚇 Friesenplatz AX, DC, MC, VI

Päffgen in der Altstadt $$
This pub, belonging to Cologne's smallest brewery, is centrally located and convenient to the city's main attractions. Tasty regional dishes and *Kölsch* beer are served in a congenial atmosphere.

➕ 225 B2   ✉ Heumarkt 62   ☎ 0221 257 7765   🕐 Closed Mon.   🚋 Tram 1, 7, 9 No credit cards

Paul's Restaurant $$$
Located in a former pub in a typical quarter of Cologne, Paul's serves traditional, international and modern cuisine. A good selection of German wines is available.

➕ 225 B3   ✉ Bülowstrasse 2   ☎ 0221 766 839   🕐 Closed Mon.   🚋 Tram 6, 12, 18 MC

MUNICH HOTELS
Price guide: (double room with breakfast for two people)
$ up to €75
$$ €75–€150
$$$ over €150

Englischer Garten Hotel $–$$
This hotel, at the edge of the English Garden in Schwabing, is housed in a converted water mill. You'll really feel as if you're in the heart of the country, especially when eating the breakfast buffet, served in the garden in summer.

➕ 230 Off the map   ✉ Liebergesellstrasse 8   ☎ 089 383 9410; fax 089 38 39 41 33   🚇 Münchener Freiheit AX, DC, MC, VI

Mandarin Oriental Munich $$$
Celebrity guests including Madonna and Prince Charles have stayed at the city's newest luxury hotel, with 73 rooms including luxurious suites.

➕ 231 D2   ✉ Neuturmstrasse 1   ☎ 089 29 09 80; fax 089 22 25 39   🚇 Marienplatz   🚋 Tram 19 AX, DC, MC, VI

Opera $$$
This 56-bed hotel, set in an old mansion with elegant arcades and a Renaissance courtyard, is convenient to upscale shopping.

➕ 231 D2   ✉ St. Anna-Strasse 10   ☎ 089 210 4940; fax 089 2104 9477   🚇 Lehel   🚋 Tram 19 AX, MC, VI

Splendid $$
Rooms at this small bed and breakfast in the city center are decorated in a range of styles, from baroque to Bavarian.

➕ 230 D2   ✉ Tierstrasse 49   ☎ 089 23 80 80; fax 089 23 80 83 65   🚇 Lehel AX, DC, MC, VI

Torbräu $$$
Munich's oldest hotel has been in the heart of the Old Town for more than five centuries. On the premises are an Italian restaurant, café and 86 quiet, individually styled rooms.

➕ 231 C2   ✉ Tal 41   ☎ 089 24 23 40; fax 089 24 23 42 35   🚇 Marienplatz or Isartor AX, MC, VI

MUNICH RESTAURANTS
Price guide: (dinner per person, excluding drinks)
$ up to €15
$$ €15–€30
$$$ over €30

Augustiner Restaurant $
Munich's oldest surviving brewery was producing its own beer until 1897, and now serves Bavarian dishes in the large dining hall. There's a beer garden in the courtyard.

➕ 231 B2   ✉ Neuhauser Strasse 27   ☎ 089 23 18 32 57   🚇 Marienplatz or Karlsplatz AX, DC, MC, VI

Halali $$$
Unpretentious regional cooking, focusing on game dishes such as venison, is served with special touches like cranberry or wild mushroom sauce.

➕ 231 D3   ✉ Schönfeldstrasse 22   ☎ 089 28 59 09   🕐 Closed Sun.   🚇 Odeonsplatz AX, MC, VI

Ratskeller $$
Hearty local dishes are served in the Ratskeller tavern, situated in

---

the New Town Hall's impressive vaulted cellars.

➕ 231 C2   ✉ Marienplatz 8   ☎ 089 21 99 89-0   🚇 Marienplatz AX, MC, VI

Schlosscafé Palmenhaus $$–$$$
This elegant café is located in the palm house at Nymphenburg Palace.

➕ 230 Off the map   ✉ Schloss Nymphenburg, entrance 43   ☎ 089 17 53 09   🕐 Closes at 5 (winter) and 6 (summer)   🚋 Tram 12, 17 VI

Spatenhaus an der Oper $$$
The atmosphere is relaxed and the service good at this favored after-theater restaurant, which serves a Bavarian menu as well as other regional and international dishes.

➕ 230 C3   ✉ Residenzstrasse 12   ☎ 089 290 7060   🚇 Marienplatz, Odeonsplatz; tram 19 AX, MC, VI

ATHENS HOTELS
Price guide: (double room with breakfast for two people)
$ €40–€60
$$ €60–€120
$$$ over €120

Acropolis House $
This clean and simple family-run hotel on the edge of the Plaka is a good mid-range choice, although not all rooms have baths.

➕ 244 B2   ✉ 6–8 Kodrou Plaka   ☎ 210 322 2344; fax 210 324 4143   🚋 11, 18 AX, DC, VI

Art Gallery Hotel $$
This welcoming small hotel is a short distance south of the Acropolis. It has a pleasant, old-fashioned ambience, but with modern conveniences.

➕ Off the map   ✉ 5 Erehthiou   ☎ 210 923 8376; fax 210 923 3025   🚋 1, 22, 23, 035, 230 AX, MC, VI

Grande Bretagne $$$
Athens' most historic, grandest and very traditional hotel, offering the highest level of service and amenities. It has retained its sense of history even after recent renovations.

➕ 244 C2   ✉ Syntagmatos   ☎ 210 333 0000; fax 01 322 8034   🚋 1, 18, 15 AX, DC, MC, VI

Phaedra $
A location at the quieter end of Plaka makes up for one or two fairly small rooms at this pleasant hotel.

➕ 244 C2   ✉ Adrianou/Lisicratous

KEY TO SYMBOLS

✚ map page number and
coordinates
✉ address
☎ telephone number
🕐 days/times closed
Ⓜ nearest subway station
🚌 nearest bus/trolley
bus/tram/funicular route
⛴ ferry
$$$ expensive
$$ moderate
$ inexpensive
AX American Express
DC Diners Club
MC MasterCard
VI VISA

& Cherefontos 16 Street ☎ 210 323
8461; fax 210 322 7795 Ⓜ Akropoli
🚌 9, 11, 15 AX, DC, VI

Saint George Lycabettus $$$

Beautifully situated on the quiet,
shady slopes of Lycabettus hill, this
first-class hotel offers lovely views
from its rooftop restaurant.
✚ 244 D3 ✉ 2 Kleomenous-
Dexamini ☎ 210 729 0711; fax 210
721 0439 🚌 3, 8, 13 AX, DC, MC, VI

Price guide: (dinner per person,
excluding drinks)
$ €6–€12
$$ €12–€20
$$$ over €20

Archeon Gefsis $$$

Dine at this imaginative restaurant
that offers meat and fish dishes
prepared from classical recipes.
✚ 244 A4 ✉ Kodratou 22 ☎ 210
523 9661 Ⓜ Metaxourghio
AX, DC, VI

O Platanos $

This friendly Plaka *taverna* serves
simple and delicious food at both
indoor and outdoor tables.
✚ 244 B2 ✉ 4 Diogenous, Plaka
☎ 210 322 0666 🚌 1, 9, 11, 18
No credit cards

Psaras $$

Tucked below the Acropolis on one
of Plaka's prettiest streets is this
100-year-old *taverna,* serving home-
cooked traditional dishes.
✚ 244 B2 ✉ 16 Erekteos and
Erotokritou Plaka ☎ 210 321 8733
Ⓜ Thission 🚌 1, 9, 11, 18
AX, DC, VI

Saita $

This popular basement restaurant
in the Plaka has good food and
friendly service. (Pavement tables
close to the door belong to another
restaurant.)
✚ 244 B2 ✉ 21 Kidathineon
☎ 01 322 6671 🚌 1, 5, 9, 18
No credit cards

Symposia $$$

Located in a stylish old house, this
fine restaurant specializes in game,
such as wild boar, as well as regional
delicacies.
✚ 244 B1 ✉ Erehthiou 46
☎ 210 922 5321 Ⓜ Akropoli
🚌 5, 9, 11, 230 AX, DC, MC, VI

It's important not to waste water
in arid Greece, especially on the
islands, where it often has to be
shipped in by tankers. Although
Athens' tap water is drinkable,
bottled water is cheap and tastes
better. Greeks are water
connoisseurs, discussing the
flavor and mineral properties of
favorite spring varieties. Glasses
of water are served alongside
every drink you order in cafés:
Drink it, or pour it in your ouzo
and watch the clear spirit turn
milky white. Since it's often hot
and most places are not air-
conditioned, it's important to
drink plenty of water.

Price guide: (double room with
breakfast for two people)
$ up to Ft17,500
$$ Ft17,500–Ft44,500
$$$ over Ft44,500

Hotel Astoria $$–$$$

Set on a busy intersection in the
center of Pest, this is a splendid
hotel in an old building with a
relaxing atmosphere. It was the
headquarters of the Soviet army
during the 1956 revolution.
✚ 258 C2 ✉ Kossuth Lajos utca
19–21 ☎ 889 6000; fax 889 6091
Ⓜ Astoria AX, DC, MC, VI

Carlton $$

This is a spacious and simple hotel
at the foot of Castle Hill. Of the
95 rooms – all with excellent
facilities – only those on the upper
floor have good views.
✚ 258 B3 ✉ Apor Péter utca 3
☎ 1 224 0999 and 1 224 0998;
fax 1 224 0990 Ⓜ Battyány tér
AX, DC, MC, VI

Hilton Budapest $$$

This modern building is in a prime
position on Castle Hill,
incorporating the ruins of a 13th-
century Dominican cloister and a
17th-century Jesuit cloister. You'll
get spectacular views over the
Danube. Facilities include salons,
cafés, shops and a courtyard
concert area.
✚ 258 A3 ✉ Hess András tér 1–3
☎ 889 6600; fax 889 6644
Ⓜ Moszkva tér, then Várbusz
(Castle Bus) AX, DC, MC, VI

Kempinski Hotel Corvinus
Budapest $$$

This luxury hotel with an
unusual postmodern design includes
two presidential apartments. It's
popular with business travelers.
✚ 258 C2 ✉ Erzsébet tér 7–8
☎ 1 429 3777; fax 1 429 4777
Ⓜ Deák tér AX, DC, MC, VI

Victoria $$

Marvelous views across to the Pest
bank are a feature at this comfortable
27-room hotel on the Buda bank,
overlooking Chain Bridge and
convenient to many tourist sights.
✚ 258 B3 ✉ Bem rakpart 11
☎ 1 457 8080; fax 1 457 8088
Ⓜ Battyány tér 🚌 16; tram 19
AX, DC, MC, VI

BUDAPEST RESTAURANTS

Price guide: (dinner per person, excluding drinks)
$ up to Ft3,000
$$ Ft3,000–Ft6,000
$$$ over Ft6,000

Alabárdos $$$

This smart, formal restaurant serves Hungarian dishes in ancient vaulted dining rooms. Presentations are beautiful and the staff attentive. There are only a few tables, so reserve well in advance.
🏛 258 A3 ✉ Országház utca 2
☎ 1 356 0851 🕐 Closed Sun.
🚇 Moszkva tér, then Várbusz (Castle Bus) AX, DC, MC, VI

Empire $$

The grand restaurant in the impressive early 20th-century Hotel Astoria serves first-class Hungarian and international dishes and good wines in elegant surroundings. Gypsy bands serenade evening diners, and there's also an atmospheric café.
🏛 258 C2 ✉ Kossuth Lajos utca 19–21 ☎ 889 6000 🚇 Astoria AX, DC, MC, VI

Gundel $$$

Hungarian meals are served in this 100-year-old restaurant in City Park. The owner, George Lang, also owns the Café des Artistes in New York.
🏛 258 E4 ✉ Állatkerti út 2
☎ 1 468 4040 🚇 Hősök tere AX, DC, MC, VI

Művész Kávéház $

It's worth having refreshments at this coffeehouse, which has retained the ambience of Budapest's golden era of café society.
🏛 258 C3 ✉ Andrássy út 29 ☎ 1 352 1337 🚇 Opera No credit cards

Panorama $$

Located in the art-nouveau Danubius Hotel Gellért, this well-known restaurant rests over a thermal spring at the foot of Gellért Hill. Expect fine views of the river and specialties including pike, perch and veal.
🏛 258 C1 ✉ Gellért tér 1 ☎ 1 385 2200 🚋 Trams 18, 19, 47, 49 AX, DC, MC, VI

DUBLIN HOTELS

Price guide: (double room with breakfast for two people)
$ under €110

$$ €110–€180
$$$ over €180

Burlington Hotel $$$

This very large, top-quality hotel is located southeast of St. Stephen's Green, on the south side of the Royal Canal and about a 10-minute walk from the city center. It's best known for its stylish restaurant and bar.
🏛 274 C1 ✉ Upper Leeson Street
☎ 01 660 5222; fax 01 660 8496
🚇 Pearse Station 🚌 11A, 13A AX, DC, MC, VI

The Clarence $$$

Within walking distance of the city center, this is an individual and tasteful hotel. For sheer luxury, the two-bedroom penthouse is outstanding, and there also is a good restaurant.
🏛 274 B3 ✉ 6–8 Wellington Quay
☎ 01 407 0800; fax 01 407 0820
🚌 Most cross city buses AX, DC, MC, VI

The Fitzwilliam $$

This small, pleasant, family-run hotel on a famous Dublin Georgian street is close to the heart of things.
🏛 274 C1–C2 ✉ 41 Upper Fitzwilliam Street ☎ 01 662 5155; fax 01 676 7488 🚇 Dublin City 🚌 10A, 18 AX, MC, VI

Longfield's Hotel $$$

This town house close to the city center has a relaxed atmosphere, with an emphasis on good service and hospitality.
🏛 274C1–C2 ✉ Fitzwilliam Street
☎ 01 676 1367; fax 01 676 1542
🚇 Pearse Station 🚌 10, 18 AX, DC, MC, VI

The Shelbourne $$$

This famous central Dublin hotel opened in 1824 (although the present building dates from 1867). It is beautifully appointed and has a good restaurant and bar. It's popular for fashionable – and expensive – afternoon tea overlooking St. Stephen's Green.
🏛 274 B2 ✉ 27 St. Stephen's Green ☎ 01 663 4500; fax 01 661 6006 🚇 Pearse Station 🚌 11, 13, 44, 46, 48 AX, DC, MC, VI

DUBLIN RESTAURANTS

Price guide: (dinner per person, excluding drinks)
$ €15–€30

$$ €30–€45
$$$ over €45

Chapter One $$

This literary-themed restaurant, in the Dublin Writers Museum on Parnell Square, has fine modern Irish cuisine. Discuss Shaw over salmon or Joyce over venison.
🏛 274 B3 ✉ 18–19 Parnell Square
☎ 01 873 2266 🕐 Closed Sun.–Mon. and Sat. lunch, 🚇 DART Connolly Station 🚌 10A, 11, 11A, 11B, 13, 13A, 19A AX, DC, MC, VI

Cornucopia $

This good-value restaurant serves imaginative vegetarian food.
🏛 274 B3 ✉ 19 Wicklow Street
☎ 01 677 7583 🕐 Closed Sun.
🚇 DART Connolly Station 🚌 All cross-city buses MC, VI

Gallaghers Boxty House $$

If you want straightforward food with an Irish accent, this is the place; the name refers to *boxty*, a traditional potato pancake.
🏛 274 B3 ✉ 20 Temple Bar ☎ 01 677 2762 🚇 DART Tara Street Station 🚌 Most cross-city buses AX, MC, VI

The Lord Edward $$

This informally elegant, upstairs restaurant has a traditional menu featuring a host of seafood dishes as well as corned beef and cabbage and excellent Irish stew.
🏛 274 B2 ✉ 22 Christchurch Place (in the Liberties, near Christ Church) ☎ 01 454 2420 🕐 Closed Sun. Dec. 24–Jan. 2 🚇 DART Pearse Station 🚌 All cross city buses AX, DC, MC, VI

Restaurant Patrick Guilbaud $$$

This highly regarded French restaurant has a reputation for outstanding nouvelle cuisine. It's superbly understated, stylish and very expensive. It also contains a wonderful collection of Irish art.
🏛 274 C2 ✉ 21 Merrion Street
☎ 01 676 4192 🕐 Closed Sun. and Mon. 🚇 DART Pearse Station 🚌 11, 13A, 44 AX, DC, MC, VI

ROME HOTELS

Price guide: (double room with breakfast for two people)
$ up to €100
$$ €100–€200
$$$ over €200

Italy

KEY TO SYMBOLS

✚ map page number and coordinates
✉ address
☎ telephone number
🕐 days/times closed
Ⓜ nearest subway station
🚌 nearest bus/trolley
🚋 bus/tram/funicular route
⛴ ferry
$$$ expensive
$$ moderate
$ inexpensive
AX American Express
DC Diners Club
MC MasterCard
VI VISA

Bread, Cakes and Cookies

In Italy, bread comes from a *panificio* or *forno*, cakes and cookies from a *pasticceria*. In Tuscany there is no salt in bread, a legacy of an age when baking was done once a week and saltless bread didn't get moldy. Once you're accustomed to it, it goes well with the strong, salty flavors of prosciutto or salami. Italian cakes are outstanding: luscious creations piled with fruit, filled with cream, oozing chocolate and soaked with liqueur. Italians often buy a large cake or selection of smaller ones to eat for Sunday dessert, or a piece of *panforte*, a traditional spiced fruit confection from Siena. It's acceptable to buy a single pastry or cake and eat it on the spot in the shop.

Campo dei Fiori $$

You'll find comfortable rooms and a roof garden at this pretty, moderately priced hotel near one of Rome's liveliest squares. Good value option.
✚ 292 B3 ✉ Via del Biscione 6 ☎ 06 6880 6865; fax 06 687 6003 🚌 46, 62, 64 AX, DC, VI

Columbus $$$

This historic hotel (a favorite of visiting prelates) is housed in a former Renaissance palace a stone's throw from St. Peter's, and has many original decorative features.
✚ 292 B3 ✉ Via della Conciliazione 33 ☎ 06 686 5435; fax 06 686 4874 🚌 23, 64 AX, DC, VI

Hotel d'Inghilterra $$$

Located a few minutes from the Spanish Steps, this historic hotel has antique furniture and provides discreet and excellent service.
✚ 292 C4 ✉ Via Bocca di Leone 14 ☎ 06 699811; fax 06 679 8601 Ⓜ Spagna 🚌 119, 52, 61 AX, DC, VI

Navona $$

This comfortable, simple and friendly hotel is a few minutes' stroll from the lovely Piazza Navona. Be sure to make reservations ahead of time.
✚ 292 B3 ✉ Via dei Sediari 8 ☎ 06 686 4203; fax 06 880 3802 🚌 70, 81, 90 AX, VI

Westin Excelsior $$$

A stay at this world-class luxury hotel, with its opulent decor and high standard of service and elegance, is among Rome's most sybaritic experiences.
✚ 292 C4 ✉ Via Vittorio Veneto 125 ☎ 06 47081; fax 06 482 6205 Ⓜ Barbarini 🚌 52, 53, 95 AX, DC, VI

ROME RESTAURANTS

Price guide: (dinner per person, excluding drinks)
$ under €20
$$ €20–€35
$$$ over €35

Alberto Ciarla $$$

One of Rome's finest restaurants, this winner has an elegant atmosphere, an outstanding wine list and good fish specials.
✚ 292 B2 ✉ Piazza San Cosimato 40 ☎ 06 581 8668 🕐 Closed Sun. and for 15 days during Jan. and Aug. 🚌 44, 75, 170 AX, DC, MC, VI

Da Baffetto $$

For a quintessential Roman experience and the best pizza in town, stand in line to get a table at this tiny pizzeria. It stays open until 1 a.m.
✚ 292 B3 ✉ Via del Governo Vecchio 114 ☎ 06 686 1617 🚌 46, 62, 64 No credit cards

Checchino dal 1887 $$$

This long-established restaurant specializes in the traditional Roman dishes of tripe, brains and offal. Reservations are essential.
✚ 292 B1 ✉ Via Monte Testaccio 30 ☎ 06 574 3816 🕐 Closed Sun.–Mon., Aug. and Dec. 25 🚌 13, 23, 57 AX, DC, MC, VI

Da Lucia $

A tiny, typical Trastevere trattoria, Da Lucia has a friendly family atmosphere and great pasta.
✚ 292 B2 ✉ Vicolo del Mattonato 2b ☎ 06 580 3601 🕐 Closed Mon. and 2 weeks in Aug. 🚌 23, 65, 56 No credit cards

Da Paris $$$

You can eat outside in summer at this very popular Trastevere restaurant serving fine pasta and fish dishes.
✚ 292 B2 ✉ Piazza San Calisto 7a ☎ 06 581 5378 🕐 Closed Sun. evening, Mon. and 3 weeks in Aug. 🚌 44, 56, 60 AX, DC, MC, VI

Papà Giovanni $$$

Reservations are advised to enjoy this popular restaurant's light and innovative cooking and excellent wine list.
✚ 292 B3 ✉ Via dei Sediari 4 ☎ 06 6880 4807 🕐 Closed Sun. 🚌 70, 81, 90 MC, VI

FLORENCE HOTELS

Price guide: (double room with breakfast for two people)
$ up to €100
$$ €100–€200
$$$ over €200

Brunelleschi $$$

Reserve ahead to stay in this comfortable hotel filled with character, situated around a medieval tower in the heart of Florence.
✚ 302 C2 ✉ Piazza Santa Elisabetta 3 ☎ 055 27370; fax 055 219 653 🚌 In the pedestrian zone AX, DC, MC, VI

Firenze $

This good budget choice, located close to the center of Florence, is popular with younger travelers.
✚ 302 C2   ✉ Piazza dei Donati 4
☎ 055 214 203; fax 055 212 370
🚌 In the pedestrian zone DC, VI

Monna Lisa $$–$$$

Housed in a 15th-century palace, this hotel has grand public rooms and a tranquil garden; be sure to request a quiet bedroom.
✚ 302 E3   ✉ Borgo Pinti 27
☎ 055 247 9751; fax 055 247 9755
🚌 6, 31 AX, DC, MC, VI

Porta Rossa $$

This elegant hotel, in a 14th-century building near the Old Bridge, has wonderfully atmospheric public areas and is a good value.
✚ 302 C2   ✉ Via Porta Rossa 19
☎ 055 287 551; fax 055 282 179
🚌 In the pedestrian zone AX, DC, MC, VI

Westin Excelsior $$$

This is Florence's smartest hotel, with every comfort, exceptional service and a rooftop terrace.
✚ 302 B3   ✉ Piazza Ognissanti 3
☎ 055 27151; fax 055 210 278
🚌 C AX, DC, MC, VI

FLORENCE RESTAURANTS
Price guide: (dinner per person, excluding drinks)
$ under €20
$$ €20–€35
$$$ over €35

Cantinetta Antinori $$$

Enjoy Tuscan food with superb wine within the 15th-century Palazzo Antinori, which belongs to this great wine-producing family. Dress up to feel in place.
✚ 302 B3   ✉ Piazza Antinori 3r
☎ 055 292 234   🕐 Closed
Sat.–Sun. 🚌 In the pedestrian zone
AX, DC, MC, VI

Il Carmine $$

This family-run restaurant serves good traditional Tuscan food in a friendly atmosphere.
✚ 302 B2   ✉ Piazza del Carmine 18r
☎ 055 218 601   🕐 Closed Sun.
🚌 B AX, DC, VI

Dino $$$

This uncluttered and airy restaurant serves simple yet elegant food and is

popular with locals and tourists alike.
✚ 302 D2   ✉ Via Ghibellina 51r
☎ 055 241 452   🕐 Closed Sun.
evening and Mon. lunch 🚌 14 AX,
DC, VI

Gauguin $$

One of Florence's rare vegetarian restaurants serves imaginative dishes and is very popular with the university crowd.
✚ 302 D4   ✉ Via degli Alfani 24a
☎ 055 234 0616   🚌 6 AX, DC, VI

Ponte Vecchio $$$

Head to this restaurant for some real local cooking; it's popular with tourists, but none the worse for it.
✚ 302 C2   ✉ Lungarno
Archibusieri 8r   ☎ 055 292 289
🚌 In the pedestrian zone
AX, MC, VI

NAPLES HOTELS
Price guide: (double room with breakfast for two people)
$ up to €100
$$ €100–€200
$$$ over €200

Britannique $$

This quietly situated and comfortable hotel has a secluded garden and lovely views over the Bay of Naples.
✚ 309 B2   ✉ Corso Vittorio
Emanuele 133   ☎ 081 761 4145; fax
081 660 457   🚌 V1 AX, DC, MC, VI

Canada $$

You'll have to reserve well in advance to get one of the sea-view rooms at this small and friendly hotel, near the harbor at Mergellina.
✚ 309 Off the map   ✉ Via
Mergellina 43   ☎ 081 680 952;
fax 081 682 018   🚌 R3 AX, DC

Excelsior $$$

One of Naples' grandest hotels, in the elegant Chiaia district; rooms have period furnishings and views of Capri.
✚ 309 A1   ✉ Via Partenope 48
☎ 081 764 0111; fax 081 764 9743
🚌 R3 AX, DC, VI

Mediterraneo $$

This large, modern hotel is conveniently located near the waterfront, and has good facilities and a lovely rooftop breakfast terrace.
✚ 309 B2   ✉ Via Nuova Ponte di
Tappia 25   ☎ 081 797 0001 or 797
0111; fax 081 252 0079   🚌 R2, R3
AX, DC, VI

Santa Lucia $$$

This elegant and prestigious waterfront hotel near the Castel del'Ovo has spacious and well-furnished rooms.
✚ 309 A1   ✉ Via Partenope 46
☎ 081 764 0666; fax 081 764 8580
🚌 R3 AX, DC, MC, VI

NAPLES RESTAURANTS
Price guide: (dinner per person, excluding drinks)
$ under €20
$$ €20–€35
$$$ over €35

Al 53 $$

Naples' oldest restaurant, complete with 17th-century furnishings and original mosaic pavement, serves great hors d'oeuvres, seafood pasta and Neapolitan desserts.
✚ 309 B3   ✉ Piazza Dante 53
☎ 081 549 9372   🚌 R1, 24
DC, MC, VI

Amici Miei $$

This elegant, friendly restaurant serves excellent antipasti, risotto and pasta dishes.
✚ 309 B2   ✉ Via Monte di Dio 78
☎ 081 764 6063   🕐 Closed
Sun.–Mon. dinner 🚌 R1, R3 AX,
DC, VI

La Cantinella $$$

This seafront restaurant specializes in creative fish cooking, which you can enjoy on the terrace. The wine list is outstanding.
✚ 309 B1   ✉ Via Cuma 42
☎ 081 764 8684   🕐 Closed Sun.
(except Nov.–May) and part of Aug.
🚌 R3 AX, DC, MC, VI

Trattoria Medina $$

This cheerful restaurant, packed with locals, serves authentic Neapolitan dishes, seafood and pizzas accompanied by a variety of live music.
✚ 309 B2   ✉ Via Medina 32
☎ 081 551 5233   🚌 R3 AX, DC,
MC, VI

Trianon $

Naples' finest and most popular pizzeria, offering numerous combinations, has been in business for more than 70 years.
✚ 309 B3   ✉ Via P. Colletta 46
☎ 081 553 9426   🚌 R2, 14, 110
No credit cards

KEY TO SYMBOLS

⊞ map page number and coordinates
✉ address
☎ telephone number
◷ days/times closed
Ⓜ nearest subway station
🚌 nearest bus/trolley bus/tram/funicular route
🛳 ferry
$$$ expensive
$$ moderate
$ inexpensive
AX American Express
DC Diners Club
MC MasterCard
VI VISA

Plan Ahead for Venice

To enjoy a stress-free visit in Venice it is absolutely necessary to make hotel reservations ahead of time. Reservations for June to September should be made during the previous fall, as should those for the two weeks in February in which Carnival falls (although you may be able to get something closer to the time of your visit if you hunt around). Three months ahead should be enough time for other months. If you want to eat at a specific restaurant it's also advisable to make reservations; your hotel concierge will be happy to call and set them up.

VENICE HOTELS

Price guide: (double room with breakfast for two people)
$ up to €100
$$ €100–€200
$$$ over €200

Canada $$

This is one of the best budget bets in Venice, with a good location near the Rialto; reserve in advance.
⊞ 314 D2 ✉ Campo San Lio, Castello 5659 ☎ 041 522 9912; fax 041 523 5852 🛳 1, 82 AX, DC, MC, VI

Cipriani $$$

One of the world's most famous luxury hotels, with every comfort and impeccable service, is located amid beautiful gardens on the Giudecca (a chain of islets a short boat ride from central Venice).
⊞ 314 Off the map ✉ Giudecca 10 ☎ 041 520 7744; fax 041 520 3930 🛳 82, or use hotel's private launch service AX, DC, MC, VI

Danieli $$$

Considered to be Venice's finest hotel, the Danieli has style, elegance and class. Book a room in the older part, not in the modern annex.
⊞ 314 D2 ✉ Riva degli Schiavoni, Castello 4196 ☎ 041 522 6480; fax 041 296 1100 🛳 1 AX, DC, MC, VI

Hotel agli Alboretti $$

Book well in advance to stay at this pleasant hotel, ideally situated on a tree-lined street between the Accademia and the Záttere.
⊞ 314 C1 ✉ Rio Terrà Antonio Foscarini 884, Dorsoduro 884 ☎ 041 523 0058; fax 041 521 0158 🛳 1, 82 AX, DC, MC, VI

Pensione Seguso $$

This is a wonderfully atmospheric, old-fashioned *pension* overlooking the Giudecca Canal. Rooms feature painted ceilings, and most have water views.
⊞ 314 B1 ✉ Fondamenta ai Gesuati, Dorsoduro 779 ☎ 041 528 6858; fax 041 522 2340 🛳 52, 82 AX, DC, VI

VENICE RESTAURANTS

Price guide: (dinner per person, excluding drinks)
$ €5–€15
$$ €15–€25
$$$ over €25

Alla Madonna $$

This big, noisy fish restaurant, one of the most traditional in Venice, is hugely popular with locals, business people and tourists.
⊞ 314 D2 ✉ Calle della Madonna, San Polo 594 ☎ 041 522 3824 ◷ Closed Wed. and 2 weeks in Aug. 🛳 1, 82 AX, DC, MC, VI

Da Franz $$$

Situated near the Giardini Pubblici, this excellent fish and seafood restaurant has a summer terrace.
⊞ 314 Off the map ✉ Fondamenta San Giuseppe, Castello 745 ☎ 041 522 0861 🛳 1, 52 AX, DC, MC, VI

Dona Onesta $

The décor is simple and the Venetian dishes straightforward yet of good quality at this friendly local restaurant; reservations are advised.
⊞ 314 B2 ✉ Calle della Dona Onesta, Dorsoduro ☎ 041 710 586 ◷ Closed Sun. 🛳 1 AX, VI

Harry's Dolci $$$

This offshoot of the famous Harry's Bar offers equally good food and service, with the bonus of a waterfront terrace for summer dining; reserve in advance.
⊞ 314 Off the map ✉ Fondamenta San Biagio, Giudecca 773 ☎ 041 522 4874 ◷ Closed Tue., Nov.–Mar. 🛳 82 AX, DC, MC, VI

Taverna San Trovaso $$

This lively neighborhood restaurant and pizzeria is always busy serving Venetian families and tourists.
⊞ 314 B1 ✉ Fondamenta Priuli, Dorsoduro 1016 ☎ 041 520 3703 ◷ Closed Mon. 🛳 1 AX, DC, MC, VI

LUXEMBOURG HOTELS

Price guide: (double room with breakfast for two people)
$ €50–€75
$$ €75–€125
$$$ over €125

Français $$

Ideally located for easy strolls to the Old Town, this small hotel is at the heart of the city.
⊞ 329 B3 ✉ 14 place d'Armes ☎ 47 45 34; fax 46 42 74 🚌 All city center buses AX, DC, MC, VI

Golden Tulip Central Molitor $$–$$$

This completely modernized business

and tourist hotel is conveniently located between tourist attractions and the railway station.

🏠 329 B2   ✉ 28 avenue de la Liberté   ☎ 48 99 11; fax 48 33 82   🚌 9 AX, DC, MC, VI

Grand Hôtel Cravat $$$

Place d'Armes is a few steps away from this stylish hotel overlooking the Pétrusse valley. The property is part of the well-known restaurant association Luxembourg à la Carte, and its own restaurant offers the very best French and traditional Luxembourg cuisine.

🏠 329 B3   ✉ 29 boulevard F. D. Roosevelt   ☎ 22 19 75; fax 22 67 11   🚌 All city center buses AX, DC, MC, VI

Italia $$

Located just off the place de Paris on rue d'Anvers, this pleasant hotel is close to the city center. Its restaurant specializes in Italian cuisine.

🏠 329 B2   ✉ 15–17 rue d'Anvers   ☎ 48 66 26-1; fax 48 08 07   🚌 9 AX, DC, MC, VI

Sofitel Luxembourg $$$

This hotel is very modern, very luxurious and very expensive. It is located on the Kirchberg Plateau, next to the Centre Européen.

🏠 329 Off the map   ✉ 6 rue du Fort Niedergrünewald   ☎ 43 77 61; fax 42 50 91   🚌 18 AX, DC, MC, VI

LUXEMBOURG RESTAURANTS

Price guide: (dinner per person, excluding drinks)

$ €10–€15
$$ €15–€25
$$$ over €25

Les Caves Gourmandes $$–$$$

This popular and atmospheric restaurant in the Ilot Gastronomique complex is within part of the Old Town wall. The superb French cuisine features breast of duck with figs and *crème brûlée* for dessert.

🏠 329 C3   ✉ 32 rue de l'Eau   ☎ 46 11 24   🕐 Closed Sat. lunch and Sun.   🚌 All buses AX, DC, MC, VI

La Lorraine $$$

Located on place d'Armes, this bright, attractive restaurant offers French cuisine with excellent fish dishes. You can choose your lobster from a tank by the door.

🏠 329 B3   ✉ 7 place d'Armes   ☎ 47 14 36   🕐 Closed Sun.   🚌 All city center buses AX, DC, MC, VI

La Maison des Brasseurs $$–$$$

This popular restaurant in Grand-Rue serves classic country cooking and offers local dishes such as *Judd mat Gaardebounen* (roast and smoked pork) and vegetarian dishes.

🏠 329 B3   ✉ 48 Grand Rue   ☎ 47 13 71   🕐 Closed Sat. dinner, Sun. and public holidays   🚌 All city center buses AX, DC, MC, VI

Speltz $$$

This beautifully appointed restaurant has a pleasant outdoor eating area and an excellent wine collection to accompany the top-quality French and Luxembourg cuisine, such as turbot or scorpion fish with tomatoes, olives and basil. There is a very good cheese selection.

🏠 329 B3   ✉ 8 rue Chimay   ☎ 47 49 50   🕐 Closed Sat. lunch, Sun. and public holidays   🚌 All city center buses AX, DC, MC, VI

Via Sud $$–$$$

French cuisine is offered at this popular restaurant, where you can eat outside on nice evenings. Try the red mullet in olive oil.

🏠 329 B3   ✉ 22–24 rue du Curé   ☎ 22 82 50   🕐 Closed Sun.   🚌 All city center buses AX, DC, MC, VI

AMSTERDAM HOTELS

Price guide: (double room with breakfast for two people)

$ €75–€150
$$ €150–€300
$$$ over €300

Ambassade Hotel $$

Located on the splendid Herengracht, the city's most elegant canal, this beautifully furnished hotel offers a good breakfast.

🏠 342 B2   ✉ Herengracht 335–353   ☎ 020 555 0222; fax 020 555 0277   🚌 Tram 1, 2, 5, AX, MC, VI

Amstel Botel $

For a different experience, and waterside views from some rooms, stay in this permanently moored hotel boat near Centraal Station.

🏠 342 D3   ✉ Oosterdokskade 2–4   ☎ 020 626 4247; fax 020 639 1952   🚌 22, 326 AX, MC, VI

Hotel de L'Europe $$$

The private boat landing at this expensive luxury hotel overlooking the Amstel river says it all. A Victorian exterior welcomes the traveler into the renovated interior, where there is every modern amenity – including the finest *haute cuisine* and wine list at the hotel's Excelsior restaurant.

🏠 342 C2   ✉ Nieuwe Doelenstraat 2–8   ☎ 020 531 1777; fax 020 531 1778   🚌 Tram 4, 9, 14, 16, 24, 25 AX, MC, VI

Nova Hotel $

This family-run hotel has a central location but is sheltered from street noise. Spotless en-suite rooms and friendly, efficient service make this a good budget choice.

🏠 342 C3   ✉ Nieuwezijds Voorburgwal 276   ☎ 020 623 0066; fax 020 627 2026   🚌 Tram 1, 2, 5 AX, MC, VI

Hotel Pulitzer $$$

This stylish luxury hotel recaptures some of the spirit of old Amsterdam within its unified complex of 25 17th-century canal houses on the handsome Prinsengracht. Relax in the art nouveau Garden Room or the 17th-century Saxenburg Room.

🏠 342 B2   ✉ Prinsengracht 315–331   ☎ 020 523 5235; fax 020 627 6753   🚌 Tram 6, 13, 14, 17 AX, MC, VI

AMSTERDAM RESTAURANTS

Price guide: (dinner per person, excluding drinks)

$ €10–€20
$$ €20–€30
$$$ over €30

Claes Claesz $$

This friendly restaurant is situated in the attractive Jordaan district, on the banks of the Egelantiergracht. Good Dutch food is served, and there is often live music.

🏠 342 B3   ✉ Egelantiersstraat 24–26   ☎ 020 625 5306   🕐 Closed Mon.   🚌 10; tram 7, 10, 17 MC, VI

Dorrius $$$

Located inside the Crowne Plaza Amsterdam City Centre, Dorrius is the place for a taste of real Dutch cuisine with a dash of French flair. Try delicious oysters and eel or

Netherlands

KEY TO SYMBOLS

✚	map page number and coordinates
✉	address
☎	telephone number
🕐	days/times closed
Ⓜ	nearest subway station
🚌	nearest bus/trolley
	bus/tram/funicular route
⛴	ferry
$$$	expensive
$$	moderate
$	inexpensive
AX	American Express
DC	Diners Club
MC	MasterCard
VI	VISA

Weekend Treats

As in other Scandinavian cities, Oslo hotels cater to business people on weekdays. This makes room rates some of the most expensive in Europe. On weekends and during the holiday summer months fewer reservations are made, and hotels often offer discounts. You can stay in a luxury hotel from Friday night through Monday morning for a substantially reduced rate. Outside the height of summer this can also mean that there are few fellow guests, making your weekend stay seem even more exclusive. The high standard of service does not diminish with the price. Reduced rates on weekends and during holiday periods are common in many major European cities – it's always worth asking at the hotel you are interested in.

---

salted cod, cheese soufflé, and Dutch wines and liqueurs.
✚ 342 C3 ✉ Nieuwezijds Voorburgwal 5 ☎ 020 420 2224 🕐 Closed lunch Ⓜ Centraal Station 🚌 Tram 1, 2, 5,13,17 AX, DC, MC, VI

In de Waag $–$$
Come to this friendly restaurant for late-night Continental cuisine, when it is lit by hundreds of candles. The generous three-course lunch and early evening menu are good values.
✚ 342 C3 ✉ Nieuwmarkt 4 ☎ 020 422 7772 Ⓜ Nieuwmarkt AX, DC, MC, VI

De Silveren Spiegel $$$
Located in a restored, redbrick, 1614 building with yellow trim and shuttered windows, this restaurant has an excellent menu ranging from Dutch cuisine to fish specialties.
✚ 342 C4 ✉ Kattengat 4–6 ☎ 020 624 6589 🕐 Closed lunch and Sun. Ⓜ Centraal Station 🚌 Tram 1, 2, 5, 6, 11, 13, 17 AX, DC, MC, VI

Toscanini $$
This stylish Jordaan district restaurant features excellent Italian food. The homemade *biscotti* is a specialty.
✚ 342 B4 ✉ Lindengracht 75 ☎ 020 623 2813 🕐 Closed lunch and Sun. 🚌 Tram 3, 10 AX, DC MC, VI

THE HAGUE HOTELS
Price guide: (double room with breakfast for two people)
$ €75–€150
$$ €150–€300
$$$ over €300

Best Western Delft Museumhotel and Residence $–$$
While in Delft, spend at least one night in this luxuriously furnished hotel, overlooking a tranquil canal.
✚ 350 Off the map ✉ Oude Delft 189, Delft ☎ 015 215 3070; fax 015 215 3079 Ⓜ Delft Railroad station 🚌 Tram 1 AX, DC, MC, VI

Carlton Ambassador Hotel $$–$$$
This luxury hotel in an elegant neighborhood is within easy walking distance of the city center.
✚ 350 B2 ✉ Sophialaan 2 ☎ 070 363 0363; fax 070 360 0535 🚌 4, 5, 22; tram 10 AX, DC, MC, VI

Hotel Cattenburch $
A comfortable hotel located some distance from the city center, but with good tram connections, this is a good budget choice. There's a restaurant on the premises.
✚ 350 B2 ✉ Laan Copes van Cattenburch 38 ☎ 070 352 2335; fax 070 354 3119 🚌 Tram 1, 9 AX, DC, MC, VI

Mercure Hotel Den Haag Central $–$$
This modern hotel is located near the railroad station and city center. It also has a restaurant.
✚ 350 C1 ✉ Spui 180 ☎ 070 363 6700; fax 070 363 9398 🚌 4, 18, 22, 25, tram 1, 9, 15, 16 AX, DC, MC, VI

Steigenberger Kurhaus Hotel $$–$$$
If you base yourself at Scheveningen and want to stay somewhere overlooking the beach, consider this Old European-style hotel, built in the 1880s.
✚ 350 A4 ✉ Gevers Deynootplein 30, Scheveningen ☎ 070 416 2636; fax 070 416 2646 🚌 14, 22, 23, tram 1, 9 AX, DC, MC, VI

THE HAGUE RESTAURANTS
Price guide: (dinner per person, excluding drinks)
$ €10–€20
$$ €20–€30
$$$ over €30

Bodega De Posthoorn $$
This restaurant is housed in an attractive building in the stylish Lange Voorhout. Reserve ahead.
✚ 350 C2 ✉ Lange Voorhout 39a ☎ 070 360 4906 🚌 4; tram 1, 9, 16 AX, MC, VI

It Rains Fishes $$$
High-quality, expensive seafood is served in this intimate restaurant. Reservations are advised.
✚ 350 B2 ✉ Noordeinde 123 ☎ 070 365 2598 🕐 Closed Sat. and Sun. lunch 🚌 Tram 7, 8 AX, DC, MC, VI

Les Ombrelles $$
Located in the attractive Denneweg area, this restaurant serves excellent seafood dishes.
✚ 350 C2 ✉ Hooistraat 4a ☎ 070 365 8789 🕐 Closed Sat. lunch and Sun. 🚌 Tram 2, 6, 8, 16 AX, DC, MC, VI

Ristorante Roma $$$

You'll find fine Italian cuisine here at the heart of The Hague's old quarter, north of the Kerkplein.
➕ 350 B1 ✉ Papestraat 22 ☎ 070 346 2345 🕐 Closed lunch and Tue. 🚋 Tram 2, 6, 8, 16 AX, DC, MC, VI

Stadsherberg 't Goude Hooft $$$

Demolished and rebuilt in the 17th century, this popular inn serves good food.
➕ 350 B1 ✉ Dagelijkse Groenmarkt 13 ☎ 070 346 9713 🚋 Tram 1, 2, 3, 6, 10, 17 MC, VI

Price guide: (double room with breakfast for two people)
$ KR800–KR1,000
$$ KR1,000–KR1,400
$$$ over KR1,400

Best Western Anker Hotel $$–$$$

A modern hotel in the city center with good-value rooms, close to Oslo's main attractions.
➕ 365 C2 ✉ Storgata 55 ☎ 22 99 75 00; fax 22 99 75 20 🚇 30, 31, 32; tram 11, 12, 13, 15, 17 🚉 Oslo Sentralstasjoen AX, DC, MC, VI

Hotel Bristol $$–$$$

This elegant hotel in the heart of Oslo has superb furnishings and decorations, as well as several bars and restaurants on the premises.
➕ 365 B1–B2 ✉ Kristian IV's gate 7 ☎ 22 82 60 00; fax 22 82 60 01 🚇 Stortinget 🚇 30, 31, 32, 37; tram 10, 11, 12, 17, 18 AX, MC, VI

Comfort Hotel Gabelshus $$$

This pleasant hotel is nestled in a quiet area, within easy reach of the city's main attractions. The service is attentive and rooms are attractive.
➕ 365 B2 ✉ Gabels gate 16 ☎ 23 27 65 00; fax 23 27 65 60 🚇 30, 32; tram 10, 13 AX, MC, VI

Continental $$$

In a prime location between the Royal Palace and City Hall, this is a top-quality, very expensive hotel. A member of "The Leading Hotels of the World," it has three good restaurants.
➕ 365 B1 ✉ Stortingsgaten 24–26 ☎ 22 82 40 00; fax 22 42 96 89 🚇 Nationaltheatret 🚇 30, 31, 32; tram 12, 15 AX, MC, VI

Grand $$–$$$

One of Oslo's most prestigious hotels is this handsome 19th-century accommodation in the heart of the city. It has well-appointed rooms, good restaurants (including the Grand Café), bars, and an inviting rooftop sauna and swimming pool.
➕ 365 B1 ✉ Karl Johans gate 31 ☎ 23 21 20 00; fax 23 21 21 00 🚇 Stortinget 🚇 30, 31, 32, 37; tram 13, 15, 19 AX, DC, MC, VI

Price guide: (dinner per person, excluding drinks)
$ KR50–KR80
$$ KR80–KR200
$$$ over KR200

Blom Kunsterernes Restaurant $$$

Excellent Norwegian food is offered at this well-established restaurant. Try *lefse*, savory pastry wrapped around reindeer meat or other fillings. Reservations are advised.
➕ 365 B1 ✉ Karl Johans gate 41B ☎ 23 13 95 00 🕐 Closed Sat. lunch and Sun. 🚇 Stortinget, 30, 31, 32, 37; tram 13, 15, 19 AX, DC, MC, VI

D/S Louise Restaurant and Bar $$$

Located in the Aker Brygge complex, where there are good views across the harbor to Akershus Castle, this nautically themed restaurant serves traditional and international dishes.
➕ 365 A1 ✉ Stranden 3 ☎ 22 83 00 60 🚋 Tram 10, 12 AX, DC, MC, VI

Engebret Café $$

Founded in 1857 by Engebret Christoffersen, this restaurant still maintains a strong tradition. Try Norwegian and international cuisine, including traditional fish dishes. There's also an excellent mid-morning sandwich buffet.
➕ 365 B1 ✉ Bankplassen 1 ☎ 22 82 25 25 🕐 Closed Sun. except during Advent 🚋 Tram 10, 12, 15 AX, DC, MC, VI

Grand Café $$$

Great tradition, including visits by Henrik Ibsen in his day, makes this restaurant inside the Grand Hotel a favorite with locals. You can sample Norwegian cuisine from elk stew to *lutefisk* (marinated dried fish).
➕ 365 B1 ✉ Karl Johans gate 31

☎ 23 21 20 00 🚇 Stortinget 30, 31, 32, 37; tram 13, 15, 19 AX, DC, MC, VI

Restaurant Det Gamle Rådhus $$

Located in the 17th-century building next to Akershus Castle, this restaurant is billed as Oslo's oldest eating establishment. International cuisine and fish specialties are served in a charming atmosphere. Reservations are strongly advised.
➕ 365 B1 ✉ Nedre Slottsgate 1 ☎ 22 42 01 07 🕐 Closed Sun. 🚋 Tram 10, 12, AX, DC, MC, VI

Price guide: (double room with breakfast for two people)
$ up to €120
$$ €120–€200
$$$ over €200

As Janelas Verdes $$$

This small hotel, housed in an 18th-century town house, has large and luxurious rooms. Its location, well west of the city center, is the only drawback.
➕ 378 Off the map ✉ Rua das Janelas Verdes 47 ☎ 21 396 8143; fax 21 396 8144 🚇 40, 49, 60 AX, DC, MC, VI

Britânia $$–$$$

Just east of Avenida da Liberdade, this friendly, Art Deco-style hotel was refurbished in the 1990s.
➕ 378 A5 ✉ Rua Rodrigues Sampaio 17 ☎ 21 315 5016; fax 21 315 5021 🚇 Avenida 🚇 9, 11, 31 AX, DC, MC, VI

Duas Nações $

Although only some rooms have private bathrooms, this hotel – housed in a 19th-century building – is a superb budget choice, located in the heart of the historic Baixa district.
➕ 378 B2–C2 ✉ Rua da Vitória 41 ☎ 21 346 0710; fax 21 347 0206 🚇 Rossio No credit cards

Metrópole $$

The Metrópole is located on Rossio, Lisbon's busiest and noisiest square. If you would prefer a quieter stay, ask for a room at the back to avoid the noise.
➕ 378 B3 ✉ Praça do Pedro IV 30 ☎ 21 321 9030; fax 21 346 9166 🚇 Rossio AX, DC, MC, VI

Portugal

KEY TO SYMBOLS

➕ map page number and coordinates
✉ address
☎ telephone number
🕐 days/times closed
Ⓜ nearest subway station
🚌 nearest bus/trolley
　 bus/tram/funicular route
🚢 ferry
$$$ expensive
$$ moderate
$ inexpensive
AX American Express
DC Diners Club
MC MasterCard
VI VISA

Eating in Portugal

The Portuguese do not eat at the same hours as their Spanish neighbors, so you won't have to wait until 10 p.m. for dinner. Many people eat dinner as early as 7:30, and restaurants remain open until about 10:30; they tend to close all day on Sunday. Breakfast is usually a light meal, and the lunch hour starts around 12:30. The daily menu (*ementa turística*) is an excellent value and normally offers a decent variety. Meals often start with a selection of appetizers, which arrive automatically and are added to your bill if you eat them. Portuguese helpings are big, but you can ask for a half portion.

Ritz Four Seasons $$$

One of Lisbon's most luxurious hotels, the Ritz opened in the 1950s. Sumptuously decorated, it has large rooms and suites and provides exceptional service.
➕ 378 Off the map ✉ Rua Rodrigo da Fonseca 88 ☎ 21 381 1400; fax 21 383 1783 Ⓜ Rotonda 🚌 1, 9, 11 AX, DC, MC, VI

LISBON RESTAURANTS

Price guide: (dinner per person, excluding drinks)
$ up to €20
$$ €20–€30
$$$ over €30

Bota Alta $$$

For large portions of authentic Portuguese food, go to this popular restaurant in the Upper Town, which has an attractive, rustic ambience.
➕ 378 B2 ✉ Travessa da Queimada 35/37 ☎ 21 342 7959 🕐 Closed Sat. lunch and Sun. Ⓜ Restauradores AX, DC, MC, VI

Fidalgo $

This welcoming restaurant in the Upper Town serves fish and seafood. It has a trendy clientele.
➕ 378 B2 ✉ Rua da Barroca 27/31 ☎ 21 342 2900 🕐 Closed Sun. Ⓜ Rossio 🚌 1, 11; tram 28 AX, DC, VI

Gambrinus $$$

There's an old-fashioned ambience at this deluxe, formal restaurant, where fish and seafood are the specialties; reservations advised.
➕ 378 A4 ✉ Rua das Portas de Santo Antão 23 ☎ 21 342 1466 Ⓜ Rossio AX, MC, VI

São Jerónimo $$$

Stop at this modern restaurant, close to the Jerónimo monastery, for fish and seafood.
➕ 378 map inset ✉ Rua dos Jerónimo 12 ☎ 21 364 8797 🕐 Closed Sat. lunch and Sun. 🚌 28, 49, 51; tram 15 AX, DC, MC, VI

Tágide $$$

Great views, atmosphere and excellent food are what make this one of Lisbon's classiest restaurants.
➕ 378 C3 ✉ Largo da Academia Nacional de Belas Artes 12/20 ☎ 21 346 0570 Ⓜ Rossio 🚌 58, 100 AX, DC, MC, VI

Via Graça $$

You'll find traditional Portuguese cooking and great views of the city at this candlelit restaurant.
➕ 378 D5 ✉ Rua Damasceno Monteiro 9b ☎ 21 887 0830 🕐 Closed Sat. lunch and Sun. Ⓜ Intendente 🚌 Tram 28 AX, DC, MC, VI

PORTO HOTELS

Price guide: (double room with breakfast for two people)
$ up to €100
$$ €100–€180
$$$ over €180

Boavista $$

This peaceful, quiet hotel in the suburb of Foz is very comfortable and has great ocean views.
➕ 387 Off the map ✉ Esplanada do Castelo 58 ☎ 22 532 0020; fax 22 617 3818 🚌 24; tram 18 AX, DC, MC, VI

Hotel da Bolsa $$

Friendly service and spacious rooms await at this comfortable hotel in the heart of the historic center.
➕ 387 B2 ✉ Rua Ferreira Borges 101 ☎ 22 202 6768; fax 22 205 8888 🚌 21, 22 AX, DC, MC, VI

Infante de Sagres $$$

Porto's best and classiest hotel has elegant public rooms filled with antiques, a pretty terrace and lovely bedrooms.
➕ 387 B3 ✉ Praça Filipa de Lencastre 62 ☎ 22 339 8500; fax 22 339 8599 🚌 20, 21, 22 AX, DC, MC, VI

Internacional $

Located just off the Praça de Liberdade, this friendly hotel has been pleasantly refurbished.
➕ 387 B3 ✉ Rua do Almada 131 ☎ 22 200 5032; fax 22 200 9063 🚌 20, 21, 22 AX, DC, MC, VI

Hotel Malaposta $$

Smart, modern hotel that is conveniently located to the Old Town, the Upper Town and the downtown tourist information center.
➕ 387 B3 ✉ Rua da Conceição 80 ☎ 22 200 6278; fax 22 200 6295 🚌 7, 54, 71, 72, 91, 95 AX, DC, MC, VI

PORTO RESTAURANTS

Price guide: (dinner per person, excluding drinks)

$ up to €15
$$ €15–€25
$$$ over €25

Dona Filipa $$$
The restaurant at the Hotel Infante Sagres is one of Porto's best, serving Portuguese and international dishes in elegant surroundings.
🚩 387 B3 ✉ Praça Filipa de Lencastre 62 ☎ 22 339 8500
🚌 21, 22 AX, DC, MC, VI

Filha da Mãe Preta $$
There are lovely river views from this restaurant specializing in regional dishes such as squid, octopus, eel and *bacalhau* (dried, salted cod).
🚩 387 B1 ✉ Cais da Ribeira 40 ☎ 22 205 5515 🕒 Closed Sun. AX, DC, MC, VI

Mercearia $$$
This traditional restaurant on the riverbank in Old Porto specializes in fish, seafood, soup and *bacalhau* recipes.
🚩 387 B1 ✉ Cais da Ribeira 32–33A ☎ 22 200 4389 AX, DC, MC, VI

Porto Ibérico $$
If you're visiting the port warehouses across the river, this restaurant – serving a range of northern Portuguese and Spanish dishes – is a good choice.
🚩 387 B1 ✉ Rua do Rei Ramiro 697 ☎ 22 370 6674 🕒 Closed Sun. 🚌 57, 91 AX, DC, MC, VI

Taberna de Bêbobos $$
Traditional Porto dishes are served at this atmospheric, historic tavern on the waterfront, in the oldest part of town.
🚩 387 B1 ✉ Cais da Ribeira 24 ☎ 22 205 3565 🕒 Closed Sun. AX, MC, VI

Price guide: (double room with breakfast for two people)
$ €50–€100
$$ €100–€150
$$$ over €150

Asturias $
This conveniently located budget choice has a friendly staff and pleasant, clean rooms.
🚩 402 C2 ✉ Sevilla 2 ☎ 91 429 6676; fax 91 429 4036 🚇 Sevilla AX, DC, MC, VI

Carlos V Best Western $$
To be sure of a room, you'll want to reserve in advance at this good-value hotel in an excellent location near the Puerta del Sol.
🚩 402 B2 ✉ Maestro Vitoria 5 ☎ 91 531 4100; fax 91 531 3761 🚇 Sol, Callao AX, DC, MC, VI

Ritz $$$
Madrid's Ritz opened in 1910 and offers a high level of luxury, service and facilities. There's a terrace-restaurant from spring to autumn.
🚩 402 D2 ✉ Plaza de la Lealtad 5 ☎ 91 701 6767; fax 91 701 6776 🚇 Banco de España AX, DC, MC, VI

Suecia $$$
This quiet hotel is located between the Prado Museum and Puerta del Sol square.
🚩 402 C2 ✉ Marqués de Casa Riera 4 ☎ 91 531 6900; fax 91 521 7141 🚇 Sevilla AX, DC, MC, VI

Westin Palace $$$
This grand, high-tech hotel, with fitness center, sauna and solarium, is ideally situated within walking distance of Madrid's main attractions.
🚩 402 C2 ✉ Plaza Cortes 7 ☎ 91 360 8000; fax 91 360 8100 🚇 Banco de España AX, DC, MC, VI

Price guide: (dinner per person, excluding drinks)
$ €10–€25
$$ €25–€50
$$$ over €50

El Bodegon $$$
Many people think this is Madrid's best restaurant. El Bodegon offers a set menu at dinner and an à la carte lunch menu, with superb service.
🚩 402 C4 ✉ Pinar 15 ☎ 91 562 8844 🕒 Closed Sun. and Aug. 🚇 Gregorio Marañón AX, DC, MC, VI

La Bola $$
This long-established restaurant specializes in Madrid *cocido*, different stews cooked slowly in traditional pots. It also offers friendly service.
🚩 402 B2 ✉ Bola 5 ☎ 91 547 6930 🕒 Closed Sun. dinner 🚇 Santo Domingo No credit cards

Botín $$
Immensely popular with visitors, this restaurant, founded in 1725, serves

good traditional grills and other meat dishes.
🚩 402 B2 ✉ Cuchilleros 17 ☎ 91 366 3026 🚇 Sol AX, DC, MC, VI

Los Galayos $$–$$$
Located on the Plaza Mayor, this elegant restaurant, with a terrace and bar, serves Castilian dishes cooked in wood-fired ovens.
🚩 402 B2 ✉ Botoneras 5 (Plaza Mayor) ☎ 91 366 3028 🚇 Sol AX, DC, MC, VI

Hylogui $
This traditional restaurant, popular with locals, offers straightforward home cooking and a huge menu.
🚩 402 C2 ✉ Ventura de la Vega 3 ☎ 91 429 7357 🕒 Closed Sun. dinner and Aug. 🚇 Sevilla AX, MC, VI

El Pescador $$–$$$
This restaurant takes full advantage of the seafood that arrives fresh in Madrid each day.
🚩 402 E3 ✉ José Ortega y Gasset, 75 ☎ 91 402 1290 🕒 Closed Sun. and Sat. lunch 🚇 Lista AX, DC, MC, VI

Price guide: (double room with breakfast for two people)
$ €50–€100
$$ €100–€150
$$$ over €150

Arts $$$
This 44-story, luxury waterfront hotel, with superb views across the city, epitomizes modern Barcelona.
🚩 411 Off the map ✉ Carrer de la Marina 19–21 ☎ 93 221 1000; fax 93 221 1070 🚇 Ciutadella/Vila Olímpica AX, DC, MC, VI

Colón $$$
Situated opposite the cathedral, this refurbished hotel combines a friendly and old-fashioned atmosphere with lots of comfort.
🚩 411 C2 ✉ Avenida de la Catedral 7 ☎ 93 301 1404; fax 93 317 2915 🚇 Jaume I AX, DC, MC, VI

Internacional $$
A good budget choice, this hotel is located on La Rambla and has simple rooms (but not all with bath).
🚩 411 B2 ✉ La Rambla 78–80 ☎ 93 302 2566; fax 93 317 6190 🚇 Liceu AX, DC, MC, VI

Spain

KEY TO SYMBOLS

⊞ map page number and coordinates
✉ address
☎ telephone number
🕓 days/times closed
🚇 nearest subway station
🚌 nearest bus/trolley bus/tram/funicular route
⛴ ferry
$$$ expensive
$$ moderate
$ inexpensive
AX American Express
DC Diners Club
MC MasterCard
VI VISA

Andalucian Cuisine

Simplicity is all in Andalucian cooking, in which the superb quality of the ingredients, combined with a Moorish legacy of spices, almonds and oranges, has created one of Spain's most enjoyable cuisines. *Tapas* originated here, as did *gazpacho*, the cold summer soup, and sherry, a fortified wine that is drunk and used in cooking. There are tasty stews and soups, both thickened with lentils and potatoes, and every dish is redolent with olive oil, garlic and tomatoes. Excellent bread and rich Arab-inspired pastries and desserts complete the picture.

Rivoli Ramblas $$$
This popular hotel with excellent facilities is housed in a restored Art Deco building on La Rambla.
⊞ 411 B2 ✉ La Rambla 128
☎ 93 302 6643; fax 93 317 5053
🚇 Catalunya AX, DC, MC, VI

Hotel Suizo $$
This comfortable and old-fashioned hotel is a five-minute walk from the cathedral and the historic Gothic Quarter.
⊞ 411 C2 ✉ Plaza del Angel 12
☎ 93 310 6108; fax 93 315 0461
🚇 Jaume I 🚌 17, 19, 45 AX, DC, MC, VI

BARCELONA RESTAURANTS
Price guide: (dinner per person, excluding drinks)
$ €10–€25
$$ €25–€50
$$$ over €50

Ca la Lluisa $$
This waterfront restaurant serves excellent *fideua* (a dish similar to paella) and delicious changing daily specials.
⊞ 411 C2 ✉ Passeig Joan de Borbó 12, La Barceloneta ☎ 93 225 0695 🕓 Closed Tue.–Wed. dinner 🚇 Barceloneta AX, MC, VI

El Rodizio $$
This very popular restaurant features Brazilian-style meat dishes and also offers a huge self-service buffet at good prices.
⊞ 411 B3 ✉ Carrer Consell de Cent 403 ☎ 93 265 5112
🕓 Closed Sun. evening 🚇 Girona AX, MC, VI

Neichel $$$
Locally considered the finest restaurant in Barcelona, Neichel is noted for its service, daily specials, cheeses and desserts.
⊞ 411 Off the map ✉ Beltran i Rózpide 1–5 ☎ 93 205 6369
🕓 Closed Sun.–Mon. and Aug.
🚇 Palau Reial AX, DC, MC, VI

Nou Celler $
This friendly and unpretentious neighborhood restaurant serves good traditional Catalan dishes at reasonable prices.
⊞ 411 C2 ✉ Carrer de la Princessa 16 ☎ 93 310 4773
🕓 Closed Sat., and Sun. dinner
🚇 Jaume I AX, DC, VI

Set Portes $$–$$$
One of Barcelona's best and most historic restaurants serves a wide range of excellent Catalan food and fine wines.
⊞ 411 C2 ✉ Passeig de Isabel II 14 ☎ 93 319 3033 🚇 Barceloneta AX, DC, MC, VI

SANTIAGO HOTELS
Price guide: (double room with breakfast for two people)
$ €50–€100
$$ €100–€150
$$$ over €150

Hesperia Compostela $$
This comfortable and spacious hotel outside the historic center offers superb views of the heart of the city.
⊞ 418 Off the map ✉ Hórreo 1
☎ 981 585 700; fax 981 585 290
AX, DC, MC, VI

Hogar San Francisco $
This is a simple and peaceful hotel, housed in the old convent of St. Francis in the historic center, only a five-minute stroll from the cathedral.
⊞ 418 A2 ✉ Campillo del Convento de San Francisco
☎ 90 215 3321; fax 981 571 916
AX, MC, VI

Hostal El Rápido $
An example of a simple, clean pilgrim hostel, El Rapido is on one of the historic center's main streets.
⊞ 418 A1 ✉ Rua do Franco 22
☎ 981 584 983 AX, DC, MC, VI

Hotel dos Reis Católicos $$$
This *parador is* considered by many to be the finest deluxe hotel in Spain. The hotel is magnificently located on the cathedral square and is housed in a beautiful 15th-century cloistered building.
⊞ 418 A2 ✉ Plaza del Obradoiro 1
☎ 981 582 300; fax 981 563 094
AX, DC, MC, VI

San Carlos $$
This first-class hotel, facing the Galician parliament buildings, is conveniently located only a few minutes' walk from the town center.
⊞ 418 Off the map ✉ Hórreo 106
☎ 981 560 505; fax 981 560 506
AX, DC, MC, VI

SANTIAGO RESTAURANTS

Price guide: (dinner per person, excluding drinks)
$ €10–€25
$$ €25–€50
$$$ over €50

Botafumeiro $
This simple, unpretentious local restaurant just behind the cathedral serves inexpensive shellfish and other Galician specialties.
➕ 418 A2 ✉ Azabachería 16 ☎ 981 584 439 🚫 Closed Sat. MC, VI

Don Gaiferos $$
In the heart of the old center, this restaurant serves wonderful shellfish, seafood and other Galician dishes.
➕ 418 A1 ✉ Rua Nueva 23 ☎ 981 583 894 🚫 Closed Sun. dinner AX, DC, MC, VI

El Estanco del Hórreo $$
Located just outside the historic center, this spacious restaurant is a good place to try local shellfish.
➕ 418 Off the map ✉ Hórreo 26 ☎ 981 563 808 🚫 Closed Sun.–Mon. dinner evenings AX, DC, MC, VI

Toñi Vicente $$$
Probably Santiago's most famous and elegant restaurant, Toñi Vicente specializes in the imaginative use of local ingredients.
➕ 418 Off the map ✉ Rosalía de Castro 24 ☎ 981 594 100 🚫 Closed Sun. AX, DC, MC, VI

SEVILLE HOTELS

Price guide: (double room with breakfast for two people)
$ €50–€100
$$ €100–€150
$$$ over €150

Alfonso XIII $$$
Seville's top hotel, set in an attractive palm-shaded garden, has every comfort and an exceptional level of service.
➕ 425 B2 ✉ San Fernando 2 ☎ 95 491 7000; fax 95 491 7099 🚌 21, 23, C3, C4 AX, DC, MC, VI

Best Western Hotel Bécquer $$
This hotel is conveniently located between the river and the center of town and offers excellent service.
➕ 425 A3 ✉ Reyes Católicos 4 ☎ 95 422 8900; fax 95 421 4400 🚌 43 AX, DC, MC, VI

Casas de la Judería $$–$$$
This atmospheric hotel, located in the heart of Santa Cruz, features peaceful courtyards with fountains.
➕ 425 B3 ✉ Callejón de dos Hermanas 7 ☎ 95 441 5150; fax 95 442 2170 🚌 5, C3, C4 AX, DC, MC, VI

Meliá Sevilla $$$
A modern hotel, located near lovely Maria Luisa Park. It has many facilities, including a pool.
➕ 425 B2 ✉ Dr. Pedro de Castro 1 ☎ 95 441 4551; fax 95 442 2977 🚌 30, 31, 33 AX, DC, MC, VI

San Gil $$–$$$
This attractive and spacious hotel is in a lovely old building complete with interior courtyards.
➕ 425 B4 ✉ Parras 28 ☎ 95 490 6811; fax 95 490 6939 🚌 C1, 14 AX, DC, MC, VI

SEVILLE RESTAURANTS

Price guide: (dinner per person, excluding drinks)
$ €10–€25
$$ €25–€50
$$$ over €50

Becerrita $$
This long-established restaurant serves traditional Andalucian food and prides itself on its desserts.
➕ 425 B3 ✉ Recaredo 9 ☎ 95 441 2057 🚫 Closed Sun. dinner 🚌 10, 11, C1, C2 AX, DC, MC, VI

La Madrata $
There's an excellent variety of Spanish tapas at this traditional restaurant, decorated in rustic style. Prices are economical.
➕ 425 B4 ✉ Peris Mancheta, Alameda de Hercules ☎ 95 490 8188 🚌 C1, C2, C3, C4, 43 MC, VI

Enrique Becerra $$$
This restaurant serves well-prepared Andalucian dishes and remains a favorite with American visitors.
➕ 425 B2 ✉ Gamazo 2 ☎ 95 421 3049 🚫 Closed Sun. 🚌 10, 11, 12 AX, MC, VI

El Giraldillo $$
A pretty, tiled restaurant opposite the cathedral, El Giraldillo serves fresh fish and local specialties.
➕ 425 B2 ✉ Virgen de los Reyes 2 ☎ 95 421 4525 🚌 41, 40, 42 DC, MC, VI

El 3 de Oro $$
This lively and friendly restaurant in Santa Cruz is always packed with locals. The menu consists of straightforward, traditional but delicious Andalucian dishes.
➕ 425 B3 ✉ Santa María la Blanca 34 ☎ 95 442 6820 🚌 1, C3, C4 AX, MC, VI

STOCKHOLM HOTELS

Price guide: (double room with breakfast for two people)
$ 800Kr–1,500SKr
$$ 1,500Kr–2,200SKr
$$$ over 2,200SKr

Diplomat $$–$$$
This comfortable hotel in a handsome early 20th-century building overlooks the waterfront on the road to Djurgården. The Diplomat Tea House is a delightful place to stop for afternoon tea and tasty treats.
➕ 437 C2 ✉ Strandvägen 7C ☎ 08 459 68 00; fax 08 459 68 22 🚌 47, 69 AX, MC, VI

First Hotel Reisen $–$$$
A popular and well-appointed hotel on the east side of the Old Town, within easy walking distance of the city center.
➕ 437 B2–C2 ✉ Skeppsbron 12–14 ☎ 08 22 32 60; fax 08 20 15 59 🚌 43, 46, 55, 59, 76 AX, MC, VI

Grand Hôtel Stockholm $$$
The handsome facade of this top-quality hotel stands across the Norrström from the Royal Palace. Facilities are luxurious; the restaurants serve international as well as local cuisine, and the hotel is famous for its *smörgåsbord*.
➕ 437 C2 ✉ Sodra Blasieholmshamnen 8 ☎ 08 679 35 00; fax 08 611 86 86 🚌 65 AX, MC, VI

Mälardrottningen $–$$
Once owned by Woolworth heiress Barbara Hutton, this 1920s converted luxury yacht is a hotel with a difference. It's moored on the west side of the Old Town. The restaurant serves excellent international and Swedish cuisine.
➕ 437 B2 ✉ Riddarholmen ☎ 08 545 187 80; fax 08 24 36 76 🚇 Gamla Stan 🚌 3, 53 AX, MC, VI

Sweden, Switzerland

KEY TO SYMBOLS

- ✚ map page number and coordinates
- ✉ address
- ☎ telephone number
- ◷ days/times closed
- Ⓜ nearest subway station
- 🚌 nearest bus/trolley
- 🚋 bus/tram/funicular route
- ⛴ ferry
- **$$$** expensive
- **$$** moderate
- **$** inexpensive
- AX American Express
- DC Diners Club
- MC MasterCard
- VI VISA

Radisson SAS Strand Hotel $$

This comfortable hotel with modern facilities is in a fine old building on the southwest side of Nybroviken inlet. Enjoy views across the water from the top-floor restaurant.

✚ 437 B2 ✉ Nybrokajen 9
☎ 08 50 66 4000; fax 08 50 66 4001
Ⓜ Kungsträdgården 🚌 65 AX, MC, VI

STOCKHOLM RESTAURANTS

Price guide: (dinner per person, excluding drinks)
$ 50SKr–150SKr
$$ 150SKr–250SKr
$$$ 250SKr–300SKr

Den Gyldene Freden $$$

Established in 1722, this famous Old Town restaurant has long attracted the rich and famous, including Nobel Prize selection committee members. Even the restroom has 18th-century poetry on the wall. The cuisine is outstanding. Reservations required.

✚ 437 B2 ✉ Österlånggatan 51
☎ 08 24 97 60 ◷ Closed Mon.–Fri. lunch, Sun. and public holidays Ⓜ Gamla Stan 🚌 46, 55 AX, DC, MC, VI

KB $$$

Near the Royal Drama Theater and traditionally the haunt of writers and artists, this excellent but pricey restaurant serves Swedish and French cuisine (a special menu often lists less expensive dishes). Reservations are strongly advised, even for lunch.

✚ 437 C2 ✉ Smålandsgatan 7
☎ 08 679 60 32 ◷ Closed Sun. and late Jun.–early Aug. Ⓜ Östermalmstorg 🚌 46, 47, 62, 69 AX, DC, MC, VI

Kungshallens $

This big food outlet, arranged on several levels in the heart of modern Stockholm, offers every kind of fast and ethnic food from kebabs to Thai.

✚ 437 B3 ✉ Kungsgatan 44
☎ 08 21 80 05 Ⓜ Hötorget 🚌 41, 53 No credit cards

Pontus in the Green House $$$

Another Old Town institution, Pontus in the Green House is expensive and always busy, but superb fish dishes, specialty sauces and great service make it worth the money. Reservations are advised.

✚ 437 B2 ✉ Österlånggatan 17
☎ 08 23 85 00 ◷ Closed Sat. lunch and Sun. Ⓜ Gamla Stan 🚌 46, 55 AX, DC, MC, VI

Zum Franziskaner $$–$$$

Located in Gamla Stan, this is the oldest restaurant in Stockholm, founded in 1421. Swedish and German home cooking is served in authentic *Jugendstil* surroundings.

✚ 437 C2 ✉ Skeppsbron 44
☎ 08 411 83 30 ◷ Closed Sun.
Ⓜ Gamla Stan AX, DC, MC, VI

GENEVA HOTELS

Price guide: (double room with breakfast for two people)
$ SF100–SF250
$$ SF250–SF400
$$$ over SF400

Edelweiss Manotel $–$$

A popular choice with tourists, this chalet-style hotel near the lakeside has attractive, comfortable rooms and stages frequent folklore evenings.

✚ 451 B3 ✉ 2 place de la Navigation 2 ☎ 022 544 5151; fax 022 544 5199 🚌 1 AX, DC, MC, VI

Eden $–$$

In a quiet area near Mon Repos park and the lake, this comfortable hotel has a good restaurant and a friendly, relaxed atmosphere.

✚ 451 Off the map ✉ rue de Lausanne 135 ☎ 022 716 3700; fax 022 731 5260 🚌 4, 18 AX, DC, MC, VI

Beau-Rivage $$$

Founded in 1865 on the shore of Lake Leman, the Beau-Rivage is one of the most famous and luxurious hotels of the world. Its distinguished elegance and perfect service embody in every sense the dream and the qualities of "Old Europe."

✚ 451 B3 ✉ quai de Mont Blanc 13 ☎ 022 7166 6666; fax 022 716 6060 🚌 5, 8, 11 AX, DC, MC, VI

Hôtel Central $

This is a friendly, family-run hotel in the heart of the city and at the foot of the old town, just a three-minute walk from Lake Geneva.

✚ 451 B2 ✉ rue de la Rôtisserie 2 ☎ 022 818 8100; fax 022 818 8101 🚌 10; tram 16 AX, DC, MC, VI

Rio $

This traditional, centrally located hotel, housed in an early 20th-century building, is an excellent budget choice.

✚ 451 A3 ✉ place Isaac-Mercier 1 ☎ 022 732 3264; fax 022 732 8264 🚌 7 DC, MC, VI

Switzerland

Tiffany $$–$$$

This newly renovated hotel in the heart of Geneva is furnished in *belle époque* style, with comfortable rooms, a bar and a restaurant.

⊞ 451 A2 ⊠ rue des Marbriers 1 ☎ 022 708 1616; fax 022 708 1617 🚊 13 AX, DC, MC, VI

GENEVA RESTAURANTS

Price guide: (dinner per person, excluding drinks)
$ SF25–SF45
$$ SF45–SF60
$$$ over SF60

Auberge de Coutance $$$

This elegant French restaurant provides exceptional service and offers dishes such as foie gras and duck specialties.

⊞ 451 A3 ⊠ rue Coutance 25 ☎ 022 732 7919 🕐 Closed Mon. 🚊 13, 16 AX, DC, MC, VI

Auberge de Savièse $$

Enjoy a selection of Swiss specialties at this friendly restaurant, which features different types of fondue.

⊞ 451 B3 ⊠ rue des Pâquis 20 ☎ 022 732 8330 🚊 1 AX, DC, MC, VI

Brasserie Lipp $$

This popular French restaurant in the Confédération-Centre shopping complex on the Left Bank is named after a famous brasserie in Paris.

⊞ 451 B2 ⊠ rue de la Confédération 8 ☎ 022 311 1011 🚊 12 AX, DC, MC, VI

La Coupole $$

Choose from classic French rotisserie specials or traditional Tuscan cuisine at this large, stylish restaurant on the Left Bank.

⊞ 451 B2 ⊠ rue du Rhone 116 ☎ 022 787 5010 🚊 2, 9, 22; tram 12 AX, DC, VI

Patara $$

This is the best Thai restaurant in Geneva. Expect impeccable service in tasteful surroundings.

⊞ 451 B3 ⊠ quai du Mont-Blanc 13 ☎ 022 731 5566 🚊 6, 33 AX, DC, MC, VI

Restaurant des Vieux Grenadiers $$

This typical Genevan restaurant specializes in regional dishes and fondues. It has a pretty summer terrace and occasional live jazz.

⊞ 451 B3 ⊠ rue de Carouge 92 ☎ 022 320 1327 🕐 Closed Sun. and Thu. evenings 🚊 12, 13 AX, MC, VI

ZURICH HOTELS

Price guide: (double room with breakfast for two people)
$ SF150–SF250
$$ SF250–SF400
$$$ over SF400

Bristol $

This is a friendly and comfortable hotel near the railroad station, with modern and functional rooms.

⊞ 456 B4 ⊠ Stampfenbachstrasse 34 ☎ 01 258 4444 🚊 3, 31, 46 AX, DC, MC, VI

Dolder Waldhaus Hotel $$–$$$

Situated high above Zurich, with wide views from the terraces, this luxury hotel offers every comfort as well as excellent service.

⊞ 456 Off the map ⊠ Kurhausstrasse 20 ☎ 044 269 1000; fax 044 269 1001 🚊 3, 8, 15 AX, DC, MC, VI

Eden au Lac $$$

Stay at this elegant lakeside hotel, built in 1909, for the ultimate in comfort, luxury and service.

⊞ 456 B1 ⊠ Utoquai 45 ☎ 01 266 2525; fax 01 266 2500 🚊 4 AX, DC, MC, VI

Franziskaner $$

This reasonably priced hotel, overlooking a pretty square, has comfortable rooms and a restaurant.

⊞ 456 B2 ⊠ Niederdorferstrasse 1 ☎ 01 250 5300; fax 01 250 5301 🚊 4, 15 AX, DC, MC, VI

Krone Unterstrass $–$$

This well-equipped, comfortable hotel caters to business travelers and is located in a quiet residential area 10 minutes fom the city center.

⊞ 456 Off the map ⊠ Schaffhauserstrasse 1 ☎ 01 360 5656; fax 01 360 5600 🚊 7, 14 AX, DC, MC, VI

Rössli $$

The inconspicuous exterior of the Rössli hides a comfortable and imaginatively designed hotel with well-equipped rooms.

⊞ 456 B2 ⊠ Rössligasse 7 ☎ 01 256 7050; fax 01 256 7051 🚊 4, 15 AX, DC, MC, VI

ZURICH RESTAURANTS

Price guide: (dinner per person, excluding drinks)
$ SF25–SF45
$$ SF45–SF60
$$$ over SF60

Adler's Swiss Chuchi $

This friendly restaurant in the Hotel Adler serves meat and cheese fondue as well as local veal specialties.

⊞ 456 B2 ⊠ Rosengasse 10 ☎ 01 266 9666 🚊 4, 15 AX, DC, MC, VI

Haus Zum Rüden $$$

Overlooking the Limmat river, this historic restaurant serves the best of Swiss specialties in an elegant atmosphere.

⊞ 456 B2 ⊠ Limmatquai 42 ☎ 01 261 9566 🕐 Closed Sat.–Sun. 🚊 4, 15 AX, DC, MC, VI

Kronenhalle $$–$$$

This long-established restaurant offers traditional dishes beneath artworks by Picasso and Matisse.

⊞ 456 B2 ⊠ Rämistrasse 4 ☎ 01 251 6669 🚊 2, 4, 5, 9, 11, 15 AX, DC, MC, VI

Mère Cathérine $

This centrally located garden restaurant serves fish and seafood, with an accent on Mediterranean and Provençal dishes.

⊞ 456 B2 ⊠ Nägelihof 3 ☎ 01 250 5940 🚊 4, 15 AX, MC, VI

Münsterhof $$

Historic Münsterhof serves traditional Swiss specialties at good prices and also has a garden.

⊞ 456 A2 ⊠ Münsterhof 6 ☎ 01 211 4340 🚊 4, 15 AX, DC, MC, VI

Restaurant Kropf $$

This cheerful restaurant with sumptuously decorated rooms has been serving local dishes since 1888.

⊞ 456 A2 ⊠ In Gassen 16 ☎ 01 221 1805 🕐 Closed Sun. 🚊 2, 8, 9, 11 MC , VI

Walliser Kanne $$

This friendly restaurant features every imaginable type of fondue – meat, cheese, *chinoise* – as well as raclette and Swiss specialties such as *rösti* (a potato pancake).

⊞ 456 A3 ⊠ Lintheschergasse 21 ☎ 01 211 3133 🚊 10, 11, 13 AX, DC, MC, VI

European Distance Chart

EUROPEAN DISTANCE CHART

Road distances, in kilometers (km), are calculated by the shortest or quickest routes (highways, main roads) from center to center and do not take into account seasonal weather conditions.

Miles	Km
1	1.6
10	16
20	32
30	48
40	64
50	80
100	160
200	320
300	480
400	640
500	800
1000	1600

Amsterdam (NL)
Barcelona (E)
Berlin (D)
Bruges (B)
Brussels (B)
The Hague (NL)
Dublin (IRL)
Edinburgh (GB)
Florence (I)
Geneva (CH)
Ghent (B)
Innsbruck (A)
Cologne (D)
Copenhagen (DK)
Lisbon (P)
London (GB)
Lyon (F)
Madrid (E)
Munich (D)
Naples (I)
Nice (F)
Odense (DK)
Oxford (GB)
Paris (F)
Porto (P)
Rome (I)
Salzburg (A)

```
1582
656 1865
249 1422 809
203 1382 768 103
63 1558 699 215 179
959 1958 1522 704 791 930
1092 2091 1655 837 924 1063 538
1385 1078 1238 1342 1228 1406 2001 2134
997 764 1110 769 729 905 1355 1488 608
219 1427 776 57 56 195 742 875 1298 774
1004 1369 755 1068 960 1025 1751 1884 485 567 1021
263 1371 566 322 214 284 1005 1138 1137 749 275 753
926 2313 397 1132 1073 970 1822 1955 1899 1543 1084 1421 886
2463 1257 2984 2246 2250 2439 2747 2880 2320 2006 2250 2616 2431 3225
482 1481 1045 227 314 453 463 665 1524 878 265 1274 528 1345 2270
938 629 1238 778 738 914 1365 1498 696 148 783 715 728 1656 1871 888
1828 627 2350 1611 1615 1804 2186 2319 1690 1377 1616 1986 1796 2663 628 1709 1241
838 1339 588 901 793 859 1584 1717 647 587 854 164 586 1254 2581 1107 735 1951
1861 1553 1713 1817 1703 1882 2473 2606 472 1083 1770 961 1609 2371 2795 1996 1171 2166 1122
1396 656 1346 1267 1227 1403 1853 1986 422 540 1271 718 1144 1935 1898 1376 473 1268 807 897
765 2151 599 971 911 809 1660 1793 1737 1381 922 1260 724 165 3063 1183 1495 2502 1093 2209 1774
589 1588 1152 334 421 560 396 598 1631 985 372 1381 635 1452 2377 90 995 1816 1214 2103 1483 1290
520 1043 1042 303 307 496 888 1021 1158 536 308 956 488 1364 1938 411 464 1305 836 1634 952 1202 518
2181 1211 2702 1964 1968 2157 2547 2680 2164 1851 1968 2460 2149 3025 323 2070 1715 615 2425 2640 1742 2863 2177 1658
1661 1353 1513 1617 1503 1682 2277 2410 272 883 1570 761 1409 2175 2595 1800 971 1966 922 227 697 2014 1907 1434 2440
981 1475 731 1044 936 1002 1727 1860 662 723 997 179 723 1397 2717 1250 871 2087 140 1137 889 1236 1347 992 2561 947
2060 1270 2582 1843 1847 2036 2454 2587 2044 1730 1848 2340 2028 2933 549 1977 1595 674 2305 2519 1622 2771 2084 1537 233 2329 2441
2367 1046 2889 2150 2154 2343 2733 2866 2120 1807 2155 2416 2335 3209 480 2256 1671 538 2381 2596 1698 3047 2363 1844 780 2406 2517
1542 2929 1013 1748 1689 1586 2438 2571 2515 2159 1700 2037 1502 620 3841 1961 2273 3279 1870 2986 2552 781 2068 1982 3641 2791 2013
607 1135 758 546 432 608 1213 1346 785 397 499 478 355 1177 2377 736 508 1748 369 1260 795 1015 843 488 2197 1070 524
1340 1225 1090 1295 1181 1361 1959 2092 252 574 1248 338 1088 1797 2467 1482 694 1838 499 728 569 1636 1589 1103 2312 538 433
1150 1816 877 1213 1105 1171 1907 2040 843 1013 1166 469 898 1577 3058 1430 1161 2429 431 1319 1160 1415 1537 1232 2881 1129 296
805 1804 1368 550 637 776 322 311 1847 1201 588 1597 851 1668 2593 339 1211 2032 1430 2319 1699 1506 295 734 2393 2123 1573
822 1029 839 788 674 843 1446 1579 596 277 741 293 571 1370 2271 969 425 1641 312 1072 607 1209 1076 662 2115 882 448
```

European Distance Chart

	Oxford (GB)	Paris (F)	Porto (P)	Praha (Prague) (CZ)	Roma (Rome) (I)	Salzburg (A)	Santiago de Compostela (E)	Sevilla (Seville) (E)	Stockholm (S)	Strasbourg (F)	Venézia (Venice) (I)	Wien (Vienna) (A)	York (GB)	Zürich (CH)
	518													
	2177	1656												
	1347	1049	2695											
	1907	1419	2437	1303										
	1347	987	2591	377	934									
	2084	1564	231	2603	2345	2499								
	2363	1840	679	2762	2389	2543	910							
	2068	1982	3641	1377	2791	2013	3548	3827						
	843	489	2135	618	1060	516	2042	2157	1793					
	1589	1119	2312	816	532	436	2219	2266	2413	742				
	1537	1238	2884	294	1119	297	2791	2853	2193	807	605			
	295	734	2393	1563	2123	1573	2300	2579	2284	1059	1805	1753		
	1076	664	2151	712	867	445	2058	2105	1986	229	548	740	1292	

Index

Index

Acknowledgements

Abbreviations for terms appearing below: (t) top; (b) bottom; (l) left; (r) right; (c) centre

The Automobile Assocation wishes to thank the following photographers and libraries for their assistance in the preparation of this book. Alamy 229, 455; Mary Evans Picture Library 45(t), 278(t); Ghent Altarpiece, Central Panel, 1432: Lord in Majesty between Virgin Mary and St. John the Baptist; below – Adoration of the Lamb by Jan van Eyck (c.1390–1441) St. Bavo Cathedral, Ghent, Belgium/Bridgeman Art Library 75; Bruce Coleman Collection 193; Corbis/Layne Kennedy 152; Des Hannigan 71, 163(c), 439, 440, 441, 467(t), 479(b), 483(t), 483(b), 511(t), 515(t), 515(b), 519(t), 519(b), 531(t), 531(b); Embassy of the Czech Republic 121; John Heseltine Archive 308, 312, 313; Innsbruck Tourism 39; Mri Bankers Guide To Foreign Currency 470, 474, 478, 498, 518, 530, 534; Pictures Colour Library 47(c), 157, 189, 192, 364, 456(t); Spanish Tourist Office 526; Spectrum Colour Library 73, 154, 197, 201, 331, 351, 463(t), 491(t); World Pictures 38, 43, 44, 45(b), 47(b), 48, 55, 61, 69, 74, 155, 162, 163(t), 169, 187, 191(t), 199, 202, 203(t), 203(c), 205, 224, 322, 324, 327, 332, 333, 341(b), 353, 354, 355, 356, 360, 361, 368, 369, 375, 391(t), 418, 420, 421, 422, 423, 435, 438, 443, 450, 452, 454, 456(b), 458, 460; Carol Weitz 463(t), 535(t), 535(b); www.euro.ecb.int/ (euro notes) 462, 466, 482, 486, 490, 494, 502, 506, 510, 514, 522, 526.

The remaining photographs are held in the Association's own library (AA Photo Library) and were taken by the following photographers: AA Photo Library 57, 83, 93, 109, 110, 117, 281(b), 363, 390; Adrian Baker 34, 211, 449, 538; Dave Austin 491(t); Peter Baker 18, 22, 32, 37, 97(t); M Birkitt 471(t); Liam Blake 270; Jamie Blandford 266; Jim Carnie 82; Michelle Chaplow 399, 417(b), 527(t), 527(b); Douglas Corrance 101, 102; Steve Day 274, 401(t), 413, 414, 415, 444; J Edmanson 168, 307(t), 406(b); Richard Elliott 105; Philip Enticknap 409; Derek Forss 76, 132, 137, 139, 145, 148, 150; Terry Harris 246, 247, 249; A Hemmison 227; Stephen Hill 503(b); Jim Holmes 5, 507(t); JW Jorgensen 135, 144, 151(tl), 151(tr), 479(t); Max Jourdan 429; Alex Kouprianoff 52, 53, 58, 59(t), 59(b), 63, 64, 65(b), 66, 67, 68, 374, 377, 381, 383(t), 383(b), 384, 385, 391(b), 467(b), 511(b), 523(t); Andrew Lawson 106; S McBride 269, 300; S&O Mathews 471(b), 495(t), 495(b); Eric Meacher 81, 191(b), 262, 417(t); Dario Miterdiri 294, 299(c); Anna Mockford & Nick Bonetti 388; Andrew Molyneux 392, 397, 424, 427; Rob Moore 487(t), 487(b); George Munday 271; Kim Naylor 430; Rich Newton 112, 115; D Noble 23, 25, 30, 33, 181(t); Ken Paterson 98, 104, 170, 176, 178, 179, 185, 238, 257, 261, 263, 264, 265, 287, 334, 338/339, 339, 341(t), 345, 346, 347, 348, 499(t); Bertrand Rieger 181(c); Douglas Robertson 396; Clive Sawyer 29, 126, 130, 164, 212, 215, 219, 220, 222, 234, 235(t), 237(b), 282, 289, 291, 296, 297, 298, 299(t), 301, 305, 307(b), 317, 319, 320, 321(t), 321(b); Michael Short 278; M Siebert 31(c), 31(c); Slide File 277, 280; Barrie Smith 90, 94, 97(b), 507(b); Antony Souter 118, 171(b), 173, 180, 182, 183, 221(t), 221(c), 223, 233, 235(b), 236, 237(t), 491(b); Rick Strange 171(t), 198, 401(b), 405(t), 405(b), 406(t), 407, 408; R Surman 251; JA Tims 2, 96; D Traverso 206; Jonathon Welsh 111; Stephen Whitehorn 276, 279, 281(t), 503(t); Peter Wilson 116/117, 243, 248, 250, 252, 260, 370, 412, 416, 523(b); TimWoodcock 85; Gregory Wrona 499(b); John Wyand 123, 127, 128, 129(t), 129(c), 131(t), 131(b), 475(t), 475(b); Wyn Voysey 95.